Chevrolet & GMC Pick-ups Automotive Repair Manual

by Jeff Killingsworth and John H Haynes

Member of the Guild of Motoring Writers

ABCDE
FGHIJ
KLMNO
PQRS

Models covered:

Chevrolet Silverado and GMC Sierra
1500 models - 2014 through 2016
2500/3500 models - 2015 through 2016
Includes 2015 and 2016 Chevrolet Suburban and Tahoe, GMC Yukon, Yukon XL and Cadillac Escalade

Does not include 2014 Chevrolet Silverado/GMC Sierra 2500/3500 models or 2014 SUV models, or information specific to diesel engine models

Haynes Publishing Group

Sparkford Nr Yeovil
Somerset BA22 7JJ England

Haynes North America, Inc

859 Lawrence Drive
Newbury Park
California 91320 USA
www.haynes.com

Acknowledgements

Technical writers who contributed to this project include Demian Hurst and Scott "Gonzo" Weaver.

© Haynes North America, Inc. 2016

With permission from J.H. Haynes & Co. Ltd.

A book in the Haynes Automotive Repair Manual Series

Printed in Malaysia

ISBN-13: 978-1-62092-254-5
ISBN-10: 1-62092-254-1

Library of Congress Control Number: 2016954674

Contents

Haynes mechanic and photographer with a 2015 Chevrolet 1500 pick-up

About this manual

Its purpose

The purpose of this manual is to help you get the best value from your vehicle. It can do so in several ways. It can help you decide what work must be done, even if you choose to have it done by a dealer service department or a repair shop; it provides information and procedures for routine maintenance and servicing; and it offers diagnostic and repair procedures to follow when trouble occurs.

We hope you use the manual to tackle the work yourself. For many simpler jobs, doing it yourself may be quicker than arranging an appointment to get the vehicle into a shop and making the trips to leave it and pick it up. More importantly, a lot of money can be saved by avoiding the expense the shop must pass on to you to cover its labor and overhead costs. An added benefit is the sense of satisfaction and accomplishment that you feel after doing the job yourself.

Using the manual

The manual is divided into Chapters. Each Chapter is divided into numbered Sections, which are headed in bold type between horizontal lines. Each Section consists of consecutively numbered paragraphs.

The reference numbers used in illustration captions pinpoint the pertinent Section and the Step within that Section. That is, illustration 3.2 means the illustration refers to Section 3 and Step (or paragraph) 2 within that Section.

Procedures, once described in the text, are not normally repeated. When it's necessary to refer to another Chapter, the reference will be given as Chapter and Section number. Cross references given without use of the word "Chapter" apply to Sections and/or paragraphs in the same Chapter. For example, "see Section 8" means in the same Chapter.

References to the left or right side of the vehicle assume you are sitting in the driver's seat, facing forward.

Even though we have prepared this manual with extreme care, neither the publisher nor the author can accept responsibility for any errors in, or omissions from, the information given.

NOTE

A **Note** provides information necessary to properly complete a procedure or information which will make the procedure easier to understand.

CAUTION

A **Caution** provides a special procedure or special steps which must be taken while completing the procedure where the Caution is found. Not heeding a Caution can result in damage to the assembly being worked on.

WARNING

A **Warning** provides a special procedure or special steps which must be taken while completing the procedure where the Warning is found. Not heeding a Warning can result in personal injury.

Introduction

The chassis layout on the models covered by this manual is conventional with the engine mounted at the front and the power being transmitted through either a six-speed or eight-speed automatic transmission or driveshaft to the rear axle. On 4WD models, a transfer case transmits the power to the front differential and then to the front wheels through independent driveaxles.

Engines are either V6 or V8, equipped with electronic, sequential multi-port fuel injection.

These models feature independent front suspension with coil-over shock absorbers (1500 models) or torsion bars and shock absorbers (2500 and 3500 models). At the rear, all models have a solid rear axle supported by leaf springs and shock absorbers on pick-ups, and coil springs, upper and lower control arms and shock absorbers on SUV models.

The power-assisted steering is either rack-and-pinion or conventional recirculating ball type. The rack-and-pinion steering unit is mounted in front of the engine and the conventional steering box is located on the left-side frame rail.

Vehicle identification numbers

Modifications are a continuing and unpublicized process in vehicle manufacturing. Since spare parts manuals and lists are compiled on a numerical basis, the individual vehicle numbers are essential to correctly identify the component required.

Vehicle Identification Number (VIN)

The Vehicle Identification Number (VIN), which appears on the Vehicle Certificate of Title and Registration, is also embossed on a gray plate located on the upper left (driver's side) corner of the dashboard, near the windshield (see illustration). The VIN tells you when and where a vehicle was manufactured, its country of origin, make, type, passenger safety system, line, series, body style, engine and assembly plant.

VIN engine and model year codes

Two particularly important pieces of information found in the VIN are the engine code and the model year code. Counting from the left, the engine code letter designation is the 8th character and the model year code is the 10th character.

On the model years covered by this manual the engine codes are:

H 4.3L V6 (LV3)
P 4.3L V6 (LV1)
C 5.3L V8 (L83)
B 6.0L V8 (LC8)
G 6.0L V8 (L96)
J 6.2L V8 (L86)

On the models covered by this manual the model year codes are:

E 2014
F 2015
G 2016

Vehicle Safety Certification label

The Vehicle Safety Certification label is attached to the rear edge of the driver's door (see illustration). The label contains the name of the manufacturer, the month and year of production, the Gross Vehicle Weight Rating (GVWR), the Gross Axle Weight Rating (GAWR) and the certification statement. On most models, the label also includes the OEM tire sizes and pressures.

Engine Identification Number (EIN)

The Engine Identification Number (EIN) is stamped into the rear of the engine block just below the left cylinder head.

The VIN plate is visible from the outside of the vehicle, through the driver's side of the windshield

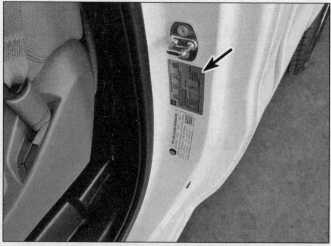

The Vehicle Safety Certification label is affixed to the driver's side door end or post

The service parts identification label is located in the glove box

Service parts identification or Regular Production Option (RPO) code label

This label is located in the glove box (see illustration). It lists the VIN, paint number, options and other information specific to the vehicle. You may sometimes need to refer to this label when you order parts.

Recall information

Vehicle recalls are carried out by the manufacturer in the rare event of a possible safety-related defect. The vehicle's registered owner is contacted at the address on file at the Department of Motor Vehicles and given the details of the recall. Remedial work is carried out free of charge at a dealer service department.

If you are the new owner of a used vehicle which was subject to a recall and you want to be sure that the work has been carried out, it's best to contact a dealer service department and ask about your individual vehicle - you'll need to furnish them your Vehicle Identification Number (VIN).

The table below is based on information provided by the National Highway Traffic Safety Administration (NHTSA), the body which oversees vehicle recalls in the United States. The recall database is updated constantly. For the latest information on vehicle recalls, check the NHTSA website at www.nhtsa.gov, www.safercar.gov, or call the NHTSA hotline at 1-888-327-4236.

Recall date	Recall campaign number	Model(s) affected	Concern
Jul 19, 2013	13V315000	2014 Silverado, Sierra	Certain model trucks may have welding on the passenger airbag inflator that may fracture when the airbag is deployed, allowing some gas from the airbag inflator to vent behind the instrument panel, instead of into the airbag. As a result, the airbag may not fully inflate, increasing the risk of injury.
Aug 06, 2013	13V342000	2014 Suburban, Tahoe, Yukon, Yukon XL	On some models, the rear brake caliper bolts may not be fully tightened. Loose caliper bolts may cause reduced braking performance and result in lengthened stopping distances, increasing the risk of a crash.

Recall date	Recall campaign number	Model(s) affected	Concern
Oct 17, 2013	13V488000	2014 Silverado, Sierra 1500	On some models with manual reclining seatbacks, either of the front seatbacks may have play. If the vehicle is struck from behind, the head restraint may not properly protect occupants, increasing the risk of injury.
Jan 13, 2014	14V007000	2014 2015 Silverado 1500, HD, Sierra 1500, HD, Yukon, Yukon XL, Cadillac Escalade	On some models equipped with the 4.3L and 5.3L engine, the exhaust components, when overheated, may melt nearby plastic parts and may result in an engine fire.
Mar 31, 2014	14V152000	2014 Siverado, Sierra, 1500 series, 2015 Suburban, Tahoe, Yukon, Yukon XL	GM is recalling certain vehicles equipped with a 6-Speed Automatic Transmission (RPO code MYC). The subject vehicles may have a transmission oil cooler line that is not securely seated in the fitting. If the line is not securely seated and transmission oil leaks from the fitting, the oil could contact a hot surface and cause a fire.
May 14, 2014	14V246000	2014 Silverado, Sierra, 2015 Tahoe	On some models the tie-rod threaded attachment may not be properly tightened to the steering gear rack. An improperly tightened tie-rod attachment may allow the tie-rod to separate from the steering rack, resulting in a loss of steering, increasing the risk of a crash.
May 16, 2014	14V259000	2015 Cadillac Escalade	On some models, the airbag module is secured to a chute adhered to the backside of the instrument panel with an insufficiently heated infrared weld. This may result in only a partial deployment of the front passenger airbag, increasing the risk of occupant injury.
Jun 06, 2014	14V301000	2014 Silverado, Sierra, 2015 Silverado, Sierra, Tahoe, Suburban	On some models with a base radio and an internal amplifier, the radio may become inoperative, and as a result, there would be no audible chime to notify the driver if the door is opened with the key in the ignition or no audible seat belt warning indicating the seat belts were not buckled. Without an audible indicator, the driver may not be aware that the driver's door is open while the key is in the ignition, increasing the risk of a vehicle rollaway. Additionally, there would be no reminder that the driver's or front seat passenger's seat belt is not buckled, which could increase the risk of injury in a crash.
Jun 18, 2014	14V345000	2014 Silverado, Sierra	Some models with both optional accessory all-weather floor mats (RPO VAV) and optional vinyl flooring (RPO BG9), do not have the retention features necessary to properly secure the floor mat on the driver's side. The floor mat could shift such that it could interfere with the accelerator pedal, preventing its return to an idle position, which could result in unintended vehicle speeds, increasing the risk of a crash.

Recall date	Recall campaign number	Model(s) affected	Concern
Jun 27, 2014	14V374000	2014 Silverado, Sierra, 2015 Silverado, Sierra, Yukon, Suburban, Tahoe	On some models, an electrical signal short may cause the transfer case to shift to neutral without the driver's input. If the transfer case switches to neutral while the vehicle is parked and the parking brake is not in use, the vehicle may roll away increasing the risk of injury to bystanders. If the transfer case switches to neutral while the vehicle is being driven, the vehicle would lose drive power, increasing the risk of a crash.
Jul 23, 2014	14V446000	2014, 2015 Silverado, Sierra	Some models may have had an incomplete weld on the seat hook bracket assembly. The front seats in the affected vehicles may not stay secured in place during a high load condition such as a crash. A seat that does not stay secured increases the risk of occupant injury in a crash.
Jul 23, 2014	14V451000	2015 Suburban, Tahoe, Yukon, Yukon XL	Some models have roof rail airbags (RRAB) that were not reinforced at the points where the bags contact the hardware used to attach the roof carrier. During deployment, the RRAB may be punctured or torn by the roof carrier hardware, reducing its performance and increasing the risk of occupant injury in the event of a crash.
Oct 01, 2014	14V614000	2014 Silverado, Suburban, Tahoe, Yukon, Yukon XL, Silverado HD, Sierra HD, Cadillac Escalade	Some models may have a chassis electronic module with internal contamination, resulting in an electrical short. If the module experiences an electrical short, the vehicle could stall, increasing the risk of a crash.
Oct 06, 2014	14V624000	2015 Cadillac Escalade	On some models, the passenger side instrument panel top cover may have been manufactured using an incorrect spacer fabric, causing a reduction of adhesion between the spacer fabric and the vinyl show surface. This reduced adhesion may result in inconsistent passenger airbag deployment, which increases the risk of injury in the event of a crash necessitating airbag deployment.
Nov 10, 2014	14V719000	2015 Silverado, Suburban, Tahoe, Sierra, Yukon XL	Some models with Electric Power Steering (EPS) may experience a sudden loss of power steering assist during operation. An unexpected loss of power steering increases the risk of a crash.
Dec 24, 2014	14V819000	2015 Silverado 1500, Sierra 1500	On some models, due to an improper heat-treatment, the rear axleshaft may fracture while the vehicle is being driven. If the rear axle shaft fractures, the rear wheel may separate from the axleshaft, increasing the risk of a crash.

Recall date	Recall campaign number	Model(s) affected	Concern
Oct 09, 2015	15V640000	2014 Silverado, Sierra, Suburban, Tahoe, 2015 Silverado, Suburban, Sierra	Some models have an ignition lock actuator that may bind, making turning the key difficult or causing the ignition to get stuck in the "Start" position. If stuck in the "Start" position, the ignition may suddenly snap back into the "Accessory" position, causing a loss of engine, steering, and braking power, increasing the risk of a crash. If the vehicle is in a crash, the airbags may not deploy, increasing the risk of occupant injury.
Dec 10, 2015	15V830000	2016 Silverado, Sierra	On some models, a mounting stud used to secure the airbag Sensing and Diagnostic Module (SDM) may be incorrectly positioned. As a result, the SDM housing could fracture. If the SDM housing fractures, water may get into SDM causing it to malfunction and hinder the proper deployment of the airbags in the event of a crash, thereby increasing the risk of occupant injury.
Feb 05, 2016	16V069000	2015, 2016 Siverado 2500, 3500, Sierra 2500, 3500	On some models, the brake pedal pivot nut may loosen, causing the brake pedal to be loose or inoperative. If the brake pedal becomes loose or inoperative, the driver may be unable to stop the vehicle by using the brake pedal. Additionally, a loose pedal may also interfere with the accelerator pedal. Either condition may increase the risk of a crash.
Feb 11, 2016	16V084000	2016 Silverado, Sierra	On some models, the radio may intermittently fail to provide an audio warning when the key has been left in the ignition and the door is opened or when the driver does not fasten their seat belt. An unbelted driver is at a greater risk of injury in a crash.
Apr 12, 2016	16V209000	2014, 2015 Silverado 1500, Sierra 1500	When entering the vehicle on some models, the seat belt tensioner cable may be positioned such that the driver slides over it. This movement may result in the fatigue and separation of the cable. If the tensioner cable separates, the driver may not be properly restrained in the event of a crash, increasing their risk of injury.
Apr 28, 2016	16V256000	2016 Silverado, Suburban, Tahoe, Sierra, Yukon, Yukon XL, Cadillac Escalade	On some models, the front upper control arms may have inadequate welds near the control arm bushing. Inadequate welds may allow the control arm to separate from the bushing, compromising steering and increasing the risk of a crash.

Buying parts

Replacement parts are available from many sources, which generally fall into one of two categories - authorized dealer parts departments and independent retail auto parts stores. Our advice concerning these parts is as follows.

Retail auto parts stores: Good auto parts stores will stock frequently needed components which wear out relatively fast, such as clutch components, exhaust systems, brake parts, tune-up parts, etc. These stores often supply new or reconditioned parts on an exchange basis, which can save a considerable amount of money. Discount auto parts stores are often very good places to buy materials and parts needed for general vehicle maintenance such as oil, grease, filters, spark plugs, belts, touch-up paint, bulbs, etc. They also usually sell tools and general accessories, have convenient hours, charge lower prices and can often be found not far from home.

Authorized dealer parts department: This is the best source for parts which are unique to the vehicle and not generally available elsewhere (such as major engine parts, transmission parts, trim pieces, etc.).

Warranty information: If the vehicle is still covered under warranty, be sure that any replacement parts purchased - regardless of the source - do not invalidate the warranty!

To be sure of obtaining the correct parts, have engine and chassis numbers available and, if possible, take the old parts along for positive identification.

Maintenance techniques, tools and working facilities

Maintenance techniques

There are a number of techniques involved in maintenance and repair that will be referred to throughout this manual. Application of these techniques will enable the home mechanic to be more efficient, better organized and capable of performing the various tasks properly, which will ensure that the repair job is thorough and complete.

Fasteners

Fasteners are nuts, bolts, studs and screws used to hold two or more parts together. There are a few things to keep in mind when working with fasteners. Almost all of them use a locking device of some type, either a lockwasher, locknut, locking tab or thread adhesive. All threaded fasteners should be clean and straight, with undamaged threads and undamaged corners on the hex head where the wrench fits. Develop the habit of replacing all damaged nuts and bolts with new ones. Special locknuts with nylon or fiber inserts can only be used once. If they are removed, they lose their locking ability and must be replaced with new ones.

Rusted nuts and bolts should be treated with a penetrating fluid to ease removal and prevent breakage. Some mechanics use turpentine in a spout-type oil can, which works quite well. After applying the rust penetrant, let it work for a few minutes before trying to loosen the nut or bolt. Badly rusted fasteners may have to be chiseled or sawed off or removed with a special nut breaker, available at tool stores.

If a bolt or stud breaks off in an assembly, it can be drilled and removed with a special tool commonly available for this purpose. Most automotive machine shops can perform this task, as well as other repair procedures, such as the repair of threaded holes that have been stripped out.

Flat washers and lockwashers, when removed from an assembly, should always be replaced exactly as removed. Replace any damaged washers with new ones. Never use a lockwasher on any soft metal surface (such as aluminum), thin sheet metal or plastic.

Fastener sizes

For a number of reasons, automobile manufacturers are making wider and wider use of metric fasteners. Therefore, it is important to be able to tell the difference between standard (sometimes called U.S. or SAE) and metric hardware, since they cannot be interchanged.

All bolts, whether standard or metric, are sized according to diameter, thread pitch and length. For example, a standard 1/2 - 13 x 1 bolt is 1/2 inch in diameter, has 13 threads per inch and is 1 inch long. An M12 - 1.75 x 25 metric bolt is 12 mm in diameter, has a thread pitch of 1.75 mm (the distance between threads) and is 25 mm long. The two bolts are nearly identical, and easily confused, but they are not interchangeable.

In addition to the differences in diameter, thread pitch and length, metric and standard bolts can also be distinguished by examining the bolt heads. To begin with, the distance across the flats on a standard bolt head is measured in inches, while the same dimension on a metric bolt is sized in millimeters (the same is true for nuts). As a result, a standard wrench should not be used on a metric bolt and a metric wrench should not be used on a standard bolt. Also, most standard bolts have slashes radiating out from the center of the head to denote the grade or strength of the bolt, which is an indication of the amount of torque that can be applied to it. The greater the number of slashes, the greater the strength of the bolt. Grades 0 through 5 are commonly used on automobiles. Metric bolts have a property class (grade) number, rather than a slash, molded into their heads to indicate bolt strength. In this case, the higher the number, the stronger the bolt. Property class numbers 8.8, 9.8 and 10.9 are commonly used on automobiles.

Strength markings can also be used to distinguish standard hex nuts from metric hex nuts. Many standard nuts have dots stamped into one side, while metric nuts are marked with a number. The greater the number of

dots, or the higher the number, the greater the strength of the nut.

Metric studs are also marked on their ends according to property class (grade). Larger studs are numbered (the same as metric bolts), while smaller studs carry a geometric code to denote grade.

It should be noted that many fasteners, especially Grades 0 through 2, have no distinguishing marks on them. When such is the case, the only way to determine whether it is standard or metric is to measure the thread pitch or compare it to a known fastener of the same size.

Standard fasteners are often referred to as SAE, as opposed to metric. However, it should be noted that SAE technically refers to a non-metric fine thread fastener only. Coarse thread non-metric fasteners are referred to as USS sizes.

Since fasteners of the same size (both standard and metric) may have different

strength ratings, be sure to reinstall any bolts, studs or nuts removed from your vehicle in their original locations. Also, when replacing a fastener with a new one, make sure that the new one has a strength rating equal to or greater than the original.

Tightening sequences and procedures

Most threaded fasteners should be tightened to a specific torque value (torque is the twisting force applied to a threaded component such as a nut or bolt). Overtightening the fastener can weaken it and cause it to break, while undertightening can cause it to eventually come loose. Bolts, screws and studs, depending on the material they are made of and their thread diameters, have specific torque values, many of which are noted in the Specifications at the beginning of each Chapter. Be sure to follow the torque recommen-

Grade 1 or 2   Grade 5   Grade 8

Bolt strength marking (standard/SAE/USS; bottom - metric)

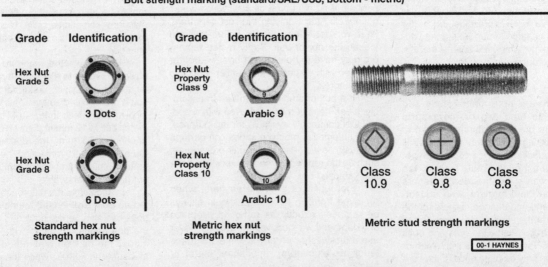

Grade	Identification
Hex Nut Grade 5	3 Dots
Hex Nut Grade 8	6 Dots

Standard hex nut strength markings

Grade	Identification
Hex Nut Property Class 9	Arabic 9
Hex Nut Property Class 10	Arabic 10

Metric hex nut strength markings

Class 10.9   Class 9.8   Class 8.8

Metric stud strength markings

00-1 HAYNES

dations closely. For fasteners not assigned a specific torque, a general torque value chart is presented here as a guide. These torque values are for dry (unlubricated) fasteners threaded into steel or cast iron (not aluminum). As was previously mentioned, the size and grade of a fastener determine the amount of torque that can safely be applied to it. The figures listed here are approximate for Grade 2 and Grade 3 fasteners. Higher grades can tolerate higher torque values.

Fasteners laid out in a pattern, such as cylinder head bolts, oil pan bolts, differential cover bolts, etc., must be loosened or tightened in sequence to avoid warping the component. This sequence will normally be shown in the appropriate Chapter. If a specific pattern is not given, the following procedures can be used to prevent warping.

Initially, the bolts or nuts should be assembled finger-tight only. Next, they should be tightened one full turn each, in a criss-cross or diagonal pattern. After each one has been tightened one full turn, return to the first one and tighten them all one-half turn, following the same pattern. Finally, tighten each of them one-quarter turn at a time until each fastener has been tightened to the proper torque. To loosen and remove the fasteners, the procedure would be reversed.

Metric thread sizes

	Ft-lbs	Nm
M-6	6 to 9	9 to 12
M-8	14 to 21	19 to 28
M-10	28 to 40	38 to 54
M-12	50 to 71	68 to 96
M-14	80 to 140	109 to 154

Pipe thread sizes

1/8	5 to 8	7 to 10
1/4	12 to 18	17 to 24
3/8	22 to 33	30 to 44
1/2	25 to 35	34 to 47

U.S. thread sizes

1/4 - 20	6 to 9	9 to 12
5/16 - 18	12 to 18	17 to 24
5/16 - 24	14 to 20	19 to 27
3/8 - 16	22 to 32	30 to 43
3/8 - 24	27 to 38	37 to 51
7/16 - 14	40 to 55	55 to 74
7/16 - 20	40 to 60	55 to 81
1/2 - 13	55 to 80	75 to 108

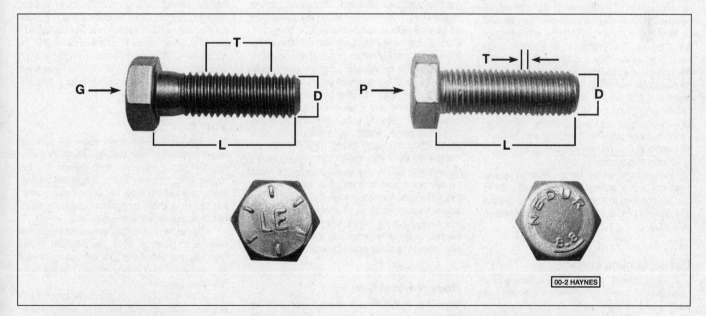

Standard (SAE and USS) bolt dimensions/grade marks	Metric bolt dimensions/grade marks
G Grade marks (bolt strength)	P Property class (bolt strength)
L Length (in inches)	L Length (in millimeters)
T Thread pitch (number of threads per inch)	T Thread pitch (distance between threads in millimeters)
D Nominal diameter (in inches)	D Diameter

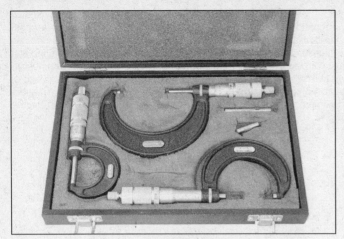

Micrometer set

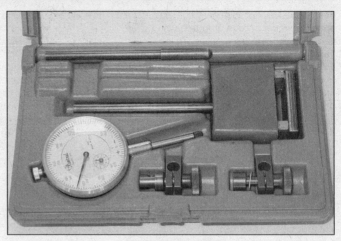

Dial indicator set

Component disassembly

Component disassembly should be done with care and purpose to help ensure that the parts go back together properly. Always keep track of the sequence in which parts are removed. Make note of special characteristics or marks on parts that can be installed more than one way, such as a grooved thrust washer on a shaft. It is a good idea to lay the disassembled parts out on a clean surface in the order that they were removed. It may also be helpful to make sketches or take instant photos of components before removal.

When removing fasteners from a component, keep track of their locations. Sometimes threading a bolt back in a part, or putting the washers and nut back on a stud, can prevent mix-ups later. If nuts and bolts cannot be returned to their original locations, they should be kept in a compartmented box or a series of small boxes. A cupcake or muffin tin is ideal for this purpose, since each cavity can hold the bolts and nuts from a particular area (i.e. oil pan bolts, valve cover bolts, engine mount bolts, etc.). A pan of this type is especially helpful when working on assemblies with very small parts, such as the carburetor, alternator, valve train or interior dash and trim pieces. The cavities can be marked with paint or tape to identify the contents.

Whenever wiring looms, harnesses or connectors are separated, it is a good idea to identify the two halves with numbered pieces of masking tape so they can be easily reconnected.

Gasket sealing surfaces

Throughout any vehicle, gaskets are used to seal the mating surfaces between two parts and keep lubricants, fluids, vacuum or pressure contained in an assembly.

Many times these gaskets are coated with a liquid or paste-type gasket sealing compound before assembly. Age, heat and pressure can sometimes cause the two parts to stick together so tightly that they are very difficult to separate. Often, the assembly can

be loosened by striking it with a soft-face hammer near the mating surfaces. A regular hammer can be used if a block of wood is placed between the hammer and the part. Do not hammer on cast parts or parts that could be easily damaged. With any particularly stubborn part, always recheck to make sure that every fastener has been removed.

Avoid using a screwdriver or bar to pry apart an assembly, as they can easily mar the gasket sealing surfaces of the parts, which must remain smooth. If prying is absolutely necessary, use an old broom handle, but keep in mind that extra clean up will be necessary if the wood splinters.

After the parts are separated, the old gasket must be carefully scraped off and the gasket surfaces cleaned. Stubborn gasket material can be soaked with rust penetrant or treated with a special chemical to soften it so it can be easily scraped off. **Caution:** *Never use gasket removal solutions or caustic chemicals on plastic or other composite components.* A scraper can be fashioned from a piece of copper tubing by flattening and sharpening one end. Copper is recommended because it is usually softer than the surfaces to be scraped, which reduces the chance of gouging the part. Some gaskets can be removed with a wire brush, but regardless of the method used, the mating surfaces must be left clean and smooth. If for some reason the gasket surface is gouged, then a gasket sealer thick enough to fill scratches will have to be used during reassembly of the components. For most applications, a non-drying (or semi-drying) gasket sealer should be used.

Hose removal tips

Warning: *If the vehicle is equipped with air conditioning, do not disconnect any of the A/C hoses without first having the system depressurized by a dealer service department or a service station.*

Hose removal precautions closely parallel gasket removal precautions. Avoid scratching or gouging the surface that the

hose mates against or the connection may leak. This is especially true for radiator hoses. Because of various chemical reactions, the rubber in hoses can bond itself to the metal spigot that the hose fits over. To remove a hose, first loosen the hose clamps that secure it to the spigot. Then, with slip-joint pliers, grab the hose at the clamp and rotate it around the spigot. Work it back and forth until it is completely free, then pull it off. Silicone or other lubricants will ease removal if they can be applied between the hose and the outside of the spigot. Apply the same lubricant to the inside of the hose and the outside of the spigot to simplify installation.

As a last resort (and if the hose is to be replaced with a new one anyway), the rubber can be slit with a knife and the hose peeled from the spigot. If this must be done, be careful that the metal connection is not damaged.

If a hose clamp is broken or damaged, do not reuse it. Wire-type clamps usually weaken with age, so it is a good idea to replace them with screw-type clamps whenever a hose is removed.

Tools

A selection of good tools is a basic requirement for anyone who plans to maintain and repair his or her own vehicle. For the owner who has few tools, the initial investment might seem high, but when compared to the spiraling costs of professional auto maintenance and repair, it is a wise one.

To help the owner decide which tools are needed to perform the tasks detailed in this manual, the following tool lists are offered: *Maintenance and minor repair, Repair/overhaul* and *Special.*

The newcomer to practical mechanics should start off with the *maintenance and minor repair* tool kit, which is adequate for the simpler jobs performed on a vehicle. Then, as confidence and experience grow, the owner can tackle more difficult tasks, buying additional tools as they are needed. Eventually the basic kit will be expanded into the *repair and overhaul* tool set. Over a period of time, the

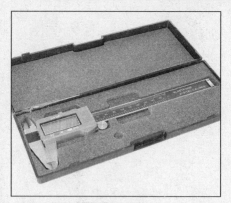

Dial caliper

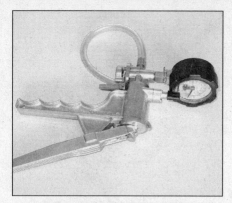

Hand-operated vacuum pump

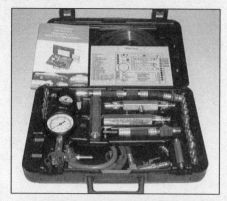

Fuel pressure gauge set

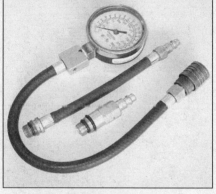

Compression gauge with spark plug hole adapter

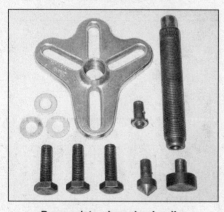

Damper/steering wheel puller

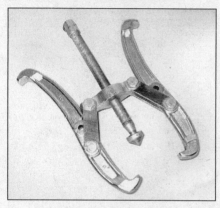

General purpose puller

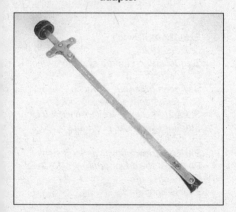

Hydraulic lifter removal tool

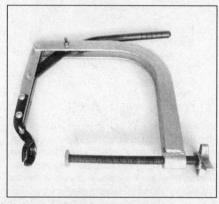

Valve spring compressor

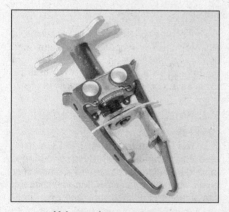

Valve spring compressor

Ridge reamer

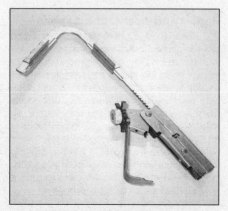

Piston ring groove cleaning tool

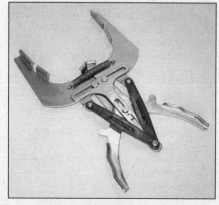

Ring removal/installation tool

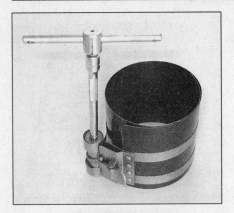

Ring compressor

Cylinder hone

Brake hold-down spring tool

Torque angle gauge

Clutch plate alignment tool

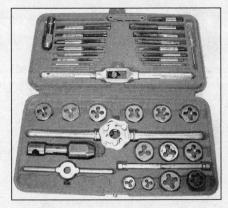

Tap and die set

experienced do-it-yourselfer will assemble a tool set complete enough for most repair and overhaul procedures and will add tools from the special category when it is felt that the expense is justified by the frequency of use.

Maintenance and minor repair tool kit

The tools in this list should be considered the minimum required for performance of routine maintenance, servicing and minor repair work. We recommend the purchase of combination wrenches (box-end and open-end combined in one wrench). While more expensive than open end wrenches, they offer the advantages of both types of wrench.

*Combination wrench set (1/4-inch to
    1 inch or 6 mm to 19 mm)*
Adjustable wrench, 8 inch
Spark plug wrench with rubber insert
Spark plug gap adjusting tool
Feeler gauge set
Brake bleeder wrench
*Standard screwdriver (5/16-inch x
    6 inch)*
Phillips screwdriver (No. 2 x 6 inch)
Combination pliers - 6 inch
Hacksaw and assortment of blades
Tire pressure gauge
Grease gun
Oil can
Fine emery cloth

Wire brush
Battery post and cable cleaning tool
Oil filter wrench
Funnel (medium size)
Safety goggles
Jackstands (2)
Drain pan

Note: *If basic tune-ups are going to be part of routine maintenance, it will be necessary to purchase a good quality stroboscopic timing light and combination tachometer/dwell meter. Although they are included in the list of special tools, it is mentioned here because they are absolutely necessary for tuning most vehicles properly.*

Repair and overhaul tool set

These tools are essential for anyone who plans to perform major repairs and are in addition to those in the maintenance and minor repair tool kit. Included is a comprehensive set of sockets which, though expensive, are invaluable because of their versatility, especially when various extensions and drives are available. We recommend the 1/2-inch drive over the 3/8-inch drive. Although the larger drive is bulky and more expensive, it has the capacity of accepting a very wide range of large sockets. Ideally, however, the mechanic should have a 3/8-inch drive set and a 1/2-inch drive set.

Socket set(s)
Reversible ratchet

Extension - 10 inch
Universal joint
*Torque wrench (same size drive as
    sockets)*
Ball peen hammer - 8 ounce
Soft-face hammer (plastic/rubber)
Standard screwdriver (1/4-inch x 6 inch)
*Standard screwdriver (stubby -
    5/16-inch)*
Phillips screwdriver (No. 3 x 8 inch)
Phillips screwdriver (stubby - No. 2)
Pliers - vise grip
Pliers - lineman's
Pliers - needle nose
Pliers - snap-ring (internal and external)
Cold chisel - 1/2-inch
Scribe
*Scraper (made from flattened copper
    tubing)*
Centerpunch
Pin punches (1/16, 1/8, 3/16-inch)
Steel rule/straightedge - 12 inch
*Allen wrench set (1/8 to 3/8-inch or
    4 mm to 10 mm)*
A selection of files
Wire brush (large)
Jackstands (second set)
Jack (scissor or hydraulic type)

Note: *Another tool which is often useful is an electric drill with a chuck capacity of 3/8-inch and a set of good quality drill bits.*

Special tools

The tools in this list include those which are not used regularly, are expensive to buy, or which need to be used in accordance with their manufacturer's instructions. Unless these tools will be used frequently, it is not very economical to purchase many of them. A consideration would be to split the cost and use between yourself and a friend or friends. In addition, most of these tools can be obtained from a tool rental shop on a temporary basis.

This list primarily contains only those tools and instruments widely available to the public, and not those special tools produced by the vehicle manufacturer for distribution to dealer service departments. Occasionally, references to the manufacturer's special tools are included in the text of this manual. Generally, an alternative method of doing the job without the special tool is offered. However, sometimes there is no alternative to their use. Where this is the case, and the tool cannot be purchased or borrowed, the work should be turned over to the dealer service department or an automotive repair shop.

Valve spring compressor
Piston ring groove cleaning tool
Piston ring compressor
Piston ring installation tool
Cylinder compression gauge
Cylinder ridge reamer
Cylinder surfacing hone
Cylinder bore gauge
Micrometers and/or dial calipers
Hydraulic lifter removal tool
Balljoint separator
Universal-type puller
Impact screwdriver
Dial indicator set
Stroboscopic timing light (inductive
*   pick-up)*
Hand operated vacuum/pressure pump
Tachometer/dwell meter
Universal electrical multimeter
Cable hoist
Brake spring removal and installation
*   tools*
Floor jack

Buying tools

For the do-it-yourselfer who is just starting to get involved in vehicle maintenance and repair, there are a number of options available when purchasing tools. If maintenance and minor repair is the extent of the work to be done, the purchase of individual tools is satisfactory. If, on the other hand, extensive work is planned, it would be a good idea to purchase a modest tool set from one of the large retail chain stores. A set can usually be bought at a substantial savings over the individual tool prices, and they often come with a tool box. As additional tools are needed, add-on sets, individual tools and a larger tool box can be purchased to expand the tool selection. Building a tool set gradually allows the cost of the tools to be spread over a longer period of time and gives the mechanic the freedom to choose only those tools that will actually be used.

Tool stores will often be the only source of some of the special tools that are needed, but regardless of where tools are bought, try to avoid cheap ones, especially when buying screwdrivers and sockets, because they won't last very long. The expense involved in replacing cheap tools will eventually be greater than the initial cost of quality tools.

Care and maintenance of tools

Good tools are expensive, so it makes sense to treat them with respect. Keep them clean and in usable condition and store them properly when not in use. Always wipe off any dirt, grease or metal chips before putting them away. Never leave tools lying around in the work area. Upon completion of a job, always check closely under the hood for tools that may have been left there so they won't get lost during a test drive.

Some tools, such as screwdrivers, pliers, wrenches and sockets, can be hung on a panel mounted on the garage or workshop wall, while others should be kept in a tool box or tray. Measuring instruments, gauges, meters, etc. must be carefully stored where they cannot be damaged by weather or impact from other tools.

When tools are used with care and stored properly, they will last a very long time. Even with the best of care, though, tools will wear out if used frequently. When a tool is damaged or worn out, replace it. Subsequent jobs will be safer and more enjoyable if you do.

How to repair damaged threads

Sometimes, the internal threads of a nut or bolt hole can become stripped, usually from overtightening. Stripping threads is an all-too-common occurrence, especially when working with aluminum parts, because aluminum is so soft that it easily strips out.

Usually, external or internal threads are only partially stripped. After they've been cleaned up with a tap or die, they'll still work. Sometimes, however, threads are badly damaged. When this happens, you've got three choices:

1) *Drill and tap the hole to the next suitable oversize and install a larger diameter bolt, screw or stud.*
2) *Drill and tap the hole to accept a threaded plug, then drill and tap the plug to the original screw size. You can also buy a plug already threaded to the original size. Then you simply drill a hole to the specified size, then run the threaded plug into the hole with a bolt and jam nut. Once the plug is fully seated, remove the jam nut and bolt.*
3) *The third method uses a patented thread repair kit like Heli-Coil or Slimsert. These easy-to-use kits are designed to repair damaged threads in straight-through holes and blind holes. Both are available as kits which can handle a variety of sizes and thread patterns. Drill the hole, then tap it with the special included tap. Install the Heli-Coil and the hole is back to its original diameter and thread pitch.*

Regardless of which method you use, be sure to proceed calmly and carefully. A little impatience or carelessness during one of these relatively simple procedures can ruin your whole day's work and cost you a bundle if you wreck an expensive part.

Working facilities

Not to be overlooked when discussing tools is the workshop. If anything more than routine maintenance is to be carried out, some sort of suitable work area is essential.

It is understood, and appreciated, that many home mechanics do not have a good workshop or garage available, and end up removing an engine or doing major repairs outside. It is recommended, however, that the overhaul or repair be completed under the cover of a roof.

A clean, flat workbench or table of comfortable working height is an absolute necessity. The workbench should be equipped with a vise that has a jaw opening of at least four inches.

As mentioned previously, some clean, dry storage space is also required for tools, as well as the lubricants, fluids, cleaning solvents, etc. which soon become necessary.

Sometimes waste oil and fluids, drained from the engine or cooling system during normal maintenance or repairs, present a disposal problem. To avoid pouring them on the ground or into a sewage system, pour the used fluids into large containers, seal them with caps and take them to an authorized disposal site or recycling center. Plastic jugs, such as old antifreeze containers, are ideal for this purpose.

Always keep a supply of old newspapers and clean rags available. Old towels are excellent for mopping up spills. Many mechanics use rolls of paper towels for most work because they are readily available and disposable. To help keep the area under the vehicle clean, a large cardboard box can be cut open and flattened to protect the garage or shop floor.

Whenever working over a painted surface, such as when leaning over a fender to service something under the hood, always cover it with an old blanket or bedspread to protect the finish. Vinyl covered pads, made especially for this purpose, are available at auto parts stores.

Booster battery (jump) starting

1   Observe these precautions when using a booster battery to start a vehicle:

a) *Before connecting the booster battery, make sure the ignition switch is in the Off position.*

b) *Turn off the lights, heater and other electrical loads.*

c) *Your eyes should be shielded. Safety goggles are a good idea.*

d) *Make sure the booster battery is the same voltage as the dead one in the vehicle.*

e) *The two vehicles MUST NOT TOUCH each other!*

f) *Make sure the transmission is in Park (automatic).*

g) *If the booster battery is not a maintenance-free type, remove the vent caps and lay a cloth over the vent holes.*

2   The main battery on these vehicles (some models have an optional second battery) is located in the right-rear corner of the engine compartment.

3   Connect the red jumper cable to the positive (+) terminals of each battery.

Note: *The positive terminal on the battery in these vehicles is located under a protective red cover which must be flipped up.*

4   Connect one end of the black cable to the negative (-) terminal of the booster battery. The other end of this cable should be connected to a good ground on the engine, such as a bracket, or a bolt on the body (see illustration). Make sure the cable will not come into contact with the fan, drivebelts or other moving parts of the engine.

5   Start the engine using the booster battery, then run the booster vehicle at a fast idle for a few minutes to instill some charge in the dead battery. Let the engine idle, then disconnect the jumper cables in the reverse order of connection. The vehicle with the dead battery may have to be driven for 20 minutes or more to sufficiently recharge the battery for independent starting.

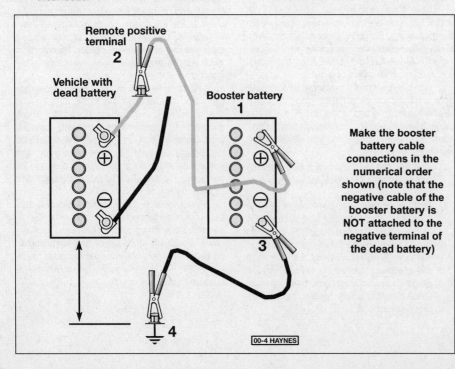

Remote positive terminal

2

Vehicle with dead battery

Booster battery

1

Make the booster battery cable connections in the numerical order shown (note that the negative cable of the booster battery is NOT attached to the negative terminal of the dead battery)

3

4

00-4 HAYNES

Jacking and towing

Jacking

1   The jack supplied with the vehicle should only be used for raising the vehicle when changing a tire or placing jackstands under the frame. NEVER work under the vehicle or start the engine when the vehicle is supported only by a jack.

2   The vehicle should be parked on level ground with the wheels blocked, the parking brake applied and the transmission in Park (automatic) or Reverse (manual). If the vehicle is parked alongside the roadway, or in any other hazardous situation, turn on the emergency hazard flashers. If a tire is to be changed, loosen the lug nuts one-half turn before raising off the ground.

3   Place the jack under the vehicle in the indicated positions (see illustrations). Operate the jack with a slow, smooth motion until the wheel is raised off the ground. Remove the lug nuts, pull off the wheel, install the spare and thread the lug nuts back on with the beveled side facing in. Tighten the lug nuts snugly, lower the vehicle until some weight is on the wheel, tighten them completely in a criss-cross pattern and remove the jack.

Towing

4   Equipment specifically designed for towing should be used and attached to the main structural members of the vehicle. Optional tow hooks may be attached to the frame at both ends of the vehicle; they are intended for emergency use only, for rescuing a stranded vehicle. Do not use the tow hooks for highway towing. Stand clear when using tow straps or chains (they may break, causing serious injury.)

5   Safety is a major consideration when towing and all applicable state and local laws must be obeyed. In addition to a tow bar, a safety chain must be used for all towing.

6   The manufacturer states that the best way to tow these vehicles is with wheel lift equipment or a flatbed car carrier.

7   Two-wheel drive vehicles may be towed from the rear with the rear wheels on a towing dolly. They should NOT be towed with the rear wheels on the ground, as this could damage the transmission.

8   Four-wheel drive models with a two-speed transfer case that has Neutral and 4-wheel drive Low ranges can be towed with all four wheels on the ground and the transfer case in Neutral. The following preliminary actions must be taken:

a)   Chock the wheels and release the parking brake.
b)   Shift the transfer case to Neutral.
c)   Start the engine, shift the transmission into Drive, the turn the engine off and place the shifter in Park.
d)   Wait at least ten seconds, then start the engine, shift into Drive, then turn the engine off.
e)   Disconnect the cable from the negative terminal of the battery. Make sure the cable cannot come into contact with the battery negative post.
f)   Place the shifter back into the Park position.
g)   Make sure the steering column is not locked (make sure the key is in the ACC position).

9   If any vehicle is to be towed with the front wheels on the ground and the rear wheels raised, the ignition key must be turned to the OFF position to unlock the steering column and a steering wheel clamping device designed for towing must be used or damage to the steering column lock may occur.

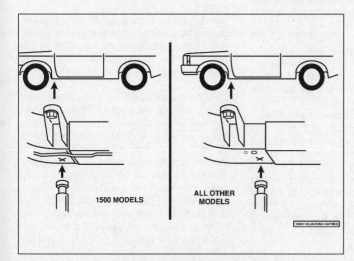

8.3a Front jacking position

8.3b Rear jacking position

Automotive chemicals and lubricants

A number of automotive chemicals and lubricants are available for use during vehicle maintenance and repair. They include a wide variety of products ranging from cleaning solvents and degreasers to lubricants and protective sprays for rubber, plastic and vinyl.

Cleaners

Carburetor cleaner and choke cleaner is a strong solvent for gum, varnish and carbon. Most carburetor cleaners leave a dry-type lubricant film which will not harden or gum up. Because of this film it is not recommended for use on electrical components.

Brake system cleaner is used to remove brake dust, grease and brake fluid from the brake system, where clean surfaces are absolutely necessary. It leaves no residue and often eliminates brake squeal caused by contaminants.

Electrical cleaner removes oxidation, corrosion and carbon deposits from electrical contacts, restoring full current flow. It can also be used to clean spark plugs, carburetor jets, voltage regulators and other parts where an oil-free surface is desired.

Demoisturants remove water and moisture from electrical components such as alternators, voltage regulators, electrical connectors and fuse blocks. They are non-conductive and non-corrosive.

Degreasers are heavy-duty solvents used to remove grease from the outside of the engine and from chassis components. They can be sprayed or brushed on and, depending on the type, are rinsed off either with water or solvent.

Lubricants

Motor oil is the lubricant formulated for use in engines. It normally contains a wide variety of additives to prevent corrosion and reduce foaming and wear. Motor oil comes in various weights (viscosity ratings) from 0 to 50. The recommended weight of the oil depends on the season, temperature and the demands on the engine. Light oil is used in cold climates and under light load conditions. Heavy oil is used in hot climates and where high loads are encountered. Multi-viscosity oils are designed to have characteristics of both light and heavy oils and are available in a number of weights from 0W-20 to 20W-50.

Gear oil is designed to be used in differentials, manual transmissions and other areas where high-temperature lubrication is required.

Chassis and wheel bearing grease is a heavy grease used where increased loads and friction are encountered, such as for wheel bearings, balljoints, tie-rod ends and universal joints.

High-temperature wheel bearing grease is designed to withstand the extreme temperatures encountered by wheel bearings in disc brake equipped vehicles. It usually contains molybdenum disulfide (moly), which is a dry-type lubricant.

White grease is a heavy grease for metal-to-metal applications where water is a problem. White grease stays soft under both low and high temperatures (usually from -100 to +190-degrees F), and will not wash off or dilute in the presence of water.

Assembly lube is a special extreme pressure lubricant, usually containing moly, used to lubricate high-load parts (such as main and rod bearings and cam lobes) for initial start-up of a new engine. The assembly lube lubricates the parts without being squeezed out or washed away until the engine oiling system begins to function.

Silicone lubricants are used to protect rubber, plastic, vinyl and nylon parts.

Graphite lubricants are used where oils cannot be used due to contamination problems, such as in locks. The dry graphite will lubricate metal parts while remaining uncontaminated by dirt, water, oil or acids. It is electrically conductive and will not foul electrical contacts in locks such as the ignition switch.

Moly penetrants loosen and lubricate frozen, rusted and corroded fasteners and prevent future rusting or freezing.

Heat-sink grease is a special electrically non-conductive grease that is used for mounting electronic ignition modules where it is essential that heat is transferred away from the module.

Sealants

RTV sealant is one of the most widely used gasket compounds. Made from silicone, RTV is air curing, it seals, bonds, waterproofs, fills surface irregularities, remains flexible, doesn't shrink, is relatively easy to remove, and is used as a supplementary sealer with almost all low and medium temperature gaskets.

Anaerobic sealant is much like RTV in that it can be used either to seal gaskets or to form gaskets by itself. It remains flexible, is solvent resistant and fills surface imperfections. The difference between an anaerobic sealant and an RTV-type sealant is in the curing. RTV cures when exposed to air, while an anaerobic sealant cures only in the absence of air. This means that an anaerobic sealant cures only after the assembly of parts, sealing them together.

Thread and pipe sealant is used for sealing hydraulic and pneumatic fittings and vacuum lines. It is usually made from a Teflon compound, and comes in a spray, a paint-on liquid and as a wrap-around tape.

Chemicals

Anti-seize compound prevents seizing, galling, cold welding, rust and corrosion in fasteners. High-temperature ant-seize, usually made with copper and graphite lubricants, is used for exhaust system and exhaust manifold bolts.

Anaerobic locking compounds are used to keep fasteners from vibrating or working loose and cure only after installation, in the absence of air. Medium strength locking compound is used for small nuts, bolts and screws that may be removed later. High-strength locking compound is for large nuts, bolts and studs which aren't removed on a regular basis.

Oil additives range from viscosity index improvers to chemical treatments that claim to reduce internal engine friction. It should be noted that most oil manufacturers caution against using additives with their oils.

Gas additives perform several functions, depending on their chemical makeup. They usually contain solvents that help dissolve gum and varnish that build up on carburetor, fuel injection and intake parts. They also serve to break down carbon deposits that form on the inside surfaces of the combustion chambers. Some additives contain upper cylinder lubricants for valves and piston rings, and others contain chemicals to remove condensation from the gas tank.

Miscellaneous

Brake fluid is specially formulated hydraulic fluid that can withstand the heat and pressure encountered in brake systems. Care must be taken so this fluid does not come in contact with painted surfaces or plastics. An opened container should always be resealed to prevent contamination by water or dirt.

Weatherstrip adhesive is used to bond weatherstripping around doors, windows and trunk lids. It is sometimes used to attach trim pieces.

Undercoating is a petroleum-based, tar-like substance that is designed to protect metal surfaces on the underside of the vehicle from corrosion. It also acts as a sound-deadening agent by insulating the bottom of the vehicle.

Waxes and polishes are used to help protect painted and plated surfaces from the weather. Different types of paint may require the use of different types of wax and polish. Some polishes utilize a chemical or abrasive cleaner to help remove the top layer of oxidized (dull) paint on older vehicles. In recent years many non-wax polishes that contain a wide variety of chemicals such as polymers and silicones have been introduced. These non-wax polishes are usually easier to apply and last longer than conventional waxes and polishes.

Conversion factors

Length (distance)
Inches (in)	X	25.4	= Millimeters (mm)	X 0.0394	= Inches (in)
Feet (ft)	X	0.305	= Meters (m)	X 3.281	= Feet (ft)
Miles	X	1.609	= Kilometers (km)	X 0.621	= Miles

Volume (capacity)
Cubic inches (cu in; in^3)	X	16.387	= Cubic centimeters (cc; cm^3)	X 0.061	= Cubic inches (cu in; in^3)
Imperial pints (Imp pt)	X	0.568	= Liters (l)	X 1.76	= Imperial pints (Imp pt)
Imperial quarts (Imp qt)	X	1.137	= Liters (l)	X 0.88	= Imperial quarts (Imp qt)
Imperial quarts (Imp qt)	X	1.201	= US quarts (US qt)	X 0.833	= Imperial quarts (Imp qt)
US quarts (US qt)	X	0.946	= Liters (l)	X 1.057	= US quarts (US qt)
Imperial gallons (Imp gal)	X	4.546	= Liters (l)	X 0.22	= Imperial gallons (Imp gal)
Imperial gallons (Imp gal)	X	1.201	= US gallons (US gal)	X 0.833	= Imperial gallons (Imp gal)
US gallons (US gal)	X	3.785	= Liters (l)	X 0.264	= US gallons (US gal)

Mass (weight)
Ounces (oz)	X	28.35	= Grams (g)	X 0.035	= Ounces (oz)
Pounds (lb)	X	0.454	= Kilograms (kg)	X 2.205	= Pounds (lb)

Force
Ounces-force (ozf; oz)	X	0.278	= Newtons (N)	X 3.6	= Ounces-force (ozf; oz)
Pounds-force (lbf; lb)	X	4.448	= Newtons (N)	X 0.225	= Pounds-force (lbf; lb)
Newtons (N)	X	0.1	= Kilograms-force (kgf; kg)	X 9.81	= Newtons (N)

Pressure
Pounds-force per square inch (psi; lbf/in^2; lb/in^2)	X	0.070	= Kilograms-force per square centimeter (kgf/cm^2; kg/cm^2)	X 14.223	= Pounds-force per square inch (psi; lbf/in^2; lb/in^2)
Pounds-force per square inch (psi; lbf/in^2; lb/in^2)	X	0.068	= Atmospheres (atm)	X 14.696	= Pounds-force per square inch (psi; lbf/in^2; lb/in^2)
Pounds-force per square inch (psi; lbf/in^2; lb/in^2)	X	0.069	= Bars	X 14.5	= Pounds-force per square inch (psi; lbf/in^2; lb/in^2)
Pounds-force per square inch (psi; lbf/in^2; lb/in^2)	X	6.895	= Kilopascals (kPa)	X 0.145	= Pounds-force per square inch (psi; lbf/in^2; lb/in^2)
Kilopascals (kPa)	X	0.01	= Kilograms-force per square centimeter (kgf/cm^2; kg/cm^2)	X 98.1	= Kilopascals (kPa)

Torque (moment of force)
Pounds-force inches (lbf in; lb in)	X	1.152	= Kilograms-force centimeter (kgf cm; kg cm)	X 0.868	= Pounds-force inches (lbf in; lb in)
Pounds-force inches (lbf in; lb in)	X	0.113	= Newton meters (Nm)	X 8.85	= Pounds-force inches (lbf in; lb in)
Pounds-force inches (lbf in; lb in)	X	0.083	= Pounds-force feet (lbf ft; lb ft)	X 12	= Pounds-force inches (lbf in; lb in)
Pounds-force feet (lbf ft; lb ft)	X	0.138	= Kilograms-force meters (kgf m; kg m)	X 7.233	= Pounds-force feet (lbf ft; lb ft)
Pounds-force feet (lbf ft; lb ft)	X	1.356	= Newton meters (Nm)	X 0.738	= Pounds-force feet (lbf ft; lb ft)
Newton meters (Nm)	X	0.102	= Kilograms-force meters (kgf m; kg m)	X 9.804	= Newton meters (Nm)

Vacuum
Inches mercury (in. Hg)	X	3.377	= Kilopascals (kPa)	X 0.2961	= Inches mercury
Inches mercury (in. Hg)	X	25.4	= Millimeters mercury (mm Hg)	X 0.0394	= Inches mercury

Power
Horsepower (hp)	X	745.7	= Watts (W)	X 0.0013	= Horsepower (hp)

Velocity (speed)
Miles per hour (miles/hr; mph)	X	1.609	= Kilometers per hour (km/hr; kph)	X 0.621	= Miles per hour (miles/hr; mph)

Fuel consumption*
Miles per gallon, Imperial (mpg)	X	0.354	= Kilometers per liter (km/l)	X 2.825	= Miles per gallon, Imperial (mpg)
Miles per gallon, US (mpg)	X	0.425	= Kilometers per liter (km/l)	X 2.352	= Miles per gallon, US (mpg)

Temperature
Degrees Fahrenheit = (°C x 1.8) + 32   Degrees Celsius (Degrees Centigrade; °C) = (°F - 32) x 0.56

*It is common practice to convert from miles per gallon (mpg) to liters/100 kilometers (l/100km),
where mpg (Imperial) x l/100 km = 282 and mpg (US) x l/100 km = 235

DECIMALS to MILLIMETERS

Decimal	mm	Decimal	mm
0.001	0.0254	0.500	12.7000
0.002	0.0508	0.510	12.9540
0.003	0.0762	0.520	13.2080
0.004	0.1016	0.530	13.4620
0.005	0.1270	0.540	13.7160
0.006	0.1524	0.550	13.9700
0.007	0.1778	0.560	14.2240
0.008	0.2032	0.570	14.4780
0.009	0.2286	0.580	14.7320
0.010	0.2540	0.590	14.9860
0.020	0.5080		
0.030	0.7620		
0.040	1.0160	0.600	15.2400
0.050	1.2700	0.610	15.4940
0.060	1.5240	0.620	15.7480
0.070	1.7780	0.630	16.0020
0.080	2.0320	0.640	16.2560
0.090	2.2860	0.650	16.5100
0.100	2.5400	0.660	16.7640
0.110	2.7940	0.670	17.0180
0.120	3.0480	0.680	17.2720
0.130	3.3020	0.690	17.5260
0.140	3.5560		
0.150	3.8100		
0.160	4.0640	0.700	17.7800
0.170	4.3180	0.710	18.0340
0.180	4.5720	0.720	18.2880
0.190	4.8260	0.730	18.5420
0.200	5.0800	0.740	18.7960
0.210	5.3340	0.750	19.0500
0.220	5.5880	0.760	19.3040
0.230	5.8420	0.770	19.5580
0.240	6.0960	0.780	19.8120
0.250	6.3500	0.790	20.0660
0.260	6.6040		
0.270	6.8580	0.800	20.3200
0.280	7.1120	0.810	20.5740
0.290	7.3660	0.820	21.8280
		0.830	21.0820
0.300	7.6200	0.840	21.3360
0.310	7.8740	0.850	21.5900
0.320	8.1280	0.860	21.8440
0.330	8.3820	0.870	22.0980
0.340	8.6360	0.880	22.3520
0.350	8.8900	0.890	22.6060
0.360	9.1440		
0.370	9.3980		
0.380	9.6520		
0.390	9.9060	0.900	22.8600
0.400	10.1600	0.910	23.1140
0.410	10.4140	0.920	23.3680
0.420	10.6680	0.930	23.6220
0.430	10.9220	0.940	23.8760
0.440	11.1760	0.950	24.1300
0.450	11.4300	0.960	24.3840
0.460	11.6840	0.970	24.6380
0.470	11.9380	0.980	24.8920
0.480	12.1920	0.990	25.1460
0.490	12.4460	1.000	25.4000

FRACTIONS to DECIMALS to MILLIMETERS

Fraction	Decimal	mm	Fraction	Decimal	mm
1/64	0.0156	0.3969	33/64	0.5156	13.0969
1/32	0.0312	0.7938	17/32	0.5312	13.4938
3/64	0.0469	1.1906	35/64	0.5469	13.8906
1/16	0.0625	1.5875	9/16	0.5625	14.2875
5/64	0.0781	1.9844	37/64	0.5781	14.6844
3/32	0.0938	2.3812	19/32	0.5938	15.0812
7/64	0.1094	2.7781	39/64	0.6094	15.4781
1/8	0.1250	3.1750	5/8	0.6250	15.8750
9/64	0.1406	3.5719	41/64	0.6406	16.2719
5/32	0.1562	3.9688	21/32	0.6562	16.6688
11/64	0.1719	4.3656	43/64	0.6719	17.0656
3/16	0.1875	4.7625	11/16	0.6875	17.4625
13/64	0.2031	5.1594	45/64	0.7031	17.8594
7/32	0.2188	5.5562	23/32	0.7188	18.2562
15/64	0.2344	5.9531	47/64	0.7344	18.6531
1/4	0.2500	6.3500	3/4	0.7500	19.0500
17/64	0.2656	6.7469	49/64	0.7656	19.4469
9/32	0.2812	7.1438	25/32	0.7812	19.8438
19/64	0.2969	7.5406	51/64	0.7969	20.2406
5/16	0.3125	7.9375	13/16	0.8125	20.6375
21/64	0.3281	8.3344	53/64	0.8281	21.0344
11/32	0.3438	8.7312	27/32	0.8438	21.4312
23/64	0.3594	9.1281	55/64	0.8594	21.8281
3/8	0.3750	9.5250	7/8	0.8750	22.2250
25/64	0.3906	9.9219	57/64	0.8906	22.6219
13/32	0.4062	10.3188	29/32	0.9062	23.0188
27/64	0.4219	10.7156	59/64	0.9219	23.4156
7/16	0.4375	11.1125	15/16	0.9375	23.8125
29/64	0.4531	11.5094	61/64	0.9531	24.2094
15/32	0.4688	11.9062	31/32	0.9688	24.6062
31/64	0.4844	12.3031	63/64	0.9844	25.0031
1/2	0.5000	12.7000	1	1.0000	25.4000

Safety first!

Regardless of how enthusiastic you may be about getting on with the job at hand, take the time to ensure that your safety is not jeopardized. A moment's lack of attention can result in an accident, as can failure to observe certain simple safety precautions. The possibility of an accident will always exist, and the following points should not be considered a comprehensive list of all dangers. Rather, they are intended to make you aware of the risks and to encourage a safety conscious approach to all work you carry out on your vehicle.

Essential DOs and DON'Ts

DON'T rely on a jack when working under the vehicle. Always use approved jackstands to support the weight of the vehicle and place them under the recommended lift or support points.

DON'T attempt to loosen extremely tight fasteners (i.e. wheel lug nuts) while the vehicle is on a jack - it may fall.

DON'T start the engine without first making sure that the transmission is in Neutral (or Park where applicable) and the parking brake is set.

DON'T remove the radiator cap from a hot cooling system - let it cool or cover it with a cloth and release the pressure gradually.

DON'T attempt to drain the engine oil until you are sure it has cooled to the point that it will not burn you.

DON'T touch any part of the engine or exhaust system until it has cooled sufficiently to avoid burns.

DON'T siphon toxic liquids such as gasoline, antifreeze and brake fluid by mouth, or allow them to remain on your skin.

DON'T inhale brake lining dust - it is potentially hazardous (see *Asbestos* below).

DON'T allow spilled oil or grease to remain on the floor - wipe it up before someone slips on it.

DON'T use loose fitting wrenches or other tools which may slip and cause injury.

DON'T push on wrenches when loosening or tightening nuts or bolts. Always try to pull the wrench toward you. If the situation calls for pushing the wrench away, push with an open hand to avoid scraped knuckles if the wrench should slip.

DON'T attempt to lift a heavy component alone - get someone to help you.

DON'T rush or take unsafe shortcuts to finish a job.

DON'T allow children or animals in or around the vehicle while you are working on it.

DO wear eye protection when using power tools such as a drill, sander, bench grinder, etc. and when working under a vehicle.

DO keep loose clothing and long hair well out of the way of moving parts.

DO make sure that any hoist used has a safe working load rating adequate for the job.

DO get someone to check on you periodically when working alone on a vehicle.

DO carry out work in a logical sequence and make sure that everything is correctly assembled and tightened.

DO keep chemicals and fluids tightly capped and out of the reach of children and pets.

DO remember that your vehicle's safety affects that of yourself and others. If in doubt on any point, get professional advice.

Steering, suspension and brakes

These systems are essential to driving safety, so make sure you have a qualified shop or individual check your work. Also, compressed suspension springs can cause injury if released suddenly - be sure to use a spring compressor.

Airbags

Airbags are explosive devices that can **CAUSE** injury if they deploy while you're working on the vehicle. Follow the manufacturer's instructions to disable the airbag whenever you're working in the vicinity of airbag components.

Asbestos

Certain friction, insulating, sealing, and other products - such as brake linings, brake bands, clutch linings, torque converters, gaskets, etc. - may contain asbestos or other hazardous friction material. Extreme care must be taken to avoid inhalation of dust from such products, since it is hazardous to health. If in doubt, assume that they do contain asbestos.

Fire

Remember at all times that gasoline is highly flammable. Never smoke or have any kind of open flame around when working on a vehicle. But the risk does not end there. A spark caused by an electrical short circuit, by two metal surfaces contacting each other, or even by static electricity built up in your body under certain conditions, can ignite gasoline vapors, which in a confined space are highly explosive. Do not, under any circumstances, use gasoline for cleaning parts. Use an approved safety solvent.

Always disconnect the battery ground (-) cable at the battery before working on any part of the fuel system or electrical system. Never risk spilling fuel on a hot engine or exhaust component. It is strongly recommended that a fire extinguisher suitable for use on fuel and electrical fires be kept handy in the garage or workshop at all times. Never try to extinguish a fuel or electrical fire with water.

Fumes

Certain fumes are highly toxic and can quickly cause unconsciousness and even death if inhaled to any extent. Gasoline vapor falls into this category, as do the vapors from some cleaning solvents. Any draining or pouring of such volatile fluids should be done in a well ventilated area.

When using cleaning fluids and solvents, read the instructions on the container carefully. Never use materials from unmarked containers.

Never run the engine in an enclosed space, such as a garage. Exhaust fumes contain carbon monoxide, which is extremely poisonous. If you need to run the engine, always do so in the open air, or at least have the rear of the vehicle outside the work area.

The battery

Never create a spark or allow a bare light bulb near a battery. They normally give off a certain amount of hydrogen gas, which is highly explosive.

Always disconnect the battery ground (-) cable at the battery before working on the fuel or electrical systems.

If possible, loosen the filler caps or cover when charging the battery from an external source (this does not apply to sealed or maintenance-free batteries). Do not charge at an excessive rate or the battery may burst.

Take care when adding water to a non maintenance-free battery and when carrying a battery. The electrolyte, even when diluted, is very corrosive and should not be allowed to contact clothing or skin.

Always wear eye protection when cleaning the battery to prevent the caustic deposits from entering your eyes.

Household current

When using an electric power tool, inspection light, etc., which operates on household current, always make sure that the tool is correctly connected to its plug and that, where necessary, it is properly grounded. Do not use such items in damp conditions and, again, do not create a spark or apply excessive heat in the vicinity of fuel or fuel vapor.

Secondary ignition system voltage

A severe electric shock can result from touching certain parts of the ignition system (such as the spark plug wires) when the engine is running or being cranked, particularly if components are damp or the insulation is defective. In the case of an electronic ignition system, the secondary system voltage is much higher and could prove fatal.

Hydrofluoric acid

This extremely corrosive acid is formed when certain types of synthetic rubber, found in some O-rings, oil seals, fuel hoses, etc. are exposed to temperatures above 750-degrees F (400-degrees C). The rubber changes into a charred or sticky substance containing the acid. *Once formed, the acid remains dangerous for years. If it gets onto the skin, it may be necessary to amputate the limb concerned.*

When dealing with a vehicle which has suffered a fire, or with components salvaged from such a vehicle, wear protective gloves and discard them after use.

Troubleshooting

Contents

This section provides an easy reference guide to the more common problems which may occur during the operation of your vehicle. These problems and their possible causes are grouped under headings denoting various components or systems, such as Engine, Cooling system, etc. They also refer you to the chapter and/or section which deals with the problem.

Remember that successful troubleshooting is not a mysterious black art practiced only by professional mechanics. It is simply the result of the right knowledge combined with an intelligent, systematic approach to the problem. Always work by a process of elimination, starting with the simplest solution and working through to the most complex - and never overlook the obvious. Anyone can run the gas tank dry or leave the lights on overnight, so don't assume that you are exempt from such oversights.

Finally, always establish a clear idea of why a problem has occurred and take steps to ensure that it doesn't happen again. If the electrical system fails because of a poor connection, check the other connections in the system to make sure that they don't fail as well. If a particular fuse continues to blow, find out why - don't just replace one fuse after another. Remember, failure of a small component can often be indicative of potential failure or incorrect functioning of a more important component or system.

Engine

1 Engine will not rotate when attempting to start

1   Battery terminal connections loose or corroded. Check the cable terminals at the battery. Tighten the cable or remove corrosion as necessary.
2   Battery discharged or faulty. If the cable connections are clean and tight on the battery posts, turn the key to the On position and switch on the headlights and/or windshield wipers. If they fail to function, the battery is discharged.
3   Automatic transmission not completely engaged in Park.
4   Broken, loose or disconnected wiring in the starting circuit. Inspect all wiring and connectors at the battery, starter solenoid and ignition switch.
5   Starter motor pinion jammed in driveplate ring gear. Remove starter and inspect pinion and driveplate (Chapter 5).
6   Starter solenoid faulty (Chapter 5).
7   Starter motor faulty (Chapter 5).
8   Ignition switch faulty (Chapter 12).
9   Starter relay faulty.
10 Body Control Module (BCM) or Powertrain Control Module (PCM) faulty.

2 Engine rotates but will not start

1   Fuel tank empty, fuel filter plugged or fuel line restricted.
2   Fault in the fuel injection system (Chapter 4).
3   Battery discharged (engine rotates slowly). Check the operation of electrical components as described in the previous Section.
4   Battery terminal connections loose or corroded (see previous Section).
5   Fuel pump faulty (Chapter 4).
6   Ignition system faulty (see Chapter 5).
7   Worn, faulty or incorrectly gapped spark plugs (Chapter 1).
8   Broken, loose or disconnected wires at the ignition coils (Chapter 5).

3 Starter motor operates without rotating engine

1   Starter pinion sticking. Remove the starter (Chapter 5) and inspect.
2   Starter pinion or driveplate teeth worn or broken. Remove the driveplate access cover and inspect.

4 Engine hard to start when cold

1   Discharged or low battery. Check as described in Section 2.
2   Fault in the fuel or ignition systems (Chapters 4 and 5).
3   Injector(s) leaking (Chapter 4).

5 Engine hard to start when hot

1   Air filter clogged (Chapter 1).
2   Fault in the fuel or ignition systems (Chapters 4 and 5).
3   Fuel not reaching the injectors (see Chapter 4).
4   Low cylinder compression (Chapter 2A).

6 Starter motor noisy or excessively rough in engagement

1   Pinion or flywheel gear teeth worn or broken. Remove the cover at the rear of the engine (if equipped) and inspect.
2   Starter motor mounting bolts loose or missing.

7 Engine starts but stops immediately

1   Fault in the fuel or ignition systems (Chapters 4 and 5).
2   Vacuum leak at the gasket surfaces of the intake manifold or throttle body. Make sure all mounting bolts/nuts are tightened securely and all vacuum hoses connected to the manifold are positioned properly and in good condition.

3   Restricted intake or exhaust systems (Chapter 4).

8 Engine lopes while idling or idles erratically

1   Vacuum leakage. Check the mounting bolts/nuts at the throttle body and intake manifold for tightness. Make sure all vacuum hoses are connected and in good condition. Use a stethoscope or a length of fuel hose held against your ear to listen for vacuum leaks while the engine is running. A hissing sound will be heard. A soapy water solution will also detect leaks.
2   Fault in the fuel or ignition systems (Chapters 4 and 5).
3   Plugged PCV valve or hose (see Chapter 1).
4   Air filter clogged (Chapter 1).
5   Fuel pump not delivering sufficient fuel to the fuel injectors (see Chapter 4).
6   Leaking head gasket. Perform a compression check (Chapter 2C).
7   Camshaft lobes worn (Chapter 2A).
8   Faulty valve lifter (Chapter 2A).

9 Engine misses at idle speed

1   Spark plugs worn, fouled or not gapped properly (Chapter 1).
2   Fault in the fuel or ignition systems (Chapters 4 and 5).
3   Vacuum leaks at intake manifold or hose connections. Check as described in Section 9.
4   Uneven or low cylinder compression. Check compression as described in Chapter 2C.

10 Engine misses throughout driving speed range

1   Fuel filter clogged and/or impurities in the fuel system (Chapter 1).
2   Faulty or incorrectly gapped spark plugs (Chapter 1).
3   Fault in the fuel or ignition systems (Chapters 4 and 5).

4   Faulty emissions system components (Chapter 6).
5   Low or uneven cylinder compression pressures. Remove the spark plugs and test the compression with a gauge (Chapter 2C).
6   Vacuum leaks at the throttle body, intake manifold or vacuum hoses (see Section 9).

11   Engine stalls

1   Fuel filter clogged and/or water and impurities in the fuel system (Chapter 1).
2   Fault in the fuel system or sensors (Chapters 4 and 6).
3   Faulty emissions system components (Chapter 6).
4   Faulty or incorrectly gapped spark plugs (Chapter 1).
5   Vacuum leak at the throttle body, intake manifold or vacuum hoses. Check as described in Section 9.

12   Engine lacks power

1   Fault in the fuel or ignition systems (Chapters 4 and 5).
2   Faulty or incorrectly gapped spark plugs (Chapter 1).
3   Faulty coils (Chapter 5).
4   Brakes binding (Chapter 1).
5   Automatic transmission fluid level incorrect (Chapter 1).
6   Fuel filter clogged and/or impurities in the fuel system (Chapter 1).
7   Emissions control system not functioning properly (Chapter 6).
8   Use of substandard fuel. Fill the tank with the proper fuel.
9   Low or uneven cylinder compression pressures. Test with a compression tester, which will detect leaking valves and/or a blown head gasket (Chapter 2A).
10   Restriction in the intake or exhaust system (Chapter 4).

13   Engine backfires

1   Emissions system not functioning properly (Chapter 6).
2   Fault in the fuel or ignition systems (Chapters 4 and 5).
3   Vacuum leak at the throttle body, intake manifold or vacuum hoses. Check as described in Section 9.
4   Valves sticking (Chapter 2A).

14   Pinging or knocking engine sounds during acceleration or uphill

1   Incorrect grade of fuel. Fill the tank with fuel of the proper octane rating.

2   Fault in the fuel or ignition systems (Chapters 4 and 5).
3   Improper spark plugs. Check the plug type against the VECI label located in the engine compartment. Also check the plugs for damage (Chapter 1).
4   Faulty emissions system (Chapter 6).
5   Vacuum leak. Check as described in Section 10.

15   Engine continues to run after switching off

Faulty ignition switch (Chapter 12).

Engine electrical system

16   Battery will not hold a charge

1   Drivebelt or tensioner defective (Chapter 1).
2   Electrolyte level low or battery discharged (Chapter 1).
3   Battery terminals loose or corroded (Chapter 1).
4   Alternator not charging properly (Chapter 5).
5   Loose, broken or faulty wiring in the charging circuit (Chapter 5).
6   Battery defective internally.

17   Alternator light fails to go out

1   Fault in the alternator or charging circuit (Chapter 5).
2   Drivebelt or tensioner defective (Chapter 1).

18   Alternator light fails to come on when key is turned on

1   Instrument cluster warning light bulb defective (Chapter 12).
2   Alternator faulty (Chapter 5).
3   Fault in the instrument cluster printed circuit, dashboard wiring or bulb holder (Chapter 12).

Fuel system

19   Excessive fuel consumption

1   Dirty or clogged air filter element (Chapter 1).
2   Emissions system not functioning properly (Chapter 6).
3   Fault in the fuel or ignition systems (Chapters 4 and 5).

4   Low tire pressure or incorrect tire size (Chapter 1).
5   Restricted exhaust system (Chapter 4).
6   Brakes binding (Chapter 9).

20   Fuel leakage and/or fuel odor

1   Leak in a fuel feed or vent line (Chapter 4).
2   Tank overfilled. Fill only to automatic shut-off.
3   Evaporative emissions system canister clogged (Chapter 6).
4   Vapor leaks from system lines or injectors (Chapter 4).

Cooling system

21   Overheating

1   Insufficient coolant in the system (Chapter 1).
2   Drivebelt or tensioner defective (Chapter 1).
3   Radiator core blocked or radiator grille dirty and restricted (see Chapter 3).
4   Thermostat faulty (Chapter 3).
5   Fan blades broken or cracked (Chapter 3).
6   Expansion tank cap not maintaining proper pressure. Have the cap pressure tested by a gas station or repair shop.
7   Fault in electrical circuit for cooling fans (Chapter 3).

22   Overcooling

1   Thermostat faulty (Chapter 3).
2   Inaccurate temperature gauge (Chapter 12).
3   Fault in electrical circuit for cooling fans (Chapter 3).

23   External coolant leakage

1   Deteriorated or damaged hoses or loose clamps. Replace hoses and/or tighten the clamps at the hose connections (Chapter 1).
2   Water pump seals defective. If this is the case, water will drip from the weep hole in the water pump body (Chapter 3).
3   Leakage from the radiator core or side tank(s). This will require the radiator to be professionally repaired (see Chapter 3 for removal procedures).
4   Engine drain plug(s) leaking (Chapter 1) or water jacket core plugs leaking.
5   Leakage at the heater core. Signs of leakage should show up on interior carpeting (Chapter 3).

24 Internal coolant leakage

Note: *Internal coolant leaks can usually be detected by examining the oil. Check the dipstick and inside of the valve cover for water deposits and an oil consistency like that of a milkshake.*

1 Leaking cylinder head gasket. Have the cooling system pressure tested.
2 Cracked cylinder bore or cylinder head. Remove the head(s) and inspect (Chapter 2A).
3 Leaking intake manifold gasket (Chapter 2A).

25 Coolant loss

1 Too much coolant in the system (Chapter 1).
2 Coolant boiling away due to overheating (Chapter 3).
3 External or internal leakage (see Sections 23 and 24 above).
4 Faulty expansion tank cap. Have the cap pressure tested.

26 Poor coolant circulation

1 Inoperative water pump. A quick test is to pinch the top radiator hose closed with your hand while the engine is idling, then let it loose. You should feel the surge of coolant if the pump is working properly (see Chapter 1).
2 Restriction in the cooling system. Drain, flush and refill the system (Chapter 1). If necessary, remove the radiator (Chapter 3) and have it reverse flushed.
3 Drivebelt or tensioner defective (Chapter 1).
4 Thermostat sticking (Chapter 3).
5 Drivebelt incorrectly routed, causing the pump to turn backward (Chapter 1).

Automatic transmission

27 General shift mechanism problems

1 Chapter 7A deals with checking and adjusting the shift cable on automatic transmissions. Common problems that may be attributed to poorly adjusted cable are:

a) *Engine starting in gears other than Park or Neutral.*
b) *Indicator on shifter pointing to a gear other than the one actually being selected.*
c) *Vehicle moves when in Park.*

2 Refer to Chapter 7A to adjust the linkage.
3 Problem with the electronic shift solenoid. Check for Diagnostic Trouble Codes (Chapter 6).

28 Transmission will not downshift with accelerator pedal pressed to the floor

Transmission pressure control solenoid valve faulty. Check for Diagnostic Trouble Codes (Chapter 6).

29 Transmission slips, shifts rough, is noisy or has no drive in forward or reverse gears

1 Of the many probable causes for the above problems, the home mechanic should be concerned with only one possibility - fluid level.
2 Before taking the vehicle to a repair shop, check the level and condition of the fluid as described in Chapter 1. Correct fluid level as necessary or change the fluid and filter if needed. If the problem persists, have a professional diagnose the probable cause.
3 If the transmission shifts late and the shifts are harsh, suspect a faulty transmission pressure control solenoid valve. Check for Diagnostic Trouble Codes (Chapter 6).

30 Fluid leakage

1 Automatic transmission fluid is a deep red color. Fluid leaks should not be confused with engine oil, which can easily be blown by airflow to the transmission.
2 To pinpoint a leak, first remove all built-up dirt and grime from around the transmission. Degreasing agents and/or steam cleaning will achieve this. With the underside clean, drive the vehicle at low speeds so airflow will not blow the leak far from its source. Raise the vehicle and determine where the leak is coming from. Common areas of leakage are:

a) *Pan: Tighten the mounting bolts and/ or replace the pan gasket as necessary (see Chapter 1).*
b) *Filler pipe: Replace the rubber seal where the pipe enters the transmission case.*
c) *Transmission oil lines: Tighten the connectors where the lines enter the transmission case and/or replace the lines.*
d) *Vent pipe: Transmission overfilled and/or water in fluid (Chapter 1).*
e) *Speed sensor connector: Replace the O-ring where the vehicle speed sensor enters the transmission case (Chapter 6).*

Transfer case

31 Transfer case is difficult to shift into the desired range

1 Speed may be too great to permit engagement. Stop the vehicle and shift into the desired range.
2 Shift linkage loose, bent or binding. Check the linkage for damage or wear and replace or lubricate as necessary (Chapter 7B).
3 If the vehicle has been driven on a paved surface for some time, the driveline torque can make shifting difficult. Stop and shift into two-wheel drive on paved or hard surfaces.
4 Insufficient or incorrect grade of lubricant. Drain and refill the transfer case with the specified lubricant (Chapter 1).
5 Worn or damaged internal components. Disassembly and overhaul of the transfer case, by a qualified shop, may be necessary.
6 Fault in the electrical system of the front axle or automatic transfer case. Check for Diagnostic Trouble Codes (Chapter 6).

32 Transfer case noisy in all gears

Insufficient or incorrect grade of lubricant. Drain and refill (Chapter 1).

33 Noisy or jumps out of four-wheel drive Low range

1 Transfer case not fully engaged. Stop the vehicle, shift into Neutral and then engage 4L.
2 Shift linkage loose, worn or binding. Tighten, repair or lubricate linkage as necessary.
3 Shift fork cracked, inserts worn or fork binding on the rail. Disassemble and repair as necessary (Chapter 7B).
4 Fault in the electrical system of the front axle or automatic transfer case. Check for Diagnostic Trouble Codes (Chapter 6).

34 Lubricant leaks from the vent or output shaft seals

1 Transfer case is overfilled. Drain to the proper level (Chapter 1).
2 Vent is clogged or jammed closed. Clear or replace the vent.
3 Output shaft seal incorrectly installed or damaged. Replace the seal and check contact surfaces for nicks and scoring.

Driveshaft

35 Oil leak at seal end of driveshaft

Defective transmission or transfer case oil seal. See Chapter 7A for replacement procedures. While this is done, check the splined yoke for burrs or a rough condition that may be damaging the seal. Burrs can be removed with crocus cloth or a fine whetstone.

36 Knock or clunk when the transmission is under initial load (just after transmission is put into gear)

1   Loose or disconnected rear suspension components. Check all mounting bolts, nuts and bushings (see Chapter 10).
2   Loose driveshaft bolts. Inspect all bolts and nuts and tighten them to the specified torque.
3   Worn or damaged universal joint bearings. Check for wear (see Chapter 8).

37 Metallic grinding sound consistent with vehicle speed

Pronounced wear in the universal joint bearings. Check as described in Chapter 8.

38 Vibration

Note: *Before assuming that the driveshaft is at fault, make sure the tires are perfectly balanced and perform the following test.*
1   Install a tachometer inside the vehicle to monitor engine speed as the vehicle is driven. Drive the vehicle and note the engine speed at which the vibration (roughness) is most pronounced. Now shift the transmission to a different gear and bring the engine speed to the same point.
2   If the vibration occurs at the same engine speed (rpm) regardless of which gear the transmission is in, the driveshaft is NOT at fault since the driveshaft speed varies.
3   If the vibration decreases or is eliminated when the transmission is in a different gear at the same engine speed, refer to the following probable causes.
4   Bent or dented driveshaft. Inspect and replace as necessary (see Chapter 8).
5   Undercoating or built-up dirt, etc., on the driveshaft. Clean the shaft thoroughly and recheck.
6   Worn universal joint bearings (see Chapter 8).
7   Driveshaft and/or companion flange out of balance. Check for missing weights on the shaft. Remove the driveshaft (see Chapter 8) and reinstall 180-degrees from original position, then retest. Have the driveshaft professionally balanced if the problem persists.

Axles

39 Noise

1   Road noise. No corrective procedures available.
2   Tire noise. Inspect tires and check tire pressures (Chapter 1).
3   Rear wheel bearings worn or damaged (Chapter 8).

40 Vibration

See probable causes under Driveshaft. Proceed under the guidelines listed for the driveshaft. If the problem persists, check the rear wheel bearings by raising the rear of the vehicle and spinning the rear wheels by hand. Listen for evidence of rough (noisy) bearings. Remove and inspect (see Chapter 8).

41 Oil leakage

1   Pinion seal damaged (see Chapter 8).
2   Axleshaft oil seals damaged (see Chapter 8).
3   Differential inspection cover leaking. Tighten the bolts or replace the gasket as required (see Chapter 8).

Driveaxles (4WD)

42 Clicking noise on turns

Worn or damaged outboard CV joints (Chapter 8).

43 Shudder or vibration during acceleration

1   Excessive toe-in. Have alignment checked.
2   Incorrect spring heights (Chapter 10).
3   Worn or damaged inboard or outboard CV joints (Chapter 8).
4   Sticking inboard CV joint assembly (Chapter 8).

44 Vibration at highway speeds

1   Out-of-balance front wheels and/or tires (Chapters 1 and 10).
2   Out-of-round front tires (Chapters 1 and 10).
3   Worn CV joints (Chapter 8).

Brakes

45 Vehicle pulls to one side during braking

1   Defective, damaged or oil contaminated disc brake pads on one side. Inspect as described in Chapter 9.
2   Excessive wear of brake pad material or disc on one side. Inspect and correct as necessary.
3   Loose or disconnected front suspension components. Inspect and tighten all bolts to the specified torque (Chapter 10).
4   Defective brake caliper assembly. Remove the caliper and inspect for a stuck piston or other damage (Chapter 9).
5   Inadequate lubrication of front brake caliper slide pins. Remove caliper and lubricate slide pins (Chapter 9).

46 Noise (grinding or high-pitched squeal with the brakes applied)

1   Brake pads worn out. Replace the pads with new ones immediately (Chapter 9).
2   Linings contaminated with dirt or grease. Replace pads.
3   Scored disc or drum (Chapter 9).

47 Excessive brake pedal travel

1   Partial brake system failure. Inspect the entire system (Chapter 9) and correct as required.
2   Insufficient fluid in the master cylinder. Check (Chapter 1), add fluid and bleed the system if necessary (Chapter 9).

48 Brake pedal feels spongy when depressed

1   Air in the hydraulic lines. Bleed the brake system (Chapter 9).
2   Faulty flexible hoses. Inspect all system hoses and lines. Replace parts as necessary.
3   Master cylinder mounting bolts/nuts loose.
4   Master cylinder defective (Chapter 9).

49 Excessive effort required to stop vehicle

1   Power brake booster not operating properly (see check in Chapter 1, repairs in Chapter 9).
2   Excessively worn pads or shoes. Inspect and replace if necessary (Chapter 9).
3   One or more caliper or wheel cylinder pistons seized or sticking. Inspect and replace as required (Chapter 9).

4   Brake pads contaminated with oil or grease. Inspect and replace as required (Chapter 9).

5   New pads installed and not yet seated. It will take a while for the new material to seat against the disc.

50 Pedal travels to the floor with little resistance

1   Little or no fluid in the master cylinder reservoir caused by leaking caliper piston(s), loose, damaged or disconnected brake lines. Inspect the entire system and correct as necessary.

2   Faulty master cylinder (Chapter 9).

51 Brake pedal pulsates during brake application

Disc(s) warped. Check for excessive lateral runout and parallelism. Have the discs resurfaced or replace them with new ones (Chapter 9).

Suspension and steering systems

52 Vehicle pulls to one side

1   Tire pressures uneven or tires mismatched (Chapter 1).

2   Defective tire (Chapter 1).

3   Excessive wear in suspension or steering components (Chapter 10).

4   Front end in need of alignment.

5   Front brakes dragging. Inspect the brakes as described in Chapter 9.

53 Shimmy, shake or vibration

1   Tire or wheel out-of-balance or out-of-round. Have professionally balanced.

2   Loose, worn or out-of-adjustment front wheel bearings (Chapter 1).

3   Shock absorbers and/or suspension components worn or damaged (Chapter 10).

54 Excessive pitching and/or rolling around corners or during braking

1   Defective shock absorbers. Replace as a set (Chapter 10).

2   Broken or weak springs and/or suspension components. Inspect as described in Chapters 1 and 10.

55 Excessively stiff steering

1   Lack of fluid in power steering fluid reservoir (Chapter 1).

2   Incorrect tire pressures (Chapter 1).

3   Lack of lubrication at steering joints (see Chapter 1).

4   Front end out of alignment.

5   Lack of power assistance (Chapter 10).

56 Excessive play in steering

1   Worn front wheel bearings (Chapter 10).

2   Excessive wear in suspension or steering components (Chapter 10).

3   Steering gear worn (Chapter 10).

57 Lack of power assistance

1   Drivebelt or tensioner faulty (Chapter 1).

2   Fluid level low (Chapter 1).

3   Hoses or lines restricted. Inspect and replace parts as necessary.

4   Air in power steering system. Bleed the system (Chapter 10).

58 Excessive tire wear (not specific to one area)

1   Incorrect tire pressures (Chapter 1).

2   Tires out-of-balance. Have professionally balanced.

3   Wheels damaged. Inspect and replace as necessary.

4   Suspension or steering components excessively worn (Chapter 10).

59 Excessive tire wear on outside edge

1   Inflation pressures incorrect (Chapter 1).

2   Excessive speed in turns.

3   Front-end alignment incorrect. Have the front end professionally aligned.

4   Suspension arm bent (Chapter 10).

60 Excessive tire wear on inside edge

1   Inflation pressures incorrect (Chapter 1).

2   Front-end alignment incorrect. Have the front end professionally aligned.

3   Loose or damaged steering components (Chapter 10).

61 Tire tread worn in one place

1   Tires out-of-balance.

2   Damaged or buckled wheel. Inspect and replace if necessary.

3   Defective tire (Chapter 1).

Service record

Date	Mileage	Work performed

Service record

Date	Mileage	Work performed

Service record

Date	Mileage	Work performed

Service record

Date	Mileage	Work performed

Notes

Chapter 1
Tune-up and routine maintenance

Contents

Specifications

Recommended lubricants and fluids

Note: *Listed here are manufacturer recommendations at the time this manual was written. Manufacturers occasionally upgrade their fluid and lubricant specifications, so check with your local auto parts store for current recommendations.*

Engine oil	Engine oil that meets GM dexos1 standard (AC Delco dexos1 synthetic blend, or equivalent)
Viscosity	
4.3L V6 and 6.0L V8 engines	SAE 5W-30
5.3L and 6.2L V8 engines	SAE 0W-20
Fuel	Unleaded gasoline, 87 octane minimum
Automatic transmission fluid	
6-speed transmission	DEXRON VI automatic transmission fluid
8-speed transmission	DEXRON HP automatic transmission fluid
Transfer case	DEXRON VI automatic transmission fluid
Differential	
Front	SAE 75W90 synthetic gear oil
Rear	
8.6/9.5/9.76-inch axles	SAE 75W-85 synthetic gear oil
10.5/11.5-inch axles	SAE 75W-90 synthetic gear oil

Recommended lubricants and fluids (continued)

Note: *Listed here are manufacturer recommendations at the time this manual was written. Manufacturers occasionally upgrade their fluid and lubricant specifications, so check with your local auto parts store for current recommendations.*

Power steering fluid	GM power steering fluid
Brake fluid	DOT 3 brake fluid
Engine coolant	50/50 mixture of DEX-COOL coolant and demineralized water
Parking brake mechanism grease	White lithium-based grease NLGI no. 2
Chassis lubrication grease	NLGI Grade 2 LB or GC-LB chassis grease
Hood, door and trunk hinge lubricant	Lubriplate, lubricant aerosol spray
Door hinge and check spring grease	NLGI no. 2 multi-purpose grease or equivalent
Key lock cylinder lubricant	Graphite spray
Hood latch assembly lubricant	NLGI no. 2 multi-purpose grease or equivalent
Door latch lubricant	NLGI no. 2 multi-purpose grease or equivalent

Capacities*

Engine oil (including filter)	
V6 engine	6.0 quarts
V8 engines	
All models, except 5.3L VIN C (L83) and 6.2L VIN J (L86) models	6.0 quarts
5.3L VIN C (L83) and 6.2L VIN J (L86) models	8.0 quarts
Automatic transmission (fluid and filter change)	
4L80-E/6L90	6.0 quarts
6L50/6L80	6.0 quarts
8L90	7.4 quarts
Differential	
Front (4WD models)	Up to 2.0 quarts
Rear	
8.6-inch axle	2.2 quarts
9.5-inch 9.76-inch and 10.5-inch axles	2.75 quarts
11.5-inch axle	3.2 quarts
Transfer case	1.6 quarts
Cooling system**	
V6 engine	16.5 quarts
V8 engines	
Without rear A/C	16.9 quarts
With rear A/C	
4.3L	16.5 quarts
5.3L and 6.2L	16.9 quarts
6.0L (LC8) and (L96) with oil cooler	16.3 quarts
6.0L (L96) with oil cooler	17.2 quarts

Note: **All capacities approximate. Add as necessary to bring to appropriate level.*
Note: ***Cooling system capacities vary depending on engine/transmission package, radiator and A/C system type. Add coolant as necessary to bring to appropriate level.*

Brakes

Disc brake pad wear limit	3/32 inch
Parking brake shoe wear limit	1/16 inch

Ignition system

Spark plug type	AC Delco 41-114 or equivalent
Spark plug gap	0.037 - 0.043 inch
Firing order	
V6 engine	1-6-5-4-3-2
V8 engines	1-8-7-2-6-5-4-3

V6 engine cylinder numbering diagram

24068-2A-0.0a HAYNES

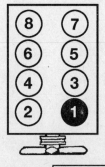

V8 engine cylinder numbering diagram

24017-1-B HAYNES

Torque specifications

Ft-lbs (unless otherwise indicated)

Note: *One foot-pound (ft-lb) of torque is equivalent to 12 inch-pounds (in-lbs) of torque. Torque values below approximately 15 ft-lbs are expressed in inch-pounds, since most foot-pound torque wrenches are not accurate at these smaller values.*

Spark plugs	132 in-lbs
Drivebelt tensioner bolts	
V6 engine	43
V8 engines	
5.3L and 6.2L engines	43
6.0L engine	37
Drivebelt idler pulley bolt	
V6 engine	15
6.0L V8 engine	37
Wheel lug nuts	140
Automatic transmission pan bolts	
6L80/6L90	80 in-lbs
8L90	89 in-lbs
Engine oil drain plug	18
Transfer case drain/fill plug	156 in-lbs
Differential drain and fill plugs	
Front differential	24
Rear differential	
Drain plug (if equipped)	24
Fill plug	
8.6-inch and 9.5-inch	24
10.5-inch	55
11.5-inch	44
Differential cover bolts	
8.6-inch, 9.5-inch and 9.76-inch	
Step 1	15
Step 2	Tighten an additional 20 degrees
10.5-inch and 11.5-inch	30

Engine compartment components (V6 engine)

1	Engine oil filler cap
2	Engine oil dipstick
3	Brake fluid reservoir
4	Underhood fuse/relay box
5	Windshield washer fluid reservoir
6	Upper radiator hose
7	Air filter housing
8	Coolant expansion tank
9	Automatic transmission fluid dipstick
10	Battery

Typical engine compartment underside components (V6, 2WD 1500 pick-up)

1 Automatic transmission fluid pan	4 Oil filter	7 Steering gear boot
2 Exhaust pipe/catalytic converter	5 Front brake caliper	8 Steering knuckle
3 Stabilizer bar	6 Shock absorber/coil spring assembly	9 Lower radiator hose

Typical rear underside components

1	Driveshaft	4	Leaf spring	7	Differential cover
2	Muffler	5	Brake caliper	8	Parking brake cable
3	Fuel tank	6	Shock absorber		

Engine compartment components (V8 engine, Suburban)

1	Engine oil filler cap	5	Windshield washer fluid reservoir	8	Coolant expansion tank
2	Engine oil dipstick	6	Upper radiator hose	9	Automatic transmission fluid dipstick
3	Brake fluid reservoir	7	Air filter housing	10	Battery
4	Underhood fuse/relay box				

Typical engine compartment underside components (V8, 4WD Suburban)

1	Splash shield	4	Outer driveaxle boot	6	Engine oil drain plug
2	Steering gear boots	5	Inner driveaxle boot	7	Oil filter
3	Shock absorber/coil spring assembly				

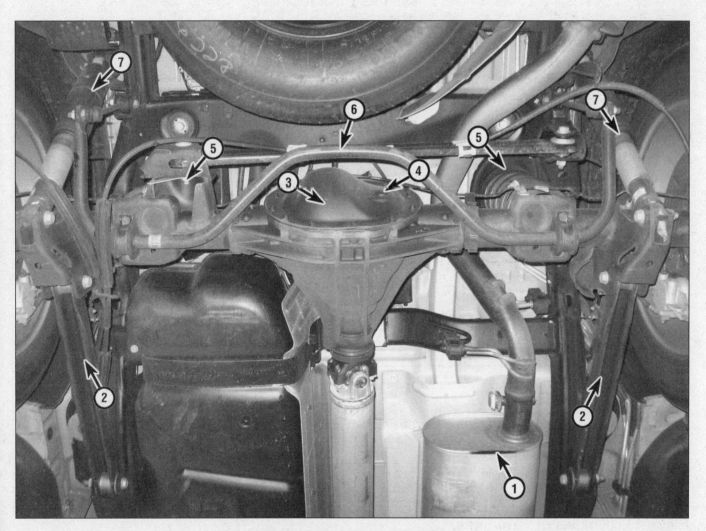

Typical rear underside components (V8, 4WD Suburban)

1 Muffler	4 Differential check/fill plug	6 Stabilizer bar
2 Trailing arm (lower)	5 Coil spring	7 Shock absorber
3 Differential cover		

1 Maintenance schedule

1   The following maintenance intervals are based on the assumption that the vehicle owner will be doing the maintenance or service work, as opposed to having a dealer service department do the work. These are the minimum maintenance intervals recommended by the factory for vehicles that are driven daily. If you wish to keep your vehicle in peak condition at all times, you may wish to perform some of these procedures even more often. Because frequent maintenance enhances the efficiency, performance and resale value of your car, we encourage you to do so. If you drive in dusty areas, tow a trailer, idle or drive at low speeds for extended periods or drive for short distances (less than four miles) in below freezing temperatures, shorter intervals are also recommended.

2   When the vehicle is new, follow the maintenance schedule to the letter, record the maintenance performed in your owner's manual and keep all receipts to protect the new vehicle warranty. In many cases the initial maintenance check is done at no cost to the owner (check with your dealer service department for more information).

Every 250 miles or weekly, whichever comes first

Check the engine oil level (Section 4)
Check the coolant level (Section 4)
Check the windshield washer fluid level (Section 4)
Check the brake fluid level (Section 4)
Check the tires and tire pressures (Section 5)

Every 3000 miles or 3 months, whichever comes first

All items listed above, plus . . .
Check the power steering fluid level (Section 6)
Check the automatic transmission fluid level (Section 7)
Change the engine oil and filter (Section 8)

Every 6000 miles or 6 months, whichever comes first

All items listed above, plus . . .
Check the seat belts (Section 9)
Inspect the windshield wiper blades (Section 10)
Check and service the battery (Section 11)
Check the drivebelt(s) (Section 12)
Inspect underhood hoses (Section 13)
Check the cooling system (Section 14)
Rotate the tires (Section 15)

Every 15,000 miles or 12 months, whichever comes first

All items listed above, plus . . .
Check the differential lubricant level in the front (4WD) and rear axles (Section 16)
Lubricate the chassis (Section 17)
Check the fuel system (Section 18)
Check the brake system (Section 19)*
Check the exhaust system (Section 20)
Check the transfer case lubricant level (4WD models) (Section 21)
Check the air filter (Section 24)*

Every 30,000 miles or 30 months, whichever comes first

All items listed above, plus . . .
Change the brake fluid (Section 23)
Replace the air filter (Section 24)*
Replace the spark plugs (conventional, non-platinum or non-iridium type) (Section 25)**
Service the cooling system (drain, flush and refill) (green-colored ethylene glycol antifreeze only) (Section 26)
Check the steering, suspension and driveaxle boots (Section 27)
Change the automatic transmission fluid and filter (Section 28)**

Every 60,000 miles or 48 months, whichever comes first

Change the transfer case lubricant (Section 29)
Change the differential lubricant (Section 30)**
Replace the Positive Crankcase Ventilation (PCV) valve (V6 engine) (Section 31)

Every 100,000 miles or 60 months, whichever comes first

Replace the spark plugs (platinum or iridium type) (Section 25)
Inspect/replace the spark plug wires (Section 32)
Service the cooling system (drain, flush and refill) (orange-colored DEX-COOL antifreeze only) (Section 26)

* This item is affected by "severe" operating conditions, as described below. If the vehicle is operated under severe conditions, perform all maintenance indicated with an asterisk (*) at half the indicated intervals. Severe conditions exist if you mainly operate the vehicle . . .

a) in dusty areas
b) towing a trailer
c) idling for extended periods
d) driving at low speeds when outside temperatures remain below freezing and most trips are less than four miles long

** Perform this procedure at half the recommended interval if operated under one or more of the following conditions:

a) in heavy city traffic where the outside temperature regularly reaches 90-degrees F or higher in hilly or mountainous terrain
b) frequent trailer towing
c) if the vehicle has been driven through deep water

2 Introduction

1 This chapter is designed to help the home mechanic maintain the Chevrolet/GMC pickup or Avalanche/Tahoe/Yukon/Suburban with the goals of maximum performance, economy, safety and reliability in mind.

2 Included is a master maintenance schedule, followed by procedures dealing specifically with each item on the schedule. Visual checks, adjustments, component replacement and other helpful items are included. Refer to the accompanying illustrations of the engine compartment and the underside of the vehicle for the locations of various components.

3 Servicing your vehicle in accordance with the mileage/time maintenance schedule and the step-by-step procedures will result in a planned maintenance program that should produce a long and reliable service life. Keep in mind that it's a comprehensive plan, so maintaining some items but not others at the specified intervals will not produce the same results.

4 As you service your vehicle, you will discover that many of the procedures can - and should - be grouped together because of the nature of the particular procedure you're performing or because of the close proximity of two otherwise unrelated components to one another.

5 For example, if the vehicle is raised for chassis lubrication, you should inspect the exhaust, suspension, steering and fuel systems while you're under the vehicle. When you're rotating the tires, it makes good sense to check the brakes since the wheels are already removed. Finally, let's suppose you have to borrow or rent a torque wrench. Even if you only need it to tighten the spark plugs, you might as well check the torque of as many critical fasteners as time allows.

6 The first step in this maintenance program is to prepare yourself before the actual work begins. Read through all the procedures you're planning to do, then gather up all the parts and tools needed. If it looks like you might run into problems during a particular job, seek advice from a mechanic or an experienced do-it-yourselfer.

Owner's manual and VECI label information

7 Your vehicle owner's manual was written for your year and model and contains very specific information on component locations, specifications, fuse ratings, part numbers, etc. The owner's manual is an important resource for the do-it-yourselfer to have; if one was not supplied with your vehicle, it can generally be ordered from a dealer parts department.

8 Among other important information, the Vehicle Emissions Control Information (VECI) label contains specifications and procedures for tune-up adjustments (if applicable) and, in some cases, spark plugs (see Chapter 6 for more information on the VECI label). The information on this label is the exact maintenance data recommended by the manufac-turer. This data often varies by intended operating altitude, local emissions regulations, month of manufacture, etc.

9 This chapter contains procedural details, safety information and more ambitious maintenance intervals than you might find in the manufacturer's literature. However, you may also find procedures and specifications in your owner's manual or VECI label that differ with what's printed here. In these cases, the owner's manual or VECI label can be considered correct, since it is specific to your particular vehicle.

3 Tune-up general information

1 The term tune-up is used in this manual to represent a combination of individual operations rather than one specific procedure that will maintain a gasoline engine in proper tune.

2 If, from the time the vehicle is new, the routine maintenance schedule is followed closely and frequent checks are made of fluid levels and high wear items, as suggested throughout this manual, the engine will be kept in relatively good running condition and the need for additional work will be minimized.

3 More likely than not, however, there may be times when the engine is running poorly due to lack of regular maintenance. This is even more likely if a used vehicle, which has not received regular and frequent maintenance checks, is purchased. In such cases, an engine tune-up will be needed outside of the regular routine maintenance intervals.

4 The first step in any tune-up or diagnostic procedure to help correct a poor running engine is a cylinder compression check. A compression check (see Chapter 2C) will help determine the condition of internal engine components and should be used as a guide for tune-up and repair procedures. If, for instance, the compression check indicates serious internal engine wear, a conventional tune-up won't improve the performance of the engine and would be a waste of time and money. Because of its importance, the compression check should be done by someone with the proper equipment and the knowledge to use it properly.

5 The following procedures are those most often needed to bring a generally poor running engine back into a proper state of tune.

Minor tune-up

Check all engine related fluids (Section 4)
Clean, inspect and test the battery (Section 11)
Check the drivebelt(s) (Section 12)
Check all underhood hoses (Section 13)
Check the cooling system (Section 14)
Check the air filter (Section 24)
Inspect the spark plug wires (Section 31)

Major tune-up

6 All items listed under Minor tune-up, plus . . .

Replace the air filter (Section 24)
Replace the spark plugs (Section 25)
Replace the PCV valve (Section 31)
Replace the spark plug wires (Section 32)
Check the ignition system (Chapter 5)
Check the charging system (Chapter 5)

4 Fluid level checks (every 250 miles or weekly)

Note: *The following are fluid level checks to be done on a 250 mile or weekly basis. Additional fluid level checks can be found in specific maintenance procedures that follow. Regardless of intervals, be alert to fluid leaks under the vehicle, which would indicate a fault to be corrected immediately.*

1 Fluids are an essential part of the lubrication, cooling, brake, clutch and windshield washer systems. Because the fluids gradually become depleted and/or contaminated during normal operation of the vehicle, they must be periodically replenished. See *Recommended lubricants and fluids* in this Chapter's Specifications before adding fluid to any of the following components.

Note: *The vehicle must be on level ground when fluid levels are checked.*

Engine oil

2 The engine oil level is checked with a dipstick that extends through a tube and into the oil pan at the bottom of the engine (see illustration).

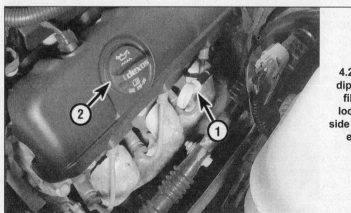

4.2 The engine oil dipstick (A) and oil filler cap (B) are located on the left side of the engine (V6 engine shown, V8 similar)

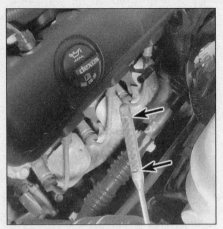

4.4 The oil level must be maintained in the cross-hatched area, but not above it

4.10 The coolant expansion tank is located on the right side, near the air filter - make sure the level is up to the COLD mark when the engine is cold

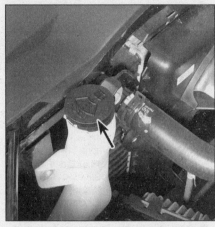

4.15 Location of the windshield washer fluid reservoir

3   The oil level should be checked before the vehicle has been driven, or about 5 minutes after the engine has been shut off. If the oil is checked immediately after driving the vehicle, some of the oil will remain in the upper engine components, resulting in an inaccurate reading on the dipstick.

4   Pull the dipstick out of the tube and wipe all the oil from the end with a clean rag or paper towel. Insert the clean dipstick all the way back into the tube, then pull it out again. Note the oil at the end of the dipstick. Add oil as necessary to keep the level between the cross-hatched area on the dipstick (see illustration).

5   Do not overfill the engine by adding too much oil since this may result in oil-fouled spark plugs, oil leaks or oil seal failures.

6   Oil is added to the engine after unscrewing the cap from the valve cover (see illustration 4.2).

Note: *Always make sure the area around the opening is clean before removing the cap to prevent dirt from contaminating the engine.*

7   Checking the oil level is an important preventive maintenance step. A consistently low oil level indicates oil leakage through damaged seals, defective gaskets or past worn rings or valve guides. If the oil looks milky or has water droplets in it, the cylinder head gasket(s) may be blown or the head(s) or block may be cracked. The engine should be checked immediately. The condition of the oil should also be checked. Whenever you check the oil level, slide your thumb and index finger up the dipstick before wiping off the oil. If you see small dirt or metal particles clinging to the dipstick, the oil should be changed (see Section 8).

Engine coolant

Warning: *Do not allow antifreeze to come in contact with your skin or painted surfaces of the vehicle. Rinse off spills immediately with plenty of water. Antifreeze is highly toxic if ingested. Never leave antifreeze lying around in an open container or in puddles on the floor;*

children and pets are attracted by its sweet smell and may drink it. Check with local authorities on disposing of used antifreeze. Many communities have collection centers that will see that antifreeze is disposed of safely.

Caution: *Never mix green-colored ethylene glycol antifreeze and orange-colored DEX-COOL silicate-free coolant because doing so will destroy the efficiency of the DEX-COOL coolant which is designed to last for 100,000 miles or five years.*

Note: *Non-toxic antifreeze is now manufactured and available at local auto parts stores, but even this type should be disposed of properly.*

8   All vehicles covered by this manual are equipped with a pressurized coolant expansion tank, located at the right side of the engine compartment, and connected by hoses to the radiator and cooling system.

9   The coolant level in the expansion tank should be checked regularly.

Warning: *Do not remove the pressure cap to check the coolant level when the engine is warm.*

10   The level of coolant in the expansion tank varies with the temperature of the engine. When the engine is cold, the coolant level should be at or slightly above the COLD mark on the expansion tank (see illustration). To add coolant, slowly unscrew the cap, then add coolant until it is up to the COLD mark (see the Caution at the beginning of this section).

Warning: *If coolant or steam escapes as you unscrew the cap, let the engine cool down longer, then remove the cap.*

11   Install the cap, start the engine and run it at approximately 2000 rpm until the coolant temperature gauge reads approximately 195-degrees F. If the coolant level drops, let the engine cool, then add more until it is up to the COLD mark. In order to maintain the proper ratio of antifreeze and water, always top up the coolant level with the correct mixture. Do not use rust inhibitors or additives.

12   If the coolant level drops consistently,

there may be a leak in the system. Inspect the radiator, hoses, pressure cap, drain plugs and water pump (see Section 14).

13   If no leaks are noted, have the pressure cap tested by a service station.

14   Check the condition of the coolant as well. It should be relatively clear. If it is brown or rust colored, the system should be drained, flushed and refilled. Even if the coolant appears to be normal, the corrosion inhibitors wear out, so it must be replaced at the specified intervals. If the system is filled with standard green coolant/water, it must be flushed and replaced more frequently than if the original DEX-COOL coolant is retained.

Windshield washer fluid

15   Fluid for the windshield washer system is located in a plastic reservoir in the left side of the engine compartment (see illustration).

16   In milder climates, plain water can be used in the reservoir, but it should be kept no more than 2/3 full to allow for expansion if the water freezes. In colder climates, use windshield washer system antifreeze, available at any auto parts store, to lower the freezing point of the fluid. Mix the antifreeze with water in accordance with the manufacturer's directions on the container.

Caution: *Don't use cooling system antifreeze - it will smear the windshield and damage the vehicle's paint.*

17   To help prevent icing in cold weather, warm the windshield with the defroster before using the washer.

Battery electrolyte

18   These vehicles are equipped with a battery which is permanently sealed (except for vent holes) and has no filler caps. Water doesn't have to be added to these batteries at any time. If a maintenance-type battery is installed, the caps on the top of the battery should be removed periodically to check for a low electrolyte level. This check is most critical during the warm summer months. Add only distilled water to any battery.

4.20 Never let the brake fluid level drop below the MIN mark

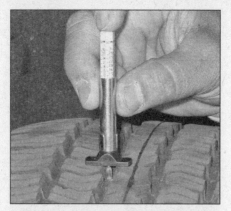

5.2 Use a tire tread depth indicator to monitor tire wear

Brake fluid

19   The brake master cylinder is mounted on the upper left of the engine compartment firewall.

20   The translucent plastic reservoir allows the fluid inside to be checked without removing the cap (see illustration). Be sure to wipe the top of reservoir cap with a clean rag to prevent contamination of the brake system before removing the cover.

21   When adding fluid, pour it carefully into the reservoir to avoid spilling it on surrounding painted surfaces. Be sure the specified fluid is used, since mixing different types of brake fluid can cause damage to the system. See Recommended lubricants and fluids in this Chapter's Specifications or your owner's

manual.

Warning: *Brake fluid can harm your eyes and damage painted surfaces, so use extreme caution when handling or pouring it. Do not use brake fluid that has been standing open or is more than one year old. Brake fluid absorbs moisture from the air. Moisture in the system can cause a dangerous loss of brake performance.*

22   At this time, the fluid and master cylinder can be inspected for contamination. The system should be drained and refilled if deposits, dirt particles or water droplets are seen in the fluid.

23   After filling the reservoir to the proper level, make sure the cover or cap is on tight to prevent fluid leakage.

24   The brake fluid level in the master cylinder will drop slightly as the pads at the front wheels wear down during normal operation. If the master cylinder requires repeated additions to keep it at the proper level, it's an indication of leakage in the brake system, which should be corrected immediately. Check all brake lines and connections (see Section 19 for more information).

25   If, upon checking the master cylinder fluid level, you discover the reservoir is empty or nearly empty, the brake system should be bled and thoroughly inspected (see Chapter 9).

5   Tire and tire pressure checks (every 250 miles or weekly)

1   Periodic inspection of the tires may spare you the inconvenience of being stranded with a flat tire. It can also provide you with vital information regarding possible problems in the steering and suspension systems before major damage occurs.

2   The original tires on this vehicle are equipped with 1/2-inch wide wear bands that will appear when tread depth reaches 1/16-inch, at which point the tires can be considered worn out. Tread wear can be monitored with a simple, inexpensive device known as a tread depth indicator (see illustration).

3   Note any abnormal tread wear (see illustration). Tread pattern irregularities such as cupping, flat spots and more wear on one side than the other are indications of front end

UNDERINFLATION

CUPPING

Cupping may be caused by:
- Underinflation and/or mechanical irregularities such as out-of-balance condition of wheel and/or tire, and bent or damaged wheel.
- Loose or worn steering tie-rod or steering idler arm.
- Loose, damaged or worn front suspension parts.

OVERINFLATION

INCORRECT TOE-IN OR EXTREME CAMBER

FEATHERING DUE TO MISALIGNMENT

5.3 This chart will help you determine the condition of the tires and the probable cause(s) of abnormal wear

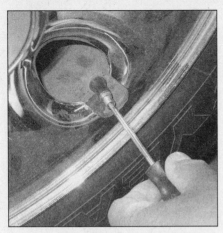

5.4a If a tire loses air on a steady basis, check the valve stem core first to make sure it's snug (valve core drivers are commonly available at auto parts stores)

5.4b If the valve stem core is tight, raise the corner of the vehicle with the low tire and spray a soapy water solution onto the tread as the tire is turned slowly - leaks will cause small bubbles to appear

5.8 To extend the life of the tires, check the air pressure at least once a week with an accurate gauge (don't forget the spare!)

alignment and/or balance problems. If any of these conditions are noted, take the vehicle to a tire shop or service station to correct the problem.

4   Look closely for cuts, punctures and embedded nails or tacks. Sometimes a tire will hold air pressure for a short time or leak down very slowly after a nail has embedded itself in the tread. If a slow leak persists, check the valve stem core to make sure it's tight (see illustration). Examine the tread for an object that may have embedded itself in the tire or for a plug that may have begun to leak (radial tire punctures are repaired with a plug that's installed in a puncture). If a puncture is suspected, it can be easily verified by spraying a solution of soapy water onto the puncture area (see illustration). The soapy solution will bubble if there's a leak. Unless the puncture is unusually large, a tire shop or service station can usually repair the tire.

5   Carefully inspect the inner sidewall of each tire for evidence of brake fluid leakage. If

you see any, inspect the brakes immediately.

6   Correct air pressure adds miles to the lifespan of the tires, improves mileage and enhances overall ride quality. Tire pressure cannot be accurately estimated by looking at a tire, especially if it's a radial. A tire pressure gauge is essential. Keep an accurate gauge in the vehicle. The pressure gauges attached to the nozzles of air hoses at gas stations are often inaccurate.

7   Always check tire pressure when the tires are cold. Cold, in this case, means the vehicle has not been driven over a mile in the three hours preceding a tire pressure check. A pressure rise of four to eight pounds is not uncommon once the tires are warm.

8   Unscrew the valve cap protruding from the wheel or hubcap and push the gauge firmly onto the valve stem (see illustration). Note the reading on the gauge and compare the figure to the recommended tire pressure shown on the placard on the driver's side door pillar. Be sure to reinstall the valve cap to

keep dirt and moisture out of the valve stem mechanism. Check all four tires and, if necessary, add enough air to bring them up to the recommended pressure.

9   Don't forget to keep the spare tire inflated to the specified pressure (see your owner's manual or the tire sidewall).

6   Power steering fluid level check (every 3000 miles or 3 months)

1   The hydraulic power steering system relies on fluid which may, over a period of time, require replenishing.

2   On all models equipped with hydraulic power steering, the fluid reservoir for the power steering pump is located on the pump body at the front of the engine (see illustration).

3   For the check, the front wheels should be pointed straight ahead and the engine should be off.

4   Use a clean rag to wipe off the reservoir cap and the area around the cap. This will help prevent any foreign matter from entering the reservoir during the check.

5   Twist off the cap and check the temperature of the fluid at the end of the dipstick with your finger.

6   Wipe off the fluid with a clean rag, reinsert the dipstick, then withdraw it and read the fluid level. The fluid should be at the proper level, depending on whether it was checked hot or cold (see illustration). Never allow the fluid level to drop below the lower mark on the dipstick.

7   If additional fluid is required, pour the specified type into the reservoir, a little at a time to avoid overfilling.

8   If the reservoir requires frequent fluid additions, all power steering hoses, hose connections, steering gear and the power steering pump should be carefully checked for leaks.

6.2 The power steering fluid dipstick is located in the power steering pump reservoir - turn the cap counterclockwise to remove it

6.6 The power steering fluid dipstick has marks on it so the fluid can be checked hot or cold

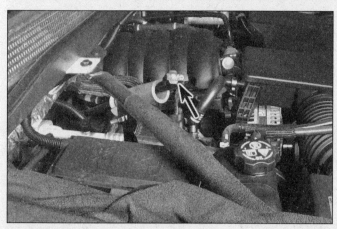

7.4 The automatic transmission dipstick is located at the right rear of the engine compartment - flip up the handle before pulling out the dipstick

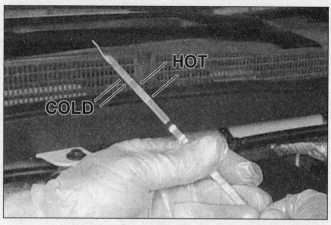

7.7 The automatic transmission fluid must be kept in the regions marked, depending on the fluid temperature

7   Automatic transmission fluid level check (every 3000 miles or 3 months)

1   The automatic transmission fluid level should be carefully maintained. Low fluid level can lead to slipping or loss of drive, while overfilling can cause foaming. Either condition can damage the transmission.
Note: *Incorrect fluid level readings will result if the vehicle has just been driven at high speeds for an extended period, in hot weather in city traffic, or if it has been pulling a trailer. If any of these conditions apply, wait until the fluid has cooled (about 30 minutes).*

6-speed (6L80/6L90) models
2   With the parking brake set, start the engine, then move the shift lever through all the gear ranges, ending in Park. The fluid level must be checked with the vehicle level and the engine running at idle.
3   Press the Trip/Fuel button or the trip odometer reset button to display the transmission fluid temperature on the speedometer or on the Driver Information Center (DIC). If the fluid temperature is between 80 and 90-degrees F, you'll be using the COLD markings on the dipstick. If it's between 160 and 200-degrees F, you'll be using the HOT markings on the dipstick. If it's above 200-degrees F, wait until the fluid has cooled back down and falls into the "hot" temperature range. If it's between 90 and 160-degrees F, operate the vehicle until warms up to the "hot" range.
4   With the transmission at the proper temperature, remove the dipstick from the filler tube. The dipstick is located at the rear of the engine compartment on the passenger's side (see illustration).
5   Wipe the fluid from the dipstick with a clean rag and push it back into the filler tube until the cap seats.
6   Pull the dipstick out again and note the fluid level.
7   If the fluid is cold or slightly warm (80 to 90-degrees F), the level should be in the

COLD range on the dipstick (see illustration). If it's hot (160 to 200-degrees F), the level should be in the crosshatched HOT range. If additional fluid is required, add it into the dipstick tube using a funnel. Add the fluid a little at a time and keep checking the level until it's correct. It is important to not overfill the transmission.
8   The condition of the fluid should also be checked along with the level. If the fluid at the end of the dipstick is a dark reddish-brown color, or if it smells burned, it should be changed. If you are in doubt about the condition of the fluid, purchase some new fluid and compare the two for color and smell.

8-speed (8L90) model
Warning: *Never get underneath the vehicle when it is supported only by a jack. The jack provided with your vehicle is designed solely for raising the vehicle to remove and install a wheel. Always use jackstands to support the vehicle when it becomes necessary to place your body underneath the vehicle.*
Note: *The vehicle must be level to accurately check the automatic transmission fluid, so it will be necessary to raise both the front and rear of the vehicle.*
Warning: *These transmissions do not have a dipstick to check fluid level. The fluid level is checked at the transmission fluid check plug at the bottom of the transmission pan. To accurately check the fluid level, the engine must be running in Park and the vehicle has to be raised off the ground. There is a risk of personal injury from hot transmission fluid and also from the nearby exhaust system. Therefore if attempting this procedure, wear heat-proof gloves and position yourself beneath the vehicle so you are not at risk of being splashed by any transmission fluid. Do not remove the check plug unless the engine is running at idle and in Park, as the transmission fluid drains from the torque converter once the engine is switched off and flows back to the transmission pan. If removed with the engine Off, a large amount of transmission fluid will be expelled from the plug hole.*

7.12 Locate the automatic transmission fluid level check plug and remove it - typical check plug shown

9   With the parking brake set, start the engine, then move the shift lever through all the gear ranges, ending in Park. The fluid level must be checked with the vehicle level and the engine running at idle. The automatic transmission must be at the proper temperature to obtain an accurate fluid level reading.
10   Press the Trip/Fuel button or the trip odometer reset button to display the transmission fluid temperature on the speedometer or on the Driver Information Center (DIC). The transmission fluid temperature should be between 95 and 113-degrees F.
11   Raise the vehicle and support it securely on jackstands.
Warning: *Position your body far enough away from the filler plug hole or oil level check plug hole as hot transmission fluid can cause burns. Also take care as the exhaust is positioned close to the filler plug.*
12   Make sure the engine is idling in Park. Place a drain pan under the transmission fluid level check plug, then remove the check plug from the transmission fluid pan (see illustration).
13   Allow the fluid to drain until it starts to just drip from the hole. If no fluid comes out when

7.15 Use angled needle-nose pliers to lift the plunger on the top of the fill plug to unlock the plug

7.17 Use a hand pump with a long hose to fill the transmission through the fill plug hole

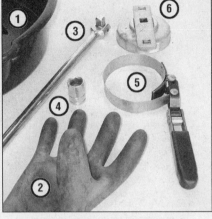

8.3 These tools are required when changing the engine oil and filter

1   *Drain pan* - It should be fairly shallow in depth, but wide to prevent spills
2   *Rubber gloves* - When removing the drain plug and filter, you will get oil on your hands (the gloves will prevent burns)
3   *Breaker bar* - Sometimes the oil drain plug is tight, and a long breaker bar is needed to loosen it
4   *Socket* – To be used with the breaker bar or a ratchet (must be the correct size to fit the drain plug - six-point preferred)
5   *Filter wrench* - This is a metal band-type wrench, which requires clearance around the filter to be effective
6   *Filter wrench* - This type fits on the bottom of the filter and can be turned with a ratchet or breaker bar (different-size wrenches are available for different types of filters)

the check plug is removed, fluid will have to be added until it begins to drip from the hole.

Adding fluid
14   Clean around the top of the fill plug to prevent anything from falling into the transmission.
Note: *The fill plug is located on the right side of the transmission case.*
15   Use a pair of long needle-nose pliers with a 90-degree bend to unlock the fill plug (see illustration).
16   With the plug unlocked, use the pliers to lift the plug out of the hole.
17   Add fluid through the fill plug hole using a hand pump with a long hose (see illustration) until fluid starts running out of the fluid level check plug hole.
18   Install the check plug into the transmission pan and tighten it temporarily.
19   Install the fill plug and depress the plunger to lock it in place.
20   Check the fluid level (see Steps 12 and 13).
21   Install the check plug and tighten it to the torque listed in this Chapter's Specifications.
22   The condition of the fluid should also be checked along with the level. If the fluid is a dark reddish-brown color, or if the fluid has a burned smell, the fluid should be changed. If you're in doubt about the condition of the fluid, purchase some new fluid and compare the two for color and smell.

8   Engine oil and filter change (every 3000 miles or 3 months)

Note: *These vehicles are equipped with an oil life indicator system that illuminates a light or message on the instrument panel when the system deems it necessary to change the oil. A number of factors are taken into consideration to determine when the oil should be considered worn out. Generally, this system will*

allow the vehicle to accumulate more miles between oil changes than the traditional 3000-mile interval, but we believe that frequent oil changes are cheap insurance and will prolong engine life. If you do decide not to change your oil every 3000 miles and rely on the oil life indicator instead, make sure you don't exceed 7,500 miles before the oil is changed, regardless of what the oil life indicator shows.
1   Frequent oil changes are the most important preventive maintenance procedures that can be done by the home mechanic. As engine oil ages, it becomes diluted and contaminated, which leads to premature engine wear.
2   Although some sources recommend oil filter changes every other oil change, we feel that the minimal cost of an oil filter and the relative ease with which it is installed dictate that a new filter be installed every time the oil is changed.
3   Gather together all necessary tools and materials before beginning this procedure (see illustration). You should also have plenty of clean rags and newspapers handy to mop up any spills.
4   Warm the engine to normal operating temperature. If the new oil or any tools are needed, use this warm-up time to gather everything necessary for the job. The correct type of oil for your application can be found in *Recommended lubricants and fluids* in this Chapter's Specifications.
5   Raise the vehicle and support it securely on jackstands then remove the splash shield (see illustration).
Warning: *Do not work under a vehicle which is supported only by a jack.*
6   If this is your first oil change, familiarize yourself with the locations of the oil drain plug and the oil filter.
7   Set the drain pan under the drain plug. Keep in mind that the oil will initially flow from the pan with some force; position the pan accordingly.

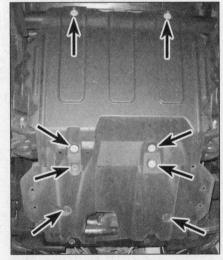

8.5 Splash shield fastener locations

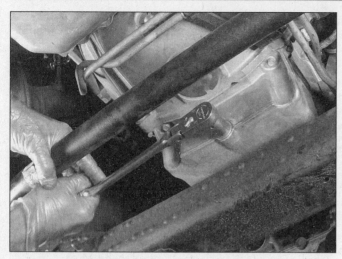

8.8 Use a proper size box-end wrench or socket to remove the oil drain plug and avoid rounding it off

8.10 Since the oil filter is on very tight, you'll need a special wrench for removal - DO NOT use the wrench to tighten the new filter

8   Being careful not to touch any of the hot exhaust components, use a wrench to remove the drain plug near the bottom of the oil pan (see illustration). Depending on how hot the oil is, you may want to wear gloves while unscrewing the plug the final few turns.

9   After all the oil has drained, wipe off the drain plug with a clean rag. Clean the area around the drain plug opening and reinstall the plug. Tighten the plug securely with the wrench. If a torque wrench is available, use it to tighten the plug to the torque listed in this Chapter's Specifications.

10   Move the drain pan into position under the oil filter, then use the oil filter wrench to loosen the oil filter (see illustration).

11   Completely unscrew the old filter. Be careful: it's full of oil. Empty the oil inside the filter into the drain pan.

12   Compare the old filter with the new one to make sure they're the same type.

13   Clean the area where the oil filter mounts to the engine. Check the old filter to make sure the rubber gasket isn't stuck to the engine. If the gasket is stuck to the engine (use a flashlight if necessary), remove it.

14   Apply a light coat of clean oil to the rubber gasket on the new oil filter (see illustration).

15   Attach the new filter to the engine, following the tightening directions printed on the filter canister or packing box. Most filter manufacturers recommend against using a filter wrench due to the possibility of overtightening and damage to the seal.

16   Lower the vehicle, open the hood and locate the oil filler cap.

17   Refer to the engine oil capacity in this Chapter's Specifications and add the proper amount of fresh oil into the engine. Wait a few minutes to allow the oil to drain into the pan, then check the level on the oil dipstick (see Section 4). If the oil level is above the hatched area, start the engine and allow the new oil to circulate.

18   Run the engine for only about a minute and then shut it off. Immediately look under the vehicle and check for leaks at the oil pan drain plug and around the oil filter.

19   Wait about five minutes, then recheck the level on the dipstick. Add more oil as necessary.

20   During the first few trips after an oil change, make it a point to check frequently for leaks and proper oil level.

21   The old oil drained from the engine cannot be reused in its present state and should be disposed of. Check with your local auto parts store, disposal facility or environmental agency to see if they will accept the oil for recycling. After the oil has cooled it can be drained into a container (capped plastic jugs, topped bottles, milk cartons, etc.) for transport to one of these disposal sites. Don't dispose of the oil by pouring it on the ground or down a drain!

Oil Life Monitor

22   The Oil Life Monitor is a function of the PCM that tracks engine operating temperature and rpm. If the PCM determines that your engine's oil has been used long enough, an indicator that shows "CHANGE ENGINE OIL SOON" will light on the instrument panel.

23   When you change your engine oil and filter, whether you change it at the interval recommended in this chapter or only when the light comes on, you will have to reset the system to make the indicator go out and allow the system to accurately calculate when the next oil change is due.

24   To reset, turn the ignition key to the Run position (not Start) with the engine off, then fully depress and let up the accelerator pedal three times within a five-second period. Turn the key to Off, then start the engine. If the "CHANGE ENGINE OIL SOON" message still appears, repeat the resetting procedure.

8.14 Lubricate the oil filter gasket with clean engine oil before installing the filter on the engine

9   Seat belt check (every 6000 miles or 6 months)

1   Check seat belts, buckles, latch plates and guide loops for obvious damage and signs of wear.

2   Where the seat belt receptacle bolts to the floor of the vehicle, check that the bolts are secure.

3   See if the seat belt reminder light comes on when the key is turned to the Run or Start position. A chime should also sound.

10   Wiper blade inspection and replacement (every 6000 miles or 6 months)

1   The windshield wiper blade elements should be checked periodically for cracks and deterioration.

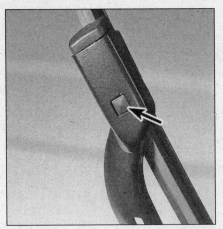

10.3 Depress the button and and slide the blade outward

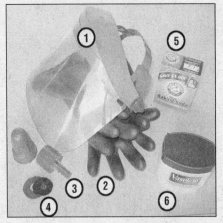

11.1 Tools and materials required for battery maintenance

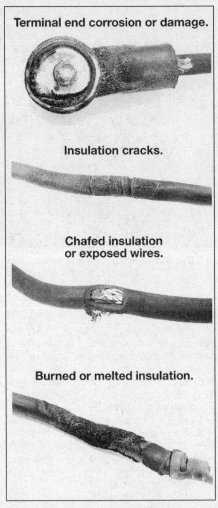

11.5 Typical battery cable problems

2   Lift the wiper blade assembly away from the glass.

3   Press the button down (see illustration) to allow the blade to slide out and disengage the first lock.

4   Rotate the blade upward and unhook the blade from the arm.

5   Compare the new blade with the old for length, design, etc.

6   Install the new blade by reversing the removal procedure.

7   Check to be sure the wiper blade is properly secured, a click should be heard when the blade is properly locked, then wet the windshield and test for proper operation.

11   Battery check, maintenance and charging (every 6000 miles or 6 months)

Warning: *Certain precautions must be followed when checking and servicing the battery. Hydrogen gas, which is highly flammable, is always present in the battery cells, so keep lighted tobacco and all other open flames and sparks away from the battery. The electrolyte inside the battery is actually dilute sulfuric acid, which will cause injury if splashed on your skin or in your eyes. It will also ruin clothes and painted surfaces. When removing the battery cables, always detach the negative cable first and hook it up last!*

1   A routine preventive maintenance program for the battery in your vehicle is the only way to ensure quick and reliable starts. But before performing any battery maintenance, make sure that you have the proper equipment necessary to work safely around the battery (see illustration).

Note: *Some models have an auxiliary battery in addition to the standard battery. All of the following care and maintenance should be applied to both batteries.*

2   There are also several precautions that should be taken whenever battery mainte-

1   Face shield/safety goggles - When removing corrosion with a brush, the acidic particles can easily fly up into your eyes

2   Rubber gloves - Another safety item to consider when servicing the battery; remember that's acid inside the battery!

3   Battery terminal/ cable cleaner - This wire brush cleaning tool will remove all traces of corrosion from the battery and cable

4   Treated felt washers - Placing one of these on each terminal, directly under the cable end, will help prevent corrosion (be sure to get the correct type for side terminal batteries)

5   Baking soda - A solution of baking soda and water can be used to neutralize corrosion

6   Petroleum jelly - A layer of this on the battery terminal bolts will help prevent corrosion

nance is performed. Before servicing the battery, always turn the engine and all accessories off and disconnect the cable from the negative terminal of the battery.

3   The battery produces hydrogen gas, which is both flammable and explosive. Never create a spark, smoke or light a match around the battery. Always charge the battery in a ventilated area.

4   Electrolyte contains poisonous and corrosive sulfuric acid. Do not allow it to get in your eyes, on your skin or on your clothes. Never ingest it. Wear protective safety glasses when working near the battery. Keep children away from the battery.

5   Note the external condition of the battery. If the positive terminal and cable clamp on your vehicle's battery is equipped with a rubber protector, make sure that it's not torn or damaged. It should completely cover the terminal. Look for any corroded or loose connections, cracks in the case or cover or loose hold-down clamps. Also check the entire length of each cable for cracks and frayed conductors (see illustration).

6   If corrosion, which looks like white, fluffy

deposits is evident, particularly around the terminals, the battery should be removed for cleaning. Loosen the cable bolts with a wrench, being careful to remove the ground cable first, and slide them off the terminals. Then disconnect the hold-down clamp bolt and nut, remove the clamp and lift the battery from the engine compartment.

7   Clean the cable ends thoroughly with a battery brush or a terminal cleaner and a solution of warm water and baking soda. Wash the terminals and the side of the battery case with the same solution but make sure that the solution doesn't get into the battery. When cleaning the cables, terminals and battery case, wear safety goggles and rubber gloves to prevent any solution from coming in contact with your eyes or hands. Wear old clothes too - even diluted, sulfuric acid splashed onto clothes will burn holes in them. If the terminals have been corroded, clean them up with a terminal cleaner (see illustrations). Thoroughly wash all cleaned areas with plain water.

8   Make sure that the battery tray is in good condition and the hold-down clamp bolts are tight. If the battery is removed from the tray, make sure no parts remain in the bottom of

Terminal end corrosion or damage.

Insulation cracks.

Chafed insulation or exposed wires.

Burned or melted insulation.

11.7a A tool like this one (available at auto parts stores) is used to clean the side-terminal type battery-cable contact area

11.7b Use the brush side of the tool to finish the job

11.7c Regardless of the type of tool used on the battery and cables, a clean, shiny surface should be the result

the tray when the battery is reinstalled. When reinstalling the hold-down clamp bolts, do not overtighten them.

9   Any metal parts of the vehicle damaged by corrosion should be covered with a zinc-based primer, then painted.

10   Information on removing and installing the battery can be found in Chapter 5. Information on jump-starting can be found at the front of this manual. For more detailed battery checking procedures, refer to the Haynes Automotive Electrical Manual.

Charging

Warning: *When batteries are being charged, hydrogen gas, which is very explosive and flammable, is produced. Do not smoke or allow open flames near a charging or a recently charged battery. Wear eye protection when near the battery during charging. Also, make sure the charger is unplugged before connecting or disconnecting the battery from the charger.*

Note: *The manufacturer recommends the battery be removed from the vehicle for charging because the gas that escapes during this procedure can damage the paint. Fast charging with the battery cables connected can result in damage to the electrical system.*

11   Slow-rate charging is the best way to restore a battery that's discharged to the point where it will not start the engine. It's also a good way to maintain the battery charge in a vehicle that's only driven a few miles between starts. Maintaining the battery charge is particularly important in the winter when the battery must work harder to start the engine and electrical accessories that drain the battery are in greater use.

12   It's best to use a one- or two-amp battery charger (sometimes called a "trickle" charger). They are the safest and put the least strain on the battery. They are also the least expensive. For a faster charge, you can use a higher amperage charger, but don't use one rated more than 1/10th the amp/hour rating of

the battery. Rapid boost charges that claim to restore the power of the battery in one to two hours are hardest on the battery and can damage batteries not in good condition. This type of charging should only be used in emergency situations.

13   The average time necessary to charge a battery should be listed in the instructions that come with the charger. As a general rule, a trickle charger will charge a battery in 12 to 16 hours.

14   Remove all the cell caps (if equipped) and cover the holes with a clean cloth to prevent spattering electrolyte. Disconnect the negative battery cable and hook the battery charger cable clamps up to the battery posts (positive to positive, negative to negative), then plug in the charger. Make sure it is set at 12-volts if it has a selector switch.

15   If you're using a charger with a rate higher than two amps, check the battery regularly during charging to make sure it doesn't overheat. If you're using a trickle charger, you can safely let the battery charge overnight after you've checked it regularly for the first couple of hours.

16   If the battery has removable cell caps, measure the specific gravity with a hydrometer every hour during the last few hours of the charging cycle. Hydrometers are available inexpensively from auto parts stores - follow the instructions that come with the hydrometer. Consider the battery charged when there's no change in the specific gravity reading for two hours and the electrolyte in the cells is gassing (bubbling) freely. The specific gravity reading from each cell should be very close to the others. If not, the battery probably has a bad cell(s).

17   Some batteries with sealed tops have built-in hydrometers on the top that indicate the state of charge by the color displayed in the hydrometer window. Normally, a bright-colored hydrometer indicates a full charge and a dark hydrometer indicates the battery still needs charging.

18   If the battery has a sealed top and no built-in hydrometer, you can hook up a digital voltmeter across the battery terminals to check the charge. A fully charged battery should read 12.5 volts or higher.

19   Further information on the battery and jump-starting can be found in Chapter 5 and at the front of this manual.

12   Drivebelt check and replacement (every 30,000 miles or 24 months)

1   The drivebelt(s) are located at the front of the engine and play an important role in the overall operation of the engine and its components. Depending on the year and engine used, several configurations are available ranging from a single belt to multiple belts. Due to their function and material make up, the belts are prone to wear and should be periodically inspected. The belt(s) drive the alternator, power steering pump, water pump, vacuum pump and air conditioning compressor. Although the belts should be inspected at the recommended intervals, replacement may not be necessary for more than 100,000 miles.

Check

2   The tension of the belt for the alternator, power steering and water pump is automatically adjusted by the belt tensioner and does not require any adjustments. The drivebelt for the air conditioning compressor or vacuum pump has no tensioner, it uses a "stretchy" belt.

3   With the engine stopped, inspect the full length of the drivebelt(s) for cracks and separation of the belt plies. It will be necessary to turn the engine (using a wrench or socket and breaker bar on the crankshaft pulley bolt, working clockwise only) in order to move the belt from the pulleys so that the belt can be inspected thoroughly. Check for fraying, and

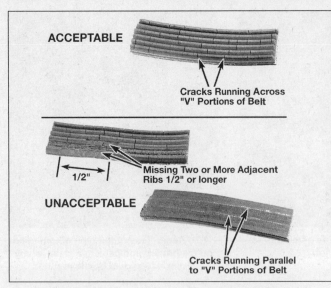

12.4 Small cracks in the underside of a V-ribbed belt are acceptable - lengthwise cracks, or missing pieces that cause the belt to make noise, are cause for replacement

12.6a V6 engine accesory drivebelt tensioner details

1 *Square drive*
2 *Rotate counterclockwise to release tension*
3 *Tensioner mounting bolt*

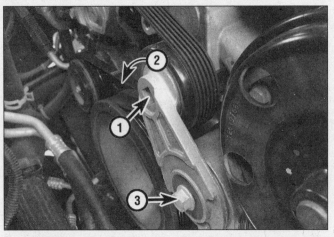

12.6b V8 engine accessory drivebelt tensioner details

1 *Square drive*   3 *Tensioner mounting bolt*
2 *Rotate counterclockwise*
   to release tension

12.13 Install the belt installation tool and rotate the crankshaft pulley until the belt is lifted onto the pulley

glazing which gives the belt a shiny appearance. Check the pulleys for nicks, cracks, distortion and corrosion.

4   Note that it is not unusual for a ribbed belt to exhibit small cracks in the edges of the belt ribs, and unless these are extensive or very deep, belt replacement is not essential (see illustration).

Replacement

Accessory drivebelt (alternator, water pump and power steering pump, if equipped)

5   Remove the air intake duct (see Chapter 4, Section 12).

6   Note how the drivebelt is routed, then insert a 1/2-inch square drive breaker bar into the tensioner pulley square hole. Rotate

the tensioner counterclockwise (see illustrations) to release the drivebelt tension. Once tension has been released, remove the belt from the pulleys. Once the outer belt has been removed, the air conditioning belt and vacuum pump belt can be accessed.

7   Install the new drivebelt onto the crankshaft, idler, alternator, power steering pump and water pump pulleys, then turn the tensioner back and locate the drivebelt on the tensioner pulley. Make sure that the drivebelt is correctly seated in all of the pulley grooves, then release the tensioner. Reinstall the air filter duct.

Air conditioning compressor drivebelt

8   Remove the accessory drivebelt (see Steps 5 and 6).

9   Remove the engine splash shield (see Section 8).

10   Using a pair of diagonal cutting pliers, cut the air conditioning belt to remove it.

Note: *Some tool manufacturers make air conditioning compressor belt removal tools that can remove the belt without cutting it off. We only recommend using this type of tool if the belt if relatively new. Always check the belt for damage after the removal process.*

11   Place the new belt on the crankshaft pulley, making sure the belt is fully seated in the pulley grooves.

12   Place the installation tool on the compressor pulley, then loop the belt over the tool.

13   Rotate the crankshaft pulley and allow the tool to turn, which will lift the belt onto the pulley (see illustration).

12.17 Cut the vacuum pump belt to remove it

12.18 Place an angled scraping tool between the belt and the top of the pulley

12.20 Install the belt onto the pulley while pressing toward the pulley and rotate the crankshaft pulley until the belt is lifted over the lip of the pulley

12.23a Drivebelt tensioner (accessory) mounting bolt location-4.3L models shown, 5.3L and 6.2L models similar

12.23b Drivebelt tensioner (accessory) mounting bolts - 6.0L models

14   The remainder of installation is the reverse of removal.

Vacuum pump drivebelt
15   Remove the accessory drivebelt (see Steps 5 and 6).

16   Remove the air conditioning compressor pump belt (see Steps 9 and 10).

17   Using a pair of diagonal cutting pliers (see illustration), cut the vacuum pump belt to remove it.

18   An alternative way to remove the belt without cutting it off is to place an angled scraping tool between the belt and the pulley (see illustration), then rotate the crankshaft pulley until the belt is removed from the pulley. We only recommend trying this if the belt if relatively new. Always check the belt for damage after the removal process.

19   Place the new belt on the crankshaft pulley, making sure the belt is fully seated in the pulley grooves.

20   Start the belt on the lower edge of the vacuum pump, then rotate the crankshaft pulley and allow the belt to be pulled onto the pulley (see illustration).

21   The remainder of installation is the reverse of removal.

Drivebelt tensioners

Drivebelt tensioner
22   Remove the drivebelt (see Steps 5 and 6).

23   Remove the bolt(s) securing the tensioner to the engine (see illustrations), then detach the tensioner from the engine.

24   Installation is the reverse of removal. Tighten the tensioner bolts to the torque listed in this Chapter's Specifications.

13   Underhood hose check and replacement (every 6000 miles or 6 months)

General
Caution: *Replacement of air conditioning hoses must be left to a dealer service depart-*

ment or air conditioning shop that has the equipment to depressurize the system safely and recover the refrigerant. Never remove air conditioning components or hosesuntil the system has been depressurized.

1   High temperatures in the engine compartment can cause the deterioration of the rubber and plastic hoses used for engine, accessory and emission systems operation. Periodic inspection should be made for cracks, loose clamps, material hardening and leaks. Information specific to the cooling system hoses can be found in Section 14.

2   Some, but not all, hoses are secured to their fittings with clamps. Where clamps are used, check to be sure they haven't lost their tension, allowing the hose to leak. If clamps aren't used, make sure the hose has not expanded and/or hardened where it slips over the fitting, allowing it to leak.

Vacuum hoses
3   It's quite common for vacuum hoses, especially those in the emissions system, to be color-coded or identified by colored stripes

molded into them. Various systems require hoses with different wall thickness, collapse resistance and temperature resistance. When replacing hoses, be sure the new ones are made of the same material.

4   Often the only effective way to check a hose is to remove it completely from the vehicle. If more than one hose is removed, be sure to label the hoses and fittings to ensure correct installation.

5   When checking vacuum hoses, be sure to include any plastic T-fittings in the check. Inspect the fittings for cracks and the hose where it fits over the fitting for distortion, which could cause leakage.

6   A small piece of vacuum hose (1/4-inch inside diameter) can be used as a stethoscope to detect vacuum leaks. Hold one end of the hose to your ear and probe around vacuum hoses and fittings, listening for the hissing sound characteristic of a vacuum leak. **Warning:** *When probing with the vacuum hose stethoscope, be very careful not to come into contact with moving engine components such as the drivebelt, cooling fan, etc.*

Fuel hose

Warning: *Gasoline is extremely flammable, so take extra precautions when you work on any part of the fuel system. Don't smoke or allow open flames or bare light bulbs near the work area, and don't work in a garage where a gas-type appliance (such as a water heater or clothes dryer) is present. Since gasoline is carcinogenic, wear latex gloves when there's a possibility of being exposed to fuel, and, if you spill any fuel on your skin, rinse it off immediately with soap and water. Mop up any spills immediately and do not store fuel-soaked rags where they could ignite. When you perform any kind of work on the fuel system, wear safety glasses and have a Class B type fire extinguisher on hand. The fuel system is under pressure, so if any lines must be disconnected, the pressure in the system must be relieved first (see Chapter 4 for more information).*

7   Check all rubber fuel lines for deterioration and chafing. Check especially for cracks in areas where the hose bends and just before fittings, such as where a hose attaches to the fuel filter and fuel injection unit.

8   High quality fuel line, specifically designed for high-pressure fuel injection applications, must be used for fuel line replacement. Never, under any circumstances, use regular fuel line, unreinforced vacuum line, clear plastic tubing or water hose for fuel lines.

9   Spring-type (pinch) clamps are commonly used on fuel lines. These clamps often lose their tension over a period of time, and can be sprung during removal. Replace all spring-type clamps with screw clamps whenever a hose is replaced.

Metal lines

10   Sections of metal line are routed along the frame, between the fuel tank and the engine. Check carefully to be sure the line has not been bent or crimped and no cracks have started in the line.

11   If a section of metal fuel line must be replaced, only seamless steel tubing should be used, since copper and aluminum tubing don't have the strength necessary to withstand normal engine vibration.

12   Check the metal brake lines where they enter the master cylinder and brake proportioning unit for cracks in the lines or loose fittings. Any sign of brake fluid leakage calls for an immediate and thorough inspection of the brake system.

---

14   Cooling system check (every 6000 miles or 6 months)

Warning: *Wait until the engine is completely cool before beginning this procedure.*
Caution: *Never mix green-colored ethylene glycol antifreeze and orange-colored DEX-COOL silicate-free coolant because doing so will destroy the efficiency of the DEX-COOL coolant, which is designed to last for 100,000 miles or five years.*

1   Many major engine failures can be attributed to a faulty cooling system. The cooling system also cools the transmission fluid and thus plays an important role in prolonging transmission life.

2   The cooling system should be checked with the engine cold. Do this before the vehicle is driven for the day or after it has been shut off for at least three hours.

3   Remove the coolant pressure cap on the expansion tank by slowly unscrewing it. If you hear any hissing sounds (indicating there is still pressure in the system), wait until it stops. Thoroughly clean the cap, inside and out, with clean water. Also clean the filler neck on the expansion tank. All traces of corrosion should be removed. The coolant inside the expansion tank should be relatively transparent. If it is rust colored, the system should be drained and refilled (see Section 26). If the coolant level is not up to the Cold mark, add additional antifreeze/coolant mixture (see Section 4).

4   Carefully check the large upper and lower radiator hoses along with any smaller diameter heater hoses that run from the engine to the firewall. Inspect each hose along its entire length, replacing any hose that is cracked, swollen or shows signs of deterioration. Cracks may become more apparent if the hose is squeezed (see illustration).

5   Make sure all hose connections are tight. A leak in the cooling system will usually show up as white or rust-colored deposits on the areas adjoining the leak. If wire-type clamps are used at the ends of the hoses, it may be wise to replace them with more secure, screw-type clamps.

6   Use compressed air or a soft brush to remove bugs, leaves, etc., from the front of the radiator or air conditioning condenser. Be careful not to damage the delicate cooling fins or cut yourself on them.

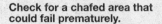
Check for a chafed area that could fail prematurely.

Check for a soft area indicating the hose has deteriorated inside.

Overtightening the clamp on a hardened hose will damage the hose and cause a leak.

Check each hose for swelling and oil-soaked ends. Cracks and breaks can be located by squeezing the hose.

14.4 Hoses, like drivebelts, have a habit of failing at the worst possible time - to prevent the inconvenience of a blown radiator or heater hose, inspect them carefully as shown here

7   Every other inspection, or at the first indication of cooling system problems, have the cap and system pressure tested. If you don't have a pressure tester, most gas stations and repair shops will do this for a minimal charge.

Overheat Protection Operating Mode

8   These engines have a system to protect the engine from damage caused by severe overheating. When the computer senses an overheat condition, an instrument panel warning light comes on that says "reduced power." In this mode, the computer switches the firing of the individual coils on and off at each cylinder to allow cooling cycles between the firing cycles. The engine will have a dramatic loss of power, but will allow vehicle operation in an emergency.

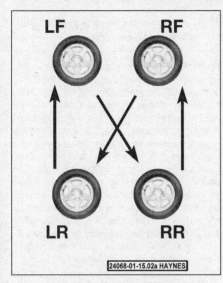

15.2a The recommended four-tire rotation pattern for non-directional tires

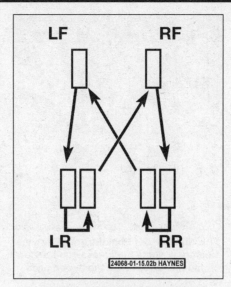

15.2b The recommended tire rotation pattern for vehicles with dual rear wheels (except models with polished aluminum wheels)

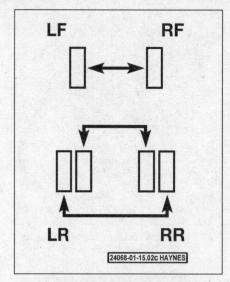

15.2c The recommended tire rotation pattern for vehicles with dual rear wheels and polished aluminum rims

9   If this light is on, find a safe place to get off the road as soon as possible, and allow the engine to cool thoroughly.

10   Check the coolant level and inspect for a split hose or other obvious signs of coolant leakage.

11   The engine oil will be ruined after this mode has operated, since unburned fuel will get into the oil. After fixing the overheating problem, change the oil and filter right away and reset the Oil Life Monitor (see Section 8).

15 Tire rotation (every 6000 miles or 6 months)

1   The tires should be rotated at the specified intervals and whenever uneven wear is noticed.

2   Tires must be rotated in the recommended pattern (see illustrations).

3   Refer to the information in Jacking and towing at the front of this manual for the proper procedures to follow when raising the vehicle and changing a tire. If the brakes are to be checked, don't apply the parking brake as stated. Make sure the tires are blocked to prevent the vehicle from rolling as it's raised.

4   Preferably, the entire vehicle should be raised at the same time. This can be done on a hoist or by jacking up each corner, then lowering the vehicle onto jackstands placed under the frame rails and rear axle. Always use four jackstands and make sure the vehicle is safely supported.

5   After rotation, check and adjust the tire pressures as necessary. Tighten the lug nuts to the torque listed in this Chapter's Specifications.

16 Differential lubricant level check (every 15,000 miles or 12 months)

Note: *4WD vehicles have two differentials - one in the center of each axle. 2WD vehicles have one differential in the center of the rear axle. On 4WD vehicles, be sure to check the lubricant level in both differentials.*

1   If the vehicle is raised to gain access to the plug, be sure to support it safely on jackstands - DO NOT crawl under the vehicle when only the jack supports it. Be sure the vehicle is level or the check may not be accurate. If you're checking the front differential lubricant, remove the splash shield or rock guard, if equipped.

2   Remove the plug from the filler hole in the differential housing or cover (see illustrations).

16.2a On some models, the rear differential filler plug is on the differential cover. On this particular model, the cover must be removed to drain the lubricant

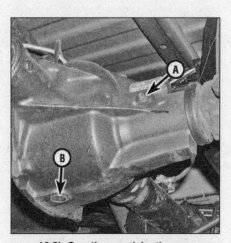

16.2b On other models, the rear differential filler plug (A) is on the side of the housing. (B) is the drain plug

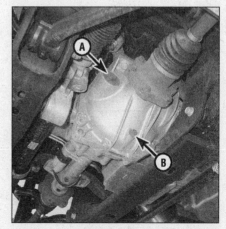

16.2c Front differential filler plug (A) and drain plug (B)

17.1 Materials required for chassis and body lubrication

1   **Engine oil** - Light engine oil in a can like this can be used for door and hood hinges

2   **Graphite spray** - Used to lubricate lock cylinders

3   **Grease** - Grease, in a variety of types and weights, is available for use in a grease gun. Check the Specifications for your requirements

4   **Grease gun**- A common grease gun, shown here with a detachable hose and nozzle, is needed for chassis lubrication. After use, clean it thoroughly!

3   The lubricant level should be within the specified range from the bottom of the filler hole:

4   Front axle - 0 to 1/4-inch

5   Rear axle

a) 8.6-inch axle = 3/64 to 3/4-inch

b) 9.5-inch and 9.76-inch axle = 5/8 to 1-9/16 inch

c) 10.5-inch axle = 0 to 3/8-inch

d) 11.5-inch axle = 5/8 to 3/4-inch

6   If the level is low, use a pump or squeeze bottle to add the recommended lubricant until it is up to the proper level.

7   Install the plug into the filler hole and tighten it to the torque listed in this Chapter's Specifications.

17   Chassis lubrication (every 15,000 miles or 12 months)

1   Refer to *Recommended lubricants and fluids* in this Chapter's Specifications to obtain the necessary grease, etc. You'll also need a grease gun (see illustration). If a suspension component has no grease fitting in place, this indicates the part is sealed and doesn't require periodic lubrication. Some components on 4WD models have fittings that aren't on 2WD versions, and vice versa.

2   Look under the vehicle and locate the grease fittings (see illustration).

3   For easier access under the vehicle,

17.2 Wipe the dirt from the grease fittings before pushing the grease gun nozzle onto the fitting - lube the tie-rod ends

raise it with a jack and place jackstands under the frame. Make sure it's safely supported by the stands. If the wheels are to be removed at this interval for tire rotation or brake inspection, loosen the lug nuts slightly while the vehicle is still on the ground.

4   Before beginning, force a little grease out of the nozzle to remove any dirt from the end of the gun. Wipe the nozzle clean with a rag.

5   With the grease gun and plenty of clean rags, crawl under the vehicle and begin lubricating the components.

6   Wipe one of the grease fittings clean and push the nozzle firmly over it. Pump the gun until the component is completely lubricated. On balljoints, stop pumping when the rubber seal is firm to the touch. Do not pump too much grease into the fitting as it could rupture the seal. For all other suspension and steering components, continue pumping grease into the fitting until it oozes out of the joint between the two components. If it escapes around the grease gun nozzle, the fitting is clogged or the nozzle is not completely seated on the fitting. Resecure the gun nozzle to the fitting and try again. If necessary, replace the fitting with a new one.

7   Wipe the excess grease from the components and the grease fitting. Repeat the procedure for the remaining fittings.

8   Clean the fitting and pump grease into the driveline universal joints until the grease can be seen coming out of the contact points. The other U-joints are sealed and do not require lubrication.

Note: *Most replacement driveshaft U-joints aren't permanently sealed, and are sold with grease fittings. If your U-joints have been replaced, make sure you include them in your routine chassis lubrication.*

9   Also clean and lubricate the parking brake cable guides and levers.

Caution: *Do not use chassis lubrication on the brake cables themselves. The grease will cause the cable housings to deteriorate.*

18   Fuel system check (every 15,000 miles or 12 months)

Warning: *Gasoline is extremely flammable, so take extra precautions when you work on any part of the fuel system. Don't smoke or allow open flames or bare light bulbs near the work area, and don't work in a garage where a gas-type appliance (such as a water heater or clothes dryer) is present. Since gasoline is carcinogenic, wear fuel-resistant gloves when there's a possibility of being exposed to fuel, and, if you spill any fuel on your skin, rinse it off immediately with soap and water. Mop up any spills immediately and do not store fuel-soaked rags where they could ignite. When you perform any kind of work on the fuel system, wear safety glasses and have a Class B type fire extinguisher on hand. The fuel system is under constant pressure, so, before any lines are disconnected, the fuel system pressure must be relieved (see Chapter 4).*

Note: *These vehicles are not equipped with fuel filters. A filter is integral with the fuel pump/fuel level sensor module and requires no maintenance.*

1   If you smell gasoline while driving or after the vehicle has been sitting in the sun, inspect the fuel system immediately.

2   Remove the gas filler cap and inspect if for damage and corrosion. The gasket should have an unbroken sealing imprint. If the gasket is damaged or corroded, install a new cap.

3   Inspect the fuel feed and return lines for cracks. Make sure that the connections between the fuel lines and the fuel injection system are tight.

Warning: *Your vehicle is fuel injected, so you must relieve the fuel system pressure before servicing fuel system components. The fuel system pressure relief procedure is outlined in Chapter 4.*

4   If the fuel injectors are visible, look for signs of fuel leakage (wet spots) around any of the injectors (see Chapter 4), they may need new O-rings.

5   Since some components of the fuel system - the fuel tank and part of the fuel feed and return lines, for example - are underneath the vehicle, they can be inspected more easily with the vehicle raised on a hoist. If that's not possible, raise the vehicle and support it on jackstands.

6   With the vehicle raised and safely supported, inspect the gas tank and filler neck for punctures, cracks and other damage. The connection between the filler neck and the tank is particularly critical. Sometimes a rubber filler neck will leak because of loose clamps or deteriorated rubber. Inspect all fuel tank mounting brackets and straps to be sure that the tank is securely attached to the vehicle.

Warning: *Do not, under any circumstances, try to repair a fuel tank (except rubber components). A welding torch or any open flame can easily cause fuel vapors inside the tank to explode.*

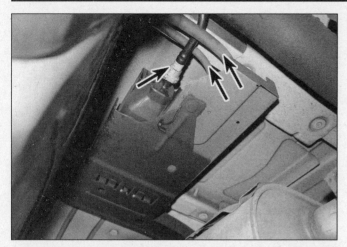

18.9 Check the evaporative emissions system canister and its lines for damage

19.7 With the wheel off, check the thickness of the inner pad through the inspection holes (front caliper)

7   Carefully check all rubber hoses and metal lines leading away from the fuel tank. Check for loose connections, deteriorated hoses, crimped lines and other damage. Repair or replace damaged sections as necessary (see Chapter 4).

8   The evaporative emissions control system can also be a source of fuel odors. The function of the system is to store fuel vapors from the fuel tank in a charcoal canister until they can be routed to the intake manifold where they mix with incoming air before being burned in the combustion chambers.

9   The most common symptom of a faulty evaporative emissions system is a strong odor of fuel. If a fuel odor has been detected, and you have already checked the areas described above, check the charcoal canister, located under the rear of the vehicle, and the hoses connected to it (see illustration).

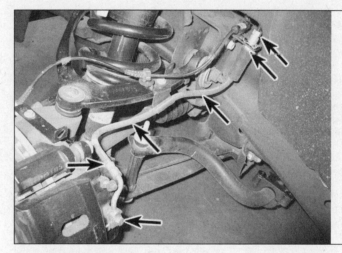

19.11 Check along the brake hoses and at each fitting for deterioration, cracks and leakage

19   Brake system check (every 15,000 miles or 12 months)

Warning: *The dust created by the brake system is harmful to your health. Never blow it out with compressed air and don't inhale any of it. An approved filtering mask should be worn when working on the brakes. Do not, under any circumstances, use petroleum-based solvents to clean brake parts. Use brake system cleaner only! Try to use non-asbestos replacement parts whenever possible.*
Note: *For detailed photographs of the brake system, refer to Chapter 9.*

1   In addition to the specified intervals, the brakes should be inspected every time the wheels are removed or whenever a defect is suspected.

2   Any of the following symptoms could indicate a potential brake system defect: The vehicle pulls to one side when the brake pedal is depressed, the brakes make squealing or dragging noises when applied, brake pedal travel is excessive, the pedal pulsates, or brake fluid leaks, usually onto the

inside of the tire or wheel.

3   Loosen the wheel lug nuts.

4   Raise the vehicle and place it securely on jackstands.

5   Remove the wheels (see *Jacking and towing* at the front of this book, or your owner's manual, if necessary).

Disc brakes

6   There are two pads (an outer and an inner) in each caliper. The pads are visible with the wheels removed. Most vehicles covered by this manual have disc brakes front and rear, with a mechanical, drum-type parking brake mechanism inside the rear discs.

7   Check the pad thickness by looking at each end of the caliper and through the inspection window in the caliper body (see illustration). If the lining material is less than the thickness listed in this Chapter's Specifications, replace the pads.
Note: *Keep in mind that the lining material is riveted or bonded to a metal backing plate and the metal portion is not included in this measurement.*
Note: *The outer pad on front calipers (and both pads on rear calipers) is checked at the edge of the caliper.*

8   If it is difficult to determine the exact thickness of the remaining pad material by the above method, or if you are at all concerned about the condition of the pads, remove the caliper(s), then remove the pads from the calipers for further inspection (see Chapter 9).

9   Once the pads are removed from the calipers, clean them with brake cleaner and re-measure them with a ruler or a vernier caliper.

10   Measure the disc thickness with a micrometer to make sure that it still has service life remaining. If any disc is thinner than the specified minimum thickness, replace it (see Chapter 9). Even if the disc has service life remaining, check its condition. Look for scoring, gouging and burned spots. If these conditions exist, remove the disc and have it resurfaced (see Chapter 9).

11   Before installing the wheels, check all brake lines and hoses for damage, wear, deformation, cracks, corrosion, leakage, bends and twists, particularly in the vicinity of the rubber hoses at the calipers (see illustration). Check the clamps for tightness and the connections for leakage. Make sure that all hoses and lines are clear of sharp edges, moving parts and the exhaust system. If any

20.2a Inspect the muffler and all hangers for signs of deterioration

20.2b Inspect all flanged joints and slip joints (shown) for signs of exhaust gas leakage

of the above conditions are noted, repair, reroute or replace the lines and/or fittings as necessary (see Chapter 9).

Brake booster check

12   Sit in the driver's seat and perform the following sequence of tests.

13   With the brake fully depressed, start the engine - the pedal should move down a little when the engine starts.

14   With the engine running, depress the brake pedal several times - the travel distance should not change.

15   Depress the brake, stop the engine and hold the pedal in for about 30 seconds - the pedal should neither sink nor rise.

16   Restart the engine, run it for about a minute and turn it off. Then firmly depress the brake several times - the pedal travel should decrease with each application.

17   If your brakes do not operate as described, the brake booster has failed. Refer to Chapter 9 for the replacement procedure.

Parking brake

18   One method of checking the parking

brake is to park the vehicle on a steep hill with the parking brake set and the transmission in Neutral (be sure to stay in the vehicle for this check). If the parking brake cannot prevent the vehicle from rolling, it's in need of attention (see Chapter 9).

20   Exhaust system check (every 15,000 miles or 12 months)

1   With the engine cold (at least three hours after the vehicle has been driven), check the complete exhaust system from the manifold to the end of the tailpipe. Be careful around the catalytic converter, which may be hot even after three hours. The inspection should be done with the vehicle on a hoist to permit unrestricted access. If a hoist isn't available, raise the vehicle and support it securely on jackstands.

2   Check the exhaust pipes and connections for signs of leakage and/or corrosion indicating a potential failure. Make sure that all brackets and hangers are in good condi-

tion and tight (see illustrations).

3   Inspect the underside of the body for holes, corrosion, open seams, etc., which may allow exhaust gases to enter the passenger compartment. Seal all body openings with silicone sealant or body putty.

4   Rattles and other noises can often be traced to the exhaust system, especially the hangers, mounts and heat shields. Try to move the pipes, mufflers and catalytic converter. If the components can come in contact with the body or suspension parts, secure the exhaust system with new brackets and hangers.

21   Transfer case lubricant level check (4WD models) (every 15,000 miles or 12 months)

1   The transfer case lubricant level is checked by removing the upper plug located at the rear of the case (see illustration).

2   After removing the plug, reach inside the hole with your finger. The lubricant level should be just at the bottom of the hole. If not, add the appropriate lubricant through the opening.

22   Interior ventilation filter replacement (every 15,000 miles [24,000 km] or 12 months)

1   These models are equipped with an air filtering element for the interior ventilation system. The access panel is located behind the glove box.

2   Remove the glove box door (see Chapter 11).

3   Release the tabs on the filter cover (see illustration), then lower the cover for access to the filter.

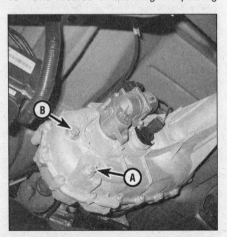

21.1 The drain plug (A) and fill plug (B) are on the rear of the transfer case

22.3 Pull the tabs back to release them

22.4 Slide the filter out, noting the direction of the filter

24.3a Disconnect the electrical connector to the MAF sensor . . .

24.3b . . . then use a prying tool to remove the harness fastener from the filter housing

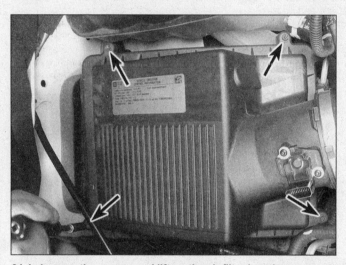

24.4a Loosen the screws and lift up the air filter housing cover . . .

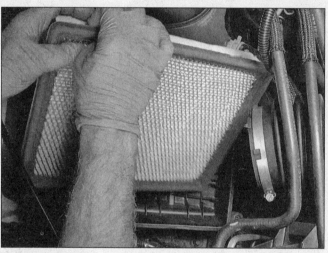

24.4b . . . then remove the filter element

4   Slide the filter straight out (see illustration).

5   Clean out any leaves or other debris from the housing.

6   Installation is the reverse of the removal procedure.

23 Brake fluid change (every 30,000 miles or 24 months)

Warning: *Brake fluid can harm your eyes and damage painted surfaces, so use extreme caution when handling or pouring it. Do not use brake fluid that has been standing open or is more than one year old. Brake fluid absorbs moisture from the air. Excess moisture can cause a dangerous loss of braking effectiveness.*

1   At the specified intervals, the brake fluid should be drained and replaced. Since the brake fluid may drip or splash when pouring it, place plenty of rags around the master cylinder to protect any surrounding painted surfaces.

2   Before beginning work, purchase the specified brake fluid (see Recommended lubricants and fluids in this Chapter's Specifications).

3   Remove the cap from the master cylinder reservoir.

4   Using a hand suction pump or similar device, withdraw the fluid from the master cylinder reservoir.

5   Add new fluid to the master cylinder until it rises to the line indicated on the reservoir.

6   Bleed the brake system as described in Chapter 9 at all four brakes until new and uncontaminated fluid is expelled from the bleeder screw. Be sure to maintain the fluid level in the master cylinder as you perform the bleeding process. If you allow the master cylinder to run dry, air will enter the system.

7   Refill the master cylinder with fluid and check the operation of the brakes. The pedal should feel solid when depressed, with no sponginess.

Warning: *Do not operate the vehicle if you are in doubt about the effectiveness of the brake system.*

24 Air filter replacement (every 30,000 miles or 24 months)

1   At the specified intervals, the air filter element should be replaced with a new one.

2   On all models, the air filter is housed in a black plastic box mounted on the inner fenderwell on the right side of the engine compartment. If you drive in conditions that are particularly dusty, the need for a filter change may be necessary before the normally recommended mileage interval.

3   Disconnect the Mass Air Flow (MAF) sensor electrical connector, then disengage the harness retaining clip from the top cover (see illustrations).

4   Loosen the screws and pull the housing cover up, then lift the air filter element out of the housing (see illustrations). Wipe out the inside of the air filter housing with a clean rag.

5   Place the new filter element in the air filter housing. Make sure it seats properly in the groove of the housing.

6   Installation is the reverse of removal. After installing the new filter, push in on the top of the filter indicator to reset it.

25   Spark plug replacement (see maintenance schedule for service intervals)

1   The spark plugs are threaded into the sides of the cylinder heads, adjacent to the exhaust ports.
2   In most cases, the tools necessary for

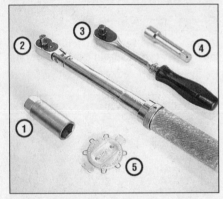

25.2 Tools required for changing the spark plugs

1   Spark plug socket - This will have special padding inside to protect the spark plug's porcelain insulator
2   Torque wrench - Although not mandatory, using this tool is the best way to ensure the plugs are tightened properly
3   Ratchet - Standard hand tool to fit the spark plug socket
4   Extension - Depending on model and accessories, you may need special extensions and universal joints to reach one or more of the plugs
5   Spark plug gap gauge - This gauge for checking the gap comes in a variety of styles. Make sure the gap for your engine is included

spark plug replacement include a spark plug socket, which fits onto a ratchet (spark plug sockets are padded inside to prevent damage to the porcelain insulators on the new plugs), various extensions and a gap gauge to check and adjust the gaps on the new plugs (see illustration). A special plug wire removal tool is available for separating the wire boots from the spark plugs, but it isn't absolutely necessary. A torque wrench should be used to tighten the new plugs.
3   The best approach when replacing the spark plugs is to purchase the new ones in advance, adjust them to the proper gap and replace them one at a time. When buying the new spark plugs, be sure to obtain the correct plug type for your particular engine. This information can be found in the factory owner's manual and this Chapter's Specifications.
4   Allow the engine to cool completely before attempting to remove any of the plugs. While you're waiting for the engine to cool, check the new plugs for defects and adjust the gaps.
5   The gap is checked by inserting the proper-thickness gauge between the electrodes at the tip of the plug (see illustration). The gap

25.5 When checking the spark plug gap, the wire should slide between the electrodes with a slight drag

between the electrodes should be as listed in this Chapter's Specifications. The gauge should just slide between the electrodes with a slight amount of drag.
6   Remove the spark plug wire from one spark plug. Pull only on the rubber boot on the end of the wire - do not pull on the wire. A plug wire removal tool should be used, if available (see illustration).
7   If compressed air is available, use it to blow any dirt or foreign material away from the spark plug hole. This will eliminate the possibility of debris falling into the cylinder as the spark plug is removed.
8   Place the spark plug socket over the plug and remove it from the engine by turning it in a counterclockwise direction (see illustration).
9   Compare the spark plug to those shown in the photos located on the inside back cover of this book to get an indication of the general running condition of the engine.
10   Before installing the new plugs, it is a good idea to apply a thin coat of anti-seize compound to the threads (see illustration).
11   Thread one of the new plugs into the hole until you can no longer turn it with your fingers, then tighten it with a torque wrench (if

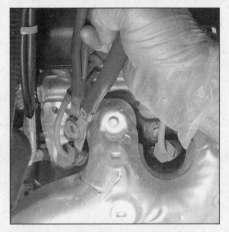

25.6 A tool like this one makes the job of removing the spark plug boot easier - twist it back-and-forth and pull only on the boot

25.8 Use a socket and extension to unscrew the spark plugs - various length extensions and perhaps a flex-joint may be required to reach some plugs

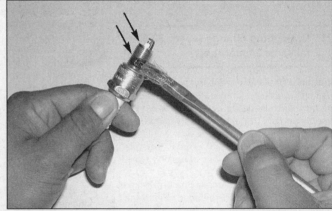

25.10 Apply a thin coat of anti-seize compound to the spark plug threads, being careful not to get any near the lower threads

available) or the ratchet. Where plugs are at the rear of the engine and harder to reach, it might be a good idea to slip a short length of rubber hose over the end of the plug to use as a tool to thread it into place (see illustration). The hose will grip the plug well enough to turn it, but will start to slip if the plug begins to cross-thread in the hole - this will prevent damaged threads and the accompanying repair costs.

12 Attach the plug wire to the new spark plug, again using a twisting motion on the boot until it's seated on the spark plug.

13 Repeat the procedure for the remaining spark plugs, replacing them one at a time to prevent mixing up the spark plug wires.

26 Cooling system servicing (draining, flushing and refilling) (see maintenance schedule for interval)

Warning: *Do not allow antifreeze to come in contact with your skin or painted surfaces of the vehicle. Rinse off spills immediately with plenty of water. Antifreeze is highly toxic if ingested. Never leave antifreeze lying around in an open container or in puddles on the floor; children and pets are attracted by its sweet smell and may drink it. Check with local authorities on disposing of used antifreeze. Many communities have collection centers that will see that antifreeze is disposed of safely. Antifreeze is flammable under certain conditions - be sure to read the precautions on the container.*

Caution: *Never mix green-colored ethylene glycol antifreeze and orange-colored DEX-COOL silicate-free coolant because doing so will destroy the efficiency of the DEX-COOL coolant, which is designed to last for 100,000 miles or five years.*

Draining

1 Periodically, the cooling system should be drained, flushed and refilled to replenish the antifreeze mixture and prevent formation of rust and corrosion, which can impair the performance of the cooling system and cause engine damage. When the cooling system is serviced, all hoses and the expansion tank cap should be checked and replaced if necessary.

2 Apply the parking brake and block the wheels.

Warning: *If the vehicle has just been driven, wait several hours to allow the engine to cool down before beginning this procedure.*

3 Move a drain pan under the lower right side of the radiator. Attach a length of hose to the drain fitting below the drain valve, direct it into the pan, then unscrew the drain valve (see illustration). Remove the expansion tank cap and allow the coolant to drain.

4 After coolant stops flowing out of the radiator and hose, move the container under the engine block drain plugs - there's one on each side of the block (see illustration).

Note: *On some models, a block heater is installed in place of a plug.*

5 Remove the plugs and allow the coolant in the block to drain (see illustration).

6 While the coolant is draining, check the condition of the radiator hoses, heater hoses and clamps.

7 Replace any damaged clamps or hoses. Reinstall the drain plugs and tighten them securely, using Permatex 2 sealant on the threads of the plugs. Tighten the radiator drain valve.

Flushing

8 Fill the cooling system with clean water, following the Refilling procedure (see Step 14).

9 Start the engine and allow it to reach normal operating temperature, then rev up the engine a few times.

10 Turn the engine off and allow it to cool completely, then drain the system as described earlier.

11 Repeat Steps 8 through 10 until the water being drained is free of contaminants.

12 In severe cases of contamination or clogging of the radiator, remove the radiator (see Chapter 3) and have a radiator repair facility clean and repair it if necessary.

13 Many deposits can be removed by the chemical action of a cleaner available at auto parts stores. Follow the procedure outlined in the manufacturer's instructions.

Note: *When the coolant is regularly drained and the system refilled with the correct antifreeze/water mixture, there should be no need to use chemical cleaners or descalers.*

Refilling

14 Tighten the radiator drain fitting.

15 Place the heater temperature control in the maximum heat position.

16 Slowly add new coolant (a 50/50 mixture of water and DEX-COOL antifreeze) to the radiator until the level is up to the bottom of the filler neck.

17 Install the radiator cap and run the engine at idle for two minutes, periodically raising the engine rpm to 2500 to 3000 rpm.

18 Turn the engine off and let it cool. Add more coolant mixture to bring the level up to the bottom of the radiator filler neck.

19 Repeat Steps 17 and 18 as necessary.

20 Start the engine, allow it to reach normal operating temperature and check for leaks. Also, set the heater and blower controls to the maximum setting and check to see that the heater output from the air ducts is warm. This is a good indication that all air has been purged from the cooling system.

21 Check the level of coolant in the coolant reservoir, adding as necessary (see Section 4).

25.11 A length of snug-fitting rubber hose will save time and prevent damaged threads when installing the spark plugs

26.3 The radiator drain valve is located on the lower right corner of the radiator

1   Drain valve
2   Length of hose attached to the drain fitting

26.5 Cylinder block drain plug - there is one on each side of the block (on some models it may be necessary to remove the starter for access to the plug)

27   Suspension, steering and driveaxle boot check (every 30,000 miles or 30 months)

Note: *The steering linkage and suspension components should be checked periodically. Worn or damaged suspension and steering linkage components can result in excessive and abnormal tire wear, poor ride quality and vehicle handling and reduced fuel economy. For detailed illustrations of the steering and suspension components, refer to Chapter 10.*

Shock absorber check

1   Park the vehicle on level ground, turn the engine off and set the parking brake. Check the tire pressures.

2   Push down at one corner of the vehicle, then release it while noting the movement of the body. It should stop moving and come to rest in a level position within one or two bounces.

3   If the vehicle continues to move up-and-down or if it fails to return to its original posi-tion, a worn or weak shock absorber is prob-ably the reason.

4   Repeat the above check at each of the three remaining corners of the vehicle.

5   Raise the vehicle and support it securely on jackstands.

6   Check the shock absorbers for evidence of fluid leakage (see illustration). A light film of fluid is no cause for concern. Make sure that any fluid noted is from the shocks and not from some other source. If leakage is noted, replace the shocks as a set.

7   Check the shocks to be sure that they are securely mounted and undamaged. Check the upper mounts for damage and wear. If damage or wear is noted, replace the shocks as a set (front or rear).

8   If the shocks must be replaced, refer to Chapter 10 for the procedure.

Steering and suspension check

9   Visually inspect the steering and suspen-sion components (front and rear) for damage and distortion. Look for damaged seals, boots and bushings and leaks of any kind. Examine the bushings where the control arms meet the chassis (see illustrations).

10   Clean the lower end of the steering knuckle. Have an assistant grasp the lower edge of the tire and move the wheel in and out while you look for movement at the steer-ing knuckle-to-control arm balljoint. If there is any movement the suspension balljoint(s) must be replaced.

11   Grasp each front tire at the front and rear edges, push in at the front, pull out at the rear and feel for play in the steering system com-ponents. If any freeplay is noted, check the idler arm and the tie-rod ends for looseness (see illustration).

12   Additional steering and suspension sys-tem information and illustrations can be found in Chapter 10.

Driveaxle boot check (4WD models)

13   The driveaxle boots are very important because they prevent dirt, water and foreign material from entering and damaging the con-

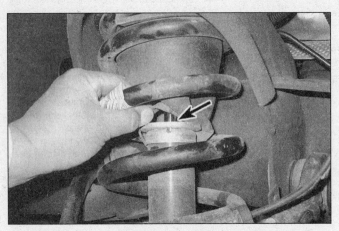

27.6 Check for signs of fluid leakage at this point on shock absorbers (front shock shown)

27.9a Examine the bushings for the upper . . .

27.9b . . . and lower control arms on the front suspension

27.11 With the steering wheel in the locked position and the vehicle raised, grasp the front tire as shown and try to move it back-and-forth - if any play is noted, check the steering gear mounts and tie-rod ends for looseness

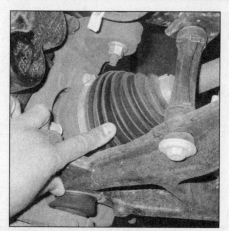

27.14 Inspect the inner and outer driveaxle boots on 4WD models for loose clamps, cracks or signs of leaking lubricant (inner boot shown)

28.5 Remove the bolts from three sides and allow the pan to drain from the front of the pan - 6-speed models shown, 8-speed models similar

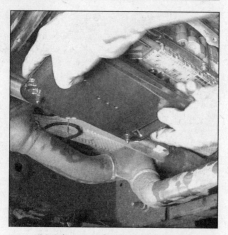

28.9 Remove the filter from the transmission by pulling it straight down

28.10a Use a seal puller and slide hammer to remove the transmission filter seal

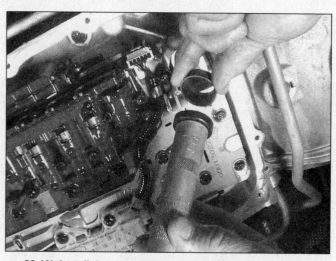

28.10b Install the new seal into its bore with a hammer and seal driver

stant velocity (CV) joints. Oil and grease can cause the boot material to deteriorate prematurely, so it's a good idea to wash the boots with soap and water. Because it constantly pivots back and forth following the steering action of the front hub, the outer CV boot wears out sooner and should be inspected regularly.

14   Inspect the boots for tears and cracks as well as loose clamps (see illustration). If there is any evidence of cracks or leaking lubricant, they must be replaced as described in Chapter 8.

28   Automatic transmission fluid and filter change (every 30,000 miles or 30 months)

1   At the specified intervals, the transmission fluid should be drained and replaced. Since the fluid will remain hot long after driv-

ing, perform this procedure only after the engine has cooled down completely.

2   Before beginning work, purchase the specified transmission fluid (see *Recommended lubricants and fluids* in this Chapter's Specifications) and a new filter and pan gasket.

3   Other tools necessary for this job include a floor jack, jackstands to support the vehicle in a raised position, a drain pan capable of holding at least eight quarts, newspapers and clean rags.

4   Raise the vehicle and support it securely on jackstands. Remove the front portion of the exhaust system if it will interfere with removal of the transmission fluid pan.

5   Place the drain pan underneath the transmission pan. Remove the bolts from three sides of the pan (see illustration), then loosen the remaining bolts and allow the pan to drop down to drain the fluid. Once most of the fluid has been drained, remove the bolts

and carefully lower the pan and drain the rest of the fluid.

6   Remove the transmission pan mounting bolts, then carefully pry the transmission pan loose with a screwdriver.

Warning: *There will still be some transmission fluid in the pan.*

7   Carefully clean the gasket surface of the transmission to remove all traces of the old gasket and sealant.

8   Clean the pan with solvent and dry it with compressed air, if available.

Note: *Some models are equipped with magnets in the transmission pan to catch metal debris. Clean the magnet thoroughly. A small amount of metal material is normal at the magnet. If there is considerable debris, consult a dealer or transmission specialist.*

9   Remove the filter from the valve body inside the transmission (see illustration).

10   Install a new seal and filter (see illustrations).

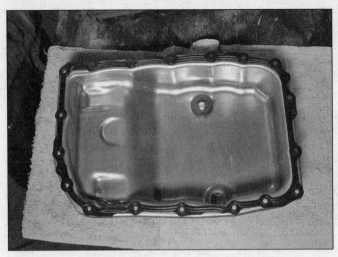

28.11 Clean the transmission pan, position the magnet back in place, and install the new pan gasket

31.2 PCV valve location - V6 engine

11   Make sure the gasket surface on the transmission pan is clean, then install a new gasket on the pan (see illustration). Put the pan in place against the transmission and install all of the bolts. Working around the pan, tighten each bolt a little at a time to the torque listed in this Chapter's Specifications.

12   Add new fluid to the transmission (see Section 7). Check the specifications in this Chapter for the proper quantity.

13   With the transmission in Park and the parking brake set, run the engine at a fast idle, but don't race it.

14   Move the gear selector through each range and back to Park, then let the engine idle. Check the fluid level; it will probably be low at this point. Add enough fluid to bring the level to the proper mark on the dipstick. Be careful not to overfill.

15   Check under the vehicle for leaks during the first few trips. Check the fluid level again when the transmission is hot (see Section 7).

16   The old fluid drained from the transmission cannot be reused in its present state and should be disposed of. Check with your local auto parts store, disposal facility or environmental agency to see if they will accept the fluid for recycling. After the fluid has cooled it can be drained into a container (capped plastic jugs, topped bottles, milk cartons, etc.) for transport to one of these disposal sites. Don't dispose of the fluid by pouring it on the ground or down a drain!

29   Transfer case lubricant change (4WD models) (every 60,000 miles or 48 months)

1   This procedure should be performed after the vehicle has been driven so the lubricant will be warm and therefore will flow out of the transfer case more easily.

2   Raise the vehicle and support it securely

on jackstands.

3   Remove the filler plug from the case (see illustration 21.1).

4   Remove the drain plug from the lower part of the case and allow the lubricant to drain completely.

5   After the case is completely drained, carefully clean and install the drain plug. Tighten the plug securely.

6   Fill the case with the specified lubricant until it is level with the lower edge of the filler hole.

7   Install the filler plug and tighten it securely.

8   Drive the vehicle for a short distance and recheck the lubricant level. In some instances a small amount of additional lubricant will have to be added.

9   The old lubricant cannot be reused in its present state and should be disposed of. Check with your local auto parts store, disposal facility or environmental agency to see if they will accept the lubricant for recycling. After the lubricant has cooled it can be drained into a container (capped plastic jugs, topped bottles, milk cartons, etc.) for transport to one of these disposal sites. Don't dispose of the lubricant by pouring it on the ground or down a drain!

30   Differential lubricant change (every 60,000 miles or 48 months)

1   This procedure should be performed after the vehicle has been driven, so the lubricant will be warm and therefore will flow out of the differential more easily.

2   Raise the vehicle and support it securely on jackstands. You'll be draining the lubricant by removing the drain plug, so move a drain pan, rags, newspapers and wrenches under the vehicle.

3   Remove the filler plug and the drain plug and allow the lubricant to drain into the pan,

then clean and reinstall the drain plug (see Section 16).

Note: *On differentials not equipped with a drain plug, the differential cover must be removed to drain the lubricant (see Chapter 8).*

4   Use a hand pump, syringe or squeeze bottle to fill the differential housing with the specified lubricant until it's at the level specified in Section 16. Reinstall the drain plug.

5   The old lubricant cannot be reused in its present state and should be disposed of. Check with your local auto parts store, disposal facility or environmental agency to see if they will accept the lubricant for recycling. After the lubricant has cooled it can be drained into a container (capped plastic jugs, topped bottles, milk cartons, etc.) for transport to one of these disposal sites. Don't dispose of the lubricant by pouring it on the ground or down a drain!

31   Positive Crankcase Ventilation (PCV) valve replacement (V6 engine) (every 60,000 miles or 48 months)

1   The PCV valve is located in the left valve cover on 4.3L V6 and 6.0L V8 engines and in the valve lifter oil manifold (between the cylinder heads) on 5.3L and 6.2L V8 models.

Note: *On 5.3L and 6.2L models, the intake manifold is mounted above the valve lifter oil manifold but the PCV valve is accessible at the left front corner of the manifold.*

2   Detach the hose from the valve and remove it from the valve cover (see illustration) or the valve lifter oil manifold.

3   When purchasing a replacement PCV valve, make sure it's for your particular vehicle and engine size. Compare the old valve with the new one to make sure they're the same.

4   Reverse the removal procedure to install the valve, then reconnect the hose.

32 Spark plug wire check and replacement (every 100,000 miles or 60 months)

1   The spark plug wires should be checked at the recommended intervals and whenever new spark plugs are installed in the engine. V6 engines have spark plug wires that go from the spark plugs all the way to an ignition coil assembly. V8 engines have individual coils for each cylinder and short spark plug wires from each coil to the corresponding spark plug.

2   Begin this procedure by making a visual check of the spark plug wires while the engine is running. In a darkened garage (make sure there is adequate ventilation) start the engine and observe each plug wire. Be careful not to come into contact with any moving engine parts. If there is a break in the wire, you will see arcing or a small spark at the damaged area. If arcing is noticed, make a note to obtain new wires.

3   Disconnect the plug wire from one spark plug (with the engine off). To do this, grab the rubber boot, twist slightly and pull the wire free. Do not pull on the wire itself, only on the rubber boot. A boot-pulling tool is helpful.

4   Check inside the boot for corrosion, which will look like a white crusty powder. Push the wire and boot back onto the end of the spark plug. It should be a tight fit on the plug. If it isn't, remove the wire and use a pair of pliers to carefully crimp the metal connector inside the boot until it fits securely on the end

32.6 Use a spark plug boot pulling tool to remove each end of a spark plug wire - never pull on the wire itself

of the spark plug.

5   Using a clean rag, wipe the entire length of the wire to remove any built-up dirt and grease. Once the wire is clean, check for holes, burned areas, cracks and other damage. Don't bend the wire excessively or the conductor inside might break.

6   Disconnect the wire from the coil. Pull the wire straight out of the coil. Pull only on the rubber boot during removal (see illustration). Check for corrosion and a tight fit in the same manner as the spark plug end. Reattach the wire to the ignition coil.

7   Check the remaining spark plug wires one at a time, making sure they are securely fastened at both ends when the check is complete.

8   If new spark plug wires are required, purchase a new set for your specific engine model. Wire sets are available pre-cut, with the rubber boots already installed. Remove and replace the wires one at a time to avoid mix-ups in the firing order. The wire routing is extremely important, so be sure to note exactly how each wire is situated before removing it. On V6 engines, release the ignition wire loom clamps to exchange the wires, then snap the clamps back in place on the new wires.

Notes

Chapter 2 Part A V6 engine

Contents

Specifications

General

Displacement	262 cubic inches (4.3 liters)
VIN	
H	RPO LV3
P	RPO LV1
Bore and stroke	3.92 x 3.622 inches
Cylinder numbers	
Left bank	1-3-5
Right bank	2-4-6
Firing order	1-6-5-4-3-2

Camshaft

Journal diameter	2.164 to 2.166 inches
Journal-to-bearing clearance	0.0002 to 0.0038 inch
Endplay	0.001 to 0.012 inch
Lobe lift	
Intake	
Non Active Fuel Management (AFM)	0.278 inch
Active Fuel Management (AFM)	0.283 inch
Exhaust	
Non Active Fuel Management (AFM)	0.274 inch
Active fuel management (AFM)	0.279 inch
Fuel pump lobe	0.224 inch
Runout, maximum	0.002 inch

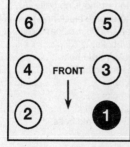

24068-2A-0.0a HAYNES

V6 cylinder numbering diagram

Torque specifications   Ft-lbs (unless otherwise indicated)

Note: *One foot-pound (ft-lb) of torque is equivalent to 12 inch-pounds (in-lbs) of torque. Torque values below approximately 15 foot-pounds are expressed in inch-pounds, because most foot-pound torque wrenches are not accurate at these smaller values.*

Balance shaft driven gear bolt	43
Balance shaft idler sprocket bolt	43
Balance shaft chain guide bolts	89 in-lbs
Balance shaft retainer bolts	89 in-lbs
Camshaft position actuator magnet bolt*	89 in-lbs
Camshaft position actuator solenoid valve*	
Step 1	48
Step 2	Tighten an additional 90 degrees
Camshaft retainer bolts - Torx	132 in-lbs
Crankshaft balancer bolt*	
Installation pass with old bolt, to insure the balancer is completely seated	240
New flange head bolt	
Step 1	89
Step 2	Loosen 360 degrees
Step 3	59
Step 4	Tighten an additional 125 degrees
New bolt with retained rotating washer	
Step 1	15
Step 2	Loosen 360 degrees
Step 3	15
Step 4	Tighten an additional 200 degrees
Cylinder head bolts* (in sequence - see illustration 9.19)	
Step 1	59
Step 2	Tighten an additional 90 degrees
Step 3	Tighten an additional 60 degrees
Driveplate-to-crankshaft bolts* (automatic transmission)	
Step 1	132 in-lbs
Step 2	22
Step 3	Tighten an additional 45 degrees
Flywheel bolts* (manual transmission)	
Step 1	132 in-lbs
Step 2	22
Step 3	Tighten an additional 30 degrees
Exhaust manifold bolt/studs	
Original cylinder head	17
New cylinder head	20
Exhaust manifold heat shield bolts	89 in-lbs
Intake manifold cover bolts/studs	40 in-lbs
Intake manifold bolts	
Step 1	44 in-lbs
Step 2	89 in-lbs
Engine oil cooler adapter	106 in-lbs
Oil pan cover bolts	89 in-lbs
Oil pan bolts (in sequence, see illustration 15.15)	
Oil pan-to-rear housing bolts (A)	106 in-lbs
Oil pan-to-engine block and timing chain cover bolts	18
Lower oil pan-to-upper oil pan bolts	89 in-lbs
Oil pan baffle bolts	89 in-lbs
Oil pump pickup tube bolts	89 in-lbs
Oil pump mounting bolts	18
Rocker arm bolts	22
Valve cover bolts	89 in-lbs
Valve lifter guide bolts	106 in-lbs
Valve lifter oil manifold bolts	
Step 1	132 in-lbs
Step 2	22
Valve lifter oil manifold filter plug	22
Timing chain cover-to-block bolts	18
Timing chain tensioner bolts	18
Rear main seal housing bolts	18

Use NEW cylinder head bolts. Used ones should be discarded.

1 General information

1   This Part of Chapter 2 is devoted to in-vehicle repair procedures for the 4.3L V6 engine. These engines utilize cast-aluminum blocks with six cylinders arranged in a "V" shape at a 90-degree angle between the two banks. The overhead valve cast aluminum cylinder heads are equipped with powdered-metal valve guides and seats. Hydraulic roller lifters actuate the valves through tubular pushrods and rocker arms. A balance shaft has been incorporated into this engine to smooth vibration. The balance shaft is located mounted to the engine block valley cover directly above the camshaft and is driven by a chain off the camshaft. The oil pump is mounted to the front of the block and is driven by the crankshaft.

2   To positively identify this engine, locate the Vehicle Identification Number (VIN) on the left front corner of the instrument panel. The VIN is visible from the outside of the vehicle through the windshield. The eighth character in the sequence is the engine designation:

3   Information concerning engine removal and installation and engine overhaul can be found in Part C of this Chapter. The following repair procedures are based on the assumption that the engine is installed in the vehicle. If the engine has been removed from the vehicle and mounted on a stand, many of the steps outlined in this Part of Chapter 2 will not apply.

2 Repair operations possible with the engine in the vehicle

1   Many major repair operations can be accomplished without removing the engine from the vehicle.

2   Clean the engine compartment and the exterior of the engine with some type of pressure washer before any work is done. It will make the job easier and help keep dirt out of the internal areas of the engine.

3   Remove the hood, if necessary, to improve access to the engine as repairs are performed (see Chapter 11 if necessary).

4   If vacuum, exhaust, oil or coolant leaks develop, indicating a need for gasket or seal replacement, the repairs can generally be made with the engine in the vehicle. The intake and exhaust manifold gaskets, timing chain cover gasket, oil pan gasket, crankshaft oil seals and cylinder head gaskets are all accessible with the engine in place.

5   Exterior engine components, such as the intake and exhaust manifolds, the oil pan and oil pump, the water pump, the starter motor, the alternator and the fuel system components can be removed for repair with the engine in place.

6   Since the cylinder heads can be removed without pulling the engine, valve component servicing can also be accomplished with the engine in the vehicle. Replacement of the timing chain and sprockets is also possible with the engine in the vehicle.

3 Top Dead Center (TDC) for number one piston - locating

1   Top Dead Center (TDC) is the highest point in the cylinder that each piston reaches as it travels up the cylinder bore. Each piston reaches TDC on the compression stroke and again on the exhaust stroke, but TDC generally refers to piston position on the compression stroke.

2   Positioning the piston(s) at TDC is an essential part of many procedures such as timing chain/sprocket removal.

3   Before beginning this procedure, be sure to place the transmission in Neutral and apply the parking brake or block the rear wheels. Also, disable the ignition system by disconnecting the primary electrical connectors at the ignition coil packs, then remove the spark plugs (see Chapter 1).

4   In order to bring any piston to TDC, the crankshaft must be turned using a socket and ratchet or breaker bar attached to the crankshaft pulley bolt. When looking at the front of the engine, normal crankshaft rotation is clockwise.

5   Install a compression gauge in the no. 1 cylinder spark plug hole or place your finger partially over the number one spark plug hole and rotate the crankshaft until air pressure is felt. Air pressure at the spark plug hole indicates that the cylinder has started the compression stroke. Once the compression stroke has begun, TDC for the number one cylinder is obtained when the piston reaches the top of the cylinder on the compression stroke.

6   To bring the piston to the top of the cylinder, insert a long screwdriver into the number one spark plug hole until it touches the top of the piston.

Note: *Wrap the tip of the screwdriver with tape to avoid scratching the top of the piston and the cylinder walls.*

7   Use the screwdriver as a feeler gauge to tell where the top of the piston is located in the cylinder while slowly rotating the crankshaft. As the piston rises the screwdriver will be pushed out. The point at which the screwdriver stops moving outward is TDC.

Note: *Always hold the screwdriver upright while the engine is being rotated so that the screwdriver will not get wedged as the piston travels upward.*

8   If you go past TDC, rotate the crankshaft counterclockwise until the piston is approximately 1/2-inch below TDC, then slowly rotate the crankshaft clockwise again until TDC is reached.

9   After the number one piston has been positioned at TDC on the compression stroke, TDC for any of the remaining pistons can be located by repeating the procedure described above and following the firing order.

4 Valve covers - removal and installation

Removal

1   Disconnect the cable from the negative terminal of the battery (see Chapter 5).

2   Disconnect the PCV hose quick connect fitting from the valve covers (see illustration).

3   On the left valve cover remove the oil filler cap (see illustration).

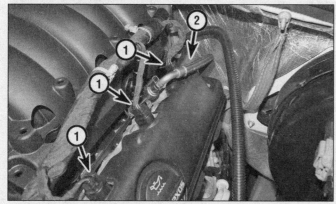

4.2 Disconnect the electrical connectors (1) to the ignition coils, then disconnect the PCV hose quick connector (2) - left side shown, right side similar

4.3 Remove the oil filler cap

4.4 Pull the valve cover insulator up from the ends

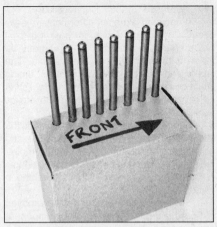

5.4 A perforated cardboard box can be used to store the pushrods to ensure that they're installed in their original positions - note the label indicating the front of the engine

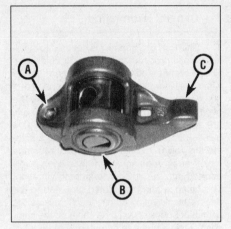

5.5 Rocker arm wear points

A   *Pushrod socket*
B   *Pivot bearing*
C   *Valve stem contact point*

4   Pull the valve cover insulator off the valve cover (see illustration).
5   If you're removing the left-side valve cover, remove the oil dipstick tube mounting bolt and pivot the tube out of the way.
6   If you're removing the right-side valve cover, remove the air intake duct (see Chapter 4).
7   Disconnect the spark plug wires from the coils by first twisting them a half turn to loosen them. Pull only on the boot - not on the wire.
8   Remove the ignition coils (see Chapter 5).
9   Disconnect the interfering engine wiring harnesses and move them aside.
10   Remove the valve cover bolts, then detach the cover from the cylinder head.
Note: *If the cover is stuck to the cylinder head, bump one end with a block of wood and a hammer to jar it loose. If that doesn't work, try to slip a flexible putty knife between the cylinder head and cover to break the gasket seal. Don't pry at the cover-to-head joint or damage to the sealing surfaces may occur (leading to oil leaks in the future).*

Installation

11   The mating surfaces of each cylinder head and valve cover must be perfectly clean when the covers are installed. Use a gasket scraper to remove all traces of sealant and old gasket material, then clean the mating surfaces with brake system cleaner. If there's sealant or oil on the mating surfaces when the cover is installed, oil leaks may develop.
12   Clean the mounting bolt threads with a die to remove any corrosion and restore damaged threads. Make sure the threaded holes in the cylinder head are clean - run a tap into them to remove corrosion and restore damaged threads.
13   Position the gasket inside the cover lip. If the gasket will not stay in place in the cover lip, apply a thin coat of RTV sealant to the cover flange, then allow the sealant to set up so the gasket adheres to the cover.

14   Tighten the bolts a little at a time, starting with the center bolts and working outward, to the torque listed in this Chapter's Specifications.
15   The remainder of installation is the reverse of removal. Use thread locking material on the ignition coil bracket studs and nuts.
16   Start the engine and check carefully for oil leaks as the engine warms up.

5   Rocker arms and pushrods - removal, inspection and installation

Removal

1   Remove the valve cover(s) from the cylinder head(s) (see Section 4).
2   Beginning at the front of one cylinder head, loosen and remove the rocker arms.
3   Keep track of the component positions, since they must be returned to the same locations. Store each set of components separately in a marked container to ensure that they're reinstalled in their original locations.
4   Remove the pushrods and store them separately to make sure they don't get mixed up during installation (see illustration).

Inspection

5   Check each rocker arm for wear, cracks and other damage, especially where the pushrods and valve stems contact the rocker arm (see illustration).
6   Check the roller bearings in the rocker arms for free rotation. Make sure the hole at the pushrod end of each rocker arm is open.
7   Inspect the pushrods for cracks and excessive wear at the ends. Roll each pushrod across a piece of plate glass to see if it's bent (if it wobbles, it's bent).

Installation

8   Lubricate the lower end of each pushrod with clean engine oil or engine assembly lube

and install them in their original locations. Make sure each pushrod seats completely in the lifter socket.
9   Apply engine assembly lube to the ends of the valve stems and to the upper ends of the pushrods to prevent damage to the mating surfaces on initial start-up. Also apply clean engine oil to the pivot shaft and bearing of each rocker arm and install the rocker arms loosely in their original locations. DO NOT tighten the bolts at this time!
10   Rotate the crankshaft until the number one piston is at TDC on the compression stroke (see Section 3). Both pushrods for the number one cylinder should be in the lowered position. When the number one piston is at TDC, tighten the intake valve rocker arms for the Number 1, 3 and 2 cylinders and the exhaust rocker arms for the Number 1, 5 and 6 cylinders. Tighten each of the specified rocker arm bolts to the torque listed in this Chapter's Specifications.
11   Rotate the crankshaft 360 degrees. Tighten the intake valve rocker arms for the Number 5, 4 and 6 cylinders and the exhaust rocker arms for the Number 3, 2 and 4 cylinders. Tighten each of the rocker arm bolts to the torque listed in this Chapter's Specifications.
12   Refer to Section 4 and install the valve covers. Start the engine, listen for unusual valve train noses and check for oil leaks at the valve cover gaskets.

6   Valve springs, retainers and seals - replacement

Note: *Broken valve springs and defective valve stem seals can be replaced without removing the cylinder heads. Two special tools and a compressed air source are normally required to perform this operation, so read through this Section carefully and rent or buy the tools before beginning the job.*
1   Remove the valve cover from the cylin-

6.5 Use compressed air to hold the valve closed when the springs are removed - the air hose adapter (arrow) threads into the spark plug hole and accepts the hose from the compressor

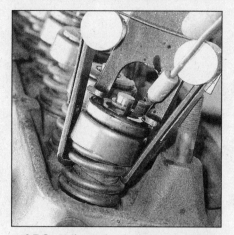

6.7 Once the spring is depressed, the keepers can be removed with a small magnet or needle-nose pliers (a magnet is preferred to prevent dropping the keepers)

6.13 Using a deep socket and hammer, gently tap the new seals onto the valve guide - don't bottom the seal against the valve guide

der head (see Section 4). If all of the valve stem seals are being replaced, remove both valve covers.

2   Remove the spark plug from the cylinder which has the defective component. If all of the valve stem seals are being replaced, all of the spark plugs should be removed.

3   Turn the crankshaft until the piston in the affected cylinder is at Top Dead Center on the compression stroke (see Section). If you are replacing all of the valve stem seals, begin with cylinder number 1 and work on the valves for one cylinder at a time. Move from cylinder-to-cylinder following the firing order sequence (1-6-5-4-3-2). Each cylinder in the firing order is 120-degrees of crankshaft rotation (clockwise) from the previous one.

4   Remove all of the rocker arms, pushrods and support bar from the cylinder head on which you're working.

5   Thread an adapter into the spark plug hole (see illustration) and connect an air hose from a compressed air source to it. Most auto parts stores can supply the air hose adapter. **Note:** *Many cylinder compression gauges utilize a screw-in fitting that may work with your air hose quick-disconnect fitting.*

6   Apply 90 to 100 psi of compressed air to the cylinder. The valves should be held in place by the air pressure. **Warning:** *If the cylinder isn't exactly at TDC, air pressure may cause the engine to rotate. Do not leave a socket or wrench on the vibration damper bolt; damage or personal injury may result.*

7   Stuff shop rags into the cylinder head holes to prevent parts and tools from falling into the engine, then use a valve spring compressor to compress the valve spring and the valve spring retainer. Remove the keepers with small needle-nose pliers or a magnet (see illustration).

8   Remove the spring retainer or rotator and valve spring assembly (on some models there is both an inner and outer valve spring for each valve - the inner is called a spring

damper), then remove the valve stem seal from the valve guide.

Note: *If air pressure fails to hold the valve in the closed position during this operation, the valve face and/or seat is probably damaged. If so, the cylinder head will have to be removed for additional repair operations.*

9   Wrap a rubber band or tape around the top of the valve stem so the valve won't fall into the combustion chamber, then release the air pressure.

10   Inspect the valve stem for damage. Rotate the valve in the guide and check the end for eccentric movement, which would indicate that the valve is bent.

11   Move the valve up-and-down in the guide and make sure it does not bind. If the valve stem binds, either the valve is bent or the guide is damaged. In either case, the cylinder head will have to be removed for repair.

12   Reapply air pressure to the cylinder to retain the valve in the closed position, then remove the tape or rubber band from the valve stem.

13   Lubricate the valve stems with engine oil and install the new valve stem seals. Using the stem of the valves as a guide, slide the seals down to the top of each valve guide, then use a hammer and a deep socket or seal installation tool to gently tap each seal into place until it's positioned to the specified depth (see illustration).

14   Install the valve spring and damper (if equipped) over the valve, with the more closely-wound spring coils toward the cylinder head.

15   Install the valve spring retainer or rotator. Compress the valve springs and carefully position the valve stem keepers in the groove. Apply a small dab of grease to the inside of each keeper to hold it in place (see illustration).

16   Disconnect the air hose and remove the adapter from the spark plug hole.

17   Repeat the above procedure on the remaining cylinders, following the firing order

6.15 Apply a small dab of grease to each keeper as shown here before installation - it will hold them in place on the valve stem as the spring is released

sequence (see the Specifications). Bring each piston to Top Dead Center on the compression stroke before applying air pressure.

18   Install the rocker arms, support bars and pushrods (see Section 5).

19   Install the valve cover(s) (see Section 4).

20   Install the spark plug(s) and hook up the wire(s).

21   Start and run the engine, then check for oil leaks and unusual sounds coming from the valve cover area.

7   Intake manifold and Valve Lifter Oil Manifold (VLOM) - removal and installation

Warning: *Wait until the engine is completely cool before starting this procedure.*

Removal

Intake manifold

1   Disconnect the cable from the negative terminal of the battery (see Chapter 5).

7.6a Loosen the bolts in 1/4-turn increments on the left side . . .

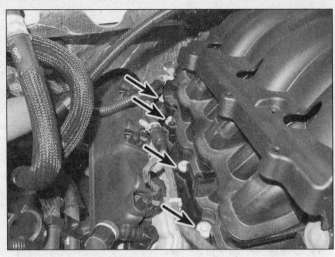

7.6b . . . then on the right side until all the bolts can be removed by hand

7.8 Remove the insulator from the top of the valve lifter oil manifold

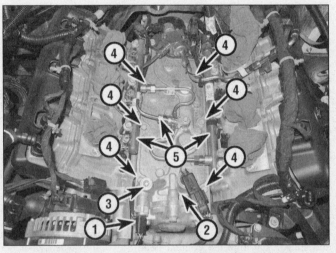

7.11a Valve Lifter Oil Manifold (VLOM) assembly details

1	Oil pressure sensor	4	Mounting bolts
2	Valve Lifter Oil Manifold	5	High-pressuer fuel lines
3	Valve lifter oil filter plug		and fuel rails

Relieve the fuel system pressure (see Chapter 4).

2   Refer to Chapter 4 and remove the air filter housing outlet duct.

3   Label, then disconnect all of the engine wiring harnesses that interfere with intake manifold removal. Also detach all the harness retainers and clips. Move the detached harnesses aside and secure them out of the way. **Note:** *Clear labeling will make the assembly procedure go smoothly and quickly.*

4   Disconnect the hose from the canister purge solenoid (see Chapter 6). Disconnect the fuel line from the fuel rail (see Chapter 4). Disconnect the PCV hose from the intake manifold.

5   Disconnect any remaining electrical connectors or vacuum hoses connected to the intake manifold or throttle body.

6   Loosen the intake manifold mounting bolts in 1/4-turn increments until they can be

removed by hand (see illustrations).
Caution: *Do not pry between the manifold and the heads or damage to the gasket sealing surfaces may result and vacuum leaks could develop. Also, don't use too much force - the manifold is made of a plastic composite and could crack.*

7   Remove the intake manifold. As the manifold is lifted from the engine, be sure to check for and disconnect anything still attached.

Valve Lifter Oil Manifold (VLOM)

8   Remove the fuel pump insulator (see illustration).

9   Remove the fuel rail and injectors (see Chapter 4).

10   Remove the balance shaft sprocket (see Section 14).

11   Remove the Valve Lifter Oil Manifold (VLOM) assembly mounting bolts (see illustrations).

Note: *Removing the manifold will be easier if you have an assistant hold the wiring harnesses out of the way.*

Installation

Note: *The mating surfaces of the cylinder heads, block and manifold must be perfectly clean when the manifold is installed.*

12   Carefully remove all traces of old gasket material. Note that the intake manifold is made of a composite material and the cylinder heads on some engines are made of aluminum; therefore aggressive scraping is not suggested and will damage the sealing surfaces. After the gasket surfaces are cleaned and free of any gasket material, wipe the mating surfaces with a cloth saturated with safety solvent. If there is old sealant or oil on the mating surfaces when the manifold is installed, oil or vacuum leaks may develop. Use a vacuum cleaner to remove any gasket

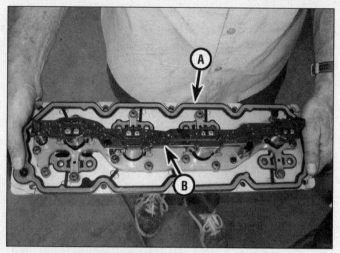

7.11b The Valve Lifter Oil Manifold (VLOM) gasket (A) can be re-used if it's in good condition. Don't pick up the assembly by the electrical lead frame (B)

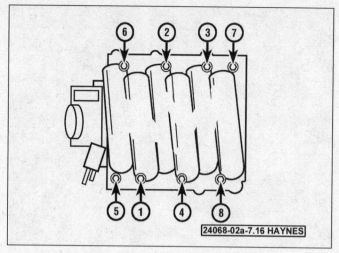

7.16 Intake manifold bolt tightening sequence

8.5 Access the exhaust pipe bolts/nuts from underneath the vehicle - on some models it may be easier to remove the wheel and work through the fenderwell opening

8.7 Exhaust manifold mounting bolts (heat shield removed for clarity) - right side shown, left side similar

material that falls into the intake ports in the heads.

13   Position the new gasket on the cylinder block then install the VLOM, if removed, and tighten the bolts to the torque listed in this Chapter's Specifications.

Warning: *Wear safety glasses or a face shield to protect your eyes when using compressed air.*

14   Position the new gaskets on the intake manifold. Note that the gaskets are equipped with installation tabs that must snap into place on the intake manifold. The words "Manifold Side" may appear on the gasket. If so, this will ensure proper installation. Make sure the gaskets snap into place and all intake port openings align.

15   Carefully set the manifold in place.

16   Install the bolts and tighten them following the recommended sequence (see illustration) to the torque listed in this Chapter's Specifications. Do not overtighten the bolts or

gasket leaks may develop.

17   The remainder of installation is the reverse of removal. Start the engine and check carefully for vacuum leaks at the intake manifold joints.

8   Exhaust manifolds - removal and installation

Removal

Warning: *Use caution when working around the exhaust manifolds, the sheet metal heat shields can be sharp on the edges. Also, the engine should be cold when this procedure is followed.*

1   Disconnect the cable from the negative terminal of the battery (see Chapter 5).

2   Raise the vehicle and support it securely on jackstands.

3   If you're removing the left side manifold, use a dab of paint to mark the alignment of the upper section of the steering intermediate shaft to the lower part of the steering column. Remove the fasteners, then separate the shafts so they can be moved aside (see Chapter 10).

Caution: *Don't move the wheels or the steering wheel after disconnecting the shafts. The airbag system clockspring could be damaged.*

4   Working under the vehicle, apply penetrating oil to the exhaust pipe-to-manifold studs and nuts (they're usually rusty).

5   Remove the nuts retaining the exhaust pipe(s) to the manifold(s) (see illustration).

6   Refer to Chapter 1 and disconnect the spark plug wires.

7   Remove the exhaust manifold fasteners (see illustration).

8   Remove the manifolds along with the heat shields. Throw the gaskets away. The heat shields can be removed at this time.

9.8 Alternator and air conditioning bracket mounting bolt/stud locations - right side cylinder removal only

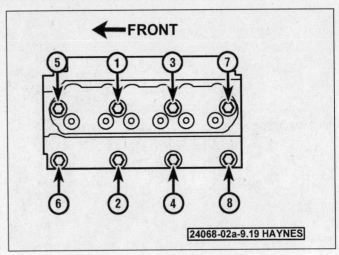

9.19 Cylinder head bolt TIGHTENING sequence

Installation

9   Check the manifold for cracks and make sure the bolt threads are clean and undamaged. The manifold and cylinder head mating surfaces must be clean before the manifolds are reinstalled - use a gasket scraper to remove all carbon deposits.

10   Position the manifold on a bench and install the heat shields, bolts and gaskets onto the manifold. Retaining tabs surrounding the gasket bolt holes will hold the assembly together as the manifold is installed. Place the manifold on the cylinder head and install the mounting bolts finger tight.

11   When tightening the mounting bolts, work from the center to the ends and be sure to use a torque wrench. Tighten the bolts in two steps to the torque listed in this Chapter's Specifications. If equipped, bend the locking tabs back against the bolt heads.

12   The remainder of installation is the reverse of removal.

13   Start the engine and check for exhaust leaks.

9   Cylinder heads - removal and installation

Warning: *Wait until the engine is completely cool before beginning this procedure.*

Removal

1   Drain the cooling system (see Chapter 1).

2   Remove the intake manifold (see Section 7).

3   Remove the fuel rail(s) from the cylinder head(s) (see Chapter 4).

4   Remove the valve covers (see Section 4).

5   Remove the rocker arms and pushrods (see Section 5).

6   Refer to Section 8 and disconnect

the exhaust manifold(s) from the cylinder head(s).

7   If you're working on the right cylinder head, remove the drivebelt, air conditioning compressor belt (see Chapter 1) then the alternator (see Chapter 5).

8   If you're working on the right cylinder head, remove the idler pulley bolt then remove the alternator and air conditioning compressor bracket (see illustration).

9   Remove the spark plugs.

10   Loosen the cylinder head bolts in 1/4-turn increments until they can be removed by hand. Work from bolt-to-bolt in a pattern that's the reverse of the tightening sequence shown in illustration 9.25.

Caution: *Discard the bolts and obtain new ones for installation.*

11   Lift the cylinder head(s) off the engine. If resistance is felt, DO NOT pry between the cylinder head and block as damage to the mating surfaces will result. To dislodge the cylinder head, place a block of wood against the end of it and strike the wood block with a hammer. Store the cylinder heads on wood blocks to prevent damage to the gasket sealing surfaces.

Installation

12   The mating surfaces of the cylinder heads and block must be perfectly clean when the cylinder heads are installed.

13   Use a gasket scraper to remove all traces of carbon and old gasket material, then clean the mating surfaces with brake system cleaner. If there's oil on the mating surfaces when the cylinder heads are installed, the gaskets may not seal correctly and leaks may develop. When working on the block, cover the lifter valley with shop rags to keep debris out of the engine. Use a vacuum cleaner to remove any debris that falls into the cylinders.

Caution: *The cylinder head and cylinder block are made of aluminum and can easily be dam-*

aged by using a scraper or sanding the surfaces.

14   Check the block and cylinder head mating surfaces for nicks, deep scratches and other damage. If damage is slight, it can be removed with a file - if it's excessive, machining may be the only alternative.

15   Use a tap of the correct size to chase the threads in the cylinder head bolt holes. Dirt, corrosion, sealant and damaged threads will affect torque readings.

16   Position the new gaskets over the dowel pins in the block with the marks UP on top.

Note: *Composition-type gaskets are used on most engines, with a thin sheet metal core. Be very careful when handling because the edges may be very sharp. Composition gaskets do not require sealant.*

17   Carefully position the cylinder heads on the block without disturbing the gaskets.

18   Purchase NEW cylinder head bolts.

19   Install the new bolts and tighten them finger tight. Follow the recommended sequence and tighten the bolts in several steps to the torque and angle of rotation listed in this Chapter's Specifications (see illustration).

20   The remainder of installation is the reverse of removal.

21   Change the engine oil and filter and fill the cooling system with the proper coolant (see Chapter 1), then start the engine and check carefully for oil and coolant leaks.

10   Crankshaft balancer - removal and installation

Note: *This procedure requires a special balancer installation tool and a new crankshaft balancer bolt. Read through the entire procedure and obtain the tool and materials before proceeding.*

1   Disconnect the cable from the negative terminal of the battery (see Chapter 5).

2   Raise the front of the vehicle and sup-

10.5 Driveplate holding tool bolted in place

10.6 The use of a three-jaw puller will be necessary to remove the crankshaft balancer - always place the puller jaws around the hub, not the outer ring

10.9 Before the new crankshaft bolt is installed and tightened, the balancer must be measured for proper installation - when properly installed, the balancer hub should extend 3/32 to 11/64-inch past the crankshaft snout

port it securely on jackstands. Then apply the parking brake.

3   Remove the drivebelt, air conditioning compressor belt and the vacuum pump belt (see Chapter 1). Remove the cooling fan and shroud assembly (see Chapter 3).

4   Working under the vehicle, remove the stone shield from below the engine (if equipped).

5   Remove the starter motor (see Chapter 5). Install a driveplate holding tool into the ring gear teeth and bolt it to the engine block (see illustration).

6   Pull the balancer off the crankshaft with a puller (see illustration).

Caution: *The jaws of the puller must only contact the hub of the balancer - not the outer ring.*

Caution: *The proper adapter EN-41815-2 or a long Allen-head bolt should be inserted into the crankshaft nose for the puller's tapered tip to push against to prevent damage to the crankshaft threads.*

7   Position the crankshaft pulley/balancer on the crankshaft and slide it on as far as it will go.

8   Using a crankshaft balancer installation tool, press the crankshaft pulley/balancer onto the crankshaft.

9   Install the old crankshaft balancer bolt and tighten the crankshaft bolt to the Step 1 torque listed in this Chapter's Specifications. Remove the old bolt and measure the distance from the snout of the crankshaft to the balancer hub (see illustration). When properly installed, the balancer hub should extend 3/32 to 11/64-inch past the crankshaft snout. If the measurement is incorrect, reinstall the balancer installation tool and press the balancer on the crankshaft until the measurement is correct.

10   Install a new crankshaft balancer bolt and tighten it to the torque and angle of rotation listed in this Chapter's Specifications.

11   The remainder of installation is the reverse of removal.

11   Crankshaft front oil seal - removal and installation

1   Remove the crankshaft balancer (see Section 10).

2   Note how the seal is installed - the new one must be installed to the same depth and facing the same way. Carefully pry the oil seal out of the cover with a seal puller or a large screwdriver (see illustration). Be very careful not to distort the cover or scratch the crankshaft! Wrap electrician's tape around the tip of the screwdriver to avoid damage to the crankshaft.

3   If the seal is being replaced with the timing chain cover removed, support the cover on top of two blocks of wood and drive the seal out from the rear with a hammer and punch.

Caution: *Be careful not to scratch, gouge or distort the area that the seal fits into or a leak will develop.*

4   Apply clean engine oil or multi-purpose grease to the outer edge of the new seal, then install it in the cover with the lip (spring side) facing IN and the words on the seal ***THIS SIDE OUT*** facing outward. Drive the seal into place with a seal driver or a large socket and a hammer. Make sure the seal enters the bore squarely and stops when the front face is at the proper depth.

5   Check the surface on the balancer hub that the oil seal rides on. If the surface has been grooved from long-time contact with the seal, replace the crankshaft balancer.

6   Lubricate the balancer hub with clean engine oil and reinstall the crankshaft balancer as described in Section 10.

7   The remainder of installation is the reverse of removal.

11.2 Carefully pry the old seal out of the timing chain cover - don't damage the crankshaft in the process

12   Timing chain and sprockets - removal and installation

Warning: *Wait until the engine is completely cool before beginning this procedure.*

Caution: *The timing system is complex, and severe engine damage will occur if you make any mistakes. Do not attempt this procedure unless you are highly experienced with this type of repair. If you are at all unsure of your abilities, be sure to consult an expert. Double-check all your work and be sure everything is correct before you attempt to start the engine.*

Removal

1   Disconnect the cable from the negative terminal of the battery (see Chapter 5). Drain the cooling system (see Chapter 1).

2   Remove the drivebelts (see Chapter 1).

3   Remove the cooling fan and coolant manifold (see Chapter 3).

12.10 Disconnect the electrical connectors to the camshaft position sensor (1) and the camshaft position actuator magnet (2), then remove the wiring harness-to-cover bolts (3)

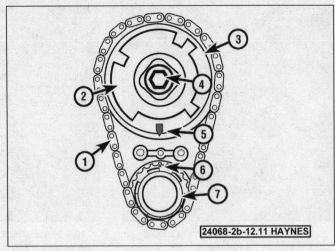

12.14 Timing chain alignment marks - when properly aligned, the crankshaft gear should be in the 12 o'clock position, the camshaft gear should be in the 6 o'clock position and the number one piston should be at TDC

1   Timing chain
2   Reluctor wheel
3   Camshaft/actuator sprocket
4   Camshaft position actuator solenoid valve
5   Camshaft sprocket timing mark (6 o'clock position)
6   Crankshaft sprocket timing mark (12 o'clock position)
7   Crankshaft sprocket

12.15 Camshaft position actuator system components - the "bolt" is the solenoid valve (it must be replaced with a new one whenever it's removed); don't try to disassemble the actuator mechanism

4   Remove the crankshaft balancer (see Section 10).
5   Remove the vacuum pump (see Chapter 9).
6   Remove the air conditioning compressor mounting bolts, then reposition the compressor and secure it out of the way, without disconnecting the compressor lines.
7   Remove the oil pan (see Section 15) and the oil pump (see Section 16).
8   Remove the starter (see Chapter 5).
9   Position the number one piston at TDC on the compression stroke (see Section 3).
10   Disconnect the electrical connectors to the camshaft position sensor and camshaft position actuator magnet, then remove the sensor bolts and the bolts retaining the wiring harness to the front cover (see illustration).
11   Remove the oil pan (see Section 15).
12   Remove the cover bolts and separate the timing chain cover from the block. It may be stuck - if so, use a putty knife or screwdriver to break the RTV gasket seal.
Caution: *The timing chain cover bolts are different lengths and sizes; be sure to mark them and keep them in order. They must be installed in their original locations.*
13   Remove the balance shaft chain, tensioner and sprocket (see Section 14).
14   If the timing marks aren't perfectly aligned, screw the crankshaft balancer bolt into the end of the crankshaft and rotate the crankshaft as necessary until the timing marks

are aligned at the 12 o'clock and 6 o'clock positions (see illustration).
Caution: *Once the timing marks are aligned and the timing chain has been removed, DO NOT turn the camshaft or the crankshaft until the chain has been reinstalled!*
15   Remove the solenoid valve from the center of the upper sprocket assembly and discard it (see illustration). It must be replaced with a new one.
16   Loosen the actuator from the front of the camshaft by putting your fingers around the rear of the chain and sprocket while pulling it off (see illustration).
Warning: *Don't grasp the reluctor wheel or any other parts of the assembly. The actuator could pop apart, injure you and become damaged.*
17   Remove the actuator assembly along with the chain, then separate the chain.
Warning: *Do not push or pull on the reluctor wheel on the camshaft position actuator/ sprocket at any time. The reluctor wheel is attached to the actuator by three small roll pins. If you push or pull on the reluctor it may separate from the front of the actuator. The actuator has a return spring that is under very high tension. If the reluctor wheel is separate from the actuator, the return spring can cause it to spin, which can cause serious personal injury.*
Caution: *Do not turn the crankshaft or the camshaft while the chain is off. Damage to the pistons and/or the valves could result.*

12.16 Place your fingers as shown when pulling the actuator from the end of the camshaft - don't pull on the reluctor ring as it could pop apart and be destroyed

12.18 Secure the actuator with a wire tie or something similar to ensure that it doesn't come apart

12.21 The sprocket on the crankshaft can be removed with a two- or three-jaw puller

18   Tie the actuator assembly together for safety (see illustration).
19   Remove the timing chain tensioner and inspect it for wear and damage.
20   Also inspect the camshaft and crankshaft sprockets for wear and damage.
21   If replacement of the timing chain is necessary, remove the sprocket from the crankshaft with a two- or three-jaw puller, but be careful not to damage the threads in the end of the crankshaft (see illustration).

Installation

Caution: *Timing chains must be replaced as a set with the camshaft and crankshaft sprockets. Never put a new chain on old sprockets.*
22   Use a gasket scraper to remove all traces of old RTV gasket material and sealant from the cover and engine block.
23   Align the crankshaft sprocket with the Woodruff key and press the sprocket onto the crankshaft (if removed) with the vibration damper bolt, a large socket and some washers or tap it gently into place until it is completely seated.
Caution: *If resistance is encountered, do not hammer the sprocket onto the crankshaft. It may eventually move onto the shaft, but it may be cracked in the process and fail later, causing extensive engine damage.*
24   Loop the new chain over the camshaft sprocket, then turn the sprocket until the timing mark is at the bottom (if you're working on an engine with the camshaft position actuator system, you'll be installing the actuator/ sprocket assembly rather than the sprocket). Mesh the chain with the crankshaft sprocket and position the camshaft sprocket on the end of the camshaft. If necessary, turn the camshaft so the dowel in the camshaft fits into the hole in the sprocket with the timing mark in the 6 o'clock position. When the chain is installed, the timing marks MUST align as shown in illustration 12.14.
Caution: *When installing the camshaft*

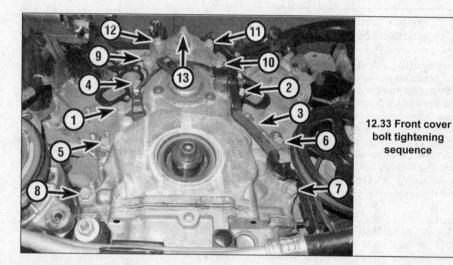

12.33 Front cover bolt tightening sequence

sprocket/actuator, be careful not to push the camshaft back into the engine block.
25   Lay a straightedge across the front of the block and verify that the timing chain does not protrude in front of the face of the engine block.
26   Tighten the NEW camshaft position actuator valve (sprocket bolt) to the torque listed in this Chapter's Specifications.
27   Compress the timing chain tensioner and temporarily insert a pin in the hole to secure it in the retracted position.
28   Install the tensioner and tighten the bolts to the torque listed in this Chapter's Specifications. Remove the pin to allow the tensioner to extend.
29   Install the balance shaft tensioner, chain and sprocket (see Section 14).
Caution: *Carefully and slowly rotate the crankshaft by hand through at least two full revolutions (use a socket and breaker bar on the crankshaft pulley center bolt). If you feel any resistance, STOP! There is something wrong - most likely valves are contacting the pistons. You must find the problem before proceeding.*

30   Install the oil pump (see Section 16).
31   Clean all sealing areas of the timing chain cover and remove all traces of old RTV sealant. Clean the area with brake system cleaner to remove oily residue. Remove the crankshaft oil seal and purchase a new one.
32   Apply a 0.118 inch (3 mm) bead of RTV sealant to the sealing surfaces of the timing cover and 0.197 inch (5 mm) bead to the bottom inch of the cover and the flats on the upper sides of the cover.
33   Install the timing chain cover on the engine loosely, making sure the mounting bolts are in their original locations. Tighten the bolts, in sequence (see illustration) to the torque listed in this Chapter's Specifications.
34   Install a new crankshaft oil seal (see Section 11).
35   The remainder of installation is the reverse of removal.
36   Refill the cooling system and engine oil, and replace the engine oil filter (see Chapter 1). Run the engine and check for oil and coolant leaks.

13.18 Remove the bolts and take off the camshaft retainer plate, noting which side faces the block

13.21a Lobe lift can be obtained by measuring camshaft lobe height . . .

13.21b . . . and the camshaft base circle - the difference between the two measurements equals lobe lift

13   Camshaft and lifters - removal, inspection and installation

Warning: *Wait until the engine is completely cool before beginning this procedure.*
Warning: *The air conditioning system is under high pressure. DO NOT loosen any fittings or remove any components until after the system has been discharged. Air conditioning refrigerant must be properly discharged into an EPA-approved container at a dealership service department or an automotive air conditioning repair facility. Always wear eye protection when disconnecting air conditioning system fittings.*
Caution: *If the camshaft is being replaced, always install new lifters as well. Do not use old lifters on a new camshaft.*
Note: *The manufacturer states that the engine should be removed for this procedure.*

Removal

1   Have the air conditioning system discharged by an automotive air conditioning technician (see the Warning above).
2   Relieve the fuel system pressure (see Chapter 4), then disconnect the cable from the negative battery terminal (see Chapter 5).
3   Drain the cooling system (see Chapter 1), then remove the radiator (see Chapter 3).
4   Refer to Chapter 3 and remove the air conditioning condenser.
5   Remove the auxiliary automatic transmission fluid cooler, if equipped.
6   Remove the valve covers (see Section 4).
7   Remove the intake manifold and valve lifter oil manifold (see Section 7).
8   Remove the valve lifter follower guide mounting bolt and lift the guide out from the valley.
9   Remove the rocker arms and pushrods (see Section 5).
10   Remove the oil pump (see Section 16).

11   Remove the balance shaft chain (see Section 14).
12   Remove the timing chain and camshaft position actuators (see Section 12).
13   Remove the cylinder heads (see Section 9).
14   Before removing the lifters, arrange to store them in a clearly labeled box to ensure that they're reinstalled in their original locations.
15   Remove the lifter retainers and lifters and store them where they won't get dirty (see Chapter 2B, Section 13). DO NOT attempt to withdraw the camshaft with the lifters in place.
Note: *The roller lifters are held in place by retainers - remove the retainer bolts and remove the retainers and the lifters as an assembly. Note the front retainer houses two lifters and the rear retainer houses four lifters; they must be installed back in their original locations if they're going to be reused.*
16   Once the lifters and retainers are removed from the block they can be marked (for location and installation purposes) and inspected.
17   If the lifters are built up with gum and varnish they may not come out with the retainer. If so, there are several ways to extract the lifters from the bores. A special tool designed to grip and remove lifters is manufactured by many tool companies and is widely available, but it may not be required in every case. On newer engines without a lot of varnish buildup, the lifters can often be removed with a small magnet or even with your fingers. A machinist's scribe with a bent end can be used to pull the lifters out by positioning the point under the retainer ring in the top of each lifter.
Caution: *Don't use pliers to remove the lifters unless you intend to replace them with new ones. The pliers will damage the precision machined and hardened lifters, rendering them useless.*
18   Remove the bolts and the camshaft retainer plate, noting which direction faces the

block (see illustration).
19   Thread a bolt into the camshaft sprocket bolt hole to use as a handle when removing the camshaft from the block.
20   Carefully and slowly pull the camshaft out. Support the cam near the block so the lobes don't nick or gouge the bearings as it's withdrawn.

Inspection

Camshaft lobe lift check

21   Measure the camshaft lobe height and the base circle (see illustrations). The difference between the two measurements is the lobe lift (lobe height - base circle = lobe lift). Record this figure for future reference and repeat the check on the remaining camshaft lobes.
22   After the lobe lift check is complete, compare the results to the values listed in this Chapter's Specifications. If the lobe lift is 0.002 inch less than specified, cam lobe wear has occurred and a new camshaft should be installed.

Camshaft bearing journals, lobes and bearings

23   After the camshaft has been removed from the engine, cleaned with solvent and dried, inspect the bearing journals for uneven wear, pitting and evidence of seizure. If the journals are damaged, the bearing inserts in the block are probably damaged as well. Both the camshaft and bearings will have to be replaced.
Note: *Camshaft bearing replacement requires special tools and expertise that place it beyond the scope of the average home mechanic. The tools for bearing removal and installation are available at stores that carry automotive tools, possibly even found at a tool rental business. It is advisable though, if the bearings are bad and the procedure is beyond your ability, take the engine block to an automotive machine shop to ensure that the job is done correctly.*

13.24 Check the diameter of each camshaft bearing journal to pinpoint excessive wear and out-of-round conditions

13.26 Check the pushrod seat in the top of each lifter for wear

13.27 The roller on the lifters must turn freely - check for wear and excessive play as well

24   Measure the bearing journals with a micrometer to determine if they are excessively worn or out-of-round (see illustration).
25   Check the camshaft lobes for heat discoloration, score marks, chipped areas, pitting and uneven wear. If the lobes are in good condition and if the lobe lift measurements recorded earlier are as specified, the camshaft can be reused.

Lifters

26   Clean the lifters with solvent and dry them thoroughly without mixing them up. Check each lifter wall and pushrod seat and for score marks and uneven wear (see illustration). If the lifter walls are damaged or worn (which is not very likely), inspect the lifter bores in the engine block as well. If the pushrod seats are worn, check the pushrod ends.
27   Check the rollers carefully for wear and damage and make sure they turn freely without excessive play (see illustration).
28   Used roller lifters cannot be reinstalled with a new camshaft, but the original camshaft can be used if new lifters are installed. Always use new lifters when installing a new camshaft.

Installation

29   Lubricate the camshaft bearing journals and cam lobes with camshaft and lifter assembly lube (see illustration).
30   Slide the camshaft into the engine. Support the cam near the block and be careful not to scrape or nick the bearings.
31   Apply a non-hardening thread-locking compound to two thirds of the threads on the camshaft retainer bolts, then allow to cure for ten minutes before installing the bolts.
32   Turn the camshaft until the dowel pin is in the 3 o'clock position. Iinstall the camshaft thrust plate and tighten the bolts to the torque listed in this Chapter's Specifcations. Make sure the gasket surface on the camshaft thrust plate and the engine block are free from oil and dirt.
33   Install the timing chain and sprockets

(see Section 12).
34   Install the balance shaft chain (see Section 14) and the oil pump (see Section 16).
35   Lubricate the lifters with clean engine oil and install them in the lifter retainers. Be sure to align the flats on the lifters with the flats in the lifter retainers. Install the retainer and lifters into the engine block as an assembly. If the original lifters are being reinstalled, be sure to return them to their original locations. If a new camshaft is being installed, install new lifters as well. Tighten the lifter retainer bolts to the torque listed in this Chapter's Specifications.
36   The remainder of installation is the reverse of removal.
37   Before starting and running the engine, refill the cooling system, change the oil and install a new oil filter (see Chapter 1).
38   Have the air conditioning system evacuated, recharged and leak tested by the shop that discharged it.

---

14   Balance shaft, chain and sprockets - removal and installation

---

Removal

1   Disconnect the cable from the negative terminal of the battery (see Chapter 5).
2   Raise the vehicle and support it securely on jackstands, then refer to Chapter 1 and drain the engine oil and remove the oil filter.
3   Remove the oil pan skid plate if equipped.
4   There is an engine wiring harness at the front of the oil pan. Disconnect the harness bracket.
5   Remove the starter motor (see Chapter 5). Also remove the plastic bellhousing side covers (see Chapter 7A). Disconnect the transmission cooler line bracket from the side of the oil pan.
6   Position the number one piston at TDC on the compression stroke (see Section 3) to

13.29 Be sure to apply camshaft assembly lube to the cam lobes and bearing journals before installing the camshaft

align the sprocket timing marks (see illustration 12.14). It may be easiest to wait until you remove the front cover to do this.
7   Remove the oil pump (see Section 16).
8   Remove the timing chain cover (see Section 12).
9   Push downwards on the balance shaft thrust plate spring and insert special tool EN-46330 to hold the spring in the down position.
10   Loosen the balance shaft sprocket bolt and the idler shaft sprocket bolt.
11   Remove the balance shaft chain guide retainer bolts and chain guide from the side of the chain.
12   Remove the balance shaft driven sprocket bolt, sprocket and chain as a unit from the camshaft actuator sprocket.
13   Remove the balance shaft retainer mounting bolts and retainer from the front of the engine block.
14   Carefully and slowly pull the balance shaft out. Support the balance shaft near the block so the counterweights don't nick or gouge the bearings as it's withdrawn.

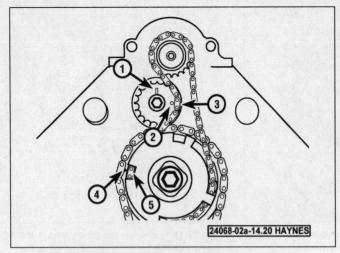

14.20 Balance shaft chain timing marks locations

1   *Driven sprocket 20th tooth (vertical cast line)*
2   *Balance shaft driven sprocket timing mark (dot)*
3   *Balance shaft chain upper plate colored link (blue)*
4   *Camshaft actuator timing mark (triangle)*
5   *Balance shaft chain lower plate colored link (blue)*

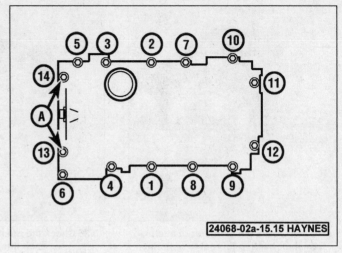

15.15 Oil pan tightening bolt sequence - bolts marked "A" have a lower torque

Installation

15   Lubricate the balance shaft bearing journals and balance shaft journals with camshaft and lifter assembly lube.
16   Insert the balance shaft retainer on to the end of the balance shaft. Carefully insert the balance shaft into the cylinder block making sure the flat spot of the end of the balance shaft is facing toward the 3 o'clock position.
17   Install the balance shaft retainer bolts and tighten the bolts to the torque listed in this Chapter's Specifications.
18   Loop the balance shaft chain around the camshaft actuator sprocket, the driven sprocket and the balance shaft idler sprocket.
19   Install the driven sprocket bolt and tighten it by hand.
Caution: *The flat spot on the balance shaft must be facing the 3 o'clock position.*
20   Check that the timing marks are properly aligned. The lower blue link plate of the balance shaft chain must align with the camshaft actuator triangle mark and the upper blue link plate of the balance shaft chain must align with the dot on the balance shaft driven sprocket (see illustration).
Note: *The 20th tooth on the driven sprocket will have a cast-in vertical line pointing at the 12 o'clock position.*
21   Place a 0.04 inch (1.1mm) feeler gauge between the balance shaft guide and the chain, then install the bolts and tighten the bolts to the torque listed in this Chapter's Specifications.
22   Tighten the balance shaft driven sprocket bolt to the torque listed in this Chapter's Specifications.
23   The idler sprocket should still be able to move up and down. Remove special tool EN-46330 or equivalent from the tensioner and tighten the idler sprocket bolt to the torque

listed in this Chapter's Specifications.
24   The balance shaft chain should now be tight. If it is, remove the feeler gauge (Step 21) and the chain should now have a slight amount of play.
25   The remainder of installation is the reverse of removal.
26   Add the proper type and quantity of oil (see Chapter 1). Start the engine and check for leaks before placing the vehicle back in service.

15   Oil pan - removal and installation

Removal

1   Disconnect the cable from the negative terminal of the battery (see Chapter 5).
2   Raise the vehicle and support it securely on jackstands, then drain the engine oil and remove the oil filter (see Chapter 1).
3   Remove the oil pan skid plate if equipped.
4   Remove the crossmember from below the oil pan.
5   On 4WD models, remove the front differential carrier (see Chapter 8).
6   There is an engine wiring harness at the front of the oil pan. Disconnect the harness bracket.
7   Remove the starter motor (see Chapter 5). Also remove the plastic bellhousing side covers (see Chapter 7A). Disconnect the transmission cooler line bracket from the side of the oil pan.
8   Disconnect the remaining wiring harness brackets.
9   Disconnect the electrical connector from the oil level sensor, if equipped.
10   Remove the transmission-to-oil pan bolts

(see Chapter 7A).
11   Remove the oil pan bolts, then lower the pan from the engine. The pan will probably stick to the engine, so strike the pan with a rubber mallet until it breaks the gasket seal. Carefully slide the oil pan out, to the rear.
Caution: *Before using force on the oil pan, be sure all the bolts have been removed.*

Installation

12   Wash out the oil pan with solvent. Thoroughly clean the mounting surfaces of the oil pan and engine block of old gasket material and sealer. Wipe the gasket surfaces clean with a rag soaked in brake system cleaner.
Note: *On models with a low-oil-level sensor, remove the sensor and install a new sensor upon assembly.*
13   Install new O-ring seals to the oil pan.
14   Apply a 3/16-inch wide, one inch long bead of RTV sealant to the corners where the front cover meets the block and at the rear where the rear main cap meets the block. Then attach the new gasket to the pan, install the pan and tighten the bolts/studs finger-tight.
Note: *The original oil pan gasket was RTV bead of sealant, but aftermarket gaskets may be available. If there is no gasket, apply a 3/16 (5 mm) wide bead around the sealing surface of the oil pan.*
15   Tighten the oil pan bolts to the torque listed in this Chapter's Specifications (see illustration).
16   The remainder of installation is the reverse of removal.
17   Add the proper type and quantity of oil (see Chapter 1). Start the engine and check for leaks before placing the vehicle back in service.

16   Oil pump - removal, inspection and installation

Removal

1   Remove the timing chain cover (see Section 12).
2   Remove the oil pan (see Section 15).
3   Install special tool EN-51257 to the engine block by placing the one piece of the tool against the timing chain tensioner and the other piece against the edge of the oil pump body. Then tighten the mounting bolts securely.
4   Remove the oil pump mounting bolts and slide the pump off of the crankshaft.
Caution: *If the oil pump is being removed and not replaced, special tool EN-51267 (oil pump alignment tool) must be installed to the engine block and against the pump before the oil pump is removed, and remain in place until the pump is reinstalled. If the alignment tool is not installed prior to removal, a new oil pump must be installed.*

Inspection

5   Remove the oil pump cover and withdraw the rotors from the pump body. Clean the components with solvent, dry them thoroughly and inspect for any obvious damage. Also check the bolt holes for damaged threads and the splined surfaces on the crankshaft sprocket for any apparent damage. If any of the components are scored, scratched or worn, replace the entire oil pump assembly. There are no serviceable parts currently available.

Installation

6   Prime the pump by pouring clean engine oil into the pick-up tube hole, while turning the pump by hand.
7   Position the oil pump over the end of the crankshaft. Align the teeth on the crank-shaft sprocket with the teeth on the oil pump drive gear, making sure the pump is fully seated against the block.
8   Push the pump body upward so that the pump body contacts the tool and hold it in this position while tightening the bolts. Constant contact between the oil pump body and the oil pump alignment tool must be maintained. There can be no gap between the oil pump housing and the tool. If there is a gap, loosen the oil pump bolts and push the pump against the tool and tighten the pump bolts again.
9   Install the oil pump mounting bolts and tighten them to the torque listed in this Chapter's Specifications.
10   Install and align the timing chain cover (see Section 12), then install the oil pan (see Section 15).
11   The remainder of installation is the reverse of removal.
12   Add oil and coolant as necessary. Run

17.2 Before removing the driveplate, mark its relationship to the crankshaft

the engine and check for oil and coolant leaks. Also check the oil pressure as described in Chapter 2C.

17   Driveplate - removal and installation

Removal

1   Raise the vehicle and support it securely on jackstands, then remove the transmission (see Chapter 7A).
2   Mark the relationship between the driveplate and the crankshaft with a marker or similar device, then remove the bolts that secure the driveplate to the crankshaft (see illustration). If the crankshaft turns, wedge a screwdriver in the ring gear teeth to jam the driveplate.
3   Remove the driveplate from the crankshaft. Since the driveplate is fairly heavy, be sure to support it while removing the last bolt.
4   Clean the driveplate to remove grease and oil. Inspect the surface for cracks, and check for cracked and broken ring gear teeth. Lay the driveplate on a flat surface to check for warpage.
5   Clean and inspect the mating surfaces of the driveplate and the crankshaft. If the rear main oil seal is leaking, replace it before reinstalling the driveplate (see Section 18).

Installation

6   Position the driveplate against the crankshaft. Be sure to align the marks made during removal. Note that some engines have an alignment dowel or staggered bolt holes to ensure correct installation. Before installing the bolts, apply thread locking compound to the threads and place the retaining ring (if equipped) in position on the driveplate.
7   Wedge a screwdriver through the ring gear teeth to keep the driveplate from turning as you tighten the bolts to the torque listed in this Chapter's Specifications. If the transmis-

sion front pump seal/O-ring is leaking, now would be a very good time to replace it.
8   The remainder of installation is the reverse of removal.

18   Rear main oil seal - replacement

1   Remove the transmission (see Chapter 7A).
2   Remove the driveplate (see Section 17).
3   Pry the oil seal from the rear cover with a screwdriver. Be careful not to nick or scratch the crankshaft or the seal bore. Be sure to note how far it's recessed into the housing bore before removal so the new seal can be installed to the same depth. Thoroughly clean the seal bore in the block with a shop towel. Remove all traces of oil and dirt.
4   Don't lubricate the seal or touch the sealing lip. Make sure the seal is installed in the correct orientation (it has a reverse-lip design). The marking on the seal (. . . THIS SIDE OUT . . .) must be visible when it's installed. Preferably, a seal installation tool (available at most auto parts stores) should be used to press the new seal back into place. If the proper seal installation tool is unavailable, use a large drift and carefully drive the new seal squarely into the seal bore and flush with the rear cover.
5   Install the driveplate (see Section 17).
6   Install the transmission (see Chapter 7A).

19   Engine mounts - check and replacement

1   The engine mount replacement for V6 engines is identical to the engine mount replacement procedure for the V8 engines. Refer to Chapter 2B for the procedure.

Notes

Chapter 2 Part B V8 engines

Contents

Specifications

General

Displacement
5.3L engine	323 cubic inches
6.0L engine	364 cubic inches
6.2L engine	376 cubic inches

VIN
5.3L engine (C)	RPO L83
6.0L engine	
B	RPO LC8
G	RPO L96
6.2L engine (J)	RPO L86

Bore and stroke
5.3L engine	3.779 x 3.622 inches
6.0L engine	4.0017 x 3.622 inches
6.2L engine	4.055 x 3.622 inches

Cylinder numbers (front-to-rear)
Left (driver's) side	1-3-5-7
Right side	2-4-6-8
Firing order	1-8-7-2-6-5-4-3

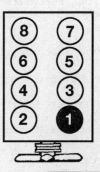

**Cylinder numbering -
V8 engines**

24017-1-B HAYNES

Camshaft

Journal diameters	2.164 to 2.166 inches
Camshaft endplay	0.001 to 0.012 inch

Lobe lift
4.8L engine	0.283 inch

5.3L engine
  Active fuel management cylinders
Intake	0.283 inch
Exhaust	0.279 inch

  Non-active fuel management cylinders
Intake	0.278 inch
Exhaust	0.2741 inch

6.0L engine
Intake	0.274 inch
Exhaust	0.281 inch

6.2L engine
  Active fuel management cylinders
Intake	0.311 inch
Exhaust	0.295 inch

  Non-active fuel management cylinders
Intake	0.306 inch
Exhaust	0.290 inch

Torque specifications*

Ft-lbs (unless otherwise indicated)

Note: *One foot-pound (ft-lb) of torque is equivalent to 12 inch-pounds (in-lbs) of torque. Torque values below approximately 15 foot-pounds are expressed in inch-pounds, because most foot-pound torque wrenches are not accurate at these smaller values.*

Camshaft sprocket bolt - 6.0L engine	55
Camshaft position actuator magnet bolts	89 in-lbs
Camshaft position actuator solenoid valve* - 5.3L and 6.2L engines	
Step 1	48
Step 2	Tighten an additional 90 degrees
Camshaft retainer bolts	
Hex head (6.0L engine)	18
Torx head	132 in-lbs
Crankshaft balancer bolt	
Installation pass with used bolt, to insure the balancer	
is completely seated	240
6.0L engine (use new bolt)	
Step 1	110
Step 2	Loosen 360 degrees
Step 3	59
Step 4	Tighten an additional 125 degrees
5.3L and 6.2L engines	
New bolt with flanged head	
Step 1	89
Step 2	Loosen 360 degrees
Step 3	59
Step 4	125
New bolt with captive rotating washer	
Step 1	15
Step 2	Loosen 360 degrees
Step 3	15
Step 4	200
Crankshaft rear oil seal retainer bolts	
5.3L and 6.2L engines	18
6.0L engine	22
Cylinder head bolts* (in sequence - see illustration 9.22a or 9.22b)	
5.3L and 6.2L engines	

Note: *The left-side cylinder head uses an internal-hex bolt located at the front.*

Step 1	59
Step 2	Tighten an additional 90 degrees
Step 3	
Left-side cylinder head internal hex bolt	Tighten an additional 40 degrees
All other bolts	Tighten an additional 60 degrees
6.0L engine	
Step 1	
All 11 mm bolts (1 through 10)	22
Step 2	
All 11 mm bolts (1 through 10)	Tighten an additional 90 degrees
Step 3	
All 11 mm bolts (1 through 10)	Tighten an additional 70 degrees
Step 4	
All 8 mm bolts (11 through 15)	22
Driveplate bolts	
5.3L and 6.2L engines*	
Step 1	132 in-lbs
Step 2	22
Step 3	Tighten an additional 45 degrees
6.0L engine	
Step 1	15
Step 2	37
Step 3	74
Engine mount fasteners	
To engine	37
To frame	48
Engine mount bracket through-bolt - 6.0L (L96) engine	74
Engine cover to cross bar bolts	15

Torque specifications* (continued)   Ft-lbs (unless otherwise indicated)

Note: *One foot-pound (ft-lb) of torque is equivalent to 12 inch-pounds (in-lbs) of torque. Torque values below approximately 15 foot-pounds are expressed in inch-pounds, because most foot-pound torque wrenches are not accurate at these smaller values.*

Exhaust manifold bolts	
5.3L and 6.2L engines	
Existing manifold	17
New manifold	20
6.0L engine	
Step 1	132 in-lbs
Step 2	15
Exhaust manifold heat shield bolt	
5.3L and 6.2L engines	89 in-lbs
6.0L engine	80 in-lbs
Exhaust pipe flange nuts	20 to 25
Intake manifold cover bolts	40 to 44 in-lbs
Intake manifold bolts	
Step 1	44 in-lbs
Step 2	89 in-lbs
Crankshaft oil deflector/baffle	
5.3L and 6.2L engines - bolts	89 in-lbs
6.0L engine - nuts	18
Oil pan drain plug	18
Oil pan rear access plugs	80 in-lbs
Oil pan bolts	
To engine and front cover	18
To rear cover	100 in-lbs
Lower oil pan to upper oil pan - 5.3L and 6.2L engines	89 in-lbs
Oil pump cover bolts	
5.3L and 6.2L engines	89 in-lbs
6.0L engine	80 in-lbs
Oil pump mounting bolts	18
Oil pump pickup tube/screen to oil pump - bolts/nuts	
5.3L and 6.2L engines (bolts)	89 in-lbs
6.0L engine (nuts)	106 in-lbs
Rocker arm bolts	22
Timing chain tensioner bolts	22
Timing chain cover bolts	18
Valley cover bolts	18
Valve cover bolts	
5.3L and 6.2L engines	89 in-lbs
6.0L engine	106 in-lbs
Valve lifter guide bolts	106 in-lbs

Refer to Part C for additional specifications.

1   General Information

1   This Part of Chapter 2 is devoted to in-vehicle repair procedures for the 5.3L, 6.0L and 6.2L V8 engines. These engines utilize either aluminum or cast-iron blocks with eight cylinders arranged in a "V" shape at a 90-degree angle between the two banks. The cylinder heads utilize an overhead valve arrangement. Engines with aluminum cylinder heads use pressed-in valve guides and valve seats, while engines with cast iron cylinder heads have integral valve guides and hardened valve seats. Hydraulic roller lifters actuate the valves through tubular pushrods and rocker arms. The oil pump is mounted at the front of the engine behind the timing chain cover and is driven by the crankshaft.

2   To positively identify these engines, locate the Vehicle Identification Number (VIN) on the left front corner of the instrument panel. The VIN is visible from the outside of the vehicle through the windshield. The eighth character in the sequence is the engine designation:

    C = 5.3L V8 engine
    B, G = 6.0L V8 engine
    J= 6.2L V8 engine

3   Information concerning engine removal and installation and engine overhaul can be found in Part C of this Chapter. The following repair procedures are based on the assumption that the engine is installed in the vehicle. If the engine has been removed from the vehicle and mounted on a stand, many of the steps outlined in this Part of Chapter 2 will not apply.

2   Repair operations possible with the engine in the vehicle

1   Many major repair operations can be accomplished without removing the engine from the vehicle.

2   Clean the engine compartment and the exterior of the engine with some type of pressure washer before any work is done. A clean engine will make the job easier and will help keep dirt out of the internal areas of the engine.

3   Depending on the components involved, it may be a good idea to remove the hood to improve access to the engine as repairs are performed (refer to Chapter 11 if necessary).

4   If oil or coolant leaks develop, indicating a need for gasket or seal replacement, the repairs can generally be made with the engine in the vehicle. The oil pan gasket, the cylinder head gaskets, intake and exhaust manifold gaskets, timing chain cover gaskets and the crankshaft oil seals are all accessible with the engine in place.

5   Exterior engine components, such as the water pump, the starter motor, the alternator and the fuel injection components, as well as the intake and exhaust manifolds, can be removed for repair with the engine in place.

6   Since the cylinder heads can be removed without removing the engine, valve component servicing can also be accomplished with the engine in the vehicle.

7   Replacement of, repairs to or inspection of the timing chain and sprockets and the oil pump are all possible with the engine in place.

8   In extreme cases caused by a lack of necessary equipment, repair or replacement of piston rings, pistons, connecting rods and rod bearings is possible with the engine in the vehicle. However, this practice is not recommended because of the cleaning and preparation work that must be done to the components involved.

3   Top Dead Center (TDC) for number one piston - locating

1   Top Dead Center (TDC) is the highest point in the cylinder that each piston reaches as it travels up the cylinder bore. Each piston reaches TDC on the compression stroke and again on the exhaust stroke, but TDC generally refers to piston position on the compression stroke.

2   Positioning the piston(s) at TDC is an essential part of many procedures such as timing chain/sprocket removal.

3   Before beginning this procedure, be sure to place the transmission in Neutral and apply the parking brake or block the rear wheels. Also, disable the ignition system by disconnecting the primary electrical connectors at the ignition coil packs, then remove the spark plugs (see Chapter 1).

4   In order to bring any piston to TDC, the crankshaft must be turned using a socket and ratchet or breaker bar attached to the crankshaft pulley bolt. When looking at the front of the engine, normal crankshaft rotation is clockwise.

5   Install a compression gauge in the no. 1 cylinder spark plug hole or place your finger partially over the number one spark plug hole and rotate the crankshaft until air pressure is felt. Air pressure at the spark plug hole indicates that the cylinder has started the compression stroke. Once the compression stroke has begun, TDC for the number one cylinder is obtained when the piston reaches the top of the cylinder on the compression stroke.

6   To bring the piston to the top of the cylinder, insert a long screwdriver into the number one spark plug hole until it touches the top of the piston.

Note: *Wrap the tip of the screwdriver with tape to avoid scratching the top of the piston and the cylinder walls.*

7   Use the screwdriver as a feeler gauge to tell where the top of the piston is located in the cylinder while slowly rotating the crankshaft. As the piston rises the screwdriver will be pushed out. The point at which the screwdriver stops moving outward is TDC.

Note: *Always hold the screwdriver upright while the engine is being rotated so that the*

screwdriver will not get wedged as the piston travels upward.

8   If you go past TDC, rotate the crankshaft counterclockwise until the piston is approximately 1/2-inch below TDC, then slowly rotate the crankshaft clockwise again until TDC is reached.

9   After the number one piston has been positioned at TDC on the compression stroke, TDC for any of the remaining pistons can be located by repeating the procedure described above and following the firing order.

4   Valve covers - removal and installation

Removal

1   Disconnect the cable from the negative terminal of the battery (see Chapter 5).

5.3L and 6.2L engines

2   Disconnect the PCV quick connect fitting (see Chapter 6) from the air filter housing and the valve covers.

3   Pull the valve cover insulator off the valve cover.

4   If you remove the left side valve cover, remove the oil dipstick tube mounting bolt and pivot the tube out of the way.

5   If you remove the right side valve cover, remove the air cleaner duct (see Chapter 4).

6   Disconnect the spark plug wires from the coils by first twisting them a half turn to loosen them. Pull only on the boot - not on the wire.

7   Remove the ignition coils (see Chapter 5).

8   Disconnect the interfering engine wiring harnesses and move them aside.

9   Remove the valve cover bolts, then detach the cover from the cylinder head.

Note: *If the cover is stuck to the cylinder head, bump one end with a block of wood and a hammer to jar it loose. If that doesn't work, try to slip a flexible putty knife between the cylinder head and cover to break the gasket seal. Don't pry at the cover-to-head joint or damage to the sealing surfaces may occur (leading to oil leaks in the future).*

6.0L engine

10   Pull the intake manifold cover up and off of the ballstuds.

11   If you're working on the right valve cover, detach the heater hoses from the hose bracket on the valve cover (see illustrations). Remove the heater hose bracket.

12   Disconnect the spark plug wires from the coils by first twisting them a half turn to loosen them. Pull only on the boot - not on the wire.

13   Remove the ignition coil bracket along with the coils (see Chapter 5).

14   Remove the PCV tube or hose from the valve cover (see Chapter 6).

15   Remove the valve cover bolts, then detach the cover from the cylinder head (see illustration).

4.11a The main wiring harness restricts access to the left valve cover - it must be released from its retainers and moved aside

4.11b The heater hoses can be unclipped from their retainer to remove the right valve cover

4.15 Valve cover mounting bolts (6.0L engine)

4.18 Position the new gasket in the valve cover lip

Installation

16   The mating surfaces of each cylinder head and valve cover must be perfectly clean when the covers are installed. Use a gasket scraper to remove all traces of sealant and old gasket material, then clean the mating surfaces with brake system cleaner. If there's sealant or oil on the mating surfaces when the cover is installed, oil leaks may develop.

17   Clean the mounting bolt threads with a die to remove any corrosion and restore damaged threads. Make sure the threaded holes in the cylinder head are clean - run a tap into them to remove corrosion and restore damaged threads.

18   Position the gasket inside the cover lip (see illustration). If the gasket will not stay in place in the cover lip, apply a thin coat of RTV sealant to the cover flange, then allow the sealant to set up so the gasket adheres to the cover.

19   Tighten the bolts in three or four steps to the torque listed in this Chapter's Specifications.

20   The remainder of installation is the reverse of removal. Use thread locking material on the ignition coil bracket studs and nuts.

21   Start the engine and check carefully for oil leaks as the engine warms up.

5   Rocker arms and pushrods - removal, inspection and installation

Removal

1   Refer to Section 4 and remove the valve covers from the cylinder heads.

2   Loosen the rocker arm pivot bolts one at a time and remove the rocker arms and bolts, then remove the pivot support pedestal (see illustration). Keep track of the component positions, since they must be returned

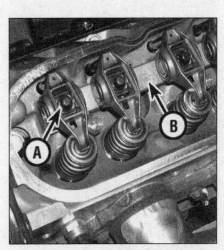

5.2 Remove the mounting bolts (A) and rocker arms, then remove the pivot support pedestal (B)

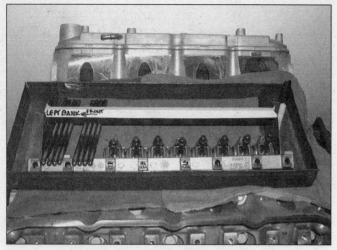

5.3 Store the pushrods and rocker arms in order to ensure they are reinstalled in their original locations

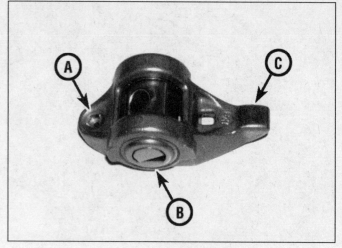

5.4 Rocker arm wear points

A   Pushrod socket   C   Valve stem contact point
B   Pivot bearing

5.9 Lubricate the pushrod ends and the valve stems with engine assembly lube before installing the rocker arms

to the same locations. Store each set of components separately in a marked container to ensure that they're reinstalled in their original locations. This includes the rocker arms and the pivot support.

3   Remove the pushrods and store them in order to make sure they don't get mixed up during installation (see illustration).

Inspection

4   Check each rocker arm for wear, cracks and other damage, especially where the pushrods and valve stems contact the rocker arm (see illustration).

5   Check the pivot bearings for binding and roughness. If the bearings are worn or damaged, replacement of the entire rocker arm will be necessary. Also check the rocker arm pivot support pedestal for cracks and other obvious damage.

Note: *Keep in mind that there is no valve adjustment on these engines, so excessive wear or damage in the valve train can easily result in excessive valve clearance, which in*

turn will cause valve noise when the engine is running.

6   Make sure the hole at the pushrod end of each rocker arm is open.

7   Inspect the pushrods for cracks and excessive wear at the ends, also check that the oil hole running through each pushrod is not clogged. Roll each pushrod across a piece of plate glass to see if it's bent (if it wobbles, it's bent).

Installation

8   Lubricate the lower end of each pushrod with clean engine oil or engine assembly lube and install them in their original locations. Make sure each pushrod seats completely in the lifter socket.

9   Apply engine assembly lube to the ends of the valve stems and to the upper ends of the pushrods to prevent damage to the mating surfaces on initial start-up (see illustration). Also apply clean engine oil to the pivot shaft and bearing of each rocker arm and install the rocker arms loosely in their original locations.

DO NOT tighten the bolts at this time!

10   Rotate the crankshaft until the number one piston is at TDC on the compression stroke (see Section). Both pushrods for the number one cylinder should be in the lowered position. When the number one piston is at TDC, tighten the intake valve rocker arms for the Number 1, 3, 4, and 5 cylinders and the exhaust rocker arms for the Number 1, 2, 7, and 8 cylinders. Tighten each of the specified rocker arm bolts to the torque listed in this Chapter's Specifications.

11   Rotate the crankshaft 360 degrees. Tighten the intake valve rocker arms for the Number 2, 6, 7, and 8 cylinders and the exhaust rocker arms for the Number 3, 4, 5, and 6 cylinders. Tighten each of the rocker arm bolts to the torque listed in this Chapter's Specifications.

12   Refer to Section 4 and install the valve covers. Start the engine, listen for unusual valve train noises and check for oil leaks at the valve cover gaskets.

6   Valve springs, retainers and seals - replacement

Note: *Broken valve springs and defective valve stem seals can be replaced without removing the cylinder head. Two special tools and a compressed air source are normally required to perform this operation, so read through this section carefully and rent or buy the tools before beginning the job.*

1   Remove the spark plugs (see Chapter 1).

2   Remove the valve covers (see Section 4).

3   Rotate the crankshaft until the number one piston is at Top Dead Center on the compression stroke (see Section 3).

4   Remove the rocker arms for the number one piston.

6.5 This is what the air hose adapter that fits into the spark plug hole looks like - they're commonly available from auto parts stores

6.8 Once the spring is depressed, the keepers can be removed with a small magnet or needle-nose pliers (a magnet is preferred to prevent dropping the keepers)

6.10 Use a pair of needle-nose pliers to remove the valve seals

5   Thread an adapter into the spark plug hole and connect an air hose from a compressed air source to it (see illustration). Most auto parts stores can supply the air hose adapter.
Note: *Many cylinder compression gauges utilize a screw-in fitting that may work with your air hose quick-disconnect fitting. If a cylinder compression gauge fitting is used, it will be necessary to remove the Schrader valve from the end of the fitting before using it in this procedure.*
6   Apply compressed air to the cylinder. The valves should be held in place by the air pressure.
Warning: *If the cylinder isn't exactly at TDC, air pressure may force the piston down, causing the engine to quickly rotate. DO NOT leave a wrench on the crankshaft balancer bolt or you may be injured by the tool.*
7   Stuff shop rags into the cylinder head holes around the valves to prevent parts and tools from falling into the engine.
8   Using a socket and a hammer, gently tap on the top of each valve spring retainer several times (this will break the seal between the valve keeper and the spring retainer and allow the keeper to separate from the valve spring retainer as the valve spring is compressed), then use a valve-spring compressor to compress the spring. Remove the keepers with small needle-nose pliers or a magnet (see illustration).
Note: *Several different types of tools are available for compressing the valve springs with the head in place. One type grips the lower spring coils and presses on the retainer as the knob is turned, while the lever-type shown here utilizes the rocker arm bolt for leverage. Both types work very well, although the lever type is usually less expensive.*
9   Remove the valve spring and retainer.
Note: *If air pressure fails to retain the valve in the closed position during this operation, the valve face or seat may be damaged. If so,*

the cylinder head will have to be removed for repair.
10   Remove the old valve stem seals, noting differences between the intake and exhaust seals (see illustration).
11   Wrap a rubber band or tape around the top of the valve stem so the valve won't fall into the combustion chamber, then release the air pressure.
12   Inspect the valve stem for damage. Rotate the valve in the guide and check the end for eccentric movement, which would indicate that the valve is bent.
13   Move the valve up-and-down in the guide and make sure it does not bind. If the valve stem binds, either the valve is bent or the guide is damaged. In either case, the head will have to be removed for repair.
14   Reapply air pressure to the cylinder to retain the valve in the closed position, then remove the tape or rubber band from the valve stem.
15   Install a new valve stem seal over the valve stem and press it down over the valve guide to the specified depth. Don't force the valve seal against the top of the guide.
16   Install the spring and retainer in position over the valve.
17   Compress the valve spring assembly only enough to install the keepers in the valve stem.
18   Position the keepers in the valve stem groove. Apply a small dab of grease to the inside of each keeper to hold it in place if necessary (see illustration). Remove the pressure from the spring tool and make sure the keepers are seated.
19   Disconnect the air hose and remove the adapter from the spark plug hole.
20   Repeat the above procedure on the remaining cylinders, following the firing order sequence (see this Chapter's Specifications). Bring each piston to Top Dead Center on the compression stroke before applying air pressure (see Section 3).

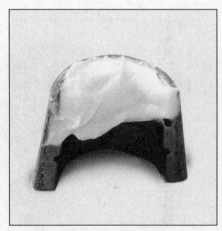

6.18 Apply a small dab of grease to each keeper as shown here before installation - it'll hold them in place on the valve stem as the spring is released

21   Reinstall the rocker arm assemblies and the valve covers (see Sections 4 and 5).
22   Start the engine, then check for oil leaks and unusual sounds coming from the valve cover area. Allow the engine to idle for at least five minutes before revving the engine.

7   Intake manifold and Valve Lifter Oil Manifold (VLOM) - removal and installation

Warning: *Wait until the engine is completely cool before starting this procedure.*

Removal

1   Disconnect the cable from the negative terminal of the battery (see Chapter 5). Relieve the fuel system pressure (see Chapter 4).
2   Refer to (see Chapter 4) and remove the

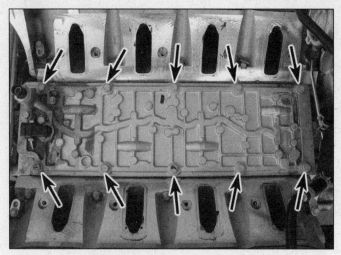

7.9a Valve Lifter Oil Manifold (VLOM) assembly mounting bolts

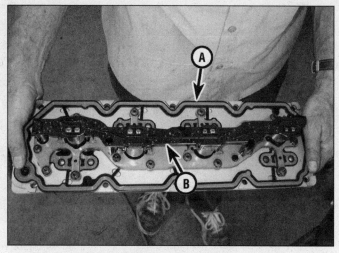

7.9b The Valve Lifter Oil Manifold (VLOM) gasket (A) can be re-used if it's in good condition. Don't pick up the assembly by the electrical lead frame (B)

7.13 Align the tabs on the intake gaskets with the tabs on the manifold and snap the gasket into place

air filter housing outlet duct.

3   Refer to (see Chapter 5) and remove the alternator.

4   Label, then disconnect all of the engine wiring harnesses that interfere with intake manifold removal. Also detach all the harness retainers and clips. Move the detached harnesses aside and secure them out of the way. **Note:** *Clear labeling will make the assembly procedure go smoothly and quickly.*

5   Disconnect the power brake vacuum hose from the booster.

6   Disconnect the hose from the canister purge solenoid (see Chapter 6). Disconnect the fuel line from the fuel rail (see Chapter 4). Disconnect the PCV hose from the intake manifold.

7   Disconnect any remaining electrical connectors or vacuum hoses connected to the intake manifold or throttle body.

8   Loosen the intake manifold mounting bolts in 1/4-turn increments in the reverse order of the tightening sequence until they can be removed by hand (see illustrations

7.15a or 7.15b). The manifold will probably be stuck to the cylinder heads and force may be required to break the gasket seal. A pry bar can be positioned between the front of the manifold and the valley tray to break the bond made by the gasket.

Caution: *Do not pry between the manifold and the heads or damage to the gasket sealing surfaces may result and vacuum leaks could develop. Also, don't use too much force - the manifold is made of a plastic composite and could crack.*

9   Slide the manifold forward and disconnect the wiring harness fasteners, then remove the intake manifold. As the manifold is lifted from the engine, be sure to check for and disconnect anything still attached to the manifold. The Valve Lifter Oil Manifold (VLOM) assembly can be removed at this time (see illustrations).

10   On 6.0L models, if the manifold is being replaced, remove the fuel rail and injectors from the intake manifold (see Chapter 4).

Installation

Note: *The mating surfaces of the cylinder heads, block and manifold must be perfectly clean when the manifold is installed.*

11   Carefully remove all traces of old gasket material. Note that the intake manifold is made of a composite material and the cylinder heads on some engines are made of aluminum; therefore aggressive scraping is not suggested and will damage the sealing surfaces. After the gasket surfaces are cleaned and free of any gasket material, wipe the mating surfaces with a cloth saturated with safety solvent. If there is old sealant or oil on the mating surfaces when the manifold is installed, oil or vacuum leaks may develop. Use a vacuum cleaner to remove any gasket material that falls into the intake ports in the heads.

12   Use a tap of the correct size to chase the threads in the bolt holes, then use compressed air (if available) to remove the debris from the holes.

Warning: *Wear safety glasses or a face shield to protect your eyes when using compressed air.*

13   Position the new gaskets on the intake manifold (see illustration). Note that the gaskets are equipped with installation tabs that must snap into place on the intake manifold. The words "Manifold Side" may appear on the gasket. If so, this will ensure proper installation. Make sure the gaskets snap into place and all intake port openings align.

14   Carefully set the manifold in place.

15   Install the bolts and tighten them following the recommended sequence (see illustrations) to the torque listed in this Chapter's Specifications. Do not overtighten the bolts or gasket leaks may develop.

16   The remainder of installation is the reverse of removal. Start the engine and check carefully for vacuum leaks at the intake manifold joints.

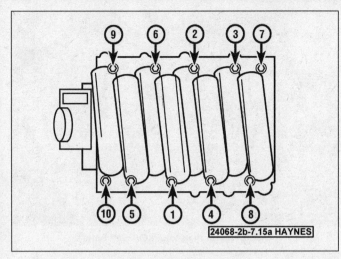

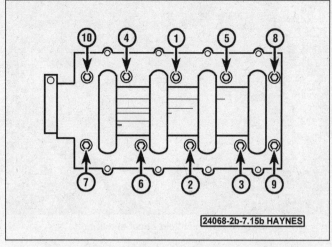

7.15a Intake manifold bolt tightening sequence - 5.3L and 6.2L engines

7.15b Intake manifold bolt tightening sequence - 6.0L engine

8 Exhaust manifolds - removal and installation

Removal

Warning: *Use caution when working around the exhaust manifolds - the sheetmetal heat shields can be sharp on the edges. Also, the engine should be cold when this procedure is followed.*

1 Disconnect the cable from the negative terminal of the battery (see Chapter 5).

2 Raise the vehicle and support it securely on jackstands.

3 Working under the vehicle, apply penetrating oil to the exhaust pipe-to-manifold studs and nuts (they're usually rusty) (see illustration).

4 Remove the inner fender splash shield (see Chapter 11).

5 Disconnect the exhaust pipe/catalytic converter pipe from the exhaust manifold.

6 Remove the spark plug wires (see Chapter 1).

Caution: *Twist the boots to loosen them, then pull on the boots only - not the wires.*

Left side

7 Use a dab of paint to mark the alignment of the upper section of the steering intermediate shaft to the lower part of the steering column (see illustration). Remove the fasteners, then separate the shafts so they can be moved aside.

Caution: *Don't move the wheels or the steering wheel after disconnecting the shafts. The airbag system clockspring could be damaged.*

Note: *On 6.0L models, install special tool J-42640 (steering column anti-rotation pin) into the steering column lower access hole to prevent the column from rotating.*

Right side

8 On 6.0L models, remove the oil dipstick tube.

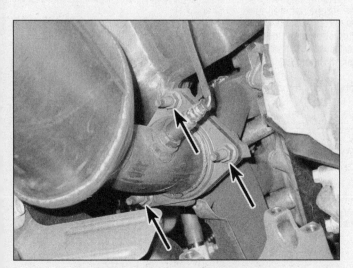

8.3 Typical exhaust pipe-to-manifold nuts

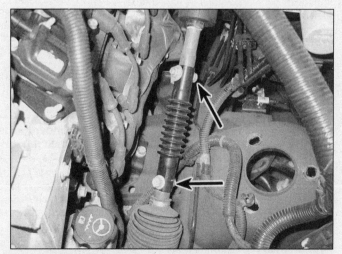

8.7 The steering shaft should be disconnected for access to the left exhaust manifold; don't turn the steering wheel or the front wheels after separating it

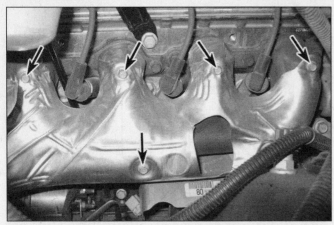

8.9a Exhaust manifold - heat shield bolts

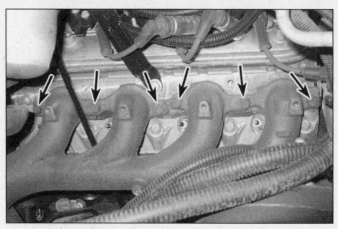

8.9b Exhaust manifold mounting bolts

9.8 The alternator bracket can be unbolted and moved forward as a complete assembly - 6.0L model shown

9.11 Label, then disconnect the ground wires that are bolted to the right cylinder head

Both sides

9   If a new manifold is to be installed, remove the heat shield (see illustration). Remove the manifold mounting bolts, then lift off the exhaust manifold and its gasket (see illustration).

Installation

10   Check the manifold for cracks and make sure the bolt threads are clean and undamaged. The manifold and cylinder head mating surfaces must be clean before the manifolds are reinstalled - use a gasket scraper to remove all carbon deposits and gasket material.
Note: *The cylinder heads are made of aluminum; therefore aggressive scraping is not suggested and will damage the sealing surfaces.*
11   Install the heat shields, then install the bolts and gaskets onto the manifold. Retaining tabs surrounding the gasket bolt holes should hold the assembly together as the manifold is installed.
12   Starting at the fourth thread, apply a 1/4-inch wide band of medium-strength threadlocking compound to the threads of the bolts.
Note: *The manufacturer recommends not applying threadlocking compound on the first three threads.*

13   Place the manifold on the cylinder head and install the mounting bolts finger tight.
14   When tightening the mounting bolts, work from the center to the ends. Tighten the bolts in two steps to the torque listed in this Chapter's Specifications. If required, bend the exposed end of the exhaust manifold gasket back against the cylinder head.
15   The remainder of installation is the reverse of removal.
16   Start the engine and check for exhaust leaks.

---

9   Cylinder heads - removal and installation

Warning: *Wait until the engine is completely cool before beginning this procedure.*
Note: *It will be necessary to purchase a new set of 11 mm cylinder head bolts for this procedure.*

Removal

1   Relieve the fuel system pressure (see Chapter 4). Disconnect the cable from the negative terminal of the battery (see Chapter 5) and drain the cooling system (see Chapter 1).

2   Remove the intake manifold (see Section 7).
3   On 5.3L and 6.2L engines, remove the fuel rail(s) from the cylinder head(s) (see Chapter 4).
4   Detach the exhaust manifold(s) from the cylinder head(s) (see Section 8). It is not necessary to disconnect the manifold(s) from the exhaust pipe(s).
5   Remove the valve cover(s) (see Section 4).
6   Remove the rocker arms and pushrods (see Section 5).
Caution: *Again, as mentioned in Section 5, keep all the parts in order so they can be reinstalled in the same locations.*
7   Remove the coolant air bleed pipe.

Left cylinder head

8   Remove the alternator and its bracket (see Chapter 5) (see illustration).
9   Disconnect the ground strap at the back of the cylinder head.

Right cylinder head

10   On 6.0L models, remove the dipstick tube.
11   Disconnect the ground cables from the front of the cylinder head (see illustration).

Both cylinder heads

12   Loosen the head bolts in 1/4-turn increments in the reverse order of the tightening sequence (see illustration 9.22a or 9.22b) until they can be removed by hand.

Note: *There will be different length and size head bolts for different locations. Make a note of the different sizes and lengths and where they go when removing the bolts to ensure correct installation of the new bolts.*

13   Lift the head (s) off the engine. If resistance is felt, do not pry between the head and block as damage to the mating surfaces will result. To dislodge the head, place a pry bar or long screwdriver into the intake port and carefully pry the head off the engine (see illustration).

14   Store the heads on blocks of wood to prevent damage to the gasket sealing surfaces.

Installation

15   The mating surfaces of the cylinder heads and block must be perfectly clean when the heads are installed. Gasket removal solvents are available at auto parts stores and may prove helpful.

16   Use a gasket scraper to remove all traces of carbon and old gasket material, then wipe the mating surfaces with a cloth saturated with brake system cleaner. If there is oil on the mating surfaces when the heads are installed, the gaskets may not seal correctly and leaks may develop. When working on the block, use a vacuum cleaner to remove any debris that falls into the cylinders.

Note: *The cylinder heads on some engines are made of aluminum; therefore aggressive scraping is not suggested and will damage the sealing surfaces.*

17   Check the block and head mating surfaces for nicks, deep scratches and other damage. If damage is slight, it can be removed with emery cloth. If it is excessive, machining may be the only alternative.

18   Use a tap of the correct size to chase the

9.13 Using a prybar inserted into an intake port to break the head loose - do not use excessive force or damage to the head may result

9.19 Position the head gasket over the dowels at each end of the cylinder head with the mark facing the front of the vehicle

threads in the head bolt holes in the block. If a tap is not available, spray a liberal amount of brake cleaner into each hole. Use compressed air (if available) to remove the debris from the holes. All cylinder head bolts should be replaced with new bolts.

Warning: *Wear safety glasses or a face shield to protect your eyes when using compressed air.*

19   Position the new gaskets over the dowels in the block (see illustration).

20   Carefully position the heads on the block without disturbing the gaskets.

21   Before installing the 8mm head bolts, coat the threads with a medium-strength threadlocking compound. Then install the new 8mm head bolts (bolts 11 through 15).

22   Install new 11 mm head bolts (bolts 1 through 10) and tighten them finger tight. Following the recommended sequence (see illustrations), tighten the bolts in four steps to the torque listed in this Chapter's Specifications.

Caution: *DO NOT reuse head bolts - always*

replace them with new ones.

23   Install the coolant pipe, using new gaskets, onto the cylinder heads. Tighten the bolts to the torque listed in this Chapter's Specifications.

24   The remainder of installation is the reverse of removal.

25   Add coolant and change the oil and filter (see Chapter 1). Start the engine and check for proper operation and coolant or oil leaks.

10   Crankshaft balancer - removal and installation

Note: *This procedure requires a special balancer installation tool and a new crankshaft balancer bolt. Read through the entire procedure and obtain the tool and materials before proceeding.*

1   Disconnect the cable from the negative terminal of the battery (see Chapter 5).

2   Raise the front of the vehicle and sup-

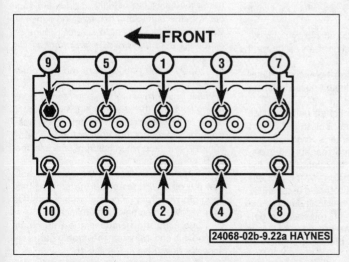

9.22a Cylinder head bolt tightening sequence - 5.3L and 6.2L engines

9.22b Cylinder head bolt tightening sequence - 6.0L engine

10.5 Driveplate holding tool bolted in place

10.6 The use of a three-jaw puller will be necessary to remove the crankshaft balancer - always place the puller jaws around the hub, not the outer ring

10.9 Before the new crankshaft bolt is installed and tightened, the balancer must be measured for proper installation - when properly installed, the balancer hub should extend 3/32 to 11/64-inch past the crankshaft snout

11.2 Carefully pry the old seal out of the timing chain cover - don't damage the crankshaft in the process

11.4 Drive the new seal into place with a large socket and hammer

port it securely on jackstands. Then apply the parking brake.

3   Remove the drivebelt, air conditioning compressor belt and on 5.3L/6.2L models the vacuum pump belt (see Chapter 1). Remove the cooling fan and shroud assembly (see Chapter 3).

4   Working under the vehicle, remove the stone shield from below the engine (if equipped).

5   Remove the starter motor (see Chapter 5). Install a driveplate holding tool into the ring gear teeth and bolt it to the engine block (see illustration).

6   Pull the balancer off the crankshaft with a puller (see illustration).

Caution: *The jaws of the puller must only contact the hub of the balancer - not the outer ring.*

Caution: *The proper adapter or a long Allen-head bolt should be inserted into the crankshaft nose for the puller's tapered tip to push*

against to prevent damage to the crankshaft threads.

7   Position the crankshaft pulley/balancer on the crankshaft and slide it on as far as it will go.

8   Using the crankshaft balancer installation tool, press the crankshaft pulley/balancer onto the crankshaft.

9   Install the old crankshaft balancer bolt and tighten the crankshaft bolt to the Step 1 torque listed in this Chapter's Specifications. Remove the old bolt and measure the distance from the snout of the crankshaft to the balancer hub (see illustration). When properly installed, the balancer hub should extend 3/32 to 11/64-inch past the crankshaft snout. If the measurement is incorrect, reinstall the balancer installation tool and press the balancer on the crankshaft until the measurement is correct.

10   Install a new crankshaft balancer bolt and tighten it to the torque and angle of rota-

tion listed in this Chapter's Specifications.

11   The remainder of installation is the reverse of removal.

---

11   Crankshaft front oil seal - removal and installation

---

1   Remove the crankshaft balancer (see Section 10).

2   Note how the seal is installed - the new one must be installed to the same depth and facing the same way. Carefully pry the oil seal out of the cover with a seal puller or a large screwdriver (see illustration). Be very careful not to distort the cover or scratch the crankshaft! Wrap electrician's tape around the tip of the screwdriver to avoid damage to the crankshaft.

3   If the seal is being replaced with the timing chain cover removed, support the cover on top of two blocks of wood and drive the seal out from the rear with a hammer and punch.

Caution: *Be careful not to scratch, gouge or distort the area that the seal fits into or a leak will develop.*

4   Apply clean engine oil or multi-purpose grease to the outer edge of the new seal, then install it in the cover with the lip (spring side) facing IN. Drive the seal into place with a seal driver or large socket and hammer (see illustration). Make sure the seal enters the bore squarely and stop when the front face is at the proper depth.

5   Check the surface on the balancer hub that the oil seal rides on. If the surface has been grooved from long-time contact with the seal, replace the crankshaft balancer.

6   Lubricate the balancer hub with clean engine oil and reinstall the crankshaft balancer as described in Section 10.

7   The remainder of installation is the reverse of removal.

12.8 Timing chain cover mounting bolts

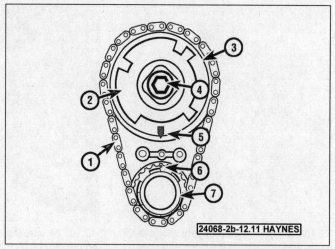

12.11 Timing chain alignment marks - when properly aligned, the crankshaft gear should be in the 12 o'clock position, the camshaft gear should be in the 6 o'clock position and the number one piston should be at TDC

1	Timing chain	5	Camshaft gear timing
2	Reluctor wheel		mark (6 o'clock position)
3	Camshaft/actuator gear	6	Crankshaft gear timing
4	Camshaft position		mark (12 o'clock position)
	actuator solenoid valve	7	Crankshaft gear

12 Timing chain and sprockets - removal, inspection and installation

Warning: *Wait until the engine is completely cool before beginning this procedure.*
Caution: *The timing system is complex, and severe engine damage will occur if you make any mistakes. Do not attempt this procedure unless you are highly experienced with this type of repair. If you are at all unsure of your abilities, be sure to consult an expert. Double-check all your work and be sure everything is correct before you attempt to start the engine.*

Removal and inspection

Note: *A special tool is recommended for aligning the timing chain cover during installation (see Step 30).*
1   Disconnect the cable from the negative terminal of the battery (see Chapter 5).
2   Refer to (see Chapter 1) and drain the cooling system and engine oil.
3   On 5.3L and 6.2L models, remove the oil pan (see Section 14), the vacuum pump (see Chapter 9) and coolant manifold (see Chapter 3).
4   Remove the air conditioning compressor mounting bolts (see Chapter 3) and secure the compressor out of the way without disconnecting the lines to the compressor.
5   On 6.0L models, remove the water pump (see Chapter 3).
6   Remove the crankshaft balancer (see Section 10).
7   Disconnect the wiring from the camshaft position sensor and the camshaft position actuator magnet (if equipped).

12.12 Camshaft position actuator system components - the "bolt" is the solenoid valve (it must be replaced with a new one whenever it's removed); don't try to disassemble the actuator mechanism

8   Remove the timing chain cover mounting bolts and separate the timing chain cover from the block (see illustration). The cover may be stuck; if so, use a putty knife to break the gasket seal. The cover can easily be damaged, so DO NOT attempt to pry it off.
9   Remove the oil pump (see Section 15).
10   Press the timing chain tensioner toward the chain until special tool EN-46330 or a 3 mm drill bit can be inserted into the tensioner.
11   Screw the crankshaft balancer bolt into the end of the crankshaft and rotate the crankshaft in the normal direction of rotation (clockwise) until the timing marks are aligned at the 12 o'clock and six o'clock positions (see illustration).

12.13 Place your fingers as shown when pulling the actuator from the end of the camshaft - don't pull on the reluctor ring as it could pop apart and be destroyed

Caution: *Once the timing marks are aligned and the timing chain has been removed, DO NOT turn the camshaft or crankshaft until the chain has been reinstalled!*
12   Remove the solenoid valve from the center of the upper sprocket assembly and discard it (see illustration). It must be replaced with a new one.
13   Loosen the actuator from the front of the camshaft by putting your fingers around the rear of the chain and sprocket while pulling it off (see illustration).
Warning: *Don't grasp the reluctor wheel or any other parts of the assembly. The actuator could pop apart, injure you and become damaged.*

12.15 Secure the actuator with a wire tie or something similar to ensure that it doesn't come apart

12.18 The sprocket on the crankshaft can be removed with a two- or three-jaw puller

12.29 Install the front cover with a new gasket onto the engine block LOOSELY - the cover must be aligned properly before final installation

14   Remove the actuator assembly along with the chain, then separate the chain.
Warning: *Do not push or pull on the reluctor wheel (see illustration 12.13) on the camshaft position actuator/sprocket at any time. The reluctor wheel is attached to the actuator by three small roll pins. If you push or pull on the reluctor it may separate from the front of the actuator. The actuator has a return spring that is under very high tension, if the reluctor wheel is separate from the actuator the return spring can cause it to spin, which can cause serous personal injury.*
Caution: *Do not turn the crankshaft or the camshaft while the chain is off. Damage to the pistons and/or the valves could result.*
15   Tie the actuator assembly together for safety (see illustration).
16   Remove the timing chain tensioner and inspect it for wear and damage.
17   Also inspect the camshaft and crankshaft sprockets for wear and damage.
18   If replacement of the timing chain is necessary, remove the sprocket from the crankshaft with a two- or three-jaw puller, but be careful not to damage the threads in the end of the crankshaft (see illustration).

Installation

Caution: *Timing chains must be replaced as a set with the camshaft and crankshaft sprockets. Never put a new chain on old sprockets.*
19   Use a gasket scraper to remove all traces of old gasket material and sealant from the cover and engine block.
20   Align the crankshaft sprocket with the Woodruff key and press the sprocket onto the crankshaft (if removed) with the vibration damper bolt, a large socket and some washers or tap it gently into place until it is completely seated.
Caution: *If resistance is encountered, do not hammer the sprocket onto the crankshaft. It may eventually move onto the shaft, but it may be cracked in the process and fail later, causing extensive engine damage.*

21   Loop the new chain over the camshaft sprocket, then turn the sprocket until the timing mark is at the bottom. Mesh the chain with the crankshaft sprocket and position the camshaft sprocket on the end of the camshaft. If necessary, turn the camshaft so the dowel in the camshaft fits into the hole in the sprocket with the timing mark in the 6 o'clock position (see illustration 12.11). When the chain is installed, the timing marks MUST align as shown.
22   Lay a straightedge across the front of the block and verify that the timing chain does not protrude in front of the face of the engine block.
23   Tighten the NEW camshaft position actuator valve to the torque listed in this Chapter's Specifications.
24   Compress the timing chain tensioner and temporarily insert a pin in the hole to secure it in the retracted position.
25   Install the tensioner and tighten the bolts to the torque listed in this Chapter's Specifications. Remove the pin to allow the tensioner to extend.
Caution: *Carefully and slowly rotate the crankshaft by hand through at least two full revolutions (use a socket and breaker bar on the crankshaft pulley center bolt). If you feel any resistance, STOP! There is something wrong - most likely valves are contacting the pistons. You must find the problem before proceeding.*
26   Install the oil pump (see Section 15).
27   Clean all sealing areas of the timing chain cover and remove all traces of old sealant. Clean the area with brake system cleaner to remove oily residue. Remove the crankshaft oil seal and purchase a new one.
28   Apply a bead of RTV sealant to the corners where the oil pan meets the engine block.
29   Install the timing chain cover on the engine loosely using a new gasket (see illustration). The bolts should be snug but not tight.

30   Align the timing chain cover as follows:
a) *Obtain a cover alignment tool GM part no. J41476. This tool is also available from other tool manufacturers.*
b) *Place the tool over the crankshaft snout with the legs registered into the slots on the front cover.*
c) *Secure the tool using the crankshaft balancer bolt but don't overtighten it.*
d) *With the timing chain cover properly aligned, tighten the cover bolts and oil pan bolts to the torque listed in this Chapter's Specifications.*
e) *Remove the tool.*
31   Install a new crankshaft oil seal (see Section 11).
32   The remainder of installation is the reverse of removal.
33   Refill the cooling system and engine oil, and replace the engine oil filter (see Chapter 1). Run the engine and check for oil and coolant leaks.

---

13   Camshaft and lifters - removal, inspection and installation

Warning: *Wait until the engine is completely cool before beginning this procedure.*
Caution: *If the camshaft is being replaced, always install new lifters as well. Do not use old lifters on a new camshaft.*
Note: *The manufacturer states that the engine should be removed for this procedure.*

Removal

1   Have the air conditioning system discharged by an automotive air conditioning technician (see the Warning above).
2   Relieve the fuel system pressure (see Chapter 4), then disconnect the cable from the negative battery terminal (see Chapter 5).
3   Remove the radiator (see Chapter 3).

13.13a The roller lifters are held in place by retainers - remove the retainer bolts and remove the retainers and the lifters as an assembly - note that each retainer houses four individual lifters and they must be installed back in their original locations if they're going to be reused

13.13b Once the lifters and retainers are removed from the block they can be marked (for location and installation purposes) and inspected

13.15 Remove the bolts and take off the camshaft retainer plate, noting which side faces the block

13.18a If the camshaft is removed from the engine, lobe lift can be obtained by measuring camshaft lobe height . . .

13.18b . . . and by measuring the camshaft base circle - the difference between the two measurements equals lobe lift

4   Remove the air conditioning condenser (see Chapter 3).

5   Remove the auxiliary automatic transmission fluid cooler, if equipped.

6   Disconnect the power steering cooler and move it aside, if equipped.

7   Remove the valve covers (see Section 4).

8   Remove the intake manifold (see Section 7).

9   Remove the rocker arms and pushrods (see Section 5).

10   Remove the timing chain and camshaft position actuator (see Section 12).

11   Remove the cylinder heads (see Section 9).

12   Before removing the lifters, arrange to store them in a clearly labeled box to ensure that they're reinstalled in their original locations.

13   Remove the lifter retainers and lifters and store them where they won't get dirty (see illustrations). DO NOT attempt to withdraw the camshaft with the lifters in place.

14   If the lifters are built up with gum and varnish they may not come out with the retainer. If so, there are several ways to extract the lifters from the bores. A special tool designed to grip and remove lifters is manufactured by many tool companies and is widely available, but it may not be required in every case. On newer engines without a lot of varnish buildup, the lifters can often be removed with a small magnet or even with your fingers. A machinist's scribe with a bent end can be used to pull the lifters out by positioning the point under the retainer ring in the top of each lifter.

Caution: *Don't use pliers to remove the lifters unless you intend to replace them with new ones. The pliers will damage the precision machined and hardened lifters, rendering them useless.*

15   Remove the bolts and the camshaft retainer plate, noting which direction faces the block (see illustration).

16   Thread a bolt into the camshaft sprocket bolt hole to use as a handle when removing the camshaft from the block.

17   Carefully and slowly pull the camshaft out. Support the cam near the block so the lobes don't nick or gouge the bearings as it's withdrawn.

Inspection

Camshaft lobe lift check

18   Measure the camshaft lobe height and the base circle (see illustrations). The difference between the two measurements is the lobe lift (lobe height - base circle = lobe lift). Record this figure for future reference and repeat the check on the remaining camshaft lobes.

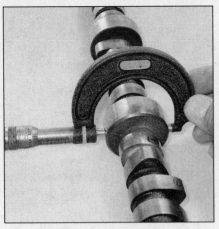

13.21 Check the diameter of each camshaft bearing journal to pinpoint excessive wear and out-of-round conditions

13.23 Check the pushrod seat in the top of each lifter for wear

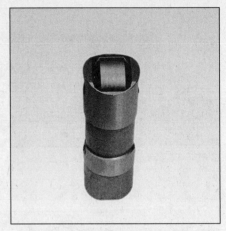

13.24 The roller on hydraulic roller lifters must turn freely - check for wear and excessive play as well

13.26 Be sure to apply camshaft assembly lube to the cam lobes and bearing journals before installing the camshaft

19   After the lobe lift check is complete, compare the results to the values listed in this Chapter's Specifications. If the lobe lift is 0.002 inch less than specified, cam lobe wear has occurred and a new camshaft should be installed.

Camshaft bearing journals, lobes and bearings

20   After the camshaft has been removed from the engine, cleaned with solvent and dried, inspect the bearing journals for uneven wear, pitting and evidence of seizure. If the journals are damaged, the bearing inserts in the block are probably damaged as well. Both the camshaft and bearings will have to be replaced.
Note: *Camshaft bearing replacement requires special tools and expertise that place it beyond the scope of the average home mechanic. The tools for bearing removal and installation are available at stores that carry automotive tools, possibly even found at a tool rental business.*

It is advisable though, if the bearings are bad and the procedure is beyond your ability, take the engine block to an automotive machine shop to ensure that the job is done correctly.
21   Measure the bearing journals with a micrometer to determine if they are excessively worn or out-of-round (see illustration).
22   Check the camshaft lobes for heat discoloration, score marks, chipped areas, pitting and uneven wear. If the lobes are in good condition and if the lobe lift measurements recorded earlier are as specified, the camshaft can be reused.

Lifters

23   Clean the lifters with solvent and dry them thoroughly without mixing them up. Check each lifter wall and pushrod seat and for score marks and uneven wear (see illustration). If the lifter walls are damaged or worn (which is not very likely), inspect the lifter bores in the engine block as well. If the pushrod seats are worn, check the pushrod ends.
24   Check the rollers carefully for wear and damage and make sure they turn freely without excessive play (see illustration).
25   Used roller lifters cannot be reinstalled with a new camshaft, but the original camshaft can be used if new lifters are installed. Always use new lifters when installing a new camshaft.

Installation

26   Lubricate the camshaft bearing journals and cam lobes with camshaft and lifter assembly lube (see illustration).
27   Slide the camshaft into the engine. Support the cam near the block and be careful not to scrape or nick the bearings.
28   Apply non-hardening thread-locking compound to two thirds of the threads on the camshaft retainer bolts, then allow to cure for ten minutes before installing the bolts.
29   Turn the camshaft until the dowel pin is in the 3 o'clock position, install the camshaft thrust plate and tighten the bolts to the torque

listed in this Chapter's Specifications. Make sure the gasket surface on the camshaft thrust plate and the engine block are free from oil and dirt.
30   Install the timing chain and sprockets (see Section 12). Also install the camshaft position sensor using a new O-ring (see Chapter 6).
31   Lubricate the lifters with clean engine oil and install them in the lifter retainers. Be sure to align the flats on the lifters with the flats in the lifter retainers. Install the retainer and lifters into the engine block as an assembly. If the original lifters are being reinstalled, be sure to return them to their original locations. If a new camshaft is being installed, install new lifters as well. Tighten the lifter retainer bolts to the torque listed in this Chapter's Specifications.
32   The remainder of installation is the reverse of removal.
33   Before starting and running the engine, refill the cooling system, change the oil and install a new oil filter (see Chapter 1).

14   Oil pan - removal and installation

Removal

1   Disconnect the cable from the negative terminal of the battery (see Chapter 5).
2   Remove the oil dipstick tube.
3   Raise the vehicle and support it securely on jackstands, then refer to Chapter 1 and drain the engine oil and remove the oil filter.
4   Remove the oil pan skid plate, if equipped.
5   On 5.3L and 6.2L models, remove the electric steering gear assembly (see Chapter 8).
6   On 4WD vehicles, remove the front differential carrier (see Chapter 8).
7   Remove the transmission bellhousing covers from the rear of the engine block.
8   Remove the crossmember bar support bolts and bar.

14.14 The manufacturer uses rivets to hold the gasket to the oil pan during assembly - carefully drill them out (it isn't necessary to rivet the new gasket to the oil pan)

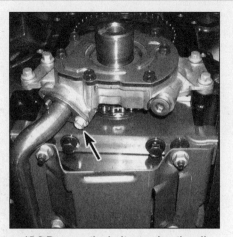

15.2 Remove the bolt securing the oil pick-up tube to the oil pump and remove the pick-up tube from the engine - 6.0L models

15.3 Oil pump mounting bolts

9   Remove the lower transmission-to-engine bolt (s). These bolts vary depending on the model of transmission used but all screw into the oil pan.
10   Disconnect the wiring from the engine oil level sensor.
11   Disconnect the wiring harness retainers from the oil pan.
12   Disconnect the oil cooler lines from the oil pan on models with automatic transmissions.
13   Remove all the oil pan bolts, then lower the pan from the engine. The pan will probably stick to the engine, so strike the pan with a rubber mallet until it breaks the gasket seal. Carefully slide the oil pan down and out, to the rear.
Caution: *Before using force on the oil pan, be sure all the bolts have been removed.*

Installation

14   On 6.0L models, drill out the rivets securing the oil pan gasket to the oil pan and remove the old gasket (see illustration). Wash out the oil pan with solvent.
15   Thoroughly clean the mounting surfaces of the oil pan and engine block of old gasket material and sealant. Wipe the gasket surfaces clean with a rag soaked in brake system cleaner.
16   Apply a 3/16-inch wide, one-inch long bead of RTV sealant to the corners of the block where the front cover and the rear cover meet the engine block. The gasket tabs protrude at these points and must have sealant around them. Attach the new gasket to the pan, install the pan and tighten the bolts finger-tight. Be sure the oil gallery passages in the pan and the gasket are aligned properly.
Note: *Oil pan gasket rivets do not need to be installed on assembly.*
17   Install all of the oil pan mounting bolts snug.
18   Install the lower transmission mounting bolts snug.
19   Tighten the oil pan bolts and the trans-

mission bolts to the torques listed in this Chapter's Specifications.
20   The remainder of installation is the reverse of removal.
21   Add the proper type and quantity of oil (see Chapter 1), start the engine and check for leaks before placing the vehicle back in service.

15   Oil pump - removal, inspection and installation

Removal

1   Remove the timing chain cover (see Section 12) and, on 6.0L models, the oil pan (see Section 14).
2   On 6.0L models, remove the oil pump pick-up tube mounting nuts and bolts and lower the pick-up tube and screen assembly from the vehicle (see illustration).
3   On 6.0L models, remove the oil pump retaining bolts and slide the pump off the end of the crankshaft (see illustration). On 5.3L and 6.2L models, install special tool EN-51257 to the engine block, by placing the one piece of the tool against the timing chain tensioner and the other piece against the edge of the oil pump body then tighten the mounting bolts securely.
Caution: *On 5.3L and 6.2L models, if the oil pump is being removed and not replaced, special tool   EN-51267 oil pump alignment tool must be installed to the engine block and against the pump before the oil pump is removed and remain in place until the pump is reinstalled. If the alignment tool is not installed prior to removal a new oil pump must be installed.*

Inspection

4   Remove the oil pump cover and withdraw the rotors from the pump body (see illustration). Clean the components with solvent, dry them thoroughly and inspect for any

15.4 Oil pump cover-to-oil pump housing mounting bolts

obvious damage. Also check the bolt holes for damaged threads and the splined surfaces on the crankshaft sprocket for any apparent damage. If any of the components are scored, scratched or worn, replace the entire oil pump assembly. There are no serviceable parts currently available.

Installation

5   Prime the pump by pouring clean engine oil into the pick-up tube hole, while turning the pump by hand.
6   Position the oil pump over the end of the crankshaft and align the teeth on the crankshaft sprocket with the teeth on the oil pump drive gear. Making sure the pump is fully seated against the block.
7   On 5.3L and 6.2L models, push the pump body upwards so that the pump body contacts the tool, then tighten the bolts. Constant contact between the oil pump body and the oil pump alignment tool must be maintained; there can be no gap between the oil pump housing and the tool. If there is a gap, loosen

15.9 Always install a new O-ring on the oil pump pick up tube

17.3 Carefully pry the old seal out with a screwdriver at the notches provided in the rear cover

17.4 The rear oil seal can be pressed into place with a seal installation tool, a section of pipe or a blunt object shown here - in any case be sure the seal is installed squarely into the seal bore and flush with the rear cover

the oil pump bolts and push the pump against the tool and tighten the pump bolts again.

8   Install the oil pump mounting bolts and tighten them to the torque listed in this Chapter's Specifications.

9   Install a new O-ring on the oil pump pick-up tube, then fasten it to the oil pump and the engine block main studs (see illustration).

Caution: *Be absolutely certain that the pick-up tube-to-oil pump bolts are properly tightened so that no air can be sucked into the oiling system at this connection.*

10   Install and align the timing chain cover (see Section 12), then install the oil pan (see Section 14) on 6.0L models.

11   The remainder of installation is the reverse of removal.

12   Add oil and coolant as necessary. Run the engine and check for oil and coolant leaks.

Also check the oil pressure as described in Chapter 2C.

16   Driveplate - removal and installation

1   The driveplate replacement for V8 engines is identical to the driveplate replacement procedure for the V6 engines. Refer to Chapter 2A for the procedure and use the torque figures in this Chapter's Specifications.

Note: *On 6.0L models, if the spacer between the driveplate and the crankshaft must be removed and it's stuck, insert bolts (M11x1.5 mm) into the two threaded holes in the spacer. Tightening the bolts will force the spacer off the crankshaft.*

17   Rear main oil seal - replacement

Note: *If the rear main seal housing is removed from the engine block, special tools must be used to properly center the housing over the end of the crankshaft. This alignment procedure is critical because a seal that is slightly off-center will leak. Refer to Chapter 2C, Section 10 for information on rear main seal housing alignment.*

1   Remove the transmission (see Chapter 7A).

2   Remove the driveplate (see Section 16).

3   Pry the oil seal from the rear cover with a screwdriver (see illustration). Be careful not to nick or scratch the crankshaft or the seal bore. Be sure to note how far it's recessed into the housing bore before removal so the new seal can be installed to the same depth. Thoroughly clean the seal bore in the block with a shop towel. Remove all traces of oil and dirt.

4   Don't lubricate the seal or touch the

sealing lip. Make sure the seal is installed in the correct orientation (it has a reverse-lip design). The seal part number must be visible when it's installed. Preferably, a seal installation tool (available at most auto parts store) should be used to press the new seal back into place. If the proper seal installation tool is unavailable, use a large drift and carefully drive the new seal squarely into the seal bore and flush with the rear cover (see illustration).

5   Install the driveplate (see Section 16).

6   Install the transmission (see Chapter 7A).

18   Engine mounts - check and replacement

1   Engine mounts seldom require attention, but broken or deteriorated mounts should be replaced immediately or the added strain placed on the driveline components may cause damage.

Check

2   During the check, the engine must be raised slightly to remove the weight from the mounts.

3   Raise the vehicle and support it securely on jackstands.

4   Check the mounts to see if the rubber is cracked, hardened or separated from the metal plates. Sometimes the rubber will split right down the center.

5   Check for relative movement between the mount plates and the engine or frame (use a large prybar to attempt to move the engine away from the mounts). If movement is noted, check the tightness of the mount fasteners first before condemning the mounts. Usually when engine mounts are broken, they are very obvious as the engine will easily move away from the mount when pried or under load.

18.12 One of the three engine mount-to-frame bolts, seen from above

18.14 Three of the four engine mount-to-block bolts

Replacement

6   Disconnect the cable from the negative terminal of the battery (see Chapter 5), then raise the vehicle and support it securely on jackstands.

7   On 5.3L and 6.2L models, remove the air cleaner inlet duct (see Chapter 4).

8   On 4WD models, remove the interfering driveaxle (see Chapter 8).

9   Remove the front stabilizer bar bushing bolts and lower the bar (see Chapter 10).

10   Remove the vacuum pump, if equipped, if you're working on the left mount.

11   If you're working on the left mount, it is necessary to remove the left inner fender splash shield and the exhaust manifold heat shield on most models.

12   Remove the engine mount-to-frame bracket bolts (see illustration). There are three bolts on each side securing the mounts to the frame bracket.

13   Attach an engine hoist to the top of the engine for lifting; do not use a jack under the oil pan to support the entire weight of the engine or the oil pump pick-up could be damaged. If a hoist is not available, a jack can be placed under the large casting lugs on each side of the engine block at the rear (near the transmission) to support the weight of the engine while the engine mounts are being replaced. To access this lug on the right side of the engine, the starter motor will have to be removed (see Chapter 5).

14   Unbolt the mount from the engine block (see illustration), and raise the engine far enough to move the mount forward, then remove the mount from between the engine and the frame.

15   Installation is the reverse of removal. Use non-hardening thread-locking compound on the mount bolts and be sure to tighten them to the torque listed in this Chapter's Specifications.

Notes

Chapter 2 Part C
General engine overhaul procedures

Contents

Specifications

General
Displacement
4.3L V6 engine	62 cubic inches
5.3L V8 engine	323 cubic inches
6.0L V8 engine	364 cubic inches
6.2L V8 engine	376 cubic inches

Bore and stroke
4.3L V6 engine	3.92 x 3.622 inches
5.3L V8 engine	3.779-3.778 x 3.622 inches
6.0L V8 engine	4.001 x 3.622 inches
6.2L V8 engine	4.065 x 3.622 inches

Compression ratio
4.3L V6 engine	11.0:1
5.3L V8 engine	11.0:1
6.0L V8 engine	9.67:1
6.2L V8 engine	11.5:1

Cylinder compression pressure
Minimum	100 psi
Maximum variation	25 percent from highest reading

Oil pressure (minimum, at operating temperature)
V6 engine
1000 rpm	22 psig
2000 rpm	30 psig
3000 rpm	33 psig

V8 engines
1000 rpm	22 psig
2000 rpm	30 psig
3000 rpm	33 psig

Torque specifications   Ft-lbs (unless otherwise indicated)

Connecting rod bearing cap bolts *
  Step 1 15
  Step 2 .... Tighten an additional 85 degrees
Main bearing cap bolts *
  All except 6.0L V8 engine - in sequence (V6 engine, see illustration 10.29; V8 engines, see illustration 10.30)
    Step 1, Inner bearing cap bolts.. 15
    Step 2, Outer bearing cap bolts.. 15
    Step 3, Inner bearing cap bolts.. Tighten an additional 110 degrees
    Step 4, Outer bearing cap bolts.. Tighten an additional 80 degrees
    Step 5, Bearing cap side bolts.. 18
    Step 6, Bearing cap side bolts.. Tighten an additional 60 degrees
  6.0L V8 engine
    Bolts 1 through 10 (M8)
      Step 1 15
      Step 2 .... Tighten an additional 80 degrees
    Studs 11 through 20 (M10)
      Step 1 15
      Step 2 .... Tighten an additional 51 degrees
    Bolts 21 through 30* 18
Transmission-to-engine bolts 37
Driveplate-to-torque converter bolts
  4L80-E transmission 44
  All other transmissions.. 47

Caution: *Must be replaced with new bolts*

1.9a An engine block being bored. An engine rebuilder will use special machinery to recondition the cylinder bores

1.9b If the cylinders are bored, the machine shop will normally hone the engine on a machine like this

1 General information - engine overhaul

1 Included in this portion of Chapter 2C are general information and diagnostic testing procedures for determining the overall mechanical condition of your engine.

2 The information ranges from advice concerning preparation for an overhaul and the purchase of replacement parts and/or components to detailed, step-by-step procedures covering removal and installation.

3 The following sections have been written to help you determine whether your engine needs to be overhauled and how to remove and install it once you've determined it needs to be rebuilt. For information concerning in-vehicle engine repair, see Chapter 2A or 2B.

4 It's not always easy to determine when, or if, an engine should be completely overhauled, because a number of factors must be considered.

5 High mileage is not necessarily an indication that an overhaul is needed, while low mileage doesn't preclude the need for an overhaul. Frequency of servicing is probably the most important consideration. An engine that's had regular and frequent oil and filter changes, as well as other required maintenance, will most likely give many thousands of miles of reliable service. Conversely, a neglected engine may require an overhaul very early in its service life.

6 Excessive oil consumption is an indication that piston rings, valve seals and/or valve guides are in need of attention. Make sure that oil leaks aren't responsible before deciding that the rings and/or guides are bad. Perform a cylinder compression check to determine the extent of the work required (see Section 3). Also check the vacuum readings under various conditions (see Section 4).

7 Check the oil pressure with a gauge installed in place of the oil pressure sending unit and compare it to this Chapter's Specifications (see Section 2). If it's extremely low,

the bearings and/or oil pump are probably worn out.

8 Loss of power, rough running, knocking or metallic engine noises, excessive valve train noise and high fuel consumption rates may also point to the need for an overhaul, especially if they're all present at the same time. If a complete tune-up doesn't remedy the situation, major mechanical work is the only solution.

9 An engine overhaul involves restoring the internal parts to the specifications of a new engine. During an overhaul, the piston rings are replaced and the cylinder walls are reconditioned (rebored and/or honed)(see illustrations 1.9a and 1.9b). If a rebore is done by an automotive machine shop, new oversize pistons will also be installed. The main bearings, connecting rod bearings and camshaft bearings are generally replaced with new ones and, if necessary, the crankshaft may be reground to restore the journals (see illustration 1.9c). Generally, the valves are serviced as well, since they're usually in less-than-perfect condition at this point. While the engine is being overhauled, other components, such

as the starter and alternator, can be rebuilt as well. The end result should be similar to a new engine that will give many trouble free miles.
Note: *Critical cooling system components such as the hoses, drivebelts, thermostat and water pump should be replaced with new parts when an engine is overhauled. The radiator should be checked carefully to ensure that it isn't clogged or leaking(see Chapter 3). If you purchase a rebuilt engine or short block, some rebuilders will not warranty their engines unless the radiator has been professionally flushed. Also, we don't recommend overhauling the oil pump - always install a new one when an engine is rebuilt.*

10 Overhauling the internal components on today's engines is a difficult and time-consuming task which requires a significant amount of specialty tools and is best left to a professional engine rebuilder (see illustrations 1.10a, 1.10b and 1.10c). A competent engine rebuilder will handle the inspection of your old parts and offer advice concerning the reconditioning or replacement of the original engine; never purchase parts or have machine work done on other components until the block

1.9c A crankshaft having a main bearing journal ground

1.10a A machinist checks for a bent connecting rod, using specialized equipment

1.10b A bore gauge being used to check the main bearing bore

1.10c Uneven piston wear like this indicates a bent connecting rod

2.2a Location of the oil pressure sending unit on V6 engines, 5.3L and 6.2L V8 engines

has been thoroughly inspected by a professional machine shop. As a general rule, time is the primary cost of an overhaul, especially since the vehicle may be tied up for a minimum of two weeks or more. Be aware that some engine builders only have the capability to rebuild the engine you bring them while other rebuilders have a large inventory of rebuilt exchange engines in stock. Also be aware that many machine shops could take as much as two weeks time to completely rebuild your engine depending on shop workload. Sometimes it makes more sense to simply exchange your engine for another engine that's already rebuilt to save time.

2   Oil pressure check

1   Low engine oil pressure can be a sign of an engine in need of rebuilding. A low oil pressure indicator (often called an "idiot light") is not a test of the oiling system. Such indicators only come on when the oil pressure is dangerously low. Even a factory oil pressure gauge in the instrument panel is only a relative indication, although much better for driver information than a warning light. A better test is with a mechanical (not electrical) oil pressure gauge.
2   Locate the engine oil pressure sending unit:
  a) *On 6.0L V8 engines, the oil pressure sender is located in the top of the valley cover near the rear of the intake manifold.*
  b) *On V6 engines, 5.3L and 6.2L V8 engines, the oil pressure sending unit is located at the front of the engine (see illustration).*

3   Unscrew the oil pressure sending unit and screw in the hose for your oil pressure gauge.
4   Connect an accurate tachometer to the

engine, according to the tachometer manufacturer's instructions.
5   Check the oil pressure with the engine running (normal operating temperature) at the specified engine speed, and compare it to this Chapter's Specifications. If it's extremely low, the bearings and/or oil pump are probably worn out.

3   Cylinder compression check

1   A compression check will tell you what mechanical condition the upper end of your engine (pistons, rings, valves, head gaskets) is in. Specifically, it can tell you if the compression is down due to leakage caused by worn piston rings, defective valves and seats or a blown head gasket.

3.5 Use a compression gauge with a threaded fitting for the spark plug hole, not the type that requires hand pressure to maintain the seal

Note: *The engine must be at normal operating temperature and the battery must be fully charged for this check.*
2   Begin by cleaning the area around the spark plugs before you remove them (compressed air should be used, if available). The idea is to prevent dirt from getting into the cylinders as the compression check is being done.
3   Remove all of the spark plugs from the engine (see Chapter 1).
4   Disable the ignition system by disconnecting the primary (low voltage) electrical connector from each ignition coil (see Chapter 5). Disable the fuel injectors by removing the INJ A and INJ B fuses from the underhood fuse/relay box.
5   Install a compression gauge in the number one cylinder spark plug hole (see illustration).
6   Have an assistent depress the accelerator pedal, then crank the engine over at least seven compression strokes and watch the gauge. The compression should build up quickly in a healthy engine. Low compression on the first stroke, followed by gradually increasing pressure on successive strokes, indicates worn piston rings. A low compression reading on the first stroke, which doesn't build up during successive strokes, indicates leaking valves or a blown head gasket (a cracked head could also be the cause). Deposits on the undersides of the valve heads can also cause low compression. Record the highest gauge reading obtained.
7   Repeat the procedure for the remaining cylinders and compare the results to this Chapter's Specifications.
8   Add some engine oil (about three squirts from a plunger-type oil can) to each cylinder, through the spark plug hole, and repeat the test.
9   If the compression increases after the oil is added, the piston rings are definitely worn.

If the compression doesn't increase significantly, the leakage is occurring at the valves or head gasket. Leakage past the valves may be caused by burned valve seats and/or faces or warped, cracked or bent valves.

10 If two adjacent cylinders have equally low compression, there's a strong possibility that the head gasket between them is blown. The appearance of coolant in the combustion chambers or the crankcase would verify this condition.

11 If one cylinder is slightly lower than the others, and the engine has a slightly rough idle, a worn lobe on the camshaft could be the cause.

12 If the compression is unusually high, the combustion chambers are probably coated with carbon deposits. If that's the case, the cylinder head(s) should be removed and decarbonized.

13 If compression is way down or varies greatly between cylinders, it would be a good idea to have a leak-down test performed by an automotive repair shop. This test will pinpoint exactly where the leakage is occurring and how severe it is.

4 Vacuum gauge diagnostic checks

1 A vacuum gauge provides inexpensive but valuable information about what is going on in the engine. You can check for worn rings or cylinder walls, leaking head or intake manifold gaskets, incorrect carburetor adjustments, restricted exhaust, stuck or burned valves, weak valve springs, improper ignition or valve timing and ignition problems.

2 Unfortunately, vacuum gauge readings are easy to misinterpret, so they should be used in conjunction with other tests to confirm the diagnosis.

3 Both the absolute readings and the rate of needle movement are important for accurate interpretation. Most gauges measure vacuum in inches of mercury (in-Hg). The following references to vacuum assume the diagnosis is being performed at sea level. As elevation increases (or atmospheric pressure decreases), the reading will decrease. For every 1,000 foot increase in elevation above approximately 2,000 feet, the gauge readings will decrease about one inch of mercury.

4 Connect the vacuum gauge directly to the intake manifold vacuum, not to ported (throttle body) vacuum. Be sure no hoses are left disconnected during the test or false readings will result.

5 Before you begin the test, allow the engine to warm up completely. Block the wheels and set the parking brake. With the transaxle in Park, start the engine and allow it to run at normal idle speed.
Warning: *Keep your hands and the vacuum gauge clear of the fans.*

6 Read the vacuum gauge; an average, healthy engine should normally produce about 17 to 22 in-Hg with a fairly steady needle (see illustration). Refer to the following vacuum gauge readings and what they indicate about the engine's condition:

7 A low steady reading usually indicates a leaking gasket between the intake manifold and cylinder head(s) or throttle body, a leaky vacuum hose, late ignition timing or incorrect camshaft timing. Check ignition timing with a timing light and eliminate all other possible causes, utilizing the tests provided in this chapter before you remove the timing chain cover to check the timing marks.

8 If the reading is three to eight inches below normal and it fluctuates at that low reading, suspect an intake manifold gasket leak at an intake port or a faulty fuel injector.

9 If the needle has regular drops of about two-to-four inches at a steady rate, the valves are probably leaking. Perform a compression check or leak-down test to confirm this.

10 An irregular drop or down-flick of the needle can be caused by a sticking valve or an ignition misfire. Perform a compression check or leak-down test and read the spark plugs.

11 A rapid vibration of about four in-Hg vibration at idle combined with exhaust smoke indicates worn valve guides. Perform a leak-down test to confirm this. If the rapid vibration occurs with an increase in engine speed, check for a leaking intake manifold gasket or head gasket, weak valve springs, burned valves or ignition misfire.

12 A slight fluctuation, say one inch up and down, may mean ignition problems. Check all the usual tune-up items and, if necessary, run the engine on an ignition analyzer.

13 If there is a large fluctuation, perform a compression or leak-down test to look for a weak or dead cylinder or a blown head gasket.

14 If the needle moves slowly through a wide range, check for a clogged PCV system, incorrect idle fuel mixture, throttle body or intake manifold gasket leaks.

15 Check for a slow return after revving the engine by quickly snapping the throttle open until the engine reaches about 2,500 rpm and let it shut. Normally the reading should drop to near zero, rise above normal idle reading (about 5 in-Hg over) and return to the previous idle reading. If the vacuum returns slowly and doesn't peak when the throttle is snapped shut, the rings may be worn. If there is a long delay, look for a restricted exhaust system (often the muffler or catalytic converter). An easy way to check this is to temporarily disconnect the exhaust ahead of the suspected part and redo the test.

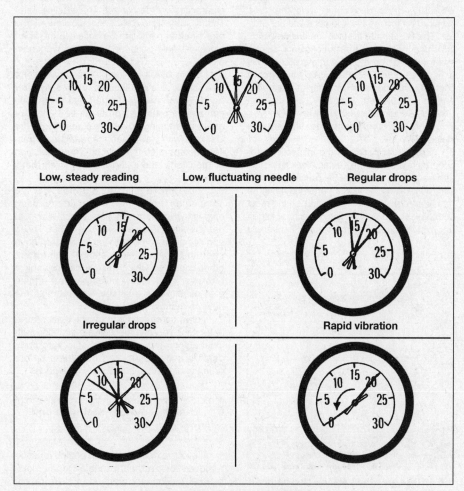

Low, steady reading   Low, fluctuating needle   Regular drops

Irregular drops   Rapid vibration

4.6 Typical vacuum gauge readings

6.3a After tightly wrapping water-vulnerable components, use a spray cleaner on everything, with particular concentration on the greasiest areas, usually around the valve cover and lower edges of the block. If one section dries out, apply more cleaner

6.3b Depending on how dirty the engine is, let the cleaner soak in according to the directions and hose off the grime and cleaner. Get the rinse water down into every area you can get at; then dry important components with a hair dryer or paper towels

5   Engine rebuilding alternatives

1   The do-it-yourselfer is faced with a number of options when purchasing a rebuilt engine. The major considerations are cost, warranty, parts availability and the time required for the rebuilder to complete the project. The decision to replace the engine block, piston/connecting rod assemblies and crankshaft depends on the final inspection results of your engine. Only then can you make a cost effective decision whether to have your engine overhauled or simply purchase an exchange engine for your vehicle.

2   Some of the rebuilding alternatives include:

3   **Individual parts** - If the inspection procedures reveal that the engine block and most engine components are in reusable condition, purchasing individual parts and having a rebuilder rebuild your engine may be the most economical alternative. The block, crankshaft and piston/connecting rod assemblies should

6.4 Make sure the hoist is rated higher than the combined weight of the engine and all its components

all be inspected carefully by a machine shop first.

4   **Short block** - A short block consists of an engine block with a crankshaft and piston/connecting rod assemblies already installed. All new bearings are incorporated and all clearances will be correct. The existing camshafts, valve train components, cylinder head and external parts can be bolted to the short block with little or no machine shop work necessary.

5   **Long block** - A long block consists of a short block plus an oil pump, oil pan, cylinder head, valve cover, camshaft and valve train components, timing sprockets and chain or gears and timing cover. All components are installed with new bearings, seals and gaskets incorporated throughout. The installation of manifolds and external parts is all that's necessary.

6   **Low mileage used engines** - Some companies now offer low mileage used engines which is a very cost effective way to get your vehicle up and running again. These engines often come from vehicles which have been in totaled in accidents or come from other countries which have a higher vehicle turn-over rate. A low mileage used engine also usually has a similar warranty like the newly remanufactured engines.

7   Give careful thought to which alternative is best for you and discuss the situation with local automotive machine shops, auto parts dealers and experienced rebuilders before ordering or purchasing replacement parts.

6   Engine removal - methods and precautions

1   If you've decided that an engine must be removed for overhaul or major repair work, several preliminary steps should be taken. Read all removal and installation procedures carefully prior to committing to this job.

2   Locating a suitable place to work is extremely important. Adequate work space, along with storage space for the vehicle, will be needed. If a shop or garage isn't available, at the very least a flat, level, clean work surface made of concrete or asphalt is required.

3   Cleaning the engine compartment and engine before beginning the removal procedure will help keep tools clean and organized (see illustrations 6.3a and 6.3b).

4   An engine hoist will also be necessary (see illustration). Make sure the hoist is rated in excess of the combined weight of the engine and its accessories. Safety is of primary importance, considering the potential hazards involved in removing the engine from the vehicle.

5   If you're a novice at engine removal, get at least one helper. One person cannot easily do all the things you need to do to remove a big heavy engine assembly from the engine compartment. Also helpful is to seek advice and assistance from someone who's experienced in engine removal.

6   Plan the operation ahead of time. Arrange for or obtain all of the tools and equipment you'll need prior to beginning the job (see illustrations). Some of the equipment necessary to perform engine removal and installation safely and with relative ease are (in addition to a vehicle hoist and an engine hoist) a heavy duty floor jack (preferably fitted with a transmission jack head adapter), complete sets of wrenches and sockets as described in the front of this manual, wooden blocks, plenty of rags and cleaning solvent for mopping up spilled oil, coolant and gasoline.

7   Plan for the vehicle to be out of use for quite a while. A machine shop can do the work that is beyond the scope of the home mechanic. Machine shops often have a busy schedule, so before removing the engine, consult the shop for an estimate of how long it will take to rebuild or repair the components that may need work.

6.6a Get an engine stand sturdy enough to firmly support the engine while you're working on it. Stay away from three-wheeled models; they have a tendency to tip over more easily, so get a four-wheeled unit

6.6b Since many of the fasteners on these engines are tightened using the angle torque method, a torque angle gauge is essential for proper assembly

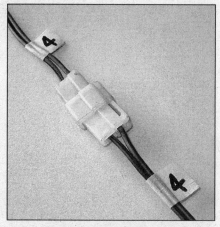

7.32 Label both ends of each wire and hose before disconnecting it

7 Engine - removal and installation

Warning: *Gasoline is extremely flammable, so take extra precautions when you work on any part of the fuel system. Don't smoke or allow open flames or bare light bulbs near the work area, and don't work in a garage where a gas-type appliance (such as a water heater or clothes dryer) is present. Since gasoline is carcinogenic, wear fuel-resistant gloves when there's a possibility of being exposed to fuel, and, if you spill any fuel on your skin, rinse it off immediately with soap and water. Mop up any spills immediately and do not store fuel-soaked rags where they could ignite. The fuel system is under constant pressure, so, if any fuel lines are to be disconnected, the fuel pressure in the system must be relieved first (see Chapter 4 for more information). When you perform any kind of work on the fuel system, wear safety glasses and have a Class B type fire extinguisher on hand.*

Warning: *The air conditioning system is under high pressure. DO NOT loosen any fittings or remove any components until after the system has been discharged. Air conditioning refrigerant should be properly discharged into an EPA-approved container at a dealer service department or an automotive air conditioning repair facility. Always wear eye protection when disconnecting air conditioning system fittings.*

Warning: *The engine must be completely cool before beginning this procedure.*

Removal

Note: *Keep in mind that during this procedure you'll have to adjust the height of the vehicle to perform certain operations.*

1   Have the air conditioning system discharged by an automotive air conditioning technician (see the Warning above).

2   Relieve the fuel system pressure (see Chapter 4).

3   Disconnect the cable from the negative terminal of the battery (see Chapter 5).

4   Remove the hood and grille (see Chapter 11).

5   Remove the upper radiator support tie bars that connect the upper front sections of the fenders.

6   Remove the headlight housings (see Chapter 12), then remove the radiator support.

7   Remove the engine cover.

8   Remove the air filter housing and air intake duct (see Chapter 4).

9   Remove the drivebelt (see Chapter 1).

10   Raise the vehicle and support it securely on jackstands. Remove the engine lower shield and the skid plate on 4WD models.

11   Drain the coolant and the engine oil (see Chapter 1). Remove the radiator hoses, the heater hoses, radiator and air conditioning condenser (see Chapter 3).

12   On 6.0L models, remove the coolant expansion tank (see Chapter 3).

13   Remove the air conditioning line bracket bolt from the alternator bracket.

14   Remove the alternator (see Chapter 5), then remove the alternator mounting bracket.

15   On 6.0L models, remove the power steering pump (see Chapter 10), then remove the pump mounting bracket.

16   Remove the intake manifold (see Chapter 2B or 2A).

17   Remove the fuel rail assembly from Bank 2 (right side) on 4.3L V6 models and Bank 1 (left side) on 5.3L and 6.2L V8 models (see Chapter 4).

18   Remove the Powertrain Control Module (PCM) (see Chapter 6).

19   Remove the engine compartment relay/junction box by rotating the two handles on each end toward each other, then lift the assembly up and out.

20   On 4WD models, remove the front driveshaft (see Chapter 8).

21   Disconnect the catalytic converter(s) from the exhaust manifolds. Wire them out of the way or remove them completely.

22   Remove the starter (see Chapter 5).

23   On 6.0L models, remove the air conditioning compressor (see Chapter 3).

24   Remove the left and right side flywheel inspection cover bolts and slide the covers down and out.

25   Disconnect the catalytic converter(s) from the exhaust manifolds. Wire them out of the way or remove them completely.

26   Remove the left and right side flywheel covers. Remove the torque converter bolts. You'll have to rotate the crankshaft with a socket and a breaker bar to access all of the bolts.

27   Support the transmission with a jack, then raise it slightly to take the pressure off of the mount and remove the rear transmission crossmember (see Chapter 7A or 7B).

28   Remove the transmission-to-engine bolts (see Chapter 7A), then temporarily reinstall the transmission rear crossmember and lower the vehicle.

Note: *It will be necessary to lower the rear of the transmission slightly to gain access to the transmission-to-engine top bolts.*

29   Disconnect the transmission cooler lines from the oil pan.

30   On 6.0L models, remove the automatic transmission dipstick tube.

31   Remove the transfer case vent hose if you're working on a 4WD model.

32   Label, then disconnect each wiring connection from the engine (see illustration). Also detach all wiring clips, brackets and retainers. Make notes of the positions of wiring harnesses as necessary.

33   Check all sides of the engine to make

7.34 It will be necessary to attach the chains to the cylinder heads

7.35 Pull the engine forward as far as possible to clear the transmission and the cowl, then lift the engine high enough to clear the body

9.1 Before you try to remove the pistons, use a ridge reamer to remove the raised material (ridge) from the top of the cylinders

sure that all components are disconnected and that hoses as well as wires are labeled.

34   Attach lengths of chain to the engine (see illustration). There are lifting brackets on some of the engines but not all. If you can't find a lifting bracket, be sure to attach the chains to secure points such as the cylinder heads.

35   Roll the engine hoist into position and connect the chains to it (see illustration). Take up the slack in the chain, but don't lift the engine yet.

Warning: *DO NOT place any part of your body under the engine when only a hoist or other lifting device supports it.*

36   Place a floor jack under the front of the transmission to support it while the engine is removed.

37   Remove the engine mount-to-frame bracket bolts.

38   Raise the engine slightly. Work it away from the transmission, being sure that the converter stays in the automatic transmission (clamp vise-grips to the bellhousing to keep

the converter from sliding out).

39   Carefully raise the engine from the engine compartment. Check as you go to make sure nothing is hanging up. Remove the driveplate and mount the engine on an engine stand.

Installation

40   Installation is the reverse of the removal procedure, noting the following points:

a) *Check the engine and transmission mounts. If they're worn, replace them.*

b) *Tighten the torque converter bolts to the torque listed in this Chapter's Specifications.*

c) *Refill the cooling system with the proper mixture of coolant and refill the engine with the recommended oil (see Chapter 1).*

d) *Check the transmission fluid level and add fluid as necessary.*

e) *Have the air conditioning system recharged by the shop that discharged it.*

8   Engine overhaul - disassembly sequence

1   It's much easier to remove the external components if the engine is mounted on a portable engine stand. A stand can often be rented quite cheaply from an equipment rental yard. Before the engine is mounted on a stand, the driveplate should be removed from the engine.

2   If a stand isn't available, it's possible to remove the external engine components with it blocked up on the floor. Be extra careful not to tip or drop the engine when working without a stand.

3   If you're going to obtain a rebuilt engine, all external components must come off first, to be transferred to the replacement engine. These components include:

Driveplate
Ignition system components
Emissions-related components
Engine mounts and mount brackets
Engine rear cover (spacer plate between driveplate and engine block), if equipped
Intake/exhaust manifolds
Fuel injection components
Oil filter
Ignition coils and spark plugs
Thermostat and housing assembly
Water pump

Note: *When removing the external components from the engine, pay close attention to details that may be helpful or important during installation. Note the installed position of gaskets, seals, spacers, pins, brackets, washers, bolts and other small items.*

4   If you're going to obtain a short block (assembled engine block, crankshaft, pistons and connecting rods), then remove the timing chain or belt, cylinder head(s), oil pan, oil pump pick-up tube, oil pump and water pump from your engine so that you can turn in your old short block to the rebuilder as a core. See *Engine rebuilding alternatives* for additional information regarding the different possibilities to be considered.

9   Pistons and connecting rods - removal and installation

Removal

Note: *Prior to removing the piston/connecting rod assemblies, remove the cylinder head and oil pan (see Chapter 2A or 2B).*

1   Use your fingernail to feel if a ridge has formed at the upper limit of ring travel (about 1/4-inch down from the top of each cylinder). If carbon deposits or cylinder wear have produced ridges, they must be completely removed with a special tool (see illustration). Follow the manufacturer's instructions provided with the tool. Failure to remove the

9.3 Checking the connecting rod endplay (side clearance)

9.4 If the connecting rods and caps are not marked, use paint to mark the caps to the rods by cylinder number (for example, this would be the No. 4 connecting rod)

9.13 Install the piston ring into the cylinder then push it down into position using a piston so the ring will be square in the cylinder

ridges before attempting to remove the piston/connecting rod assemblies may result in piston breakage.

2   After the cylinder ridges have been removed, turn the engine so the crankshaft is facing up.

3   Before the connecting rods are removed, check the connecting rod endplay with feeler gauges. Slide them between the first connecting rod and the crankshaft throw until the play is removed (see illustration). Repeat this procedure for each connecting rod. The endplay is equal to the thickness of the feeler gauge(s). Check with an automotive machine shop for the endplay service limit (a typical endplay limit should measure between 0.005 to 0.015 inch [0.127 to 0.396 mm]). If the play exceeds the service limit, new connecting rods will be required. If new rods (or a new crankshaft) are installed, the endplay may fall under the minimum allowable. If it does, the rods will have to be machined to restore it. If necessary, consult an automotive machine shop for advice.

4   Check the connecting rods and caps for identification marks. If they aren't plainly marked, use paint or marker to clearly identify each rod and cap (1, 2, 3, etc., depending on the cylinder they're associated with) (see illustration).

5   Remove the connecting rod cap bolts. Obtain new bolts for installation, but keep the old bolts (they will be used during the oil clearance check).

6   Remove the number one connecting rod cap and bearing insert. Don't drop the bearing insert out of the cap.

7   Remove the bearing insert and push the connecting rod/piston assembly out through the top of the engine. Use a wooden or plastic hammer handle to push on the upper bearing surface in the connecting rod. If resistance is felt, double-check to make sure that all of the ridge was removed from the cylinder.

8   Repeat the procedure for the remaining cylinders.

9   After removal, reassemble the connecting rod caps and bearing inserts in their

respective connecting rods and install the fasteners finger tight. Leaving the old bearing inserts in place until reassembly will help prevent the connecting rod bearing surfaces from being accidentally nicked or gouged.

10   The pistons and connecting rods are now ready for inspection and overhaul at an automotive machine shop.

Piston ring installation

11   Before installing the new piston rings, the ring end gaps must be checked. It's assumed that the piston ring side clearance has been checked and verified correct.

12   Lay out the piston/connecting rod assemblies and the new ring sets so the ring sets will be matched with the same piston and cylinder during the end gap measurement and engine assembly.

13   Insert the top (number one) ring into the first cylinder and square it up with the cylinder walls by pushing it in with the top of the piston (see illustration). The ring should be near the bottom of the cylinder, at the lower limit of ring travel.

9.14 With the ring square in the cylinder, measure the ring end gap with a feeler gauge

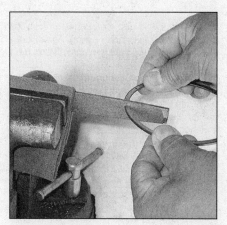

9.15 If the ring end gap is too small, clamp a file in a vise as shown and file the piston ring ends - be sure to remove all raised material

14   To measure the end gap, slip feeler gauges between the ends of the ring until a gauge equal to the gap width is found (see illustration). The feeler gauge should slide between the ring ends with a slight amount of drag. A typical ring gap should fall between 0.010 and 0.020 inch [0.25 to 0.50 mm] for compression rings and up to 0.030 inch [0.76 mm] for the oil ring steel rails. If the gap is larger or smaller than specified, double-check to make sure you have the correct rings before proceeding.

15   If the gap is too small, it must be enlarged or the ring ends may come in contact with each other during engine operation, which can cause serious damage to the engine. If necessary, increase the end gaps by filing the ring ends very carefully with a fine file. Mount the file in a vise equipped with soft jaws, slip the ring over the file with the ends contacting the file face and slowly move the ring to remove material from the ends. When performing this operation, file only by pushing the ring from the outside end of the file towards the vise (see illustration).

9.19a Installing the spacer/expander in the oil ring groove

9.19b DO NOT use a piston ring installation tool when installing the oil control side rails

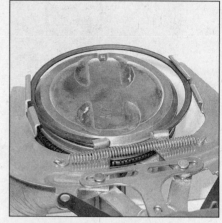

9.22 Use a piston ring installation tool to install the number 2 and the number 1 (top) rings - be sure the directional mark on the piston ring(s) is facing toward the top of the piston

16   Excess end gap isn't critical unless it's greater than 0.040 inch (1 mm). Again, double-check to make sure you have the correct ring type.

17   Repeat the procedure for each ring that will be installed in the first cylinder and for each ring in the remaining cylinders. Remember to keep rings, pistons and cylinders matched up.

18   Once the ring end gaps have been checked/corrected, the rings can be installed on the pistons.

19   The oil control ring (lowest one on the piston) is usually installed first. It's composed of three separate components. Slip the spacer/expander into the groove (see illustration). If an anti-rotation tang is used, make sure it's inserted into the drilled hole in the ring groove. Next, install the upper side rail in the same manner (see illustration). Don't use a piston ring installation tool on the oil ring side rails, as they may be damaged. Instead, place one end of the side rail into the groove between the spacer/expander and the ring land, hold it firmly in place and slide a finger around the piston while pushing the rail into

the groove. Finally, install the lower side rail.

20   After the three oil ring components have been installed, check to make sure that both the upper and lower side rails can be rotated smoothly inside the ring grooves.

21   The number two (middle) ring is installed next. It's usually stamped with a mark which must face up, toward the top of the piston. Do not mix up the top and middle rings, as they have different cross-sections.

Note: *Always follow the instructions printed on the ring package or box - different manufacturers may require different approaches.*

22   Use a piston ring installation tool and make sure the identification mark is facing the top of the piston, then slip the ring into the middle groove on the piston (see illustration). Don't expand the ring any more than necessary to slide it over the piston.

23   Install the number one (top) ring in the same manner. Make sure the mark is facing up. Be careful not to confuse the number one and number two rings.

24   Repeat the procedure for the remaining pistons and rings.

Installation

25   Before installing the piston/connecting rod assemblies, the cylinder walls must be perfectly clean, the top edge of each cylinder bore must be chamfered, and the crankshaft must be in place.

26   Remove the cap from the end of the number one connecting rod (refer to the marks made during removal). Remove the original bearing inserts and wipe the bearing surfaces of the connecting rod and cap with a clean, lint-free cloth. They must be kept spotlessly clean.

Connecting rod bearing oil clearance check

27   Clean the back side of the new upper bearing insert, then lay it in place in the connecting rod.

28   Make sure the tab on the bearing fits into the recess in the rod. Don't hammer the bearing insert into place and be very careful not to nick or gouge the bearing face. Don't lubricate the bearing at this time.

29   Clean the back side of the other bearing insert and install it in the rod cap. Again, make sure the tab on the bearing fits into the recess in the cap, and don't apply any lubricant. It's critically important that the mating surfaces of the bearing and connecting rod are perfectly clean and oil free when they're assembled.

30   Position the piston ring gaps at the specified intervals around the piston as shown (see illustration).

31   Lubricate the piston and rings with clean engine oil and attach a piston ring compressor to the piston. Leave the skirt protruding about 1/4-inch to guide the piston into the cylinder. The rings must be compressed until they're flush with the piston.

32   Rotate the crankshaft until the number one connecting rod journal is at BDC (Bottom Dead Center) and apply a liberal coat of engine oil to the cylinder walls.

33   With the arrow on top of the piston facing the front (timing chain) of the engine, gently

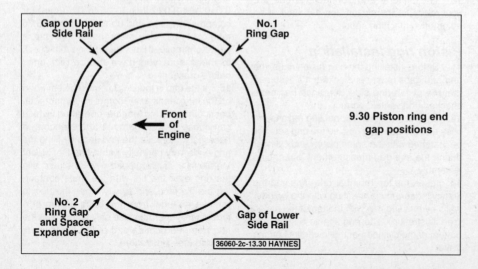

9.30 Piston ring end gap positions

Gap of Upper Side Rail

No.1 Ring Gap

Front of Engine

No. 2 Ring Gap and Spacer Expander Gap

Gap of Lower Side Rail

36060-2c-13.30 HAYNES

9.35 Use a plastic or wooden hammer handle to push the piston into the cylinder

9.37 Place Plastigage on each connecting rod bearing journal parallel to the crankshaft centerline

9.41 Use the scale on the Plastigage package to determine the bearing oil clearance - be sure to measure the widest part of the Plastigage and use the correct scale; it comes with both standard and metric scales

insert the piston/connecting rod assembly into the number one cylinder bore and rest the bottom edge of the ring compressor on the engine block.

34   Tap the top edge of the ring compressor to make sure it's contacting the block around its entire circumference.

35   Gently tap on the top of the piston with the end of a wooden or plastic hammer handle (see illustration) while guiding the end of the connecting rod into place on the crankshaft journal. The piston rings may try to pop out of the ring compressor just before entering the cylinder bore, so keep some downward pressure on the ring compressor. Work slowly, and if any resistance is felt as the piston enters the cylinder, stop immediately. Find out what's hanging up and fix it before proceeding. Do not, for any reason, force the piston into the cylinder - you might break a ring and/or the piston.

36   Once the piston/connecting rod assembly is installed, the connecting rod bearing oil clearance must be checked before the rod cap is permanently installed.

37   Cut a piece of the appropriate size Plastigage slightly shorter than the width of the connecting rod bearing and lay it in place on the number one connecting rod journal, parallel with the journal axis (see illustration).

38   Clean the connecting rod cap bearing face and install the rod cap. Make sure the mating mark on the cap is on the same side as the mark on the connecting rod (see illustration 9.4).

39   Install the OLD rod bolts and tighten them to the torque listed in this Chapter's Specifications.

Note: *Use a thin-wall socket to avoid erroneous torque readings that can result if the socket is wedged between the rod cap and the bolt. If the socket tends to wedge itself between the fastener and the cap, lift up on it slightly until it no longer contacts the cap. DO NOT rotate the crankshaft at any time during this operation.*

40   Remove the fasteners and detach the rod cap, being very careful not to disturb the Plastigage.

41   Compare the width of the crushed Plastigage to the scale printed on the Plastigage envelope to obtain the oil clearance (see illustration). The connecting rod oil clearance is usually about 0.001 to 0.002 inch. Consult an automotive machine shop for the clearance specified for the rod bearings on your engine.

42   If the clearance is not as specified, the bearing inserts may be the wrong size (which means different ones will be required). Before deciding that different inserts are needed, make sure that no dirt or oil was between the bearing inserts and the connecting rod or cap when the clearance was measured. Also, recheck the journal diameter. If the Plastigage was wider at one end than the other, the journal may be tapered. If the clearance still exceeds the limit specified, the bearing will have to be replaced with an undersize bearing.

Caution: *When installing a new crankshaft, always use a standard size bearing.*

Final installation

43   Carefully scrape all traces of the Plastigage material off the rod journal and/or bearing face. Be very careful not to scratch the bearing - use your fingernail or the edge of a plastic card.

44   Make sure the bearing faces are perfectly clean, then apply a uniform layer of clean moly-base grease or engine assembly lube to both of them. You'll have to push the piston into the cylinder to expose the face of the bearing insert in the connecting rod.

45   Slide the connecting rod back into place on the journal, install the rod cap, install the NEW bolts and tighten them to the torque listed in this Chapter's Specifications.

46   Repeat the entire procedure for the remaining pistons/connecting rods.

47   The important points to remember are:

a)   *Keep the back sides of the bearing inserts and the insides of the connecting rods and caps perfectly clean when assembling them.*

b)   *Make sure you have the correct piston/ rod assembly for each cylinder.*

c)   *The arrow on the piston must face the front (timing chain end) of the engine.*

d)   *Lubricate the cylinder walls liberally with clean oil.*

e)   *Lubricate the bearing faces when installing the rod caps after the oil clearance has been checked.*

48   After all the piston/connecting rod assemblies have been correctly installed, rotate the crankshaft a number of times by hand to check for any obvious binding.

49   As a final step, check the connecting rod endplay as described in Step 3. If it was correct before disassembly and the original crankshaft and rods were reinstalled, it should still be correct. If new rods or a new crankshaft were installed, the endplay may be inadequate. If so, the rods will have to be removed and taken to an automotive machine shop for resizing.

10   Crankshaft - removal and installation

Removal

Note: *The crankshaft can be removed only after the engine has been removed from the vehicle. It's assumed that the driveplate, crankshaft pulley, timing chain, oil pan, oil pump body, oil filter and piston/connecting rod assemblies have already been removed. The rear main oil seal retainer must be unbolted and separated from the block before proceeding with crankshaft removal.*

1   Before the crankshaft is removed, measure the endplay. Mount a dial indicator with

10.1 Checking crankshaft endplay with a dial indicator

10.3 Checking the crankshaft endplay with feeler gauges at the thrust bearing journal

the indicator in line with the crankshaft and just touching the end of the crankshaft as shown (see illustration).

2   Pry the crankshaft all the way to the rear and zero the dial indicator. Next, pry the crankshaft to the front as far as possible and check the reading on the dial indicator. The distance traveled is the endplay. A typical crankshaft endplay will fall between 0.003 to 0.010 inch (0.076 to 0.254 mm). If it is greater than that, check the crankshaft thrust surfaces for wear after it's removed. If no wear is evident, new main bearings should correct the endplay.

3   If a dial indicator isn't available, feeler gauges can be used. Gently pry the crankshaft all the way to the front of the engine. Slip feeler gauges between the crankshaft and the front face of the thrust bearing or washer to determine the clearance (see illustration).

4   Loosen the main bearing cap bolts 1/4-turn at a time each, until they can be removed by hand. Obtain new bolts for installation (but keep the old bolts - they will be used during the oil clearance check).

5   Remove the main bearing caps. Pull the

main bearing cap straight up and off the cylinder block. Removing the caps may require a special slide-hammer removal tool that threads into the caps. Gently tap the main bearing cap with a soft-face hammer, if necessary.

6   Carefully lift the crankshaft out of the engine. It may be a good idea to have an assistant available, since the crankshaft is quite heavy and awkward to handle. With the bearing inserts in place inside the engine block and main bearing caps, reinstall the main bearing caps onto the engine block and tighten the bolts finger tight. Make sure the caps are in the exact order they were removed with the arrow pointing toward the front (timing chain and front cover) of the engine.

Installation

7   Crankshaft installation is the first step in engine reassembly. It's assumed at this point that the engine block and crankshaft have been cleaned, inspected and repaired or reconditioned.

8   Position the engine block with the bottom facing up.

9   Remove the bolts and lift off the main bearing caps.

10   If they're still in place, remove the original bearing inserts from the block and from the main bearing caps. Wipe the bearing surfaces of the block and main bearing cap assembly with a clean, lint-free cloth. They must be kept spotlessly clean. This is critical for determining the correct bearing oil clearance.

Main bearing oil clearance check

11   Without mixing them up, clean the back sides of the new upper main bearing inserts (with grooves and oil holes) and lay one in each main bearing saddle in the engine block. Each upper bearing (engine block) has an oil groove and oil hole in it. The thrust washer or thrust bearing insert must be installed in the correct location. Clean the back sides of the

lower main bearing inserts and lay them in the corresponding location in the main bearing caps. Make sure the tab on the bearing insert fits into the recess in the block or main bearing caps.

Caution: *The oil holes in the block must line up with the oil holes in the engine block inserts.*

Note: *The thrust bearing is located on the third journal in the main bearing cap journals (counting from the front).*

Caution: *Do not hammer the bearing insert into place and don't nick or gouge the bearing faces. DO NOT apply any lubrication at this time.*

12   Clean the faces of the bearing inserts in the block and the crankshaft main bearing journals with a clean, lint-free cloth.

13   Check or clean the oil holes in the crankshaft, as any dirt here can go only one way - straight through the new bearings.

14   Once you're certain the crankshaft is clean, carefully lay it in position in the cylinder block.

15   Before the crankshaft can be permanently installed, the main bearing oil clearance must be checked.

16   Cut several strips of the appropriate size of Plastigage. They must be slightly shorter than the width of the main bearing journal.

17   Place one piece on each crankshaft main bearing journal, parallel with the journal axis as shown (see illustration).

18   Clean the faces of the bearing inserts in the main bearing caps or lower crankcase. Install the caps without disturbing the Plastigage.

19   Apply clean engine oil to all bolt threads prior to installation, install the OLD bolts finger-tight, then tighten them to the torque listed in this Chapter's Specifications. DO NOT rotate the crankshaft at any time during this operation.

Note: *Follow the correct torque sequence (see illustrations 10.29 or 10.30), but note that it isn't necessary to install the side bolts at this time.*

10.17 Place the Plastigage onto the crankshaft bearing journal as shown

10.21 Use the scale on the Plastigage package to determine the bearing oil clearance - be sure to measure the widest part of the Plastigage and use the correct scale; it comes with both standard and metric scales

20 Remove the bolts and carefully lift the main bearing caps straight up and off the block. Do not disturb the Plastigage or rotate the crankshaft.

21 Compare the width of the crushed Plastigage on each journal to the scale printed on the Plastigage envelope to determine the main bearing oil clearance (see illustration). Check with an automotive machine shop for the crankshaft bearing oil clearance for your engine.

22 If the clearance is not as specified, the bearing inserts may be the wrong size (which means different ones may be required). Before deciding if different inserts are needed, make sure that no dirt or oil was between the bearing inserts and the caps or block when the clearance was measured. If the Plastigage was wider at one end than the other, the crankshaft journal may be tapered. If the clearance still exceeds the limit specified, the bearing insert(s) will have to be replaced with an undersize bearing insert(s).

Caution: *When installing a new crankshaft, always install a standard bearing insert set.*

23 Carefully scrape all traces of the Plastigage material off the main bearing journals and/or the bearing insert faces. Be sure to remove all residue from the oil holes. Use your fingernail or the edge of a plastic card - don't nick or scratch the bearing faces.

Final installation

24 Carefully lift the crankshaft out of the cylinder block.

25 Clean the bearing insert faces in the cylinder block, then apply a thin, uniform layer of moly-base grease or engine assembly lube to each of the bearing surfaces. Be sure to coat the thrust faces as well as the journal face of the thrust bearing.

26 Make sure the crankshaft journals are clean, then lay the crankshaft back in place in the cylinder block.

27 Clean the bearing insert faces and apply the same lubricant to them. Clean the engine block and the bearing cap mating surfaces thoroughly. The surfaces must be free of oil residue.

28 Prior to installation, apply clean engine oil to the NEW bolt threads, wiping off any excess, then install all bolts finger-tight.

29 On V6 engines, tighten bolts one through sixteen to the torque listed in Step 1 of this Chapter's Specifications. Be sure to follow the correct sequence (see illustration). Tap the crankshaft to the rear and then to the front to align the thrust bearing. The last tap must be in the forward direction. Proceed with the rest of the fastener tightening steps listed in this Chapter's Specifications for the V6 engine, ending with the tightening of the side bolts.

Caution: *On 4.3L V6 models, 5.3L and 6.2L V8 models, there are two design versions of the inner and outer crankshaft bearing cap bolts. Always install new bolts that match the correct design. If the wrong design bolts are used during installation the final torque output which may result in lower engine noise and/or damage to the engine.*

Note: *On 4.3L V6 models, 5.3L and 6.2L V8 models, the first design outer crankshaft bolts have an "M" marked in the center of the bolt and the second design outer crankshaft bolts have an "MNP 10.9" marked in the center of the bolt. The first design inner crankshaft bolts have an "M 109" marked in the center of the bolt and the second design inner crankshaft bolts have an "MNP 10.9" marked in the center of the bolt.*

30 On V8 engines, tighten bolts one through ten to the torque listed in Step 1 of this Chapter's Specifications. Be sure to follow the correct sequence (see illustration). Tap the crankshaft to the rear and then to the front to align the thrust bearing on V8 engines. The last tap must be in the forward direction.

31 Proceed with the rest of the fastener tightening steps listed in this Chapter's Specifications for the V8 engine, ending with the tightening of the NEW side bolts.

Note: *Using old side bolts may result in oil leaks as the bolts have a sealing compound on them.*

32 Recheck the crankshaft endplay with a feeler gauge or a dial indicator. The endplay should be correct if the crankshaft thrust faces aren't worn or damaged and if new bearings have been installed.

33 Rotate the crankshaft a number of times by hand to check for any obvious binding. It should rotate with a running torque of 50 in-lbs or less. If the running torque is too high, correct the problem at this time.

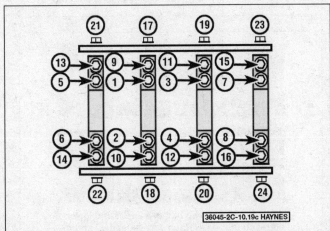
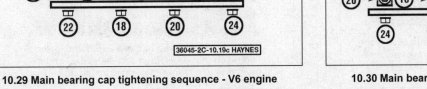

10.29 Main bearing cap tightening sequence - V6 engine

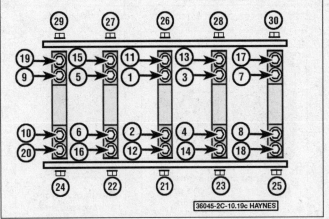

10.30 Main bearing cap tightening sequence - V8 engine

ENGINE BEARING ANALYSIS

Debris

Babbitt bearing embedded with debris from machinings

Microscopic detail of debris

Microscopic detail of gouges

Overplated copper alloy bearing gouged by cast iron debris

Aluminum bearing embedded with glass beads

Microscopic detail of glass beads

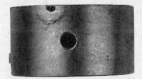

Damaged lining caused by dirt left on the bearing back

Misassembly

Result of a lower half assembled as an upper - blocking the oil flow

Excessive oil clearance is indicated by a short contact arc

Polished and oil-stained backs are a result of a poor fit in the housing bore

Result of a wrong, reversed, or shifted cap

Overloading

Damage from excessive idling which resulted in an oil film unable to support the load imposed

Damaged upper connecting rod bearings caused by engine lugging; the lower main bearings (not shown) were similarly affected

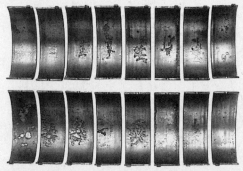

The damage shown in these upper and lower connecting rod bearings was caused by engine operation at a higher-than-rated speed under load

Misalignment

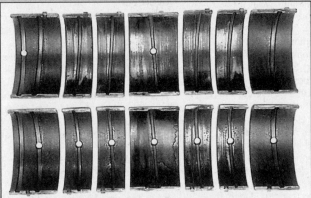

A warped crankshaft caused this pattern of severe wear in the center, diminishing toward the ends

A poorly finished crankshaft caused the equally spaced scoring shown

A tapered housing bore caused the damage along one edge of this pair

A bent connecting rod led to the damage in the "V" pattern

Lubrication

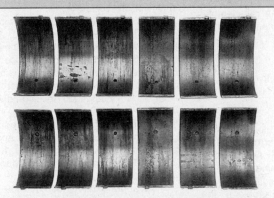

Result of dry start: The bearings on the left, farthest from the oil pump, show more damage

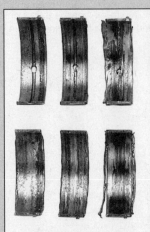

Result of a low oil supply or oil starvation

Severe wear as a result of inadequate oil clearance

Corrosion

Microscopic detail of corrosion

Corrosion is an acid attack on the bearing lining generally caused by inadequate maintenance, extremely hot or cold operation, or inferior oils or fuels

Microscopic detail of cavitation

Example of cavitation - a surface erosion caused by pressure changes in the oil film

Damage from excessive thrust or insufficient axial clearance

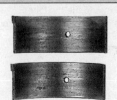

Bearing affected by oil dilution caused by excessive blow-by or a rich mixture

Rear main oil seal retainer installation

V6 models, 5.3L and 6.2L V8 models

34   Install the rear seal retainer with a new gasket. Tighten the fasteners to the torque listed in this Chapter's Specifications.

35   Refer to Chapter 2A for information regarding installing the seal into the retainer.

6.0L V8 models

Without a seal in the retainer - first and second design

36   Install the rear seal retainer with a new gasket but only tighten the bolts snug.

37   Install the proper alignment tool (GM part J 41480 or an equivalent) to the rear of the engine block oil pan rail. Tighten the bolts to 18 ft-lbs.

38   On 6.0L models with first design rear housings, the seal must be removed before installing the housing and requires alignment tool (GM part J 41476 or an equivalent) to be installed to the rear of the crankshaft. The two mounting bolts should be parallel to the oil pan rail. The legs of the tool will register into the seal bore. On second design rear housings the housing can be installed with the seal in the housing and tool J 41476 is not required.

39   Snug the J 41476 mounting bolts. Tighten the J 41480 bolts that go into the retainer to 106 in-lbs.

40   Tighten the rear oil seal retainer mounting bolts to the torque listed in this Chapter's Specifications.

41   Remove the tools and lay a straightedge across the rear of the oil pan rail. Use feeler gauges to measure the clearance between the oil seal retainer and the straightedge. The clearance must be between 0 and 0.02-inch. If the clearance is not correct, repeat the installation procedure.

42   Refer to Chapter 2B for information regarding seal installation.

With a seal in the retainer - second design only

43   Check the rear oil seal retainer for two alignment tabs in the bore at the 3 o'clock and 9 o'clock positions. If the retainer doesn't have these tabs, it must be installed without the seal - refer to Step 36. If it does have the tabs, continue to the next step.

44   Install the proper alignment tool (GM part

J 41479-2A or an equivalent) to the rear of the crankshaft. Tighten the bolts snug.

45   Install the oil seal retainer (with a seal in it) with a new gasket and finger-tighten the bolts.

46   Remove the alignment tool.

47   Install the proper alignment tool (GM part J 41480 or an equivalent) to the rear of the engine block. Tighten the bolts to 18 ft-lbs.

48   Tighten the tool bolts that go into the seal retainer to 106 in-lbs.

49   Tighten the oil seal retainer bolts to the torque listed in this Chapter's Specifications.

50   Remove the tool and lay a straightedge across the rear of the oil pan rail. Use feeler gauges to measure the clearance between the oil seal retainer and the straightedge. The clearance must be between 0 and 0.02-inch. If the clearance is not correct, repeat the installation procedure.

51   Refer to Chapter 2B for information regarding seal installation.

11   Engine overhaul - reassembly sequence

1   Before beginning engine reassembly, make sure you have all the necessary new parts, gaskets and seals as well as the following items on hand:

  Common hand tools
  A 1/2-inch drive torque wrench
  New engine oil
  Gasket sealant
  Thread locking compound

2   If you obtained a short block it will be necessary to install the cylinder head, the oil pump and pick-up tube, the oil pan, the water pump, the timing belt and timing cover, and the valve cover (see Chapter 2A or 2B). In order to save time and avoid problems, the external components must be installed in the following general order:

  Thermostat and housing cover
  Water pump
  Intake and exhaust manifolds
  Fuel injection components
  Emission control components
  Spark plugs
  Ignition coils or coil pack and spark
   plug wires
  Oil filter
  Engine mounts and mount brackets
  Driveplate

12   Initial start-up and break-in after overhaul

Warning: *Have a fire extinguisher handy when starting the engine for the first time.*

1   Once the engine has been installed in the vehicle, double-check the engine oil and coolant levels.

2   With the spark plugs out of the engine and the ignition system and fuel injectors disabled (see Section 3, Step 4) crank the engine until oil pressure registers on the gauge or the light goes out.

3   Install the spark plugs, hook up the plug wires and restore the ignition system and fuel injector functions.

4   Start the engine. It may take a few moments for the fuel system to build up pressure, but the engine should start without a great deal of effort.

5   After the engine starts, it should be allowed to warm up to normal operating temperature. While the engine is warming up, make a thorough check for fuel, oil and coolant leaks.

6   Shut the engine off and recheck the engine oil and coolant levels.

7   Drive the vehicle to an area with minimum traffic, accelerate from 30 to 50 mph, then allow the vehicle to slow to 30 mph with the throttle closed. Repeat the procedure 10 or 12 times. This will load the piston rings and cause them to seat properly against the cylinder walls. Check again for oil and coolant leaks.

8   Drive the vehicle gently for the first 500 miles (no sustained high speeds) and keep a constant check on the oil level. It is not unusual for an engine to use oil during the break-in period.

9   At approximately 500 to 600 miles, change the oil and filter.

10   For the next few hundred miles, drive the vehicle normally. Do not pamper it or abuse it.

11   After 2,000 miles, change the oil and filter again and consider the engine broken in.

COMMON ENGINE OVERHAUL TERMS

B

Backlash - The amount of play between two parts. Usually refers to how much one gear can be moved back and forth without moving the gear with which it's meshed.

Bearing Caps - The caps held in place by nuts or bolts which, in turn, hold the bearing surface. This space is for lubricating oil to enter.

Bearing clearance - The amount of space left between shaft and bearing surface. This space is for lubricating oil to enter.

Bearing crush - The additional height which is purposely manufactured into each bearing half to ensure complete contact of the bearing back with the housing bore when the engine is assembled.

Bearing knock - The noise created by movement of a part in a loose or worn bearing.

Blueprinting - Dismantling an engine and reassembling it to EXACT specifications.

Bore - An engine cylinder, or any cylindrical hole; also used to describe the process of enlarging or accurately refinishing a hole with a cutting tool, as to bore an engine cylinder. The bore size is the diameter of the hole.

Boring - Renewing the cylinders by cutting them out to a specified size. A boring bar is used to make the cut.

Bottom end - A term which refers collectively to the engine block, crankshaft, main bearings and the big ends of the connecting rods.

Break-in - The period of operation between installation of new or rebuilt parts and time in which parts are worn to the correct fit. Driving at reduced and varying speed for a specified mileage to permit parts to wear to the correct fit.

Bushing - A one-piece sleeve placed in a bore to serve as a bearing surface for shaft, piston pin, etc. Usually replaceable.

C

Camshaft - The shaft in the engine, on which a series of lobes are located for operating the valve mechanisms. The camshaft is driven by gears or sprockets and a timing chain. Usually referred to simply as the cam.

Carbon - Hard, or soft, black deposits found in combustion chamber, on plugs, under rings, on and under valve heads.

Cast iron - An alloy of iron and more than two percent carbon, used for engine blocks and heads because it's relatively inexpensive and easy to mold into complex shapes.

Chamfer - To bevel across (or a bevel on) the sharp edge of an object.

Chase - To repair damaged threads with a tap or die.

Combustion chamber - The space between the piston and the cylinder head, with the piston at top dead center, in which air-fuel mixture is burned.

Compression ratio - The relationship between cylinder volume (clearance volume) when the piston is at top dead center and cylinder volume when the piston is at bottom dead center.

Connecting rod - The rod that connects the crank on the crankshaft with the piston. Sometimes called a con rod.

Connecting rod cap - The part of the connecting rod assembly that attaches the rod to the crankpin.

Core plug - Soft metal plug used to plug the casting holes for the coolant passages in the block.

Crankcase - The lower part of the engine in which the crankshaft rotates; includes the lower section of the cylinder block and the oil pan.

Crank kit - A reground or reconditioned crankshaft and new main and connecting rod bearings.

Crankpin - The part of a crankshaft to which a connecting rod is attached.

Crankshaft - The main rotating member, or shaft, running the length of the crankcase, with offset throws to which the connecting rods are attached; changes the reciprocating motion of the pistons into rotating motion.

Cylinder sleeve - A replaceable sleeve, or liner, pressed into the cylinder block to form the cylinder bore.

D

Deburring - Removing the burrs (rough edges or areas) from a bearing.

Deglazer - A tool, rotated by an electric motor, used to remove glaze from cylinder walls so a new set of rings will seat.

E

Endplay - The amount of lengthwise movement between two parts. As applied to a crankshaft, the distance that the crankshaft can move forward and back in the cylinder block.

F

Face - A machinist's term that refers to removing metal from the end of a shaft or the face of a larger part, such as a flywheel.

Fatigue - A breakdown of material through a large number of loading and unloading cycles. The first signs are cracks followed shortly by breaks.

Feeler gauge - A thin strip of hardened steel, ground to an exact thickness, used to check clearances between parts.

Free height - The unloaded length or height of a spring.

Freeplay - The looseness in a linkage, or an assembly of parts, between the initial application of force and actual movement. Usually perceived as slop or slight delay.

Freeze plug - See Core plug.

G

Gallery - A large passage in the block that forms a reservoir for engine oil pressure.

Glaze - The very smooth, glassy finish that develops on cylinder walls while an engine is in service.

H

Heli-Coil - A rethreading device used when threads are worn or damaged. The device is installed in a retapped hole to reduce the thread size to the original size.

I

Installed height - The spring's measured length or height, as installed on the cylinder head. Installed height is measured from the spring seat to the underside of the spring retainer.

J

Journal - The surface of a rotating shaft which turns in a bearing.

K

Keeper - The split lock that holds the valve spring retainer in position on the valve stem.

Key - A small piece of metal inserted into matching grooves machined into two parts fitted together - such as a gear pressed onto a shaft - which prevents slippage between the two parts.

Knock - The heavy metallic engine sound, produced in the combustion chamber as a result of abnormal combustion - usually detonation. Knock is usually caused by a loose or worn bearing. Also referred to as detonation, pinging and spark knock. Connecting rod or main bearing knocks are created by too much oil clearance or insufficient lubrication.

L

Lands - The portions of metal between the piston ring grooves.

Lapping the valves - Grinding a valve face and its seat together with lapping compound.

Lash - The amount of free motion in a gear train, between gears, or in a mechanical assembly, that occurs before movement can begin. Usually refers to the lash in a valve train.

Lifter - The part that rides against the cam to transfer motion to the rest of the valve train.

M

Machining - The process of using a machine to remove metal from a metal part.

Main bearings - The plain, or babbit, bearings that support the crankshaft.

Main bearing caps - The cast iron caps, bolted to the bottom of the block, that support the main bearings.

O

O.D. - Outside diameter.

Oil gallery - A pipe or drilled passageway in the engine used to carry engine oil from one area to another.

Oil ring - The lower ring, or rings, of a piston; designed to prevent excessive amounts of oil from working up the cylinder walls and into the combustion chamber. Also called an oil-control ring.

Oil seal - A seal which keeps oil from leaking out of a compartment. Usually refers to a dynamic seal around a rotating shaft or other moving part.

O-ring - A type of sealing ring made of a special rubberlike material; in use, the O-ring is compressed into a groove to provide the sealing action.

Overhaul - To completely disassemble a unit, clean and inspect all parts, reassemble it with the original or new parts and make all adjustments necessary for proper operation.

P

Pilot bearing - A small bearing installed in the center of the flywheel (or the rear end of the crankshaft) to support the front end of the input shaft of the transmission.

Pip mark - A little dot or indentation which indicates the top side of a compression ring.

Piston - The cylindrical part, attached to the connecting rod, that moves up and down in the cylinder as the crankshaft rotates. When the fuel charge is fired, the piston transfers the force of the explosion to the connecting rod, then to the crankshaft.

Piston pin (or wrist pin) - The cylindrical and usually hollow steel pin that passes through the piston. The piston pin fastens the piston to the upper end of the connecting rod.

Piston ring - The split ring fitted to the groove in a piston. The ring contacts the sides of the ring groove and also rubs against the cylinder wall, thus sealing space between piston and wall. There are two types of rings: Compression rings seal the compression pressure in the combustion chamber; oil rings scrape excessive oil off the cylinder wall.

Piston ring groove - The slots or grooves cut in piston heads to hold piston rings in position.

Piston skirt - The portion of the piston below the rings and the piston pin hole.

Plastigage - A thin strip of plastic thread, available in different sizes, used for measuring clearances. For example, a strip of plastigage is laid across a bearing journal and mashed as parts are assembled. Then parts are disassembled and the width of the strip is measured to determine clearance between journal and bearing. Commonly used to measure crankshaft main-bearing and connecting rod bearing clearances.

Press-fit - A tight fit between two parts that requires pressure to force the parts together. Also referred to as drive, or force, fit.

Prussian blue - A blue pigment; in solution, useful in determining the area of contact between two surfaces. Prussian blue is commonly used to determine the width and location of the contact area between the valve face and the valve seat.

R

Race (bearing) - The inner or outer ring that provides a contact surface for balls or rollers in bearing.

Ream - To size, enlarge or smooth a hole by using a round cutting tool with fluted edges.

Ring job - The process of reconditioning the cylinders and installing new rings.

Runout - Wobble. The amount a shaft rotates out-of-true.

S

Saddle - The upper main bearing seat.

Scored - Scratched or grooved, as a cylinder wall may be scored by abrasive particles moved up and down by the piston rings.

Scuffing - A type of wear in which there's a transfer of material between parts moving against each other; shows up as pits or grooves in the mating surfaces.

Seat - The surface upon which another part rests or seats. For example, the valve seat is the matched surface upon which the valve face rests. Also used to refer to wearing into a good fit; for example, piston rings seat after a few miles of driving.

Short block - An engine block complete with crankshaft and piston and, usually, camshaft assemblies.

Static balance - The balance of an object while it's stationary.

Step - The wear on the lower portion of a ring land caused by excessive side and back-clearance. The height of the step indicates the ring's extra side clearance and the length of the step projecting from the back wall of the groove represents the ring's back clearance.

Stroke - The distance the piston moves when traveling from top dead center to bottom dead center, or from bottom dead center to top dead center.

Stud - A metal rod with threads on both ends.

T

Tang - A lip on the end of a plain bearing used to align the bearing during assembly.

Tap - To cut threads in a hole. Also refers to the fluted tool used to cut threads.

Taper - A gradual reduction in the width of a shaft or hole; in an engine cylinder, taper usually takes the form of uneven wear, more pronounced at the top than at the bottom.

Throws - The offset portions of the crankshaft to which the connecting rods are affixed.

Thrust bearing - The main bearing that has thrust faces to prevent excessive endplay, or forward and backward movement of the crankshaft.

Thrust washer - A bronze or hardened steel washer placed between two moving parts. The washer prevents longitudinal movement and provides a bearing surface for thrust surfaces of parts.

Tolerance - The amount of variation permitted from an exact size of measurement. Actual amount from smallest acceptable dimension to largest acceptable dimension.

U

Umbrella - An oil deflector placed near the valve tip to throw oil from the valve stem area.

Undercut - A machined groove below the normal surface.

Undersize bearings - Smaller diameter bearings used with re-ground crankshaft journals.

V

Valve grinding - Refacing a valve in a valve-refacing machine.

Valve train - The valve-operating mechanism of an engine; includes all components from the camshaft to the valve.

Vibration damper - A cylindrical weight attached to the front of the crankshaft to minimize torsional vibration (the twist-untwist actions of the crankshaft caused by the cylinder firing impulses). Also called a harmonic balancer.

W

Water jacket - The spaces around the cylinders, between the inner and outer shells of the cylinder block or head, through which coolant circulates.

Web - A supporting structure across a cavity.

Woodruff key - A key with a radiused backside (viewed from the side).

Notes

Notes

Chapter 3
Cooling, heating and air conditioning systems

Contents

Specifications

General
Coolant capacity..	See Chapter 1
Refrigerant type...	R-134a or R-1234yf (refer to HVAC specification tag)
Refrigerant capacity...	Refer to HVAC specification tag

Torque specifications

Ft-lbs (unless otherwise indicated)

Note: *One foot-pound (ft-lb) of torque is equivalent to 12 inch-pounds (in-lbs) of torque. Torque values below approximately 15 foot-pounds are expressed in inch-pounds, because most foot-pound torque wrenches are not accurate at these smaller values.*

Air conditioning compressor bolt/nuts...	16
Air conditioning pressure sensor	53 in-lbs
Coolant manifold bolts..	18
Radiator mounting bolts...	18
Thermostat housing bolts	
4.3L V6, 5.3L and 6.2L V8 engines	89 in-lbs
6.0L V8 engines	132 in-lbs
Water pump bolts	
4.3L V6, 5.3L and 6.2L V8 engines	89 in-lbs
6.0L V8 engines	
Step 1	132 in-lbs
Step 2	22

1   General information

Engine cooling system

1   The cooling system consists of a radiator, a coolant expansion tank, a pressure cap (located on the expansion tank), a thermostat, an electric cooling fan, and a water pump.
2   When the engine is cold, the thermostat restricts the circulation of coolant to the engine. When the minimum operating temperature is reached, the thermostat begins to open, allowing coolant to flow through the radiator.

Transmission cooling system

3   Vehicles with an automatic transmission are equipped with a transmission fluid cooler, located inside the radiator. An auxiliary transmission fluid cooler is located in front of the radiator.

Engine oil cooling system

4   Besides the engine and transmission cooling systems described above, engine heat is also dissipated through an external oil cooler that's integrated into the lubrication system. The oil cooler helps keep engine and oil temperatures within design limits under extreme load conditions.

Heating system

5   The heating system consists of the heater controls, the heater core, the heater blower assembly (which houses the blower motor and the blower motor resistor), and the hoses connecting the heater core to the engine cooling system. Hot engine coolant is circulated through the heater core. When the heater mode is activated, a flap door opens to expose the heater box to the passenger compartment. A fan switch on the heater control panel activates the blower motor, which forces air through the core, heating the air.

Air conditioning system

6   The air conditioning system consists of the condenser, which is mounted in front of the radiator, the evaporator case assembly under the dash, a compressor mounted on the engine, and the plumbing connecting all of the above components.
7   A blower fan forces the warmer air of the passenger compartment through the evaporator core (sort of a radiator-in-reverse), transferring the heat from the air to the refrigerant. The liquid refrigerant boils off into low pressure vapor, taking the heat with it when it leaves the evaporator.

2   Troubleshooting

Coolant leaks

1   A coolant leak can develop anywhere in the cooling system, but the most common causes are:

a)   A loose or weak hose clamp
b)   A defective hose
c)   A faulty pressure cap
d)   A damaged radiator
e)   A bad heater core
f)   A faulty water pump
g)   A leaking gasket at any joint that carries coolant

2   Coolant leaks aren't always easy to find. Sometimes they can only be detected when the cooling system is under pressure. Here's where a cooling system pressure tester comes in handy. After the engine has cooled completely, the tester is attached in place of the pressure cap, then pumped up to the pressure value equal to that of the pressure cap rating (see illustration). Now, leaks that only exist when the engine is fully warmed up will become apparent. The tester can be left connected to locate a nagging slow leak.

Coolant level drops, but no external leaks

3   If you find it necessary to keep adding coolant, but there are no external leaks, the probable causes include:

a)   A blown head gasket
b)   A leaking intake manifold gasket (only on engines that have coolant passages in the manifold)
c)   A cracked cylinder head or cylinder block

4   Any of the above problems will also usually result in contamination of the engine oil, which will cause it to take on a milkshake-like appearance. A bad head gasket or cracked head or block can also result in engine oil contaminating the cooling system.
5   Combustion leak detectors (also known as block testers) are available at most auto parts stores. These work by detecting exhaust gases in the cooling system, which indicates a compression leak from a cylinder into the coolant. The tester consists of a large bulb-type syringe and bottle of test fluid (see illustration). A measured amount of the fluid is added to the syringe. The syringe is placed over the cooling system filler neck and, with the engine running, the bulb is squeezed and a sample of the gases present in the cooling system are drawn up through the test fluid (see illustration). If any combustion gases are present in the sample taken, the test fluid will change color.
6   If the test indicates combustion gas is present in the cooling system, you can be sure that the engine has a blown head gasket or a crack in the cylinder head or block, and will require disassembly to repair.

Pressure cap

Warning: *Wait until the engine is completely cool before beginning this check.*
7   The cooling system is sealed by a spring-loaded cap, which raises the boiling

2.2 The cooling system pressure tester is connected in place of the pressure cap on the coolant expansion tank, then pumped up to pressurize the system

2.5a The combustion leak detector consists of a bulb, syringe and test fluid

2.5b Place the tester over the cooling system filler neck and use the bulb to draw a sample into the tester

point of the coolant. If the cap's seal or spring are worn out, the coolant can boil and escape past the cap. With the engine completely cool, remove the cap and check the seal; if it's cracked, hardened or deteriorated in any way, replace it with a new one.

8   Even if the seal is good, the spring might not be; this can be checked with a cooling system pressure tester (see illustration). If the cap can't hold a pressure within approximately 1-1/2 lbs of its rated pressure (which is marked on the cap), replace it with a new one.

9   The cap is also equipped with a vacuum relief spring. When the engine cools off, a vacuum is created in the cooling system. The vacuum relief spring allows air back into the system, which will equalize the pressure and prevent damage to the radiator (the radiator tanks could collapse if the vacuum is great enough). If, after turning the engine off and allowing it to cool down you notice any of the cooling system hoses collapsing, replace the pressure cap with a new one.

Thermostat

10   Before assuming the thermostat (see illustration) is responsible for a cooling system problem, check the coolant level (see Chapter 1), drivebelt tension (see Chapter 1) and temperature gauge (or light) operation.

11   If the engine takes a long time to warm up (as indicated by the temperature gauge or heater operation), the thermostat is probably stuck open. Replace the thermostat with a new one.

12   If the engine runs hot or overheats, a thorough test of the thermostat should be performed.

13   Definitive testing of the thermostat can only be made when it is removed from the vehicle. If the thermostat is stuck in the open position at room temperature, it is faulty and must be replaced.

Caution: *Do not drive the vehicle without a thermostat. The computer may stay in open loop and emissions and fuel economy will suffer.*

14   To test a thermostat, suspend the (closed) thermostat on a length of string or wire in a pot of cold water.

15   Heat the water on a stove while observing the thermostat. The thermostat should fully open before the water boils.

16   If the thermostat doesn't open and close as specified, or sticks in any position, replace it.

Cooling fan

Electric cooling fan

17   If the engine is overheating and the cooling fan is not coming on when the engine temperature rises to an excessive level, unplug the fan motor electrical connector(s) and connect the motor directly to the battery with fused jumper wires. If the fan motor doesn't come on, replace the motor.

18   If the radiator fan motor is okay, but it isn't coming on when the engine gets hot, the fan relay might be defective. A relay is used to control a circuit by turning it on and off in response to a control decision by the Powertrain Control Module (PCM). These control circuits are fairly complex, and checking them should be left to a qualified automotive technician. Sometimes, the control system can be fixed by simply identifying and replacing a bad relay.

19   Locate the fan relays in the engine compartment fuse/relay box.

20   Test the relay (see Chapter 12).

21   If the relay is okay, check all wiring and connections to the fan motor. Refer to the wiring diagrams at the end of Chapter 12. If no obvious problems are found, the problem could be the Engine Coolant Temperature (ECT) sensor or the Powertrain Control Module (PCM). Have the cooling fan system and

circuit diagnosed by a dealer service department or repair shop with the proper diagnostic equipment.

Belt-driven cooling fan

22   Disconnect the cable from the negative terminal of the battery and rock the fan back and forth by hand to check for excessive bearing play.

23   With the engine cold (and not running), turn the fan blades by hand. The fan should turn freely.

24   Visually inspect for substantial fluid leakage from the clutch assembly. If problems are noted, replace the clutch assembly.

25   With the engine completely warmed up, turn off the ignition switch and disconnect the negative battery cable from the battery. Turn the fan by hand. Some drag should be evident. If the fan turns easily, replace the fan clutch.

Water pump

26   A failure in the water pump can cause serious engine damage due to overheating.

Drivebelt-driven water pump

27   There are two ways to check the operation of the water pump while it's installed on the engine. If the pump is found to be defective, it should be replaced with a new or rebuilt unit.

28   Water pumps are equipped with weep (or vent) holes (see illustration). If a failure occurs in the pump seal, coolant will leak from the hole.

29   If the water pump shaft bearings fail, there may be a howling sound at the pump while it's running. Shaft wear can be felt with the drivebelt removed if the water pump pulley is rocked up and down (with the engine off). Don't mistake drivebelt slippage, which causes a squealing sound, for water pump bearing failure.

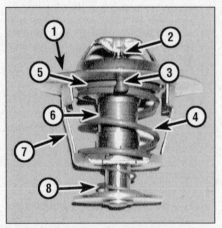

2.8 Checking the cooling system pressure cap with a cooling system pressure tester

2.10 Typical thermostat:

1	Flange	5	Valve seat
2	Piston	6	Valve
3	Jiggle valve	7	Frame
4	Main coil spring	8	Secondary coil spring

2.28 The water pump weep hole is generally located on the underside of the pump

Timing belt-driven water pump

30   Water pumps driven by the timing belt are located underneath the timing belt cover.

31   Checking the water pump is limited because of where it is located. However, some basic checks can be made before deciding to remove the water pump. If the pump is found to be defective, it should be replaced with a new or rebuilt unit.

32   One sign that the water pump may be failing is that the heater (climate control) may not work well. Warm the engine to normal operating temperature, confirm that the coolant level is correct, then run the heater and check for hot air coming from the ducts.

33   Check for noises coming from the water pump area. If the water pump impeller shaft or bearings are failing, there may be a howling sound at the pump while the engine is running.

34   It you suspect water pump failure due to noise, wear can be confirmed by feeling for play at the pump shaft. This can be done by rocking the drive sprocket on the pump shaft up and down. To do this you will need to remove the tension on the timing chain or belt as well as access the water pump.

All water pumps

35   In rare cases or on high-mileage vehicles, another sign of water pump failure may be the presence of coolant in the engine oil. This condition will adversely affect the engine in varying degrees.

Note: *Finding coolant in the engine oil could indicate other serious issues besides a failed water pump, such as a blown head gasket or a cracked cylinder head or block.*

36   Even a pump that exhibits no outward signs of a problem, such as noise or leakage, can still be due for replacement. Removal for close examination is the only sure way to tell. Sometimes the fins on the back of the impeller can corrode to the point that cooling efficiency is diminished significantly.

Heater system

37   Little can go wrong with a heater. If the fan motor will run at all speeds, the electrical part of the system is okay. The three basic heater problems fall into the following general categories:

a) *Not enough heat*
b) *Heat all the time*
c) *No heat*

38   If there's not enough heat, the control valve or door is stuck in a partially open position, the coolant coming from the engine isn't hot enough, or the heater core is restricted. If the coolant isn't hot enough, the thermostat in the engine cooling system is stuck open, allowing coolant to pass through the engine so rapidly that it doesn't heat up quickly enough. If the vehicle is equipped with a temperature gauge instead of a warning light, watch to see if the engine temperature rises to the normal operating range after driving for a reasonable distance.

39   If there's heat all the time, the control valve or the door is stuck wide open.

40   If there's no heat, coolant is probably not reaching the heater core, or the heater core is plugged. The likely cause is a collapsed or plugged hose, core, or a frozen heater control valve. If the heater is the type that flows coolant all the time, the cause is a stuck door or a broken or kinked control cable.

Air conditioning system

41   If the cool air output is inadequate:

a) *Inspect the condenser coils and fins to make sure they're clear.*
b) *Check the compressor clutch for slippage.*
c) *Check the blower motor for proper operation.*
d) *Inspect the blower discharge passage for obstructions.*
e) *Check the system air intake filter for clogging.*

42   If the system provides intermittent cooling air:

a) *Check the circuit breaker, blower switch and blower motor for a malfunction.*
b) *Make sure the compressor clutch isn't slipping.*
c) *Inspect the plenum door to make sure it's operating properly.*
d) *Inspect the evaporator to make sure it isn't clogged.*
e) *If the unit is icing up, it may be caused by excessive moisture in the system, incorrect super heat switch adjustment or low thermostat adjustment.*

43   If the system provides no cooling air:

a) *Inspect the compressor drivebelt. Make sure it's not loose or broken.*
b) *Make sure the compressor clutch engages. If it doesn't, check for a blown fuse.*
c) *Inspect the wire harness for broken or disconnected wires.*
d) *If the compressor clutch doesn't engage, bridge the terminals of the air conditioning pressure switch(es) with a jumper wire; if the clutch now engages, and the system is properly charged, the pressure switch is bad.*
e) *Make sure the blower motor is not disconnected or burned out.*
f) *Make sure the compressor isn't partially or completely seized.*
g) *Inspect the refrigerant lines for leaks.*
h) *Check the components for leaks.*
i) *Inspect the receiver-drier/accumulator or expansion valve/tube for clogged screens.*

44   If the system is noisy:

a) *Look for loose panels in the passenger compartment.*
b) *Inspect the compressor drivebelt. It may be loose or worn.*
c) *Check the compressor mounting bolts. They should be tight.*
d) *Listen carefully to the compressor. It may be worn out.*

e) *Listen to the idler pulley and bearing and the clutch. Either may be defective.*
f) *The winding in the compressor clutch coil or solenoid may be defective.*
g) *The compressor oil level may be low.*
h) *The blower motor fan bushing or the motor itself may be worn out.*
i) *If there is an excessive charge in the system, you'll hear a rumbling noise in the high pressure line, a thumping noise in the compressor, or see bubbles or cloudiness in the sight glass.*
j) *If there's a low charge in the system, you might hear hissing in the evaporator case at the expansion valve, or see bubbles or cloudiness in the sight glass.*

---

3   Air conditioning and heating system - check and maintenance

---

Air conditioning system

Warning: *The air conditioning system is under high pressure. DO NOT loosen any fittings or remove any components until after the system has been discharged. Air conditioning refrigerant must be properly discharged into an EPA-approved container at a dealership service department or an automotive air conditioning repair facility. Always wear eye protection when disconnecting air conditioning system fittings.*

Warning: *R-1234yf refrigerant is easily contaminated, and is toxic and flammable.*

Caution: *On R-1234yf systems, the desiccant in the receiver-drier must be replaced if the oil has been contaminated or the air conditioning refrigerant system has been open to atmosphere for more than four hours. Damage to the system will result if the desiccant is not replaced.*

Caution: *All 2014 models covered by this manual use environmentally friendly R-134a. 2015 and later models use either R-134a or R-1234yf; these refrigerants are not compatible with each other (nor are their appropriate refrigerant oils) and must never be mixed or the components will be damaged.*

Caution: *When replacing entire components, additional refrigerant oil should be added equal to the amount that is removed with the component being replaced. Be sure to read the can before adding any oil to the system, to make sure it is compatible with either R-134a or R-1234yf, as applicable.*

1   The following maintenance checks should be performed on a regular basis to ensure that the air conditioning continues to operate at peak efficiency.

a) *Inspect the condition of the compressor drivebelt. If it is worn or deteriorated, replace it (see Chapter 1).*
b) *Check the drivebelt tension (see Chapter 1).*
c) *Inspect the system hoses. Look for cracks, bubbles, hardening and deterioration. Inspect the hoses and all fittings for oil bubbles or seepage. If there is any*

3.1 The evaporator drain hose is located on the passenger's side of the firewall

3.9 Insert a thermometer in the center vent, turn on the air conditioning system and wait for it to cool down; depending on the humidity, the output air should be 35 to 40 degrees cooler than the ambient air temperature

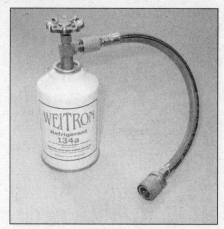

3.11 R-134a automotive air conditioning charging kit

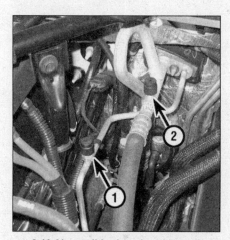

3.13 Air conditioning charging port locations

1   High-side charging port
2   Low-side charging port

evidence of wear, damage or leakage, replace the hose(s).

d) *Inspect the condenser fins for leaves, bugs and any other foreign material that may have embedded itself in the fins. Use a fin comb or compressed air to remove debris from the condenser.*

e) *Make sure the system has the correct refrigerant charge.*

f) *If you hear water sloshing around in the dash area or have water dripping on the carpet, check the evaporator housing drain tube (see illustration) and insert a piece of wire into the opening to check for blockage.*

2   It's a good idea to operate the system for about ten minutes at least once a month. This is particularly important during the winter months because long term non-use can cause hardening, and subsequent failure, of the seals. Note that using the Defrost function operates the compressor.

3   If the air conditioning system is not working properly, proceed to Step 6 and perform the general checks outlined below.

4   Because of the complexity of the air conditioning system and the special equipment necessary to service it, in-depth troubleshooting and repairs beyond checking the refrigerant charge and the compressor clutch operation are not included in this manual. However, simple checks and component replacement procedures are provided in this chapter. For more complete information on the air conditioning system, refer to the Haynes Automotive Heating and Air Conditioning Manual.

5   The most common cause of poor cooling is simply a low system refrigerant charge. If a noticeable drop in system cooling ability occurs, one of the following quick checks will help you determine if the refrigerant level is low.

Checking the refrigerant charge

6   Warm the engine up to normal operating temperature.

7   Place the air conditioning temperature selector at the coldest setting and put the blower at the highest setting.

8   After the system reaches operating temperature, feel the larger pipe exiting the evaporator at the firewall. The outlet pipe should be cold (the tubing that leads back to the compressor). If the evaporator outlet pipe is warm, the system probably needs a charge.

9   Insert a thermometer in the center air distribution duct (see illustration) while operating the air conditioning system at its maximum setting - the temperature of the output air should be 35 to 40 degrees F below the ambient air temperature (down to approximately 40 degrees F). If the ambient (outside) air temperature is very high, say 110 degrees F, the duct air temperature may be as high as 60 degrees F, but generally the air conditioning is 35 to 40 degrees F cooler than the ambient air.

10   Further inspection or testing of the system requires special tools and techniques and is beyond the scope of the home mechanic.

Adding refrigerant

Caution: *Make sure any refrigerant, refrigerant oil or replacement component you purchase is designated as compatible with the type of system being serviced.*

Note: *At the time of this manual's release, R-1234yf refrigerant charging kits were not available for purchase unless you are an EPA certified HVAC technician.*

11   Purchase an automotive air conditioning charging kit at an auto parts store (see illustration). A charging kit includes a can of refrigerant, a tap valve and a short section of hose that can be attached between the tap valve and the system low side service valve.

Caution: *Never add more than one can of refrigerant to the system. If more refrigerant than that is required, the system should be evacuated and leak tested.*

12   Back off the valve handle on the charging kit and screw the kit onto the refrigerant can, making sure first that the O-ring or rub-

ber seal inside the threaded portion of the kit is in place.

13   Remove the dust cap from the low-side charging port and attach the hose's quick-connect fitting to the port (see illustration). The fittings on the charging kit are designed to fit only on the low side of the system.

Warning: *DO NOT hook the charging kit hose to the system high side!*

Warning: *Wear protective eyewear when dealing with pressurized refrigerant cans.*

14   Warm up the engine and turn On the air conditioning. Keep the charging kit hose away from the fan and other moving parts.

Note: *The charging process requires the compressor to be running. If the clutch cycles off, you can put the air conditioning switch on High and leave the car doors open to keep the clutch on and compressor working. The compressor can be kept on during the charging by removing the connector from the pressure switch and bridging it with a paper clip or jumper wire during the procedure.*

15   Turn the valve handle on the kit until the stem pierces the can, then back the handle

4.4 Detach the expansion tank and radiator hoses from the thermostat housing cover

4.5 Thermostat bolt locations - 4.3L V6, 5.3L and 6.2L V8 models

out to release the refrigerant. You should be able to hear the rush of gas. Keep the can upright at all times, but shake it occasionally. Allow stabilization time between each addition.

Note: *The charging process will go faster if you wrap the can with a hot-water-soaked rag to keep the can from freezing up.*

16   If you have an accurate thermometer, you can place it in the center air conditioning duct inside the vehicle and keep track of the output air temperature. A charged system that is working properly should cool down to approximately 40 degrees F. If the ambient (outside) air temperature is very high, say 110 degrees F, the duct air temperature may be as high as 60 degrees F, but generally the air conditioning is 35 to 40 degrees F cooler than the ambient air.

17   When the can is empty, turn the valve handle to the closed position and release the connection from the low-side port. Reinstall the dust cap.

18   Remove the charging kit from the can and store the kit for future use with the piercing valve in the UP position, to prevent inadvertently piercing the can on the next use.

Heating systems

19   If the carpet under the heater core is damp, or if antifreeze vapor or steam is coming through the vents, the heater core is leaking. Remove it (see Section 12) and install a new unit (most radiator shops will not repair a leaking heater core).

20   If the air coming out of the heater vents isn't hot, the problem could stem from any of the following causes:

a) *The thermostat is stuck open, preventing the engine coolant from warming up enough to carry heat to the heater core. Replace the thermostat (see Section 4).*

b) *There is a blockage in the system, preventing the flow of coolant through the heater core. Feel both heater hoses at the firewall. They should be hot. If one of them is cold, there is an obstruction in*

one of the hoses or in the heater core, or the heater control valve is shut. Detach the hoses and back flush the heater core with a water hose. If the heater core is clear but circulation is impeded, remove the two hoses and flush them out with a water hose.

c) *If flushing fails to remove the blockage from the heater core, the core must be replaced (see Section 12).*

Eliminating air conditioning odors

21   Unpleasant odors that often develop in air conditioning systems are caused by the growth of a fungus, usually on the surface of the evaporator core. The warm, humid environment there is a perfect breeding ground for mildew to develop.

22   The evaporator core on most vehicles is difficult to access, and factory dealerships have a lengthy, expensive process for eliminating the fungus by opening up the evaporator case and using a powerful disinfectant and rinse on the core until the fungus is gone. You can service your own system at home, but it takes something much stronger than basic household germ-killers or deodorizers.

23   Aerosol disinfectants for automotive air conditioning systems are available in most auto parts stores, but remember when shopping for them that the most effective treatments are also the most expensive. The basic procedure for using these sprays is to start by running the system in the RECIRC mode for ten minutes with the blower on its highest speed. Use the highest heat mode to dry out the system and keep the compressor from engaging by disconnecting the wiring connector at the compressor.

24   The disinfectant can usually comes with a long spray hose. Insert the nozzle into an intake port inside the cabin, and spray according to the manufacturer's recommendations. Try to cover the whole surface of the evaporator core, by aiming the spray up, down and sideways. Follow the manufacturer's recom-

mendations for the length of spray and waiting time between applications.

Note: *Remove the cabin air filter (see Chapter 1) and insert the nozzle of the disinfectant can into the housing.*

25   Once the evaporator has been cleaned, the best way to prevent the mildew from coming back again is to make sure your evaporator housing drain tube is clear.

Automatic heating and air conditioning systems

26   Some vehicles are equipped with an optional automatic climate control system. This system has its own computer that receives inputs from various sensors in the heating and air conditioning system. This computer, like the PCM, has self-diagnostic capabilities to help pinpoint problems or faults within the system. Vehicles equipped with automatic heating and air conditioning systems are very complex and considered beyond the scope of the home mechanic. Vehicles equipped with automatic heating and air conditioning systems should be taken to dealer service department or other qualified facility for repair.

4   Thermostat - replacement

Warning: *Wait until the engine is completely cool before beginning this procedure.*

1   Disconnect the cable from the negative terminal of the battery (see Chapter 5).

2   Drain the cooling system (see Chapter 1).

4.3L V6, 5.3L and 6.2L V8 models

Note: *The thermostat and thermostat housing are replaced as a unit on these models.*

3   Remove the air intake duct and resonator assembly (see Chapter 4).

4   Squeeze the hose clamps and slide them up the hoses, then detach the radiator hose and the expansion tank hose from the thermostat housing cover. If the hose sticks, grasp it near the end with a pair of adjustable pliers and twist it to break the seal, then pull it off. If the hose is old or deteriorated, cut it off and install a new one.

5   Remove the bolts and detach the thermostat housing/thermostat assembly (see illustration). If the housing is stuck, tap it with a soft-face hammer to jar it loose. Be prepared for some coolant to spill as the gasket seal is broken.

6   Clean the mating surfaces of the coolant manifold and thermostat housing cover.

7   Install a new O-ring seal to the thermostat housing (see illustration).

8   Install the thermostat/housing to the coolant manifold and install the bolts, tightening them to the torque listed in this Chapter's Specifications.

9   Reconnect the hoses to the thermostat housing.

4.7 Replace the thermostat housing O-ring with a new one

4.13 Thermostat housing cover bolts - 6.0L V8 engines

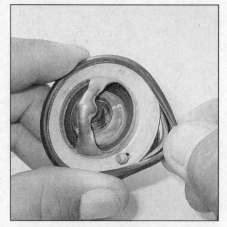

4.16 Install a new rubber seal around the thermostat

10   Refill the cooling system (see Chapter 1).

6.0L V8 models

11   Remove the air intake duct and resonator assembly (see Chapter 4).
12   Follow the lower radiator hose to the engine, then disconnect it. If the outer surface of the thermostat housing cover that mates with the hose is deteriorated (corroded, pitted, etc.) it may be damaged further by hose removal. If it is, the thermostat housing cover will have to be replaced.
13   Remove the thermostat housing cover from the engine (see illustration).
14   Note how it's installed (which end is facing out), then remove the thermostat.
15   Clean the sealing surfaces on the water pump housing and the thermostat housing cover.
16   Install a new rubber O-ring around the thermostat (see illustration). Install the thermostat into the coolant manifold, spring-end first.
17   Place the thermostat housing onto the coolant manifold and install the bolts. Tighten the bolts to the torque listed in this Chapter's Specifications.
18   The remainder of installation is the reverse of the removal procedure.
19   Refill the cooling system (see Chapter 1).

---

5   Engine cooling fans and clutch - replacement

Warning: *Wait until the engine is completely cool before beginning this procedure.*
Warning: *To avoid possible injury or damage, DO NOT operate the engine with a damaged fan. Do not attempt to repair fan blades - replace a damaged fan with a new one.*
1   Disconnect the cable from the negative terminal of the battery (see Chapter 5).
2   Remove the plastic cover over the radiator support (see Chapter 11, Section 10).

6.0L V8 models

3   Partially drain the cooling system (see Chapter 1).
4   Remove the air filter housing assembly and intake duct (see Chapter 4).
5   Detach any hoses attached to the upper fan shroud and position them aside; the expansion tank hose will have to be detached from the radiator. Remove the upper fan shroud (see illustration). It's only necessary to remove the upper portion for many service operations.
6   Use a large wrench to remove the fan clutch retaining nut and detach the fan and clutch assembly from the engine. The drivebelt should keep the pulley from turning as the fan nut is loosened. If the water pump pulley slips on the belt it will be necessary to remove the drivebelt(s) (see Chapter 1) and use a strap wrench to hold the pulley (see illustration).
Note: *The clutch hub nut has regular, right-hand threads (turn the nut counterclockwise to loosen).*
7   Remove the bolts securing the fan to the fan clutch (see illustration).
8   Installation is the reverse of removal. Be sure to tighten all fasteners to the torques listed in this Chapter's Specifications.
9   Refill the cooling system (see Chapter 1).

5.5 Detach the retaining clips (A) and, if equipped, the bolts (B) on each side of the shroud

5.6 Loosening the fan clutch hub nut while holding the pulley with a strap wrench

5.7 Fan retaining bolts

5.13 Disconnect the transmission cooler lines (1) then remove the fan shroud right side mounting bolt (2)

5.14 Disconnect the engine oil cooler lines (1) then remove the fan shroud left side mounting bolt (2)

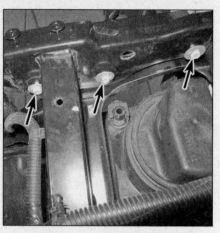

6.10a Remove the mounting bolts from under the radiator support, on each side . . .

6.10b . . . then remove the center bolt (1) and support rod bolts (2) and lift the radiator support up and off

4.3L V6 and 5.3L/6.2L V8 models

Warning: *Wait until the engine is completely cool before beginning this procedure.*

10   Drain the cooling system (see Chapter 1).

11   Remove the intake air duct and resonator assembly (see Chapter 4).

12   Disconnect the upper radiator hose and expansion tank hose.

13   Disconnect the transmission cooler lines, then remove the fan shroud mounting bolt from the right side of the radiator (see illustration).

14   Disconnect the engine oil cooler lines, then remove the fan shroud mounting bolt from the left side of the radiator (see illustration).

15   Disconnect the fan motor electrical connectors. Remove any hoses or wiring harnesses that may be attached to the fan shroud.

16   Remove the cooling fan/shroud assembly by lifting it up and out of the engine compartment.

17   Remove the mounting bolts and separate the cooling fan motor(s) from the shroud.

Caution: *Before removing the fans from the shroud, be sure to mark them. The left and right side fans are different, but it's possible to*

install them on the wrong side.

18   Put tape over any openings on good motors when either one of them is removed to protect them from debris.

19   After thoroughly cleaning all debris from the shroud, remove the protective tape from the motor(s).

20   Install the fan motor mounting bolts and tighten them securely.

21   Turn the fan blade and confirm that it is correctly installed.

22   The remainder of installation is the reverse of the removal procedure. Tighten all fasteners securely.

23   Refill the cooling system and check the engine oil and transmission fluid levels (see Chapter 1).

---

6   Radiator and coolant expansion tank - removal and installation

Warning: *Wait until the engine is completely cool before beginning this procedure.*

Radiator

Note: *The vehicles covered by this manual use spring type radiator hose clamps. If you decide to reuse them, make sure that the hose*

is installed on a connection that is clean and dry. Don't try to reuse these clamps on aftermarket hoses. Replace them with conventional worm drive type clamps.

1   Disconnect the cable from the negative terminal of the battery (see Chapter 5).

2   Drain the cooling system (see Chapter 1).

3   Remove the plastic cover over radiator support (see Chapter 11, Section 10).

4   Remove the cooling fan shroud (see Section 5).

5   Disconnect the surge tank hose at the radiator and surge tank.

6   Disconnect and remove the upper radiator hose.

7   Remove the plastic cover over radiator support (see Chapter 11, Section 10).

4.3L V6, 5.3L and 6.2L V8 models

8   Remove the headlight housings (see Chapter 12).

9   Remove the condenser upper mounting bolts and bracket retaining nut (see Section 14) from the radiator.

10   Remove the upper radiator support (see illustrations).

11   Unclip and detach the remove the radiator air baffle (see illustration).

12   Remove the radiator mounting bolts.

13   Depress the condenser retaining tabs and carefully lift the condenser off of the radiator, without disconnecting the condenser lines.

14   Tilt the radiator away from the condenser, then unclip the lower baffle from the bottom of the radiator and remove the radiator out of the engine compartment.

6.0L V8 models

15   Disconnect the transmission cooler lines and engine oil cooler lines from the radiator (see illustrations 5.13 and 5.14), then unclip the lower section of the fan shroud. Lift the shroud around the fan and out of the engine compartment.

16   Remove the radiator mounting bolts and

6.11 Unclip each side of the air baffle then lift the baffle off of the radiator

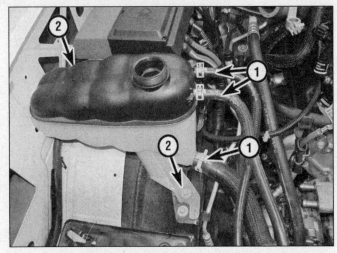

6.23 Expansion tank mounting details

1   *Expansion tank coolant hoses*
2   *Expansion tank fasteners*

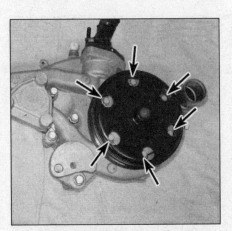

7.4 Water pump mounting bolt locations - coolant manifold removed for clarity

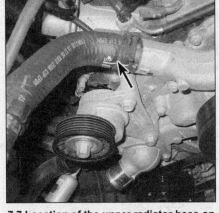

7.7 Location of the upper radiator hose on the water pump

7.8 Disconnect the expansion tank hose (A) and the heater hose (B)

lift the radiator out of the engine compartment.

All models

17   Prior to installation of the radiator, replace any damaged radiator hoses and hose clamps.
18   Radiator installation is the reverse of removal. Tighten the bolts to the torque listed in this Chapter's Specifications. When installing the radiator, make sure that the radiator seats properly in the lower saddles and that the upper brackets are secure. Install the cooler line retaining clips onto the quick connect fitting before installing the lines, then snap the cooler lines into place on the quick connect fittings. Be sure to reinstall the plastic collars on the quick connect fittings as they lock the retaining clip in place.
19   After installation, refill the cooling system (see Chapter 1), then check the engine oil and automatic transmission fluid levels.

Coolant expansion tank

20   Disconnect the cable from the negative

terminal of the battery (see Chapter 5).
21   Drain the cooling system as described in Chapter 1 until the expansion tank is empty.
22   Remove the air filter housing (see Chapter 4).
23   Detach the coolant hoses from the expansion tank. Unscrew the mounting fasteners, then remove the expansion tank (see illustration).
24   Prior to installation, make sure the tank is clean and free of debris which could be drawn into the radiator (wash it with soapy water and a brush if necessary, then rinse thoroughly).
25   Installation is the reverse of removal. Refill the cooling system (see Chapter 1) and check for leaks.

7   Water pump - replacement

Warning: *Wait until the engine is completely cool before beginning this procedure.*
1   Disconnect the cable from the negative terminal of the battery (see Chapter 5).
2   Drain the coolant (see Chapter 1).

Remove the air intake duct and resonator assembly (see Chapter 4).
3   Remove the drivebelt (see Chapter 1).

4.3L V6, 5.3L and 6.2L V8 engines

4   Center the water pump pulley holes over the water pump mounting bolts (see illustration), then remove the water pump mounting bolts.
5   Remove the water pump and gasket from the coolant manifold.

6.0L V8 engines

6   Remove the fan and fan clutch (see Section 5).
7   Remove the water pump inlet hose (see illustration).
8   Remove the water pump outlet hose at the thermostat (see Section 4) and the heater and expansion tank hoses (see illustration).
9   If necessary for access, detach the coolant air bleed hose from the engine.
10   If a new water pump is to be installed, remove the thermostat housing (see Section 4).

7.11 Water pump mounting bolts

8.7 Use pliers to squeeze the spring clamps open, then disconnect the hoses

8.8a Remove the bracket mounting bolt from the side of coolant manifold

8.8b Coolant manifold bolt locations

11   Unbolt the water pump (see illustration). It may be necessary to tap the pump with a soft-face hammer to break the gasket seal.

All models

12   Remove all traces of the old gasket seal from the mounting surface on the engine. Do the same on the water pump if the same pump is going to be re-installed.

13   Clean the mounting bolt threads and threaded holes on the mounting surface to remove corrosion and sealant, if necessary.

14   Compare the replacement pump with the old one to make sure that they're identical.

15   Place the gaskets and water pump into position. Use caution to ensure that the gasket doesn't slip out of position. Install the mounting bolts until they are all finger tight.

16   Tighten the bolts to the torque listed in this Chapter's Specifications.

17   The remainder of installation is the reverse of the removal procedure.

18   Refill the engine with coolant (see Chapter 1). Run the engine and check for leaks.

8   Coolant manifold (4.3L V6, 5.3L and 6.2L V8 models) - removal and installation

Warning: *Wait until the engine is completely cool before beginning this procedure.*

Removal

1   Disconnect the cable from the negative terminal of the battery (see Chapter 5).

2   Drain the coolant (see Chapter 1). Remove the air intake duct and resonator assembly (see Chapter 4).

3   Remove the drivebelt (see Chapter 1).

4   Disconnect the electrical connector to the coolant temperature sensor (see Chapter 6).

5   Remove the alternator and alternator

bracket (see Chapter 5).

6   Disconnect the expansion tank and radiator hoses from the thermostat housing (see illustration 4.4).

7   Disconnect the heater hoses from the coolant manifold (see illustration).

8   Remove the coolant manifold bolts (see illustrations), then remove manifold and gaskets. It may be necessary to tap the housing with a soft-face hammer to break the gasket's seal.

Note: *It is not necessary to remove the water pump from the coolant manifold to remove the coolant manifold.*

Installation

9   Remove all traces of the old gaskets from the mounting surface on the engine. Do the same on the coolant manifold.

10   Clean the mounting bolt threads and threaded holes on the mounting surface to remove corrosion and sealant, then apply

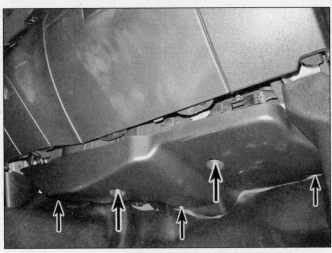

10.1 Lower trim panel screw locations

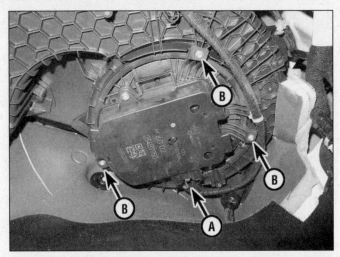

10.2 Blower motor electrical connector (A) and mounting screws (B)

10.11 Disengage the module retainer

10.12 Locate the electrical connector, then disconnect the connector from the control module

thread locking sealant to the bolt threads.

11   Place the gaskets and coolant manifold into position. Use caution to ensure that the gaskets don't slip out of position. Install the mounting bolts until they are all finger-tight.

12   Tighten the bolts to the torque listed in this Chapter's Specifications.

13   The remainder of installation is the reverse of the removal procedure.

14   Refill the engine with coolant (see Chapter 1). Run the engine and check for leaks.

9   Coolant temperature gauge sending unit - check and replacement

1   The coolant temperature indicator system consists of a warning light or a temperature gauge on the dash and a coolant temperature sending unit mounted on the engine. On the models covered by this manual, the Engine Coolant Temperature (ECT) sensor is an information sensor for the Powertrain Control Module (PCM) and also functions as

the coolant temperature sending unit for the temperature gauge. Information on the ECT sensor can be found in Chapter 6.

10   Blower motor and control module - removal and installation

Warning: *These models have airbags. Always disable the airbag system before working in the vicinity of any airbag system component to avoid the possibility of accidental deployment of the airbag, which could cause personal injury (see Chapter 12).*

Note: *These models are equipped with a control module that controls activation and fan blower speeds. The control module is mounted on the HVAC housing near the blower fan. Some models are equipped with rear auxiliary heating and air conditioning systems that have the control module mounted on the HVAC housing in the rear of the vehicle. Fuses for this system can be checked, but due to the*

use of an integrated electronic control module and Body Control Module that can only be tested with specialized equipment, it will be necessary to take these vehicles to a dealer service department or other qualified repair shop to have the blower motor circuit checked in the event of a problem.

Blower motor

Front blower motor (all models)

1   Disconnect the cable from the negative terminal of the battery (see Chapter 5). Working under the instrument panel on the passenger's side, remove the trim panel screws and lower the panel (see illustration).

2   Disconnect the electrical connector from the blower motor (see illustration).

3   Remove the mounting screws and lower the motor from the housing.

4   Installation is the reverse of removal.

Rear auxiliary blower motor

5   Remove the right-side quarter trim panels from the right rear of the vehicle for access to the rear HVAC unit (see Chapter 11).

6   Disconnect the electrical connector from the blower motor.

7   Remove the retaining screws and pull the blower motor from the case.

8   Installation is the reverse of removal.

Control module

Front blower motor control module (all models)

9   Disconnect the cable from the negative terminal of the battery (see Chapter 5).

10   Working under the instrument panel on the passenger's side, remove the trim panel screws and lower the panel (see illustration 10.1).

11   Using a screwdriver or pick, unclip the module retainer from the cover (see illustration).

12   Disconnect the control module harness connector (see illustration).

10.13 Rotate the control module to the side, then remove the module

11.3 Radio, heater and air conditioning control assembly mounting bolts (standard dash shown, premium dash similar)

11.4 Disconnect the electrical connectors to the radio/heater, air conditioning controller

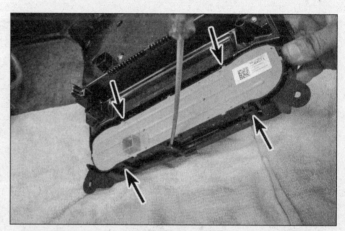

11.5 Disengage the controller retaining clips and separate the controller from the instrument panel

13   Maneuver the control module out from the blower housing (see illustration).

14   Installation is the reverse of removal.

Rear auxiliary blower motor module

15   Remove the right rear quarter trim panel (see Chapter 11).

16   Disconnect the control module harness connector.

17   Remove the control module mounting screws and separate the module from the blower housing.

18   Installation is the reverse of removal.

11   Heater and air conditioning control assembly - removal and installation

Warning: *These models have airbags. Always disable the airbag system before working in the vicinity of any airbag system component to avoid the possibility of accidental deployment of the airbag, which could cause personal injury (see Chapter 12).*

1   Disconnect the cable from the negative terminal of the battery (see Chapter 5).

Front control unit

2   Remove the instrument panel center trim panel to access the heater/air conditioning control mounting bolts (see Chapter 11).

3   Remove the mounting bolts from the heater and air conditioning control assembly (see illustration).

4   Pull the unit from the dash. It can be pulled out just far enough to allow disconnection of the electrical connectors (see illustration). Use a small screwdriver to release the clips.

5   Using a small screwdriver, unclip the heater and air conditioning controller from the radio controller or instrument panel center trim (see illustration).

6   Installation is the reverse of removal.

Rear auxiliary control unit

7   Remove the screws from the rear of the center console (see Chapter 11), then pull the rear panel back from the console. Disconnect

the electrical connectors and remove the control mounting screws.

8   Pry out the two side trim panels from the rear roof console, then remove the screws from the rear roof console and lower the console down. Disconnect the electrical connectors and remove the control mounting screws.

9   Installation is the reverse of removal.

12   Heater core - removal and installation

Warning: *These models have airbags. Always disable the airbag system before working in the vicinity of any airbag system component to avoid the possibility of accidental deployment of the airbag, which could cause personal injury (see Chapter 12).*

Warning: *The air conditioning system is under high pressure. DO NOT loosen any fittings or remove any components until after the system has been discharged. Air conditioning refrigerant must be properly discharged into an EPA-approved container at a dealership service*

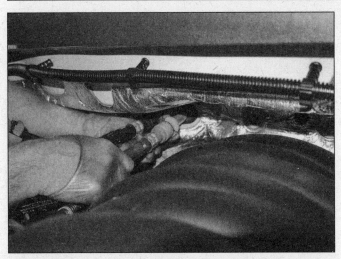

12.5 Disconnect the heater core hoses at the engine compartment firewall using a special offset disconnect tool. After the special disconnect tool is slid into the spring lock mechanism, pull the heater core hose back and off the heater core pipe

12.9 Support the heating/air conditioning unit with a block of wood to prevent it from falling once the mounting bolt/nuts are removed

12.10a Heater/air conditioning unit mounting bolt/nut locations - right side (passenger's side) of engine compartment

12.10b Heater/air conditioning unit mounting bolt/nut locations - center of engine compartment

department or an automotive air conditioning facility. Always wear eye protection when disconnecting air conditioning system fittings.
Warning: *Wait until the engine is completely cool before beginning this procedure.*

1   Have the air conditioning system discharged by a dealership service department or an automotive air conditioning facility (see the Warning above).

Front heater core

2   Disconnect the cable from the negative terminal of the battery (see Chapter 5).
3   Remove the battery and battery tray (see Chapter 5).
4   Drain the cooling system (see Chapter 1). Detach the air conditioning lines from the evaporator core fittings at the firewall (see illustration 17.2). Be sure to plug each refrigerant line to avoid contamination of the air conditioning system.
5   Disconnect the heater hoses from the

heater core pipes on the engine side of the firewall (see illustration). Plug the open fittings.
6   Remove the intake manifold (see Chapter 2A or 2B).
7   Remove the dash and dash carriage (see Chapter 11).
8   Disconnect the drain tube at the firewall (see illustration 3.1).
9   Support the heating/air conditioning unit with a block of wood inside the vehicle (see illustration).
10   Working in the engine compartment, remove the fasteners securing the heating/air conditioning unit to the firewall (see illustrations).
11   Working back inside the passenger compartment, remove the electrical connectors and any ground straps, then remove the heating/air conditioning unit from the vehicle.
12   Remove the temperature valve actuator screws (see illustration) and lift the actuator off of the case.

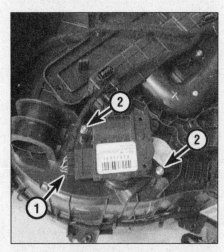

12.12 Temperature valve actuator details;

1   *Electrical connector*
2   *Mounting screws*

12.13a Locate the plastic stakes (rivets) around the perimeter of the cover . . .

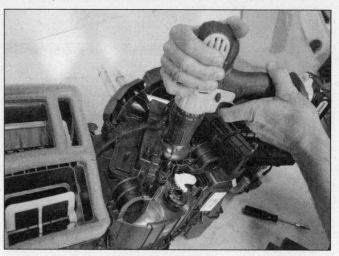

12.13b . . . then use a drill to cut the head of the stake off without drilling into the cover

12.14 Release the tabs and lift the control module off of the housing

12.15 The heater core cover is at the top of the heater/air conditioning unit

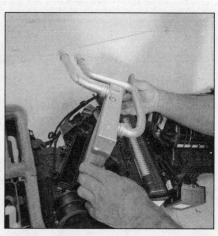

12.16 Remove the heater core from the housing

13 The heater core/evaporator core cover has melted plastic stakes where the mounting screws would normally be installed. To remove the melted stakes, use a drill bit and carefully cut the heads of the plastic stakes off (see illustrations).

14 Disconnect the control module harness connectors, then depress the tabs and remove the blower motor control module (see illustration).

15 Remove the heater core cover (see illustration).

16 Carefully lift the heater core out of the housing (see illustration).

17 Installation is the reverse of removal.

Note: *When reinstalling the heater core, make sure any original insulating/sealing materials are in place around the heater core pipes, heater core and heating/air conditioning unit.*

18 Refill the cooling system (see Chapter 1). Have the air conditioning system charged by the shop that discharged it.

19 Start the engine and check for proper operation and leaks.

Rear (auxiliary) heater core

20 Remove the right rear quarter trim panel (see Chapter 11).

21 Detach the air conditioning lines from the rear evaporator core fittings on the underside of the vehicle. Be sure to plug each refrigerant line to avoid contamination of the air conditioning system. Use special release tools to remove the quick-connect fittings.

22 Also working from the underside of the vehicle, clamp off the heater hoses leading to the rear heater core, then disconnect the hoses from the inlet and outlet fittings and plug the open fittings. To disconnect the hose fittings, squeeze the plastic retainer tabs, then pull off the hoses.

23 Remove the upper auxiliary air duct.

24 Remove the rear heating/air conditioning unit lower mounting nuts from under the vehicle.

25 Remove the electrical connectors and wiring harness retaining straps, then unscrew the rear heating/air conditioning unit mounting

upper screws and remove the housing from the vehicle. Follow the remaining steps to remove the heater core from the rear heating/air conditioning unit.

26 On long wheel base models, remove the heater core cover located on the bottom of the heater/air conditioning unit.

27 On short wheel base models, remove the blower/heater core case mounting screws and separate the two case halves.

28 Remove the heater core from the housing.

29 Installation is the reverse of removal.

Note: *When reinstalling the heater core, make sure any original insulating/sealing materials are in place around the heater core pipes, heater core and housing.*

30 Check the coolant level, adding coolant as necessary (see Chapter 1).

31 Start the engine and check for proper operation. Recheck the coolant level. Have the air conditioning system charged by the shop that discharged it.

13.8a Air conditioning compressor mounting details - V6 engine shown, others similar

1 *Compressor clutch electrical connector*
2 *Refrigerant line fitting nut*

13.8b Compressor pressure sensor electrical connector location

14.8 Push the tab forward, then lift the baffle out of the clip

13 Air conditioning compressor removal and installation

Removal

Warning: *The air conditioning system is under high pressure. DO NOT loosen any fittings or remove any components until after the system has been discharged. Air conditioning refrigerant must be properly discharged into an EPA-approved container at a dealership service department or an automotive air conditioning repair facility. Always wear eye protection when disconnecting air conditioning system fittings.*

Note: *The compressor is mounted on the lower right side (passenger side) of the engine and is driven by a separate drivebelt that can be accessed after the engine drivebelt is removed.*

Note: *The refrigerant desiccant (see Section 16) should be replaced whenever the compressor is replaced.*

1 Have the air conditioning system discharged by an automotive air conditioning technician (see Warning above).
2 Disconnect the cable from the negative terminal of the battery (see Chapter 5).
3 Raise the vehicle and support it securely on jackstands, then remove the splash shield (see Chapter 1, Section 8).
4 Remove the skid plate mounting bolts and plate, if equipped.
5 Remove the air intake duct and resonator assembly (see Chapter 4).
6 Remove the serpentine (accessory) drivebelt, and the air conditioning compressor drivebelt (see Chapter 1).
7 Disconnect the electrical connector(s) from the air conditioning compressor.
8 Clean the compressor thoroughly around the refrigerant line fittings. Disconnect the suction and discharge lines from the compressor (see illustrations). Plug the open fittings to prevent the entry of dirt and moisture, and discard the O-rings between the refrigerant lines and compressor.
9 Remove the compressor mounting bolt/nuts. Detach the compressor from the mounting bracket and remove the compressor from the engine compartment.

Installation

10 If a new compressor is being installed, follow the directions with the compressor regarding the measuring and adding of oil prior to installation.
11 Installation is the reverse of removal. When installing the line fitting bolt to the compressor, use new seals lubricated with clean refrigerant oil, and tighten the bolt securely.
12 Reconnect the cable to the negative terminal of the battery.
13 Have the system evacuated, recharged and leak tested by the shop that discharged it.

Oil balancing

14 With the old compressor removed, remove the compressor drain plug and allow the oil to drain into a graduated container. Tilt the compressor over to allow both ports to drain into the same container.
Note: *Turn the compressor shaft to make sure all of the oil drains out.*
15 Once all the oil is drained from the compressor, record the amount that you measured and add the total to any amount measured when the system was evacuated in Step 1.
16 A new compressor has 1.4 oz (40 ml) of oil in it. If the total amount of oil drained is less than 1.4 oz (40 ml) no balancing is required. Install the compressor and have the system evacuated, recharged and leak tested by the shop that discharged it.
17 If the total amount of oil drained is more than 1.4 oz (40 ml), oil will have to be added.
18 To balance the system, subtract 1.4 oz (40 ml) from the amount of drained oil and add the difference to the new compressor.

Install the compressor and have the system evacuated, recharged and leak tested by the shop that discharged it.

14 Air conditioning condenser - removal and installation

Warning: *The air conditioning system is under high pressure. DO NOT loosen any fittings or remove any components until after the system has been discharged. Air conditioning refrigerant must be properly discharged into an EPA-approved container at a dealership service department or an automotive air conditioning repair facility. Always wear eye protection when disconnecting air conditioning system fittings.*

Note: *The refrigerant desiccant should be replaced if the condenser was damaged, causing the system to be open for some time (see Section 16).*

1 Have the air conditioning system discharged by an automotive air conditioning technician (see Warning above).
2 Remove the plastic cover over radiator support (see Chapter 11, Section 10).
3 Remove the headlight housings (see Chapter 12).
4 Remove the condenser upper mounting bolts and bracket retaining nut (see Section 14) from the radiator.
5 (See illustration) Remove the radiator support (see illustrations 6.10a and 6.10b).
6 Unclip, then remove the radiator air baffle (see illustration 6.11).
7 Remove the condenser bracket mounting nut and pull the bracket off of the stud.
8 Unclip the left and right side air baffles from the condenser (see illustration).
9 Disconnect the air conditioning lines to the condenser. Plug the open fittings to prevent the entry of dirt and moisture, and discard the O-rings between the refrigerant lines and condenser.

15.1 The air conditioning pressure sensor is located on the refrigerant line attached to the right-side frame rail, near the air conditioning compressor

16.4 Typical air conditioning refrigerant desiccant cap

17.2 The front Thermostatic Expansion Valve is located on the firewall

10   Depress the condenser retaining tabs and carefully lift the condenser off of the radiator.

11   If a new condenser is being installed, pour two ounces of R-134a or R-1234yf-compatible refrigerant oil into it prior to installation.

Caution: *The oil used must be labeled as compatible with R-134a or R-1234yf refrigerant systems.*

12   Installation is the reverse of removal. When installing the lines to the condenser, use new seals lubricated with clean refrigerant oil, and tighten the bolt securely.

13   Have the system evacuated, recharged and leak tested by the shop that discharged it.

15 Air conditioning pressure sensor - removal and installation

Warning: *The air conditioning system is under high pressure. Do not loosen any hose fittings or remove any components until the system has been discharged. Air conditioning refrigerant should be properly discharged into an EPA-approved recovery/recycling unit by a dealer service department or an automotive air conditioning repair facility. Always wear eye protection when disconnecting air conditioning system fittings.*

1   Working near the air conditioning compressor, unplug the electrical connector from the pressure sensor (see illustration).

2   Remove the sensor from the air conditioning line fitting. Be sure to hold the fitting using an open-end wrench to prevent deforming the pressure line.

3   Install the new pressure sensor, then tighten it securely.

4   Reconnect the electrical connector.

16 Air conditioning refrigerant desiccant - replacement

Warning: *The air conditioning system is under high pressure. DO NOT loosen any fittings or remove any components until after the system has been discharged. Air conditioning refrigerant must be properly discharged into an EPA-approved container at a dealer service department or an automotive air conditioning repair facility. Always wear eye protection when servicing the air conditioning system.*

Note: *These vehicles are not equipped with a traditional receiver-drier. Instead, a desiccant cartridge is built into the left side of the condenser. It should be replaced whenever the compressor is replaced or whenever a component has been replaced because of a leak in the system.*

1   Have the air conditioning system discharged by a dealer service department or by an automotive air conditioning shop before proceeding (see Warning above).

2   Remove the condenser (see Section 14).

3   Remove the splash guard between the bumper cover and the subframe.

4   Using a large Allen wrench or hex bit, unscrew the cap from the desiccant tube on the left side of the condenser (see illustration).

5   Pull the desiccant cartridge from the tube.

6   Installation is the reverse of removal. Be sure to use a new O-ring on the cap.

7   Have the system evacuated, recharged and leak tested by the shop that discharged it.

17 Air conditioning thermostatic expansion valve (TXV) - general information

Warning: *The air conditioning system is under high pressure. DO NOT loosen any hose fittings or remove any components until the system has been discharged. Air conditioning refrigerant must be properly discharged into an EPA-approved recovery/recycling unit by a dealer service department or an automotive air conditioning repair facility. Always wear eye protection when disconnecting air conditioning system fittings.*

1   There are several ways that air conditioning systems convert the high-pressure liquid refrigerant from the compressor to lower-pressure vapor. The conversion takes place at the air conditioning evaporator. The evaporator is chilled as the refrigerant passes through, cooling the airflow through the evaporator for delivery to the vents. The conversion is usually accomplished by a sudden change in the tubing size. Many vehicles have a removable controlled orifice in one of the refrigerant lines at the firewall.

2   The models covered by this manual use a Thermostatic Expansion Valve (TXV) that accomplishes the same thing as a controlled orifice (see illustration) for the front and auxiliary air conditioning systems. To remove the TXV, have the air conditioning system discharged by a licensed air conditioning technician, then disconnect the refrigerant lines from the TXV at the firewall or rear air conditioning unit. Remove the two bolts securing the valve, then remove the valve and replace the four O-rings. Installation is the reverse of removal.

Notes

Notes

Chapter 4
Fuel and exhaust systems

Contents

Specifications

Fuel pressure

Ignition key turned to ON, engine OFF (on use scan tool to command pump ON)	50 to 60 psi
6.0L models	50 to 60 psi
Non-6.0L models	
Fuel pump running	46 to 84 psi
Fuel pump off (after running)	68 to 79 psi
Vehicle at cruising speed, during acceleration or hard cornering maneuvers	
6.0L models	Fuel pressure should not drop off (decrease dramatically) below 50 psi
Non-6.0L models	Fuel pressure should not drop off (decrease dramatically) below 46 psi
Fuel pressure leakdown	
One minute after turning key to OFF (all models)	No more than 5 psi drop
Five minutes after turning key to OFF	
Non-6.0L models	No more than 2 psi drop
6.0L models	Not available
Fuel injector coil resistance	
Between each injector terminal and injector body	Infinite (no resistance)
Between injector terminals	
6.0L models	11 to 14 ohms (approximate)
Non-6.0L models	0.95 to 1.17 ohms

Torque specifications

Ft-lbs (unless otherwise indicated)

Note: *One foot-pound (ft-lb) of torque is equivalent to 12 inch-pounds (in-lbs) of torque. Torque values below approximately 15 ft-lbs are expressed in inch-pounds, since most foot-pound torque wrenches are not accurate at these smaller values.*

Fuel pressure sensor
    Fuel line .... 132 in-lbs
    Fuel rail 18
High-pressure fuel feed pipe (to high-pressure fuel pump and fuel rails) 21
High-pressure fuel pump mounting bolts... 18
Throttle body mounting fasteners... 89 in-lbs
Fuel tank strap bolts 30
Fuel rail fasteners
    Non-6.0L models 18
    6.0L models... 89 in-lbs

1 General information and precautions

Fuel system warnings

1   Gasoline is extremely flammable and repairing fuel system components can be dangerous. Consider your automotive repair knowledge and experience before attempting repairs, which may be better suited for a professional mechanic.

a) *Don't smoke or allow open flames or bare light bulbs near the work area*
b) *Don't work in a garage with a gas-type appliance (water heater, clothes dryer)*
c *Use fuel-resistant gloves. If any fuel spills on your skin, wash it off immediately with soap and water*
d) *Clean up spills immediately*
e) *Do not store fuel-soaked rags where they could ignite*
f) *Prior to disconnecting any fuel line, you must relieve the fuel pressure (see Section 3)*
g *Wear safety glasses*
h) *Have a proper fire extinguisher on hand*

Fuel system

2   This chapter covers the removal and installation procedures for the important parts of the air intake, fuel and exhaust systems. Because emission control systems are integral parts of the engine management system, there are many cross-references to Chapter 6. (Information on the engine management system, information sensors and output actuators is in that chapter.)
3   The air intake system consists of the air filter housing, the air intake duct, the throttle body, and the intake manifold. Incoming air passes through the air filter element, the Mass Air Flow (MAF) sensor, the air intake duct, the throttle body, the intake manifold plenum and the intake manifold runners before being mixed with fuel sprayed into the intake ports by the fuel injectors.

4   On 6.0L V8 models, the Sequential Fuel Injection (SFI) system consists of the fuel tank, an electric fuel pump/fuel level sending unit module mounted inside the tank, the fuel pressure regulator (integral with the fuel pump module), a fuel pump flow control module, the fuel rail, the fuel injectors, and the metal and flexible fuel lines that connect the various components of the SFI system.
5   On all models except those equipped with the 6.0L V8, the Direct Injection (DI) system consists of the fuel tank, an electric fuel pump/fuel level sending unit module mounted inside the tank, the fuel pressure regulator (integral with the fuel pump module), a fuel pump flow control module, a high pressure fuel pump, the fuel rail, the fuel injectors, and the metal and flexible fuel lines that connect the various components of the DI system.
6   Fuel is circulated from the fuel pump to the fuel rail through fuel lines running along the underside of the vehicle. Various sections of the fuel line are either rigid metal or nylon, or flexible fuel hose. The various sections of the fuel hose are connected either by quick-connect fittings or threaded metal fittings.

Exhaust system

7   The exhaust system consists of the exhaust manifold, catalytic converter, muffler, tailpipe and all connecting pipes, flanges and clamps. The catalytic converter is an emission control device added to the exhaust system to reduce pollutants.

2 Troubleshooting

Fuel pump

1   The fuel pump is located inside the fuel tank. Sit inside the vehicle with the windows closed, turn the ignition key to ON (not START) and listen for the sound of the fuel pump as it's briefly activated. You will only hear the sound for a second or two, but that

sound tells you that the pump is working. Alternatively, have an assistant listen at the fuel filler cap.
2   If the pump does not come on, check the fuel pump control module fuses and ignition main relay (fuel pump relay) (see illustration). If the fuse and relay are okay, check the wiring back to the fuel pump. If the fuse, relay and wiring are okay, the fuel pump is probably defective. If the pump runs continuously with the ignition key in the ON position, the Powertrain Control Module (PCM) is probably defective. Have the PCM checked by a professional mechanic.
Note: *The fuel pump control module is also referred to as the fuel pump driver control module or fuel pump flow control module.*

Fuel injection system

Note: *The following procedure is based on the assumption that the fuel pump is working and the fuel pressure is adequate (see).*
3   Check all electrical connectors that are related to the system. Check the ground wire connections for tightness.
4   Verify that the battery is fully charged (see Chapter 1, Section 11).
5   Inspect the air filter element (see Chapter 1).
6   Check all fuses related to the fuel system (see Chapter 12).
7   Check the air induction system between the throttle body and the intake manifold for air leaks. Also inspect the condition of all vacuum hoses connected to the intake manifold and to the throttle body.
8   Remove the air intake duct from the throttle body and look for dirt, carbon, varnish, or other residue in the throttle body, particularly around the throttle plate. If it's dirty, clean it with carb cleaner, a toothbrush and a clean shop towel.
9   With the engine running, place an automotive stethoscope against each injector, one at a time, and listen for a clicking sound that indicates operation (see illustration).
Warning: *Stay clear of the drivebelt and any rotating or hot components.*

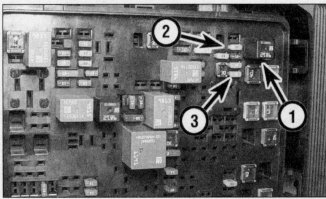

2.2 Fuel system-related underhood fuse/relay box details (2015 1500 model shown. Be sure to check the underside of the fusebox cover on your vehicle for fuse/relay identification)

1   *Ignition main relay (supplies power to the fuel pump control module)*
2   *Fuel pump control module fuse (receives power from the ignition main relay when the key is in the RUN position)*
3   *Fuel pump control module fuse (always hot)*

2.9 An automotive stethoscope is used to listen to the fuel injectors in operation

4.4 Disconnect the fuel feed hose from the fuel feed pipe, and, using the proper fittings, connect a fuel pressure gauge (V6 models shown, V8 models similar)

10   If you can hear the injectors operating, but the engine is misfiring, the electrical circuits are functioning correctly, but the injectors might be dirty or clogged. Try a commercial injector cleaning product (available at auto parts stores). If cleaning the injectors doesn't help, replace the injector(s).
11   If an injector is not operating (it makes no sound), disconnect the injector electrical connector and measure the resistance across the injector terminals with an ohmmeter. Compare this measurement to the other injectors. If the resistance of the non-operational injector is quite different from the other injectors, replace it.
12   If the injector is not operating, but the resistance reading is within the range of resistance of the other injectors, the PCM or the circuit between the PCM and the injector might be faulty.

---

3   Fuel pressure relief procedure

Warning: *Gasoline is extremely flammable, so take extra precautions when you work on any part of the fuel system. Don't smoke or allow open flames or bare light bulbs near the work area, and don't work in a garage where a gas-type appliance (such as a water heater or clothes dryer) is present. Since gasoline is carcinogenic, wear fuel-resistant gloves when there's a possibility of being exposed to fuel, and, if you spill any fuel on your skin, rinse it off immediately with soap and water. Mop up any spills immediately and do not store fuel-soaked rags where they could ignite. The fuel system is under constant pressure, so, if any fuel lines are to be disconnected, the fuel pressure in the system must be relieved first. When you perform any kind of work on the fuel system, wear safety glasses and have a Class B type fire extinguisher on hand.*
Caution: *After the fuel pressure has been relieved, it's a good idea to lay a shop towel over any fuel connection to be disassembled,*

to absorb the residual fuel that may leak out when servicing the fuel system.
1   Unscrew the fuel filler cap to relieve any built-up vapor pressure in the fuel tank.

All except 6.0L V8 engines

Warning: *The fuel delivery system on these models is made up of a low-pressure system (from the fuel pump in the tank to the high-pressure fuel pump on the engine) and a high-pressure system (high-pressure fuel pump, fuel rail and injectors). Once the pressure on the low-pressure side of the system has been relieved, wait at least two hours before loosening any fuel line fittings in the high-pressure portion of the system.*
2   Remove the fuel pump control module fuses from the underhood electrical center (see Chapter 12, Section 3).
3   Start the engine and allow to idle until it stops.
4   Attempt to start the vehicle two or three more times.
5   Turn the ignition off and disconnect the cable from the negative terminal of the battery (see Chapter 5).

6.0L models

6   Disconnect the cable from the negative terminal of the battery (see Chapter 5).
7   Unscrew the cap on the fuel pressure test port.
8   Surround and cover the test port with shop rags, then depress the Schrader valve inside the test port with a small screwdriver until the pressure in the fuel system is relieved. Properly dispose of the rags.

---

4   Fuel pump/fuel pressure - check

Warning: *Gasoline is extremely flammable, so take extra precautions when you work on any part of the fuel system. See the Warning in Section 3.*

Fuel pump operation check

1   Sit inside the vehicle with the windows closed, turn the ignition key to ON (not START) and listen carefully for the sound made by the fuel pump as it's briefly turned on by the PCM to pressurize the fuel system prior to starting the engine. You will only hear a whirring sound for a second or two, but that sound tells you that the pump is working. If you can't hear the pump, remove the fuel filler cap, then have an assistant turn the ignition switch to ON while you listen for the sound of the pump operating for a couple of seconds.
2   If the pump does not come on when the ignition key is turned to ON, check the fuel pump fuse(s) and relay (see illustration 2.2). If the fuse(s) and relay are okay, check the wiring back to the fuel pump. If the fuse, relay and wiring are okay, the fuel pump is probably defective. If the pump runs continuously with the ignition key in its ON position, the Powertrain Control Module (PCM) is probably

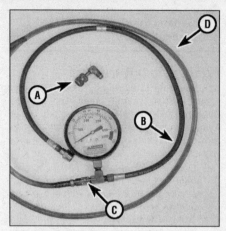

4.7 A typical fuel pressure gauge set up

A   *Screw-on adapter for the Schrader valve on the fuel rail*
B   *Hose with fitting to connect to the adapter*
C   *Bleeder valve (optional)*
D   *Bleeder hose (optional)*

defective. Have the PCM checked by a dealer service department or other qualified repair shop.

Fuel pressure check

Warning: *The fuel delivery system is made up of a low-pressure system and a high-pressure system. The following procedure only measures the fuel pressure in the low-pressure fuel system (in-tank fuel pump). The high-pressure fuel system operates at extremely high pressures and can cause injury. Only a qualified service center should perform diagnostics on the high pressure fuel system.*

Connecting a fuel pressure gauge - non-6.0L models

3   Relieve the fuel pressure (see Section 3).
4   Disconnect the quick connect fitting (see Section 5) for the fuel feed hose from the fuel feed pipe at the rear of the driver's side cylinder head (see illustration). Use a shop towel in order to catch any fuel that may leak.
5   Install a fuel pressure gauge test adapter between the fuel feed pipe and the fuel feed hose. Connect the gauge to the adapter.
6   Cycle the ignition to run the fuel pump, and check for leaks prior to performing the fuel pressure check.

Connecting a fuel pressure gauge - 6.0L models

7   To measure the fuel pressure, you'll need a fuel pressure gauge, and a hose and fitting suitable for connecting the gauge to the Schrader valve-type test port on the fuel feed line (see illustration).
8   Locate the fuel pressure test port, unscrew the cap and connect a fuel pressure gauge (see illustrations).

4.8a The fuel pressure test port on V8 models is located on the right fuel rail

4.8b The fuel pressure gauge connected to the test port on the fuel rail (V8 model shown)

9   Cycle the ignition to run the fuel pump, and check for leaks prior to performing the fuel pressure check.

Fuel pressure check

10   Start the engine and allow it to idle. Note the gauge reading as soon as the pressure stabilizes, and compare it with the pressure listed in this Chapter's Specifications.

   a) *If the pressure is lower than specified, suspect a restricted fuel filter (the fuel filter is an integral part of the fuel pump/ fuel level sensor module; to replace it you must replace the fuel pump). Also check the fuel lines and hoses for kinks, blockages and leaks.*

   b) *Except 6.0L models: If there are no restrictions and you changed the fuel filter but the pressure is still lower than specified, the regulator (which is an integral component of the fuel pump module) might be stuck in the open position, which will prevent the fuel system from reaching its normal operating pressure range. The regulator is not serviceable separately; if it's defective you must replace the fuel pump module.*

   c) *It's possible that one or more of the fuel injectors might be leaking or stuck open (but if this is happening the engine will be running very poorly and will most likely have set a trouble code). Remove and inspect the injectors (see Section 14).*

   d) *Except 6.0L models: If the fuel pressure is higher than specified, the fuel pressure regulator might be stuck in the closed position. The regulator is an integral component of the fuel pump module, and is not serviceable separately; if it's defective, you must replace the fuel pump module.*

11   Drive the vehicle and monitor fuel pressure. If fuel pressure dramatically decreases at cruise speed, during acceleration or hard cornering maneuvers, check for a restricted fuel filter (the fuel filter is an integral part of the fuel pump/fuel level sensor module; to replace it you must replace the fuel pump). Also check the fuel lines and hoses for kinks, blockages and leaks.

12   Turn off the engine. Verify that the fuel pressure loses no more than the specified pressure for one minute after the engine is turned off.

Tip: *If pressure leaks down too quickly, check for a leaky check valve in the fuel pump by pinching off the line to the fuel tank and retesting. If pressure still drops, check for a leaking fuel injector.*

Tip: *If pressure holds, the check valve in the fuel pump may be at fault, requiring fuel pump replacement.*

13   On 6.0L models, disconnect the fuel pressure gauge and screw on the test port cap. On all models except 6.0L, remove the fuel pressure gauge and adapter and reconnect the fuel line fitting. Clean up any spilled gasoline.

14   Start the engine and verify that there are no fuel leaks.

5   Fuel lines and fittings - general information and disconnection

Warning: *Gasoline is extremely flammable, so take extra precautions when you work on any part of the fuel system. See Fuel system warnings in Section 1.*

1   Relieve the fuel pressure before servicing fuel lines or fittings (see Section 3). Disconnect the cable from the negative battery terminal (see Chapter 5) before proceeding.

2   The fuel supply line connects the fuel pump in the fuel tank to the fuel rail on the engine. The Evaporative Emissions Control (EVAP) system lines connect the fuel tank to the EVAP canister and connect the canister to the intake manifold.

3   Whenever you're working under the vehicle, be sure to inspect all fuel and evaporative emission lines for leaks, kinks, dents and other damage. Always replace a damaged fuel or EVAP line immediately.

4   If you find signs of dirt in the lines during disassembly, disconnect all lines and blow them out with compressed air. Inspect the fuel strainer on the fuel pump pick-up unit for damage and deterioration.

Steel tubing

5   It is critical that the fuel lines be replaced with lines of equivalent type and specification.

6   Some steel fuel lines have threaded fittings. When loosening these fittings, hold the stationary fitting with a wrench while turning the tube nut.

Plastic tubing

7   When replacing fuel system plastic tubing, use only original equipment replacement plastic tubing.

Caution: *When removing or installing plastic fuel line tubing, be careful not to bend or twist it too much, which can damage it. Also, plastic fuel tubing is NOT heat resistant, so keep it away from excessive heat.*

Flexible hoses

8   When replacing fuel system flexible hoses, use only original equipment replacements.

9   Don't route fuel hoses (or metal lines) within four inches of the exhaust system or within ten inches of the catalytic converter. Make sure that no rubber hoses are installed directly against the vehicle, particularly in places where there is any vibration. If allowed to touch some vibrating part of the vehicle, a hose can easily become chafed and it might start leaking. A good rule of thumb is to maintain a minimum of 1/4-inch clearance around a hose (or metal line) to prevent contact with the vehicle underbody.

Disconnecting Fuel Line Fittings

Two-tab type fitting; depress both tabs with your fingers, then pull the fuel line and the fitting apart

On this type of fitting, depress the two buttons on opposite sides of the fitting, then pull it off the fuel line

Threaded fuel line fitting; hold the stationary portion of the line or component (A) while loosening the tube nut (B) with a flare-nut wrench

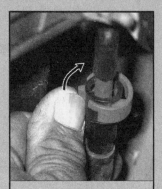

Plastic collar-type fitting; rotate the outer part of the fitting

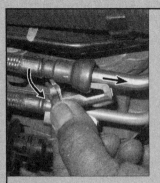

Metal collar quick-connect fitting; pull the end of the retainer off the fuel line and disengage the other end from the female side of the fitting . . .

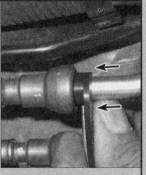

. . . insert a fuel line separator tool into the female side of the fitting, push it into the fitting and pull the fuel line off the pipe

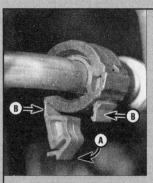

Some fittings are secured by lock tabs. Release the lock tab (A) and rotate it to the fully-opened position, squeeze the two smaller lock tabs (B) . . .

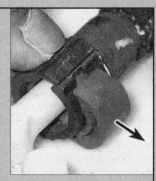

. . . then push the retainer out and pull the fuel line off the pipe

Spring-lock coupling; remove the safety cover, install a coupling release tool and close the tool around the coupling . . .

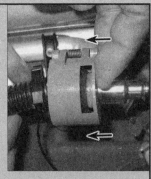

. . . push the tool into the fitting, then pull the two lines apart

Hairpin clip type fitting: push the legs of the retainer clip together, then push the clip down all the way until it stops and pull the fuel line off the pipe

6 Exhaust system servicing - general information

Warning: *Allow exhaust system components to cool before inspection or repair. Also, when working under the vehicle, make sure it is securely supported on jackstands.*

1   The exhaust system consists of the exhaust manifolds, catalytic converter, muffler, tailpipe and all connecting pipes, flanges and clamps. The exhaust system is isolated from the vehicle body and from chassis components by a series of rubber hangers (see illustration). Periodically inspect these hangers for cracks or other signs of deterioration, replacing them as necessary.

2   Conduct regular inspections of the exhaust system to keep it safe and quiet. Look for any damaged or bent parts, open seams, holes, loose connections, excessive corrosion or other defects which could allow exhaust fumes to enter the vehicle. Do not repair deteriorated exhaust system components; replace them with new parts.

3   If the exhaust system components are extremely corroded, or rusted together, a cutting torch is the most convenient tool for removal. Consult a properly-equipped repair shop. If a cutting torch is not available, you can use a hacksaw, or if you have compressed air, there are special pneumatic cutting chisels that can also be used. Wear safety goggles to protect your eyes from metal chips and wear work gloves to protect your hands.

4   Here are some simple guidelines to follow when repairing the exhaust system:

a) *Work from the back to the front when removing exhaust system components.*

b) *Apply penetrating oil to the exhaust system component fasteners to make them easier to remove.*

c) *Use new nuts, gaskets, hangers and clamps.*

d) *Apply anti-seize compound to the threads of all exhaust system fasteners during reassembly.*

e) *Be sure to allow sufficient clearance between newly installed parts and all points on the underbody to avoid overheating the floor pan and possibly damaging the interior carpet and insulation. Pay particularly close attention to the catalytic converter and heat shield.*

7 Fuel tank - removal and installation

Warning: *Gasoline is extremely flammable, so take extra precautions when you work on any part of the fuel system. See the Warning in Section 3.*

Warning: *Before disconnecting or opening any part of the fuel system, relieve the fuel system pressure (see Section 3), and equalize the pressure inside the fuel tank by removing the fuel filler cap.*

1   Relieve the fuel system pressure (see Section 3).

2   Disconnect the cable from the negative battery terminal (see Chapter 5, Section 3).

3   Raise the vehicle and support it securely on jackstands.

4   Remove the fuel tank rock guard, if equipped.

5   Locate the fuel tank filler neck hose (see illustration) and disconnect the filler neck hose from the tank pipe.

6   Locate the EVAP line that goes from the tank to the EVAP canister and disconnect it from the EVAP canister. Disconnect the EVAP vent line from the EVAP canister. Disconnect any EVAP line clips attaching the line to the chassis.

7   Locate the fuel line quick-connect fittings (see Section 5) and disconnect them from the

chassis lines (see illustration).

8   It's easier to remove the fuel tank when it's nearly empty. But there is no fuel tank drain plug, so if there's still a lot of fuel in the tank, siphon or hand-pump the remaining fuel, from the tank through the tank filler neck pipe, into an approved gasoline container.

Warning: *Don't start the siphoning action by mouth! Use a siphoning kit (available at most auto parts stores).*

9   Detach any clips that secure the fuel pump/fuel level sending unit harness to the crossmember or frame rail and detach it/them.

Caution: *Failure to detach these clips will result in damage to the fuel pump/fuel level sending unit harness when the tank is lowered.*

10   Support the fuel tank.

11   The fuel tank is retained by two transverse straps. The outer end of each fuel tank

6.1 Typical exhaust system hangers. Inspect regularly and replace at the first sign of damage or deterioration

7.5 Loosen the hose clamp on the fuel tank filler neck hose (at the tank), then work the hose off the pipe

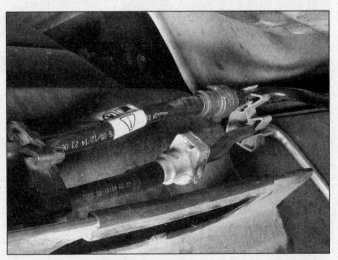

7.7 Disconnect the fuel and EVAP line quick-connect fittings

strap is secured to the vehicle by a bolt (see illustrations). The inner end of each strap is secured to a mounting bracket by a hinge. Remove the two fuel tank strap bolts, then disengage each strap hinge from its mounting bracket and remove the straps.

12   Carefully lower the tank just far enough to access the fuel pump/fuel level sensor module, then disconnect the electrical connectors from the pump module and from the fuel tank fuel pressure sensor (see illustration).

13   Lower the tank the rest of the way.

14   Installation is the reverse of removal.

8   Fuel pump module - removal and installation

Warning: *Gasoline is extremely flammable, so take extra precautions when you work on any part of the fuel system. See the Warning in Section 3.*

1   Relieve the system fuel pressure (see Section 3).

2   Disconnect the cable from the negative battery terminal (see Chapter 5).

3   Remove the fuel tank (see Section 7).

4   Clean the top of the fuel pump module.

5   Disconnect the quick-connect fittings from the fuel pump module (see illustration).

6   Note the orientation of the pump mounting flange and mark the orientation of the fuel pump in relation to the fuel tank (see illustration) to ensure that the fuel pump is correctly realigned when you install it again. If you're going to install a new pump, note the location of your alignment mark on the old pump and make a mark at the same spot on the new unit.

7   Using a pair of large water pump pliers, unscrew the fuel pump module lock ring by turning it counterclockwise (see illustration).

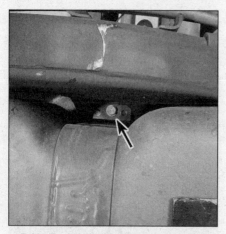

7.11a To detach the fuel tank from the vehicle, remove the front fuel tank strap bolt . . .

7.11b . . . and the rear fuel tank strap bolt

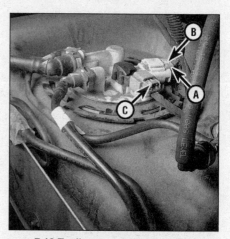

7.12 To disconnect the electrical connector from the fuel pump/fuel level sending unit module, slide the connector lock out (A), then depress the tab (B) and pull off the connector. To disconnect the electrical connector from the fuel tank pressure sensor, depress the tab (C) and pull off the connector

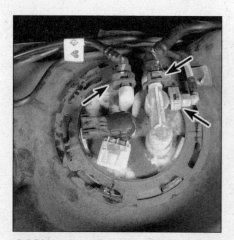

8.5 Disconnect the quick-connect fittings from the fuel pump module

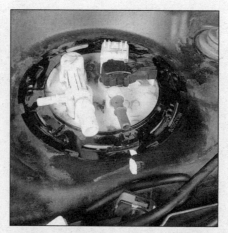

8.6 To ensure that the pipes for the EVAP vent line, fuel tank vent line and fuel supply line are oriented correctly when you install the fuel pump module, make alignment marks on the tank and the pump flange at this wider part of the flange

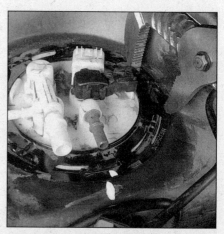

8.7 Use a large pair of water pump pliers to unscrew the fuel pump lock ring; if the lock ring is too tight to loosen this way, carefully tap it loose with a hammer and a brass punch

If the lock ring is tight or pliers will not work, use a hammer and a brass punch to loosen it (don't use a steel punch, which could produce sparks when struck by the hammer).

8   Remove the pump assembly (see illustration), taking care not to damage the fuel level sensor float arm and float.

9   Before installing the pump, inspect the O-ring (see illustration) for cracks, tears and deterioration. If it isn't in perfect condition, replace it.

10   The float arm may need to be installed onto the new fuel pump module. Note the installed position of the float arm on the old module and snap the float arm onto the new module in the same position.

11   Insert the fuel pump/fuel level sensor module into the fuel tank, align the mark that you made on the fuel pump/fuel level sending unit flange with the mark you made on the tank and carefully seat the pump flange on the tank. Make sure that you don't damage the float arm or the float during installation. If the float arm is bent, the fuel level that is indicated on the fuel level gauge on the instrument cluster will be incorrect.

12   Remaining installation is reverse of removal.

9   Fuel level sending unit - component replacement

Warning: *Gasoline is extremely flammable, so take extra precautions when you work on any part of the fuel system. See the Warning in Section 3.*

Note: *You can purchase the complete fuel pump/fuel level sending unit module, or you can purchase either the fuel pump or the fuel level sending unit separately. If only one component fails, use this procedure to separate the two components, then reassemble the good component and the new replacement component.*

1   Remove the fuel pump/fuel level sending

unit (see Section 8).

2   Place the fuel pump/fuel level sending unit on a clean workbench surface.

3   Disconnect the fuel level sending unit electrical connector from the fuel pump mounting flange.

4   Disengage the fuel level sensor wiring harness from the top of the fuel pump module.

5   Remove the fuel level sensor unit from the fuel pump module (see illustration).

6   No further disassembly of the fuel pump module is possible. If any component of the fuel pump module is defective, replace the fuel pump module.

7   To install the fuel level sending unit on the fuel pump module, slide the sensor unit into place until you hear a click, then pull on the sensor unit to verify that it's locked into place.

8   The float arm snaps into the fuel level sending unit.

9   Remaining installation is reverse of removal.

10   High-pressure fuel pump and fuel rail fuel pressure sensor - removal and installation

Warning: *Gasoline is extremely flammable. See* Fuel system warnings *in Section 1.*

Warning: *The fuel delivery system is made up of a low-pressure system and a high-pressure system. Once the pressure on the low-pressure side of the system has been relieved, wait at least two hours before loosening any fuel line fittings in the engine compartment.*

1   Remove the engine covers.

2   Relieve the fuel system pressure (see Section 3).

3   Disconnect the cable from the negative battery terminal (see Chapter 5).

4   Remove the intake manifold (see Chapter 2A or 2B) and the fuel pump/fuel rail insulator (see Section 14).

Fuel rail fuel pressure sensor

Note: *The fuel rail fuel pressure sensor is located at the rear of the left-side fuel rail.*

5   Disconnect the fuel pressure sensor electrical connector (see illustration).

6   Unscrew and remove the sensor from the end of the fuel rail.

Caution: *The manufacturer states that the sensor must be replaced if it has been removed.*

7   Clean the threads in the fuel rail of any gasoline. Place a single drop of oil on the new sensor threads, then install the sensor and hand tighten.

8   Remove the sensor, place another drop of clean engine oil on the threads, then reinstall the sensor and tighten it to the torque listed in this Chapter's Specifications.

9   Connect the sensor electrical connector.

10   The remainder of installation is reverse of removal.

8.8 Carefully remove the fuel pump/ fuel level sensor module from the fuel tank; once the module has cleared the mounting hole in the tank, angle it as shown to work the float arm through the mounting hole without damaging anything

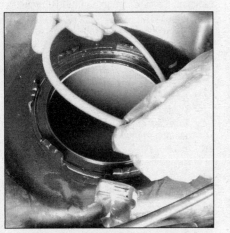

8.9 Remove and inspect the O-ring seal for the fuel pump mounting flange; if it's cracked, torn or deteriorated, replace it

9.5 Pry these two retaining tangs on the locking lugs of the sending unit, then slide the sending unit up and remove it from the pump module

10.5 Fuel rail pressure sensor electrical connector

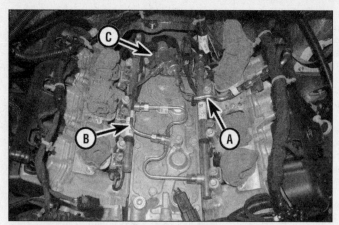

10.12 Disconnect the feed line (A) and the high-pressure line (B) from the fuel pump (C)

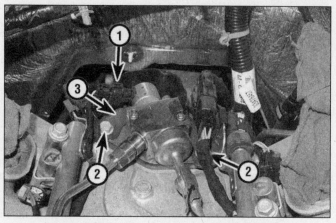

10.14 High-pressure fuel pump mounting details

1	Electrical connector	3	Pump cover
2	Mounting bolts		

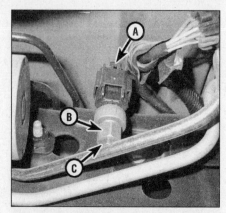

11.3 To disconnect the electrical connector from the fuel pressure sensor, depress the release tab (A). To remove the sensor (B) from the fuel supply line, hold the flats on the fuel line (C) with a wrench (to prevent twisting the line), then unscrew the sensor

High-pressure fuel pump

11   Remove the low pressure fuel feed line bracket bolt and disconnect the feed line at the pump.

12   Using a flare-nut wrench, unscrew the high-pressure line fittings between the fuel rail and fuel pump and discard the pipe as a new one must be used (see illustration).
Caution: *The manufacturer states that the pipe must be replaced whenever it has been removed.*

13   Disconnect the electrical connector from the high-pressure fuel pump.

14   Remove the high-pressure fuel pump bolts (see illustration), then remove the cover, pump and gasket. Always replace the bolts and pump gasket with new ones.
Caution: *Unscrew the bolts one turn at a time, alternating between the two of them. If this is not done, the pump plunger will be damaged.*

15   With the pump removed, rotate the engine by hand and make sure the camshaft lobe is at its base circle (lowest point) before

trying to install the pump.

16   Lubricate the pump roller with engine oil.

17   Using a NEW gasket, set the pump and cover into position on the valley cover and tighten the bolts evenly, one turn at a time, side-to-side.
Caution: *Alternately hand-tighten the fuel pump bolts one turn at a time until the pump is fully seated. Attempting to tighten down the pump unevenly may result in pump plunger damage. As the pump bolts are tightened, it will get harder to tighten the bolts until the spring in the pump is compressed.*

18   Tighten the bolts to the torque listed in this Chapter's Specifications.

19   The remainder of installation is the reverse of removal. Clean the high-pressure fuel line fittings on the pump and crossover pipe, then apply a drop of clean engine oil to the threads of each fitting. Install the NEW high-pressure fuel line, tightening the fittings to the torque listed in this Chapter's Specifications.

20   The remainder of installation is the reverse of the removal procedure.

21   Reconnect the cable to the negative battery terminal (see Chapter 5), then start the engine and check for fuel leaks.

---

11   Fuel pressure sensor and fuel pump flow control module - replacement

Fuel pressure sensor
Warning: *Gasoline is extremely flammable, so take extra precautions when you work on any part of the fuel system. See the Warning in Section 3.*
Note: *The fuel pressure sensor is located under the vehicle, on the fuel supply line.*

1   Relieve the system fuel pressure (see Section 3).

2   Raise the vehicle and support it securely on jackstands.

3   Disconnect the electrical connector from the fuel pressure sensor (see illustration).

11.8 FPFCM location, above the spare tire

4   Unscrew the fuel pressure sensor from the fuel supply line.
Warning: *Be prepared for fuel spillage.*

5   Remove and discard the old fuel pressure sensor O-ring. Coat a new O-ring with a little clean engine oil, then install it on the fuel pressure sensor.

6   Installation is otherwise the reverse of removal. Be sure to tighten the fuel pressure sensor securely.

7   Before lowering the vehicle, test for leaks as follows:

a) *Turn the ignition switch key to the ON position (don't start the engine) for two seconds.*

b) *Turn the ignition switch key to the OFF position for ten seconds.*

c) *Turn the ignition switch key to the ON position (don't start the engine).*

d) *Inspect the area around the fuel pressure sensor for leaks.*

Fuel Pump Flow Control Module (FPFCM)
Note: *The FPFCM is also referred to as the Fuel Pump Power Control Module.*

8   The fuel pump flow control module is located under the vehicle, above the spare tire (see illustration). Remove the spare tire from the vehicle.

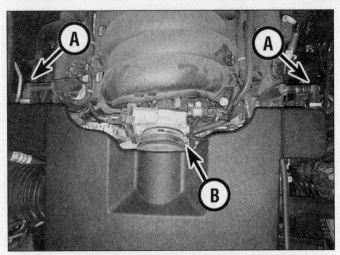

12.2 Disconnect PCV fresh air inlet hoses (A) and loosen the throttle body hose clamp (B) (non-6.0L V8 model shown)

12.3 MAF sensor hose clamps (V8 model shown)

13.3 Disconnect the throttle body electrical connector

9   Raise the rear of the vehicle and support it securely on jackstands.
10   Remove the spare tire.
11   Disconnect the electrical connector from the FPFCM.
12   Remove the FPFCM mounting bolts (see illustration) and remove the module from its mounting bracket.
13   Installation is the reverse of removal.

12 Air intake duct and air filter housing - removal and installation

Air intake duct

1   On 6.0L models, remove the intake manifold cover.
2   Disconnect the PCV fresh air inlet hose from the air intake duct and loosen the hose clamp screw at the throttle body (see illustration).

3   Loosen the hose clamp screw at the Mass Air Flow (MAF) sensor (see illustration).
4   On 6.0L models, detach the radiator hose clip from the air intake duct. Pull upwards to disconnect the grommet from the duct at the top of the intake manifold.
5   On all models, remove the air duct by disconnecting from the MAF and the throttle body.
6   Installation is the reverse of removal.

Air filter housing

7   Remove the air intake duct.
8   Disconnect the electrical connector from the Mass Air Flow (MAF) sensor.
9   Grasp the air filter housing firmly and pull it straight up to disengage the locator pins from their insulator grommets.
10   While the air filter housing is out, inspect the rubber mounting grommets. If a grommet is cracked, torn or otherwise damaged, replace it.
11   Installation is the reverse of removal.

13 Throttle body - inspection, removal and installation

Inspection

1   Remove the air intake duct from the throttle body, open the throttle plate and inspect the throttle body bore for carbon and residue build-up. If it's dirty, clean it with solvent or carburetor cleaner. Make sure that the solvent or carb cleaner is safe for oxygen sensor systems and catalytic converters.
Caution: *Do not clean the Throttle Position (TP) sensor or the throttle motor with solvent. Also, do NOT use a metal brush to clean the bore of the throttle body, which is protected by a special coating. Scrubbing the bore with a stiff brush could ruin the coating. Instead, wipe out the bore with a clean shop rag and a little carburetor cleaner.*

13.4 To detach the throttle body from the intake manifold, remove the four fasteners

Removal and installation

Warning: *Wait until the engine is completely cool before beginning this procedure.*
Note: *The photos accompanying this section depict the throttle body on a V6 model, but the throttle body used on V8 models is virtually identical, except that it's mounted on top of the intake manifold instead of the front of the manifold.*

2   Remove the air intake duct (see Section 12).
3   Pull out the lock, then depress the release tab and pull off the electrical connector for the throttle body (see illustration).
4   Remove the throttle body mounting fasteners (see illustration) and remove the throttle body.
5   Remove the old throttle body O-ring gasket and discard it.
6   Installation is the reverse of removal. Be sure to use a new gasket and tighten the throttle body mounting fasteners to the torque listed in this Chapter's Specifications.

14.5 Remove the foam insulator covering the injector rails

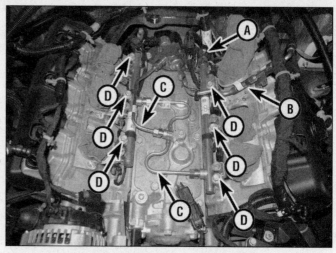

14.8 Remove the following items in order:

A   Fuel rail fuel pressure sensor electrical connector
B   Fuel feed line
C   High-pressure fuel lines
D   Fuel rail bolts

14.10 Use snap-ring pliers to open up the retaining clip, then remove it

14.11 Remove the injectors from the fuel rail

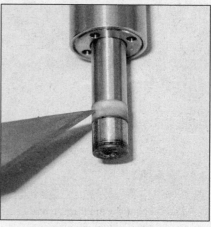

14.12 To remove the Teflon sealing ring, cut it off with a hobby knife (be careful not to scratch the injector groove)

7   Start the engine, then verify that the throttle body operates correctly and that there are no air leaks.

14 Fuel rail and injectors - removal and installation

Warning: *Gasoline is extremely flammable. See* Fuel system warnings *in Section 1.*
Note: *Even if you only removed the fuel rail assembly to replace a single injector or a leaking O-ring, it's a good idea to remove all of the injectors from the fuel rail and replace all of the O-rings at the same time.*

1   Relieve the fuel system pressure (see Section 3).
2   Disconnect the cable from the negative battery terminal (see Chapter 5).
3   Remove the air intake duct (see Section 12).

Non-6.0L models

Warning: *The fuel delivery system is made up of a low-pressure system and a high-pressure system. Once the pressure on the low-pressure side of the system has been relieved, wait at least two hours before loosening any fuel line fittings in the engine compartment.*
Caution: *The manufacturer recommends replacing all of the seals on the injectors whenever they are removed from the cylinder head.*

4   Remove the intake manifold (see Chapter 2A or 2B).
5   Remove the fuel pump/fuel rail insulator (see illustration).
6   Remove the fuel feed and high-pressure fuel line from the pump and fuel rails (see illustration).
7   Disconnect the fuel injector electrical connectors and position the harness out of the way.

8   Remove the mounting bolts from both fuel rails (see illustration).
9   Install the center bolts, leaving several threads exposed, then evenly pry the driver's side fuel rail and injectors out of the cylinder head. Repeat the same procedure for the other fuel rail.
10   Using external snap-ring pliers, carefully spread the retaining clip open, then remove the clip (see illustration).
11   Remove each injector from the fuel rail (see illustration).
12   Remove the old combustion chamber Teflon sealing ring and the upper O-ring and support ring from each injector (see illustration).
Caution: *Be extremely careful not to damage the groove for the seal or the rib in the floor of the groove. If you damage the groove or the rib, you must replace the injector.*
13   Before installing the new Teflon seal on

14.17 Slide the new Teflon seal onto the end of a socket that's the same diameter as the end of the fuel injector . . .

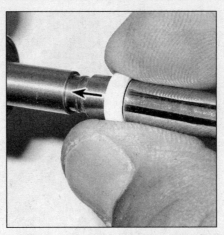

14.18 . . . align the socket with the end of the injector and slide the seal onto the injector and into its mounting groove

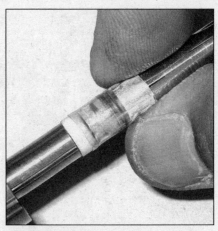

14.19a Use the socket to push a short section of plastic tubing onto the end of the injector and over the new seal . . .

14.19b . . . then leave the plastic tubing in place for several hours to compress the new seal

14.20 Note that the upper O-ring (1) is installed above the support ring (2)

each injector, thoroughly clean the groove for the seal and the injector shaft. Remove all combustion residue and varnish with a clean shop rag.

Teflon seal installation using the special tools

14   The manufacturer recommends that you use the tools included in the special injector tool set described above to install the Teflon lower seals on the injectors: Install the special seal assembly cone on the injector, install the special sleeve on the injector and use the sleeve to push on the assembly cone, which pushes the Teflon seal into place on its groove. Do NOT use any lubricants to do so.

15   Pushing the Teflon seal into place in its groove expands it slightly. There is a two-sided sizing sleeve in the special tool set with two different inside diameters. Using a clockwise rotating motion of about 180 degrees, install the slightly larger sleeve onto the injector and over the Teflon seal until the sleeve hits its stop, then carefully turn the sleeve counterclockwise as you pull it off the injector. Use the slightly smaller sizing sleeve the

same way. The seal is now sized. Repeat this step for each injector.

Teflon seal installation without special tools

16   If you don't have the special injector tool set, the Teflon seal can be installed using this method: First, find a socket that is equal or very close in diameter to the diameter of the end of the fuel injector.

17   Work the new Teflon seal onto the end of the socket (see illustration).

18   Place the socket against the end of the injector (see illustration) and slide the seal from the socket onto the injector. Do NOT use any lubricants to do so. Continue pushing the seal onto the injector until it seats into its mounting groove.

19   Because the inside diameter of the seal has to be stretched open to fit over the bore of the socket and the injector, its outside diameter is now slightly too large - it is no longer flush with the surface of the injector. It must be shrunk it back to its original size. To do so, push a piece of plastic tubing with an interference fit onto the end of the socket; a

plastic straw that fits tightly on the injector will work. After pushing the plastic tubing onto the socket about an inch, snip off the rest of the tubing, then use the socket to push the tubing onto the end of the injector (see illustration) and slide it onto the injector until it completely covers the new seal (see illustration). Leave the tubing on for a few hours, then remove it. The seal should now be shrunk back to its original outside diameter, or close to it.

Injector and fuel rail installation

20   Install the new support ring at the upper end of the injector. Lubricate the new upper O-ring with clean engine oil and install it on the injector. Do NOT oil the new Teflon seal. Note that the seal is installed above the spacer (see illustration).

21   Thoroughly clean the injector bores with a small nylon brush.

22   Install the new compensation element and retaining ring to the bottom of each injector.

23   Install the fuel injectors in the fuel rail and secure them with new retainers, then install the fuel rail and injectors. The bores in

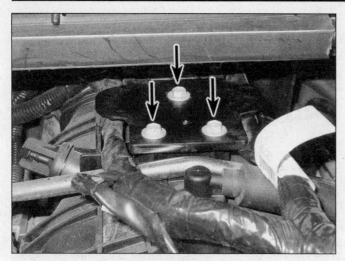

14.30 To detach the intake manifold cover bracket, remove these three bolts

14.31 To detach the engine wiring harness bracket, remove this nut

14.33 To disconnect the electrical connector from each fuel injector, pull up the retainer, then depress the lower end of the retainer and pull off the connector

14.35 To detach the PCV hose from the intake manifold, grasp it firmly and pull it straight up

the cylinder head are slightly tapered, so you will encounter some resistance as the Teflon seal nears the bottom of the bore.

24   Apply a drop of non-hardening thread locking compound to the fuel rail bolts. Install the bolts, tightening them alternately until they are seated, then tighten them to the torque listed in this Chapter's Specifications.

25   The remainder of installation is the reverse of removal. Clean the high-pressure fuel line fittings on the fuel rails, then apply a little clean engine oil to the threads. Install the new high-pressure fuel line, tightening the fittings to the torque listed in this Chapter's Specifications. Install a new fuel rail fuel pressure sensor (see Section 10).

6.0L models

26   Remove the intake manifold cover.

27   Relieve the fuel system pressure (see Section 3).

28   Disconnect the cable from the negative battery terminal (see Chapter 5).

29   Remove the air intake duct (see Section 12).

30   Remove the intake manifold cover bracket bolts (see illustration) and remove the manifold cover bracket.

31   Remove the nut that secures the engine wiring harness bracket to the intake manifold (see illustration) and detach the harness bracket.

32   Trace each electrical lead in the engine wiring harness to its corresponding electrical connector and disconnect the electrical connectors from the following components:

a) Alternator (see Chapter 5) - also detach the engine wiring harness clip from the alternator
b) EVAP purge solenoid (see Chapter 6)
c) Ignition coils (see Chapter 5)

d) Manifold Absolute Pressure (MAP) sensor (see Chapter 6)
e) Throttle body (see Section 13)

33   Disconnect the electrical connectors from the fuel injectors (see illustration).

34   Detach all engine wiring harness clips (including the clip on the alternator) and set the engine wiring harness aside.

35   Disconnect the PCV crankcase ventilation hose (PCV hose) from the intake manifold (see illustration) and set the PCV hose aside.

36   Disconnect the fuel line from the fuel rail (see illustration).

37   Disconnect the EVAP canister purge solenoid from the intake manifold and remove it from the fuel rail (see Chapter 6).

38   Remove the fuel rail mounting bolts (see illustration).

39   Carefully disengage the injectors from the intake manifold and lift the fuel rail and all six injectors from the engine as a single

14.36 Disconnect the fuel supply line quick-connect fitting at the fuel rail (if you're unfamiliar with metal-collar type quick-connect fittings, see Section 4).

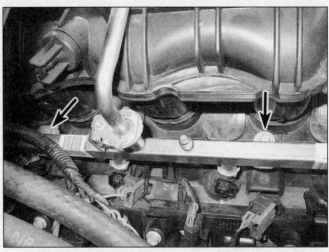

14.38 To detach the fuel rail, remove the four mounting bolts (two bolts on right side fuel rail shown)

14.39 Disengage the fuel injectors from the intake manifold, then lift the fuel rail and the injectors as a single assembly

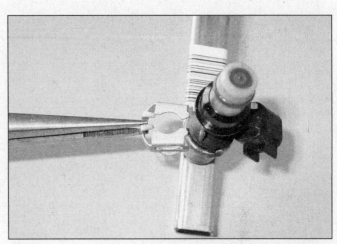

14.40 Pull off each injector retaining clip with needle nose pliers, then pull the injector out of the fuel rail

assembly (see illustration).

40   Remove each injector retainer (see illustration) and remove the injectors from the fuel rail.

41   Remove and discard the old injector O-rings (see illustration). Always install new O-rings on the injectors before reassembling the injectors and the fuel rail.

42   To ensure that the new injector O-rings are not damaged when the injectors are installed into the fuel rail and into the intake manifold, lubricate them with clean engine oil.

43   When installing the injector retainers, make sure that they're aligned properly and fit tightly (see illustration). If a retainer is damaged, replace it.

44   Installation is otherwise the reverse of removal. Be sure to tighten the fuel rail mounting bolts to the torque listed in this Chapter's Specifications.

45   Turn the ignition key to the On position to pressurize the fuel system and verify that there are no fuel leaks.

14.41 Remove the O-rings from each fuel injector, then install new O-rings. Coat the O-rings with a little clean engine oil to protect them from damage

14.43 When installing each injector retainer, make sure that it's aligned properly and fits tightly

Notes

Chapter 5
Engine electrical systems

Contents

Specifications

General

Firing order

V6 engines 1-6-5-4-3-2

V8 engines 1-8-7-2-6-5-4-3

Cylinder numbering

V6 engines

Left bank 1-3-5

Right bank 2-4-6

V8 engines

Left bank 1-3-5-7

Right bank 2-4-6-8

Ignition timing .... Not adjustable

Torque specifications Ft-lbs (unless otherwise indicated)

Note: *One foot-pound (ft-lb) of torque is equivalent to 12 inch-pounds (in-lbs) of torque. Torque values below approximately 15 ft-lbs are expressed in inch-pounds, since most foot-pound torque wrenches are not accurate at these smaller values.*

Engine compartment brace .... 80 in-lbs

Alternator mounting bolts 37

Alternator cable nut 11

Starter motor mounting bolts 37

Starter solenoid cable nut .... 80 in-lbs

1   General information and precautions

General information

Ignition system

1   The ignition system consists of the ignition coils, the spark plugs, the Camshaft Position (CMP) sensor, the Crankshaft Position (CKP) sensor, the knock sensor, and the Powertrain Control Module (PCM).

2   The CKP, CMP and knock sensors are information sensors used by the PCM to control ignition timing and other engine operating parameters. The PCM also uses a number of other information sensors to make decisions regarding the correct ignition timing. These other sensors include the Throttle Position (TP) sensor, the Engine Coolant Temperature (ECT) sensor, the Mass Air Flow (MAF) sensor, the Intake Air Temperature (IAT) sensor, the Vehicle Speed Sensor (VSS) and the transmission gear position sensor or Transmission Range (TR) switch. For more information on these and other sensors, refer to Chapter 6.

Charging system

3   The charging system includes the alternator (with an integral voltage regulator), the Powertrain Control Module (PCM), the Body Control Module (BCM), a charge indicator light on the dash, the battery, a fuse or fusible link and the wiring connecting all of these components. The charging system supplies electrical power for the ignition system, the lights, the radio, etc. The alternator is driven by a drivebelt.

Starting system

4   The starting system consists of the battery, the ignition switch, the starter relay, the Powertrain Control Module (PCM), the Body Control Module (BCM), the Transmission Range (TR) switch, the starter motor and solenoid assembly, and the wiring connecting all of these components.

Precautions

5   Always observe the following precautions when working on the electrical system:

a)   *Be extremely careful when servicing engine electrical components. They are easily damaged if checked, connected or handled improperly.*

b)   *Never leave the ignition switched on for long periods of time when the engine is not running.*

c)   *Never disconnect the battery cables while the engine is running.*

d)   *Maintain correct polarity when connecting battery cables from another vehicle during jump starting - see the "Booster battery (jump) starting" in Chapter 0.*

e)   *Always disconnect the cable from the negative battery terminal before working on the electrical system, but read the battery disconnection procedure first (see Section 3).*

6   It's also a good idea to review the safety-related information regarding the engine electrical systems located in the Safety first! Section at the front of this manual before beginning any operation included in this chapter.

2   Troubleshooting

Ignition system

1   If a malfunction occurs in the ignition system, do not immediately assume that any particular part is causing the problem. First, check the following items:

a)   *Make sure that the cable clamps at the battery terminals are clean and tight.*

b)   *Test the condition of the battery (see Steps 19 through 22). If it doesn't pass all the tests, replace it.*

c)   *Check the ignition coil or coil pack connections.*

d)   *Check any relevant fuses in the engine compartment fuse and relay box (see Chapter 12). If they're burned, determine the cause and repair the circuit.*

Check

Warning: *Because of the high voltage generated by the ignition system, use extreme care when performing a procedure involving ignition components.*
Note: *The ignition system components on these vehicles are difficult to diagnose. In the event of ignition system failure that you can't diagnose, have the vehicle tested at a dealer service department or other qualified auto repair facility.*
Note: *For the following test, you'll need a spark tester (available at auto parts stores).*
2   If the engine turns over but won't start, verify that there is sufficient secondary ignition voltage to fire the spark plug as follows:
3   Disconnect a spark plug wire from a spark plug and install the tester between the spark plug wire boot and the spark plug (see illustration).

All models

4   Crank the engine while watching the tester. If the tester flashes, sufficient voltage is reaching the spark plug to fire it.
Caution: *Do NOT crank the engine or allow it to run for more than five seconds; running the engine for more than five seconds may set a Diagnostic Trouble Code (DTC) for a cylinder misfire.*
5   Repeat this test on the remaining cylinders.
6   Proceed on this basis until you have verified that there's a good spark from each coil. If there is, then you have verified that the coils are functioning correctly.
7   If there is no spark, then either the coil is bad or the spark plug wire is bad.
8   Also inspect the coil electrical connector. Make sure that it's clean, tight and in good condition.
9   If all the coils are firing correctly, but the engine misfires when the spark plug wires are connected to the spark plugs, then one or more of the plugs might be fouled. Remove and check the spark plugs or install new ones (see Chapter 1).
10   Also inspect the boots carefully for corrosion (high resistance) or deterioration of the insulation (low resistance). If any of the boots look damaged or deteriorated, replace them as a set.
11   No further testing of the ignition system is possible without special tools. If the problem persists, have the ignition system tested by a dealer service department or other qualified repair shop.

Charging system

12   If a malfunction occurs in the charging system, do not automatically assume the alternator is causing the problem. First check the following items:

a)   *Check the drivebelt tension and condition, as described in Chapter 1. Replace it if it's worn or deteriorated.*

b)   *Make sure the alternator mounting bolts are tight.*

c)   *Inspect the alternator wiring harness and the connectors at the alternator and voltage regulator. They must be in good condition, tight and have no corrosion.*

d)   *Check the fuses in the underhood fuse/relay box. If any are burned, determine the cause, repair the circuit and replace the fuse (the vehicle will not start and/or the accessories will not work if the main fuse is blown).*

e)   *Start the engine and check the alternator for abnormal noises (a shrieking or squealing sound indicates a bad bearing).*

f)   *Check the battery. Make sure it's fully charged and in good condition (one bad cell in a battery can cause overcharging by the alternator).*

g)   *Disconnect the battery cables (negative first, then positive). Inspect the battery posts and the cable clamps for corrosion. Clean them thoroughly if necessary (see Chapter 1). Reconnect the cables (positive first, negative last).*

2.3 Here's the setup used for checking to see if the ignition coil is sending power to the spark plug. If the coil is delivering power to the plug, the tester will flash

2.19 To test the open circuit voltage of the battery, touch the black probe of the voltmeter to the negative terminal and the red probe to the positive terminal of the battery; a fully charged battery should be at least 12.6 volts

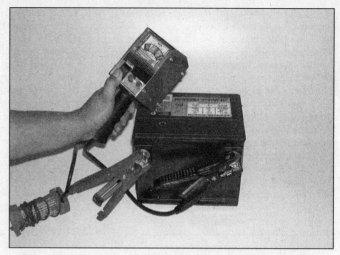

2.21 Connect a battery load tester to the battery and check the battery condition under load following the tool manufacturer's instructions

Alternator - check

13   Use a voltmeter to check the battery voltage with the engine off. It should be at least 12.6 volts (see illustration 2.19).

14   Start the engine and check the battery voltage again. It should now be approximately 13.5 to 15 volts.

15   If the voltage reading is more or less than the specified charging voltage, the voltage regulator is probably defective, which will require replacement of the alternator (the voltage regulator is not replaceable separately). Remove the alternator and have it bench tested (most auto parts stores will do this for you).

16   The charging system (battery) light on the instrument cluster lights up when the ignition key is turned to ON, but it should go out when the engine starts.

17   If the charging system light stays on after the engine has been started, there is a problem with the charging system. Before replacing the alternator, check the battery condition, alternator belt tension and electrical cable connections.

18   If replacing the alternator doesn't restore voltage to the specified range, have the charging system tested by a dealer service department or other qualified repair shop.

Battery - check

19   Check the battery state of charge. Visually inspect the indicator eye on the top of the battery (if equipped with one); if the indicator eye is black in color, charge the battery as described in Chapter 1. Next perform an open circuit voltage test using a digital voltmeter. With the engine and all accessories Off, touch the negative probe of the voltmeter to the negative terminal of the battery and the positive probe to the positive terminal of the battery (see illustration). The battery voltage should be 12.6 volts or slightly above. If the battery is less than the specified voltage, charge the

battery before proceeding to the next test. Do not proceed with the battery load test unless the battery charge is correct.

Note: *The battery's surface charge must be removed before accurate voltage measurements can be made. Turn on the high beams for ten seconds, then turn them off and let the vehicle stand for two minutes.*

20   Disconnect the negative battery cable, then the positive cable from the battery.

21   Perform a battery load test. An accurate check of the battery condition can only be performed with a load tester (see illustration). This test evaluates the ability of the battery to operate the starter and other accessories during periods of high current draw. Connect the load tester to the battery terminals. Load test the battery according to the tool manufacturer's instructions. This tool increases the load demand (current draw) on the battery.

22   Maintain the load on the battery for 15 seconds and observe that the battery voltage does not drop below 9.6 volts. If the battery condition is weak or defective, the tool will indicate this condition immediately.

Note: *Cold temperatures will cause the minimum voltage reading to drop slightly. Follow the chart given in the manufacturer's instructions to compensate for cold climates. Minimum load voltage for freezing temperatures (32 degrees F) should be approximately 9.1 volts.*

Starting system

The starter rotates, but the engine doesn't

23   Remove the starter (see Section 8). Check the overrunning clutch and bench test the starter to make sure the drive mechanism extends fully for proper engagement with the flywheel ring gear. If it doesn't, replace the starter.

24   Check the flywheel ring gear for missing teeth and other damage. With the igni-

tion turned off, rotate the flywheel so you can check the entire ring gear.

The starter is noisy

25   If the solenoid is making a chattering noise, first check the battery (see Steps 21 through 24). If the battery is okay, check the cables and connections.

26   If you hear a grinding, crashing metallic sound when you turn the key to Start, check for loose starter mounting bolts. If they're tight, remove the starter and inspect the teeth on the starter pinion gear and flywheel ring gear. Look for missing or damaged teeth.

27   If the starter sounds fine when you first turn the key to Start, but then stops rotating the engine and emits a zinging sound, the problem is probably a defective starter drive that's not staying engaged with the ring gear. Replace the starter.

The starter rotates slowly

28   Check the battery (see Steps 19 through 22).

29   If the battery is okay, verify all connections (at the battery, the starter solenoid and motor) are clean, corrosion-free and tight. Make sure the cables aren't frayed or damaged.

30   Check that the starter mounting bolts are tight so it grounds properly. Also check the pinion gear and flywheel ring gear for evidence of a mechanical bind (galling, deformed gear teeth or other damage).

The starter does not rotate at all

31   Check the battery (see Steps 19 through 22).

32   If the battery is okay, verify all connections (at the battery, the starter solenoid and motor) are clean, corrosion-free and tight. Make sure the cables aren't frayed or damaged.

33   Check all of the fuses in the underhood fuse/relay box.

34   Check that the starter mounting bolts are tight so it is grounded properly.

35   Check for voltage at the starter solenoid "S" terminal when the ignition key is turned to the start position. If voltage is present, replace the starter/solenoid assembly. If no voltage is present, the problem could be the starter relay, the Transmission Range (TR) switch (see Chapter 6), or with an electrical connector somewhere in the circuit (see the wiring diagrams). Also, on many modern vehicles, the Powertrain Control Module (PCM) and the Body Control Module (BCM) control the voltage signal to the starter solenoid; on such vehicles a special scan tool is required for diagnosis.

3   Battery - disconnection and reconnection

Warning: *On models with OnStar, make absolutely sure the ignition key is in the Off position and Retained Accessory Power (RAP) has been depleted before disconnecting the cable from the negative battery terminal. Also, never remove the OnStar fuse with the ignition key in any position other than Off. If these precautions are not taken, the OnStar system's back-up battery will be activated, and remain activated, until it goes dead. If this happens, the OnStar system will not function as it should in the event that the main vehicle battery power is cut off (as might happen during a collision).*
Note: *To disconnect the battery for service procedures requiring power to be cut from the vehicle, first open the driver's door to disable Retained Accessory Power (RAP), then loosen the cable end bolt and disconnect the cable from the negative battery terminal. Isolate the cable end to prevent it from coming into accidental contact with the battery terminal.*

1   The battery is located in the right side of the engine compartment on all vehicles covered by this manual. To disconnect the battery for service procedures that require battery disconnection, simply disconnect the cable from the negative battery terminal (see Section 4). Make sure that you isolate the cable to prevent it from coming into contact with the battery negative terminal.
Caution: *If both battery cables are to be disconnected, to prevent damage to any electrical components, always disconnect the negative battery cable first, then the positive battery cable second. When reconnecting the battery cables, always connect the positive battery cable first, then the negative battery cable second.*
2   Some vehicle systems (radio, alarm system, power door locks, etc.) require battery power all the time, either to enable their operation or to maintain control unit memory (Powertrain Control Module, automatic transaxle control module, etc.), which would be lost if the battery were to be disconnected. So before you disconnect the battery, note the following points:

a)   *Before connecting or disconnecting the cable from the negative battery terminal, make sure that you turn the ignition key and the lighting switch to their OFF positions. Failure to do so could damage semiconductor components.*
b)   *On a vehicle with power door locks, it is a wise precaution to remove the key from the ignition and to keep it with you, so that it does not get locked inside if the power door locks should engage accidentally when the battery is reconnected!*
c)   *After the battery has been disconnected, then reconnected (or a new battery has been installed) on vehicles with an automatic transaxle, the Transaxle Control Module (TCM) will need some time to relearn its adaptive strategy. As a result, shifting might feel firmer than usual. This is a normal condition and will not adversely affect the operation or service life of the transaxle. Eventually, the TCM will complete its adaptive learning process and the shift feel of the transaxle will return to normal.*
d)   *The engine management system's PCM has some learning capabilities that allow it to adapt or make corrections in response to minor variations in the fuel system in order to optimize drivability and idle characteristics. However, the PCM might lose some or all of this information when the battery is disconnected. The PCM must go through a relearning process before it can regain its former drivability and performance characteristics. Until it relearns this lost data, you might notice a difference in drivability, idle and/or (if you have an automatic) shift "feel." To facilitate this relearning process, refer to "Enabling the PCM to relearn" below.*

Memory savers

3   Devices known as memory savers (typically, small 9-volt batteries) can be used to avoid some of the above problems. A memory saver is usually plugged into the cigarette lighter, and then you can disconnect the vehicle battery from the electrical system. The memory saver will deliver sufficient current to maintain security alarm codes and - maybe, but don't count on it! - PCM memory. It will also run unswitched (always on) circuits such as the clock and radio memory, while isolating the car battery in the event that a short circuit occurs while the vehicle is being serviced.
Warning: *If you're going to work around any airbag system components, disconnect the battery and do not use a memory saver. If you do, the airbag could accidentally deploy and cause personal injury.*
Caution: *Because memory savers deliver current to operate unswitched circuits when the battery is disconnected, make sure that the circuit that you're going to service is actually open before working on it!*

Enabling the PCM to relearn

4   After the battery has been reconnected, perform the following procedure in order to facilitate PCM relearning:

5   Start the engine and allow it to warm up to its normal operating temperature.

6   Drive the vehicle at part-throttle, under moderate acceleration and idle conditions, until normal performance returns.

7   Park the vehicle and apply the parking brake with the engine running.

8   Depress the brake pedal and put the shift lever in Drive.

9   Allow the engine to idle for about two minutes, or until the idle stabilizes. Make sure that the engine is at its normal operating temperature.

Resetting power windows, sunroof, and Electric Power Steering (EPS)

10   Power windows: Sit in the vehicle with all of the doors closed. Operate each window (one at a time) to the fully open position, then raise the window until it is closed and hold the switch in the UP position for two seconds.

11   Sunroof: Open the sunroof completely, then close it completely.

12   Electric Power Steering (EPS): Sit in the driver's seat and start the engine. Turn the steering wheel completely counterclockwise, then completely clockwise, then back to center.

4   Battery and battery tray - removal and installation

Note: *Battery straps and handlers are available at most auto parts stores for reasonable prices. They make it easier to remove and carry the battery.*
1   Remove the engine compartment brace from over the battery (see illustration).

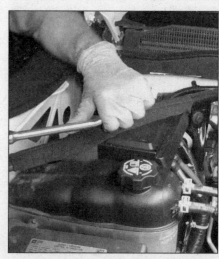

4.1 Remove the brace above the battery

2   Disconnect the cable from the negative terminal of the battery (see illustration).

3   Disconnect the cable from the positive terminal of the battery (see illustration).

4   Flip the mega-fuse box and back out of the way and remove the hold-down clamp (see illustration).

5   Lift out the battery. Be careful - it's heavy.

6   To remove the battery tray, remove the coolant expansion tank screws and position it to allow removal of the battery tray.

7   Remove the battery tray fasteners and remove the battery tray (see illustration).

8   If you are replacing the battery, make sure you get one that's identical, with the same dimensions, amperage rating, cold cranking rating, etc.

9   Installation is the reverse of removal. Connect the cable to the positive battery terminal first, then connect the ground cable to the negative battery terminal.

5   Battery cables - replacement

1   When removing the cables, always disconnect the cable from the negative battery terminal first and hook it up last, or you might accidentally short out the battery with the tool you're using to loosen the cable clamps. Even if you're only replacing the cable for the positive terminal, be sure to disconnect the negative cable from the battery first.

2   Disconnect the old cables from the battery or the mega-fuse terminal, then trace each of them to their opposite ends and disconnect them. Be sure to note the routing of each cable before disconnecting it to ensure correct installation.

3   If you are replacing any of the old cables, take them with you when buying new cables. It is vitally important that you replace the cables with identical parts.

4   Clean the threads of the solenoid or ground connection with a wire brush to remove rust and corrosion. Apply a light coat

4.2 Disconnect the negative terminal first

of battery terminal corrosion inhibitor or petroleum jelly to the threads to prevent future corrosion.

5   Attach the cable to the solenoid or ground connection and tighten the mounting nut/bolt securely.

6   Before connecting a new cable to the battery, make sure that it reaches the battery post without having to be stretched.

7   Connect the cable to the positive battery terminal first, then connect the ground cable to the negative battery terminal.

6   Ignition coil - removal and installation

1   Disconnect the cable from the negative battery terminal (see Section 4).

2   Remove the air intake duct (see Chapter 4, Section 12).

3   On 6.0L models, remove the engine cover. On all other models, remove the engine cover from the side of the engine from which you wish to remove the ignition coil (see illustration).

4.3 Disconnect the positive terminal second

4.4 Rotate the mega-fuse box back out of the way, then remove the hold-down clamp bolt

Note: *For the driver's side cover, remove the oil filler cap to remove the cover. On V8 models, you may have to disconnect the PCV hoses to remove the engine covers.*

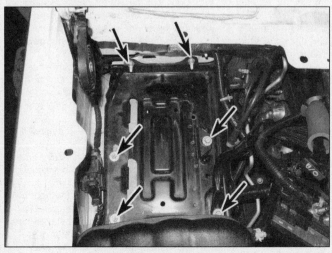

4.7 Battery tray fasteners

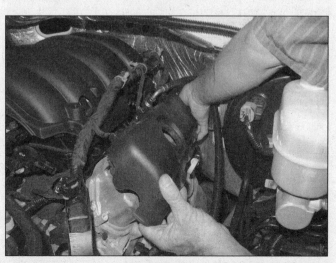

6.3 Removing the driver's side engine cover (V6 model shown, V8 models similar)

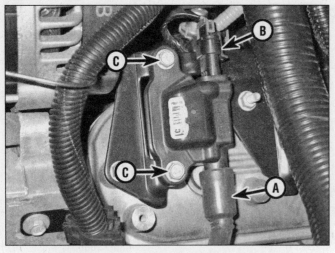

6.5 Coil mounting details (V8 engine, V6 similar)

A　Spark plug wire　　　C　Mounting bolts
B　Electrical connector

**7.7a Alternator mounting details
(V6 and non-6.0L V8 engines shown)**

1　B+ terminal　　　　　　3　Mounting bolts
2　Electrical connector

7.7b To detach the alternator from 6.0L models, remove these two bolts

8.6 To remove the heat shield (if equipped) from the starter motor, simply pull it off (6.0L model shown, others similar)

4　Reposition any harnesses or EVAP tubing to allow access to the desired ignition coil.
5　Disconnect the electrical connector from the ignition coil to be removed (see illustration).
6　Disconnect the spark plug wire boot from the spark plug (see Chapter 1).
7　Remove the two ignition coil mounting bolts and remove the coil.
8　Before installing the plug wire on the ignition coil, coat the interior of the boot with silicone dielectric compound. Installation is otherwise the reverse of removal.

7　Alternator - removal and installation

1　Disconnect the cable from the negative battery terminal (see Section 3).
2　Remove the air intake duct (see Chapter 4, Section 12).

3　Remove the drivebelt (see Chapter 1).
4　On 6.0L models, remove the engine cover.
5　Peel back the weather boot from the B+ terminal, remove the nut and disconnect the battery cable from the alternator (see illustration 7.7a).
6　Disconnect the electrical connector from the alternator.
7　Remove the two alternator mounting bolts (see illustrations).
8　Remove the alternator.
9　Installation is the reverse of removal. Be sure to tighten the alternator mounting bolts to the torque listed in this Chapter's Specifications.

8　Starter motor - removal and installation

Note: The photos accompanying this sec-

tion depict the starter motor assembly on a V8 model, but the starter motor used on V6 models is in the same location and is similar to what is shown here.

1　Disconnect the cable from the negative battery terminal (see Section 3).
2　On 6.0L models, loosen the wheel lug nuts for the right front wheel. On all models, raise the front of the vehicle and place it securely on jackstands. On 6.0L models, remove the right front wheel.
3　Remove any skid plates, if equipped, to allow access to the starter.
4　On non-6.0L models with 4WD, remove the right front differential carrier bracket under the starter, if equipped.
5　On 6.0L models, remove the right front wheel well splash shield (see Chapter 11).
6　On all models, remove the starter motor heat shield, if equipped (see illustration).
7　Disconnect the battery cable (the larger cable) and the starter control cable (the smaller cable) from the starter motor solenoid

8.7 Remove the smaller nut (A) and disconnect the cable from the starter solenoid terminal, then remove the larger nut (B) and disconnect the battery cable from the starter

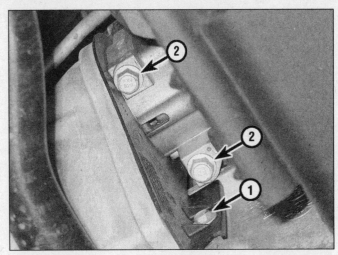

8.8 On 6.0L engines, remove the transmission cover bolt (1). On all engines, remove these two bolts (2) to remove the starter

terminals (see illustration).

Note: *If you're unable to remove the nuts that secure the starter cable and starter control cable nuts with the starter bolted in place (particularly on 6.0L models), skip this step for now, then remove the nuts and disconnect the two electrical cables after the starter has been*

unbolted *(but be sure to support the starter; don't allow the starter to hang by the cables!)*

8   On 6.0L models, remove the transmission cover bolt (see illustration).

9   On all models, remove the starter motor mounting bolts and remove the starter motor.

10   You can remove the starter motor from

underneath the vehicle on non 6.0L models. On 6.0L models, remove the starter motor through the right wheel well opening.

11   Installation is the reverse of removal. Be sure to tighten the starter motor mounting bolts to the torque listed in this Chapter's Specifications.

Notes

Chapter 6
Emissions and engine control systems

Contents

Specifications

Torque specifications   Ft-lbs (unless otherwise indicated)   Nm

Note: *One foot-pound (ft-lb) of torque is equivalent to 12 inch-pounds (in-lbs) of torque. Torque values below approximately 15 ft-lbs are expressed in inch-pounds, since most foot-pound torque wrenches are not accurate at these smaller values.*

Accelerator pedal position sensor bolts	80 in-ilbs
Camshaft position actuator/solenoid valve	
Step 1	48
Step 2	Additional 90 degrees
Camshaft position sensor bolts	
6.0L models	106 in-lbs
Non-6.0L models	18
Crankshaft position sensor bolts	18
Engine coolant temperature sensor	15
Engine oil pressure sensor	26
Knock sensor retaining bolt	18
Manifold Absolute Pressure sensor bolt	40 in-lbs
Oxygen sensors	31
PCV valve	53 in-lbs
TR switch mounting bolts	106 in-lbs
Vacuum pump bolts	18
Valve Lifter Oil Manifold (VLOM) assembly mounting bolts	18

1   General Information

1   To prevent pollution of the atmosphere from incompletely burned and evaporating gases, and to maintain good driveability and fuel economy, a number of emission control systems are incorporated. They include the:

Catalytic converter

2   A catalytic converter is an emission control device in the exhaust system that reduces certain pollutants in the exhaust gas stream. There are two types of converters: oxidation converters and reduction converters.

3   Oxidation converters contain a monolithic substrate (a ceramic honeycomb) coated with the semi-precious metals platinum and palladium. An oxidation catalyst reduces unburned hydrocarbons (HC) and carbon monoxide (CO) by adding oxygen to the exhaust stream as it passes through the substrate, which, in the presence of high temperature and the catalyst materials, converts the HC and CO to water vapor (H_2O) and carbon dioxide (CO_2).

4   Reduction converters contain a monolithic substrate coated with platinum and rhodium. A reduction catalyst reduces oxides of nitrogen (NOx) by removing oxygen, which in the presence of high temperature and the catalyst material produces nitrogen (N) and carbon dioxide (CO_2).

5   Catalytic converters that combine both types of catalysts in one assembly are known as "three-way catalysts" or TWCs. A TWC can reduce all three pollutants.

Evaporative Emissions Control (EVAP) system

6   The Evaporative Emissions Control (EVAP) system prevents fuel system vapors (which contain unburned hydrocarbons) from escaping into the atmosphere. On warm days, vapors trapped inside the fuel tank expand until the pressure reaches a certain threshold. Then the fuel vapors are routed from the fuel tank through the fuel vapor vent valve and the fuel vapor control valve to the EVAP canister, where they're stored temporarily until the next time the vehicle is operated. When the conditions are right (engine warmed up, vehicle up to speed, moderate or heavy load on the engine, etc.) the PCM opens the canister purge valve, which allows fuel vapors to be drawn from the canister into the intake manifold. Once in the intake manifold, the fuel vapors mix with incoming air before being drawn through the intake ports into the combustion chambers where they're burned up with the rest of the air/fuel mixture. The EVAP system is complex and virtually impossible to troubleshoot without the right tools and training.

Secondary Air Injection (AIR) system

7   Some models are equipped with a Secondary Air Injection (AIR) system. The secondary air injection system is used to reduce tailpipe emissions on initial engine start-up. The system uses an electric motor/pump assembly, relay, vacuum valve/solenoid, air shut-off valve, check valves and tubing to inject fresh air directly into the exhaust manifolds. The fresh air (oxygen) reacts with the exhaust gas in the catalytic converter to reduce HC and CO levels. The air pump and solenoid are controlled by the PCM through the AIR relay. During initial start-up, the PCM energizes the AIR relay, the relay supplies battery voltage to the air pump and the vacuum valve/solenoid, engine vacuum is applied to the air shut-off valve which opens and allows air to flow through the tubing into the exhaust manifolds. The PCM will operate the air pump until closed loop operation is reached (approximately four minutes). During normal operation, the check valves prevent exhaust backflow into the system.

Powertrain Control Module (PCM)

8   The Powertrain Control Module (PCM) is the brain of the engine management system. It also controls a wide variety of other vehicle systems. In order to program the new PCM, the dealer needs the vehicle as well as the new PCM. If you're planning to replace the PCM with a new one, there is no point in trying to do so at home because you won't be able to program it yourself.

Positive Crankcase Ventilation (PCV) system

9   The Positive Crankcase Ventilation (PCV) system reduces hydrocarbon emissions by scavenging crankcase vapors, which are rich in unburned hydrocarbons. A PCV valve or orifice regulates the flow of gases into the intake manifold in proportion to the amount of intake vacuum available.

10   The PCV system generally consists of the fresh air inlet hose, the PCV valve or orifice and the crankcase ventilation hose (or PCV hose). The fresh air inlet hose connects the air intake duct to a pipe on the valve cover. The crankcase ventilation hose (or PCV hose) connects the PCV valve or orifice in the valve cover to the intake manifold.

Information Sensors

Accelerator Pedal Position (APP) sensor - as you press the accelerator pedal, the APP sensor alters its voltage signal to the PCM in proportion to the angle of the pedal, and the PCM commands a motor inside the throttle body to open or close the throttle plate accordingly

Camshaft Position (CMP) sensor - produces a signal that the PCM uses to identify the number 1 cylinder and to time the firing sequence of the fuel injectors

Crankshaft Position (CKP) sensor - produces a signal that the PCM uses to calculate engine speed and crankshaft position, which enables it to synchronize ignition timing with fuel injector timing, and to detect misfires

Engine Coolant Temperature (ECT) sensor - a thermistor (temperature-sensitive variable resistor) that sends a voltage signal to the PCM, which uses this data to determine the temperature of the engine coolant

Fuel tank pressure sensor - measures the fuel tank pressure and controls fuel tank pressure by signaling the EVAP system to purge the fuel tank vapors when the pressure becomes excessive

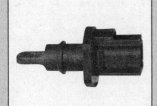

Intake Air Temperature (IAT) sensor - monitors the temperature of the air entering the engine and sends a signal to the PCM to determine injector pulse-width (the duration of each injector's on-time) and to adjust spark timing (to prevent spark knock)

Knock sensor - a piezoelectric crystal that oscillates in proportion to engine vibration which produces a voltage output that is monitored by the PCM. This retards the ignition timing when the oscillation exceeds a certain threshold

Manifold Absolute Pressure (MAP) sensor - monitors the pressure or vacuum inside the intake manifold. The PCM uses this data to determine engine load so that it can alter the ignition advance and fuel enrichment

Mass Air Flow (MAF) sensor - measures the amount of intake air drawn into the engine. It uses a hot-wire sensing element to measure the amount of air entering the engine

Oxygen sensors - generates a small variable voltage signal in proportion to the difference between the oxygen content in the exhaust stream and the oxygen content in the ambient air. The PCM uses this information to maintain the proper air/fuel ratio. A second oxygen sensor monitors the efficiency of the catalytic converter

Throttle Position (TP) sensor - a potentiometer that generates a voltage signal that varies in relation to the opening angle of the throttle plate inside the throttle body. Works with the PCM and other sensors to calculate injector pulse width (the duration of each injector's on-time)

Photos courtesy of Wells Manufacturing, except APP and MAF sensors.

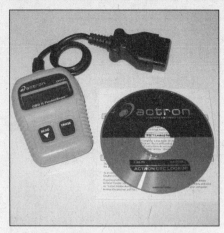

2.4a Simple code readers are an economical way to extract trouble codes when the CHECK ENGINE light comes on

2.4b Hand-held scan tools like these can extract computer codes and also perform diagnostics

2.6 The 16-pin Data Link Connector (DLC), also referred to as the diagnostic connector, is located under the left part of the dash

2   On Board Diagnosis (OBD) system and diagnostic trouble codes

General description

1   All models are equipped with the second generation OBD-II system. This system consists of an on-board computer known as the Powertrain Control Module (PCM), and information sensors, which monitor various functions of the engine and send data to the PCM. This system incorporates a series of diagnostic monitors that detect and identify fuel injection and emissions control system faults and store the information in the computer memory. This system also tests sensors and output actuators, diagnoses drive cycles, freezes data and clears codes.

2   The PCM is the brain of the electronically controlled fuel and emissions system. It receives data from a number of sensors and other electronic components (switches, relays, etc.). Based on the information it receives, the PCM generates output signals to control various relays, solenoids (fuel injectors) and other actuators. The PCM is specifically calibrated to optimize the emissions, fuel economy and driveability of the vehicle.

3   It isn't a good idea to attempt diagnosis or replacement of the PCM or emission control components at home while the vehicle is under warranty. Because of a federally-mandated warranty which covers the emissions system components and because any owner-induced damage to the PCM, the sensors and/or the control devices may void this warranty, take the vehicle to a dealer service department if the PCM or a system component malfunctions.

Scan tool information

4   Because extracting the Diagnostic Trouble Codes (DTCs) from an engine management system is now the first step in troubleshooting many computer-controlled systems and components, a code reader, at the very least, will be required (see illustration). More powerful scan tools can also perform many of the diagnostics once associated with expensive factory scan tools (see illustration). If you're planning to obtain a generic scan tool for your vehicle, make sure that it's compatible with OBD-II systems. If you don't plan to purchase a code reader or scan tool and don't have access to one, you can have the codes extracted by a dealer service department or an independent repair shop.

Note: *Some auto parts stores even provide this service.*

Obtaining and clearing Diagnostic Trouble Codes (DTCs)

5   Before outputting any DTCs stored in the PCM, thoroughly inspect ALL electrical connectors and hoses. Make sure that all electrical connections are tight, clean and free of corrosion. Make sure that all hoses are correctly connected, fit tightly and are in good condition (no cracks or tears). Also, make sure that the engine is tuned up. A poorly running engine is probably one of the biggest causes of emission-related malfunctions. Often, simply giving the engine a good tune-up will correct the problem.

Accessing the DTCs

6   On these models, all of which are equipped with On-Board Diagnostic II (OBD-II) systems, the Diagnostic Trouble Codes (DTCs) can only be accessed with a code reader or a scan tool (see illustrations 2.4a and 2.4b). Simply plug the connector of the tool into the Data Link Connector (DLC) or diagnostic connector (see illustration), which is located under the lower edge of the dash, just to the right of the steering column. Then follow the instructions included with the scan tool to extract the DTCs.

7   Once you have outputted all of the stored DTCs, look them up on the accompanying DTC chart.

8   After troubleshooting the source of each DTC, make any necessary repairs or replace the defective component(s).

Clearing the DTCs

9   Clear the DTCs with the scan tool in accordance with the instructions provided by the scan tool's manufacturer.

Diagnostic Trouble Codes (DTCs)

10   The accompanying tables are a list of the Diagnostic Trouble Codes (DTCs) that can be accessed by a do-it-yourselfer working at home (there are many, many more DTCs available to dealerships with proprietary scan tools and software, but those codes cannot be accessed by a generic scan tool). If, after you have checked and repaired the connectors, wire harness and vacuum hoses (if applicable) for an emission-related system, component or circuit, the problem persists, have the vehicle checked by a dealer service department.

OBD-II trouble codes

Note: *Not all trouble codes apply to all models.*

Code	Probable cause
P0006	High Pressure Fuel Cut-Off Solenoid Valve Control Circuit Low Voltage
P0007	High Pressure Fuel Cut-Off Solenoid Valve Control Circuit High Voltage
P0010	Camshaft Position (CMP) actuator solenoid control circuit
P0011	Camshaft Position (CMP) system performance
P0016	Crankshaft Position (CKP) sensor/Camshaft Position (CMP) sensor correlation
P0030	Oxygen sensor heater control circuit (bank 1, sensor 1)
P0031	Oxygen sensor heater control circuit low voltage (bank 1, sensor 1)
P0032	Oxygen sensor heater control circuit high voltage (bank 1, sensor 1)
P0036	Oxygen sensor heater control circuit (bank 1, sensor 2)
P0037	Oxygen sensor heater control circuit low voltage (bank 1, sensor 2)
P0038	Oxygen sensor heater control circuit high voltage (bank 1, sensor 2)
P0050	Oxygen sensor heater control circuit (bank 2, sensor 1)
P0051	Oxygen sensor heater control circuit low voltage (bank 2, sensor 1)
P0052	Oxygen sensor heater control circuit high voltage (bank 2, sensor 1)
P0053	Oxygen sensor heater resistance (bank 1, sensor 1)
P0054	Oxygen sensor heater resistance (bank 1, sensor 2)
P0056	Oxygen sensor heater control circuit (bank 2, sensor 2)
P0059	Oxygen sensor heater resistance (bank 2, sensor 1)
P0060	Oxygen sensor heater resistance (bank 2, sensor 2)
P0068	Throttle body air flow performance
P0071	Ambient Air Temperature Sensor Performance
P0072	Ambient Air Temperature Sensor Circuit Low Voltage
P0073	Ambient Air Temperature Sensor Circuit High Voltage
P0074	Ambient Air Temperature Sensor Circuit Intermittent
P0089	Fuel pressure regulator performance
P0090	Fuel pressure regulator control circuit
P0091	Fuel Pressure Regulator Control Circuit Low Voltage
P0092	Fuel Pressure Regulator Control Circuit High Voltage
P0096	Intake Air Temperature (IAT) sensor 2 performance

OBD-II trouble codes (continued)

Note: *Not all trouble codes apply to all models.*

Code	Probable cause
P0097	Intake Air Temperature (IAT) sensor 2, circuit low voltage
P0098	Intake Air Temperature (IAT) sensor 2, circuit high voltage
P0099	Intake Air Temperature (IAT) sensor 2, circuit intermittent
P00C6	Fuel Rail Pressure Low During Engine Cranking
P00C7	Intake Air Pressure Measurement System - Multiple Sensors Not Plausible
P00C8	Fuel Pressure Regulator High Control Circuit Open
P00C9	Fuel Pressure Regulator High Control Circuit Low Voltage
P00CA	Fuel Pressure Regulator High Control Circuit High Voltage
P00F4	Intake Air Humidity Sensor Circuit Low Voltage
P00F5	Intake Air Humidity Sensor Circuit High Voltage
P00F6	Intake Air Humidity Sensor Circuit Erratic
P0101	Mass Air Flow (MAF) sensor performance
P0102	Mass Air Flow (MAF) sensor circuit, low frequency
P0103	Mass Air Flow (MAF) sensor circuit, high frequency
P0106	Manifold Absolute Pressure (MAP) sensor performance
P0107	Manifold Absolute Pressure (MAP) sensor circuit, low voltage
P0108	Manifold Absolute Pressure (MAP) sensor circuit, high voltage
P0111	Intake Air Temperature (IAT) sensor 1 performance
P0112	Intake Air Temperature (IAT) sensor circuit, low voltage
P0113	Intake Air Temperature (IAT) sensor circuit, high voltage
P0114	Intake Air Temperature (IAT) sensor circuit intermittent
P0116	Engine Coolant Temperature (ECT) sensor performance
P0117	Engine Coolant Temperature (ECT) sensor circuit, low voltage
P0118	Engine Coolant Temperature (ECT) sensor circuit, high voltage
P0119	Engine Coolant Temperature (ECT) sensor circuit intermittent
P0121	Throttle Position (TP) sensor 1 performance
P0122	Throttle Position (TP) sensor 1 circuit, low voltage
P0123	Throttle Position (TP) sensor 1 circuit, high voltage
P0128	Engine coolant temperature below thermostat-regulating temperature

Code	Probable cause
P0131	Oxygen sensor circuit, low voltage (bank 1, sensor 1)
P0132	Oxygen sensor circuit, high voltage (bank 1, sensor 1)
P0133	Oxygen sensor slow response (bank 1, sensor 1)
P0134	Oxygen sensor circuit, insufficient activity (bank 1, sensor 1)
P0135	Oxygen sensor heater performance (bank 1, sensor 1)
P0136	Oxygen sensor circuit (bank 1, sensor 2)
P0137	Oxygen sensor circuit, low voltage (bank 1, sensor 2)
P0138	Oxygen sensor circuit, high voltage (bank 1, sensor 2)
P013A	Oxygen sensor, rich-to-lean response too slow (bank 1, sensor 2)
P013B	Oxygen sensor, lean-to-rich response too slow (bank 1, sensor 2)
P013C	Oxygen sensor, lean-to-rich response too slow (bank 2, sensor 2)
P013D	Oxygen sensor, lean-to-rich response too slow (bank 2, sensor 2)
P013E	Oxygen sensor, delayed rich-to-lean response (bank 1, sensor 2)
P013F	Oxygen sensor, delayed lean-to-rich response (bank 1, sensor 2)
P0140	Oxygen sensor circuit, insufficient activity (bank 1, sensor 2)
P0141	Oxygen sensor heater performance (bank 1, sensor 2)
P014A	Oxygen sensor, delayed rich-to-lean response (bank 2, sensor 2)
P014B	Oxygen sensor, delayed lean-to-rich response (bank 2, sensor 2)
P0151	Oxygen sensor circuit, low voltage (bank 2, sensor 1)
P0152	Oxygen sensor circuit, high voltage (bank 2, sensor 1)
P0153	Oxygen sensor, slow response (bank 2, sensor 1)
P0154	Oxygen sensor circuit, insufficient activity (bank 2, sensor 1)
P0155	Oxygen sensor heater performance (bank 2, sensor 1)
P0156	Oxygen sensor performance (bank 2, sensor 2)
P0157	Oxygen sensor circuit, low voltage (bank 2, sensor 2)
P0158	Oxygen sensor circuit, high voltage (bank 2, sensor 2)
P015A	Oxygen sensor circuit, Delayed Response Rich to Lean Bank 1 Sensor 1
P015B	Oxygen sensor circuit, Delayed Response Lean to Rich Bank 1 Sensor 1
P015C	Oxygen sensor circuit, Delayed Response Rich to Lean Bank 2 Sensor 1
P015D	Oxygen sensor circuit, Delayed Response Lean to Rich Bank 2 Sensor 1
P0160	Oxygen sensor circuit, insufficient activity (bank 2, sensor 2)

OBD-II trouble codes (continued)

Note: *Not all trouble codes apply to all models.*

Code	Probable cause
P0161	Oxygen sensor heater performance (bank 2, sensor 2)
P0171	Fuel trim system lean (bank 1)
P0172	Fuel trim system rich (bank 1)
P0174	Fuel trim system lean (bank 2)
P0175	Fuel trim system rich (bank 2)
P0178	Fuel Composition Sensor Circuit Low Frequency
P0179	Fuel Composition Sensor Circuit High Frequency
P018B	Fuel temperature sensor performance
P018C	Fuel temperature sensor circuit, low voltage
P018D	Fuel temperature sensor circuit, high voltage
P0191	Fuel Rail Pressure (FRP) sensor performance
P0192	Fuel Rail Pressure (FRP) sensor circuit, low voltage
P0193	Fuel Rail Pressure (FRP) sensor circuit, high voltage
P0200	Injector control circuit
P0201	Injector no. 1 circuit malfunction
P0202	Injector no. 2 circuit malfunction
P0203	Injector no. 3 circuit malfunction
P0204	Injector no. 4 circuit malfunction
P0205	Injector no. 5 circuit malfunction
P0206	Injector no. 6 circuit malfunction
P0207	Injector no. 7 circuit malfunction
P0208	Injector no. 8 circuit malfunction
P0218	Transmission fluid temperature too high
P0222	Throttle Position (TP) sensor 2 circuit, low voltage
P0223	Throttle Position (TP) sensor 2 circuit, high voltage
P0230	Fuel pump relay control circuit
P0231	Fuel pump control circuit, low voltage
P0232	Fuel pump control circuit, high voltage
P023F	Fuel pump control circuit

Code	Probable cause
P025A	Fuel pump control module enable circuit
P0261	Injector no. 1 circuit voltage low
P0262	Injector no. 1 circuit voltage high
P0264	Injector no. 2 circuit voltage low
P0265	Injector no. 2 circuit voltage high
P0267	Injector no. 3 circuit voltage low
P0268	Injector no. 3 circuit voltage high
P0270	Injector no. 4 circuit voltage low
P0271	Injector no. 4 circuit voltage high
P0273	Injector no. 5 circuit voltage low
P0274	Injector no. 5 circuit voltage high
P0276	Injector no. 6 circuit voltage low
P0277	Injector no. 6 circuit voltage high
P0279	Injector no. 7 circuit voltage low
P0280	Injector no. 7 circuit voltage high
P0282	Injector no. 8 circuit voltage low
P0283	Injector no. 8 circuit voltage high
P029D	Injector no. 1 leak
P02A1	Injector no. 2 leak
P02A5	Injector no. 3. Leak
P02A9	Injector no. 4 leak
P02AD	Injector no. 5 leak
P02B1	Injector no. 6 leak
P02B5	Injector no. 7 leak
P02B9	Injector no. 8 leak
P0300	Engine misfire detected
P0301	Engine misfire detected (cylinder 1)
P0302	Engine misfire detected (cylinder 2)
P0303	Engine misfire detected (cylinder 3)
P0304	Engine misfire detected (cylinder 4)
P0305	Engine misfire detected (cylinder 5)

OBD-II trouble codes (continued)

Note: *Not all trouble codes apply to all models.*

Code	Probable cause
P0306	Engine misfire detected (cylinder 6)
P0307	Engine misfire detected (cylinder 7)
P0308	Engine misfire detected (cylinder 8)
P0315	Crankshaft Position (CKP) system, system variation not learned
P0324	Knock Sensor (KS) module performance
P0325	Knock Sensor (KS) circuit (bank 1)
P0326	Knock Sensor (KS) performance (bank 1)
P0327	Knock Sensor (KS) circuit, low frequency or low voltage (bank 1)
P0328	Knock Sensor (KS) circuit, high frequency or high voltage (bank 1)
P0330	Knock Sensor (KS) circuit (bank 2)
P0331	Knock sensor (ks) performance (bank 2)
P0332	Knock Sensor (KS) circuit, low frequency or low voltage (bank 2)
P0333	Knock Sensor (KS) circuit, high frequency or high voltage (bank 2)
P0335	Crankshaft Position (CKP) sensor circuit
P0336	Crankshaft Position (CKP) sensor performance
P0340	Camshaft Position (CMP) sensor circuit
P0341	Camshaft Position (CMP) sensor performance
P0342	Camshaft Position (CMP) sensor circuit, low voltage
P0343	Camshaft Position (CMP) sensor circuit, high voltage
P0351	Ignition coil 1 control circuit
P0352	Ignition coil 2 control circuit
P0353	Ignition coil 3 control circuit
P0354	Ignition coil 4 control circuit
P0355	Ignition coil 5 control circuit
P0356	Ignition coil 6 control circuit
P0357	Ignition coil 7 control circuit
P0358	Ignition coil 8 control circuit
P0401	Exhaust Gas Recirculation (EGR) flow insufficient
P0402	Exhaust Gas Recirculation (EGR) flow excessive

Code	Probable cause
P0403	Exhaust Gas Recirculation (EGR) solenoid control circuit
P0405	Exhaust Gas Recirculation (EGR) position sensor circuit, low voltage
P0406	Exhaust Gas Recirculation (EGR) position sensor circuit, high voltage
P040C	Exhaust Gas Recirculation (EGR) temperature sensor 1 circuit, low voltage
P040D	Exhaust Gas Recirculation (EGR) temperature sensor 1 circuit, high voltage
P040F	Exhaust Gas Recirculation (EGR) temperature sensor 1 circuit-to-EGR temperature sensor 2 circuit correlation
P041C	Exhaust Gas Recirculation (EGR) temperature sensor 2 circuit, low voltage
P041D	Exhaust Gas Recirculation (EGR) temperature sensor 2 circuit, high voltage
P0420	Catalyst system, low efficiency (bank 1)
P0430	Catalyst system, high efficiency (bank 2)
P0442	Evaporative Emission (EVAP) system, small leak detected
P0443	Evaporative Emission (EVAP) system, purge solenoid control circuit
P0446	Evaporative Emission (EVAP) vent system performance
P0449	Evaporative Emission (EVAP) vent solenoid control circuit
P0451	Fuel Tank Pressure (FTP) sensor performance
P0452	Fuel Tank Pressure (FTP) sensor circuit, low voltage
P0453	Fuel Tank Pressure (FTP) sensor circuit, high voltage
P0454	Fuel Tank Pressure (FTP) sensor circuit intermittent
P0455	Evaporative Emission (EVAP) system, large leak detected
P0458	Evaporative Emission (EVAP) Purge Solenoid Valve Control Circuit Low Voltage
P0459	Evaporative Emission (EVAP) Purge Solenoid Valve Control Circuit High Voltage
P0461	Fuel level sensor circuit performance
P0462	Fuel level sensor circuit, low voltage
P0463	Fuel level sensor circuit, high voltage
P0464	Fuel level sensor circuit intermittent
P046C	Exhaust Gas Recirculation (EGR) position sensor performance
P0480	Cooling fan output circuit
P0496	EVAP system flow during non-purge
P0498	Evaporative Emission (EVAP) Vent Solenoid Valve Control Circuit Low Voltage
P0499	Evaporative Emission (EVAP) Vent Solenoid Valve Control Circuit High Voltage
P0500	Vehicle Speed Sensor (VSS) circuit

OBD-II trouble codes (continued)

Note: *Not all trouble codes apply to all models.*

Code	Probable cause
P0502	Vehicle Speed Sensor (VSS) circuit, low voltage
P0503	Vehicle Speed Sensor (VSS) circuit intermittent
P0506	Idle speed low
P0507	Idle speed high
P050D	Cold start rough idle
P0513	Theft deterrent key incorrect
P0521	Engine Oil Pressure (EOP) sensor, performance
P0522	Engine Oil Pressure (EOP) sensor circuit, low voltage
P0523	Engine Oil Pressure (EOP) sensor circuit, high voltage
P0530	Air conditioning refrigerant
P0532	Air conditioning refrigerant pressure sensor circuit, low voltage
P0533	Air conditioning refrigerant pressure sensor circuit, high voltage
P0540	Intake air heater feedback circuit
P0545	Exhaust Gas Temperature (EGT) sensor 1 circuit, low voltage
P0546	Exhaust Gas Temperature (EGT) sensor 1 circuit, high voltage
P0561	System voltage performance unstable
P0562	System voltage low
P0563	System voltage high
P0564	Cruise Control Multifunction Switch Circuit
P0565	Cruise Control Switch Circuit
P0567	Cruise control resume switch circuit
P0568	Cruise control set switch circuit
P056C	Cruise Control Cancel Switch Circuit
P0560	System Voltage Low
P0561	System Voltage Performance
P0562	System Voltage Performance
P0563	System Voltage High
P0571	Cruise control brake switch circuit
P0572	Brake switch circuit 1, low voltage

Code	Probable cause
P0573	Brake switch circuit 1, high voltage
P0575	Cruise control switch signal circuit
P057B	Brake Pedal Position Sensor Performance
P057C	Brake Pedal Position Sensor Circuit Low Voltage
P057D	Brake Pedal Position Sensor Circuit High Voltage
P0580	Cruise Control Multifunction Switch Circuit Low Voltage
P0581	Cruise Control Multifunction Switch Circuit High Voltage
P05CC	Cold Start Intake Camshaft Position System Performance
P0601	Powertrain or Transmission Control Module Read Only Memory (ROM)
P0602	Powertrain or Transmission Control Module not programmed
P0603	Powertrain or Transmission Control Module long-term memory reset
P0604	Powertrain or Transmission Control Module Random Access Memory
P0606 00	Powertrain Control Module (PCM) internal performance
P0606 37	Powertrain Control Module (PCM) software malfunction
P0607	Powertrain Control Module (PCM) performance
P0608	Vehicle speed output circuit
P0609	Rear wheel speed sensor
P060A	Powertrain Control Module (PCM), Monitoring Processor Performance
P060B	Powertrain Control Module (PCM), analog-to-digital performance
P060C	Powertrain Control Module (PCM), main processor performance
P060D	Powertrain Control Module (PCM), Accelerator Pedal Position (APP) system performance
P0611	Fuel Injector Control Module Performance
P0613	Transmission Control Module (TCM) processor
P0615	Starter relay control circuit
P0616	Starter relay control circuit, low voltage
P0617	Starter relay control circuit, high voltage
P061C	Powertrain Control Module (PCM), engine speed performance
P0621	Alternator L-terminal circuit
P0622	Alternator F-terminal circuit
P0628	Fuel Pump Relay Control Circuit Low Voltage
P0629	Fuel Pump Relay Control Circuit High Voltage

OBD-II trouble codes (continued)

Note: *Not all trouble codes apply to all models.*

Code	Probable cause
P062B	Powertrain Control Module (PCM), Fuel Injector Control Performance
P062C	Powertrain Control Module (PCM), vehicle speed performance
P062F	Powertrain Control Module (PCM) long-term memory performance
P062F	Transmission Control Module (TCM) EEPROM error
P0630	VIN Not Programmed or Mismatched - Engine Control Module (ECM)
P0633	Theft deterrent key not programmed
P0634	Transmission Control Module (TCM), internal temperature too high
P0641	5-volt reference 1 circuit
P0642	5-volt reference 1 circuit, low voltage
P0643	5-volt reference 1 circuit, high voltage
P0645	Air conditioning clutch relay control circuit
P0646	Air conditioning clutch relay control circuit, low voltage
P0647	Air conditioning clutch relay control circuit, high voltage
P064A	Fuel pump control module driver temperature too high
P064F	Powertain Control Module (PCM) or Transmission Control Module (TCM) Long Term Memory Performance
P0650	Malfunction Indicator Light (MIL) control circuit
P0651	5-volt reference 2 circuit
P0652	5-volt reference 2 circuit, low voltage
P0653	5-volt reference 2 circuit, high voltage
P0654	Engine speed output circuit
P0658	Actuator supply voltage 1 low
P0659	Actuator supply voltage 1 high
P0667	Transmission Control Module (TCM) temperature sensor performance
P0668	Transmission Control Module (TCM) temperature sensor circuit, low voltage
P0669	Transmission Control Module (TCM) temperature sensor circuit, high voltage
P0685	Engine controls ignition relay control circuit
P0686	Engine Controls Ignition Relay Control Circuit Low Voltage
P0687	Engine Controls Ignition Relay Control Circuit High Voltage
P0689	Engine controls ignition relay feedback circuit, low voltage

Code	Probable cause
P0690	Engine controls ignition relay feedback circuit, high voltage
P0691	Cooling Fan Speed Output Circuit Low Voltage
P0692	Cooling Fan Speed Output Circuit High Voltage
P0697	5-volt reference 3 circuit
P0698	5-volt reference 3 circuit, low voltage
P0699	5-volt reference 3 circuit, high voltage
P069E	Fuel Pump Control Module (FPCM) requested MIL illumination
P06A3	5-volt reference 4 circuit
P06A6	5-volt reference circuit performance
P06AC	Transmission Control Module (TCM) Power Up Temperature Sensor Performance
P06AD	Transmission Control Module (TCM) Power Up Temperature Sensor Circuit Low Voltage
P06AE	Transmission Control Module (TCM) Power Up Temperature Sensor Circuit High Voltage
P06B6	Powertain Control Module (PCM) Knock Sensor Processor 1 Performance
P06B7	Powertain Control Module (PCM) Knock Sensor Processor 2 Performance
P0700	Transmission Control Module (TCM) requested MIL illumination
P0701	Transmission Control Module (TCM) performance
P0703	Brake switch circuit 2
P0705	Transmission Range (TR) switch circuit
P0706	Transmission Range (TR) sensor circuit, PRNDL input
P0708	Transmission Range (TR) sensor circuit, high voltage
P0711	Transmission Fluid Temperature (TFT) sensor performance or sensor circuit performance
P0712	Transmission Fluid Temperature (TFT) sensor circuit, low voltage or low input
P0713	Transmission Fluid Temperature (TFT) sensor circuit, high voltage or high input
P0716	Input Speed Sensor (ISS) performance or ISS circuit performance
P0717	Input Speed Sensor (ISS) circuit, low voltage
P0719	Brake switch circuit, low voltage
P071A	Transmission tow mode switch circuit
P0721	Output Speed Sensor (OSS) performance
P0722	Output Speed Sensor (OSS) circuit, low voltage or no signal
P0723	Output Speed Sensor (OSS) circuit, intermittent
P0724	Brake switch circuit, high voltage

OBD-II trouble codes (continued)

Note: *Not all trouble codes apply to all models.*

Code	Probable cause
P0725	Engine speed circuit
P0726	Engine speed circuit performance
P0727	No engine speed signal
P0729	Incorrect 6th gear ratio
P0730	Incorrect gear ratio
P0731	Incorrect 1st gear ratio
P0732	Incorrect 2nd gear ratio
P0733	Incorrect 3rd gear ratio
P0734	Incorrect 4th gear ratio
P0735	Incorrect 5th gear ratio
P0736	Incorrect reverse ratio
P0740	Torque Converter Clutch (TCC) enable solenoid control circuit
P0741	Torque Converter Clutch (TCC) system, stuck off
P0742	Torque Converter Clutch (TCC) system, stuck on
P0746	Clutch Pressure Control (PC) solenoid 1, stuck off
P0747	Clutch Pressure Control (PC) solenoid 1, stuck on
P0748	Pressure Control (PC) solenoid control circuit
P0751	Shift Solenoid Valve 1 Performance – Stuck Off
P0752	Shift Solenoid Valve 1 Performance – Stuck on
P0756	Shift Solenoid Valve 2 Performance – Stuck Off
P0776	Clutch Pressure Control (PC) solenoid 2, stuck off
P0777	Clutch Pressure Control (PC) solenoid 2, stuck on
P077C	Output Speed Sensor (OSS) Circuit Low Voltage
P077D	Output Speed Sensor (OSS) Circuit High Voltage
P0796	Clutch Pressure Control (PC) solenoid 3 stuck off
P0797	Clutch Pressure Control (PC) solenoid 3 stuck on
P07BF	Input Speed Sensor (ISS) Circuit Low Voltage
P07C0	Input Speed Sensor (ISS) Circuit High Voltage
P0806	Clutch Pedal Position (CPP) sensor circuit performance

Code	Probable cause
P0807	Clutch Pedal Position (CPP) sensor circuit, low voltage
P0808	Clutch Pedal Position (CPP) sensor circuit, high voltage
P080A	Clutch Pedal Position (CPP) not learned
P0815	Upshift switch circuit
P0816	Downshift switch circuit
P0826	TAP up and down shift switch circuit
P0827	TAP up and down shift switch circuit low
P0828	TAP up and down shift switch circuit high
P0833	Clutch pedal switch 2 circuit
P0842	Transmission Fluid Pressure Switch 1 Circuit Low Voltage
P0843	Transmission Fluid Pressure Switch 1 Circuit High Voltage
P0850	Park/Neutral Position (PNP) Switch Circuit
P0851	Park/Neutral Position (PNP) switch circuit, low voltage
P0852	Park/Neutral Position (PNP) switch circuit, high voltage
P0856	Traction Control Torque Request Circuit
P0872	Transmission Fluid Pressure Switch 3 Circuit Low Voltage
P0873	Transmission Fluid Pressure Switch 3 Circuit High Voltage
P0877	Transmission Fluid Pressure Switch 4 Circuit Low Voltage
P0878	Transmission Fluid Pressure Switch 4 Circuit High Voltage
P0960	Transmission Control Solenoid Valve 1 Control Circuit Open
P0961	Line Pressure Control Solenoid Valve Performance
P0962	Transmission Control Solenoid Valve 1 Control Circuit Low Voltage
P0963	Transmission Control Solenoid Valve 1 Control Circuit High Voltage
P0964	Transmission Control Solenoid Valve 2 Control Circuit Open
P0966	Transmission Control Solenoid Valve 2 Control Circuit Low Voltage
P0967	Transmission Control Solenoid Valve 2 Control Circuit High Voltage
P0968	Transmission Control Solenoid Valve 3 Control Circuit Open
P0970	Transmission Control Solenoid Valve 3 Control Circuit Low Voltage
P0971	Transmission Control Solenoid Valve 3 Control Circuit High Voltage
P0973	Shift Solenoid Valve 1 Control Circuit Low Voltage
P0974	Shift Solenoid Valve 1 Control Circuit High Voltage

OBD-II trouble codes (continued)

Note: *Not all trouble codes apply to all models.*

Code	Probable cause
P0976	Shift Solenoid Valve 2 Control Circuit Low Voltage
P0977	Shift Solenoid Valve 2 Control Circuit High Voltage
P0989	Transmission Fluid Pressure Switch 5 Circuit Low Voltage
P0990	Transmission Fluid Pressure Switch 5 Circuit High Voltage
P1101	Intake Air Flow System Performance
P1248	Cylinder 1 Injector High Control Circuit Shorted to Control Circuit
P1249	Cylinder 2 Injector High Control Circuit Shorted to Control Circuit
P124A	Cylinder 3 Injector High Control Circuit Shorted to Control Circuit
P124B	Cylinder 4 Injector High Control Circuit Shorted to Control Circuit
P124C	Cylinder 5 Injector High Control Circuit Shorted to Control Circuit
P124D	Cylinder 6 Injector High Control Circuit Shorted to Control Circuit
P124E	Cylinder 7 Injector High Control Circuit Shorted to Control Circuit
P124F	Cylinder 8 Injector High Control Circuit Shorted to Control Circuit
P1255	Fuel Pump Control Module Driver High Temperature
P127C	Fuel Rail Pressure Sensor 2 Circuit Low Voltage
P127D	Fuel Rail Pressure Sensor 2 Circuit High Voltage
P129B	Fuel Pump Driver Control Module System Voltage Low Voltage
P129C	Fuel Pump Driver Control Module System Voltage High Voltage
P129D	Fuel Pump Driver Control Module Ignition On/Start Switch Circuit Low Voltage
P129E	Fuel Pump Driver Control Module Signal Message Counter Incorrect
P12A6	Fuel Pump Driver Control Module Enable Circuit Performance
P12A8	Fuel Pump Control Signal Message Counter Incorrect
P135A	Ignition Coil Supply Voltage Circuit Bank 1
P135B	Ignition Coil Supply Voltage Circuit Bank 2
P1400	Cold Start Emission Reduction Control System
P150C	Transmission Control Module (TCM) Engine Speed Request Signal Message Counter Incorrect
P1516	Throttle Actuator Control (TAC) Module Throttle Actuator Position Performance
P155A	Cruise Control Switch State Undetermined
P155B	Cruise Control Set/Coast Switch 2 Circuit

Code	Probable cause
P155C	Cruise Control Resume/Acceleration Switch 2 Circuit
P15AE	Fuel Injector Control Module System Voltage Low Voltage
P15AF	Fuel Injector Control Module System Voltage High Voltage
P15F6	Front Object Detection Control Module Torque Request Signal Message Counter Incorrect
P15F8	Automatic Braking Engine Torque Request Signal Message Counter Incorrect
P162B	Remote Vehicle Speed Limiting Signal Message Counter Incorrect
P162C	Vehicle Speed Limiting/Warning Switch Circuit
P1631	Immobilizer Fuel Enable Signal Not Correct
P163A	Powertrain Control Module (PCM) Fuel Pressure Regulator 1 Control System Circuitry Performance
P1649	Immobilizer Security Code Not Programmed
P1682	Ignition 1 Switch Circuit 2
P16A0	Sensor Communication Circuit Low Voltage
P16A1	Sensor Communication Circuit High Voltage
P16A2	Sensor Communication Circuit Performance
P16E9	Powertrain Control Module (PCM), Serial Peripheral Interface Bus 2
P16EA	Powertrain Control Module (PCM), Serial Peripheral Interface Bus 3
P16EB	Powertrain Control Module (PCM), Serial Peripheral Interface Bus 4
P16EC	Powertrain Control Module (PCM), Serial Peripheral Interface Bus 5
P16ED	Powertrain Control Module (PCM), Serial Peripheral Interface Bus 6
P16EE	Powertrain Control Module (PCM), Serial Peripheral Interface Bus 7
P16EF	Powertrain Control Module (PCM), Serial Peripheral Interface Bus 8
P16F0	Powertrain Control Module (PCM), Serial Peripheral Interface Bus 1
P16F3	Transmission Control Module (TCM), Redundant Memory Performance
P16F4	Transmission Control Module (TCM), Transmission Range Switch Input Circuitry Performance
P16FB	Transmission Control Module (TCM), Speed Signal Analog to Digital Converter Performance
P175F	Acceleration Sensor Signal Message Counter Incorrect
P1761	Up and Down Shift Switch Signal Message Counter Incorrect
P1762	Transmission Mode Switch Signal Message Counter Incorrect
P176B	Intermediate Speed Sensor Circuit Performance
P176C	Intermediate Speed Sensor Circuit Low Voltage
P176D	Intermediate Speed Sensor Circuit High Voltage

OBD-II trouble codes (continued)

Note: *Not all trouble codes apply to all models.*

Code	Probable cause
P17D4	Transfer Case Neutral Range Detected in High or Low Range
P1824	Internal Mode Switch P Circuit Low Voltage
P182A	Internal Mode Switch A Circuit Low Voltage
P182B	Internal Mode Switch B Circuit Low Voltage
P182C	Internal Mode Switch B Circuit High Voltage
P182D	Internal Mode Switch P Circuit High Voltage
P182E	Internal Mode Switch Indicates – Invalid Range
P182F	Internal Mode Switch C Circuit High Voltage
P1838	Internal Mode Switch A Circuit High Voltage
P1839	Internal Mode Switch C Circuit Low Voltage
P1840	Internal Mode Switch S Circuit Low Voltage
P1841	Internal Mode Switch S Circuit High Voltage
P185F	Transfer Case Shift Pending Signal Not Plausible
P1876	Up and Down Shift Enable Switch Circuit Low Voltage
P18B5	Internal Mode Switch A Circuit Shorted
P18B6	Internal Mode Switch B Circuit Shorted
P18B7	Internal Mode Switch C Circuit Shorted
P18B8	Internal Mode Switch P Circuit Shorted
P18B9	Internal Mode Switch S Circuit Shorted
P18BA	Internal Mode Switch A Circuit Stuck Off – Invalid Voltage Range
P18BB	Internal Mode Switch B Circuit Stuck Off – Invalid Voltage Range
P18BC	Internal Mode Switch C Circuit Stuck Off – Invalid Voltage Range
P18BD	Internal Mode Switch P Circuit Stuck Off – Invalid Voltage Range
P18BE	Internal Mode Switch S Circuit Stuck Off – Invalid Voltage Range
P18BF	Internal Mode Switch A Circuit Stuck On – Invalid Voltage Range
P18C0	Internal Mode Switch B Circuit Stuck On – Invalid Voltage Range
P18C1	Internal Mode Switch C Circuit Stuck On – Invalid Voltage Range
P18C2	Internal Mode Switch P Circuit Stuck On – Invalid Voltage Range
P18C3	Internal Mode Switch S Circuit Stuck On – Invalid Voltage Range

Code	Probable cause
P1915	Internal Mode Switch Does Not Indicate Park/Neutral During Start
P2066	Fuel Level Sensor 2 Performance
P2067	Fuel Level Sensor 2 Low Voltage
P2068	Fuel Level Sensor 2 High Voltage
P2088	Camshaft Position Actuator Solenoid Valve Control Circuit Low Voltage
P2089	Camshaft Position Actuator Solenoid Valve Control Circuit High Voltage
P2096	Post Catalyst Fuel Trim System Low Limit Bank 1
P2097	Post Catalyst Fuel Trim System High Limit Bank 1
P2098	Post Catalyst Fuel Trim System Low Limit Bank 2
P2099	Post Catalyst Fuel Trim System High Limit Bank 2
P2101	Throttle Actuator Position Performance
P2119	Throttle Closed Position Performance
P2122	Accelerator Pedal Position (APP) Sensor 1 Circuit Low Voltage
P2123	Accelerator Pedal Position (APP) Sensor 1 Circuit High Voltage
P2127	Accelerator Pedal Position (APP) Sensor 2 Circuit Low Voltage
P2128	Accelerator Pedal Position (APP) Sensor 2 Circuit High Voltage
P2135	Throttle Position Sensors 1-2 Not Plausible
P2138	Accelerator Pedal Position (APP) Sensors 1-2 Not Plausible
P2147	Cylinder 1 Injector High Control Circuit Low Voltage
P2148	Cylinder 1 Injector High Control Circuit High Voltage
P2150	Cylinder 2 Injector High Control Circuit Low Voltage
P2151	Cylinder 2 Injector High Control Circuit High Voltage
P2153	Cylinder 3 Injector High Control Circuit Low Voltage
P2154	Cylinder 3 Injector High Control Circuit High Voltage
P2156	Cylinder 4 Injector High Control Circuit Low Voltage
P2157	Cylinder 4 Injector High Control Circuit High Voltage
P2160	Vehicle Speed Sensor (VSS) 2 Circuit Low Voltage
P2161	Vehicle Speed Sensor (VSS) 2 Circuit Intermittent
P216B	Cylinder 5 Injector High Control Circuit Low Voltage
P216C	Cylinder 5 Injector High Control Circuit High Voltage
P216E	Cylinder 6 Injector High Control Circuit Low Voltage

OBD-II trouble codes (continued)
Note: *Not all trouble codes apply to all models.*

Code	Probable cause
P216F	Cylinder 6 Injector High Control Circuit High Voltage
P2176	Minimum Throttle Position Not Learned
P217B	Cylinder 7 Injector High Control Circuit Low Voltage
P217C	Cylinder 7 Injector High Control Circuit High Voltage
P217E	Cylinder 8 Injector High Control Circuit Low Voltage
P217F	Cylinder 8 Injector High Control Circuit High Voltage
P2199	Intake Air Temperature (IAT) Sensors 1-2 Not Plausible
P219A	Fuel Trim Cylinder Balance Bank 1
P219B	Fuel Trim Cylinder Balance Bank 2
P2227	Barometric Pressure (BARO) Sensor Performance
P2228	Barometric Pressure (BARO) Sensor Circuit Low Voltage
P2229	Barometric Pressure (BARO) Sensor Circuit High Voltage
P2230	Barometric Pressure (BARO) Sensor Circuit Erratic
P2269	Water in Fuel
P2270	Oxygen sensor circuit, Signal Stuck Lean Bank 1 Sensor 2
P2271	Oxygen sensor circuit, Signal Stuck Rich Bank 1 Sensor 2
P2272	Oxygen sensor circuit, Signal Stuck Lean Bank 2 Sensor 2
P2273	Oxygen sensor circuit, Signal Stuck Rich Bank 2 Sensor 2
P228C	Fuel Pressure Regulator Control Performance - Low Pressure
P228D	Fuel Pressure Regulator Control Performance - High Pressure
P2300	Ignition Coil 1 Control Circuit Low Voltage
P2301	Ignition Coil 1 Control Circuit High Voltage
P2303	Ignition Coil 2 Control Circuit Low Voltage
P2304	Ignition Coil 2 Control Circuit High Voltage
P2306	Ignition Coil 3 Control Circuit Low Voltage
P2307	Ignition Coil 3 Control Circuit High Voltage
P2309	Ignition Coil 4 Control Circuit Low Voltage
P2310	Ignition Coil 4 Control Circuit High Voltage
P2312	Ignition Coil 5 Control Circuit Low Voltage

Code	Probable cause
P2313	Ignition Coil 5 Control Circuit High Voltage
P2315	Ignition Coil 6 Control Circuit Low Voltage
P2316	Ignition Coil 6 Control Circuit High Voltage
P2318	Ignition Coil 7 Control Circuit Low Voltage
P2319	Ignition Coil 7 Control Circuit High Voltage
P2321	Ignition Coil 8 Control Circuit Low Voltage
P2322	Ignition Coil 8 Control Circuit High Voltage
P2534	Ignition On/Start Switch Circuit Low Voltage
P2535	Ignition On/Start Switch Circuit High Voltage
P2537	Ignition Accessory Switch Circuit Low Voltage
P2544	Transmission Torque Request Circuit Message Counter Incorrect
P254F	Engine Hood Switch Circuit
P2618	Crankshaft Position Signal Output Circuit Low Voltage
P2619	Crankshaft Position Signal Output Circuit High Voltage
P262B	Powertrain Control Module (PCM), Power Off Timer Performance
P2632	Fuel Transfer Pump Relay Control Circuit
P2633	Fuel Transfer Pump Relay Control Circuit Low Voltage
P2634	Fuel Transfer Pump Relay Control Circuit High Voltage
P2635	Fuel Pump Flow Performance
P2636	Fuel Transfer Pump Flow Insufficient
P263A	Malfunction Indicator Lamp (MIL) Control Circuit Low Voltage
P263B	Malfunction Indicator Lamp (MIL) Control Circuit High Voltage
P2670	Actuator High Control Circuit Group 2 Low Voltage
P2671	Actuator High Control Circuit Group 2 High Voltage
P2714	Pressure Control Solenoid Valve 4 – Stuck Off – Transmission Hydraulic/Mechanical Performance
P2715	Pressure Control Solenoid Valve 4 – Stuck On – Transmission Hydraulic/Mechanical Performance
P2718	Transmission Control Solenoid Valve 4 Control Circuit Open
P2719	Pressure Control Solenoid 4 System Performance
P2720	Transmission Control Solenoid Valve 4 Control Circuit Low Voltage

OBD-II trouble codes (continued)
Note: *Not all trouble codes apply to all models.*

Code	Probable cause
P2721	Transmission Control Solenoid Valve 4 Control Circuit High Voltage
P2723	Pressure Control Solenoid Valve 5 – Stuck Off – Transmission Hydraulic/Mechanical Performance
P2724	Pressure Control Solenoid Valve 5 – Stuck On – Transmission Hydraulic/Mechanical Performance
P2727	Transmission Control Solenoid Valve 5 Control Circuit Open
P2728	Pressure Control (PC) Solenoid Valve 5 Performance
P2729	Transmission Control Solenoid Valve 5 Control Circuit Low Voltage
P2730	Transmission Control Solenoid Valve 5 Control Circuit High Voltage
P2736	Transmission Control Solenoid Valve 6 Control Circuit Open
P2738	Transmission Control Solenoid Valve 6 Control Circuit Low Voltage
P2739	Transmission Control Solenoid Valve 6 Control Circuit High Voltage
P2762	Torque Converter Clutch (TCC) Pressure Control Solenoid Valve Performance
P2763	Torque Converter Clutch (TCC) Pressure Control Solenoid Valve Control Circuit High Voltage
P2764	Torque Converter Clutch (TCC) Pressure Control Solenoid Valve Control Circuit Low Voltage
P2771	Four Wheel Drive (4WD) Switch Circuit
P279A	Transfer Case High Range Incorrect Ratio
P279B	Transfer Case Low Range Incorrect Ratio
P279C	Four Wheel Drive (4WD) Neutral Range Performance
P27A7	Transmission Control Solenoid Valve 1 Calibration Incorrect
P27A8	Transmission Control Solenoid Valve 2 Calibration Incorrect
P27A9	Transmission Control Solenoid Valve 3 Calibration Incorrect
P27AA	Transmission Control Solenoid Valve 4 Calibration Incorrect
P27AB	Transmission Control Solenoid Valve 5 Calibration Incorrect
P27AC	Transmission Control Solenoid Valve 6 Calibration Incorrect
P27AD	Transmission Control Solenoid Valve 7 Calibration Incorrect
P2808	Torque Converter Clutch (TCC) System Stuck Off – The TCC did not apply due to a hydraulic/mechanical condition
P2809	Torque Converter Clutch (TCC) System Stuck On – The TCC did not release due to a hydraulic/mechanical condition
P2812	Transmission Control Solenoid Valve 7 Control Circuit Open
P2814	Transmission Control Solenoid Valve 7 Control Circuit Low Voltage
P2815	Transmission Control Solenoid Valve 7 Control Circuit High Voltage

P2817	Transmission Control Solenoid Valve 8 Stuck Off – During the 3-4 upshift the transmission did not obtain 4th gear, due to a hydraulic/mechanical condition
P2818	Transmission Control Solenoid Valve 8 Stuck On – The TCC RPM slip speed is to low when commanded on in park position due to a hydraulic/mechanical condition
P281D	Transmission Control Solenoid Valve 8 Control Circuit Low Voltage
P281E	Transmission Control Solenoid Valve 8 Control Circuit High Voltage
P2824	Transmission Control Solenoid Valve 9 Control Circuit Open
P2826	Transmission Control Solenoid Valve 9 Control Circuit Low Voltage
P2827	Transmission Control Solenoid Valve 9 Control Circuit High Voltage
P3400	Cylinder Deactivation System
P3401	Cylinder 1 Deactivation Solenoid Valve Control Circuit Open
P3403	Cylinder 1 Deactivation Solenoid Valve Control Circuit Low Voltage
P3404	Cylinder 1 Deactivation Solenoid Valve Control Circuit High Voltage
P3425	Cylinder 4 Deactivation Solenoid Valve Control Circuit Open
P3427	Cylinder 4 Deactivation Solenoid Valve Control Circuit Low Voltage
P3428	Cylinder 4 Deactivation Solenoid Valve Control Circuit High Voltage
P3441	Cylinder 6 Deactivation Solenoid Valve Control Circuit Open
P3443	Cylinder 6 Deactivation Solenoid Valve Control Circuit Low Voltage
P3444	Cylinder 6 Deactivation Solenoid Valve Control Circuit High Voltage
P3449	Cylinder 7 Deactivation Solenoid Valve Control Circuit Open
P3451	Cylinder 7 Deactivation Solenoid Valve Control Circuit Low Voltage
P3452	Cylinder 7 Deactivation Solenoid Valve Control Circuit High Volage

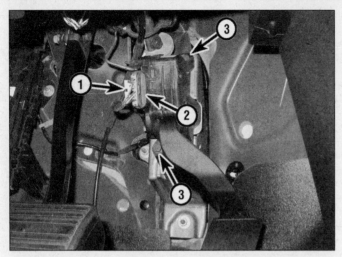

3.2 Pull the connector lock (1) out, then depress the release tab and disconnect the electrical connector (2). To detach the APP sensor/pedal assembly, remove the mounting bolts (3)

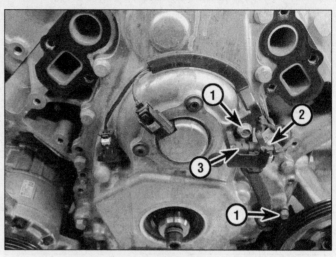

4.4 CMP sensor details - 4.3L V6 shown, others models similar (coolant crossover pipe removed for clarity)

1	Harness bracket bolts	3	CMP sensor
2	Electrical connector		

3   Accelerator Pedal Position (APP) sensor - replacement

Note: *The APP sensor is located at the top of the accelerator pedal arm. The APP sensor and the accelerator pedal are a one-piece assembly and are replaced as a unit.*

1   Remove the knee bolster (see Chapter 11).

2   Locate the APP sensor at the top of the accelerator pedal assembly (see illustration).

3   Disconnect the electrical connector from the APP sensor.

4   Unscrew the mounting bolts and remove the APP sensor and accelerator pedal as a single assembly.

5   Installation is the reverse of removal. Tighten the APP sensor assembly mounting bolts securely.

4   Camshaft Position (CMP) sensor - replacement

Note: *The CMP sensor is located on the engine front cover, at the 1 o'clock position in relation to the crankshaft pulley.*

1   Disconnect the cable from the negative terminal of the battery (see Chapter 5).

2   If you're working on a V6 or 5.3L/6.2L V8, remove the drivebelt tensioner (see Chapter 1, Section 12).

3   If you're working on a 6.0L V8 equipped with a camshaft position actuator, remove the water pump (see Chapter 3).

4   Remove the sensor harness bracket fasteners and re-position the bracket and harness (see illustration).

5   Disconnect the CMP sensor electrical connector.

6   Remove the CMP sensor from the front cover.

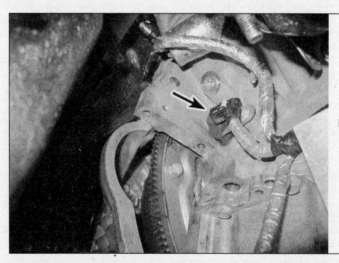

5.2 The CKP sensor is located at the right rear of the engine block, above the starter motor

7   If reusing the old sensor, remove and discard the old CMP sensor O-ring.

8   Installation is the reverse of removal. Be sure to use a new O-ring, lubricate it with a film of clean engine oil, and tighten the CMP sensor bolt to the torque listed in this Chapter's Specifications.

5   Crankshaft Position (CKP) sensor - replacement

Note: *If the Malfunction Indicator Light (MIL) comes on after replacing the CKP sensor and starting the engine, drive the vehicle to a dealer and have the service department perform a crankshaft position variation learn procedure with a factory scan tool. If a scan tool is available, follow the instructions on the scan tool to perform the relearn procedure.*

Note: *The CKP sensor is located on the right side of the engine block, near the flywheel. Access is blocked by the starter.*

1   Remove the starter motor (see Chapter 5).

2   Disconnect the electrical connector from the crankshaft position sensor (see illustration).

3   Remove the CKP sensor mounting bolt and remove the CKP sensor.

4   Installation is the reverse of removal. Be sure to tighten the CKP sensor mounting bolt to the torque listed in this Chapter's Specifications.

6   Engine Coolant Temperature (ECT) sensor - replacement

Warning: *Wait until the engine is completely cool before beginning this procedure.*

Note: *On 6.0L models, the ECT sensor is located on the left cylinder head, in front of cylinder No. 1, just below the valve cover. On non-6.0L models, the ECT sensor is located to the right of the throttle body, next to the thermostat housing.*

6.3a Location of the ECT sensor on non-6.0L models

6.3b Location of the ECT sensor on 6.0L models

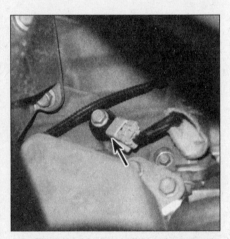

8.5a The left-side (bank 1) knock sensor is located on the engine block, in front of the oil filter housing

8.5b Right-side (bank 2) knock sensor location (4.3L V6 shown, other similar)

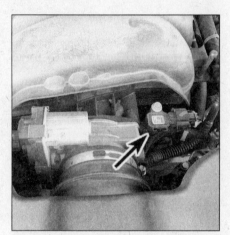

9.1 Disconnect the MAP sensor electrical connector and remove the bolt, then pull the sensor from the manifold (5.3L V8 shown)

1   Drain the cooling system to a level that's below the level of the ECT sensor (see Chapter 1).

2   On non-6.0L models, remove the air intake duct (see Chapter 4, Section 12).

3   On all models, disconnect the electrical connector from the ECT sensor (see illustrations).

4   Unscrew and remove the ECT sensor.

5   If you're installing the old sensor, apply thread sealant to the threads. The threads of a new sensor should already be coated with sealant.

6   Installation is the reverse of removal. Be sure to tighten the ECT sensor to the torque listed in this Chapter's Specifications.

7   Refill the cooling system (see Chapter 1).

7   Intake Air Temperature (IAT) sensor - replacement

1   The IAT sensor is an integral component

of the Mass Air Flow (MAF) sensor (see Section 10).

8   Knock sensor - replacement

Note: *There are two knock sensors, one on each side of the block. Knock sensor 1 is on the left side of the block; knock sensor 2 is on the right side, above the starter. Because they're located below the exhaust manifolds, you cannot access the knock sensors from above.*

1   Raise the front of the vehicle and place it securely on jackstands.

2   On non-6.0L, 4WD models, it may be necessary to remove the front driveshaft to access the knock sensor 1 for removal (see Chapter 8, Section 3).

3   On 6.0L models, to replace knock sensor 2, remove the starter (see Chapter 5, Section 8).

4   On non-6.0L models, remove the knock sensor heat shield retaining bolt and remove

the heat shield.

5   Disconnect the electrical connector from the knock sensor (see illustrations).

6   Remove the knock sensor retaining bolt and remove the knock sensor.

7   Installation is the reverse of removal. Be sure to tighten the knock sensor retaining bolt to the torque listed in this Chapter's Specifications.

9   Manifold Absolute Pressure (MAP) sensor - replacement

Non-6.0L models

Note: *The MAP sensor is located on top of the intake manifold, on the left side behind the throttle body.*

1   Disconnect the MAP sensor electrical connector (see illustration).

2   Remove the MAP sensor mounting bolt and remove the MAP sensor by pulling it straight up out of the intake manifold.

9.8a To detach the MAP sensor from the intake manifold on a V8 model, carefully pry each end of the retainer out and up and remove the retainer . . .

9.8b . . . then grasp the sensor firmly and pull it straight up and out of the manifold. Be sure to inspect the sensor grommet

10.1 Slide the connector lock (A) up and depress the release tab (B) to disconnect the electrical connector, then remove the MAF sensor screws (C)

3   Remove the old sealing grommet from the MAP sensor and inspect it. If the grommet is cracked, torn or otherwise deteriorated, replace it.

4   When installing the MAP sensor, use a little clean engine oil on the grommet so that it doesn't tear when pushing the MAP sensor into its mounting hole.

5   Installation is otherwise the reverse of removal.

6.0L models

Note: *The MAP sensor is located on top of the intake manifold, near the front.*

6   Remove the intake manifold cover.

7   Disconnect the MAP sensor electrical connector.

8   Remove the MAP sensor retainer, then remove the sensor by pulling it straight up (see illustrations).

9   Remove the old sealing grommet (see illustration 9.8b) from the MAP sensor and inspect it. If the grommet is cracked, torn or otherwise deteriorated, replace it. When installing the MAP sensor, use a little clean engine oil on the grommet so that it doesn't tear when pushing the MAP sensor into its mounting hole.

10   When installing the retainer, make sure that it snaps into place. Installation is otherwise the reverse of removal.

---

10   Mass Air Flow (MAF) sensor - replacement

Note: *The MAF sensor is located on the air filter housing.*

1   Disconnect the electrical connector from the MAF sensor (see illustration).

2   Remove the screws that secure the MAF sensor to the air filter housing.

3   Remove the MAF sensor by carefully pulling it out of the air filter housing.

4   Installation is the reverse of removal.

---

11   Oxygen sensors - general information and replacement

General information

1   An oxygen sensor is a galvanic battery that produces a very small voltage output in response to the amount of oxygen in the exhaust gases. This voltage signal is the input side of the feedback loop between the oxygen sensor and the Powertrain Control Module (PCM). Without it, the PCM would be unable to correct the injector on-time (which determines the air/fuel ratio) to maintain the perfect (known as stoichiometric) air/fuel ratio of 14.7:1 that the catalyst needs for optimal operation.

2   All vehicles covered by this manual have On-Board Diagnostics II (OBD-II) engine management systems, which means they have the ability to monitor the performance of the catalytic converter. They accomplish this by using an oxygen sensor ahead of the catalytic converter and another oxygen sensor behind the catalytic converter. By comparing the amount of oxygen in the post-catalyst exhaust gas to the oxygen content of the exhaust gas before it enters the catalyst, the PCM can determine the efficiency of the converter.

3   All models covered by this manual have four heated oxygen sensors: one upstream sensor (ahead of the catalytic converter) per cylinder bank and one downstream sensor (after the catalytic converter) per cylinder bank. The upstream sensors are located on the upper part of the front exhaust pipe assembly, above the catalytic converters. The downstream sensors are located under the vehicle, in the exhaust pipes, just behind the catalytic converters.

4   The upstream and downstream oxygen sensors are heated to speed up the warm-up time during which the sensors are unable to produce an accurate voltage signal. The circuit for each oxygen sensor heater is controlled by the PCM, which opens the ground side of the circuit to shut off the heater as soon as the sensor reaches its normal operating temperature.

5   Special care must be taken whenever a sensor is serviced.

a) *Oxygen sensors have a permanently attached pigtail and an electrical connector that cannot be removed. Damaging or removing the pigtail or electrical connector will render the sensor useless.*

b) *Keep grease, dirt and other contaminants away from the electrical connector and the louvered end of the sensor.*

c) *Do not use cleaning solvents of any kind on an oxygen sensor.*

d) *Oxygen sensors are extremely delicate. Do not drop a sensor, throw it around or handle it roughly.*

e) *Make sure that the silicone boot on the sensor is installed in the correct position. Otherwise, the boot might melt and it might prevent the sensor from operating correctly.*

Replacement

Note: *Because they're installed in the exhaust pipes, which contract as they cool down, the oxygen sensors can be very difficult to loosen when the engine is cold. Rather than risk damage to a sensor or its mounting threads, start and run the engine for a minute or two, then shut it off. Be careful not to burn yourself during the following procedure.*

Upstream oxygen sensor

Note: *The upstream oxygen sensors are located on the upper part of the front exhaust pipe assembly, just above the catalytic converters.*

11.7a Left upstream oxygen sensor (bank 1, sensor 1) location, viewed from underneath the vehicle, looking forward (V6 model shown, V8 models similar)

11.7b Right upstream oxygen sensor (bank 2, sensor 1) location, viewed from the right wheel well, with the splash shield removed (V6 model shown, V8 models similar)

11.8 Using an oxygen sensor socket, unscrew the upstream oxygen sensor from the exhaust manifold (right upstream sensor shown)

6   Raise the vehicle and place it securely on jackstands.

7   Locate the oxygen sensor (see illustrations), then trace the sensor electrical lead to the electrical connector and disconnect the connector.

8   Using an oxygen sensor socket (available at most auto parts stores), unscrew the upstream oxygen sensor (see illustration). If the sensor is difficult to loosen, spray some penetrating oil onto the sensor threads and allow it to soak in for awhile.

9   If you're going to install the old sensor, apply anti-seize compound to the threads of the sensor to facilitate future removal. If you're going to install a new oxygen sensor, it's not necessary to apply anti-seize compound to the threads. The threads on new sensors already have anti-seize compound on them.

10   Installation is otherwise the reverse of removal. Be sure to tighten the sensor to the torque listed in this Chapter's Specifications.

Downstream oxygen sensor

Note: *The downstream oxygen sensors are located on top of the exhaust pipes, just behind the catalytic converters.*

11   Raise the vehicle and place it securely on jackstands.

12   Locate the downstream oxygen sensor (see illustrations), then trace the sensor electrical lead to the connector and disconnect it.

13   Unscrew the downstream oxygen sensor with an oxygen sensor socket (see illustration 11.8). If the sensor is difficult to loosen, spray some penetrating oil onto the sensor threads and allow it to soak in for awhile.

14   If you're going to install the old sensor, apply anti-seize compound to the threads of the sensor to facilitate future removal. If you're going to install a new oxygen sensor, it's not necessary to apply anti-seize compound to the threads. The threads on new sensors already have anti-seize compound on them.

15   Installation is otherwise the reverse of removal. Be sure to tighten the sensor to the torque listed in this Chapter's Specifications.

12   Transmission Range (TR) switch - replacement

1   Drain the automatic transmission fluid and remove the fluid filter (see Chapter 1).

2   Slide out the connector lock, then unplug the TR switch connector (see illustration).

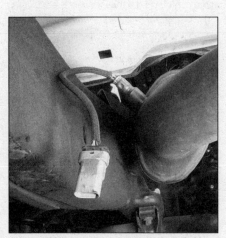

11.12a Left-side downstream oxygen sensor (bank 1, sensor 2)

11.12b Right-side downstream oxygen sensor (bank 2, sensor 2)

12.2 TR switch electrical connector

12.3 TR switch mounting bolts

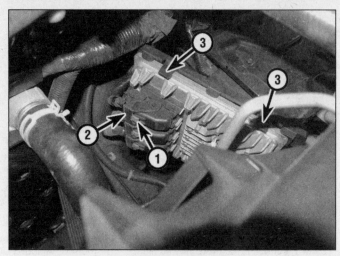

14.2 PCM mounting details

1 Connector lock	3 PCM upper mounting tabs
2 Connector lever	

3   Remove the TR switch mounting bolts and detach the switch from the valve body (see illustration).

4   Installation is the reverse of the removal procedure. Tighten the mounting bolts to the torque listed in this Chapter's Specifications. Make sure the connector lock engages securely.

5   Replace the transmission fluid filter and install the fluid pan, then refill the transmission with the proper fluid (see Chapter 1).

13   Input and output speed sensor - replacement

On these vehicles, the input and output speed sensors are located inside the transmission housing, on the valve body, requiring valve body removal for replacement of the sensors. It is recommended that the vehicle be taken to a qualified repair facility for replacment of the sensors.

14   Powertrain Control Module (PCM) - removal and installation

Caution: *To avoid electrostatic discharge damage to the PCM, handle the PCM only by its case. Do not touch the electrical terminals during removal and installation. If available, ground yourself to the vehicle with an anti-static ground strap, available at computer supply stores.*
Note: *The PCM is mounted in the left front corner of the engine compartment.*
Note: *The procedures in this section apply only to disconnecting, removing and installing the PCM that is already installed in your vehicle. If, however, you need to replace the PCM, it must be programmed with new software*

and calibrations. This procedure requires the use of GM's TECH-2 scan tool and GM's latest PCM-programming software, so you WILL NOT BE ABLE TO REPLACE THE PCM AT HOME.

1   Disconnect the cable from the negative terminal of the battery (see Chapter 5).

2   Unplug the electrical connectors from the PCM (see illustration). To unlock each PCM electrical connector, slide the red lock out, then depress it while swinging open connector lever.

3   Disengage the retaining tabs that secure the PCM to its mounting bracket and remove the PCM.

4   Installation is the reverse of removal.

15   Catalytic converters - description, check and replacement

Note: *Because of a Federally-mandated extended warranty which covers emission-related components such as the catalytic converter, check with a dealer service department before replacing the converter at your own expense.*

Description

1   A catalytic converter (or catalyst) is an emission control device in the exhaust system that reduces certain pollutants in the exhaust gas stream. There are two types of converters. An oxidation catalyst reduces hydrocarbons (HC) and carbon monoxide (CO). A reduction catalyst reduces oxides of nitrogen (NOx). Catalysts that can reduce all three pollutants are known as "three-way catalysts." The vehicles covered in this manual are equipped with two three-way catalysts.

Check

2   The test equipment for a catalytic converter (a loaded-mode dynamometer and a five-gas analyzer) is expensive. If you suspect that the converter on your vehicle is malfunctioning, take it to a dealer or authorized emission inspection facility for diagnosis and repair.

3   Whenever you raise the vehicle to service underbody components, inspect the converter for leaks, corrosion, dents and other damage. Carefully inspect the welds and/or flange bolts and nuts that attach the front and rear ends of the converter to the exhaust system. If you note any damage, replace the converter.

4   Although catalytic converters don't break too often, they can become plugged up. The easiest way to check for a restricted converter is to use a vacuum gauge to diagnose the effect of a blocked exhaust on intake vacuum.

a) *Connect a vacuum gauge to an intake manifold vacuum source (see Chapter 2A).*

b) *Warm the engine to operating temperature, place the transmission in Park (automatic models) or Neutral (manual models) and apply the parking brake.*

c) *Note the vacuum reading at idle and write it down.*

d) *Quickly open the throttle to near its wide-open position, then quickly get off the throttle and allow it to close. Note the vacuum reading and write it down.*

e) *Do this test three more times, recording your measurement after each test.*

f) *If your fourth reading is more than one in-Hg lower than the reading that you noted at idle, the exhaust system might be restricted (the catalytic converter could be plugged, OR an exhaust pipe or muffler could be restricted).*

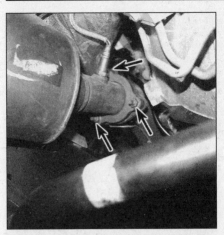

15.7a To detach the upper left end of the front exhaust pipe assembly from the left exhaust manifold, remove these nuts

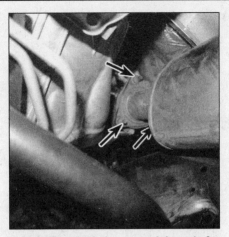

15.7b To detach the upper right end of the front exhaust pipe assembly from the right exhaust manifold, remove these nuts

15.8 To detach the rear end of the front exhaust pipe assembly from the rest of the exhaust system, remove this clamp

Replacement

Note: *The catalytic converters are integral components of the front exhaust pipe assembly, which connects the exhaust manifolds to the rest of the exhaust pipe assembly. Both catalysts are welded into the front exhaust pipe assembly, which is a one-piece assembly.*

5   Raise the vehicle and place it securely on jackstands.

6   Disconnect the electrical connectors for the upstream and downstream oxygen sensors and remove all four sensors (see Section 11).

7   Remove the three nuts at each of the upper flanges (see illustrations) that secure the front exhaust pipe assembly to the exhaust manifold flanges.

8   Remove the clamp (see illustration) that secures the rear of the front exhaust pipe assembly to the rest of the exhaust system and remove the front exhaust pipe assembly.

9   Remove and discard the old flange gaskets from the mounting flanges. Be sure to use new gaskets at both mounting flanges. Also use new fasteners at both flanges.

10   Coat the threads of the nuts and bolts with anti-seize compound to facilitate future removal. Tighten the nuts that secure the front exhaust pipe assembly to the exhaust manifold and to the rest of the exhaust system securely. Installation is otherwise the reverse of removal

16   Evaporative Emissions Control (EVAP) system - description and component replacement

Description

1   The Evaporative Emissions Control (EVAP) system prevents fuel system vapors (which contain unburned hydrocarbons) from escaping into the atmosphere. On warm days,

vapors trapped inside the fuel tank expand until the pressure reaches a certain threshold, at which point the fuel vapors are routed from the fuel tank through the fuel vapor vent valve and the fuel vapor control valve to the EVAP canister, where they're stored temporarily, until they can be consumed by the engine during normal operation. When the conditions are right (engine warmed up, vehicle up to speed, moderate or heavy load on the engine, etc.) the Powertrain Control Module (PCM) opens the canister purge solenoid, which allows the fuel vapors to be drawn from the canister into the intake manifold, where they mix with the air/fuel mixture before being consumed in the combustion chambers. This system is complex and virtually impossible to troubleshoot without the right tools and training. However, the following description should give you a good idea of how it works:

2   The EVAP canister is located under the vehicle, in front of or to the side of the fuel tank, depending on the model. The EVAP canister, which contains activated charcoal, is the repository for storing the fuel vapors, and is designed to be maintenance-free (it should last the life of the vehicle).

3   The fuel tank pressure sensor, which is located on top of the mounting flange for the in-tank fuel pump/fuel level sending unit module, monitors the pressure inside the tank, and transmits its measurement to the PCM during an OBD-II leak test.

4   The EVAP canister vent solenoid is normally open. But it seals off the EVAP system for inspection and maintenance (I/M 240) testing and for OBD-II leak and pressure tests.

5   The EVAP canister purge solenoid, which is under the control of the Powertrain Control Module (PCM), regulates the flow of vapors being purged from the EVAP canister into the intake manifold. The canister purge solenoid is normally closed. It opens only when directed to do so by the PCM, which uses the availability of intake manifold vacuum and data from various information sensor inputs

to determine when and how long to open the valve. The interval of time during which the purge valve is opened by the PCM is known as its duty cycle.

General system checks

6   The most common symptom of a faulty EVAP system is a strong fuel odor (particularly during hot weather). If you smell fuel while driving or (more likely) right after you park the vehicle and turn off the engine, check the fuel filler cap first. Make sure that it's screwed onto the fuel filler neck all the way. If the odor persists, inspect all EVAP hose connections, both in the engine compartment and under the vehicle. Be sure to inspect each hose attached to the canister for damage and leakage along its entire length. Repair or replace as necessary. Inspect the canister for damage and look for fuel leaking from the bottom. If fuel is leaking or the canister is otherwise damaged, replace it.

7   Poor idle, stalling, and poor driveability can be caused by a defective fuel vapor vent valve or canister purge solenoid, a damaged canister, cracked hoses, or hoses connected to the wrong tubes. Fuel loss or fuel odor can be caused by fuel leaking from fuel lines or hoses, a cracked or damaged canister, or a defective vapor valve.

8   To check for excessive fuel vapor pressure in the fuel tank, remove the gas cap and listen for the sound of pressure release. If the fuel tank emits a whooshing sound when you open the filler cap, fuel tank vapor pressure is excessive. Inspect the canister vapor hoses and the canister inlet port for blockage or collapsed hoses. Also inspect the vapor vent valve. A complete test can only be done with a professional-level OBD-II scan tool, which will run a series of checks to detect excessive pressure. You'll have to take the vehicle to a dealer service department or other qualified repair shop to have the EVAP system professionally diagnosed.

16.10 Canister purge solenoid location (4.3L V6 engine shown)

16.15 Canister purge solenoid details - 6.0L V8 engine

1   Canister purge valve
2   Electrical connector
3   EVAP line quick-connect fitting
4   EVAP vacuum line quick-connect fitting

16.22 Location of the EVAP canister vent solenoid (standard-bed pick-up)

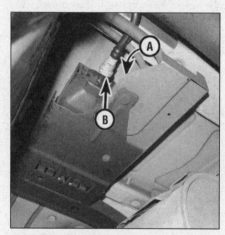

16.27 EVAP canister mounting nut (A, accessed from above) and canister vent solenoid line fitting (B)

Component replacement
EVAP canister purge solenoid

Non-6.0L models
Note: *The EVAP canister purge solenoid valve is located on the driver's side of the intake manifold, behind the throttle body.*
9   Remove the air intake duct (see Chapter 4).
10   Disconnect the canister purge solenoid electrical connector (see illustration).
11   Disconnect the EVAP purge line quick-connect fitting from the canister purge solenoid. If you're unfamiliar with quick-connect fittings, refer to Chapter 4.
12   Remove the canister purge solenoid mounting bolt and remove the purge solenoid.
13   Installation is the reverse of removal.

6.0L V8 models
Note: *The EVAP canister purge solenoid valve is located above the front end of the left fuel rail.*
14   Remove the air intake duct (see Chapter 4).
15   Disconnect the outlet purge line quick-connect fitting from the canister purge solenoid (see illustration).
16   Disconnect the electrical connector from the EVAP canister purge valve.
17   Disconnect the inlet purge line quick-connect fitting from the canister purge solenoid.
18   Cap both EVAP purge lines to prevent dirt, dust and moisture from entering the EVAP system while the line is open. If you're unfamiliar with quick-connect fittings, refer to Chapter 4, Section 4.

19   Remove the canister purge solenoid from its mounting bracket.
20   Installation is the reverse of removal.

EVAP canister vent solenoid
Note: *On some models, the EVAP canister vent solenoid is located in front of the EVAP canister. On other models, the vent solenoid is located at the back of the fuel tank.*
21   Raise the vehicle and support it securely on jackstands.
22   Disconnect the electrical connector from the vent solenoid (see illustration).
23   Follow the inlet and outlet EVAP lines from the vent solenoid to their quick-connect fittings, then disconnect the fittings. Also disconnect the lines from any clips securing them.
24   Remove the vent solenoid from its mounting bracket.
25   Installation is the reverse of removal.

EVAP canister
26   Raise the vehicle and place it securely on jackstands.
27   Clearly label all EVAP hoses connected to the EVAP canister, then disconnect the quick-connect fittings from the canister (see illustration). For more information on quick-connect fittings, see Chapter 4.
28   Remove the canister mounting nut and remove the canister from its mounting bracket.
29   Installation is the reverse of removal.

Fuel tank pressure sensor
Note: *The fuel tank pressure sensor is located on top of the mounting flange for the fuel pump/fuel level sending unit module.*
30   Raise the vehicle and place it securely on jackstands.

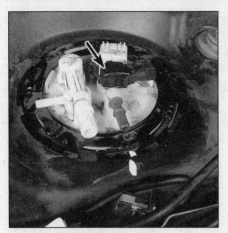

16.32 Pry the fuel tank pressure sensor out of the fuel pump/fuel level sending unit mounting flange

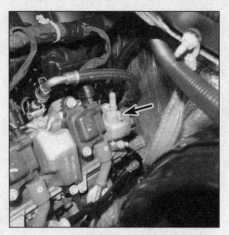

17.5 Disconnect the hose from the PCV valve (V6 shown)

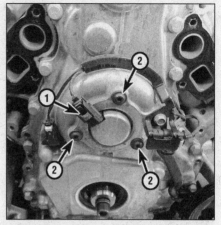

18.6 CMP actuator magnet details (coolant crossover pipe removed for clarity)

1 Electrical connector
2 Mounting bolts

31   Remove the fuel tank (see Chapter 4).
32   Remove the fuel tank pressure sensor from the fuel pump/fuel level sending unit mounting flange (see illustration).
33   Installation is the reverse of removal.

17   Positive Crankcase Ventilation (PCV) system - description and replacement

Description

1   The Positive Crankcase Ventilation (PCV) system reduces hydrocarbon emissions by scavenging crankcase vapors and burning them along with the air-fuel mixture.
2   The PCV system uses a PCV orifice (6.0L models) or a PCV valve (non-6.0L models), which are threaded into either the rear of the left valve cover (4.3L V6) or below the throttle body in the intake manifold (5.3L and 6.2L V8). There are two hoses in this system. The fresh air inlet hose carries outside air from the air intake duct to a pipe on the right valve cover, then into the crankcase, where it mixes with blow-by gases and crankcase vapors. These vapors are drawn from the crankcase through the orifice or valve, through the crankcase ventilation hose (PCV hose), then into the intake manifold, where they mix with incoming air.

Replacement

Note: *This procedure does not apply to 6.0L V8 models. On 6.0L V8 models, the orifice is part of the driver's-side valve cover and is not serviceable separately. If the orifice becomes clogged, the valve cover must be removed to clean the orifice out.*

3   On 4.3L V6 models, remove the driver's-side engine cover.

4   On models with 5.3L and 6.2L V8 engines, remove the intake air duct (see Chapter 4, Section 12).
5   Disconnect the hose from the PCV valve (see illustration).
6   Use a socket to unscrew the PCV valve from the engine.
7   To install, reverse the removal procedures.

18   Camshaft Position (CMP) Actuator System - description and component replacement

Description

1   The Camshaft Position (CMP) Actuator System is an electro-hydraulic system that changes the angle, or timing, of the camshaft relative to the crankshaft position. By controlling this, the CMP actuator system reduces emissions by using exhaust gases to help dilute the intake charge, broadens the engine torque range and increases fuel mileage.
2   The CMP actuator system consists of the Powertrain Control Module (PCM), the CMP actuator solenoid and the camshaft position actuator. The PCM controls the amount of oil that flows through an oil passage to the CMP actuator by sending a pulse-width-modulated signal to the CMP actuator solenoid. The oil flows through two passages; one passage is for advancing the camshaft and one passage is for retarding the cam. The CMP actuator is on the front end of the camshaft. When oil is directed by the solenoid through one passage, the variable cam sprocket advances the camshaft timing; when oil is directed through the other passage, the sprocket retards cam timing.
3   Any of the following factors can affect

the operation of the CMP Actuator System:

a) Aftermarket oil additives
b) Incorrect engine oil level
c) Incorrect engine oil pressure
d) Incorrect engine oil temperature
e) Incorrect engine oil viscosity

Component replacement

Camshaft Position (CMP) actuator magnet

Warning: *Wait until the engine is completely cool before beginning this procedure.*
Note: *The CMP actuator magnet is located on the timing chain cover above the balancer, on the front of the camshaft.*
4   On 6.0L models, drain the cooling system (see Chapter 1), then remove the water pump (see Chapter 3).
5   On non-6.0L models, remove the drivebelt and idler pulley (see Chapter 1, Section 12).
6   Disconnect the electrical connector from the CMP actuator magnet (see illustration).
7   Remove the three CMP actuator magnet mounting bolts and remove the magnet.
8   Remove and discard the old CMP actuator magnet gasket.
9   Make sure that the gasket surface is clean and free of all debris.
10   Installation is the reverse of removal. Be sure to use a new gasket and tighten the CMP actuator magnet mounting bolts securely.
11   On 6.0L models, refill the cooling system (see Chapter 1).

Camshaft Position (CMP) actuator/solenoid valve

12   See Chapter for the CMP actuator/solenoid valve removal and installation procedure.

19.7 Disconnect the electrical connector from the oil pressure sensor . . .

19.8 . . . unscrew the sensor with a deep socket and remove the sensor and washer . . .

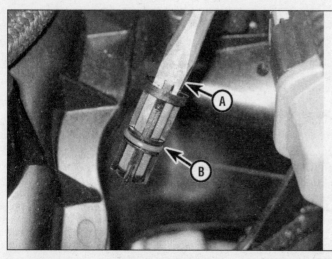

19.9 . . . then carefully wedge the tip of a screwdriver (A) into the top of the oil filter and pull out the filter. Inspect the condition of the screen and the condition of the O-ring (B). If either is damaged, replace the filter and O-ring as a set

19 Cylinder Deactivation System - description and component replacement

Description

1   The Cylinder Deactivation System (or Active Fuel Management System) improves fuel economy and lowers emissions by deactivating four of the engine's eight cylinders (V8 models) or two of the engine's six cylinders (V6 models). During starting, idling and medium or heavy throttle conditions, the engine operates normally. But during light-load cruising, the Powertrain Control Module (PCM) deactivates cylinders one and seven in the front cylinder bank and cylinders two and four in the rear cylinder bank (V8 models), or cylinder 3 on the right cylinder bank and cylinder 6 on the left cylinder bank (V6 models), effectively turning the engine into a V4.

2   The system consists of the Valve Lifter Oil Manifold (VLOM) assembly and specially designed valve lifters. The VLOM assembly consists of electrically operated solenoids. Each solenoid directs the flow of pressurized engine oil to the special intake and exhaust valve lifters. An oil pressure sensor, which is mounted on the VLOM assembly, monitors engine oil pressure and functions as an information sensor for the PCM. An oil filter, helps control contamination inside the hydraulic circuit of the Cylinder Deactivation System. An oil pressure relief valve, regulates engine oil pressure to the lubrication system and to the VLOM assembly.

3   When operating in normal V6 or V8 mode, the special valve lifters function just like conventional lifters. The solenoids in the VLOM assembly are in their closed position and no pressurized oil is directed to the valve lifters. Spring-loaded locking pins in the lifters extend outward, mechanically locking the

pin housings to the outer bodies of the valve lifters.

4   When the conditions are right, the PCM grounds the solenoid control circuits, which allows current to flow through the solenoid windings. When the solenoid windings are energized, the normally-closed solenoid valves open, which directs pressurized engine oil through the VLOM assembly into oil passages in the engine block lifter valley. The pressurized oil forces the locking pins inside the designated lifters inward, locking up the pushrods and preventing them from traveling up and down. The outer bodies of the lifters continue moving up and down independently of the pin housings. Additionally, the PCM turns off the fuel injectors to those cylinders.

5   When the PCM turns off the system, the solenoids in the VLOM assembly close, blocking the flow of pressurized oil to the valve lifters. The oil pressure within the lifters decreases and the locking pins again move out to mechanically lock up the pin housing with the outer lifter body.

Component replacement

Oil pressure sensor and oil filter

6.0L V8 engine

6   Remove the engine cover. On some models it may be necessary to remove the intake manifold (see Chapter 2B).

7   Disconnect the electrical connector from the oil pressure sensor (see illustration).

8   Remove the VLOM oil pressure sensor (see illustration) and remove the sensor washer.

9   Remove the oil filter and the filter O-ring (see illustration). If the filter is plugged or the O-ring is cracked, torn or otherwise deteriorated, replace the filter and O-ring as a set.

10   Installation is the reverse of removal.

19.11 The oil pressure sensor (A) and oil filter (B) are located under the throttle body

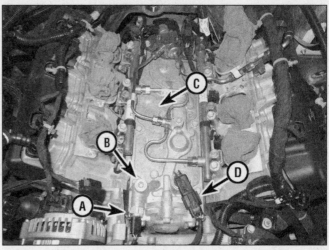

19.12 Cylinder deactivation system components (4.3L V6 shown, 5.3L/6.2L V8 V8 similar)

4.3L V6 and 5.3/6.2L V8 engines

Note: *The sensor is accessible without removing the intake manifold and fuel rail. The filter may also be accessible by removing the throttle body only.*

11   Remove the throttle body (see Chapter 4) for access to the oil pressure sensor and VLOM oil filter (see illustration).

12   Remove the sensor by unscrewing from the from the VLOM. Access the filter by removing the plug from the VLOM (see illustration).

13   Remove the oil filter plug, sealing ring, then pull out the filter. If the filter is plugged or the O-ring is cracked, torn or otherwise deteriorated, replace the filter and O-ring as a set.

14   Installation is the reverse of removal.

Valve Lifter Oil Manifold (VLOM) assembly

15   Refer to Chapter 2A (V6 engine) or Chapter 2B (V8 engines) for the VLOM removal and installation procedure.

Notes

Chapter 7 Part A
Automatic transmission

Contents

Specifications

General

Transmission fluid type .... See Chapter 1

Torque specifications

	Ft-lbs (unless otherwise indicated)	Nm

Note: *One foot-pound (ft-lb) of torque is equivalent to 12 inch-pounds (in-lbs) of torque. Torque values below approximately 15 foot-pounds are expressed in inch-pounds, because most foot-pound torque wrenches are not accurate at these smaller values.*

	Ft-lbs	Nm
Transmission fluid pan bolts	80 in-lbs	9
Fuel line brackets, dipstick tube, vent tube bracket fasteners	89 in-lbs	10
Transmission-to-engine block bolts	37	50
Driveplate-to-torque converter bolts	48	65
Transmission mount bolts		
Heavy duty models	79	107
Light duty models	40	55

1   General information

1   The models covered by this manual use either a 6L80 or 6L90 six-speed transmission or an 8L90 eight-speed transmission. They are all electronically controlled and are equipped with a torque converter clutch (TCC), which provides a direct connection between the engine and the drive wheels for improved efficiency and economy during certain operating conditions. The TCC consists of a solenoid controlled by the Powertrain Control Module (PCM) that locks the converter in third or fourth gear (four-speed transmissions) or fifth or sixth gear (six-speed transmissions) when the vehicle is cruising on level ground and the engine is fully warmed up. Some models are also equipped with an auxiliary transmission cooler that is mounted in front of the radiator and air conditioning condenser.

2   Due to the complexity of the automatic transmissions covered in this manual and the need for specialized equipment to perform most service operations, this Chapter contains only general diagnosis, adjustment and removal and installation procedures.

3   If the transmission requires major repair work, it should be left to a dealer service department or an automotive or transmission repair shop. You can, however, remove and install the transmission yourself and save the expense, even if the repair work is done by a transmission shop.

2   Diagnosis - general

Note: *Automatic transmission malfunctions may be caused by five general conditions: poor engine performance, improper adjustments, hydraulic malfunctions, mechanical malfunctions or malfunctions in the Powertrain Control Module or its signal network. Diagnosis of these problems should always begin with a check of the easily repaired items: fluid level and condition (see Chapter 1), and shift cable adjustment (see Section 3). Next, perform a road test to determine if the problem has been corrected or if more diagnosis is necessary. Because the transmission relies on many sensors in the engine control system, and since the transmission shift points are controlled by the Powertrain Control Module, you'll also want to check to see if any trouble codes have been stored in the PCM (see Chapter 6 for a list of trouble codes and how to extract them). If the problem persists after the preliminary tests and corrections are completed, additional diagnosis should be done by a dealer service department or transmission repair shop. Refer to the Troubleshooting Section at the front of this manual for transmission problem diagnosis.*

Preliminary checks

1   Drive the vehicle to warm the transmission to normal operating temperature.

2   Check the fluid level as described in Chapter 1 :
a) *If the fluid level is unusually low, add enough fluid to bring the level within the designated area of the dipstick, then check for external leaks.*
b) *If the fluid level is abnormally high, drain off the excess, then check the drained fluid for contamination by coolant. The presence of engine coolant in the automatic transmission fluid indicates that a failure has occurred in the internal radiator walls that separate the coolant from the transmission fluid (see Chapter 3).*
c) *If the fluid is foaming, drain it and refill the transmission, then check for coolant in the fluid or a high fluid level.*

3   Check the engine idle speed.
Note: *If the engine is malfunctioning, do not proceed with the preliminary checks until it has been repaired and runs normally.*

4   Inspect the shift cable (see Section 3). Make sure that it's properly adjusted and that it operates smoothly.

5   Check the Transmission Range (TR) switch adjustment (see Chapter 6).

Fluid leak diagnosis

6   Most fluid leaks are easy to locate visually. Repair usually consists of replacing a seal or gasket. If a leak is difficult to find, the following procedure may help.

7   Identify the fluid. Make sure it's transmission fluid and not engine oil or brake fluid (automatic transmission fluid is a deep red color).

8   Try to pinpoint the source of the leak. Drive the vehicle several miles, then park it over a large sheet of cardboard. After a minute or two, you should be able to locate the leak by determining the source of the fluid dripping onto the cardboard.

9   Make a careful visual inspection of the suspected component and the area immediately around it. Pay particular attention to gasket mating surfaces. A mirror is often helpful for finding leaks in areas that are hard to see.

10   If the leak still cannot be found, clean the suspected area thoroughly with a degreaser or solvent, then dry it.

11   Drive the vehicle for several miles at normal operating temperature and varying speeds. After driving the vehicle, visually inspect the suspected component again.

12   Once the leak has been located, the cause must be determined before it can be properly repaired. If a gasket is replaced but the sealing flange is bent, the new gasket will not stop the leak. The bent flange must be straightened.

13   Before attempting to repair a leak, check to make sure that the following conditions are corrected or they may cause another leak.
Note: *Some of the following conditions cannot be fixed without highly specialized tools and expertise. Such problems must be referred to a transmission shop or a dealer service department.*

Gasket leaks

14   Check the pan periodically. Make sure the bolts are tight, no bolts are missing, the gasket is in good condition and the pan is flat (dents in the pan may indicate damage to the valve body inside).

15   If the pan gasket is leaking, the fluid level or the fluid pressure may be too high, the vent may be plugged, the pan bolts may be too tight, the pan sealing flange may be warped, the sealing surface of the transmission housing may be damaged, the gasket may be damaged or the transmission casting may be cracked or porous. If sealant instead of gasket material has been used to form a seal between the pan and the transmission housing, it may be the wrong sealant.

Seal leaks

16   If a transmission seal is leaking, the fluid level or pressure may be too high, the vent may be plugged, the seal bore may be damaged, the seal itself may be damaged or improperly installed, the surface of the shaft protruding through the seal may be damaged or a loose bearing may be causing excessive shaft movement.

17   Make sure the dipstick tube seal is in good condition and the tube is properly seated. Periodically check the area around the speedometer gear or vehicle speed sensor for leakage. If transmission fluid is evident, check the O-ring for damage. Also inspect the driveshaft oil seal for leakage.

Case leaks

18   If the case itself appears to be leaking, the casting is porous and will have to be repaired or replaced.

19   Make sure the oil cooler hose fittings are tight and in good condition. The transmission oil cooler lines on these models are equipped with quick connect fittings - always inspect the O-rings if a leak is suspected.

Fluid comes out vent pipe or fill tube

20   If this condition occurs, the transmission is overfilled, there is coolant in the fluid, the case is porous, the dipstick is incorrect, the vent is plugged or the drain back holes are plugged.

3   Shift cable - replacement and adjustment

Replacement

Warning: *Models covered by this manual are equipped with a Supplemental Restraint System (SRS), more commonly known as airbags. Always disable the airbag system before working in the vicinity of any airbag system component to avoid the possibility of accidental deployment of the airbag, which could cause personal injury (see Chapter 12).*

1   Disconnect the cable from the negative

3.4 Use a screwdriver to pry the shift cable off the shift lever at the transmission

3.5 Remove the retaining clip and detach the shift cable from the bracket

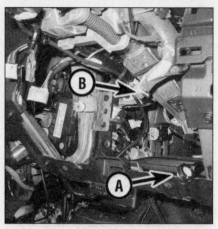

3.7 Pry the shift cable ball socket (A) from the shift lever ball pivot (B)

3.10 The cable grommet is located on the floorboard just in front of the driver's seat

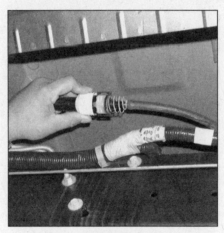

3.13 Pull the white cover back to expose the lock

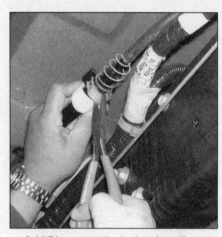

3.14 Disengage the lock using pliers

terminal of the battery (see Chapter 5, Section 3).

2   Place the transmission in PARK and apply the parking brake.

3   Block the rear wheels so the vehicle will not accidentally roll in either direction. Raise the front of the vehicle and support it securely on jackstands.

4   Disconnect the shift cable from the transmission shift lever ballstud (see illustration).

5   Unclip the cable from its retainer. Disengage the shift cable from the cable bracket on the transmission (see illustration).

6   Working inside of the vehicle, remove the knee bolster from below the steering column (see Chapter 11).

7   Pry the shift cable ball socket from the shift lever ball pivot (see illustration).

8   Remove the retainer securing the cable to the steering column bracket.

9   Remove the door sill plate and the left kick panel from the vehicle, then peel back the carpeting.

10   Trace the cable to the cable grommet (the point at which it goes through the floorboard). Pry out the grommet and pull the upper cable up through the hole in the floor to remove it (see illustration).

11   Installation is the reverse of removal.

Adjustment

12   Make sure the driver's shift lever and the transmission shift lever are in the Park position.

13   Pull the white cover back to expose the lock (see illustration).

14   Disengage the lock using pliers or similar (see illustration). The lock will pop up, and the transmission end will move slightly away from the shifter end.

15   While holding the shift lever end of the cable in one hand and the transmission end of the cable in the other hand (see illustration), line-up the outside diameter of the transmission end, with the inside diameter of the shift lever end.

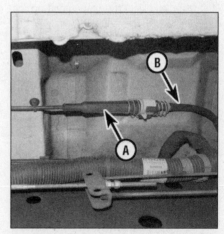

3.15 Hold the shift lever end of the cable (A) in one hand and the transmission end of the cable (B) in the other hand

4.4 Disconnect the wiring from the brake/transmission shift interlock actuator

4.5a Pry the brake/transmission shift interlock actuator from the arm . . .

4.5b . . . and from the steering column bracket

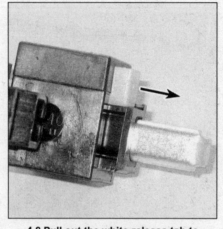

4.8 Pull out the white release tab to release the adjustment mechanism . . .

lever from being moved out of Park unless the brake pedal is depressed simultaneously. It also prevents the ignition key from being removed from the ignition switch unless the shift lever is in the Park position. When the car is started, a solenoid is energized, locking the shift lever in Park; when the brake pedal is depressed, the solenoid is de-energized, unlocking the shift lever so that it can be moved into some other gear.

Actuator replacement

Warning: *Models covered by this manual are equipped with a Supplemental Restraint System (SRS), more commonly known as airbags. Always disable the airbag system before working in the vicinity of any airbag system component to avoid the possibility of accidental deployment of the airbag, which could cause personal injury (see Chapter 12).*

Manual tilt/telescoping column

2   Park the vehicle with the shift lever in the Neutral position. Set the parking brake.

3   Disable the airbag system (see Chapter 12), then remove the driver's knee bolster (see Chapter 11, Section 28).

4   Disconnect the wiring from the shift lock actuator (see illustration).

5   Pry the shift lock actuator off of the cable shift cam and the steering column (see illustrations).

6   To install, snap the actuator onto the cable shift cam and the steering column. Connect the wiring.

7   Make sure that the shift lever clevis is still in the Neutral position.

8   Pull out the tab on the actuator (see illustration).

9   Press the adjuster block. This will disengage the internal teeth of the mechanism.

10   Slide the adjuster block away from the actuator as far as you can.

11   Push in on the tab to lock it in place (see illustration).

12   Reconnect the battery, turn the ignition

16   Push the transmission end inside the shift lever end until the blue spring on the transmission end is fully compressed; this will engage the inner wire and lock both wires together.

4.11 . . . then press the adjuster block down and slide it away from the actuator as far as possible; push the white lock tab back into place until it clicks to lock it

Caution: *DO NOT hold the transmission end during this operation, this will result in a misadjusted cable.*

17   Release the lower (transmission) end of the cable and allow the blue spring to selfadjust the cable. The blue spring must be free standing with no manual help to properly adjust the cable.

18   Pull back the white plastic collar on the shift lever end of the cable connector and insert the cable connector retaining clip (see illustration 3.6).

19   Verify that the cable connector retaining clip is fully seated and that the white plastic collar slides back over the cable connector retaining clip. Test the vehicle for proper shift operation.

---

4   Park/Lock system - description and component replacement

Description

1   The Park/Lock system prevents the shift

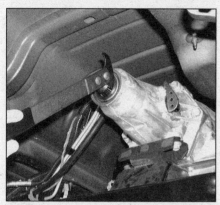

5.4 Carefully pry the old seal out of the extension housing - don't damage the splines on the output shaft

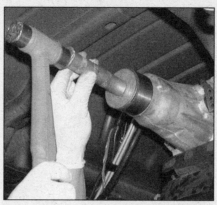

5.5 Drive the new seal into place with a seal driver or a large socket and hammer

6.2 To check the transmission mount, insert a large screwdriver or prybar between the crossmember and the transmission and try to pry the transmission up - it should move very little (2WD model shown)

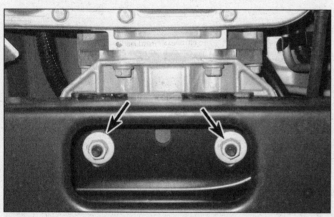

6.4a Transmission mount-to-crossmember nuts

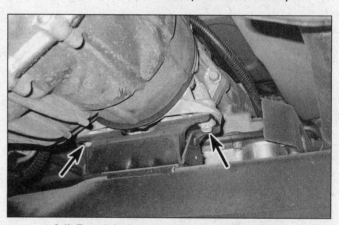

6.4b Transmission mount-to-transmission bolts

key to the On position, then check the operation of the actuator by making sure that the lever can only be moved out of Park when the brake pedal is depressed. Readjust if necessary.

13   Reinstall the knee bolster.

Power tilt/telescoping column

Note: *The shift lock actuator on power tilt/telescoping columns is part of the shifter assembly and is replaced as one unit. The shift lock actuator cannot be replaced separately.*

14   Disable the airbag system (see Chapter 12).

15   Remove the driver's knee bolster (see Chapter 11, Section 28) and the steering column covers (see Chapter 11, Section 30).

16   Disconnect the wiring from the shifter assembly.

17   Remove three fasteners from the shifter assembly near the steering wheel end, and one fastener at the opposite end.

18   To install, reverse removal procedures. Adjust the shift cable as necessary (see Section 3).

5   Extension housing oil seal (2WD) - replacement

1   Oil leaks frequently occur due to wear of the extension housing oil seal. Replacement of this seal is relatively easy, since it can be performed without removing the transmission from the vehicle.

2   The extension housing oil seal is located at the extreme rear of the transmission, where the driveshaft is attached. If leakage at the seal is suspected, raise the vehicle and support it securely on jackstands. If the seal is leaking, transmission lubricant will be built up on the front of the driveshaft and may be dripping from the rear of the transmission.

3   Remove the driveshaft (see Chapter 8).

4   Using a seal removal tool or a large screwdriver, carefully pry the oil seal out of the rear of the transmission (see illustration). Do not damage the splines on the transmission output shaft.

5   Using a seal driver or a very large deep socket as a drift, install the new oil seal (see illustration). Drive it into the bore squarely and make sure it's completely seated.

6   Lubricate the splines of the transmission output shaft and the outside of the driveshaft

yoke with lightweight grease, then install the driveshaft (see Chapter 8). Be careful not to damage the lip of the new seal.

6   Transmission mount - check and replacement

Check

1   Raise the vehicle and support it securely on jackstands.

2   Insert a large screwdriver or prybar into the space between the transmission extension housing and the crossmember and try to pry the transmission up slightly (see illustration).

3   The transmission should not move much at all - if the mount is cracked or torn, replace it.

Replacement

4   To replace the mount, remove the fasteners attaching the mount to the crossmember and to the transmission (see illustrations).

5   Raise the transmission slightly with a jack and remove the mount.

6   Installation is the reverse of the removal procedure.

7.6 Pry off the round inspection plug and mark the relationship between the torque converter and the driveplate

7.8a Passenger side bellhousing cover retaining bolt (arrow)

7.8b Driver's side bellhousing cover retaining bolt (arrow)

7.9 With a large screwdriver wedged between the teeth of the driveplate ring gear and the bellhousing, remove the torque converter-to-driveplate bolts

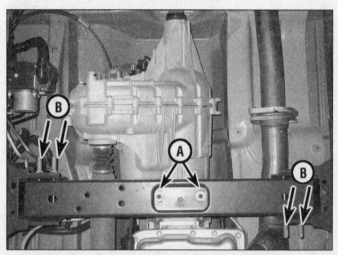

7.12 Remove the transmission mount fasteners (A) and the crossmember bolts (B) (4WD shown, 2WD similar)

7   Automatic transmission - removal and installation

Removal

Caution: *The transmission and torque converter must be removed as a single assembly. If you try to leave the torque converter attached to the driveplate, the converter driveplate, pump bushing and oil seal will be damaged. The driveplate is not designed to support the load, so none of the weight of the transmission should be allowed to rest on the plate during removal.*

1   Disconnect the cable from the negative terminal of the battery (see Chapter 5).
2   Raise the vehicle and support it securely on jackstands. Remove the skid plate and skid plate crossmember, if equipped.
3   Remove the transmission oil pan drain plug and drain the transmission fluid (see Chapter 1).
4   Remove all exhaust components that interfere with transmission removal (see Chapter 4).
5   Remove the torque converter inspection plug at the bottom of the bellhousing.
6   Working through the inspection plug hole, mark the relationship of the torque converter to the driveplate so they can be installed in the same position (see illustration).
7   Remove the starter motor (see Chapter 5).
8   Detach the covers on each side of the bellhousing (see illustrations).
9   Remove the torque converter-to-driveplate bolts (see illustration). Turn the crankshaft for access to each bolt. Turn the crankshaft in a clockwise direction only (as viewed from the front).

10   Mark the position of the yoke and remove the driveshaft (see Chapter 8). On 4WD models, remove both driveshafts.
11   Support the transmission with a jack - preferably a jack made for this purpose (available at most tool rental yards). Safety chains will help steady the transmission on the jack.
12   Remove the fasteners securing the transmission mount to the crossmember. Raise the transmission slightly, remove the crossmember bolts and the crossmember (see illustration).
13   Lower the transmission down slightly to allow access to all components, bolts and connectors.
14   Working on the left side of the transmission, disconnect the shift cable from the transmission (see Section 3) and unplug the electrical connectors from the Park/Neutral position switch. Also remove the bolt securing

7.21a Driver's side bellhousing bolts

7.21b Passenger side bellhousing bolts - there are three more bolts at the top of the bellhousing that are not visible in this photo

the wiring harness bracket to the left side of the transmission. Unbolt the fuel line support bracket from the transmission.

Note: *To disconnect the transmission electrical connector, pull the white plastic tab located on the connector circular ring outward, then rotate the circular ring of the connector counterclockwise. When the circular ring is disengaged, pull the connector straight out.*

15 Working on the right side of the transmission, remove the heat shield. Unplug the electrical connectors from the transmission solenoid and the Vehicle Speed Sensor (see Chapter 6).

16 Remove the bolts that attach the fuel line bracket to the transmission. Detach the wring harness clips and vent hose from the transmission.

17 Disconnect the transmission cooler lines from the right side of the transmission and the engine. To disconnect the lines from the transmission, simply unsnap the plastic collar from the quick connect fitting, then pry off the quick connect fitting retaining clip and remove the lines. Plug the ends of the lines to prevent fluid from leaking out after you disconnect them. Always be sure to inspect the O-rings on the cooler lines before reinstallation.

18 Remove the fill/dipstick tube bracket bolt and pull the tube out of the transmission. Don't lose the tube seal (it can be reused if it's still in good shape).

19 On 4WD models, remove the transfer case (see Chapter 7B).

Note: *If you are not planning to replace the transmission, but are removing it in order to gain access to other components such as the torque converter, flywheel or rear main oil seal, it isn't really necessary to remove the transfer case. However, the transmission and transfer case are awkward and heavy when removed and installed as a single assembly; they're much easier to maneuver off and on as separate units. If you decide to leave the transfer case attached, disconnect the shift rod (manual shift models only) from the trans-*

fer case shift lever. Also disconnect the electrical connectors from the transfer case speed sensors and detach the transfer case vent tube (see Chapter 7B).

Warning: *If you decide to leave the transfer case attached to the transmission, be sure to use safety chains to help stabilize the transmission and transfer case assembly and to prevent it from falling off the jack head, which could cause serious damage to the transmission and/or transfer case and serious bodily injury to you.*

20 Support the engine with a jack positioned under the projection on the rear of the engine block, near the transmission bellhousing.

21 Remove the bolts and/or studs securing the transmission to the engine (see illustrations). A long extension and a U-joint socket will greatly simplify this step.

22 Clamp a small pair of locking pliers on the bellhousing case through the lower inspection hole. Clamp the pliers just in front of the torque converter, behind the driveplate. The pliers will prevent the torque converter from falling out while you're removing the transmission. Move the transmission to the rear to disengage it from the engine block dowel pins and make sure the torque converter is detached from the driveplate. Lower the transmission with the jack.

Installation

23 Prior to installation, make sure the torque converter is securely engaged in the pump. If you've removed the converter, apply a small amount of transmission fluid on the torque converter rear hub, where the transmission front seal rides. Install the torque converter onto the front input shaft of the transmission while rotating the converter back and forth. It should engage into the transmission front pump in stages. Spin the converter while pushing it into place to make sure it is fully engaged in the transmission pump. Reinstall the locking pliers to hold the converter in this position.

24 With the transmission secured to the jack, raise it into position.

25 Turn the torque converter to line up the holes with the holes in the driveplate. The marks on the torque converter and driveplate made in Step 6 must line up.

26 Move the transmission forward carefully until the dowel pins and the torque converter are engaged. Make sure the transmission mates with the engine with no gap. If there's a gap, make sure there are no wires or other objects pinched between the engine and transmission and also make sure the torque converter is completely engaged in the transmission front pump. Try to rotate the converter - if it doesn't rotate easily, it's probably not fully engaged in the pump. If necessary, lower the transmission and install the converter fully.

27 Install the transmission dipstick tube and seal into the transmission housing, then install the transmission-to-engine bolts and tighten them securely. As you're tightening the bolts, make sure that the engine and transmission mate completely at all points. If not, find out why. Never try to force the engine and transmission together with the bolts or you'll break the transmission case!

28 Raise the rear of the transmission and install the transmission crossmember.

29 Remove the jacks supporting the transmission and the engine.

30 Install the torque converter-to-driveplate bolts. Tighten them to the torque listed in this Chapter's Specifications. Install the plastic bellhousing covers.

31 Install the starter motor (see Chapter 5).

32 Install new retaining rings onto the quick-connect fittings.

Note: *Don't push the retaining rings onto the fittings. Instead, hook one of the ends of the clip into a slot in the fitting, then rotate the other end of the ring into the other slot. If the retaining ring isn't installed like this, it may become spread out and won't be able to retain the cooler lines securely.*

33 Connect the transmission fluid cooler

lines to the fittings, making sure they click into place, then push the plastic caps onto the fittings.

34   Plug in the transmission electrical connectors and install the heat shield.

35   Connect the shift cable (see Section 3).

36   Install the torque converter inspection cover.

37   On 4WD models, install the transfer case, if removed (see Chapter 7B).

38   Install the driveshaft(s) (see Chapter 8).

39   Adjust the shift cable (see Section 3).

40   Install any exhaust system components that were removed or disconnected (see Chapter 4).

41   Remove the jackstands and lower the vehicle.

42   Fill the transmission with the specified fluid (see Chapter 1). Run the engine and check for fluid leaks.

Chapter 7B
Transfer case

Contents

Specifications

Torque specifications

Note: *One foot-pound (ft-lb) of torque is equivalent to 12 inch-pounds (in-lbs) of torque. Torque values below approximately 15 foot-pounds are expressed in inch-pounds, because most foot-pound torque wrenches are not accurate at these smaller values.*

	Ft-lbs (unless otherwise indicated)	Nm
Shift lever-to-floor pan bolts	97 in-lbs	11
Shift linkage adjustment bolt	132 in-lbs	15
Transfer case-to-adapter and adapter-to-transmission fasteners	37	50
Fill/drain plugs	156 in-lbs	18
2/4 wheel drive actuator (shift motor) bolts	156 in-lbs	18
Skid plate bolts	15	20

1   General information

1   Four-wheel drive (4WD) models are equipped with a transfer case mounted on the rear of the transmission. Drive is transmitted from the engine, through the transmission and the transfer case, to the front and rear axles by driveshafts.

2   Here is a list of the transfer cases available on the vehicles covered by this manual:

Manual transfer cases
MP 1222, 1225, 1226-NQG

Automatic transfer cases
MP 1625,1626-NQF
MP 3023, 3024-NQH
MP 3010-*NPO*

3   We don't recommend trying to rebuild any of these transfer cases at home. They're difficult to overhaul without special tools, and rebuilt units are available (on an exchange basis) for less than it would cost to rebuild your own.

2   Shift lever (manual-shift models) - removal and installation

1   Raise the front of the vehicle and support it securely on jackstands.

2   Remove the transfer case skid plate, if equipped.

3   Remove the front driveshaft (see Chapter 8).

4   Use a small screwdriver to release the control rod at each end. Remove the control rod.

5   Remove the knob from the lever by putting a wrench under the knob and tapping the wrench upwards with a hammer.

6   Remove the three bezel screws and remove the bezel.

7   Remove the four lever bolts and lift out the lever assembly.

8   Installation is the reverse of removal.

3   Shift linkage (manual-shift models) - replacement and adjustment

Replacement

1   Place the transmission in Park and the transfer case shift lever in the 2WD High position.

2   Raise the vehicle and support it securely on jackstands. Remove the transfer case skid plate, if equipped.

3   Remove the front driveshaft (see Chapter 8, Section 3).

4   Using a screwdriver or door panel removal tool, pry off the linkage from the ball pivots at each end of the shift linkage at the transfer case and the shift lever.

5   Remove the shift linkage from the vehicle.

Note: *Before installing the linkage, loosen the adjusting bolt so it slides with slight resistance.*

6   To install, reverse removal procedure. Adjust the shift linkage as described in the next procedure.

Adjustment

7   Place the transmission in Park and the transfer case shift lever in the 2WD High position. Have an assistant hold the lever in the indicated position.

8   Raise the vehicle and support it securely on jackstands and remove the transfer case skid plate.

9   Loosen the adjustment bolt at the center of the shift linkage.

10   Make sure the ball sockets at each end of the shift linkage are securely seated on the ball pivots at the transfer case and the shift lever.

11   Verify that the transfer case range lever is in the 2WD High position.

12   Tighten the shift linkage adjustment bolt to the torque listed in this Chapter's Specifications .

13   Lower the vehicle and check the operation of the transfer case.

6.4 Disconnect the electrical connector and remove the electric shift motor bolts

4   Transfer case control switch (manual-shift models) - replacement

1   Raise and support the vehicle on jack stands.

2   Remove the rock shield (skid plate)., if equipped.

3   Disconnect the electrical connector from the transfer case control switch located at the top of the transfer case, between the front driveshaft output and the adapter.

4   Unscrew the switch to remove.

5   Installation is reverse of removal. Lubricate the O-ring with Dextron VI (or equivalent) transmission fluid before installing.

5   Transfer case selector switch (electric-shift models) - replacement

1   Disconnect the cable from the negative terminal of the battery (see Chapter 5, Section 3).

2   Locate the selector switch and remove the trim panel from the dashboard (see Chapter 11, Section 28).

3   Unplug the electrical connector from the rear of the switch.

4   Release the retaining tabs and remove the transfer case selector switch.

5   Installation is the reverse of removal.

6   Transfer case shift motor/ actuator (electric-shift models) - replacement

1   Raise the vehicle and place it securely on jackstands.

2   Remove the stone shields from below the transfer case.

3   Unplug the shift motor electrical connector (see illustration).

4   Unscrew the retaining bolts and remove the electric shift motor/actuator assembly (see illustration).

5   Inspect the seal for damage and replace it if necessary.

6   Position the gasket and the shift motor in place on the transfer case and install the bolts. Tighten the shift motor retaining bolts to the torque listed in this Chapter's Specifications .

7   Installation is the reverse of removal.

7   Transfer case speed sensors (electric shift models) - general information

1   There are a variety of electric-shift transfer cases on the models covered by this manual and several different combinations of speed sensors available. The Vehicle Speed

9.4 The output shaft seal can be removed with a conventional seal extractor or a large screwdriver

9.6 Drive the new transfer case seals into place with a seal driver or large socket

10.7 Detach the wiring harness retaining clips and vent hose from the transfer case

Sensor (VSS) sends information to the PCM for the driveability program and is located at the rear output shaft. The procedure for checking and replacement of the output shaft speed sensor is essentially the same as the procedure for the Vehicle Speed Sensor (VSS). A scan tool must be used to access speed sensor data and trouble codes. Refer to the Vehicle Speed Sensor (VSS) replacement procedure in Chapter 6. Always use a new O-ring when installing the VSS. Lubricate the O-ring with DEXRON VI (or equivalent) transmission fluid before installing.

8 Transfer case control module (electric-shift models) - replacement

1   The transfer case control module is located under the instrument panel, to the right of the steering column. To access the control module, remove the driver's side knee bolster (see Chapter 11, Section 28). If a problem arises with the transfer case control module, it is recommended that the job be left to a dealership service department or other qualified repair shop. A new module must be programmed with a factory scan tool by a dealership service department or other shop equipped with the proper tool and software, so even if you were to replace the old module with a new unit, it wouldn't work until the vehicle was towed to a dealer (or other properly equipped repair facility) for programming

9 Oil seal - replacement

Note: *This procedure applies to both the front and rear output shaft seals.*
1   Raise the vehicle and support it securely on jackstands.

2   Remove the skid plate, if equipped.
3   If you're replacing the front seal, remove the front driveshaft; if you're replacing the rear seal, remove the rear driveshaft (see Chapter 8).
4   To remove the either output shaft seal, simply pry the seal out with a screwdriver or a seal removal tool (see illustration). Don't damage the seal bore.
5   Lubricate the new seal lips with petroleum jelly. If the new seal has a weep hole, put it at the bottom and the notch at the top.
6   Drive the seal into place with a seal driver or a large socket (see illustration). The outside diameter of the socket should be slightly smaller than the outside diameter of the seal.
7   The remainder of installation is the reverse of removal.

10 Transfer case - removal and installation

1   Disconnect the cable from the negative terminal of the battery (see Chapter 5, Section 3).
2   On models with a manually shifted transfer case, put the transfer case in the 2WD High position.
3   Raise the vehicle and support it securely on jackstands.
4   Remove the stone shields (skid plates), if equipped.
5   Drain the transfer case lubricant (see Chapter 1).
6   Remove the front and rear driveshafts (see Chapter 8).
7   Unplug all electrical connectors and detach the vent hose from the top of the transfer case (see illustration). If necessary, disconnect the transfer case vent tube.
8   On manually shifted models, disconnect the shift linkage from the transfer case. This

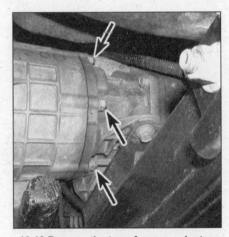

10.12 Remove the transfer case adapter-to-transmission mounting nuts

is done by simply pulling the shift linkage ball socket off the ball pivot on the transfer case shift lever.
9   Raise the transmission enough to remove the crossmember (see Chapter 7A). With the crossmember removed, support the transmission with a floor jack.
10   If necessary, remove the transmission mount from the transmission (see Chapter 7A, Section 6).
11   Support the transfer case with a jack - preferably a special jack made for this purpose. Safety chains will help steady the transfer case on the jack.
12   Remove the transfer case adapter-to-transmission mounting nuts. On some models, the fuel line bracket may be attached by the mounting nuts (see illustration).
13   Make a final check that all wires and hoses have been disconnected from the transfer case, then move the transfer case and jack toward the rear of the vehicle until it's clear of the transmission. Keep the transfer case level

as this is done. Once the input shaft is clear, rotate the transfer case as necessary, lower it and remove it from under the vehicle.

14   Remove the adapter-to-transfer case bolts and remove the adapter as needed.

Note: *Before installation of the transfer case and adapter to the transmission, on transmission/transfer case combinations where the input shaft is "dry" (not lubricated with transmission or transfer case fluid), apply lubricant (GM P/N 12345879 or equivalent) to the splines.*

15   Installation is the reverse of removal. Replace the gasket with a new one. Be sure to tighten the transmission-to-transfer case nuts to the torque listed in this Chapter's Specifications . On manually shifted models, be sure to adjust the transfer case shift linkage (see Section 3).

11   Transfer case overhaul - general information

1   Overhauling a transfer case is a difficult job for the do-it-yourselfer. It involves the disassembly and reassembly of many small parts. Numerous clearances must be precisely measured and, if necessary, changed with select-fit spacers and snap-rings. As a result, if transfer case problems arise, it can be removed and installed by a competent do-it-yourselfer, but overhaul should be left to a transmission repair shop. Rebuilt transfer cases may be available - check with your dealer parts department and auto parts stores. At any rate, the time and money involved in an overhaul is almost sure to exceed the cost of a rebuilt unit.

2   Nevertheless, it's not impossible for an inexperienced mechanic to rebuild a transfer case if the special tools are available and the job is done in a deliberate step-by-step manner so nothing is overlooked.

3   The tools necessary for an overhaul include internal and external snap-ring pliers, a bearing puller, a slide hammer, a set of pin punches, a dial indicator and possibly a hydraulic press. In addition, a large, sturdy workbench and a vise or transmission stand will be required.

4   During disassembly of the transfer case, make careful notes of how each piece comes off, where it fits in relation to other pieces and what holds it in place. Note how parts are installed when you remove them; this will make it much easier to get the transfer case back together.

Notes

Notes

Chapter 8
Driveline

Contents

Specifications

Torque specifications

Ft-lbs (unless otherwise indicated)

Note: *One foot-pound (ft-lb) of torque is equivalent to 12 inch-pounds (in-lbs) of torque. Torque values below approximately 15 foot-pounds are expressed in inch-pounds, because most foot-pound torque wrenches are not accurate at these smaller values.*

Driveshaft

Front driveshaft U-joint clamp bolts	18
Rear driveshaft	
U-joint clamp bolts	18
Center support bearing fasteners	30
Yoke nut	118

Rear axle

Pinion shaft lock screw	
8.6-inch axle	27
9.5, 9.76-inch axle	37
Full floating axle flange bolts	170
Differential cover bolts	
8.6, 9.5, 9.7-inch axle	
Step 1	15
Step 2	Tighten an additional 20 degrees
10.5, 11.5-inch axle	30

Front driveaxles (4WD models)

Driveaxle inner joint-to-differential flange bolts	58
Driveaxle/hub nut	188

Front differential carrier (4WD models)

Right axleshaft tube/shaft-to-chassis nuts	75
Right axleshaft tube/shaft-to-differential housing bolts	
8.25-inch axle	41
9.25-inch axle	48
Differential housing-to-chassis bolts/nuts	75
Front suspension frame crossmember bolts (8.25-inch axle)	
Step 1	52
Step 2	Tighten an additional 110 degrees
Shift motor	22

1   General information

1   The information in this Chapter deals with the components from the rear of the engine to the rear wheels, except for the transmission (and transfer case, if equipped), which is dealt with in the previous Chapter. For the purposes of this Chapter, these components are grouped into two categories: driveshaft and axles. Separate Sections within this Chapter offer general descriptions and checking procedures for components in each of the two groups.

2   Since nearly all the procedures covered in this Chapter involve working under the vehicle, make sure it's securely supported on sturdy jackstands or on a hoist where the vehicle can be easily raised and lowered.

2   Driveshaft and universal joints - general information and inspection

General information

1   A driveshaft is a tube, or a pair of tubes, that transmits power between the transmission (or transfer case on 4WD models) and the differential. Universal joints are located at either end of the driveshaft and in the center on two-piece driveshafts.

2   Single piece driveshafts employ a splined yoke at the front, which slips into the extension housing of the transmission. This arrangement allows the driveshaft to slide back-and-forth within the transmission during vehicle operation to compensate for changes in length due to suspension movement. An oil seal prevents leakage of fluid at this point and keeps dirt from entering the transmission. If leakage is evident at the front of the driveshaft, replace the oil seal (see Chapter 7A).

3   If a two-piece driveshaft is used, a slip joint is employed on the front of the rear driveshaft section.

4   Two-piece driveshafts also have a cen-

ter support bearing. The center bearing is a ball-type bearing mounted in a rubber cushion attached to a frame crossmember. The bearing is pre-lubricated and sealed at the factory.

5   On all models, the driveshaft assembly requires very little service. The universal joints are lubricated for life and must be replaced if problems develop. The driveshaft must be removed from the vehicle for this procedure.

6   Since the driveshaft is a balanced unit, it's important that no undercoating, mud, etc., be allowed to stay on it. When the vehicle is raised for service it's a good idea to clean the driveshaft and inspect it for any obvious damage. Also, make sure the small weights used to originally balance the driveshaft are in place and securely attached. Whenever the driveshaft is removed it must be reinstalled in the same relative position to preserve the balance.

7   Problems with the driveshaft are usually indicated by a noise or vibration while driving the vehicle. A road test should verify if the problem is the driveshaft or another component. Refer to the *Troubleshooting* Section at the front of this manual. If you suspect trouble, inspect the driveline.

Inspection

8   Raise the rear of the vehicle and support it securely on jackstands. Block the front wheels to keep the vehicle from rolling off the stands.

9   Crawl under the vehicle and visually inspect the driveshaft. Look for any dents or cracks in the tubing. If any are found, the driveshaft must be replaced.

10   Check for oil leakage at the front and rear of the driveshaft. Leakage where the driveshaft enters the transmission or transfer case indicates a defective transmission/transfer case seal (see Chapter 7A). Leakage where the driveshaft enters the differential indicates a defective pinion seal (see Section 11).

11   While under the vehicle, have an assistant rotate a rear wheel so the driveshaft will rotate. As it does, make sure the universal joints are operating properly without binding, noise or looseness. Listen for any noise from

the center bearing (if equipped), indicating it's worn or damaged. Also check the rubber portion of the center bearing for cracking or separation, which will necessitate replacement.

12   The universal joint can also be checked with the driveshaft motionless, by gripping your hands on either side of the joint and attempting to twist the joint. Any movement at all in the joint is a sign of considerable wear. Lifting up on the shaft will also indicate movement in the universal joints.

13   Finally, check the driveshaft mounting bolts at the ends to make sure they're tight.

14   On 4WD models, the above driveshaft checks should be repeated on the front driveshaft as well. In addition, check for leakage around the sleeve yoke, indicating failure of the yoke seal.

15   Check for leakage where the driveshafts connect to the transfer case and front differential. Leakage indicates worn oil seals.

16   At the same time, check for looseness in the joints of the front driveaxles. Also check for grease or oil leakage from around the driveaxles by inspecting the rubber boots and both ends of each axle. Oil leakage around the axle flanges indicates a defective axle-shaft oil seal. Grease leakage at the CV joint boots means a damaged rubber boot. For servicing of these components, see the appropriate Sections.

3   Driveshaft(s) - removal and installation

Caution: *When removing the driveshafts, do not pound on the yoke ears or use a tool between the yoke and the universal joint; the joints may fracture and may fail prematurely.*

Rear driveshaft
Removal

1   Raise the rear of the vehicle and support it securely on jackstands. Block the front wheels to prevent the vehicle from rolling.

2   Place the transmission in Neutral with the parking brake off.

3   Make reference marks on the driveshaft and the pinion flange in line with each other (see illustration). This is to make sure the driveshaft is reinstalled in the same position to preserve the balance.

4   Remove the rear universal joint bolts and retainers. Turn the driveshaft (or wheels) as necessary to bring the bolts into the most accessible position. To prevent the driveshaft from turning when you loosen the bolts, insert a large screwdriver through the driveshaft yoke (see illustration).

5   On vehicles with a two-piece driveshaft, remove the fasteners from the center support bearing.

6   On all models, tape the bearing caps to the universal joint to prevent the caps from coming off during removal.

7   Lower the rear of the driveshaft. Slide the front of the driveshaft out of the transmission or transfer case.

3.3 Mark the relationship of the rear driveshaft to the differential pinion flange

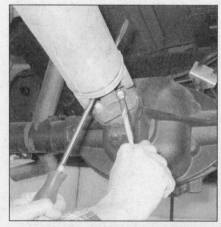

3.4 Insert a screwdriver through the driveshaft yoke to prevent the shaft from turning when you loosen the bolts

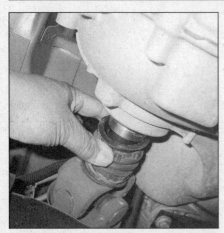

3.15 Pry up the end of the boot clamp and dislodge the boot from the transfer case output shaft

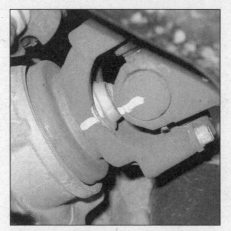

3.16 Mark the relationship of the front driveshaft to the front differential companion flange, then remove the bolts and clamps

5.3 Use a small pair of pliers to remove the snap-rings from the ends of the universal joint yokes

8   Wrap a plastic bag over the transmission or transfer case housing and hold it in place with a rubber band. This will prevent loss of fluid and protect against contamination while the driveshaft is out.

Installation
9   Remove the plastic bag from the transmission or transfer case and wipe the area clean. Inspect the oil seal carefully. Procedures for replacement of this seal can be found in Chapter 7A.
10   Slide the front of the driveshaft into the transmission or transfer case.
11   On models with a two-piece driveshaft, raise the center support bearing into position, install the fasteners and tighten them to the torque listed in this Chapter's Specifications.
12   Raise the rear of the driveshaft into position, checking to be sure the marks are in alignment. If not, turn the rear wheels to match the pinion flange and the driveshaft.
13   Remove the tape securing the bearing caps and install the clamps and bolts. Tighten all bolts to the torque listed in this Chapter's Specifications.

Front driveshaft (4WD models)
Removal
14   Raise the front of the vehicle and support it securely on jackstands. Remove the differential carrier splash shield, if equipped.
15   Pry open the clamp securing the boot at the transfer case output shaft (see illustration). Disengage the boot from the shaft and slide it forward.
16   Mark the relationship of the driveshaft to the front differential companion flange (see illustration).
17   Remove the bolts and clamps from the differential flange.
18   Push the driveshaft to the rear far enough to separate it from the differential flange, tape the bearing caps to the universal joint to prevent the caps from coming off during removal.
19   Lower the driveshaft and pull the shaft

out of the transfer case.
20   If necessary, remove the clamp and the boot from the driveshaft.

Installation
21   Slide the rear of the driveshaft into the splines in the transfer case output shaft.
22   Attach the front end of the shaft to the differential companion flange (be sure to line up the marks), remove the tape and install the clamps and bolts and tighten all of the bolts to the torque listed in this Chapter's Specifications.
23   At the rear end of the shaft, push the boot up over the transfer case output shaft and seat it into its groove. Insert a small screwdriver between the boot and the shaft to equalize pressure inside the boot, then install a new clamp and crimp it into place with a pair of clamp-crimping pliers.
24   Install the front differential carrier splash shield (if equipped).

---

4   Driveshaft center support bearing - replacement

1   Remove the driveshaft (see Section 3).
2   Mark the relationship of the front portion of the driveshaft to the rear portion of the driveshaft (it's best to make the mark on the slip yoke).
3   Remove the universal joint for the rear slip yoke and remove the rear slip yoke.
4   Secure the front of the driveshaft (with the center support bearing) in a soft-jaw vise. Remove the driveshaft yoke nut.
5   If you have access to a hydraulic press (one tall enough to accommodate the shaft) and the necessary fixtures, press the shaft out of the yoke and the center support bearing. Reverse this operation to install the new bearing (using the existing yoke).
6   If you do not have the necessary equipment, take the shaft to an automotive machine shop or other qualified repair facility to have

5.4 To remove the U-joint from the driveshaft, use a vise as a press - the small socket will push the U-joint and bearing cap into the large socket

the old bearing pressed off and the new one pressed on.

---

5   Universal joints - replacement

Note: *Always purchase a universal joint service kit for your model vehicle before beginning this procedure. Also, read through the entire procedure before beginning work.*
1   Remove the driveshaft (see Section 3).

Outer snap-ring type
2   Place the driveshaft on a bench equipped with a vise.
3   Remove the snap-rings with a small pair of pliers (see illustration).
4   Place a piece of pipe or a large socket, having an outside diameter slightly larger than the outside diameter of one of the bearing caps, over one of the bearing caps. Position a socket with an outside diameter slightly smaller than that of the opposite bearing cap against the cap (see illustration) and use the

5.5 Locking pliers can be used to remove the bearing caps from the yoke

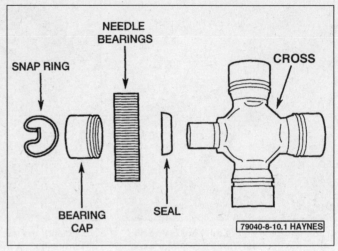

5.6 Outer snap-ring type U-joint

5.16 Remove the inner snap-rings from the U-joint by tapping them off with a screwdriver and hammer

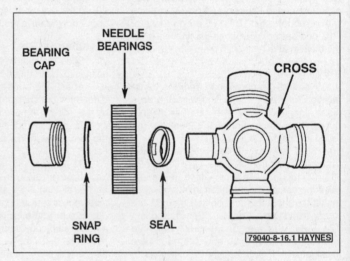

5.20 Inner snap-ring type U-joint

vise or press to force the bearing cap out (inside the pipe or large socket).

5   Press the U-joint through as far as possible, then grip the bearing cap with pliers and remove it (see illustration).

6   A universal joint repair kit will contain a new U-joint, seals, bearings, caps and snap-rings (see illustration).

7   Inspect the bearing cap bores in the yokes for wear and damage.

8   If the bearing cap bores in the yoke are so worn that the caps are a loose fit, the driveshaft will have to be replaced with a new one.

9   Make sure the dust seals are properly located on the U-joint.

10   Using a vise, press one bearing cap into the yoke approximately 1/4-inch.

11   Use chassis grease to hold the needle rollers in place in the caps.

12   Insert the U-joint into the partially installed bearing cap, taking care not to dislodge the needle rollers.

13   Hold the U-joint in correct alignment and press both caps into place by slowly and carefully closing the jaws of the vise.

14   Use a socket slightly smaller in diameter than the caps to press them into the yoke. Press in one side, install the snap-ring, then press the other side to shift the U-joint assembly tight against the installed snap-ring and install the other snap-ring.

15   Repeat the operations for the remaining two bearing caps. Proceed to Step 22.

Injected plastic (inner snap-ring) type

16   If the joint has been previously rebuilt, remove the snap-rings (bearing retainers)

located on the inner part of each bearing cap (see illustration).

17   If this is the first time the joint is being rebuilt, it will not be necessary to remove the snap-rings, since there aren't any; the pressing operation will shear the molded plastic retaining material.

Note: *It may be necessary to heat the U-joint over 500-degrees (melting the plastic retaining material) before pressing the U-joint apart.*

18   Press out the bearing caps as described in Steps 4 and 5.

19   Remove the U-joint and clean all plastic material from the yoke. Use a small punch to remove the plastic from the injection holes.

20   Reassembly is the same as for the outer snap-ring joint described in Steps 9 through 15, except the snap-rings are on the inner part of each bearing cap (see illustration).

21   When installing the bearing cap, press

5.21 Installing a snap-ring on an inner snap-ring type U-joint

5.22 Strike the yoke sharply with a hammer to spring the yoke ears, which will free-up the joint

it in until the snap-ring can be installed (see illustration).

All models

22   If the joint is stiff after assembly, strike the yoke sharply with a hammer (see illustration). This will spring the yoke ears slightly and free up the joint.

---

6   Axles - description and check

Description

1   The rear axle assembly is a hypoid (the centerline of the pinion gear is below the centerline of the ring gear), semi-floating type. When the vehicle goes around a corner, the differential allows the outer rear wheel to turn at a higher speed than the inner tire. The axleshafts are splined to the differential side gears, so when the vehicle goes around a corner, the inner wheel, which turns more slowly than the outer wheel, turns its side gear more slowly than the outer wheel turns its side gear. The differential pinion gears roll around the slower side gear, driving the outer side gear (and tire) more quickly.

2   An optional locking limited-slip rear axle is also available. This differential allows for normal operation until one wheel loses traction. A limited-slip unit is similar in design to a conventional differential, except for the addition of a pair of multi-disc clutch packs which slow the rotation of the differential case when one wheel is on a firm surface and the other on a slippery one. The difference in wheel rotational speed produced by this condition applies additional force to the pinion gears and through the cone, which is splined to the axleshafts, equalizes the rotation speed of the axleshaft driving the wheel with traction.

3   On 4WD models, a fully independent front axle assembly is used. This consists of a differential and a pair of driveaxles. Each driveaxle has an inner and outer constant velocity (CV) joint. Because the differential - like the transfer case - is offset to the left, the distance between the differential and the right front wheel is greater than the distance from the differential to the left wheel. In order to use two equal-length driveaxles, an extension axleshaft is employed on the right side to make up the difference.

Check

4   Often, a suspected axle problem lies elsewhere. Do a thorough check of other possible causes before assuming the axle is the problem.

5   The following noises are those commonly associated with axle diagnosis procedures:

a) *Road noise is often mistaken for mechanical faults. Driving the vehicle on different surfaces will show whether or not the road surface is the cause of the noise. Road noise will remain the same if the vehicle is under power or coasting.*

b) *Tire noise is sometimes mistaken for mechanical problems. Tires which are worn or low on pressure are particularly susceptible to emitting vibrations and noises. Tire noise will remain about the same during varying driving situations, where axle noise will change during coasting, acceleration, etc.*

c) *Engine and transmission noise can be deceiving because it will travel along the driveline. To isolate engine and transmission noises, make a note of the engine speed at which the noise is most pronounced. Stop the vehicle, place the transmission in Neutral and run the engine to the same speed. If the noise is the same, the axle is not at fault.*

6   Because of the special tools needed, overhauling the differential isn't cost effective for a do-it-yourselfer. The procedures included in this Chapter describe axleshaft removal and installation, axleshaft oil seal replacement, axleshaft bearing replacement and removal of the entire unit for repair or replacement. Any further work should be left to a qualified repair shop.

---

7   Axleshaft (rear) - removal and installation

Semi-floating axleshaft

Removal

1   Loosen the rear wheel lug nuts. Raise the rear of the vehicle, support it securely on jackstands and block the front wheels. Remove the wheel and brake disc (see Chapter 9).

2   Remove the rear wheel speed sensor.

3   Drain the differential lubricant (see Chapter 1). Remove the differential cover.

Note: *Only the 8.6 inch differential requires the differential cover to be removed to drain the fluid. All other models are equipped with a drain plug.*

4   Remove the pinion shaft lock screw (see illustration).

7.4 Remove the pinion shaft lock screw

7.5 Withdraw the pinion shaft for access to the C-locks (don't turn the axleshafts or differential carrier after the shaft has been pulled out, or the spider gears may become misaligned)

7.6a Push the axle flange in, then remove the C-lock from the inner end of the axleshaft

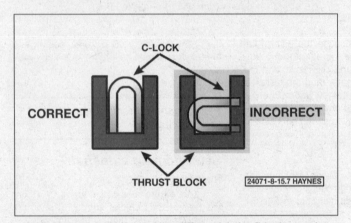

7.6b On models with a locking differential, the C-lock must be positioned as shown before it can be removed

8.2 Prying out the axleshaft oil seal with a seal removal tool

5   On models with a conventional differential (non-locking), remove the pinion shaft. On models with a locking differential, withdraw the pinion shaft part way, then rotate the differential until the shaft touches the case, providing enough clearance for access to the C-locks (see illustration).

6   Push in on the outer flanged end of the axleshaft, then remove the C-lock from the groove on the inner end of the shaft (see illustration). On models with a locking differential, use a screwdriver to rotate the C-lock until the open end points in (see illustration).

7   With the C-lock removed, withdraw the axleshaft, taking care not to damage the oil seal (but note that it is a good idea to replace the seal whenever the axleshaft is removed - see Section 8). Some models have a thrust washer in the differential; make sure it doesn't fall out when the axleshaft is removed.

Caution: *Do NOT rotate the axleshaft (and don't rotate the other axleshaft, either). The pinion (or "spider") gears in the differential will become misaligned and it will be difficult to put them back in position during reassembly.*

Installation

8   To install, carefully insert the axleshaft

into the housing until it engages with the differential side gear.

9   Install the C-lock in the axleshaft groove and pull out on the flange to lock it.

10   Insert the pinion shaft, align the hole in the shaft with the lock screw hole and install the lock screw.

Note: *Apply a non-hardening, thread-locking compound to the threads of the lock screw before installing it. Tighten the lock screw to the torque listed in this Chapter's Specifications.*

11   Install the cover and tighten the bolts to the torque listed in this Chapter's Specifications. Fill the differential with the lubricant specified in Chapter 1.

12   Install the brake disc, caliper mounting bracket and caliper, then tighten the fasteners to the torque listed in the Chapter 9 Specifications. Install the wheel and lug nuts, then lower the vehicle. Tighten the lug nuts to the torque listed in the Chapter 1 Specifications.

Full-floating axleshaft

13   Remove the bolts that attach the axleshaft flange to the hub.

14   Tap the flange with a soft-face hammer to loosen the shaft, then grip the rib in the face of the flange with a pair of locking pliers.

Twist the shaft slightly in both directions and withdraw it from the housing. Place a drip pan under the outer end of the axle to catch any lubricant which might leak out while the axle is removed.

15   Installation is the reverse of removal. Be sure to hold the axleshaft level to engage the splines at the inner end with those in the differential side gear. Always use a new gasket on the flange and keep both the flange and hub mating surfaces free of grease and oil. Tighten the axleshaft flange bolts to the torque listed in this Chapter's Specifications.

8   Axleshaft oil seal (rear, semi-floating axle) - replacement

1   Remove the axleshaft (see Section 7).

2   Pry the oil seal out of the end of the axle housing (see illustration).

3   Apply a film of multi-purpose grease to the oil seal recess and tap the new seal evenly into place with a hammer and seal installation tool (see illustration), large socket or piece of pipe so the lips are facing in and the metal face is visible from the end of the

8.3 Using a seal driver to install the axleshaft oil seal - drive the seal in until it's flush with the bore

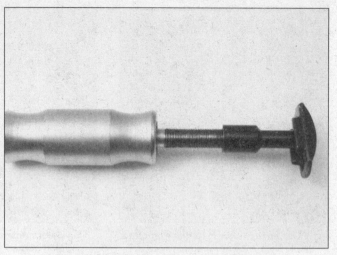

9.2 A typical slide hammer and axleshaft bearing remover attachment

9.3 Removing the axleshaft bearing with a slide hammer

9.4 Use a bearing driver or a large socket to tap the bearing evenly into the axle housing

axle housing. When correctly installed, the face of the oil seal should be flush with the end of the axle housing.
4   Install the axleshaft (see Section 7).

9   Axleshaft bearing (rear, semi-floating axle) - replacement

1   Remove the axleshaft (see Section 7) and the oil seal (see Section 8).
2   A bearing puller which grips the bearing from behind will be required for this job (see illustration).
3   Attach a slide hammer to the puller and extract the bearing from the axle housing (see illustration).
4   Clean out the bearing recess and drive in the new bearing with a bearing installer or a piece of pipe positioned against the outer bearing race (see illustration). Make sure the

bearing is tapped in to the full depth of the recess.
5   Install a new oil seal (see Section 8), then install the axleshaft (see Section 7).

10   Rear hub, wheel bearing and seal (full-floating axle) - removal, bearing/seal replacement and installation

Removal

1   Remove the axleshaft (see Section 7).
2   Loosen the rear wheel lug nuts, raise the rear of the vehicle and support it securely on jackstands. Block the front wheels and remove the rear wheels.
3   Remove the brake caliper and bracket together as an assembly. Remove the brake disc (see Chapter 9).

4   Remove the retaining ring and key (if equipped) from the end of the axle housing.
5   Remove the adjusting nut, using a special socket available at most auto parts stores.
6   Pull the hub assembly straight off the axle tube.
7   Remove and discard the oil seal from the back of the hub.
8   Use solvent to clean the bearings, hub and axle tube, then spray the bearings with brake system cleaner, which will remove the solvent and allow the bearings to dry much more rapidly.
9   Carefully inspect the bearings for cracks, wear and damage. Check the axle tube flange, studs and hub splines for damage and corrosion. Check the bearing cups (races) for pitting or scoring. Worn or damaged components must be replaced with new ones.
10   To further disassemble the hub, use a hammer and a long bar or drift punch to knock

11.3 Use an inch-pound torque wrench to check the torque required to rotate the pinion shaft

11.4 Before removing the nut, mark the position of the flange to the shaft and count the number of exposed threads

11.8 Use a seal removal tool or a large screwdriver to remove the pinion seal (be careful not to disturb the pinion while doing this)

11.9 A large socket with a diameter the same as that of the new pinion seal can be used to drive the seal into the differential housing

out the inner bearing cup (races).

11   Remove the retaining ring, then knock the outer bearing cup from the hub.

12   Clean the old sealing compound from the seal bore in the hub.

13   Inspect the brake disc (see Chapter 9).

14   Reassemble the hub by reversing the disassembly procedure. Use only the proper size bearing driver when installing the new bearing cups (races).

15   Lubricate the bearings and the axle tube contact areas with wheel bearing grease. Work the grease completely into the bearings, forcing it between the rollers, cone and cage.

Installation

16   Make sure the axle housing oil deflector is in position. Place the hub assembly on the axle tube, taking care not to damage the oil seals.

17   Install the adjusting nut and adjust the bearings.

Adjustment

18   Rotate the hub, making sure it turns freely.

19   While rotating the hub in the normal direction of rotation (forward), tighten the adjusting nut to 50 ft-lbs with a torque wrench. Again, this will require the special socket, which is available at most auto parts stores.

20   Back the nut off until it's loose, then tighten the nut hand-tight with the special socket.

21   If necessary, turn the nut counterclockwise to align the closest slot in the nut with the keyway in the spindle, then install the key.

Caution: *Don't turn the nut more than one slot to achieve alignment.*

22   Install the retaining ring.

23   Wiggle the hub assembly; you shouldn't be able to detect any play, but the hub should turn freely. There shouldn't be any preload on the bearings, but there shouldn't be any free-play, either.

24   Install the axleshaft (see Section 7) and lower the vehicle.

---

11   Pinion oil seal - replacement

Note: *This procedure applies to the front and rear pinion oil seals.*

1   Loosen the wheel lug nuts. Raise the front (for front differential) or rear (for rear differential) of the vehicle and support it securely on jackstands. Block the opposite set of wheels to keep the vehicle from rolling off the stands. Remove the wheels.

2   Disconnect the driveshaft from the differential pinion flange and fasten it out of the way (see Section 3).

3   Rotate the pinion a few times by hand. Use a beam-type or dial-type inch-pound torque wrench to check the torque required to rotate the pinion (see illustration). Record it for use later.

4   Mark the relationship of the pinion flange

to the shaft (see illustration), then count and write down the number of exposed threads on the shaft.

5   A special tool, available at most auto parts stores, can be used to keep the companion flange from moving while the self-locking pinion nut is loosened. A chain wrench can also be used to immobilize the flange.

6   Remove the pinion nut.

7   Withdraw the flange. It may be necessary to use a two-jaw puller engaged behind the flange to draw it off. Do not attempt to pry or hammer behind the flange or hammer on the end of the pinion shaft.

8   Pry out the old seal and discard it (see illustration).

9   Lubricate the lips of the new seal, then tap it evenly into position with a seal installation tool or a large socket (see illustration). Make sure it enters the housing squarely and is tapped in to its full depth.

10   Install the pinion flange, lining up the marks made in Step 4. If necessary, tighten the pinion nut to draw the flange into place. Do not try to hammer the flange into position.

11   Apply a bead of RTV sealant to the ends of the splines visible in the center of the flange so oil will be sealed in.

12   Install the washer and a new pinion nut. Tighten the nut until the number of threads recorded in Step 4 are exposed.

13   Measure the torque required to rotate the pinion and tighten the nut in small increments (no more than 5 ft-lbs) until it matches the figure recorded in Step 3. To compensate for the drag of the new oil seal, the nut should be tightened a little more until the rotational torque of the pinion exceeds the earlier recording by 3 to 5 inch-lbs.

14   Reinstall all components removed previously by reversing the removal Steps, tightening all fasteners to their specified torque values. Tighten the wheel lug nuts to the torque listed in the Chapter 1 Specifications.

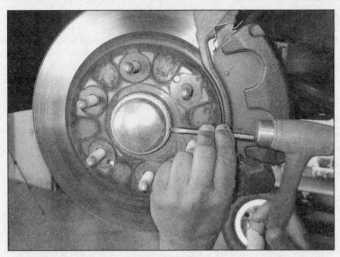

14.2 A hammer and chisel can be used to knock the cover off the hub

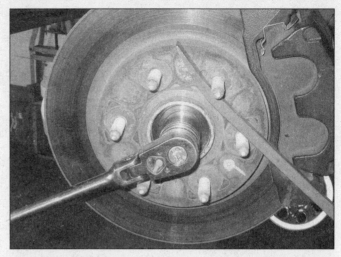

14.3 A large prybar can be used to immobilize the hub while loosening the nut, or a screwdriver can be inserted through the window in the brake caliper and into the disc cooling vanes

12 Axle assembly (rear) - removal and installation

Removal

Note: *If equipped with electronic parking brake, release the parking brake tension (see Chapter 9).*

1 Loosen the rear wheel lug nuts, raise the rear of the vehicle and support it securely on jackstands. Block the front wheels to keep the vehicle from rolling off the stands. Remove the rear wheels.
2 Position a floor jack under the rear axle differential housing.
Note: *If you have two floor jacks, place one under each axle tube.*
3 Remove the driveshaft (see Section 3).
4 Disconnect the shock absorbers at their lower mounts (see Chapter 10).
5 Disconnect the vent hose from the fitting on the axle housing.
6 Disconnect the stabilizer shaft end links from the frame.
7 Disconnect the brake line bracket bolts.
8 Remove the rear brake calipers, leaving the brake hoses connected and secure them out of the way (see Chapter 9).
9 Disconnect the parking brake cables from the brackets on the backing plates.
10 Remove the rear wheel speed sensors (see Chapter 9).

Leaf spring models

11 Remove the spring U-bolt nuts (see Chapter 10). Remove the spring plates.
12 Lower the jack under the differential, then remove the rear axle assembly from under the vehicle.

Coil spring models

13 Detach the links for the electronic suspension control sensors, if equipped, from the trailing arms.

14 Detach the track bar from the rear axle (see Chapter 10).
15 Remove the stabilizer bar (see Chapter 10).
16 Remove the coil springs (see Chapter 10).
17 Disconnect the upper and lower trailing arms from the axle assembly (see Chapter 10).
18 Lower the jack under the differential, then remove the rear axle assembly from under the vehicle.

Installation

19 Installation is the reverse of removal. Tighten the U-joint clamp bolts in a criss-cross pattern to the torque listed in this Chapter's Specifications. Tighten all suspension fasteners to the torque values listed in the Chapter 10 Specifications. Tighten the brake fasteners to the torque values listed in the Chapter 9 Specifications.
20 Install the wheels and lug nuts, then lower the vehicle and tighten the lug nuts to the torque listed in the Chapter 1 Specifications.

13 Driveaxles (4WD models) - general information and inspection

1 Power is transmitted from the front differential/axle to the front wheels through a pair of driveaxles. The inner end of each driveaxle is bolted to an axleshaft connected to the differential side gears. The outer end of each driveaxle has a stub shaft that is splined to the front hub and bearing assembly and locked in place with a large nut.
2 The inner ends of the driveaxles are equipped with sliding constant velocity (CV) joints, which are capable of both angular and

axial motion. Each inner CV joint assembly consists of a tripot-type bearing and a housing in which the joint is free to slide in-and-out as the driveaxle moves up-and-down with the wheel.
3 The outer ends of the driveaxles are equipped with ball-and-cage type CV joints, which are capable of angular but not axial movement. Each outer CV joint consists of six caged ball bearings running between an inner race and the housing.
4 The most common symptom of worn or damaged CV joints, besides lubricant leaks, is a clicking noise in turns, a clunk when accelerating after coasting and vibration at highway speeds. To check for wear in the CV joints and driveaxle shafts, grasp each axle (one at a time) and rotate it in both directions while holding the CV joint housings, feeling for play indicating worn splines or sloppy CV joints. Also check the driveaxle shafts for cracks, dents and distortion.

14 Driveaxle (4WD models) - removal and installation

Removal

1 Loosen the wheel lug nuts, raise the front of the vehicle and support it securely on jackstands. Remove the wheel.
2 If equipped, pry off the hub cover (see illustration).
3 Remove the driveaxle/hub nut. To prevent the hub from rotating, brace a large prybar across two of the wheel studs (see illustration), or insert a long punch or screwdriver through the window in the brake caliper and into the disc cooling vanes.
Caution: *Obtain a new driveaxle/hub nut for reassembly.*
4 Remove the differential carrier splash shield, if equipped.

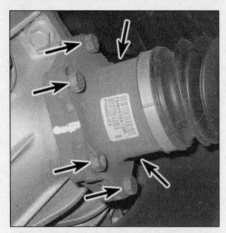

14.5 Remove the driveaxle-to-axleshaft flange bolts

5   Remove the driveaxle-to-axleshaft flange bolts (see illustration). Have an assistant apply the brake as you loosen the bolts to prevent the driveaxle from turning. Separate the driveaxle from the axleshaft flange.

6   Lower the inner end of the driveaxle, then pull the stub shaft out of the hub. Carefully guide the driveaxle out from under the vehicle.

Note: *It may be necessary to remove the stabilizer bar link to provide clearance for driveaxle removal.*

Note: *If the stub shaft sticks in the hub splines, tap on the end of the shaft with a brass punch and a hammer. If that doesn't free the splines, push the driveaxle from the hub with a puller.*

Installation

Caution: *The hub nut should not be reused. Install a new hub nut when installing the shaft.*

7   Installation is the reverse of removal. Before installing the driveaxle, lubricate the

splines on the stub shaft with multi-purpose grease. Be sure to tighten the driveaxle/hub nut (new) and the flange bolts to the torque values listed in this Chapter's Specifications. Tighten the wheel lug nuts to the torque listed in the Chapter 1 Specifications.

---

15   Front axle shift motor (4WD models) - replacement

1   Raise the front of the vehicle and support it securely on jackstands. Remove the differential carrier splash shield, if equipped.

2   Disconnect the electrical connector from the shift motor.

3   Unscrew the motor from the axle tube (see illustration).

4   Before installing the motor, coat the threads with RTV sealant. Tighten the motor securely.

---

16   Right axleshaft, tube, and bearing (4WD and AWD models) - removal, component replacement, and installation

Note: *On 9.25-inch axles, the front axle clutch gear shim adjustment is critical when replacing any parts on the right front drive axle. Proper adjustment should be made by a qualified technician, therefore, the procedure for performing the adjustment is not provided.*

Removal

1   Loosen the wheel lug nuts, raise the vehicle, place it securely on jackstands and remove the right front wheel.

2   Remove the differential carrier splash shield, if equipped.

3   Drain the lubricant from the front differential (see Chapter 1).

4   Disconnect the shift motor actuator electrical connector.

5   Disconnect the harness from the right axle shaft housing.

6   On 8.25-inch axles, remove the power steering assist motor (see Chapter 10) and the right front shock absorber (see Chapter 10, Section 2).

7   On all axles, unbolt the right driveaxle from the axleshaft flange (see Section 14). Support the driveaxle out of the way with a piece of wire - don't let it hang by the outer CV joint.

8   On 9.25-inch axles, remove the front axle shift motor (see Section 15) and the right stabilizer end link (see Chapter 10, Section 3).

9   On all axles, to prevent the differential carrier from cocking when the axle tube is removed, support it with a floor jack and a block of wood.

10   Remove the nuts that attach the axle shaft to its support bracket.

11   Remove the bolts securing the axle shaft flange to the differential carrier (see illustration).

12   Use a brass punch and hammer to tap on the axle shaft and separate it from the differential case side gear. Remove the inner axle shaft assembly and the axle shaft from the vehicle.

13   On 9.25-inch axles, take the axleshaft to a qualified technician to replace the bearing and seal.

14   On 8.25-inch axles, remove the inner seal and bearing. A special tool is required to pull the bearing from the clutch shaft. Install a new bearing and seal.

Installation

15   Using a new gasket, install the inner axle shaft housing assembly and tighten the bolts to the torque listed in this Chapter's Specifications.

16   Install the axle shaft to the support

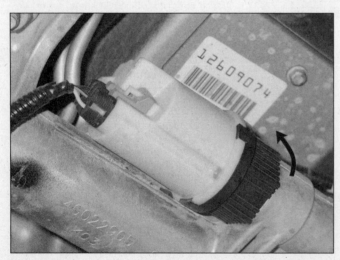

15.3 The front axle shift motor simply unscrews from the axle tube

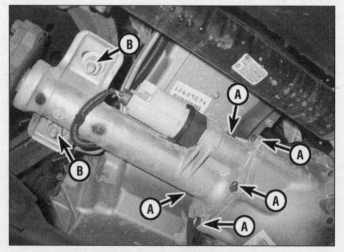

16.11 Differential carrier right axle tube

A   *Axle Tube-to-differential carrier bolts (two upper bolts are hidden from view)*

B   *Axle tube mounting nuts*

bracket, install the nuts and tighten them to the torque listed in this Chapter's Specifications.

17   On 8.25-inch axles, align the splines of the inner axle shaft with the splines on the differential side gear by slowly rotating the inner axle shaft. Tap the inner axle shaft with a mallet until the ring (clip) on the axle shaft is aligned with the groove in the differential case side gear.

18   Install the axle shaft to the inner flange. Install the axle shaft flange bolts and tighten them to the torque listed in this Chapter's Specifications.

19   Fill the differential with the proper lubricant (see Chapter 1).

20   Install the differential carrier splash shield.

21   Install the wheel and lug nuts. Lower the vehicle, tighten the lug nuts to the torque listed in the Chapter 1 Specifications, then check for proper operation.

17   Axleshaft oil seals (front, 4WD models) - replacement

Right side

1   Refer to Section 16 for the right-side axleshaft seal and bearing replacement procedure.

Left side

2   Loosen the wheel lug nuts, raise the vehicle, place it securely on jackstands and remove the left front wheel. Remove the differential carrier splash shield from under the front axle.

3   Remove the left driveaxle (see Section 14).

4   Drain the lubricant from the front differential (see Chapter 1).

5   Pull the left axleshaft out with a slide hammer and adapter.

6   Remove the deflector and seal from the differential.

7   Install a new seal and deflector. Lubricate the lips of the seal with multi-purpose grease.

8   Install the axleshaft, carefully driving it in with a soft-face hammer.

9   Fill the differential with the proper lubri-

cant (see Chapter 1).

10   Install the driveaxle (see Section 14).

11   Install the differential carrier splash shield.

12   Install the wheel and lug nuts. Lower the vehicle, tighten the lug nuts to the torque listed in the Chapter 1 Specifications, then check for proper operation.

18   Front differential carrier - removal and installation

1   Disconnect the cable from the negative terminal of the battery (see Chapter 5, Section 3).

2   Loosen the front wheel lug nuts, raise the front of the vehicle and support it securely on jackstands placed under the frame rails. Remove the wheels.

3   Remove the differential carrier splash shield, if equipped.

Note: *If you are removing the differential carrier to service other components, the fluid does not need to be drained.*

4   Drain the lubricant from the front differential (see Chapter 1, Section 30).

5   Remove the front driveshaft (see Section 3).

6   Detach the vent hose from the differential housing.

7   Disconnect the electrical connector from the shift motor and disconnect the electrical harness from the carrier.

8.25-inch axle (LD)

8   Remove the steering gear (see Chapter 10, Section 22).

9   Remove the lower control arm crossmember.

10   Detach the inner ends of the driveaxles from the axleshaft flanges (see Section 14). Suspend the driveaxles with lengths of wire - don't let them hang by the outer CV joints.

11   Support the differential carrier with a floor jack. If a transmission jack adapter is available, use it - it will hold the assembly more securely.

12   Remove the two nuts that attach the axle tube (differential carrier) to the chassis.

13   Remove the differential carrier rear mounting bolts.

14   Pivot the differential carrier forward and down and slowly lower the jack and guide the carrier out from under the vehicle.

15   Check the bushings in the front and rear mounting bosses; if they are in need of replacement, take the carrier to an automotive machine shop or other qualified repair facility to have the old bushings pressed out and the new ones pressed in.

16   Installation is the reverse of removal. Tighten all fasteners to the proper torque values. Refill the differential with the proper lubricant (see Chapter 1).

9.25-inch axle (HD)

17   Turn the steering wheel all the way to the left.

18   Remove the steering gear skid plate (if equipped).

19   Disconnect the relay rod from the idler arm and the Pitman arm (see Chapter 10). Remove the tie-rod ends from the spindles and remove the relay rod.

20   Detach the inner ends of the driveaxles from the axleshaft flanges (see Section 14). Suspend the driveaxles with lengths of wire - don't let them hang by the outer CV joints.

21   Support the differential carrier with a floor jack. If a transmission jack adapter is available, use it - it will hold the assembly more securely.

22   Remove the two nuts that attach the axle tube to the chassis.

23   Remove the differential carrier rear upper mounting bolt and nut.

24   Pivot the differential carrier down and away from the vehicle to access the lower mounting bolt and nut.

25   Slowly lower the jack and remove the lower mounting bolt. Guide the carrier out from under the vehicle.

26   Check the bushings in the front and rear mounting bosses; if they are in need of replacement, take the carrier to an automotive machine shop or other qualified repair facility to have the old bushings pressed out and the new ones pressed in.

27   Installation is the reverse of removal. Tighten all fasteners to the proper torque values. Refill the differential with the proper lubricant (see Chapter 1).

Notes

Chapter 9
Brakes

Contents

Specifications

General

Brake fluid type	See Chapter 1
Brake pedal travel (maximum)	
With vacuum power booster	2.36 inches
With hydraulic power booster	3.54 inches

Disc brakes

Minimum pad thickness	See Chapter 1
Brake disc minimum thickness	Cast into disc
Maximum disc runout	0.002 inch
Front disc maximum thickness variation	
1500 models	0.0007 inch
2500/3500 models	0.001 inch
Rear disc maximum thickness variation	
1500 models	0.0007 inch
2500/3500 models	0.001 inch

Torque specifications

Ft-lbs (unless otherwise indicated)

Note: *One foot-pound (ft-lb) of torque is equivalent to 12 inch-pounds (in-lbs) of torque. Torque values below approximately 15 foot-pounds are expressed in inch-pounds, because most foot-pound torque wrenches are not accurate at these smaller values.*

Brake booster (vacuum or hydraulic systems)	
Mounting nuts..	24
Pushrod clip bolt...	89 in-lbs
Vacuum pump mounting bolts	80 in-lbs
Brake caliper	
Caliper mounting bolts (slide pin bolts)	
Front	
1500 models..	74
2500/3500 models...	77
Rear	
1500 models..	38
2500/3500 models...	77
Caliper mounting bracket bolts	
Front	
1500 models..	170
2500/3500 models...	221
Rear	
1500 models..	148
3500 models	
JD9...	148
J90, J95, J96...	221
Hub extension nuts (heavy-duty models with RPO J96)	See Chapter 10
Rear disc-to-hub bolts (models with dual rear wheels)............................	148
Brake hose-to-caliper banjo bolt...	30
Master cylinder-to-brake booster mounting nuts	24
Wheel speed sensor mounting bolts	
Front	156 in-lbs
Rear	80 in-lbs
Wheel lug nuts..	See Chapter 1

1 General information and precautions

General

1 The vehicles covered by this manual are equipped with hydraulically operated front disc brakes. The brakes are self adjusting and automatically compensate for pad wear.

Hydraulic system

2 The hydraulic system consists of two separate circuits, split front-to-rear. The master cylinder has separate reservoirs for the two circuits, and, in the event of a leak or failure in one hydraulic circuit, the other circuit will remain operative and a warning indicator will light up on the instrument panel when a substantial amount of brake fluid is lost, showing that a failure has occurred.

Power brake booster

3 The power brake booster uses either engine manifold vacuum or hydraulic pressure from the power steering pump to provide assistance to the brakes. It is mounted on the firewall in the engine compartment, directly behind the master cylinder.

Parking brake

4 The parking brake operates the rear brakes only, through cable actuation. It's activated by a pedal mounted under the left end of the instrument panel. The parking brake cables actuate parking brake shoes mounted inside of the drum portion of each rear brake disc.

Service

5 After completing any operation involving disassembly of any part of the brake system, always test drive the vehicle to check for proper braking performance before resuming normal driving. When testing the brakes, perform the tests on a clean, dry, flat surface. Conditions other than these can lead to inaccurate test results.

6 Test the brakes at various speeds with both light and heavy pedal pressure. The vehicle should stop evenly without pulling to one side or the other.

7 Tires, vehicle load and wheel alignment are other factors which also affect braking performance.

Precautions

8 There are some general cautions and warnings involving the brake system on this vehicle:

a) Use only brake fluid conforming to DOT 3 specifications.

b) The brake pads and linings contain fibers which are hazardous to your health if inhaled. Whenever you work on brake system components, clean all parts with brake system cleaner. Do not allow the fine dust to become airborne. Also, wear an approved filtering mask.

c) Safety should be paramount whenever any servicing of the brake components is performed. Do not use parts or fasteners which are not in perfect condition, and be sure that all clearances and torque specifications are adhered to. If you are at all unsure about a certain procedure, seek professional advice. Upon completion of any brake system work, test the brakes carefully in a controlled area before putting the vehicle into normal service. If a problem is suspected in the brake system, don't drive the vehicle until it's fixed.

d) Used brake fluid is considered a hazardous waste and it must be disposed of in accordance with federal, state and local laws.

e) DO NOT pour it down the sink, into septic tanks or storm drains, or on the ground.

f) Clean up any spilled brake fluid immediately and then wash the area with large amounts of water. This is especially true for any finished or painted surfaces.

2 Troubleshooting

PROBABLE CAUSE	CORRECTIVE ACTION

No brakes - pedal travels to floor

PROBABLE CAUSE	CORRECTIVE ACTION
1 Low fluid level 2 Air in system	1 and 2 Low fluid level and air in the system are symptoms of another problem a leak somewhere in the hydraulic system. Locate and repair the leak
3 Defective seals in master cylinder	3 Replace master cylinder
4 Fluid overheated and vaporized due to heavy braking	4 Bleed hydraulic system (temporary fix). Replace brake fluid (proper fix)

Brake pedal slowly travels to floor under braking or at a stop

PROBABLE CAUSE	CORRECTIVE ACTION
1 Defective seals in master cylinder	1 Replace master cylinder
2 Leak in a hose, line, caliper or wheel cylinder	2 Locate and repair leak
3 Air in hydraulic system	3 Bleed the system, inspect system for a leak

Brake pedal feels spongy when depressed

PROBABLE CAUSE	CORRECTIVE ACTION
1 Air in hydraulic system	1 Bleed the system, inspect system for a leak
2 Master cylinder or power booster loose	2 Tighten fasteners
3 Brake fluid overheated (beginning to boil)	3 Bleed the system (temporary fix). Replace the brake fluid (proper fix)
4 Deteriorated brake hoses (ballooning under pressure)	4 Inspect hoses, replace as necessary (it's a good idea to replace all of them if one hose shows signs of deterioration)

Troubleshooting (continued)

PROBABLE CAUSE	CORRECTIVE ACTION

Brake pedal feels hard when depressed and/or excessive effort required to stop vehicle

1 Power booster faulty	1 Replace booster
2 Engine not producing sufficient vacuum, or hose to booster clogged, collapsed or cracked	2 Check vacuum to booster with a vacuum gauge. Replace hose if cracked or clogged, repair engine if vacuum is extremely low
3 Brake linings contaminated by grease or brake fluid	3 Locate and repair source of contamination, replace brake pads or shoes
4 Brake linings glazed	4 Replace brake pads or shoes, check discs and drums for glazing, service as necessary
5 Caliper piston(s) or wheel cylinder(s) binding or frozen	5 Replace calipers or wheel cylinders
6 Brakes wet	6 Apply pedal to boil-off water (this should only be a momentary problem)
7 Kinked, clogged or internally split brake hose or line	7 Inspect lines and hoses, replace as necessary

Excessive brake pedal travel (but will pump up)

1 Drum brakes out of adjustment	1 Adjust brakes
2 Air in hydraulic system	2 Bleed system, inspect system for a leak

Excessive brake pedal travel (but will not pump up)

1 Master cylinder pushrod misadjusted	1 Adjust pushrod
2 Master cylinder seals defective	2 Replace master cylinder
3 Brake linings worn out	3 Inspect brakes, replace pads and/or shoes
4 Hydraulic system leak	4 Locate and repair leak

Brake pedal doesn't return

1 Brake pedal binding	1 Inspect pivot bushing and pushrod, repair or lubricate
2 Defective master cylinder	2 Replace master cylinder

Brake pedal pulsates during brake application

1 Brake drums out-of-round	1 Have drums machined by an automotive machine shop
2 Excessive brake disc runout or disc surfaces out-of-parallel	2 Have discs machined by an automotive machine shop
3 Loose or worn wheel bearings	3 Adjust or replace wheel bearings
4 Loose lug nuts	4 Tighten lug nuts

Brakes slow to release

1 Malfunctioning power booster	1 Replace booster
2 Pedal linkage binding	2 Inspect pedal pivot bushing and pushrod, repair/lubricate
3 Malfunctioning proportioning valve	3 Replace proportioning valve
4 Sticking caliper or wheel cylinder	4 Repair or replace calipers or wheel cylinders
5 Kinked or internally split brake hose	5 Locate and replace faulty brake hose

Brakes grab (one or more wheels)

1 Grease or brake fluid on brake lining	1 Locate and repair cause of contamination, replace lining
2 Brake lining glazed	2 Replace lining, deglaze disc or drum

PROBABLE CAUSE	CORRECTIVE ACTION

Vehicle pulls to one side during braking

PROBABLE CAUSE	CORRECTIVE ACTION
1 Grease or brake fluid on brake lining	1 Locate and repair cause of contamination, replace lining
2 Brake lining glazed	2 Deglaze or replace lining, deglaze disc or drum
3 Restricted brake line or hose	3 Repair line or replace hose
4 Tire pressures incorrect	4 Adjust tire pressures
5 Caliper or wheel cylinder sticking	5 Repair or replace calipers or wheel cylinders
6 Wheels out of alignment	6 Have wheels aligned
7 Weak suspension spring	7 Replace springs
8 Weak or broken shock absorber	8 Replace shock absorbers

Brakes drag (indicated by sluggish engine performance or wheels being very hot after driving)

PROBABLE CAUSE	CORRECTIVE ACTION
1 Brake pedal pushrod incorrectly adjusted	1 Adjust pushrod
2 Master cylinder pushrod (between booster and master cylinder)	2 Adjust pushrod incorrectly adjusted
3 Obstructed compensating port in master cylinder	3 Replace master cylinder
4 Master cylinder piston seized in bore	4 Replace master cylinder
5 Contaminated fluid causing swollen seals throughout system	5 Flush system, replace all hydraulic components
6 Clogged brake lines or internally split brake hose(s)	6 Flush hydraulic system, replace defective hose(s)
7 Sticking caliper(s) or wheel cylinder(s)	7 Replace calipers or wheel cylinders
8 Parking brake not releasing	8 Inspect parking brake linkage and parking brake mechanism, repair as required
9 Improper shoe-to-drum clearance	9 Adjust brake shoes
10 Faulty proportioning valve	10 Replace proportioning valve

Brakes fade (due to excessive heat)

PROBABLE CAUSE	CORRECTIVE ACTION
1 Brake linings excessively worn or glazed	1 Deglaze or replace brake pads and/or shoes
2 Excessive use of brakes	2 Downshift into a lower gear, maintain a constant slower speed (going down hills)
3 Vehicle overloaded	3 Reduce load
4 Brake drums or discs worn too thin	4 Measure drum diameter and disc thickness, replace drums or discs as required
5 Contaminated brake fluid	5 Flush system, replace fluid
6 Brakes drag	6 Repair cause of dragging brakes
7 Driver resting left foot on brake pedal	7 Don't ride the brakes

Brakes noisy (high-pitched squeal)

PROBABLE CAUSE	CORRECTIVE ACTION
1 Glazed lining	1 Deglaze or replace lining
2 Contaminated lining (brake fluid, grease, etc.)	2 Repair source of contamination, replace linings
3 Weak or broken brake shoe hold-down or return spring	3 Replace springs
4 Rivets securing lining to shoe or backing plate loose	4 Replace shoes or pads
5 Excessive dust buildup on brake linings	5 Wash brakes off with brake system cleaner
6 Brake drums worn too thin	6 Measure diameter of drums, replace if necessary
7 Wear indicator on disc brake pads contacting disc	7 Replace brake pads
8 Anti-squeal shims missing or installed improperly	8 Install shims correctly

Troubleshooting (continued)

PROBABLE CAUSE	CORRECTIVE ACTION

Brakes noisy (scraping sound)

1 Brake pads or shoes worn out; rivets, backing plate or brake	1 Replace linings, have discs and/or drums machined (or replace) shoe metal contacting disc or drum

Brakes chatter

1 Worn brake lining	1 Inspect brakes, replace shoes or pads as necessary
2 Glazed or scored discs or drums	2 Deglaze discs or drums with sandpaper (if glazing is severe, machining will be required)
3 Drums or discs heat checked	3 Check discs and/or drums for hard spots, heat checking, etc. Have discs/drums machined or replace them
4 Disc runout or drum out-of-round excessive	4 Measure disc runout and/or drum out-of-round, have discs or drums machined or replace them
5 Loose or worn wheel bearings	5 Adjust or replace wheel bearings
6 Loose or bent brake backing plate (drum brakes)	6 Tighten or replace backing plate
7 Grooves worn in discs or drums	7 Have discs or drums machined, if within limits (if not, replace them)
8 Brake linings contaminated (brake fluid, grease, etc.)	8 Locate and repair source of contamination, replace pads or shoes
9 Excessive dust buildup on linings	9 Wash brakes with brake system cleaner
10 Surface finish on discs or drums too rough after machining	10 Have discs or drums properly machined (especially on vehicles with sliding calipers)
11 Brake pads or shoes glazed	11 Deglaze or replace brake pads or shoes

Brake pads or shoes click

1 Shoe support pads on brake backing plate grooved or	1 Replace brake backing plate excessively worn
2 Brake pads loose in caliper	2 Loose pad retainers or anti-rattle clips
3 Also see items listed under Brakes chatter	

Brakes make groaning noise at end of stop

1 Brake pads and/or shoes worn out	1 Replace pads and/or shoes
2 Brake linings contaminated (brake fluid, grease, etc.)	2 Locate and repair cause of contamination, replace brake pads or shoes
3 Brake linings glazed	3 Deglaze or replace brake pads or shoes
4 Excessive dust buildup on linings	4 Wash brakes with brake system cleaner
5 Scored or heat-checked discs or drums	5 Inspect discs/drums, have machined if within limits (if not, replace discs or drums)
6 Broken or missing brake shoe attaching hardware	6 Inspect drum brakes, replace missing hardware

Rear brakes lock up under light brake application

1 Tire pressures too high	1 Adjust tire pressures
2 Tires excessively worn	2 Replace tires
3 Defective proportioning valve	3 Replace proportioning valve

Brake warning light on instrument panel comes on (or stays on)

1 Low fluid level in master cylinder reservoir (reservoirs with fluid level sensor)	1 Add fluid, inspect system for leak, check the thickness of the brake pads and shoes
2 Failure in one half of the hydraulic system	2 Inspect hydraulic system for a leak
3 Piston in pressure differential warning valve not centered	3 Center piston by bleeding one circuit or the other (close bleeder valve as soon as the light goes out)

PROBABLE CAUSE   CORRECTIVE ACTION

Brake warning light on instrument panel comes on (or stays on) (continued)

4 Defective pressure differential valve or warning switch	4 Replace valve or switch
5 Air in the hydraulic system	5 Bleed the system, check for leaks
6 Brake pads worn out (vehicles with electric wear sensors - small	6 Replace brake pads (and sensors) probes that fit into the brake pads and ground out on the disc when the pads get thin)

Brakes do not self adjust

Disc brakes

1 Defective caliper piston seals	1 Replace calipers. Also, possible contaminated fluid causing soft or swollen seals (flush system and fill with new fluid if in doubt)
2 Corroded caliper piston(s)	2 Same as above

Drum brakes

1 Adjuster screw frozen	1 Remove adjuster, disassemble, clean and lubricate with high-temperature grease
2 Adjuster lever does not contact star wheel or is binding	2 Inspect drum brakes, assemble correctly or clean or replace parts as required
3 Adjusters mixed up (installed on wrong wheels after brake job)	3 Reassemble correctly
4 Adjuster cable broken or installed incorrectly (cable-type adjusters)	4 Install new cable or assemble correctly

Rapid brake lining wear

1 Driver resting left foot on brake pedal	1 Don't ride the brakes
2 Surface finish on discs or drums too rough	2 Have discs or drums properly machined
3 Also see Brakes drag	

---

3   Anti-lock Brake System (ABS), Traction Control (TCS) and vehicle stability control (StabiliTrak) systems - general information

1   The Anti-lock Brake System (ABS) helps to maintain vehicle maneuverability, directional stability, and optimum deceleration under severe braking conditions on most road surfaces. It does so by monitoring the rotational speed of the wheels and controlling the brake line pressure to the wheels during braking. This prevents the wheels from locking up on slippery roads or during hard braking.

Electro-Hydraulic Control Unit (EHCU)

2   The Electro-Hydraulic Control Unit (EHCU), mounted on the left-side frame rail underneath the cab, controls hydraulic pressure to the brake calipers by modulating hydraulic pressure to prevent wheel lock-up (see illustration). It is made up of the Brake

Pressure Modulator Valve (BPMV) and the Electronic Brake Control Module (EBCM). Basically, the BPMV reduces pressure in a brake line when the Electronic Brake Control Module (EBCM) detects an abnormal deceleration in the speed of a wheel (via a wheel

speed sensor signal). When the speed of the wheel is restored to normal, the modulator once again allows full pressure to the brake. This cycle is repeated as many times as necessary, which results in a pulsing of the brake pedal.

3.2 The ABS Electro-Hydraulic Control Unit (EHCU) is located along the left frame rail, underneath the driver

3   In addition to sensing and processing information received from the brake switch and wheel speed sensors to control the hydraulic line pressure and avoid wheel lock up, the EBCM also continually monitors the system and stores fault codes which indicate specific problems.

Note: *Brake fluid bleeding for the ABS control unit is only accomplished with the use of the proper type of scan tool.*

Traction Control System

4   Some models are equipped with a Traction Control System (TCS). When wheel slip is detected, the Electronic Brake Control Module (EBCM) will activate the traction control mode. A signal is sent from the EBCM to the PCM (Powertrain Control Module) commanding less torque to the drive wheels. Torque is reduced by retarding the ignition timing and by controlling the throttle control actuator (TCA).

5   The Traction Control System (TCS) is deactivated when the transmission shift lever is selected into the Low position, the driver manually selects Off on the TCS switch on the dash or the EBCM automatically shuts off the TCS during cruising or non-hazard conditions.

Stability Control System

6   Some models may be equipped with StabiliTrak, a stability control system. This system is designed to assist in correcting over/under steering. This system is integrated with the ABS and TCS systems but uses additional sensors.

Wheel speed sensors

7   Generally, there is a wheel speed sensor designated for each wheel. Each sensor generates a signal in the form of a low-voltage electrical current or a frequency when the wheel is turning. A variable signal is generated as a result of a square-toothed ring (tone-ring, exciter-ring, reluctor, etc.) that rotates very close to the sensor. The signal is directly proportional to the wheel speed and is interpreted by an electronic module (computer).

8   The front sensors are mounted to the hub and wheel bearing assemblies and the tone-rings are integrated within the assemblies (see illustration).

9   The rear sensors are mounted to the rear axle housing. The tone-rings are integrated with the rear axle shafts (see illustration).

Warning lights

10   The ABS system has self-diagnostic capabilities. Each time the vehicle is started, the EBCM runs a self-test. There are two warning lights on the instrument panel, a red BRAKE light and an amber ABS light, each with their own functions. During starting, these lights should come on briefly then go out. If the red BRAKE light stays on, it indicates a problem with the main braking system, such as low fluid level detected or the parking brake is still on. If the light stays on after the parking brake is released, check the brake fluid level in the master cylinder reservoir (see Chapter 1).

11   The amber ABS light indicates a problem with the ABS system, not the main or basic brake system. If the light stays on, it indicates that there is a problem with the ABS system, but the main system is still working. Take the vehicle to a dealer service department or other qualified repair shop for diagnosis and repair.

Diagnosis and repair

12   If a dashboard warning light comes on and stays on while the vehicle is in operation, the ABS, or other related systems require attention. Information will also be displayed in the Driver Information Center (DIC), as equipped. Although special diagnostic testing and tools are necessary to properly diagnose the system, you can perform a few preliminary checks before taking the vehicle to a dealer service department.

   a) *Check the brake fluid level in the reservoir.*
   b) *Check the electrical connectors at the EBCM and the hydraulic modulator/motor assembly.*
   c) *Check the fuses.*
   d) *Follow the wiring harness to each wheel and verify that all connections are secure and that the wiring is undamaged.*

13   If the above preliminary checks do not rectify the problem, the vehicle should be diagnosed by a qualified repair shop due to the complexity of this system. All actual repair work must be done by a qualified/certified automotive technician.

Warning: *Do NOT try to repair a wheel speed sensor wiring harness. These systems are sensitive to even the smallest changes in resistance. Repairing the harness could alter resistance values and cause the system to malfunction. If the wiring harness is damaged in any way, it must be replaced.*

Note: *Make sure the ignition is turned off before unplugging or reattaching any electrical connections.*

Wheel speed sensor - removal and installation

Warning: *The dust created by the brake system is harmful to your health. Never blow it out with compressed air and don't inhale any of it. An approved filtering mask should be worn when working on the brakes. Do not, under any circumstances, use petroleum-based solvents to clean brake parts. Use brake system cleaner only!*

14   Loosen the wheel lug nuts, raise the vehicle and support it securely on jackstands. Remove the wheel.

15   Make sure the ignition key is turned to the Off position.

16   If you're replacing a front sensor, remove the front brake disc (see Section 6).

17   Remove the mounting fastener and carefully pull the sensor out from the front hub assembly or the rear axle housing (see illustrations 3.8 and 3.9).

18   Follow the wiring harness to the electrical connector and disconnect it. Remove the harness from any brackets that may secure it to other components.

19   Installation is the reverse of the removal procedure. Tighten the mounting fastener to the torque listed in this Chapter's Specifications.

20   Install the wheel and lug nuts, lower the vehicle and tighten the lug nuts to the torque listed in the Chapter 1 Specifications.

---

4   Disc brake pads - replacement

Warning: *Disc brake pads must be replaced on both front or both rear wheels at the same time - never replace the pads on only one wheel. Also, the dust created by the brake system is harmful to your health. Never blow it out with compressed air and don't inhale any of it. An approved filtering mask should be worn when working on the brakes. Do not, under any circumstances, use petroleum-based solvents to clean brake parts. Use brake system cleaner only!*

3.8 Front wheel speed sensor location

3.9 Rear wheel speed sensor location

Note: *This procedure applies to the front and rear brake pads.*

Warning: *Brake fluid will damage paint. If any fluid is spilled, wash it off immediately with plenty of clean, cold water.*

1   Remove the cap from the brake fluid reservoir. Remove about two-thirds of the fluid from the reservoir, then reinstall the cap.

2   Loosen the front or rear wheel lug nuts, raise the front or rear of the vehicle and support it securely on jackstands. Block the wheels at the opposite end. Remove the wheels. Work on one brake assembly at a time, using the assembled brake for reference if necessary.

3   Inspect the brake disc carefully as outlined in Section 6. If machining is necessary, follow the information in that section to remove the disc.

4   Place a catch pan below the work area and clean the caliper, caliper bracket and surrounding area that you'll be working on (see illustration).

All models except 2500/3500 models with RPO J95/J96

5   Follow the accompanying photo sequence for the actual pad replacement procedure (see illustrations). Be sure to stay in order and read the caption under each illustration.

2500/3500 models with RPO J95/J96

6   Using a C-clamp, depress the pistons into the caliper bores (see illustration 4.5a).

7   Remove the caliper mounting bracket bolts and detach the caliper and brake pads from the steering knuckle. Hang the caliper with a length of wire – don't let it hang by the brake hose.

8   Remove the outer brake pad.

9   Separate the mounting bracket from the caliper.

10   Remove the pad retainers from the bracket and install new ones.

11   Remove the inner brake pad from the caliper.

12   Remove the caliper guide pin seals and boots from the caliper and install new ones.

13   Remove the upper guide pin from the mounting bracket and install a new one.

14   Lubricate the guide pins of the caliper mounting bracket with high-temperature brake grease, then install the bracket to the caliper.

15   Install new pad retainers to the mounting bracket.

16   Install the new inner and outer pads.

17   Install the caliper/bracket/brake pad

4.4 Before disassembling the brake, wash it thoroughly with brake cleaner and allow it to dry

4.5a To make room for the new pads, use a C-clamp to depress the piston(s) into the caliper before removing the caliper and pads - do this a little at a time, keeping an eye on the fluid level in the master cylinder to make sure it doesn't overflow.

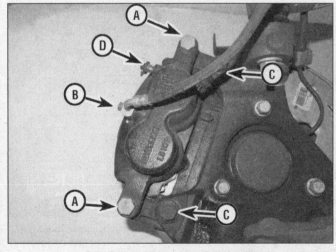

4.5b Front caliper mounting details

1	Caliper mounting bolts	3	Caliper mounting bracket bolts
2	Brake hose inlet fitting (banjo) bolt	4	Bleeder screw

4.5c If you're replacing the front brake pads, remove the lower mounting bolt and pivot the caliper up, supporting it in this position with a piece of wire

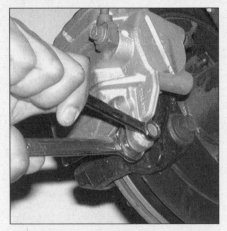

4.5d If you're replacing the rear pads, hold the caliper slide pin with an open-end wrench, loosen the lower mounting bolt with another wrench, then pivot the caliper up and support it with a piece of wire

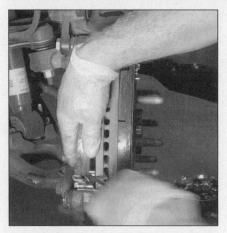

4.5e Remove the inner brake pad

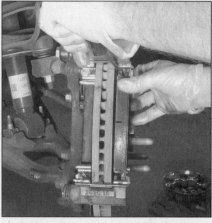

4.5f Remove the outer brake pad

4.5g Remove the upper and lower pad retainers and clean them. If they are cracked or distorted, replace them. Clean the bracket-to-pad retainer mating surface with a stiff wire brush, then wipe it clean with a rag. Apply a thin film of high-temperature brake grease to the mating surface only. DO NOT apply brake grease to the back of the pads

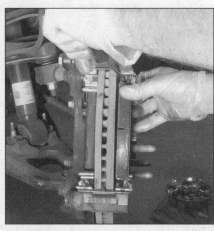

4.5h Install the upper and lower pad retainers on the caliper mounting bracket

4.5i Lubricate the retaining clips only where the brake pad will touch the retaining clips

4.5j Install the inner brake pad . . .

4.5k . . . and the outer brake pad

4.5l Inspect the caliper upper mounting bolt/slide pin for scoring and corrosion, then lubricate it with high-temperature brake grease. If it was dry, remove the caliper mounting bracket, remove the upper mounting bolt/slide pin and lubricate it too

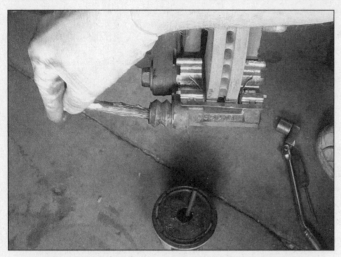

4.5m Before lowering the caliper over the pads, check the condition of the slide pin and the rubber boot, then lubricate the pin with high-temperature brake grease. Proceed to Step 18.

5.2 There is a sealing washer on either side of the brake hose inlet fitting; be sure to replace these with new ones when reconnecting the hose

assembly over the disc and install the caliper mounting bracket bolts, tightening them to the torque listed in this Chapter's Specifications.

All models

18   When reinstalling the caliper, be sure to tighten the mounting bolts to the torque listed in this Chapter's Specifications. Tighten the wheel lug nuts to the torque listed in the Chapter 1 Specifications.

19   After the job has been completed, slowly depress the brake pedal about two-thirds of its travel a few times until the pedal is firm. This will bring the pads into contact with the disc. Check the level of the brake fluid, adding some if necessary (see Chapter 1).

20   Break in the new pads by making a few low speed stops. Allow time in between each stop for the discs to cool. Listen for any grinding noise or unusual mechanical noises that could indicate a problem with the brake system. After the test drive visually reinspect the brake system for leaks or any component not reinstalled properly.

5   Brake caliper - removal and installation

Warning: *The dust created by the brake system is harmful to your health. An approved filtering mask should be worn when working on the brakes. Never blow the brake dust away with compressed air. Do not, under any circumstances, use petroleum-based solvents to clean brake parts. Use brake system cleaner only!*

Removal

1   Loosen the front or rear wheel lug nuts, raise the front or rear of the vehicle and place it securely on jackstands. Block the wheels at the opposite end. Remove the front or rear wheel.

2   Pinch off the brake line flexible rubber hose (gently). Use only enough force to prevent the fluid from coming out of the hose when it is disconnected. Remove the inlet fitting bolt and disconnect the brake hose from the caliper. Discard the old sealing washers (see illustration). Plug the brake hose immediately to keep contaminants and air out of the brake system and to prevent losing any more brake fluid than is necessary. Remove the pinch clamp off of the flexible line.

Note: *If you are simply removing the caliper for access to other components, leave the brake hose connected and suspend the caliper with a length of wire - don't let it hang by the hose.*

3   Remove the caliper mounting bolts and detach the caliper from the mounting bracket. When removing a rear caliper on a 1500 model, hold the slide pins with an open-end wrench to prevent them from turning when the mounting bolts are unscrewed.

Note: *On 2500 and 3500 models, the rear caliper mounting bracket will have to be removed in order to remove the upper caliper mounting bolt/slide pin.*

Installation

4   Installation is the reverse of removal. Don't forget to use new sealing washers on each side of the brake hose inlet fitting and be sure to tighten the fitting bolt and the caliper mounting bolts to the torque listed in this Chapter's Specifications.

5   Bleed the brake system (see Section 9).

6   Brake disc - inspection, removal and installation

Warning: *The dust created by the brake system is harmful to your health. An approved filtering mask should be worn when working on the brakes. Never blow the brake dust away*

6.2 Hang the caliper out of the way with a piece of wire - don't let it hang by the brake hose!

with compressed air. Do not, under any circumstances, use petroleum-based solvents to clean brake parts. Use brake system cleaner only!*

Inspection

1   Loosen the wheel lug nuts, raise the vehicle and support it securely on jackstands. Remove the wheel.

2   Remove the brake caliper. It isn't necessary to disconnect the brake hose. After removing the caliper bolts, suspend the caliper out of the way with a piece of wire (see illustration).

3   Visually check the disc surface for score marks, cracks and other damage. Light scratches and shallow grooves are normal after use and may not always be detrimental to brake operation. Deep score marks or cracks may require disc refinishing by an automotive machine shop, or disc replacement (see illustration). Be sure to check both sides of the disc. If the brake pedal pulsates during brake application, suspect disc runout.

6.4 The brake pads on this vehicle were obviously neglected, as they wore down completely and cut deep grooves into the disc - wear this severe means the disc must be replaced

6.5a To check disc runout, mount a dial indicator as shown and rotate the disc

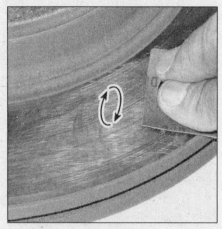

6.5b Using a swirling motion, remove the glaze from the disc with sandpaper or emery cloth

6.6a The minimum thickness is cast into the disc (typical)

6.6b Use a micrometer to measure disc thickness

6.7a Caliper mounting bracket bolts - front

6.7b Caliper mounting bracket bolts - rear

4   Drive test the vehicle and listen for any grinding or unusual mechanical noises from the brake system. If any noises are noticed perform a visual inspection. The most common symptoms of out of round discs is a pulsation felt in the steering wheel as light pressure is applied to the brakes. Check the disc for runout with a dial indicator. See this Chapter's Specifications (see illustration).

5   To check disc runout, place a dial indicator at a point about 1/2-inch from the outer edge of the disc (see illustration). Set the indicator to zero and turn the disc. Indicator readings should not exceed the specifications (see this Chapter's Specifications). If the disc is out of round and is still within the specified thickness the disc will require refinishing by an automotive machine shop or disc replacement. If disc refinishing or replacement is not necessary, you can deglaze the disc surface

with emery cloth or sandpaper (see illustration).

6   It's absolutely critical that the disc not be machined to a thickness under the specified minimum thickness. The minimum wear (or discard) thickness is cast into the underside of front discs (see illustration) and on the outside of rear discs. The disc thickness can be checked with a micrometer (see illustration).

Removal

7   Remove the two caliper mounting bracket bolts and detach the mounting bracket (see illustrations).

All except rear discs on models with dual rear wheels

8   On heavy-duty models with RPO J96, unscrew the hub extension retaining nuts and detach the hub extension.

9   If pressed-metal retaining clips are present on any of the wheel studs, cut them off (see illustration).

Note: *It is not necessary to reinstall these pressed-metal retaining clips. (The clips are installed at the factory only to hold the disc in place until the caliper is installed later on down the assembly line.)*

Rear discs on models with dual rear wheels

10   Remove the rear hub and bearing assembly (see Chapter 8).
11   Unscrew the bolts from the back side of the hub assembly and separate the disc from the hub.

Installation

12   Clean the disc and hub mating surfaces with a wire brush.
13   On all except rear discs on dual rear wheel models, place the disc in position over the threaded studs.
14   On models with dual rear wheels, place the disc onto the hub, aligning the match mark (if installing the same disc). Apply non-hardening thread locking compound to the threads of the bolts and install them, tightening them to the torque listed in this Chapter's Specifications. Install the hub and disc assembly (see Chapter 8).
15   On models with RPO J96, install the hub extension and tighten the nuts to the torque listed in this Chapter's Specifications.
16   Install the mounting bracket and tighten the bolts to the torque listed in this Chapter's Specifications. Install the brake pads.
17   Install the caliper onto the mounting bracket, tightening the bolts to the torque listed in this Chapter's Specifications.
18   Install the wheel and lug nuts. Lower the vehicle and tighten the lug nuts to the torque listed in the Chapter 1 Specifications. Depress

the brake pedal a few times to bring the brake pads into contact with the disc. Bleeding won't be necessary unless the brake hose was disconnected from the caliper. Confirm that the brakes are fully operational before resuming normal driving.

7   Master cylinder - removal, installation and reservoir/O-ring replacement

Removal

1   Disconnect the cable from the negative battery terminal (see Chapter 5).
2   Unplug the electrical connector for the fluid level warning switch (see illustration).
3   Remove as much fluid as possible from the reservoir with a suction gun, large syringe or a kitchen poultry baster used for brake fluid only.
Warning: *If a poultry baster is used, never again use it for the preparation of food.*
4   Place rags under the line fittings and prepare caps or plastic bags to cover the ends of the lines once they're disconnected. Loosen the fittings at the ends of the brake lines where they enter the master cylinder. Use a flare-nut wrench to prevent rounding off the brake line retaining nuts.
5   Pull the brake lines away from the master cylinder and plug the ends to prevent contamination.
6   Remove the nuts attaching the master cylinder to the power booster. Pull the master cylinder off the studs to remove it. Again, be careful not to spill fluid as this is done.

Installation

7   Bench bleed the new master cylinder before installing it. Mount the master cylinder in a vise, with the jaws of the vise clamping on

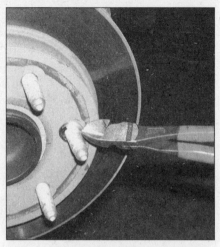

6.9 Cut off and discard the disc retaining washers, if present (it isn't necessary to reinstall them)

the mounting flange.
8   Attach a pair of master cylinder bleeder tubes to the outlet ports of the master cylinder (see illustration).
9   Fill the reservoir with brake fluid of the recommended type (see Chapter 1).
10   With the brake tubes submerged in the master cylinder, slowly push the pistons into the master cylinder (a large Phillips screwdriver can be used for this) - air will be expelled from the pressure chambers and into the reservoir. If necessary hold the tubes from coming out of the fluid to avoid air being sucked back into the lines.
11   Repeat the procedure until no more air bubbles are present.
12   Remove the bleed tubes, one at a time, and install plugs in the open ports to prevent fluid leakage and air from entering. Install the reservoir cap.

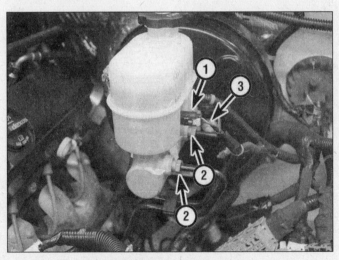

7.2 Master cylinder mounting details:

1   *Fluid level sensor electrical connector*
2   *Brake line fittings*
3   *Mounting nuts (two nuts, one on either side)*

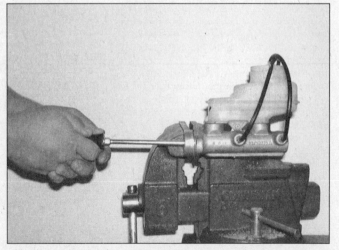

7.8 The best way to bleed air from the master cylinder before installing it on the vehicle is with a pair of bleeder tubes that direct brake fluid into the reservoir during bleeding

7.13 Install a new O-ring on the master cylinder

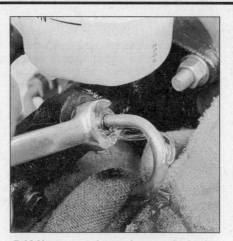

7.16 Have an assistant depress the brake pedal and hold it down, then loosen the fitting nut, allowing air and fluid to escape; repeat this procedure on both fittings until the fluid is clear of air bubbles

8.2a A front brake hose on a 4WD model (other models similar)

8.2b Rear brake hose from hard line on axle to caliper

8.2c Rear brake hoses above the rear axle housing

13   Replace the O-ring seal on the end of the master cylinder (see illustration), then install it to the booster, leaving the mounting nuts finger tight for now.

14   Thread the brake line fittings into the master cylinder. Since the master cylinder is still a bit loose, it can be moved slightly so the fittings thread in easily. Don't strip the threads as the fittings are tightened.

15   Tighten the mounting nuts to the torque listed in this Chapter's Specifications. Tighten the brake line fittings securely.

16   Fill the master cylinder reservoir with fluid, then bleed the lines at the master cylinder, followed by bleeding the remainder of the brake system (see Section 9). To bleed the lines at the master cylinder, have an assistant depress the brake pedal and hold it down. Loosen the fitting to allow air and fluid to escape (see illustration). Tighten the fitting, then allow your assistant to return the pedal to its rest position. Repeat this procedure on both fittings until the fluid is free of

air bubbles, then bleed the rest of the system. Confirm that the brakes are fully operational before resuming normal driving.

Warning: *If you do not have a firm brake pedal at the end of the bleeding procedure, or have any doubts as to the effectiveness of the brake system, DO NOT drive the vehicle. Have it towed to a dealer service department or other qualified repair shop for diagnosis.*

Reservoir/O-ring replacement

Note: *The brake fluid reservoir can be replaced separately from the master cylinder body if it becomes damaged. If there is leakage between the reservoir and the master cylinder body, the O-rings on the reservoir can be replaced.*

17   Remove as much fluid as possible from the reservoir with a suction gun, a large syringe, or a kitchen poultry baster that is used only for brake fluid.

18   Place rags under the master cylinder to absorb any fluid that may spill out once the

reservoir is detached from the master cylinder.

19   On 2500 and 3500 models, unscrew the bolts that retain the reservoir to the master cylinder. On 1500 models, carefully pry the retaining tabs outward while pulling the reservoir up to release it.

20   Pull the reservoir out of the master cylinder body.

21   If you are simply replacing the O-rings, carefully remove the old O-rings and install new ones.

22   Lubricate the reservoir O-rings with clean brake fluid, then press the reservoir into place on the master cylinder body and secure it. Use new roll pins if applicable.

23   Refill the reservoir with the recommended brake fluid (see Chapter 1) and check for leaks.

8   Brake hoses and lines - check and replacement

1   About every six months, with the vehicle raised and placed securely on jackstands, the flexible hoses which connect the steel brake lines with the front and rear brake assemblies should be inspected for cracks, chafing of the outer cover, leaks, blisters and other damage. These are important and vulnerable parts of the brake system and inspection should be complete. A light and mirror will be needed for a thorough check. If a hose exhibits any of the above defects, replace it with a new one.

Flexible hoses

Note: *The replacement hose must be an exact duplicate of the original and have all of the appropriate brackets, if equipped.*

2   Clean all dirt away from the ends of the hose (see illustrations).

3   Disconnect the brake line from the hose

fitting (see illustration). Be careful not to bend the frame bracket or line. If necessary, soak the connections with penetrating oil.

4   Remove the U-clip from the female fitting at the bracket and remove the hose from the bracket.

5   Follow the hose's path and remove any mounting fasteners for brackets that secure it to other components.

6   On models where the hose is connected directly to the caliper, disconnect the hose fitting from the caliper by removing the banjo bolt. Discard the copper washers on both sides of the fitting. Use new copper washers and attach the new brake hose to the caliper.

7   Route the hose exactly as the original one was and mount any hose brackets that secure the hose to other components, as equipped.

8   Pass the female fitting through the frame or frame bracket. With the least amount of twist in the hose, install the fitting into position.

9   Install the U-clip in the female fitting at the frame bracket.

10   Using a back-up wrench on the fitting, attach the brake line to the hose fitting. Tighten the tube nut securely.

11   Confirm that the replacement hose follows the same path as the original one. This will avoid contact with moving suspension or steering components.

12   Bleed the brake lines as described in Section 9.

Metal brake lines

13   When replacing brake lines, be sure to use the correct parts. Don't use copper tubing for any brake system components. Purchase steel brake lines from a dealer parts department or auto parts store.

14   Prefabricated brake lines, with the ends already flared and fittings installed, are available at auto parts stores and dealer service departments. If necessary, carefully bend the line to the proper shape. A tube bender is necessary for this. Do not crimp or damage the line.

15   When installing the new line, make sure it's well supported in the brackets and has plenty of clearance between moving or hot components.

16   After installation, check the brake fluid reservoir level and add fluid as necessary (see Chapter 1). Bleed the brake system as outlined in Section 9 and confirm that the brakes are fully operational before resuming normal driving.

---

9   Brake hydraulic system - bleeding

Warning: *Wear eye protection when bleeding the brake system. If the fluid comes in contact with your eyes, immediately rinse them with water and seek medical attention.*

Note: *Bleeding the hydraulic system is necessary to remove any air that manages to find*

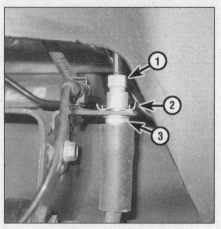

8.3 Brake hose fitting details:

1   *Metal tube nut (unscrew first - use a flare-nut wrench here)*
2   *Retaining clip (pull straight out with pliers to release the hose fitting from the bracket)*
3   *Brake hose fitting (hold with an open-end wrench while loosening the tube nut)*

its way into the system when it's been opened during removal and installation of a hose, line, caliper or master cylinder.

When to bleed the brake system

1   If air has entered it due to low fluid level.
2   If a brake line was disconnected only at a wheel, then only that caliper must be bled.
3   If a brake line is disconnected at a fitting located between the master cylinder and any of the brakes, that part of the system served by the disconnected line must be bled.

Bleeding procedure

4   Remove any residual vacuum (vacuum booster) or pressure (hydraulic booster) from the power brake booster by applying the brake several times with the engine off.

5   Remove the master cylinder reservoir cap and fill the reservoir with brake fluid. Reinstall the cap.

Note: *Check the fluid level often during the bleeding operation and add fluid as necessary to prevent the fluid level from falling low enough to allow air bubbles into the master cylinder.*

6   Have an assistant on hand, as well as a supply of new brake fluid, a clear container partially filled with clean brake fluid, a length of clear tubing to fit over the bleeder valve and a wrench to open and close the bleeder screws.

7   Beginning at the right rear wheel, (farthest brake from the master cylinder) loosen the bleeder valve slightly, then tighten it to a point where it's snug but can still be loosened quickly and easily.

8   Place one end of the tubing over the bleeder screw and submerge the other end in

9.8 When bleeding the brakes, a hose is connected to the bleed screw at the caliper and submerged in brake fluid - air will be seen as bubbles in the tube and container (all air must be expelled before moving to the next wheel)

brake fluid in the container (see illustration).

9   Have the assistant depress the brake pedal slowly and hold it in the depressed position.

Note: *Good communication between you and your helper is essential during this process. Make sure both of you can hear each other before attempting this procedure.*

10   While the pedal is held down, open the bleeder valve just enough to allow a flow of fluid to leave the screw. Watch for air bubbles to exit the submerged end of the tube. When the fluid flow slows after a couple of seconds, close the valve and then have your assistant release the pedal.

11   Repeat above steps until no more air is seen leaving the tube, then tighten the bleeder screw securely and proceed to the left rear wheel, the right front wheel and the left front wheel, in that order, and perform the same procedures again. Be sure to check the fluid in the master cylinder reservoir frequently.

Warning: *Never use old brake fluid or a bottle of brake fluid that has been left open for a long time. Brake fluid is hydroscopic, meaning it will attract moisture. Moisture in the brake fluid will cause the fluid to boil under heavy braking conditions and render the brake system inoperative.*

12   Refill the master cylinder with fluid at the end of the operation.

13   Check the operation of the brakes. The pedal should feel solid when depressed, with no sponginess. If necessary, repeat the entire process.

14   Before driving the vehicle, sit in the driver's seat and perform the following test:

a)   *Take your foot off the brake pedal*
b)   *Start the engine and let it run for a minimum of 10 seconds. Watch the amber ABS light on the dash.*
c)   *If the light comes on and does not turn off after 10 seconds, have the vehicle towed to a dealer service department*

10.10 Pull the vacuum hose fitting straight out of the grommet in the booster

10.14 Remove the retaining bolt and slide the booster pushrod off of the brake pedal assembly.

10.15 Remove the booster mounting nuts (not all nuts are visible in this photo - vicinity given)

or other qualified repair shop. A scan tool will have to be used to bleed and/or diagnose the ABS system.

d) If the ABS light goes off after three seconds or so, turn off the ignition.

e) Repeat the above steps one more time. If the ABS light turns off, test drive the vehicle in an isolated area before returning the vehicle to normal service.

Warning: *Do not operate the vehicle if you're in doubt about the effectiveness of the brake system.*

---

10   Power brake booster - check, removal and installation

Check

Vacuum booster

Operating check

1   Depress the pedal and start the engine. If the pedal goes down slightly, operation is normal.

2   Depress the brake pedal several times with the engine running and make sure that there is no change in the pedal reserve distance.

Airtightness check

3   Start the engine and turn it off after one or two minutes. Depress the brake pedal several times slowly. If the pedal goes down farther the first time but gradually rises after the second or third depression, the booster is airtight.

4   Depress the brake pedal while the engine is running, then stop the engine with the pedal depressed. If there is no change in the pedal reserve travel after holding the pedal for 30 seconds, the booster is airtight.

Hydraulic booster

5   Turn the engine off, then depress the brake pedal several times to deplete the pressure in the accumulator.

6   Push down on the brake pedal, exerting approximately 40 pounds of force, then start the engine. If the booster is working properly, the brake pedal will sink toward the floor then rise back up against your foot.

7   If the booster does not work as described, check the fluid level in the power steering fluid reservoir, adding as necessary. Also check the hoses from the power steering pump to the booster for kinks. If everything checks out OK, the booster or power steering pump is defective. Have the power steering pump output pressure checked. If the pump is developing sufficient pressure, replace the booster.

Removal

8   Disconnect the cable from the negative battery terminal.

9   Depress the brake pedal several times to deplete the pressure in the accumulator (hydraulic booster) or a few times to remove vacuum (vacuum booster).

10   If you're working on a model with a vacuum booster, detach the vacuum hose from the booster (see illustration).

11   If you're working on a model with a hydraulic booster, detach the pressure and return lines from the booster. Cap the lines to prevent fluid leakage.

12   Remove the master cylinder without detaching the brake lines. Pull it forward and position it aside. Be careful not to bend or kink the brake lines.

13   Disconnect any electrical connectors from the components mounted to the booster, as equipped.

14   Remove the retaining nut (see illustration) and slip the pushrod off the large pin on the brake pedal arm (or assembly on adjustable pedals).

15   Remove the four nuts holding the brake booster to the firewall (see illustration).

16   Slide the booster straight out from the firewall until the studs clear the holes and pull the booster and gasket from the engine compartment.

Installation

17   Installation is the reverse of removal. Be sure to use a new gasket, and tighten the booster mounting nuts and the master cylinder mounting nuts to the torque values listed in this Chapter's Specifications.

18   If you're working on a model with a hydraulic booster, bleed the power steering system as described in Chapter 10. Check the power steering fluid level and add some, if necessary, to bring it up to the appropriate level.

---

11   Vacuum pump - removal and installation

Note: *The vacuum pump is located on the lower driver's side front of the engine and is driven by a stretchy belt connected to the crankshaft pulley. Only non-6.0L models are equipped with a vacuum pump.*

1   On some models a vacuum assist pump has been added. This pump provides additional vacuum to the brake system vacuum booster to create the needed vacuum under various driving conditions.

Removal

2   Disconnect the negative battery terminal (see Chapter 5). Remove the air intake duct (see Chapter 4).

3   Disconnect the vacuum lines from the pump.

4   Remove the drivebelt from the pump (see Chapter 1).

5   Remove the bolts securing the vacuum pump to the engine.

6   Remove the pump and the gasket.

7   Installation is the reverse of removal. Install all four bolts loosely. Tighten the bolts to the torque listed in this Chapter's Specifications.

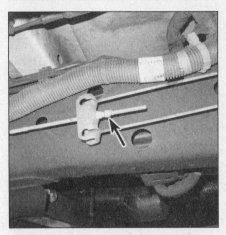

13.3 Parking brake cable adjusting nut

13.5 Insert a piece of paper between the right-side parking brake lever and backing plate

14.4 Grasp the spring with a pair of locking pliers and pull to detach the hooked ends

12   Brake pedal travel - check

Note: *On models with electrically adjustable pedals, perform the following steps with the pedals set to their lowest position (closest to the floor).*

1   The brake pedal travel should be checked if the pedal seems to go too low. You'll need a tape measure, yardstick or ruler for this procedure.

2   Depress the brake pedal several times to deplete the pressure in the accumulator (hydraulic booster) or a few times to remove vacuum (vacuum booster).

3   Measure the position of the pedal at rest. You can either measure from the floor to the pedal or from the pedal to the steering wheel. Record your reading.

4   Now, depress the pedal (exerting approximately 70 lbs. of force) and measure how far the pedal has traveled. Compare your findings with the measurement listed in this Chapter's Specifications.

5   If the pedal travel is excessive, check for air in the system (bleed the brakes - see Section 9). A failed seal in the master cylinder could also cause excessive pedal travel.

13   Parking brake - adjustment

1   Depress and release the parking brake three times.

2   Loosen the rear wheel lug nuts. Raise the rear of the vehicle and support it securely on jackstands, then remove the wheels. Release the parking brake.

3   Locate the parking brake cable equalizer adjusting nut along the outside of the left frame rail (see illustration). Loosen the adjusting nut until the parking brake cables are no longer under any tension.

4   Refer to Section 14 and adjust the park-

14.5 Turn the hold-down washer a 1/4 turn to remove it

ing brake shoes, then reinstall the brake discs and calipers.

5   Insert a piece of paper between the parking brake lever and the right-rear brake disc backing plate (see illustration).

6   Tighten the parking brake cable equalizer adjusting nut until the piece of paper falls out, then loosen the adjusting nut one turn.

7   Check the operation of the parking brake: When depressed with approximately 112-pounds of force, the pedal should travel 3 to 5 clicks. If it travels too far, tighten the adjusting nut until pedal travel is within the specified range. If it doesn't travel far enough, loosen the nut until the travel is within the specified range.

8   Install the wheels and lug nuts, then lower the vehicle. Tighten the lug nuts to the torque listed in the Chapter 1 Specifications.

14   Parking brake shoes - replacement

Warning: *The dust created by the brake sys-*

tem is harmful to your health. An approved filtering mask should be worn when working on the brakes. Never blow the brake dust away with compressed air. Do not, under any circumstances, use petroleum-based solvents to clean brake parts. Use brake system cleaner only!

1   Loosen the rear wheel lug nuts, raise the rear of the vehicle and support it securely on jackstands. Release the parking brake. Block the front wheels to prevent the vehicle from rolling, then remove the rear wheels.

2   Remove the brake caliper (see Section 5), mounting bracket and the brake disc (see Section 6).

3   Wash the brake assembly with brake system cleaner.

4   Remove the upper return spring (see illustration).

5   Hold the forward hold-down spring rod in place while applying pressure to the retaining spring. Twist the spring hold-down washer to release it (see illustration).

6   Follow the same procedure for the rear holddown spring.

14.7 Grasp the shoes from the top and tilt them away from the axle to remove

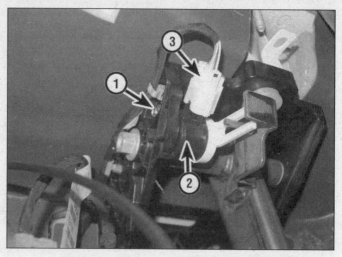

15.2 Brake light switch mounting details:

1   Retaining bolt
2   Brake light switch
3   Brake light switch electrical connector

Note: *Notice the position of the forked control arm that straddles the actuator pin on the brake pedal assembly. Make sure when reinstalling the switch that the control arm is in this same position*

7   Remove the parking brake shoes (see illustration).
8   Twist the two brake shoes across each other to release the lower return spring and adjuster.
9   Before installing the new shoes, turn the adjuster screw star wheel in, then make sure the slots in the adjusting screw and the tappet are parallel with the backing plate.
10   To install the shoes, reverse the removal procedure. Make sure the ends of the shoes seat properly in the slots in the adjuster screw and tappet.
11   When installing the new shoes, turn the adjuster screw until the shoe lining just drags on the braking surface inside the disc. Then remove the disc and back-off the adjuster screw until the shoe lining doesn't drag when the disc is installed and turned. The actual clearance between the lining surface of the shoe and the braking surface inside the disc should be 0.026-inch.
12   Installation is otherwise the reverse of the removal procedure. Be sure to tighten the caliper bracket bolts and the caliper mounting bolts to the torque listed in this Chapter's Specifications, and the wheel lug nuts to the torque listed in the Chapter 1 Specifications.
13   Adjust the parking brake (see Section 13).

15   Brake light switch - check, adjustment and replacement

1   The brake light switch is also known as the Brake Pedal Position Sensor (BPPS). However, different parts stores or even the various dealer parts departments may refer to the BPPS as the brake light switch.
Caution: *Replacing the BPPS requires the use of a scanner to properly calibrate the operation of the brake switch. See the appropriate repair facility for repair.*

Check

2   The brake light switch (see illustration) is located on the side of the brake pedal and is retained by a single bolt and an alignment hole.
3   If the brake lights are inoperative, check the fuse first (see Chapter 12).
Warning: *Do NOT apply voltage to the switch or circuit or severe damage can occur to the electrical system. The switch and circuit operate via a data signal, not a 12 volt signal.*
4   Have an assistant apply the brake pedal while you check for voltage to the brake light wires at the taillight housings. If voltage is not present, follow the wiring diagram and check all the connections and connectors for good continuity. Also, check for a good chassis ground at the tail light housing (Follow the wire diagram for ground connection location and correct routing.)
5   If voltage is present at the taillight housings and the ground is good, replace the bulb. If after replacing the bulb the lights still don't come on replace the taillight housing assembly or bulb housing fixture (Some models are serviced as a complete taillight housing only.)
6   If there is no voltage and no obvious wiring issues consult a qualified repair facility to check the BPPS system for fault codes.

Adjustment

7   The brake light switch on these vehicles is not adjustable.

Replacement

8   Unplug the electrical connector from the switch.
9   Remove the bolt that retains the switch and slip the switch off the alignment pin.
10   Installation is the reverse of removal. Have the switch calibrated by an appropriate repair facility.

Notes

Notes

Chapter 10
Suspension and steering

Contents

Specifications

General

Power steering fluid type .... See Chapter 1

Torque specifications   Ft-lbs (unless otherwise indicated)

Note: *One foot-pound (ft-lb) of torque is equivalent to 12 inch-pounds (in-lbs) of torque. Torque values below approximately 15 ft-lbs are expressed in inch-pounds, because most foot-pound torque wrenches are not accurate at these smaller values.*

Front suspension

Shock absorber	
Upper mounting nut/bolts	37
Lower mounting fastener(s)	
1500 models	37
2500/3500 models	89
Upper control arm pivot bolt nuts	
1500 models	140
2500/3500 models	192
Lower control arm pivot bolt nuts	
1500 models	129
2500/3500 models	
Step 1	133
Step 2	Tighten an additional 60 degrees

Torque specifications (continued)   Ft-lbs (unless otherwise indicated)

Note: *One foot-pound (ft-lb) of torque is equivalent to 12 inch-pounds (in-lbs) of torque. Torque values below approximately 15 ft-lbs are expressed in inch-pounds, because most foot-pound torque wrenches are not accurate at these smaller values.*

Front suspension (continued)

Upper balljoint stud nut	
1500 models	
Step 1	37
Step 2	Tighten an additional 100 degrees
2500/3500 models	37
Lower balljoint stud nut	
1500 models	
Step 1	37
Step 2	Tighten an additional 130 degrees
2500/3500 models	
Step 1	37
Step 2	Tighten an additional 100 degrees
Stabilizer bar	
Link nut	17
Clamp bolts	37
Hub/bearing assembly-to-steering knuckle bolts	133
Hub extension nuts (heavy-duty models with RPO J96)	96
Torsion bar crossmember-to-frame (bushing) bolt	92

Rear suspension

Shock absorber mounting nuts/bolts	85
Stabilizer bar	
SUV models	
Link nuts	
Step 1	48
Step 2	Tighten an additional 40 degrees
Clamp bolts	24
3500 models	
Link upper bolt/nut	70
Link lower nut	107
Clamp nuts	24
Leaf spring	
U-bolts/nuts*	
2014 models	
Step 1	85
Step 2	Tighten an additional 90 degrees
2015 and later models	
1500 models	
Step 1	59
Step 2	Loosen 180 degrees
Step 3	59
Step 4	Tighten an additional 130 degrees
2500/3500 models	
Step 1	74
Step 2	Loosen 270 degrees
Step 3	74
Step 4	Tighten an additional 180 degrees
Spring-to-frame bolt/nut (front)	
1500 models	
Step 1	125
Step 2	Tighten an additional 48 degrees
2500/3500 models	
Step 1	125
Step 2	Tighten an additional 90 degrees
Rear shackle-to-spring bolt/nut	
1500 models	
Step 1	85
Step 2	Tighten an additional 90 degrees
2500/3500 models	129

Torque specifications (continued)   Ft-lbs (unless otherwise indicated)

Note: *One foot-pound (ft-lb) of torque is equivalent to 12 inch-pounds (in-lbs) of torque. Torque values below approximately 15 ft-lbs are expressed in inch-pounds, because most foot-pound torque wrenches are not accurate at these smaller values.*

Rear suspension (continued)

Trailing arm	37
Upper arm bolt	
Step 1	74
Step 2	Tighten an additional 55 degrees
Lower arm bolts	
Step 1	63
Step 2	Tighten an additional 95 degrees
Track bar bolts/nuts	
Step 1	63
Step 2	Tighten an additional 125 degrees

*Manufacturer recommends new U-bolt nuts and washers to be used whenever they are removed.

Steering

Steering gear mounting bolts	
Rack-and pinion steering gear	
Left side	162
Right side	74
Recirculating ball steering gear	203
Tie-rod end-to-steering knuckle nut	
Step 1	26
Step 2	Tighten an additional 90 degrees
Steering linkage relay rod nut (2500/3500 models)	92
Steering linkage inner tie-rod nut (2500/3500 models)	92
Pitman arm-to-steering gear nut	273
Idler arm-to-frame nuts (2500/3500 models)	122
Electric Power Steering (EPS) assist motor bolt (requires new bolt)	89
Steering wheel nut	27
Steering column nuts/bolts	20
Intermediate shaft	
Lower shaft	
Upper bolt (to upper intermediate shaft)	37
Lower pinch bolt (to steering gear)	33
Upper shaft bolt (to steering column shaft)	46
Power steering pump fasteners	18

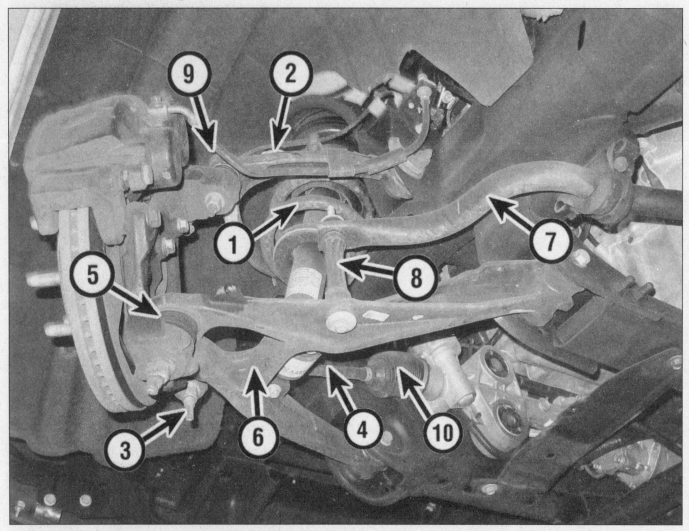

1.1a Front suspension and steering components (1500 model)

1   Shock absorber/coil spring assembly
2   Upper control arm
3   Tie-rod end
4   Tie-rod

5   Lower balljoint
6   Lower control arm
7   Stabilizer bar
8   Stabilizer bar link

9   Upper ball joint
10 Steering gear boot

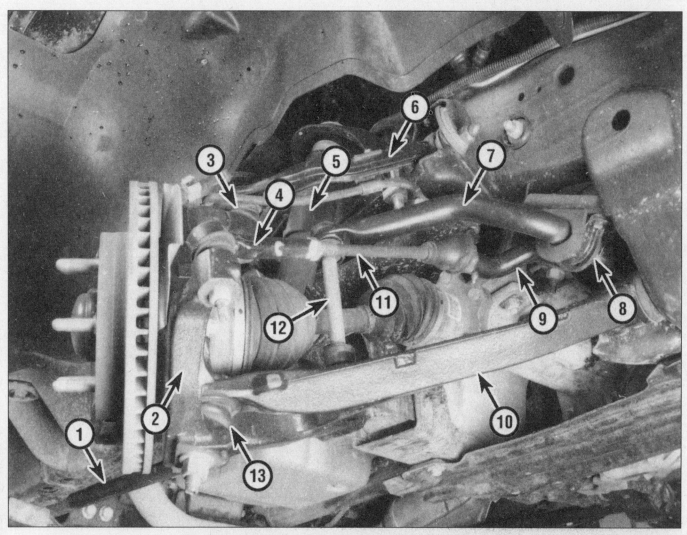

1.1b Front suspension and steering components (4WD 2500 model)

1	Torsion bar	6	Upper control arm
2	Steering knuckle	7	Stabilizer bar
3	Upper balljoint	8	Stabilizer bar clamp
4	Tie-rod end	9	Relay rod
5	Shock absorber		

10	Lower control arm
11	Tie-rod
12	Stabilizer bar link
13	Lower balljoint

1.2 Rear suspension components (1500 pick-up model shown, 2500/3500 similar)

1	Leaf spring	3	Spring plate	5	Shock absorber
2	Shackle	4	U-bolt	6	Rear axle

1.3 Rear suspension components - SUV models

1	Track bar	4	Trailing arm (lower)	7	Rear axle
2	Stabilizer bar link	5	Stabilizer bar clamp	8	Coil spring
3	Shock absorber	6	Stabilizer bar		

1   General information

Warning: *Most all the repairs regarding the suspension and steering systems requires that you work from underneath the vehicle. Extra caution should be taken when working on the underside of any vehicle while it is off the ground. Take precautions such as sturdy jackstands, block the wheels, and work only on a firm and flat surface. A lot of the components can be awkward and heavy. Use a helper when needed to avoid personal injury. Follow all the safety information for power tool usage and wear the appropriate safety equipment.*

Front suspension

1   The front suspension (see illustrations) is fully independent. Each wheel is connected to the frame by a steering knuckle, upper and lower balljoints and upper and lower control arms. All models except 4WD 2500/3500 models use coil spring/shock absorber assemblies, while 4WD 2500/3500 models are equipped with torsion bars and shock absorbers. A stabilizer bar connected to the frame and to both lower control arms reduces body roll during cornering.

Rear suspension

2   The rear suspension on pick-up models consists of a pair of multi-leaf springs and two shock absorbers (see illustrations). The rear axle assembly is attached to the leaf springs by U-bolts. The front ends of the springs are attached to the frame at the front hangers, through rubber bushings. The rear ends of the springs are attached to the frame by shackles which allow the springs to alter their length as they compress and rebound.
3   The rear suspension on SUV models is a five-link design, using coil springs, upper and lower control arms, a lateral link (track bar), two shock absorbers and a stabilizer bar (see illustration).

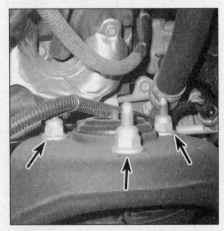

2.4 Shock absorber upper mounting nuts (1500 models)

Steering system

4   There are two types of steering systems used on these models: Belt-driven Electric Power Steering (EPS) system (light-duty models) and a hydraulic power steering system (heavy-duty models).

Belt-driven Electric Power Steering (EPS) system (1500 pick-ups and SUV models)

5   The electric steering system consists of a electronic control module, sensors, electric power steering motor, a belt drive and a ball nut mechanism, as well as a rack-and-pinion steering gear.
6   The power steering control module and power steering motor are replaced as one complete unit. The sensors are integrated into the rack-and-pinion assembly and are serviced as a complete unit.

Hydraulic power steering system

7   The hydraulic power steering system consists of a vane type power steering pump driven by a belt and a recirculating ball-type steering gear. In this system, a worm gear transfers the steering wheel movement to the Pitman arm which, in turn, moves the steering linkage arms.

Ride control systems

8   Light duty (1500) truck and SUV models may have an optional ride control system called Autoride®. This system electronically controls shock absorber damping and also incorporates an automatic leveling control system for the rear suspension. These computer controlled and fully automatic systems require no input from the driver and work in conjunction with the tow/haul mode. Autoride® is a system designed to optimize vehicle ride and handling and adjusts based on road conditions. The automatic leveling control keeps the rear of the vehicle at the proper ride height based on payload weight. It utilizes an electronically controlled air-shock system. It is likely that removing and installing any related suspension components on vehicles equipped with this option will require calibration with the use of a specialized scan tool; this will require service at a dealer service department or other qualified repair facility.

Precautions

9   Frequently, when working on the suspension or steering system components, you may come across fasteners which seem impossible to loosen. These fasteners on the underside of the vehicle are continually subjected to water, road grime, mud, etc., and can become rusted or frozen, making them extremely difficult to remove. In order to unscrew these stubborn fasteners without damaging them (or other components), be sure to use lots of penetrating oil and allow it to soak in for a while. Using a wire brush to clean exposed threads will also ease removal of the nut or bolt and prevent damage to the threads. Sometimes a sharp blow with a hammer and punch is effective in breaking the bond between a nut and bolt threads, but care must be taken to prevent the punch from slipping off the fastener and ruining the threads. Heating the stuck fastener and surrounding area with a torch sometimes helps too, but isn't recommended because of the obvious dangers associated with fire. Long breaker bars and extension, or cheater, pipes will increase leverage, but never use an extension pipe on a ratchet - the ratcheting mechanism could be damaged. Sometimes, turning the nut or bolt in the tightening (clockwise) direction first will help to break it loose. Fasteners that require drastic measures to unscrew should always be replaced with new ones.
10   Since most of the procedures that are dealt with in this Chapter involve jacking up the vehicle and working underneath it, a good pair of jackstands will be needed. A hydraulic floor jack is the preferred type of jack to lift the vehicle, and it can also be used to support certain components during various operations.
Warning: *Never, under any circumstances, rely on a floor jack to support the vehicle while working on it. Use safety jackstands whenever possible. Also, whenever any of the suspension or steering fasteners are loosened or removed they must be inspected and, if necessary, replaced with new ones of the same part number or of original equipment quality and design. Torque specifications must be followed for proper reassembly and component retention. Never attempt to heat or straighten suspension or steering components. Instead, replace bent or damaged parts with new ones.*

2   Shock absorber (front) - removal and installation

Note: *Electronically controlled shock absorbers that are part of the Autoride® system must be replaced with compatible replacement shock absorbers.*
1   Loosen the front wheel lug nuts. Raise the front of the vehicle and support it securely on jackstands, then remove the wheel.
2   Support the outer end of the lower control arm with a floor jack. The jack must remain in this position throughout the entire procedure.
3   If equipped with a ride control system, unlock and unplug the electrical connector from the top of the shock absorber.

Coil-over shock absorber models

Note: *It is possible to replace the shocks or springs individually, but the unit will have to be disassembled by a qualified repair shop with the proper equipment, and this could add considerable cost to the project. Compare the cost of replacing the complete assemblies yourself to the cost of replacing individual components (with the help of a shop).*
4   Remove the shock absorber assembly's upper mounting nuts (see illustration).
5   Working underneath the vehicle, remove the two bolts that attach the lower end of the

2.5 Shock absorber lower mounting bolts (1500 models)

3.3 Stabilizer bar bracket bolts

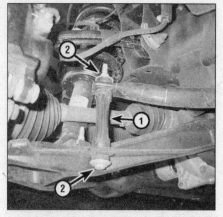

3.10 Stabilizer bar link components

1   *Stabilizer bar link*
2   *Stabilizer bar link fasteners*

shock absorber to the lower control arm (see illustration) and pull the shock out from below.
6   Installation is the reverse of removal. Be sure to tighten the mounting fasteners to the torque listed in this Chapter's Specifications.

Torsion bar models

7   Remove the two shock absorber upper mounting nuts.
8   Remove the shock absorber lower mounting nut and bolt. Note the direction in which the bolt points.
9   Remove the shock absorber.
10   Installation is the reverse of removal. Be sure to install the lower mounting bolt so it's pointing in the same direction as it was prior to removal. Tighten all fasteners to the torque listed in this Chapter's Specifications.

All models

11   If equipped with a suspension control system, reconnect the electrical connector to the top of the shock absorber.
12   Install the wheels and lug nuts, lower the vehicle and tighten the lug nuts to the torque listed in the Chapter 1 Specifications.

3   Stabilizer bar, bushings and links (front) - removal and installation

Note: *The stabilizer bar is also referred to as the sway bar. The stabilizer bar helps to maintain stability in a turn. It is connected to both of the lower control arms by way of the stabilizer bar end links. When a stabilizer bar end link fails, the vehicle will lean farther than normal and can be harder to correct from a turn.*

Stabilizer bar and bushings

1   Raise the vehicle and support it securely on jackstands. On models so equipped, remove the oil pan skid plate or engine shield.
2   Remove the top nuts from the stabilizer bar links (see Step 10).
Note: *If you're removing just the stabilizer bar,*

4.2 To ensure proper adjustment of the torsion bar upon reassembly, count the number of threads showing on the torsion bar adjuster bolt and mark the relationship of the bolt to the torsion bar adjuster nut as insurance

the links can stay in place. Just remove the top nut, washer and rubber cushion.
3   Remove the stabilizer bar bracket bolts (see illustration).
4   Remove the stabilizer bar.
5   Remove the rubber bushings.
6   Inspect all parts for wear and damage.
7   When you install the rubber bushings on the stabilizer bar, be sure to position them so the slits are facing forward.
8   Installation is otherwise the reverse of removal. Be sure to tighten all fasteners to the torque listed in this Chapter's Specifications and to use a non-hardening thread-locking compound (blue) on the threads of the bolts.

Stabilizer bar links

9   Raise the vehicle and support it securely on jackstands.
10   While securing the stabilizer bar end link bolt from turning, remove the upper nut, then drive the long bolt out of the end link (see illustration).
11   Remove the stabilzer bar link.
12   Installation is the reverse of removal. Tighten the nut to the torque listed in this Chapter's Specifications.
Be sure to use the new nuts and bushings that come with the replacement stabilizer bar

end link. Also, make sure you have the rubber bushings touching the actual stabilizer bar. The metal washers go on the outside of the rubber bushings.

4   Torsion bar - removal and installation

Note: *The torsion bars must be removed as a pair, since the torsion bar crossmember must be removed to provide clearance to slide the bars to the rear.*
1   With the vehicle unloaded, on level ground and with the wheels pointing forward, measure the ride height at the front by measuring between a point on the frame and the ground. Mark the spot on the frame from where the measurement was made so another measurement can be taken using the exact same spot. This step is crucial to establish the vehicle's ride height so that it can be restored after the torsion bars have been reinstalled.
2   Raise the front of the vehicle and support it securely on jackstands. Count the number of threads showing on the torsion bar adjuster bolt and mark the relationship of the bolt to the torsion bar adjuster nut (see illustration).

4.3 Install a two-jaw puller as shown, with the fingers hooked around the flange running along each side of the crossmember; make sure the puller bolt is centered on the dimple in the torsion bar adjuster arm. Tighten the puller bolt until all tension is removed from the adjuster bolt

4.9 Slide the torsion bar to the rear, then lower it out of the vehicle

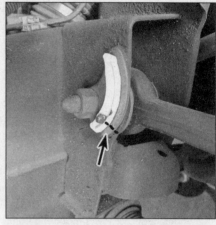

5.2 Mark the relationship of the adjusting cams to the frame brackets

3   In the torsion bar adjuster arm there's a small dimple. Install a puller with its bolt centered on this dimple (see illustration).
4   Turn the puller bolt until all tension is removed from the torsion bar adjuster bolt, then unscrew the torsion bar adjuster bolt and remove the nut. Slowly unscrew the puller bolt until the torsion bar unwinds completely and no more tension is on the adjuster arm. Remove the puller.
5   Mark the relationship of the forward end of the torsion bar to the lower control arm. Also mark the relationship of the rear end of the torsion bar to the adjuster arm.
6   Push the torsion bar forward, through the lower control arm, until the rear end of the bar clears the crossmember, then remove the torsion bar adjuster arm.
7   Repeat Steps 1 through 6 on the other torsion bar.
8   Unbolt the torsion bar crossmember and remove it. Inspect the bushings in the frame bosses where the crossmember mounts. If they're worn or otherwise deteriorated they

can be replaced. They are staked in place from behind; once unstaked, they can be driven out of their bores toward the front of the vehicle. On models equipped with a link between the crossmember and the frame, check the links for wear. If they're not in good shape, replace them.
9   Slide the torsion bar to the rear, lower the rear end of the bar down and guide it out through the hole in the frame crossmember (see illustration). If the front end of the bar hangs up in the lower control arm, drive it out of the control arm with a brass drift.
10   Installation is the reverse of removal, but if both torsion bars were removed, be sure to install them on the proper side of the vehicle (they are marked L and R on the ends). Clean out the hexagonal hole in the lower control arm and lube it with multi-purpose grease before inserting the torsion bar into the arm. Also apply some grease to the hex ends of the torsion bar, to the top of the adjuster arm and to the adjuster bolt. Make sure that the alignment marks you made on the torsion bar and the control arm and adjuster arm line up, and that the torsion bar is completely engaged with the adjuster arm.

11   Tighten the crossmember mounting fasteners to the torque values listed in this Chapter's Specifications.
12   Tighten the torsion bar adjuster bolt until the same number of threads are showing and the marks you made on the adjuster bolt and nut are lined up.
13   Lower the vehicle, jounce the front suspension a couple of times, then roll the vehicle back-and-forth a few feet to settle the suspension.
14   Repeat Steps 12 and 13 until both sides of the vehicle are set to the original ride height.
15   Have the front end alignment checked and, if necessary, adjusted. Be sure to inform the repair facility that the ride height must be inspected before any alignment procedures are performed.

---

5   Upper control arm - removal and installation

Removal

1   Loosen the wheel lug nuts, raise the front of the vehicle and support it securely on jackstands. Remove the wheel. Position a floor jack under the lower control arm in the area underneath the balljoint. Raise the jack slightly to take the spring pressure off the upper control arm.
Warning: *The jack must remain in this position throughout the entire procedure.*
2   Mark the relationship of the adjusting cams to the brackets on the frame (see illustration).
3   Remove the shock/coil spring (see Section 2).
4   Unbolt the brake hose/wheel speed sensor bracket from the upper control arm (see illustration). Also remove the wheel speed sensor (see Chapter 9), and detach the wiring harness bracket from the steering knuckle and move it aside.

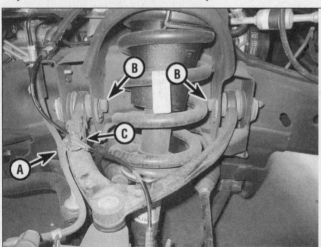

5.4 Unbolt the brake hose/wheel speed sensor bracket (A & C) from the upper control arm and note the position of the pivot bolts (B)

5.6a Separating the upper control arm balljoint from the steering knuckle using a puller

5.6b Separating the upper control arm balljoint from the steering knuckle using a picklefork type separator

6.7 A drift and a hammer can be used to loosen the ballstud from the steering knuckle if a balljoint separator isn't readily available

5   If you're working on a 4WD model, remove the driveaxle (see Chapter 8).

Note: *If you use a picklefork type balljoint separator, removal of the driveaxle is not necessary.*

6   Loosen the upper balljoint nut a few turns (don't remove it). Then install a balljoint puller or a picklefork, and break the balljoint loose from the knuckle (see illustrations). Now remove the nut.

Note: *If you don't have the proper balljoint removal tool, a hammer and a drift can sometimes be used to break the ballstud loose from the knuckle. A picklefork-type balljoint separator can also be used, but keep in mind that this type of tool will probably damage the balljoint boot.*

Note: *The manufacturer recommends replacing the balljoint nut with a new one whenever it has been removed.*

7   Remove the upper control arm pivot bolts and nuts, noting which way the bolts are installed. Remove the control arm.

Installation

8   Position the arm in the frame brackets and install the bolts and nuts, but don't tighten them yet.

9   Attach the balljoint to the steering knuckle, install a new nut and tighten it to the torque listed in this Chapter's Specifications.

10   The remainder of installation is the reverse of removal. Make sure the marks you made prior to disassembly are aligned, then tighten the nuts to the torque listed in this Chapter's Specifications.

Note: *The pivot bolt nuts should be tightened with the vehicle at normal ride height. This can be done after the vehicle has been lowered to the ground (on vehicles with adequate clearance), or it can be simulated by raising the lower control arm with a floor jack. Tighten the wheel lug nuts to the proper torque settings.*

11   Have the front end alignment checked and, if necessary, adjusted.

6   Lower control arm - removal and installation

Removal

1   Loosen the wheel lug nuts, raise the vehicle and support it securely on jackstands placed under the frame rails. Remove the wheel.

2   Disconnect the stabilizer bar link from the control arm (see Section 3).

3   Remove the shock absorber lower mounting fasteners (see Section 2).

4   On 4WD models, remove the driveaxle (see Chapter 8).

5   If you're working on a model with torsion bar front suspension, remove the torsion bar (see Section 4).

6   Using rope or wire, support the upper control arm and steering knuckle from the top of the shock absorber.

7   To disconnect the lower control arm from the steering knuckle, loosen the balljoint nut a few turns (don't remove it), install a balljoint separator and break the balljoint loose from the knuckle (see illustration). Now remove the nut.

Note: *If you don't have the proper balljoint removal tool, a hammer and a drift can sometimes be used to break the ballstud loose from the knuckle. A picklefork-type balljoint separator can also be used, but keep in mind that this type of tool will probably damage the balljoint boot.*

Note: *The manufacturer recommends replacing the balljoint nut with a new one whenever it has been removed.*

8   Remove the lower control arm pivot bolts and nuts (see illustration), noting which way the bolts are installed. Pull the lower arm from its frame brackets.

Installation

9   Position the arm in the frame brackets

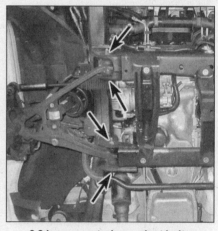

6.8 Lower control arm pivot bolts (1500 model)

and install the bolts and nuts, but don't tighten them yet.

10   Attach the balljoint to the steering knuckle, install a new nut and tighten it to the torque listed in this Chapter's Specifications.

11   The remainder of installation is the reverse of removal. Be sure to tighten all fasteners to the torque values listed in this Chapter's Specifications.

Note: *The pivot bolt nuts should be tightened with the vehicle at normal ride height. This can be done after the vehicle has been lowered to the ground (on vehicles with adequate clearance), or it can be simulated by raising the lower control arm with a floor jack.*

12   Install the wheel and lug nuts. Lower the vehicle and tighten the lug nuts to the torque listed in the Chapter 1 Specifications.

13   If you're working on a model with torsion bar front suspension, be sure to check and adjust the ride height (see Section 4).

14   Have the front end alignment checked and, if necessary, adjusted.

7   Balljoints - check and replacement

1   Inspect the control arm balljoints for looseness whenever either of them is separated from the steering knuckle. See if you can turn the ballstud in its socket with your fingers. If the balljoint is loose, or if the ballstud can be turned, replace the balljoint. You can also check the balljoints with the suspension assembled as follows.
Note: *The balljoint removal/installation tool can be rented at most parts stores. If you don't have access to the necessary equipment you can remove the control arm and take it to an automotive machine shop to have the balljoint replaced.*

Upper balljoints

Check

2   Raise the front of the vehicle and support it securely on jackstands placed under the frame rails. Place a floor jack under the lower control arm and raise it slightly.
3   Attach a dial indicator to the upper suspension arm, with the plunger of the indicator touching the steering knuckle, in line with the axle.
4   Carefully pry between the two components while observing movement from the dial indicator. There should be no more than 0.079-inch deflection. If the indicated reading exceeds this figure, replace the upper arm.

Replacement

5   For upper balljoint replacement, see Section 5. The upper balljoint is not available separately (the entire upper control arm must be replaced).

Lower balljoints

Check

6   Raise the front of the vehicle and support it securely on jackstands placed under the frame rails. Place a floor jack under the lower control arm and raise it slightly.
7   Attach a dial indicator to the lower control arm and position the indicator plunger against the steering knuckle, in line with the axle.
8   Carefully pry between the two components while observing movement from the dial indicator. There should be no more than 0.079-inch deflection. If the indicated reading exceeds this figure, replace the balljoint.

Replacement - off vehicle

9   Remove the lower control arm (see Section 6).
10   Use a hammer and punch to knock the peened tabs inward before pressing the balljoint out.
11   Using the balljoint removal tool, press the old balljoint out of the control arm. Then, press the new balljoint into the control arm. Make sure the press adapter only applies force to the flange of the balljoint. Once pressed in fully, use a hammer and punch to

8.5a The hub and bearing assembly on 1500 models is retained by three bolts - on 2500/3500 models it's retained by four bolts

crimp or stake the balljoint in place.
12   The remainder of the installation is the reverse of removal.
13   Have the front end alignment checked and, if necessary, adjusted.

Replacement - on vehicle

14   On 4WD drive models, remove the driveaxle from the steering knuckle (see Chapter 8).
Warning: *If you use a picklefork type balljoint separator, removal of the driveaxle is not necessary. However, the lower control arm on models with torsion bar front suspension MUST be supported with a floor jack.*
15   Separate the balljoint from the steering knuckle.
Note: *If you don't have the proper balljoint removal tool, a hammer and a drift can sometimes be used to break the ballstud loose from the knuckle. A picklefork-type balljoint separator can also be used, but keep in mind that this type of tool will probably damage the balljoint boot.*
16   Lower the lower control enough to allow for the balljoint removal tool to properly fit in the correct spot.
17   Use a hammer and punch to knock the peened tabs inward before pressing the balljoint out.
18   Once the balljoint removal tool is in the proper position, follow the procedure for the use of the removal tool.
19   Using the balljoint removal tool, press the old balljoint out of the control arm. Then press the new balljoint into the control arm. Make sure the press adapter only applies force to the flange of the balljoint. Once pressed in fully, use a hammer and punch to crimp or stake the balljoint in place.
20   The remainder of the installation is the reverse of removal.
21   Have the front end alignment checked and, if necessary, adjusted.

8.5b On 4WD models, there's not much room to get a wrench onto the hub bolt heads, especially when they are backed-out a few turns. As the bolts are unscrewed, push in on the driveaxle and pull the hub and bearing out of the knuckle to provide clearance

8   Hub and bearing assembly (front) - removal and installation

Warning: *The dust created by the brake system is harmful to your health. Never blow it out with compressed air and don't inhale any of it. Do not, under any circumstances, use petroleum-based solvents to clean brake parts. Use soap and water to clean the surfaces. Do not use brake cleaner. Brake cleaner will leave a residue on the surface of the components that is just as toxic as the brake dust.*
Note: *The hub and bearing assembly is sealed for life. If worn or damaged, it must be replaced as a unit.*

Removal

1   Loosen the front wheel lug nuts, raise the vehicle and support it securely on jackstands. Remove the wheel.
2   If you're working on a 4WD model, remove the hub cover, then unscrew the driveaxle/hub nut with a socket and large breaker bar see Chapter 8. Brace a large prybar across two of the wheel studs or insert a large screwdriver into the disc cooling vanes and allow it to rest against the caliper to prevent the hub from turning as the nut is loosened.
3   Remove the brake disc (see Chapter 9).
4   Remove the ABS wheel speed sensor from the hub (see Chapter 9).
5   Working from the back side of the steering knuckle, remove the hub retaining bolts (see illustrations). Remove the disc shield.
6   Remove the hub from the steering knuckle. If you're working on a 4WD model, pull the assembly off the driveaxle splines (see illustration).
Caution: *Be careful not to pull outward on the driveaxle, as this could separate the inner CV*

8.6 When removing the hub assembly on a 4WD model, don't pull out on the driveaxle; the inner CV joint could become separated

9.3 Use a small press tool such as this to push the stud out of the flange

joint components. If the driveaxle splines stick in the hub, attach a two-jaw puller to the hub flange and push the stub axle out of the hub.

7   The hub assembly should come right out of the steering knuckle, but if it doesn't, tap it from side to side to free it. If it is still stuck, try using water sprayed around the mounting area of the hub. Let the water soak in for a few minutes, then try tapping it from side to side to remove it.

Installation

8   Clean the mating surfaces on the steering knuckle, bearing flange and knuckle bore. Make sure the O-ring came out with the hub assembly, and be sure to install a new O-ring on the back of the hub before fitting the hub to the steering knuckle.

9   Insert the hub and bearing assembly into the steering knuckle and, on 4WD models, onto the end of the driveaxle.

On 4WD models, lubricate the splines of the driveaxle with multi-purpose grease before installing the hub. Position the disc shield and install the bolts, tightening them to the proper torque specifications.

10   Install the wheel speed sensor (see Chapter 9).

11   Install the brake disc, caliper mounting bracket and caliper (see Chapter 9).

12   On 4WD models, install the driveaxle/hub nut and tighten it to the torque listed in the Chapter 8 Specifications.

13   Install the wheel, lower the vehicle and tighten the lug nuts to the torque listed in the Chapter 1 Specifications.

9   Wheel studs - replacement

Note: *This procedure applies to both the front and rear wheel studs.*

1   Loosen the wheel lug nuts, raise the vehicle and support it securely on jackstands. Remove the wheel.

2   Remove the brake disc (see Chapter 9).

3   Push the stud out of the hub flange with a press tool (see illustration).

4   Insert the new stud into the hub flange from the back side and install some flat washers and a lug nut on the stud.

It's best to use an old lug nut when installing a new stud. The bottom of the nut can be damaged where it mates up with the wheel rim.

5   Tighten the lug nut until the stud is seated in the flange.

6   Reinstall the disc and caliper (see Chapter 9). Install the wheel and lug nuts. Lower the vehicle and tighten the lug nuts to the torque listed in the Chapter 1 Specifications.

10   Steering knuckle - removal and installation

1   Loosen the wheel lug nuts, raise the vehicle and support it securely on jackstands. Remove the wheel.

2   If you're working on a 4WD model, remove the driveaxle/hub nut (see Chapter 7B). Brace a large prybar across two of the wheel studs or insert a large screwdriver through the center of the brake caliper and into the disc cooling vanes to prevent the hub from turning as the nut is loosened.

Warning: *On models equipped with a torsion bar suspension, support the lower control arm with a floor jack. Raise the jack slightly. The jack must remain in this position throughout the entire procedure.*

3   Remove the brake caliper and brake disc (see Chapter 9). Hang the caliper out of the way on a piece of wire (don't disconnect the brake hose).

4   Remove the hub and bearing assembly (see Section 8).

5   Remove the disc splash shield from the steering knuckle.

6   Unbolt the brake hose bracket from the top of the steering knuckle.

7   Disconnect the tie-rod end from the steering knuckle (see Section 19).

8   Disconnect the upper and lower arms from the steering knuckle (see Section 5 and Section 6).

9   Remove the steering knuckle.

10   Installation is the reverse of removal. Be sure to tighten all the components that were removed to their proper torque specifications.

11   Shock absorber (rear) - removal and installation

Note: *Electronically controlledshock absorbers that are part of the Autoride® system must be replaced with compatible replacement shock absorbers.*

1   Raise the rear of the vehicle and support it securely on jackstands placed underneath the frame rails. Block the front wheels so the vehicle doesn't roll off the stands.

Note: *It isn't necessary to remove the rear wheels, but doing so will improve access to the shock absorbers.*

2   If the vehicle is equipped with a ride control system, disconnect the electrical connector and the air line from the shock absorber.

Warning: *Relieve the air pressure in the ride control system by loosening the line fitting to the shock a few turns and letting the air leak out over a period of time. Wear safety glasses as a precaution when removing the line completely.*

3   Support the rear axle with a floor jack placed under the axle tube closest to the

11.4 Rear shock absorber mounting fasteners

12.2 Stabilizer bar link mounting details

A   Link   C   Link-to-stabilizer bar nut
B   Link-to-frame bolt/nut

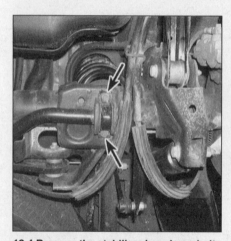

12.4 Remove the stabilizer bar clamp bolts from the axle housing

13.7 Remove the four U-bolt nuts and washers, then remove the spring plate and the two U-bolts

shock absorber being removed.
4   Remove the shock absorber upper and lower mounting fasteners (see illustration).
5   Remove the shock absorber.
6   Installation is the reverse of removal. Tighten the fasteners to the proper torque specifications.

12   Stabilizer bar and bushings (rear) - removal and installation

1   Loosen the rear wheel lug nuts, raise the rear of the vehicle and support it securely on jackstands. Block the front wheels to keep the vehicle from rolling off the stands. Remove the rear wheels.

2   Remove the stabilizer bar link-to-frame nuts/bolts (see illustration).
3   Remove the nuts from the lower ends of the links, then separate the link from the bar.
4   Remove the stabilizer bar clamp bolts (see illustration) and remove the stabilizer bar assembly.
Note: *On 3500 models, remove the right-rear shock absorber (see Section 11) and the driveshaft (see Chapter 8) to remove the bar. However, the links and bushings can be replaced with the driveshaft in place.*
5   Inspect the stabilizer bar bushings and link bushings for cracks, tears and other signs of deterioration. Replace as necessary.
6   Installation is the reverse of removal. Be sure to tighten all fasteners to the torque listed in this Chapter's Specifications.

13   Leaf spring - removal and installation

Removal

1   If you're removing the left leaf spring on a 1500 model, or either spring on a 3500 Cab-and-chassis model equipped with an auxiliary fuel tank, relieve the fuel system pressure (see Chapter 4).
2   Loosen the rear wheel lug nuts. Raise the rear of the vehicle and support it securely on jackstands placed underneath the frame rails. Block the front wheels to keep the vehicle from rolling off the stands. Remove the rear wheels.
3   Remove the trailer hitch, if so equipped.
4   If you're removing the left leaf spring on a 1500 model, remove the fuel tank (see Chapter 4).
Note: *On 3500 cab-and-chassis models, the auxiliary fuel tank must be removed to remove the rear shackle bolts on either side.*
5   If you're removing the right leaf spring, unbolt the rear portion of the exhaust system from the flange forward of the muffler, then detach the system from its rubber hangers to position it toward the center of the vehicle (this is to provide clearance for the front mounting bolt removal).
6   Support the axle with a floor jack placed under the axle tube and raise it slightly to take the weight of the axle.
7   Remove the four U-bolt nuts and washers (see illustration), the spring plate and the two U-bolts. Discard the U-bolts and nuts (the manufacturer recommends using new ones during installation).
8   At the front end of the spring, remove the

13.8 At the front end of the leaf spring, remove the nut and bolt that attach the spring to the frame bracket

13.9 At the rear end of the spring, remove the spring shackle-to-frame nut and bolt (A); the shackle-to-spring nut and bolt (B) can't be removed until the spring and shackle are removed from the vehicle

15.3a Upper trailing arm mounting fastener locations

nut and bolt from the spring-to-front bracket (see illustration).

9   At the rear end of the spring, remove the spring shackle-to-frame nut and bolt (see illustration).

10   Lower the jack slightly and remove the spring assembly. If necessary, remove the shackle from the spring. Remove the U-bolt top plate and spring spacer (if equipped) as necessary.

11   If the bushings at the ends of the spring are worn or deteriorated, an automotive machine shop or dealer service department can usually press the old ones out and press new ones in.

Installation

12   If removed, install the shackle to the spring, but don't tighten the nut yet.

13   Place the spring in position and install the forward mounting bolt and nut, but don't tighten the nut yet.

14   Raise the axle on the jack until it mates properly with the spring. Install the spring plate and new U-bolts, then install the nuts and washers. Tighten the U-bolt nuts to the torque listed in this Chapter's Specifications.

15   Tighten the front mounting bolt/nut, the shackle-to-frame bolt/nut and the spring-to-shackle bolt/nut to the torque values listed in this Chapter's Specifications.

16   The remainder of installation is the reverse of the removal procedure.

17   Install the wheel and lug nuts. Lower the vehicle and tighten the lug nuts to the torque listed in the Chapter 1 Specifications.

14 Coil spring (rear) - removal and installation

Removal

1   Loosen the rear wheel lug nuts. Raise the rear of the vehicle and support it securely on jackstands placed underneath the frame

rails. Block the front wheels to prevent the vehicle from rolling. Remove the rear wheels.

2   If your vehicle is equipped with Auto-ride®, unbolt the height sensor linkage from the bracket on the trailing arm.

Note: *Do not change the height sensor linkage adjustment or pry on it to detach it. Pivot the linkage up and support it to protect it from damage.*

3   Support the rear axle housing with a floor jack placed underneath the differential.

4   Detach the rear axle vent hose.

5   Unbolt the track bar from the bracket on the rear axle housing (see Chapter 10).

6   Disconnect the lower ends of the shock absorbers from the axle housing (see Section 11).

7   Slowly lower the floor jack in order to extend the coil springs. Do not exceed the slack in the flexible brake lines or any wire harnesses. Detach the hoses and wire harnesses if necessary.

8   When the coil springs are fully extended, remove the springs and insulators.

9   Check the condition of the insulators. If they're cracked, hardened or otherwise deteriorated, replace them.

Installation

10   Place the springs and insulators in position on the axle and raise the axle until the ends of the springs engage properly with their upper mounts (an assistant would be helpful).

11   Continue to raise the axle until the shock absorbers can be connected to the axle housing. Install the bolts and nuts, tightening them to the torque listed in this Chapter's Specifications.

12   Connect the track bar to the axle, tightening the bolt to the torque listed in this Chapter's Specifications.

13   Reattach the vent hose.

14   Reconnect the brake hoses and wire harnesses if necessary, then bleed the rear brakes (see Chapter 9).

15   If equipped with Autoride®, reattach the height sensor linkage.

15.3b Lower trailing arm mounting fastener locations

16   Install the wheels and lug nuts. Lower the vehicle and tighten the lug nuts to the torque listed in Chapter 1 Specifications.

15 Suspension arms (rear) - removal and installation

Note: *This procedure applies to models with coil spring rear suspension only.*

Trailing arms

Warning: *Remove and install only one arm at a time. This will prevent the axle housing from shifting on the jack.*

1   Loosen the rear wheel lug nuts. Raise the rear of the vehicle and support it securely on jackstands placed underneath the frame rails. Block the front wheels to prevent the vehicle from rolling. Remove the wheel(s).

2   If equipped with Autoride®, unbolt the height sensor linkage from the bracket on the trailing arm.

Note: *Do not change the height sensor linkage adjustment or pry on it to detach it. Pivot the linkage up and support it to protect it from damage.*

3   Support the rear axle with a floor jack, then remove the nuts, washers and bolts from each end of the trailing arm (see illustrations).

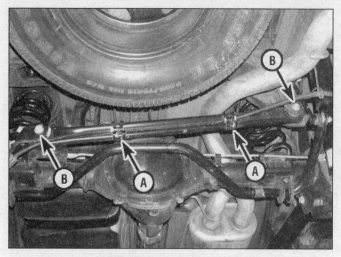

15.8 Track bar mounting details

A　*Parking brake cable clip*　　　　B　*Mounting bolt*

16.4a Insert a tool into the hole to release the airbag module from the steering wheel, one side at a time

16.4b Lift the module from the steering wheel to locate the two electrical connectors

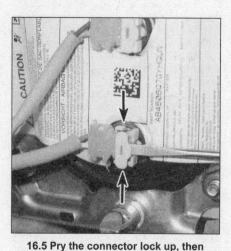

16.5 Pry the connector lock up, then squeeze the small tabs on each side of the connector to pull it out of the airbag module

4　Remove the arm. Check the bushings in the arm for cracking, hardness or other signs of deterioration. If the bushings are in need of replacement, check with your local auto parts store or dealer parts department regarding the availability of replacement bushings. If replacement bushings are available, take the arm and the bushings to an automotive machine shop or other qualified repair facility to have the old ones pressed out and the new ones pressed in.

5　Installation is the reverse of removal. Before tightening the bolts/nuts, raise the rear axle with a floor jack to simulate normal ride height, then tighten the fasteners to the torque listed in this Chapter's Specifications.

Track bar

6　Raise the rear of the vehicle and support it securely on jackstands placed underneath

the frame rails. Block the front wheels to prevent the vehicle from rolling.

7　Detach the parking brake cable from the clips on the arm.

8　Remove the nuts/bolts from each end of the bar (see illustration).

9　Remove the bar. Check the bushings in the bar for cracking, hardness or other signs of deterioration. If the bushings are in need of replacement, check with your local auto parts store or dealer parts department regarding the availability of replacement bushings. If replacement bushings are available, take the bar and the bushings to an automotive machine shop or other qualified repair facility to have the old ones pressed out and the new ones pressed in.

10　Installation is the reverse of removal. Before tightening the bolts/nuts, raise the rear axle with a floor jack to simulate normal ride

height, then tighten the fasteners to the torque listed in this Chapter's Specifications.

16　Steering wheel - removal and installation

Warning: *These models are equipped with airbags. Always disable the airbag system before working in the vicinity of any airbag system component to avoid the possibility of accidental deployment of the airbag, which could cause personal injury (see Chapter 12).*

Removal

1　Park the vehicle with the wheels pointing straight ahead. Disconnect the cable from the negative terminal of the battery.

2　Disable the airbag system (see Chapter 12).

3　Remove the steering column covers (see Chapter 11).

4　Insert a small diameter rod into the hole on one side of the steering wheel to release the airbag module on that side. Repeat the procedure for the opposite side and carefully lift the module from the steering wheel (see illustrations).

5　To disconnect the electrical connectors, pry the connector lock up, then squeeze the small tabs on each side of the connector while pulling it from the module (see illustration). Set the module aside in a safe, isolated area, with the airbag side of the module facing up.

Warning: *When carrying the airbag module, keep the driver's (trim) side of it away from your body, and when you set it down, make sure the driver's side is facing up.*

6　Unplug the electrical connector from the clockspring (see illustration).

7　Remove the steering wheel retaining nut and mark the position of the steering wheel to

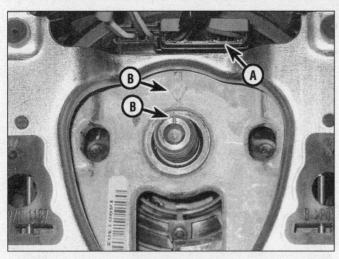

16.6 Remove the electrical connector from the clockspring (A) and note the alignment marks for the steering wheel hub and the steering shaft (B)

16.8 A puller can be used to remove the steering wheel from the steering shaft

the shaft, if marks don't already exist or don't line up.

8   Wiggle the steering wheel away from the shaft to remove it. If necessary, use a puller to release the steering wheel from the shaft (see illustration).

Caution: *Do not use a hammer to remove the steering wheel.*

9   Lift the steering wheel from the shaft while carefully guiding the airbag module harness through the steering wheel hub.

Caution: *Changing the direction of the front wheels with the steering wheel removed will rotate the steering shaft and possibly damage the clockspring.*

Installation

10   Before installing the steering wheel, make sure that the steering shaft is centered. The front wheels must be pointing straight-forward and the block tooth on the steering shaft must be pointing directly up.

Warning: *The clockspring is synchronized with the steering shaft. In the event that the steering shaft has been disconnected from the steering gear and rotated or the clockspring has been removed, the clockspring will require centering.*

Clockspring centering

11   Disconnect the electrical connectors from the bottom, remove the snap-ring from the steering shaft and carefully release any retaining tabs while lifting the clockspring off the steering column.

12   Rotate the hub clockwise until it stops (don't apply too much force). Now turn the hub 3-1/3 turns in the opposite direction until the flat-wire cable loop is visible in the window (see illustration).

Note: *New clocksprings are equipped with a centering pin which is removed after it is installed.*

13   Install the clockspring onto the steering column, aligning it with the horn tower, then

install the snap-ring. Connect the electrical connectors while making sure that the harness is in its original position.

Steering wheel installation

14   Guide the steering wheel into place while threading the wiring harness through the steering wheel hub, then align the index marks on the hub and steering shaft.

Caution: *Do not force the steering wheel onto the shaft if there is resistance. Make sure the steering wheel hub splines line up with the splines on the steering shaft.*

15   Install the steering wheel nut and tighten it to the torque listed in this Chapter's Specifications.

16   Connect the airbag connectors to the airbag module. Make sure the connector locks are securely engaged.

17   Position the airbag module on the steering wheel and push it in until the pins on the module engage with the spring retainers.

18   Reconnect the cable to the negative terminal of the battery (see Chapter 5) and enable the airbag system (see Chapter 12).

---

17   Steering column - removal and installation

Warning: *These models are equipped with airbags. Always disable the airbag systembefore working in the vicinity of any airbag system component to avoid the possibility of accidental deployment of the airbag, which could cause personal injury (see Chapter 12).*

Removal

1   Park the vehicle with the wheels pointing straight ahead. Disconnect the cable from the negative terminal of the battery. Disable the airbag system (see Chapter 12).

Warning: *With the wheels pointing straight ahead, secure the steering wheel using a steering column anti-rotation pin, the steer-*

16.12 Clockspring details

1   Block tooth on steering shaft in the 12 o'clock position
2   Centering window

ing column lock, or a strap to prevent rotation. Locking the steering column will prevent damage to the clockspring and a possible malfunction of the SIR system. The steering wheel must be secured before removing the intermediate shaft, the column, or the steering gear. DO NOT rotate the steering wheel or front wheels while the steering column is removed.

2   Secure the steering wheel in the straight ahead position using one of the following methods:

a) *Steering column lock pin - inserted from under the steering column through an access hole in the lower steering column cover. (GM tool # CH-42640)*

b) *Lock the steering column using the steering column lock (when the ignition key is removed).*

c) *Strap the steering wheel in place.*

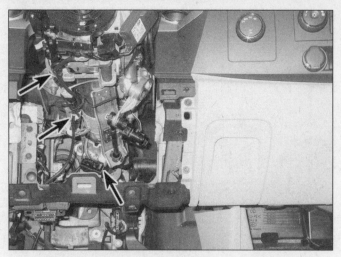

17.8 Electrical connectors and fastener locations

17.9 Match mark the intermediate shaft to the steering shaft

A   Match mark the shaft   B   Steering shaft bolt

17.10 Steering column fastener locations (same on the opposite side)

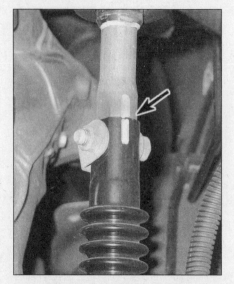

18.3 Match mark the shafts

12   Guide the steering column into position, then install the mounting nuts and bolts, but don't tighten them yet.

13   Align the upper intermediate shaft to the steering shaft and install the fasteners for the steering shaft, then tighten the bolt to the torque listed in this Chapter's Specifications.

14   Tighten the column mounting nuts and bolts to the torque listed in this Chapter's Specifications.

15   The remainder of installation is the reverse of removal. Adjust the shift cable, if necessary (see Chapter 7A).

18   Intermediate shaft and coupler - removal and installation

When disconnecting any of the steering shaft components, the main thing to keep in mind is that they must be reinstalled in the same orientation to one another so that synchronization with other components is maintained. Park the vehicle with the wheels pointing straight ahead. Disconnect the cable from the negative terminal of the battery (see Chapter 5).

1   Use one of the methods described above to prevent the steering wheel from turning.

2   Working under the hood, mark the relationship of the upper intermediate shaft to the lower intermediate shaft. Remove the fasteners securing the lower intermediate shaft to the upper intermediate shaft.

3   Mark the relationship of the intermediate shaft to the steering column shaft and remove the pinch bolt (see illustration).

Note: *The lower intermediate shaft and the intermediate shaft coupler will be removed from the steering gear as an assembly. They can be separated and replaced individually as necessary.*

4   Mark the relationship between the lower intermediate shaft and the steering gear pin-

3   Remove the steering column covers (see Chapter 11).

4   Disconnect the electrical connector to the multi-function switch.

5   Remove the knee bolster and the steel reinforcement behind it (see Chapter 11).

6   Remove the floor duct from behind the knee bolster.

7   Detach the shift cable from the column and the shift lock actuator (see Chapter 7A).

8   Disconnect all electrical connectors from the steering column and detach the related wiring fasteners (see illustration).

9   Mark the relationship of the upper intermediate shaft to the steering shaft, then remove the fasteners securing the steering shaft to the upper intermediate shaft (see illustration).

10   Remove the steering column mounting fasteners (see illustration).

11   Carefully remove the steering column from the vehicle.

Installation

Note: *If a new column is being installed, check to see if a shipping lock pin is present. If so, remove it after the column is in place.*

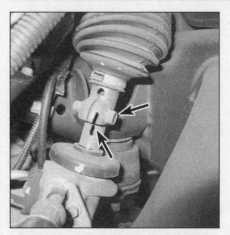

18.4 Lower intermediate shaft-to-pinion shaft match mark and retaining bolt

19.2a Loosen the tie-rod end locknut . . .

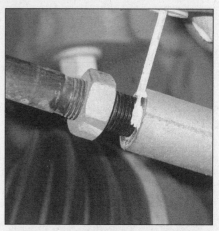

19.2b . . . then mark the position of the tie-rod end on the threaded portion of the tie-rod

19.3 Loosen (but don't remove) the castle nut from the tie-rod end ballstud, then install a balljoint separator or puller and separate the tie-rod end from the steering knuckle

20.4 The outer clamp (A) on the steering gear boot can be squeezed and removed with a pair of pliers; the inner clamp (B) must be cut off

ion shaft (see illustration).

5   Slide the lower portion of the intermediate shaft downwards and off the upper intermediate shaft, the remove then lower intermediate shaft and steering shaft coupler from the steering gear.

6   The upper intermediate shaft can easily be removed from the shaft coming from the steering column if necessary.

7   Installation is the reverse of removal. Be sure to align the matchmarks and tighten the coupler bolt/nut and the shaft-to-steering gear pinch bolt to the specified torque settings.

19 Tie-rod ends - removal and installation

1   Loosen the wheel lug nuts, raise the vehicle and place it securely on jackstands. Remove the wheel.

2   Loosen the tie-rod end locknut and mark the position of the tie-rod end on the threaded portion of the tie-rod (see illustrations).

3   Loosen the tie-rod end-to-steering knuckle nut about 1/4 inch from the tie-rod end balljoint stud, then install a balljoint separator or puller and separate the tie-rod end from the steering knuckle (see illustration). Remove the nut and detach the tie-rod end from the steering knuckle arm.

4   Unscrew the old tie-rod end and install the new one. Count each turn of the tie-rod end as you remove it. Reinstall the replacement tie-rod end to the exact number of turns. Which should line up with the mark you made on the threads of the tie-rod.

5   Installation is the reverse of removal. Be sure to tighten the tie-rod end locknut securely and the tie-rod ballstud nut to the torque listed in this Chapter's Specifications.

6   Tighten the lug nuts to the torque listed in this Chapter's Specifications.

7   Have the front end alignment checked and, if necessary, adjusted.

20 Steering gear boots - replacement

Note: *This procedure applies only to models with rack-and-pinion steering.*

1   Loosen the wheel lug nuts, raise the front of the vehicle and support it securely on jackstands. Remove the wheels.

2   Remove the tie-rod ends from the tie-rods (see Section 19).

3   Remove the tie-rod end locknuts.

4   Remove the outer boot clamps with a pair of pliers, then cut off the inner boot clamps and discard them (see illustration).

5   Mark the location of the breather tube (if used) in relation to the rack assembly, then remove the boots and the tube. Apply some grease to the exposed ends of the toothed rack before installing new boots.

6   Install a new clamp on the inner end of the boot.

7   Apply multi-purpose grease to the groove

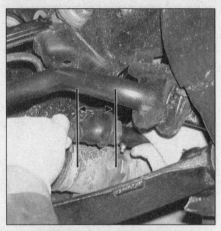

21.4 Push in and out on the relay rod (inner tie rod) and check for any movement between the relay rod and the rack and pinion

21.26 A Pitman arm puller works best

21.29 Brace the Pitman arm while tightening the nut

on the tie-rod (where the outer end of the boot will ride) and the mounting grooves on the steering gear (where the inner boot end will be clamped).

8   Line up the breather tube with the marks made during removal (if applicable) and slide the new boot onto the steering gear housing.

9   Make sure the boot isn't twisted, then tighten the new inner clamp.

10   Install the outer clamps and tie-rod end locknuts.

11   Install the tie-rod ends (see Section 19).

12   Have the front-end alignment checked and, if necessary, adjusted.

---

21 Steering linkage - inspection, removal and installation

Note: *This section applies only to models with a recirculating-ball steering gear.*

Inspection

1   The steering linkage connects the steering gear to the front wheels and keeps the wheels in proper relation to each other. The linkage consists of the Pitman arm, the idler arm, the relay rod, two adjustable tie-rods and, on some models, a steering damper. The Pitman arm, which is fastened to the steering gear shaft, moves the relay rod back and forth. The relay rod is supported on the other end by a frame-mounted idler arm. The back-and-forth motion of the relay rod is transmitted to the steering knuckles through a pair of tie-rod assemblies.

2   Unlock the steering wheel.

3   Raise the front of the vehicle and support it securely with jackstands placed underneath the frame rails.

4   Grasp the relay rod and the tie-rod and try to push them together and pull them apart. If there is more than 0.039-inch of play, replace the relay rod/tie-rod assembly. Now push up and pull down on the tie-rod end; if it

moves more than 0.039-inch, replace the tie-rod end (see illustration).

5   Push up, then pull down on the relay rod end of the idler arm, exerting a force of approximately 25 pounds each way. Measure the total distance the end of the arm travels. If the play is greater than 0.078-inch, replace the idler arm.

6   Check for torn ballstud boots and bent or damaged linkage components.

Removal and installation

Tie-rod end

7   Refer to Section 19 of this chapter for the tie-rod end replacement procedure.

Tie-rod inner (rack and pinion type)

8   Refer to the steering gear box section for removal and installation (see Section 22).

Relay rod

9   Raise the vehicle and support it securely on jackstands. Apply the parking brake.

10   Detach the tie-rod ends from the steering knuckle arms, then remove the tie-rod ends from the tie-rods (see Section 19).

11   If equipped with a steering damper, separate the damper from the relay rod.

12   Separate the relay rod from the Pitman arm.

13   Separate the relay rod from the idler arm.

14   Installation is the reverse of the removal procedure. Use new nuts on all of the ballstuds. If the ballstuds spin when attempting to tighten the nuts, force them into the tapered holes with a large pair of pliers. Be sure to tighten all of the nuts to the specified torque settings.

Idler arm

15   Raise the vehicle and support it securely on jackstands. Apply the parking brake.

16   Loosen but do not remove the idler arm-to-relay rod nut.

17   Separate the idler arm from the relay rod with a two jaw puller. Remove and discard the nut - don't reuse it.

18   Remove the idler arm-to-frame bolts.

19   To install the idler arm, position it on the frame and install the bolts, tightening them to the torque listed in this Chapter's Specifications.

20   Insert the idler arm ballstud into the relay rod and install a new nut. Tighten the nut to the torque listed in this Chapter's Specifications. If the ballstud spins when attempting to tighten the nut, force it into the tapered hole with a large pair of pliers.

Pitman arm

21   Raise the vehicle and support it securely on jackstands.

22   Remove the relay rod nut from the Pitman arm ballstud. Discard the nut - don't reuse it.

23   Using a puller, separate the relay rod from the Pitman arm ballstud.

24   Remove the steering gear (see Section 22).

25   Remove the Pitman arm nut and washer and discard the nut - use a new one during installation. Mark the Pitman arm and the steering gear shaft to ensure proper alignment at reassembly time (only if the same Pitman arm is going to be used).

26   Remove the Pitman arm with a Pitman arm puller or a two-jaw puller (see illustration).

27   Inspect the ballstud threads for damage. Inspect the ballstud seal for excessive wear. Clean the threads on the ballstud.

28   When installing the replacement pitman arm, make sure the marks you made on the Pitman arm and Pitman shaft are aligned, and be sure to use a new nut.

29   Brace the Pitman arm and tighten the nut to the proper torque settings (see illustration).

30   The remainder of the installation is the reverse of removal.

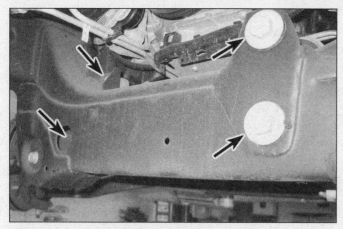

22.6 Steering gear mounting fasteners

23.2 It takes firm pressure to work the pulley off of the pump

Steering damper

31   Inspect the steering damper for fluid leakage. A slight film of fluid near the shaft seal is normal, but if there's excessive fluid present and it's obviously coming from the steering damper, replace the damper.

32   Inspect the steering damper bushing for excessive wear. If it's in bad shape, replace the damper.

33   To test the damper itself, disconnect it from the relay rod. Using as much travel as possible, extend and compress the damper. The resistance should be smooth and constant for each stroke. If any binding, dead spots or unusual noises are present, replace the damper.

34   Remove the damper ballstud-to-relay rod nut. Separate the damper from the relay rod using a small puller.

35   Remove the steering damper mounting bolt and nut, then remove the damper.

36   Installation is the reverse of removal.

---

22   Steering gear - removal and installation

Warning: *DO NOT allow the steering column shaft to rotate with the steering gear removed or damage to the airbag system could occur. As a method of preventing the shaft from turning, wrap the seat belt around the rim of the steering wheel and buckle the belt in place.*

1500 pick-ups and SUV models (rack-and-pinion steering gear)

1   Loosen the front wheel lug nuts, raise the front of the vehicle and support it securely on jackstands. Apply the parking brake. Remove the wheels.

2   Remove the under-vehicle splash shield. Also remove the skid plate bolts and the skid plate, if equipped. Refer to Section 3 in this chapter for the stabilizer bar removal.

3   Mark the relationship of the intermediate shaft coupler to the steering gear input shaft

and remove the pinch bolt.

4   Detach the tie-rod ends from the steering knuckles (see Section 19).

5   Disconnect the steering gear electrical connectors and free the harness from any wire retainers.

6   Unscrew the mounting bolts (see illustration).

7   Lower the steering gear from the vehicle.

Note: *Slide the steering gear as far to the right as possible, then when the left tie-rod end clears, tilt the entire unit downward and remove it from the vehicle.*

8   Installation is the reverse of removal. Be sure to tighten all fasteners to the torque values listed in this Chapter's Specifications. Tighten the wheel lug nuts to the torque listed in the Chapter 1 Specifications.

9   Have the front end alignment checked and, if necessary, adjusted.

2500/3500 pick-ups (recirculating-ball steering gear)

10   Raise the front of the vehicle and support it securely on jackstands. Apply the parking brake.

11   Remove the under-vehicle splash shield. Also remove the skid plate bolts and the skid plate, if equipped.

12   Mark the relationship of the intermediate shaft coupler to the steering gear input (stub) shaft, then remove the pinch bolt from the coupler.

13   Position a drain pan under the steering gear. Using a flare-nut wrench, unscrew the power steering lines from the steering gear.

14   Separate the relay rod from the Pitman arm (see Section 22).

15   Remove the steering gear retaining bolts from the frame rail, then detach the steering gear from the frame and remove it.

16   If you're installing a new steering gear or a new Pitman arm, remove the Pitman arm from the steering gear sector shaft (see Section 22).

17   Installation is the reverse of removal. Be sure to tighten all fasteners to the torque values listed in this Chapter's Specifications.

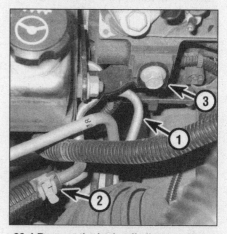

23.4 Remove the hydraulic lines and rear mounting bolt

1   *Pressure line*
2   *Return line*
3   *Rear mounting bolt*

Check the power steering fluid level and add some, if necessary then bleed the system.

---

23   Power steering pump - removal and installation

Removal

1   Remove the drivebelt (see Chapter 1).

2   Using a power steering pump pulley remover, remove the pulley from the pump (see illustration).

Note: *The pulley removal tool is available at most automotive parts or tool supply stores as a rental tool.*

3   Remove the oil pan skid plate or engine shield, if equipped.

4   Position a drain pan under the power steering pump. Disconnect the feed hose and the pressure line from the rear of the pump (see illustration). Disconnect the oil cooler hose from the pump, if equipped. Plug or cap all openings to prevent contaminants from

entering any part of the system.

5   Remove the pump mounting fasteners (see illustration) and lift the pump from the vehicle, taking care not to spill fluid on the painted surfaces.

Installation

6   Position the pump in the mounting bracket and install the mounting fasteners; tighten them to the torque listed in this Chapter's Specifications.

7   Connect the pressure line and feed hose to the pump, making sure that all connections are secure.

8   Press the pulley onto the shaft using a pulley installer tool (see illustration).

9   Install the drivebelt and engine shield (if equipped).

10   Fill the power steering reservoir with the recommended fluid and bleed the system following the procedure described in the next section.

23.5 Pump bolt locations (three bolts are only accessible with pulley off; the other one is shown by the arrow located on the back side of the pump mounting plate)

23.8 Keep tightening the tool until the tool bottoms out against the pulley and pump shaft. It has to go on until the front of the pulley is flush with the pump shaft or the pulley will not line up with the rest of the belt-driven components

24   Power steering system - bleeding

1   Following any operation in which the power steering fluid lines have been disconnected, the power steering system must be bled to remove all air and obtain proper steering performance.

2   With the front wheels in the straight ahead position, check the power steering fluid level and, if low, add fluid until it reaches the COLD mark on the dipstick or in the middle of the cross-hatched marks.

3   Raise the front of the vehicle just enough for the wheels to clear the ground and support it securely on jackstands. Apply the parking brake.

4   Turn the key to the ON position with the engine off, then turn the steering wheel fully in each direction (stop-to-stop) 12 times.

5   Check the fluid level and add more if necessary to reach the COLD fill mark.

6   Start the engine and allow it to warm up.

7   Turn the steering wheel from side to side, without hitting the stops and confirm that there is no noise coming from the system due to aeration of the fluid.

8   Road test the vehicle to be sure the steering system is functioning normally and noise free.

9   Recheck the fluid level to be sure it's up to the HOT mark on the dipstick while the engine is at normal operating temperature. Add fluid if necessary.

25   Wheels and tires - general information

1   Most vehicles covered by this manual are equipped with metric-size fiberglass or steel belted radial tires (see illustration), or inch-pattern light truck tires. Use of other size or type of tires may affect the ride and handling of the vehicle. Don't mix different types

of tires, such as radials and bias belted, on the same vehicle as handling may be seriously affected. It's recommended that tires be replaced in pairs on the same axle, but if only one tire is being replaced, be sure it's the same size, structure and tread design as the other.

2   Because tire pressure has a substantial effect on handling and wear, the pressure on all tires should be checked at least once a month or before any extended trips (see Chapter 1).

3   Wheels must be replaced if they're bent,

dented, leak air, have elongated bolt holes, are heavily rusted, out of vertical symmetry or if the lug nuts won't stay tight. Wheel repairs that use welding or peening are not recommended.

4   Tire and wheel balance is important to the overall handling, braking and performance of the vehicle. Unbalanced wheels can adversely affect handling and ride characteristics as well as tire life. Whenever a tire is installed on a wheel, the tire and wheel should be balanced by a shop with the proper equipment.

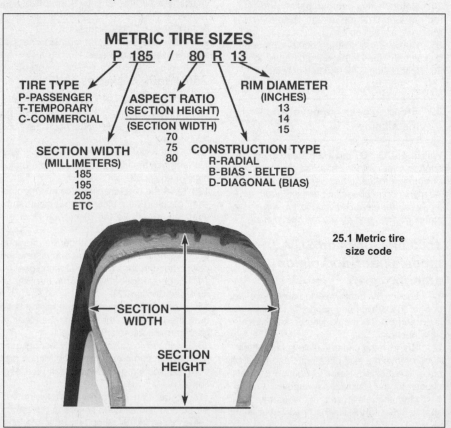

25.1 Metric tire size code

26 Front end alignment - general information

1   A front end alignment refers to the adjustments made to the front wheels so they're in proper angular relationship to the suspension and the ground (see illustration). Front wheels that are out of proper alignment not only affect steering control, but also increase tire wear.

2   Getting the proper front wheel alignment is a very exacting process, one in which complicated and expensive machines are necessary to perform the job properly. Because of this, you should have a technician with the proper equipment perform these tasks. We will, however, use this space to give you a basic idea of what is involved with front end alignment so you can better understand the process and deal intelligently with the shop that does the work.

3   Toe-in is the turning in of the front wheels. The purpose of a toe specification is to ensure parallel rolling of the front wheels. In a vehicle with zero toe-in, the distance between the front edges of the wheels will be the same as the distance between the rear edges of the wheels. The actual amount of toe-in is normally only a fraction of an inch.

Toe-in is adjusted by turning the tie-rod in the tie-rod end to lengthen or shorten the tie-rod. Incorrect toe-in will cause the tires to wear improperly by making them scrub against the road surface.

4   Camber is the tilting of the front wheels from vertical when viewed from the front of the vehicle. When the wheels tilt out at the top, the camber is said to be positive (+). When the wheels tilt in at the top the camber is negative (-). The amount of tilt is measured in degrees from the vertical and this measurement is called the camber angle. This angle affects the amount of tire tread which contacts the road and compensates for changes in the suspension geometry when the vehicle is cornering or traveling over an undulating surface. Camber is adjusted by turning the upper control arm pivot bolts, one way or the other, in equal amounts.

5   Caster is the tilting of the top of the front steering axis from vertical. A tilt toward the rear is positive caster and a tilt toward the front is negative caster. Caster is adjusted by turning the upper control arm pivot bolts, one way or the other, in opposite directions.

6   When making adjustments to the front end alignment, the caster is set first, then the camber, then the toe-in.

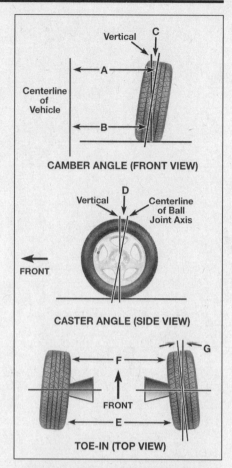

26.1 Front end alignment details

A minus B = C (degrees camber)
D = degrees caster
E minus F = toe-in (measured in inches)
G = toe-in (expressed in degrees)

Notes

Chapter 11
Body

Contents

---

1   General Information

General information

1   The vehicles covered by this manual are built with body-on-frame construction. The frame is a hydro-formed ladder-type, consisting of C-shaped center rails welded to boxed front and rear sections, with both welded-in and bolt-in crossmembers.

2   The pick-up body is in two separate sections, the cab and the bed, while the SUV body incorporates the cab, back-seat area and cargo compartment in one unitized structure.

3   Certain components are particularly vulnerable to accident damage and can be unbolted and repaired or replaced. Among these parts are the hood, doors, seats, tailgate, liftgate, bumpers and front fenders.

4   Only general body maintenance practices and body panel repair procedures within the scope of the do-it-yourselfer are included in this chapter.

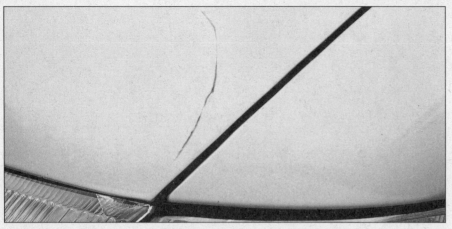

Make sure the damaged area is perfectly clean and rust free. If the touch-up kit has a wire brush, use it to clean the scratch or chip. Or use fine steel wool wrapped around the end of a pencil. Clean the scratched or chipped surface only, not the good paint surrounding it. Rinse the area with water and allow it to dry thoroughly

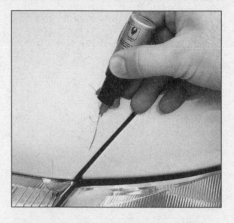

Thoroughly mix the paint, then apply a small amount with the touch-up kit brush or a very fine artist's brush. Brush in one direction as you fill the scratch area. Do not build up the paint higher than the surrounding paint

2   Repair of minor paint scratches

1   No matter how hard you try to keep your vehicle looking like new, it will inevitably be scratched, chipped or dented at some point. If the metal is actually dented, seek the advice of a professional. But you can fix minor scratches and chips yourself. Buy a touch-up paint kit from a dealer service department or an auto parts store. To ensure that you get the right color, you'll need to have the specific make, model and year of your vehicle and, ideally, the paint code, which is located on a special metal plate under the hood or in the door jamb.

3   Body repair - minor damage

Plastic body panels

1   The following repair procedures are for minor scratches and gouges. Repair of more serious damage should be left to a dealer service department or qualified auto body shop. Below is a list of the equipment and materials necessary to perform the following repair procedures on plastic body panels.
   Wax, grease and silicone removing solvent
   Cloth-backed body tape
   Sanding discs
   Drill motor with three-inch disc holder
   Hand sanding block
   Rubber squeegees
   Sandpaper
   Non-porous mixing palette
   Wood paddle or putty knife
   Curved-tooth body file
   Flexible parts repair material

Flexible panels (bumper trim)

2   Remove the damaged panel, if necessary or desirable. In most cases, repairs can be carried out with the panel installed.

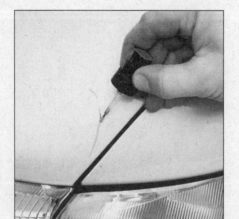

If the vehicle has a two-coat finish, apply the clear coat after the color coat has dried

3   Clean the area(s) to be repaired with a wax, grease and silicone removing solvent applied with a water-dampened cloth.
4   If the damage is structural, that is, if it extends through the panel, clean the backside of the panel area to be repaired as well. Wipe dry.
5   Sand the rear surface about 1-1/2 inches beyond the break.
6   Cut two pieces of fiberglass cloth large enough to overlap the break by about 1-1/2 inches. Cut only to the required length.
7   Mix the adhesive from the repair kit according to the instructions included with the kit, and apply a layer of the mixture approximately 1/8-inch thick on the backside of the panel. Overlap the break by at least 1-1/2 inches.
8   Apply one piece of fiberglass cloth to the adhesive and cover the cloth with additional adhesive. Apply a second piece of fiberglass cloth to the adhesive and immediately cover the cloth with additional adhesive in sufficient quantity to fill the weave.
9   Allow the repair to cure for 20 to 30 minutes at 60-degrees to 80-degrees F.

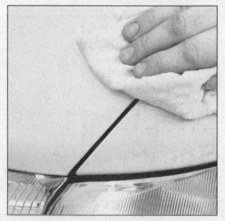

Wait a few days for the paint to dry thoroughly, then rub out the repainted area with a polishing compound to blend the new paint with the surrounding area. When you're happy with your work, wash and polish the area

10   If necessary, trim the excess repair material at the edge.
11   Remove all of the paint film over and around the area(s) to be repaired. The repair material should not overlap the painted surface.
12   With a drill motor and a sanding disc (or a rotary file), cut a "V" along the break line approximately 1/2-inch wide. Remove all dust and loose particles from the repair area.
13   Mix and apply the repair material. Apply a light coat first over the damaged area; then continue applying material until it reaches a level slightly higher than the surrounding finish.
14   Cure the mixture for 20 to 30 minutes at 60-degrees to 80-degrees F.
15   Roughly establish the contour of the area being repaired with a body file. If low areas or pits remain, mix and apply additional adhesive.
16   Block sand the damaged area with sandpaper to establish the actual contour of the surrounding surface.

17   If desired, the repaired area can be temporarily protected with several light coats of primer. Because of the special paints and techniques required for flexible body panels, it is recommended that the vehicle be taken to a paint shop for completion of the body repair.

Steel body panels

Repairing simple dents

Note: *These photos illustrate a method of repairing simple dents. They are intended to supplement Body repair - minor damage in this Chapter and should not be used as the sole instructions for body repair on these vehicles.*

18   When repairing dents, the first job is to pull the dent out until the affected area is as close as possible to its original shape. There is no point in trying to restore the original shape completely as the metal in the damaged area will have stretched on impact and cannot be restored to its original contours. It is better to bring the level of the dent up to a point that is about 1/8-inch below the level of the surrounding metal. In cases where the dent is very shallow, it is not worth trying to pull it out at all.

19   If the backside of the dent is accessible, it can be hammered out gently from behind using a soft-face hammer. While doing this, hold a block of wood firmly against the opposite side of the metal to absorb the hammer blows and prevent the metal from being stretched.

20   If the dent is in a section of the body which has double layers, or some other factor makes it inaccessible from behind, a different technique is required. Drill several small holes through the metal inside the damaged area, particularly in the deeper sections. Screw long, self-tapping screws into the holes just enough for them to get a good grip in the metal. Now pulling on the protruding heads of the screws with locking pliers can pull out the dent.

21   The next stage of repair is the removal of paint from the damaged area and from an inch or so of the surrounding metal. This is easily done with a wire brush or sanding disk in a drill motor, although it can be done just as effectively by hand with sandpaper. To complete the preparation for filling, score the surface of the bare metal with a screwdriver or the tang of a file or drill small holes in the affected area. This will provide a good grip for the filler material. To complete the repair, see the Section on filling and painting.

Repair of rust holes or gashes

22   Remove all paint from the affected area and from an inch or so of the surrounding metal using a sanding disk or wire brush mounted in a drill motor. If these are not available, a few sheets of sandpaper will do the job just as effectively.

23   With the paint removed, you will be able to determine the severity of the corrosion and decide whether to replace the whole panel, if possible, or repair the affected area. New body panels are not as expensive as most

people think and it is often quicker to install a new panel than to repair large areas of rust.

24   Remove all trim pieces from the affected area except those which will act as a guide to the original shape of the damaged body, such as headlight shells, etc. Using metal snips or a hacksaw blade, remove all loose metal and any other metal that is badly affected by rust. Hammer the edges of the hole in to create a slight depression for the filler material.

25   Wire-brush the affected area to remove the powdery rust from the surface of the metal. If the back of the rusted area is accessible, treat it with rust inhibiting paint.

26   Before filling is done, block the hole in some way. This can be done with sheet metal riveted or screwed into place, or by stuffing the hole with wire mesh.

27   Once the hole is blocked off, the affected area can be filled and painted. See the following subsection on filling and painting.

Filling and painting

28   Many types of body fillers are available, but generally speaking, body repair kits which contain filler paste and a tube of resin hardener are best for this type of repair work. A wide, flexible plastic or nylon applicator will be necessary for imparting a smooth and contoured finish to the surface of the filler material. Mix up a small amount of filler on a clean piece of wood or cardboard (use the hardener sparingly). Follow the manufacturer's instructions on the package, otherwise the filler will set incorrectly.

29   Using the applicator, apply the filler paste to the prepared area. Draw the applicator across the surface of the filler to achieve the desired contour and to level the filler surface. As soon as a contour that approximates the original one is achieved, stop working the paste. If you continue, the paste will begin to stick to the applicator. Continue to add thin layers of paste at 20-minute intervals until the level of the filler is just above the surrounding metal.

30   Once the filler has hardened, the excess can be removed with a body file. From then on, progressively finer grades of sandpaper should be used, starting with a 180-grit paper and finishing with 600-grit wet-or-dry paper. Always wrap the sandpaper around a flat rubber or wooden block, otherwise the surface of the filler will not be completely flat. During the sanding of the filler surface, the wet-or-dry paper should be periodically rinsed in water. This will ensure that a very smooth finish is produced in the final stage.

31   At this point, the repair area should be surrounded by a ring of bare metal, which in turn should be encircled by the finely feathered edge of good paint. Rinse the repair area with clean water until all of the dust produced by the sanding operation is gone.

32   Spray the entire area with a light coat of primer. This will reveal any imperfections in the surface of the filler. Repair the imperfections with fresh filler paste or glaze filler and once more smooth the surface with sandpaper. Repeat this spray-and-repair procedure

until you are satisfied that the surface of the filler and the feathered edge of the paint are perfect. Rinse the area with clean water and allow it to dry completely.

33   The repair area is now ready for painting. Spray painting must be carried out in a warm, dry, windless and dust free atmosphere. These conditions can be created if you have access to a large indoor work area, but if you are forced to work in the open, you will have to pick the day very carefully. If you are working indoors, dousing the floor in the work area with water will help settle the dust that would otherwise be in the air. If the repair area is confined to one body panel, mask off the surrounding panels. This will help minimize the effects of a slight mismatch in paint color. Trim pieces such as chrome strips, door handles, etc., will also need to be masked off or removed. Use masking tape and several thickness of newspaper for the masking operations.

34   Before spraying, shake the paint can thoroughly, then spray a test area until the spray painting technique is mastered. Cover the repair area with a thick coat of primer. The thickness should be built up using several thin layers of primer rather than one thick one. Using 600-grit wet-or-dry sandpaper, rub down the surface of the primer until it is very smooth. While doing this, the work area should be thoroughly rinsed with water and the wet-or-dry sandpaper periodically rinsed as well. Allow the primer to dry before spraying additional coats.

35   Spray on the top coat, again building up the thickness by using several thin layers of paint. Begin spraying in the center of the repair area and then, using a circular motion, work out until the whole repair area and about two inches of the surrounding original paint is covered. Remove all masking material 10 to 15 minutes after spraying on the final coat of paint. Allow the new paint at least two weeks to harden, then use a very fine rubbing compound to blend the edges of the new paint into the existing paint. Finally, apply a coat of wax

4   Body repair - major damage

1   Major damage must be repaired by an auto body shop specifically equipped to perform body and frame repairs. These shops have the specialized equipment required to do the job properly.

2   If the damage is extensive, the body must be checked for proper alignment or the vehicle's handling characteristics may be adversely affected and other components may wear at an accelerated rate.

3   Due to the fact that all of the major body components (hood, fenders, etc.) are separate and replaceable units, any seriously damaged components should be replaced rather than repaired. Sometimes the components can be found in a wrecking yard that specializes in used vehicle components, often at considerable savings over the cost of new parts.

These photos illustrate a method of repairing simple dents. They are intended to supplement *Body repair - minor damage* in this Chapter and should not be used as the sole instructions for body repair on these vehicles.

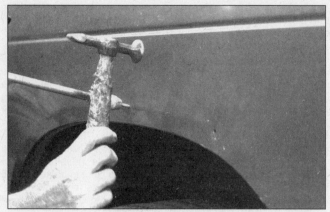

1 If you can't access the backside of the body panel to hammer out the dent, pull it out with a slide-hammer-type dent puller. Tap with a hammer near the edge of the dent to help 'pop' the metal back to its original shape, about 1/8-inch below the surface of the surrounding metal

2 Using coarse-grit sandpaper, remove the paint down to the bare metal. Clean the repair area with wax/silicone remover.

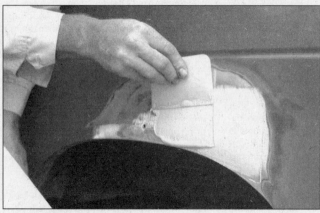

3 Following label instructions, mix up a batch of plastic filler and hardener, then quickly press it into the metal with a plastic applicator. Work the filler until it matches the original contour and is slightly above the surrounding metal

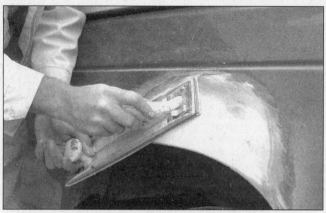

4 Let the filler harden until you can just dent it with your fingernail. File, then sand the filler down until it's smooth and even. Work down to finer grits of sandpaper - always using a board or block - ending up with 360 or 400 grit

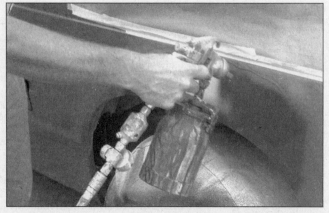

5 When the area is smooth to the touch, clean the area and mask around it. Apply several layers of primer to the area. A professional-type spray gun is being used here, but aerosol spray primer works fine

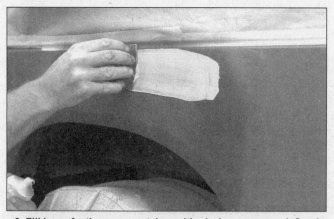

6 Fill imperfections or scratches with glazing compound. Sand with 360 or 400-grit and re-spray. Finish sand the primer with 600 grit, clean thoroughly, then apply the finish coat. Don't attempt to rub out or wax the repair area until the paint has dried completely (at least two weeks)

5 Upholstery, carpets and vinyl trim - maintenance

Upholstery and carpets

1 Every three months remove the floormats and clean the interior of the vehicle (more frequently if necessary). Use a stiff whiskbroom to brush the carpeting and loosen dirt and dust, then vacuum the upholstery and carpets thoroughly, especially along seams and crevices.

2 Dirt and stains can be removed from carpeting with basic household or automotive carpet shampoos available in spray cans. Follow the directions and vacuum again, then use a stiff brush to bring back the "nap" of the carpet.

3 Most interiors have cloth or vinyl upholstery, either of which can be cleaned and maintained with a number of material-specific cleaners or shampoos available in auto supply stores. Follow the directions on the product for usage, and always spot-test any upholstery cleaner on an inconspicuous area (bottom edge of a backseat cushion) to ensure that it doesn't cause a color shift in the material.

4 After cleaning, vinyl upholstery should be treated with a protectant.

Note: Make sure the protectant container indicates the product can be used on seats - some products may make a seat too slippery.

Warning: *Do not use protectant on vinyl-covered steering wheels. This can leave the steering wheel with an extremely slippery surface.*

5 Leather upholstery requires special care. It should be cleaned regularly with saddle-soap or leather cleaner. Never use alcohol, gasoline, nail polish remover or thinner to clean leather upholstery.

6 After cleaning, regularly treat leather upholstery with a leather conditioner, rubbed in with a soft cotton cloth. Never use car wax on leather upholstery.

7 In areas where the interior of the vehicle is subject to bright sunlight, cover leather seating areas of the seats with a sheet if the vehicle is to be left out for any length of time.

Vinyl trim

8 Don't clean vinyl trim with detergents, caustic soap or petroleum-based cleaners. Plain soap and water works just fine, with a soft brush to clean dirt that may be ingrained. Wash the vinyl as frequently as the rest of the vehicle.

9 After cleaning, application of a high-quality rubber and vinyl protectant will help prevent oxidation and cracks. The protectant can also be applied to weather-stripping, vacuum lines and rubber hoses, which often fail as a result of chemical degradation.

6 Fastener and trim removal

1 There is a variety of plastic fasteners used to hold trim panels, splash shields and other parts in place in addition to typical screws, nuts and bolts. Once you are familiar with them, they can usually be removed without too much difficulty.

2 The proper tools and approach can pre-

Fasteners

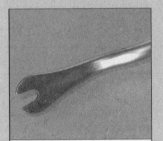

This tool is designed to remove special fasteners. A small pry tool used for removing nails will also work well in place of this tool

A Phillips head screwdriver can be used to release the center portion, but light pressure must be used because the plastic is easily damaged. Once the center is up, the fastener can easily be pried from its hole

Here is a view with the center portion fully released. Install the fastener as shown, then press the center in to set it

This fastener is used for exterior panels and shields. The center portion must be pried up to release the fastener. Install the fastener with the center up, then press the center in to set it

This type of fastener is used commonly for interior panels. Use a small blunt tool to press the small pin at the center in to release it . . .

. . . the pin will stay with the fastener in the released position

Reset the fastener for installation by moving the pin out. Install the fastener, then press the pin flush with the fastener to set it

This fastener is used for exterior and interior panels. It has no moving parts. Simply pry the fastener from its hole like the claw of a hammer removes a nail. Without a tool that can get under the top of the fastener, it can be very difficult to remove

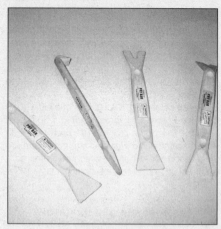

6.4 These small plastic pry tools are ideal for prying off trim panels

9.1 Cloudy headlight lenses are ugly and reduce the amount of light projected

9.3 Mask off the surrounding area and apply the compound with the buffer

9.4 The result should be a lens that is almost as clear as new

vent added time and expense to a project by minimizing the number of broken fasteners and/or parts.

3   The following illustration shows various types of fasteners that are typically used on most vehicles and how to remove and install them (see illustration). Replacement fasteners are commonly found at most auto parts stores, if necessary.

4   Trim panels are typically made of plastic and their flexibility can help during removal. The key to their removal is to use a tool to pry the panel near its retainers to release it without damaging surrounding areas or breaking-off any retainers. The retainers will usually snap out of their designated slot or hole after force is applied to them. Stiff plastic tools designed for prying on trim panels are available at most auto parts stores (see illustration). Tools that are tapered and wrapped in protective tape, such as a screwdriver or small pry tool, are also very effective when used with care.

Caution: *Age and weather as well as direct sunlight on just about any plastic or composite type trim panel can turn what used to be a pliable plastic panel into a brittle, crumbling*

and often cracking piece of faded trim. When you are trying to remove a trim section on an older vehicle with sun or weather damage to the trim, take extra precautions not to damage the trim panel any more than you have too. Make sure your trim removing tool is in the correct area to pry and listen closely for any unusual sounds that might indicate you're about to crack the plastic. Readjust your trim tool to a different area and try again. Sometimes, even with the best efforts, an old dried out plastic trim panel can't be prevented from cracking or splitting.

7   Hinges and locks - maintenance

1   Once every 3000 miles, or every three months, the hinges and latch assemblies on the doors, hood and trunk should be given a few drops of light oil or lock lubricant. The door latch strikers should also be lubricated with a thin coat of grease or white lithium lubricant to reduce wear and ensure free movement. Lubricate the door and trunk locks with spray-on graphite lubricant.

8   Windshield and fixed glass - replacement

1   Replacement of the windshield and fixed glass requires the use of special fast-setting adhesive/caulk materials and some specialized tools and techniques. These operations should be left to a shop specializing in glass replacement.

9   Headlight lens refurbishing

1   The plastic lens on most headlight assemblies is susceptible to U.V. damage from the sun as well as being out in the weather. There are several companies that make restoration kits to restore the plastic lens back to their original condition. There are also a few home remedies that have been proven somewhat effective too. Such as toothpaste buffed onto the lens as well as some bug sprays that dissolve the opaque and clouded surface of the headlight lens (see illustration).

2   Most restoration kits are a three-step process that requires a variable speed hand drill to perform the various steps. When starting a headlight restoration project, be sure to be in a well ventilated area and where you don't have anything you don't want the buffing chemicals and compounds to be sprayed on.

3   Mask off the area around the headlight assembly to avoid any painted surfaces from being damaged with the drill or the compounds in the restoration kit. Have plenty of clean rags handy to wipe up any spills and to perform the final buffing (see illustration).

4   Follow all the directions in the restoration kit as described in the instructions. We also recommend adding a top coat of wax or a suitable U.V. protectant as a final finish coat (see illustration).

10.1 Remove the plastic fasteners

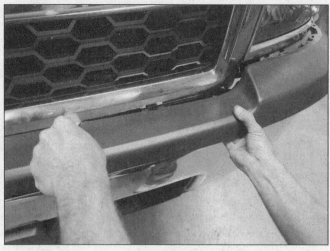

10.3 Carefully wedge the flat trim tool into the gap and pry the upper fascia off

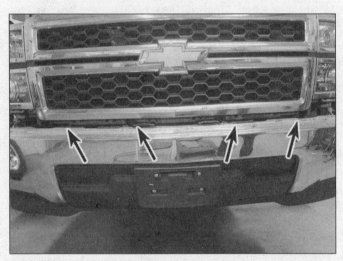

10.6a Bottom screw locations

10.6b Upper screw locations

10 Radiator grille - removal and installation

Note: *Refer to Section 6 in this chapter for fastener types and removal techniques.*

1   Open the hood and remove the plastic panel over the radiator (see illustration).
2   Remove the front bumper upper fascia by loosening the side fascia brackets first. Two screws per side.
3   Use a plastic wedge inserted between the upper fascia and the front bumper to gain access to the retaining clips (see illustration).
4   Using a flat screwdriver carefully release the clips one at a time as you pull the fascia away from the bumper.
5   Pull the fascia off and set aside.
6   Remove the grille mounting screws (see illustrations).
7   Installation is the reverse of removal.

11 Windshield washer fluid reservoir - removal and installation

1   Loosen the left front wheel lug nuts, then raise and support the front of the vehicle securely on jackstands. Remove the wheel.
2   Remove the inner fender liner (see Section 17).
3   Remove the two screws securing the wheel house forward bracket.
4   Remove the windshield washer hose and the electrical connector to the washer pump.
5   Remove the four bolts securing the reservoir (see illustration).
Note: *Two of the screws are accessed from the top side. They are attached to the battery tray.*
6   Remove the reservoir out through the wheelwell.
7   Installation is the reverse of removal.

11.5 Lower reservoir mounting screws

12.2 Mark the hood around the hinge plates to aid alignment during reinstallation

12.10 Hood latch adjustment is accomplished by loosening the hood latch bolts.

12.11 Twist the rubber bumper in or out to make fine adjustments to the hood height

13.4 Latch is shown after removal and turned upside down in this photo. To disconnect the cable from the hood latch assembly, guide the cable end off the lever and use pliers to disengage the cable housing end from the assembly

12 Hood - removal, installation and adjustment

Removal and installation

Note: *The hood is heavy and somewhat awkward to remove and install - at least two people should perform this procedure.*

1   Use blankets or pads to cover the cowl area of the body and the fenders. This will protect the body and paint as the hood is lifted off.

2   If a hood hinge is going to be replaced, or the same hood is going to be reinstalled, scribe alignment marks around the hinge flanges to insure proper hood alignment during installation (paint or a permanent-type felt-tip marker also will work for this) (see illustration). (Skip this step if the hood is going to be replaced.)

3   Disconnect any electrical connectors attached to the hood (such as the underhood light, ground wire, etc.).

4   Some models may be equipped with a hood strut. Detach the strut from the hood by removing the small clip on the end, then pull the strut end off of the ball mount.

5   Have an assistant support the weight of the hood. Remove the hinge-to-hood bolts and remove the hood.

6   Installation is the reverse of removal. Check the alignment and adjust as necessary.

Hood adjustment procedure

7   Fore-and-aft and side-to-side adjustment of the hood is done by moving the hood in relation to the hinge flanges after loosening the bolts.

8   Scribe or trace a line around the entire hinge plate so you can judge the amount of movement (paint or a permanent-type felt-tip marker also will work for this).

9   Loosen the nuts and move the hood into correct alignment. Move it only a little at a time. Tighten the hinge nuts and carefully lower the hood to check the alignment.

10   Adjust the hood latch so the hood closes securely, and check that the hood opens without binding. If the hood does bind or is hard to open readjust the hood latch as needed (see illustration).

11   Adjust the hood bumpers so that the hood is flush with the fenders when closed (see illustration).

Tip: *The hood should rest on the hood bumpers with a very slight pressure against the hood itself. Do not raise them so high that they put a great deal of pressure on the hood, as this can cause the hood to jam in the hood latch mechanism and make it harder to open. A good way to check the proper height of the hood bumpers is to remove the latch completely so it does not latch, and then raise or lower the hood bumper stops until the edge of the hood aligns perfectly with the fender*

edges. Once that is accomplished you can then reattach the latch and adjust the latch properly.

Note: *The hood latch assembly, as well as the hinges, should be periodically lubricated with white lithium-base grease to prevent sticking and wear.*

13 Hood latch and release cable - removal and installation

Warning: *The models covered by this manual are equipped with a Supplemental Restraint System (SRS), more commonly known as airbags. Always disable the airbag system before working in the vicinity of any airbag system components to avoid the possibility of accidental deployment of the airbags, which could cause personal injury (see Chapter 12).*

Latch

1   Remove the plastic panel over the radiator (see Section 10).

2   Follow the wiring harness from the latch to the electrical connector mounted nearby, then disconnect it (if applicable).

3   Mark the location of the hood latch with a scribe or suitable marking tool such as a permanent marker or paint.

4   Remove the mounting bolts and detach the latch assembly. Remove the cable from the latch (see illustration).

5   Installation is the reverse of removal. If necessary, adjust the latch so the hood engages securely when closed and the hood bumpers are in their proper position.

Release cable

6   Remove the latch and disconnect the release cable from the hood latch assembly.

7   Working in the passenger's compartment, remove the driver's kick panel to expose the hood latch release cable and handle.

8   Separate the cable end from the handle

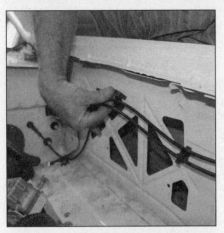

13.11 Remove the clips as needed (shown with underhood fuse box removed)

14.3 Remove the bolts from both ends of the bumper support bracket (not all bolts are shown)

14.8 Remove these bolts and nuts (left side shown) to remove the rear bumper with its brackets attached

and use pliers to release the cable housing end from the tab on the handle.

Note: *If the handle assembly must be replaced, remove its mounting bolt and detach it.*

9   On truck models, the cable is routed behind the parking brake pedal assembly. Loosen the mounting fasteners to the parking brake pedal assembly enough to allow the cable to pull through behind it.

10   Working in the engine compartment, locate the cable grommet at the firewall and pull it away from the firewall along with the cable.

11   On some models the cable is held down in different spots with plastic clips. Detach the cable from the mounting points within the engine compartment (see illustration).

12   Before pulling the cable from the passenger compartment tie a string or a piece of mechanic's wire to the end of the cable.

13   Attach the string or mechanic's wire onto the replacement cable and guide the cable through the firewall from the passenger compartment. Continue to guide the cable through the engine compartment until the grommet meets the firewall. Push the grommet into the hole in the firewall and seat it.

14   The remainder of installation is the reverse of removal.

14 Bumpers - removal and installation

Warning: *The models covered by this manual are equipped with a Supplemental Restraint System (SRS), more commonly known as airbags. Always disable the airbag system before working in the vicinity of any airbag system components to avoid the possibility of accidental deployment of the airbags, which could cause personal injury (see Chapter 12).*

Note: *Bumpers on truck models are chrome-plated steel, with black or color-matched plastic trim or a plastic one piece fascia.*

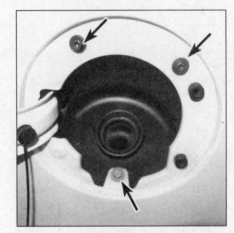

15.3 Filler neck screws

Front bumper

1   Support the bumper with a floor jack. Disconnect the electrical connectors at the fog lights, if equipped.

2   Remove the radiator grille (see Section 10). Remove the fasteners securing the fender liners to the front bumper (see Section 17).

3   With an assistant supporting the bumper, remove the bolts/nuts retaining the bumper to the frame (see illustration).

4   Disconnect any wiring harnesses or other components that would interfere with bumper removal and detach the bumper.

5   Installation is the reverse of removal.

Rear bumper

6   Support the bumper with a floor jack.

7   Disconnect the electrical connectors for the license plate lights and any other wiring harnesses or components that would interfere with the bumper removal.

8   With an assistant supporting the bumper, remove the bolts, nuts and stud plates retaining the bumper to the frame (see illustration).

15.4 Disconnect the electrical connector(s) for the rear lights

Note: *On models with a locking access hole for the spare-tire-lowering handle, pull the bumper straight back until the plastic tube on the back of the bumper clears the metal tube.*

9   Installation is the reverse of removal.

15 Truck bed - removal and installation

1   Place the truck on a flat surface with the parking brake applied.

2   Disconnect the cable from the negative battery terminal (see Chapter 5).

3   Remove the screws securing the fuel tank filler neck to the truck bed (see illustration).

4   Disconnect the rear section electrical connector running from the frame to the rear lighting (see illustration).

5   Disconnect any non-factory wiring such as an additional trailer wiring, tag light wiring, or accessory leads.

6   Disconnect the braided ground strap located near the fuel tank filler neck from the truck bed.

15.7a You'll find some of the bolts are easy to reach while others may be covered by part of a trailer hitch bracket. If so, remove the trailer hitch brackets to gain access to the bolts

15.7b Follow along the frame to find the rest of the bolts (not all the bolts are shown)

16.4 Remove the braces from both sides

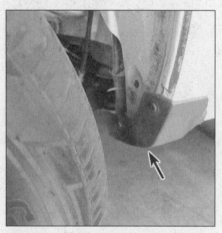

16.5 The fender protector is held on with push plastic push clips

16.6 Auxiliary battery tray location

16.8 Looking down from above the fender (with the hood removed) at the lower hood hinge bolts

7   Remove the bolts that secure the truck bed to the frame (eight bolts for the long bed, six bolts on short beds) (see illustrations). **Note:** *The truck bed bolts can be fairly stubborn to remove. Dirt and debris as well as rust can make them even harder to remove. An impact gun with an impact socket works the best rather than trying to remove them by hand.* **Tip:** *If the bolts are stuck use some rust penetrating spray on them. Leave the penetrating spray soak in for a few minutes before trying them again. If a penetrating spray isn't available a spray of plain water actually will loosen them up as well.*

8   With the aid of a few helpers (one on each corner) lift the bed off of the frame. **Tip:** *If you have access to a car hoist you can strap the truck bed to the hoist arms and use the hoist to lift the truck bed up. Then, push*

the truck out from under it.

9   Installation is the reverse of removal.

16   Front fender - removal and installation

Note: *Refer to Section 6 for fastener types and removal techniques.*

1   Disconnect the cable from the negative battery terminal (see Chapter 5). Loosen the wheel lug nuts, raise the vehicle, support it securely on jackstands and remove the front wheel.

2   Remove the headlight housing (see Chapter 12).

3   Remove the radiator grille (see Section 10).

4   Remove the upper cross braces that tie the fender to the cowling area and the fender to the core support area (see illustration).

5   Remove the lower plastic fender edge protector (located on the rear part of the fender at the edge between the rear fender well and the door opening) (see illustration).

6   For the left-side fender, remove the auxiliary battery tray (see illustration).

7   For the left-side fender, remove the windshield washer reservoir (see Section 11).

8   Remove the lower hood hinge bolts (see illustration).

Note: *If you are only changing one fender, just take the hood hinge off of that side and support the edge of the hood with a thick pile of rags and secure the hood from moving out of place. If you are taking both fenders off, remove the hood entirely.*

16.9a Underhood fuse box with support bracket removed

16.9b Lift fuse box out by rotating the lever arms on both ends of the fuse box

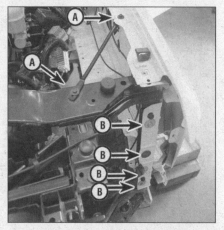

16.11a Front of the fender with grille and bumper removed

A   Front cross brace
B   Front fender bolts

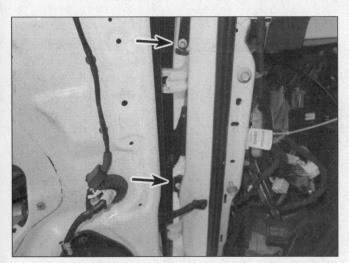

16.11b These bolts for the fender are reached with the door open

16.11c Lower fender bolt. It can be accessed after the fender protector is removed

9   On the left-side fender, remove the bracket securing the underhood fuse box to the fender (see illustrations).

10   Remove the fender liner (see Section 17).

11   Remove the bolts securing the fender to the frame (see illustrations).

12   Installation is the reverse of removal.

17   Fender liner - removal and installation

1   Loosen the lug nuts to the front wheel on the side you're going to work on.

2   Raise and support the vehicle securely on jackstands, then remove the wheel.

3   Remove the two screws securing the lower rear paint protector trim plate.

4   Remove the screws that secure the fender liner to the fender and inner body (see illustration).

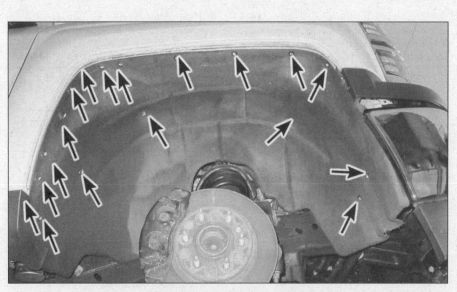

17.4 Fender liner screw locations

18.3 Cowling front fasteners

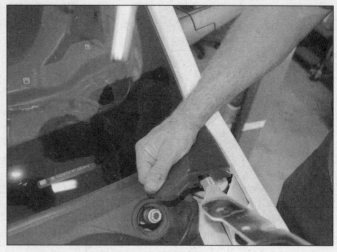

18.4 The end sections of the cowl cover snap in place without fasteners

19.2a Release handle trim removal

19.2b Grab handle trim removal

19.3 Carefully pry the trim panel off to expose the screws

5   Pull down on the lower inside edges of the liner and pull it away from the fender. Then, carefully warp the liner enough to remove it from the wheelwell.

6   Installation is the reverse of removal.

18   Cowl cover - removal and installation

1   Mark the position of both windshield wiper blades on the windshield using tape or a grease pencil. Then remove the cowling rubber gasket by pulling it off of the edge of the cowling grille.

2   Remove the wiper arms and the radio antenna on the right side, if equipped (see Chapter 12).

3   Remove the retaining clips at the front of the cowl and the plastic fastener in the center (see illustration).

4   Remove the outer edge of the cowl cover by pulling up and off (see illustration).

5   Lift up on the cowl cover to remove the windshield washer hose and coupler, then detach the cowl grille from the vehicle.

6   Installation is the reverse of removal. Make sure to align the wiper blades with the marks made during removal.

19   Door trim panels - removal and installation

Power window door panel removal

1   On models with power door locks and/or power windows, disconnect the cable from the negative battery terminal (see Chapter 5).

2   Remove the trim panel from the inside release handle and from the inside, grab handle area to expose the screws behind them. Remove the screws (see illustrations).

3   Remove the side trim from the arm rest area. Use a flat-bladed trim tool to pry the

side trim off by working around the edges of the trim until all the clips are free, then remove the side trim (see illustration).

4   After removing the side trim panel inside the arm rest trim area are the remaining screws. One in front and two near the grab handle area. Remove the screws (see illustrations).

5   On some of the models you'll find two screws at the bottom edge of the door panel near the middle section. Remove these two screws (see illustration).

6   With a flat-bladed trim tool, start to loosen the door panel from the door by working around the lower edges then up each side and across the bottom edge (see illustration).

7   Lift the door up off of the door lock stem and then tilt it out in order to gain access to the electrical connections and inside door handle release cable (see illustrations).

Note: *Before reinstalling the door panel, check that all the plastic push clips are installed on the door panel and not in the door.*

8   Installation is the reverse of removal.

19.4a Grab handle screw locations

19.4b Front door panel fastener location

19.5 Remove the lower screws securing the panel to the door

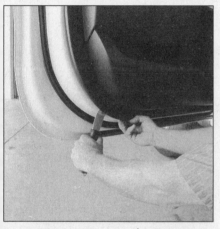

19.6 Start in the corner of the panel and work your way around until all the fasteners are free

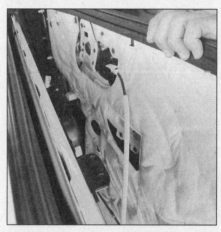

19.7a Pull the door panel away far enough to get to the electrical connectors and release cable

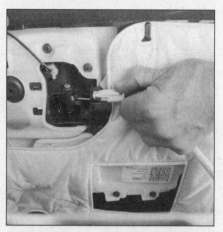

19.7b Press in on the release cable clip to remove it, then work the cable out of the slot in the inner release mechanism

Manual window door panel removal

9   All the basic steps as listed in the power window door panel are the same for the non-power window vehicles except for the manual window crank lever.

Note: *The window crank arm is held on with a retaining clip in the shape of a horseshoe. It requires a special tool to remove it or a hook to reach behind the crank lever to release the clip.*

Tip: *If you don't have access to a window crank removal tool an old mechanic's trick is to use a shop rag instead. By holding on to two corners of the shop rag slide it under the crank lever with the lever handle facing downward. Then, by using a sawing motion pull up and alternate pulling on the two corners of the shop rag. The shop rag will grab the edges of the retaining clip and pull it off of the handle. When reinstalling the crank handle put the retaining clip into the groove in the handle and push it back onto the door.*

10   After removing the window crank handle follow the same outlined procedures for the power window door panel.

11   Otherwise, installation is the reverse of removal.

Rear doors (if applicable)

12   Pry the trim covers off and remove all door trim panel retaining screws. There are two screws at the grab handle area of the armrest and one behind the inside release lever.

13   Carefully pry the power window switch out of the armrest, disconnect the electrical connector, then remove the switch, if equipped. For manual windows, remove the window crank arm.

14   On some models there are two screws on the bottom edge near the center of the door panel. Remove these screws.

15   Pry the trim panels from each side of the door by starting at the bottom corner and working your way around to the top edge.

16   Lift the door panel off of the door lock stem and tilt out far enough to gain access to any remaining electrical connectors. Disconnect them and set the door panel to the side for reinstalling later.

17   Installation is the reverse of removal.

20   Door - removal, installation and adjustment

Note: *Refer to Section 6 for general information on removing trim panels.*

1   Remove the trim panel/fuse box cover from the left side of the instrument panel.

2   On front doors, remove the appropriate door sill trim and kick panel.

3   Disconnect the electrical connectors for the door wiring harness from the passenger compartment side. Then pull the wire harness and the rubber grommet from the passenger compartment side of the door hinge area.

Tip: *You can push the grommet and wire harness into the door cavity where it can remain until you reattach or replace the door.*

4   Place a jack under the door or have an assistant on hand to support it when the hinge bolts are removed.

Note: *If a jack is used, place a rag between it and the door to protect the door's painted surfaces.*

5   Remove the door check strap retaining fastner

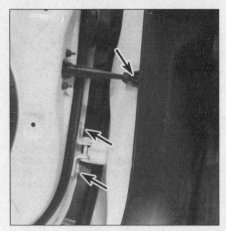

20.6 Lower door hinge bolts and door check strap locations

21.1 Peel the watershield from the door, being careful not to tear it

21.2 Remove the actuator rod

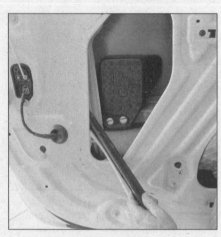

21.3a Slide the felt track guide out of the door

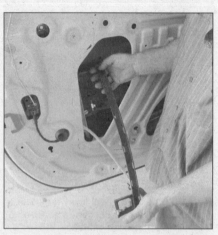

21.3b Move the regulator track out of the way to gain access to the latch housing

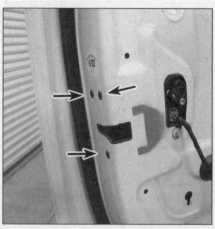

21.4 Door latch mounting fasteners

6   Remove the hinge fasteners and carefully lift off the door (see illustration).

7   Installation is the reverse of removal. All components can be transferred to a replacement door if necessary.

8   Rear doors are removed and installed as described above for front doors. The door is attached to the body B pillar; the electrical connector is just inside the pillar and can be disconnected after removing the rubber conduit. On some models the connector is under the B pillar. You'll have to remove the B pillar to gain access to the connector.

9   On access type doors for extended cab models, open the door fully and pry the plastic trim from around the hinges rearward, then remove it. Detach the rubber conduit and disconnect any electrical connectors, if equipped. Remove the hinge-to-door bolts leaving the hinges attached to the C pillar.

21   Door latch, lock cylinder and handles - removal and installation

Note: *Refer to Section 6 for general information on removing trim panels.*

Door latch

1   Raise the window completely, then remove the door trim panel and watershield (see illustration), if applicable.

2   Detach the actuator rods from the lock cylinder (see illustration).

3   To gain access to the inside of the door and the door latch connections, remove the rear window guide track. If needed, remove the rear window regulator track by unbolting it and moving it out of the way (see illustrations).

4   Remove the three Torx-head mounting

screws, then remove the latch from the door (see illustration). Disconnect the rods (if not done previously) and any electrical connectors. Detach the inside release lever cable, then separate the latch completely.

5   Installation is the reverse of the removal procedure.

Lock cylinder

6   Remove the door panel (see Section 19) and watershield.

7   Remove the door outside handle (see Step 11).

8   Remove the hidden screw that is now exposed with the outside handle removed. Reach inside the door and slip the outside latch assembly from its retainer. Then from the rear side of the latch assembly press down on the lock cylinder retainer and release the cylinder.

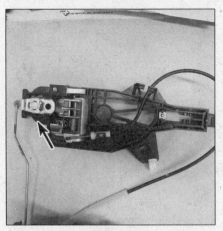

21.9 Outside latch assembly showing the door lock cylinder

21.12a Pry the protective cap off . . .

21.12b . . . then remove the screw

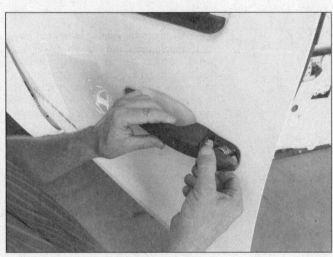

21.13 Remove the end cap

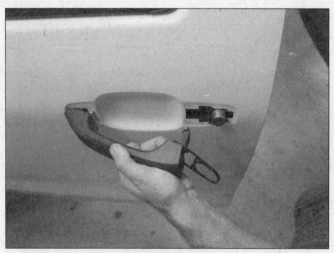

21.14 Slide the handle forward to free the front section

9   With the retainer released, pull the lock cylinder from the latch assembly (see illustration).

10   Installation is the reverse of removal.

Outside handle

11   Open the appropriate door to gain access to the edge of the door.

12   Remove the plastic protective cap and remove the screw hidden underneath (see illustrations).

13   Remove the end cap from the outside handle by prying it off (see illustration).

14   Lift the back section of the handle up slightly, then slide it forward to disengage the front hook. Then remove the handle (see illustration).

15   Installation is the reverse of the removal.

Inside release handle

16   Remove the door trim panel (see Section 19).

17   Remove any electrical connections attached to the inside door handle assembly.

18   Five screws secure the inside release handle to the door panel. Remove the screws and remove the actuator rod. Remove the inside handle assembly.

19   Transfer any switches or components from the old inside release handle to the replacement piece.

20   Installation is the reverse of removal.

Latch strikers

21   To make minor door adjustments for latch alignment, the bolts on the latch striker (which is mounted opposite the latch) can be loosened and moved up, down, or left and right. The striker should be adjusted so that the latch aligns perfectly. Re-tighten the striker mounting bolts and check for proper latch operation.

Caution: *The striker mounting plate in the body can fall if both mounting bolts are removed at the same time. If replacing the striker, make sure that one mounting bolt is in the mounting hole at all times.*

Note: *If, after adjusting the striker, the door still does not align up correctly or drags across the striker as it closes, the door is most likely sagging from the front hinges, the body alignment, or the door/a pillar is bent.*

22   On access doors (extended-cab pickups), there are two latches and strikers for each door.

23   The striker for the upper latch is attached to the vehicle's roof. To access it for removal or adjustment, remove the trim piece around it.

Note: *A common problem with the door is sagging. Over time the hinges will wear down or just from the weight of the door it will cause the door to be out of alignment with the latch. Sometimes even adjusting the latch the door still will not close properly or line up very well. There is a tool that will relocate the door to a more aligned position. The tool is very expensive but can be found at most body shops.*

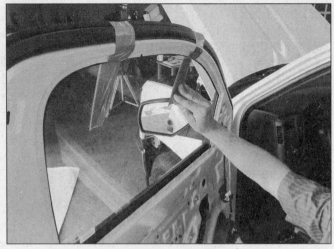

22.2 Tape the window in the fully up position

22.3 Window-to-regulator bolts

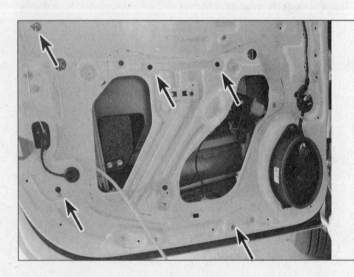

23.4 Window regulator bolts

22 Door window glass - removal and installation

Note: *Removal and installation of the window glass is essentially the same for front and rear doors, including access doors on extended-cab pick-ups.*

1   Remove the door trim panel (see Section 19) and the vapor barrier.

Tip: *Temporarily reconnect the window switch or the window crank handle on manual windows (without the retaining clip) to move the window up or down.*

2   Raise the regulator until the glass track bolts are visible in the door openings. Tape the glass securely to the window frame to support it in the raised position (see illustration).

3   Remove the bolts that secure the glass to the window tracks (see illustration).

4   Pry the inner door seal off of the door to make room for the window glass to slide out of the door. Set it aside for later reinstalling.

5   Lower the regulator to the bottom position while the glass is supported in the raised position.

6   Remove the tape and tilt the front of the glass down and then back upward to maneuver it out of the window opening.

Note: *When reinstalling the glass be sure to have the glass within the front and back felt tracks.*

7   Installation is the reverse of the removal procedure.

23 Window regulator - removal and installation

Note: *This procedure applies to front and rear door window regulators.*

Tip: *Depending on where you purchase the regulator replacement assembly it may or may not come with a new motor. Switching the motor is fairly straight forward. Just remove the three bolts from the motor and position the motor in the same location on the replacement regulator assembly.*

1   Remove the door trim panel (see Section 19) and watershield.

2   Reconnect the window switch and lower (or raise) the window to about the halfway point. Look into the door and watch the window track move to a position where you can easily reach the bolts that secure the glass to the window track. Stop the window at that point and disconnect the switch and remove the negative battery terminal.

Tip: *If you are changing out the regulator because it has jammed or the cable has snapped the window may not move electrically. In that case, use a good strong pair of wire cutters and cut the regulator drive cables. Then you should be able to manually lift the window to the desired position to remove the bolts retaining the window glass to the regulator tracks.*

Note: *The window regulator assembly consists of two guides and cables. When withdrawing the assembly from the door, push the two guides toward each other to collapse the assembly for easier removal. For access type rear doors on extended cab pick-up models, the regulator consists of one guide but removal is basically the same.*

3   Remove the door window glass (see Section 22), or tape it up out of the way.

4   Remove the five bolts that secure the window regulator to the door and the two bolts (on the top edge) that secure the track guides to the door (see illustration).

5   Remove the regulator from the door.

Note: *It's always good to remember the orientation that you used to guide the regulator assembly out of the door and to copy that same orientation when reinstalling the replacement piece.*

6   Installation is the reverse of removal.

Rear sliding window regulator replacement

7   Slide both front seats to their most forward position. Remove the rear seat (if applicable).

8   If applicable, remove the rear passenger seat belt shoulder guide by lifting it up to

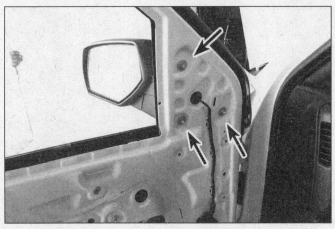

24.3 Remove the three outside mirror mounting nuts

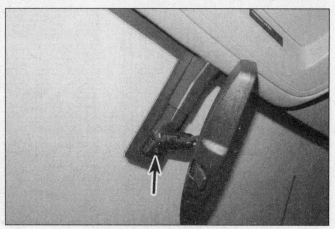

24.6 Mirror-to-base setscrew

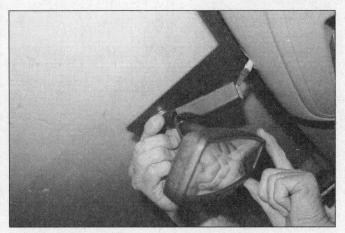

24.7a Lift up to remove the mirror from the base

24.7b Back side of the mirror assembly. Note the grooved opening for the base

release it from the molding.

9   If applicable, remove the rear passenger seat belt lower bolt that fastens the seat belt anchor plate to the body.

10   Remove the rear trim panel. (Panel is held on by pressure clips.)

11   Maneuver the seat belt through the rear trim panel and then remove the panel (if applicable).

Note: *On the four-door models, the rear panel trim is set behind the side trim panels. Remove the side trim panels also.*

12   Slide the window open about two inches. This reduces the amount of pressure on the cable ends and will make it easier to remove the cables.

Warning: *If the motor is jammed or the cable has snapped you'll need to cut the regulator cables with a strong pair of wire cutters in order to move the window.*

13   Locate the cable ends that are attached to the window track on either side of the window section. Then, by depressing the cable spring and pulling on the cable end, release the cable end from the track guide.

14   Unbolt the regulator assembly from the cab.

15   Disconnect the electrical connection to the motor and remove the regulator assembly.

16   Installation is the reverse of removal.

Slide window motor removal

17   Follow the procedure for removing the regulator assembly.

18   The motor is held onto the regulator with three screws. Remove the screws. Remember the motor-to-regulator orientation for reinstalling before lifting the motor off of the regulator assembly.

19   Installation is the reverse of removal.

---

24   Mirrors - removal and installation

Outside mirrors

1   Remove the door trim panel (see Section 19).

2   On models with power mirrors, follow the

wiring harness to the electrical connector and disconnect it.

3   Remove the nuts and detach the mirror from the door (see illustration).

Note: *Be prepared to hold onto the mirror as you remove the last nut.*

4   Installation is the reverse of removal.

Inside mirror

5   On mirrors with electronic components, disconnect the electrical connector by first removing the trim around the mirror. Push up on the trim and then away from the window.

6   Remove the setscrew (see illustration).

7   Slide the mirror assembly up and off of the base (see illustrations).

8   Installation is the reverse of removal.

Note: *If the support base for the mirror has come off the windshield, it can be reattached with a special mirror adhesive kit that is available at most auto parts stores. Clean the glass and support the base thoroughly. Follow the directions on the adhesive package, allowing the base to bond overnight before attaching the mirror.*

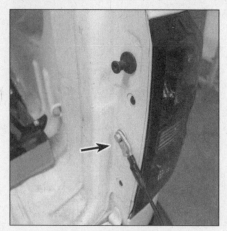

25.1 Lift the spring retainer up and slide the cable end off the pin

25.2 Lower the tailgate enough to align the open area on the right side hinge pin pocket with the straight sides of the pin, then lift the tailgate and slide it to the right and off the vehicle

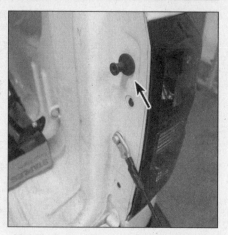

25.4 The tailgate latch strikers (right side shown) can be loosened with a Torx bit to adjust their position slightly

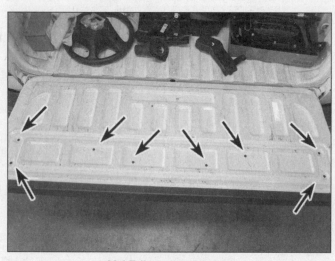

26.1 Tailgate panel screws

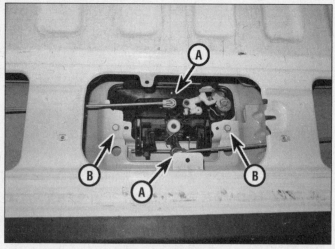

26.3 Rotate the plastic retaining clips off of the rods to detach them from the handle levers and remove the bolts

A   Plastic retaining clips for the actuator rods
B   Two bolts secure the latch handle to the tailgate

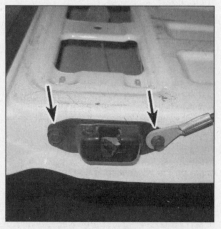

26.6 Remove the bolts to the latch

25   Tailgate - removal and installation

1   Open the tailgate and detach the retaining cables (see illustration).
2   The right-side hinge-pin aligns with a slot in the hinge pocket (about 45-degrees). Lift the tailgate out of the pocket (see illustration). With the help of an assistant to support the weight, withdraw the left hinge pin from the body and remove the tailgate from the vehicle.
3   Installation is the reverse of removal.
4   If alignment is necessary, the latches (one on each side) can be loosened and moved and/or the latch striker pins can be moved slightly for the best tailgate fit (see illustration).

26   Tailgate latch and handle - removal and installation

1   Remove the tailgate inner panel screws (see illustration).
2   Carefully pry the watershield from the inner panel enclosure.
3   Rotate the plastic retaining clips off the control rods and detach the rods from the handle (see illustration), and remove the bolts securing the latch handle to the tailgate.
4   Installation is the reverse of removal.

Tailgate latch

5   Lower the tailgate.
6   Remove the bolts securing the latch to the tailgate, then pull it out to disconnect the actuator rod from the latch (see illustration).
7   Installation is the reverse of removal.

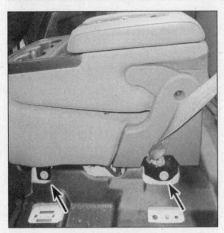

27.10 Console mounting bolts - left side (seat has been removed for clarity)

27.14 Working from a corner, gently pry the center trim from the overhead console

27.15 Turn the trim over to disconnect the electrical connectors

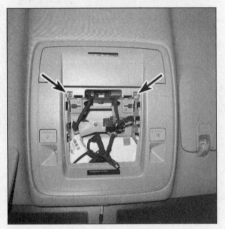

27.16a Mounting fasteners for the front overhead console

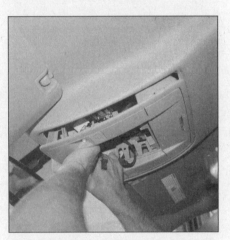

27.16b Pull down with even pressure on the left and right sides to release the remaining fasteners

27.17 Turn the overhead console over to disconnect the electrical connectors

27   Center console and overhead console - removal and installation

Note: *Refer to Section 6 for general information on removing trim panels.*

Full center floor console

1   Pry the center console trim panel off with a flat bladed trim tool. Start at a corner and work your way around until all the fasteners have been released. Then, remove the trim panel.
2   Move both seats as far forward as possible. Then, using a flat bladed trim tool pry the rear edge of the side panels loose.
3   The driver's side panel is snapped in place only in the back section. Slide the side panel rearward to remove it.
4   The passenger side panel is held in place with pressure clips in the rear section and across the top edge. Use a flat bladed trim tool to release the clips, then remove the panel.

5   Remove the two screws securing the center console to the center part of the dash panel. This is located under the upper panel trim you previously removed.
6   Pull back the carpet to expose the four screws securing the back part of the center console to the body. This is located on the rear lower section on each side.
7   Tilt the back of the console toward the dash and disconnect the electrical connectors.
8   Lift the center console and pull toward the rear of the vehicle to remove it.
9   Installation is the reverse of removal.

Half center console
Note: *The half console (or partial console) doesn't go all the way up to the dash but ends at the edge of the front seats.*
10   Slide the front seats back as far as possible and remove the front bolts (see illustration).
11   Slide the front seats as far forward as possible and remove the rear bolts.
12   Lift the console up far enough to dis-

connect the electrical connectors and then remove the console.
13   Installation is the reverse of removal.

Overhead console
Front
14   Pry the overhead console center trim off with a flat bladed trim tool (see illustration).
15   Disconnect the electrical connectors (see illustration).
16   Remove the two mounting screws, then pull the overhead console down to release the remaining clips (see illustrations).
17   Disconnect the electrical connectors (see illustration).
18   Installation is the reverse of removal.

Rear
19   If equipped with a DVD player, remove the mounting screws.
20   Pull or pry the console directly down to release its retainers.
21   Unplug the electrical connectors and remove the console.
22   Installation is the reverse of removal.

28.2a Working with two flat trim tools makes the job easier. Start in the middle where it is more flexible

28.2b Work your way to the edges by applying slight pressure on the trim with the trim tool

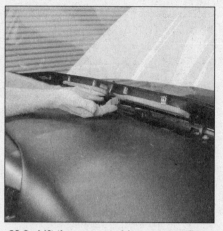

28.2c Lift the nearest side to you up first, disconnect the electrical connections and then pull it away from the windshield

28.6 A shop rag works well to keep from scratching or damaging the surfaces around the dash as you remove the instrument panel hood

28.12 Carefully pry the edges of the vent assembly to remove it

28.19 Carefully pry the center trim bezel off with a flat trim tool

28   Dash trim panels and interior trim - removal and installation

Warning: *The models covered by this manual are equipped with a Supplemental Restraint System (SRS), more commonly known as airbags. Always disable the airbag system before working in the vicinity of any airbag system components to avoid the possibility of accidental deployment of the airbags, which could cause personal injury (see Chapter 12).*
Note: *Refer to Section 6 for general information on removing trim panels.*

Defrost vent trim

1   Remove the A pillar trim from both sides of the vehicle.
2   Using a flat bladed trim tool carefully pry the corner edge of the defroster trim panel up. Then, work your way across and pry up each of the pressure clips all the way to the other side (see illustrations).
3   Disconnect the electrical connections and remove the trim panel.
4   To install, attach the electrical connec-

tions and then align the clips to their respective locations. Now press the trim back into place with firm hand pressure.
5   Reinstall the A pillar trim panels.

Instrument cluster hood

6   A flat bladed trim tool works best to pry the edges up while working around each leading edge of the instrument panel hood trim. Once all the clips are free the panel can be lifted off (see illustration).
7   To install, line up the clips and press back into place.

Driver's side switch trim plate (headlight switch bezel)

Note: *The headlight switch (bezel) trim can be removed without taking the entire vent assembly off on some models.*
8   Using a flat bladed trim tool release the pressure clips by applying pressure near the corners of the trim.
9   Disconnect the electrical connectors and remove the trim panel.
10   Installation is the reverse of removal.

Driver's side vent assembly

11   Remove the fuse box cover from the driver's side.
12   Carefully pry the trim off with a flat bladed trim tool (see illustration).
13   Disconnect the electrical connectors.
14   If replacing the trim panel, transfer all the electrical components before installing.
15   Installation is the reverse of removal.

Passenger's side dash end trim panel

16   Remove the right side fuse box cover.
17   Carefully pry the trim off with a flat bladed trim tool. The passenger's side comes off similar to the driver's side end trim.
18   Installation is the reverse of removal.

Center bezel

19   Carefully pry the trim off with a flat bladed trim tool by starting in a corner and working around the edges (see illustration).
20   Installation is the reverse of removal.

28.23 Instrument cluster trim panel screws

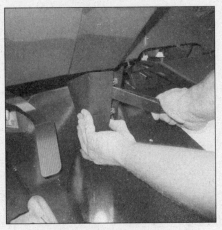

28.26 Pry the trim from the support bracket with a flat trim tool

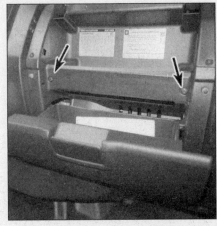

28.29 Upper screw location

28.30 Lower screw location

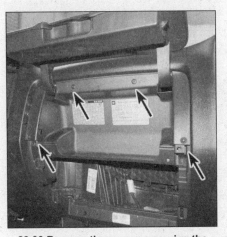

28.33 Remove the screws securing the storage box to the dash

28.34 Gently pry at the edges to free the storage box

Instrument cluster trim

21   Remove the instrument cluster hood trim (see Step 6).

22   Remove the driver's-side knee bolster trim panel (see Step 41).

23   Remove the three screws retaining the top edge of the instrument cluster trim in place (see illustration).

24   Carefully pry the bottom section free with a flat bladed trim tool.

25   Installation is the reverse of removal.

Instrument panel lower trim

26   The lower panel trim is in the center of the vehicle covering the support brackets to the dash on either side (see illustration).

27   Carefully pry the lower trim panel off with a flat bladed trim tool starting near a corner and working from the top to the bottom.

28   Installation is the reverse of removal.

Glove box

29   Open the glove box door and remove the two screws located in opposite upper corners (see illustration).

30   Close the glove box door and remove the two screws located on the underneath side of the glove box assembly (see illustration).

31   Reopen the glove box and pry the glove box assembly free with a flat bladed trim tool.

32   Installation is the reverse of removal.

Upper glove box storage

33   Open up the storage box and remove the screws (see illustration).

34   Pry the storage box out with a flat trim tool (see illustration).

35   Installation is the reverse of removal.

Instrument panel center storage area

36   Open the center storage door and remove the screw in the upper center area (see illustration).

37   Close the door and remove the two screws from the bottom section. One on each corner (see illustration).

38   Installation is the reverse of removal.

28.36 Screw location for the center storage

28.37 Lower center storage area screws plus the accessory outlet door retaining screw

28.41 Knee bolster screws

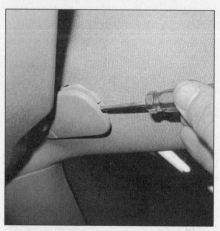

28.44a Start prying from the outside edge, then work toward the pivot point

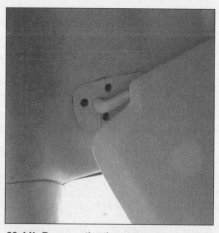

28.44b Remove the three screws securing the sun visor to the roof

28.45a A small flat screwdriver works best to remove the trim cover

Passenger's side lower closeout trim panel

39   Remove the four screws securing the trim panel to the bottom of the dash assembly.

40   Installation is the reverse of removal.

Driver's side knee bolster

41   Remove the two lower screws located near the bottom edges of the knee bolster (see illustration).

42   Carefully pry the top edge free with a flat bladed trim tool.

43   Installation is the reverse of removal.

Sun visors

44   With a flat bladed trim tool or equivalent remove the trim cap from the sun visor pivot. Then remove the screws (see illustrations).

45   Remove the trim covering the bolt to the sun visor clip. Then remove the bolt securing the sun visor clip in place (see illustrations).

Note: *On some models there may also be a clip retaining the visor clip to the headliner. If so, the headliner will have to be lowered for access to remove the retaining clip.*

46   Installation is the reverse of removal.

Door sill trim

47   Grasp the edges of the door sill and pull them free from the retaining clips (see illustration).

48   Occasionally a clip or two will stay on the body section. Pry them off and reattach them to the door sill.

49   Installation is otherwise the reverse of removal.

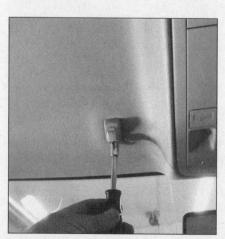

28.45b Remove the bolt, then pull the sun visor clip free

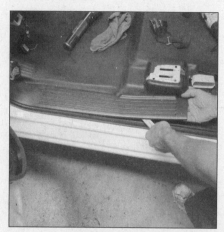

28.47 Pull the door sill trim firmly to remove

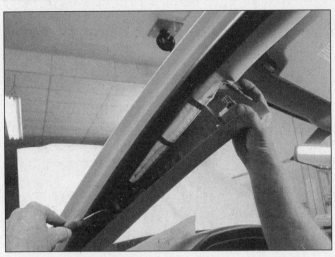

28.50 Pull straight away from the A pillar to remove the trim

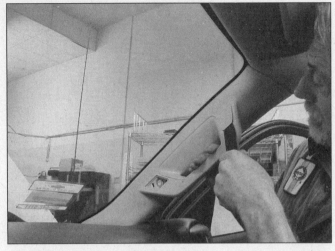

28.52 Remove the grab handle first to remove the A pillar on the passenger's side

A pillar trim

50   Driver's side A pillar is removed by grasping the edges and pulling toward the center of the vehicle (see illustration).

51   GM recommends that you replace the trim clip each time you remove the A pillar.

52   Passenger's side A pillar requires removing the grab handle first (see illustration).

53   Remove the protective caps from the grab handle and remove the two bolts securing the grab handle to the A pillar.

54   Pull the trim inwards to remove the passenger's side A pillar trim. (There is no retaining clip on this side.)

55   Installation is the reverse of removal.

B pillar trim

56   Remove the door sill trim panels (see Step 47).

57   Pull the lower B pillar trim panel off by prying along the outer edges with a flat bladed trim tool.

58   Lift the cap covering the seat belt anchor.

59   Remove the seat belt anchor bolt.

60   Pull the upper B pillar trim off by prying along the edges with a flat bladed trim tool.

61   Installation is the reverse of removal.

Rear seat side panel trim

62   Remove rear seat (see Section 33).

63   Remove the upper window garnish trim panel by prying the edge up with a flat bladed trim tool.

64   Remove the seat belt anchor bolt.

65   Pull the rear side panel off by prying near the edges with a flat bladed trim tool.

66   Slide the seat belt through the opening in the side panel and remove the panel.

67   Installation is the reverse of removal.

Liftgate interior trim

68   Remove the liftgate struts by lifting the locking tabs.

69   Remove the window trim. There are nine molding clip retainers holding it in place. Gently pry near a clip as you work your way around the molding.

70   Remove the four panel screws securing the lower section to the liftgate.

71   Pull the liftgate trim panel at the edges to release the remaining retaining fasteners.

72   There are 12 retaining clips and finish panel clips that must be removed.

73   Lift the trim panel off of the gate and disconnect the electrical connections.

74   Installation is the reverse of removal.

29   Dash - removal and installation

1   Disconnect the battery and wait about 10 minutes for any residual power to be depleted in the airbag system before disconnecting any electrical components.

Tip: *FOR COMPLETE DASH ASSEMBLY REMOVAL - A good reference tip to keep in mind when removing the entire dash as an assembly are the type of screws used. From the factory all the screws necessary to remove the entire dash assembly as one piece are brass colored. All the screws for the various subassemblies that make up the completed dash assembly such as the dash carriage, outlet vents, and crash support bar will have black screws attaching them. Black screws are also used for components as well as such components as the instrument cluster and radio. This color difference does not include the large bolts at the ends of the support bracket (bar) or for the bottom center section bolts. Those are regular bolts and will need to be unbolted to remove the dash assembly. The dash as-*

sembly was made to be installed at the factory as one complete unit and you can remove it the same way.

Dash overlay removal

Note: *The steps below are to remove the individual components that make up the dash assembly. They do not need to be separated if you are trying to get to the heater core or evaporator core. Remove the dash as an assembly rather than by sections. Just follow the tool tip above and only remove the brass screws and the main bolts for the crash support bar.*

2   Disconnect the cable from the negative terminal of the battery (see Chapter 5). Remove the center console (see Section 28).

3   Remove the center storage compartment (see Section 28).

4   Remove the instrument panel lower center trim panels (see Section 28).

5   Remove the defrost trim panel (see Section 28).

Note: *If equipped with dash speakers or the navigation system, disconnect the dash speakers and the navigation signal splitter.*

6   Remove the instrument cluster (see Chapter 12).

7   Remove the driver's side trim/vent panel (see Section 28).

8   Remove the steering column (see Chapter 10).

9   Remove the radio assembly and/or the audio disc player, whichever your vehicle is equipped with (see Chapter 12).

10   Remove the center air vents (three screws hold each of them in place). After removing the screws, pull the vents free from the radio area of the dash.

11   If applicable, remove the stability control switch (below the center vents and radio area).

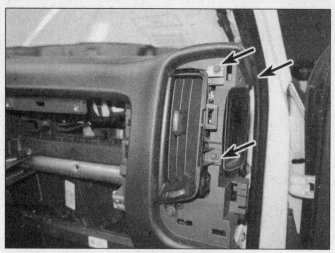

29.14 Passenger's side vent screws, dash end screws and defrost duct vent

29.16 Keep track of the screws and the various bolts for reinstalling

29.18 Center section screw locations

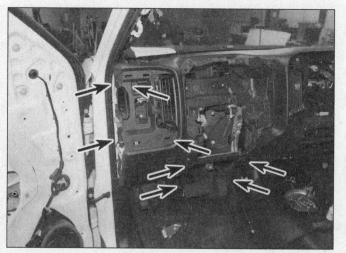

29.21 Driver's side dash end screws and knee bolster screw locations

12   Remove the upper storage compartment and the glove box (see Section 28).

13   Remove the passenger's side end trim panel (see Section 28).

14   Remove the side window defrost ducts from inside the end trim area (one per each side) (see illustration).

15   Remove the A pillars trim (see Section 28).

16   From inside the glove box area remove the seven screws securing the dash overlay assembly to the support bracket (see illustration).

17   From inside the glove box area remove the two bolts securing the passenger's side airbag to the support bracket.

18   From inside the radio area, remove the four screws that are located where the radio would be (see illustration).

19   There are also two screws located in the center storage compartment area that need to be removed.

20   From inside the instrument cluster area remove the four screws securing the dash overlay to the support bracket.

21   In the driver's side vent area there are two screws that need to be removed as well as two screws on each end of the dash. Remove these from the driver's and passenger's sides (see illustration).

22   From the knee bolster area remove the four bolts securing the dash to the support brackets.

23   While in that area, disconnect the diagnostic connector from the retainer mounted on the edge of the lower portion of the dash.

24   Remove the four screws across the top edge in the defrost trim panel area.

25   At this point a helper will be beneficial.

26   Grasp the dash and carefully jiggle it loose by about an inch or two.

27   Now look underneath for the electrical connectors that are coming out with it. One connector on the passenger's side, and one

main connector on the driver's side. There may be some wire retainers attached in the middle section that will need to be removed as well. Disconnect the connectors.

28   Pull the dash out a bit farther and check for any other connectors you may have missed.

29   Now the complete dash overlay can be removed from the vehicle.

Dash carriage removal and installation

30   Remove the dash overlay (see previous section).

31   Remove the three main carrier bolts: one on either end and one in the middle of the carriage.

32   Remove the four bolts that secure the carriage to the support bracket. You'll have to reach over the carriage to get to them.

33   Locate the remaining screw in the center of the carriage that secures the carriage to

29.35a Driver's side fasteners. Dash overlay has been removed for clarity

29.35b Passenger's side fasteners. Dash overlay has been removed for clarity

the support bar. Brace the carriage and then remove the remaining screw.

34   Installation is reverse of removal.

Support bar removal and installation

35   There are two bolts on each end and one bolt on either side of the center section (passenger's and driver's sides) near the bottom edges, and two bolts on the top edge about where the instrument cluster would be (see illustrations).

36   Remove the bolts and carefully guide the support bracket out of the car.

Caution: *Be careful removing and installing the support bracket. The edges can be extremely sharp.*

37   Installation is the reverse of removal. Tighten support bracket bolts to 16 ft. lbs. when reinstalling.

Mechanic's shortcut

Note: *If you are trying to get to the heater core or evaporator core you will need to remove the dash assembly. A mechanic's shortcut is to only remove what is needed and not take the entire assembly out of the car. The following steps are a shortcut to getting to the HVAC unit.*

38   Remove the A pillar trim from the driver's and passenger's sides (Section 28).

39   Remove the defrost trim and remove the screws across the top edge of the dash (Section 28).

40   Remove the instrument cluster, then reach in and remove the two upper bolts that secure the dash assembly to the support bracket and the frame (see Chapter 12).

41   Remove the center console (if it is the full size console). Then remove the lower center trim panels (Section 27).

42   Remove the four bolts securing the dash support bar to the lower center section brackets.

30.1 A quick but firm pull will remove the tilt lever from the steering column

43   Remove both the driver's and passenger's sides fuse box lids.

44   On the passenger's side remove the two bolts securing the support bar to the A pillar area (see Section 28).

45   On the driver's side unscrew (but do not remove) the two bolts until just a thread or two are still holding.

46   Lock the steering wheel in place so it does not move. Mark the position of the steering column shaft to the upper intermediate shaft, then remove the bolt securing the intermediate shaft. Slide the shaft up and off of the steering column shaft (see Chapter 10).

47   Disconnect the electrical connections on the driver's side and passenger's side, and the radio antenna lead coupler on the passenger's side.

48   From the passenger's side grasp the dash assembly and lift up slightly. You may have to jiggle it a bit, but if it doesn't budge you've probably missed a bolt or a screw. Go back and recheck for any screw you might have missed.

49   Once the dash assembly is lifted off of

the passenger's side bracket, the driver's side bolts that you loosened previously will act like a hinge, allowing the dash to swing out and toward the passenger seat. Move it out far enough so you can squeeze between the dash assembly and the windshield to get to the HVAC unit.

50   Installation is the reverse of removal.

---

30   Steering column covers - removal and installation

Warning: *The models covered by this manual are equipped with a Supplemental Restraint System (SRS), more commonly known as airbags. Always disable the airbag system before working in the vicinity of any airbag system components to avoid the possibility of accidental deployment of the airbags, which could cause personal injury (see Chapter 12).*

1   If equipped with a tilt-column, remove the tilt lever knob by pulling it straight out from the column (see illustration).

30.2a Removing the upper steering column cover

30.2b Removing the lower steering column cover

2   Gently pry the upper and lower halves of the steering column apart with a flat bladed trim tool or equivalent (see illustrations).
3   Installation is the reverse of removal.

31 Headliner - removal and installation

1   The models covered by this manual are equipped with a Supplemental Restraint System (SRS), more commonly known as airbags. Always disable the airbag system before working in the vicinity of any airbag system components to avoid the possibility of accidental deployment of the airbags, which could cause personal injury (see Chapter 12). **Note:** *All models are equipped with two front airbags, formally known as the Supplemental Inflatable Restraint (SIR) system. This system is designed to protect the driver and the front seat passenger from serious injury in the event of a frontal collision. It consists of an array of external and internal (inside the SDM) information sensors (decelerometers), the Inflatable Restraint Sensing and Diagnostic Module (SDM), the inflator modules (a driver's airbag in the steering wheel and a passenger's airbag in the dash) and the wiring and connectors tying all these components together. An optional pair of side-impact airbags, also known as roof rail or side curtain airbags, is available for protection against side impacts. The side-impact airbags, if equipped, are located along the left and right edges of the headliner, above the doors.*
2   Disconnect the cable from the negative battery terminal (see Chapter 5).
3   Remove the A pillar trim (see Section 28).
4   Remove the B pillar trim (see Section 28).
5   Remove the rear side trim panels (see Section 28).
6   Remove the sun visors (see Section 28).
7   Remove the roof rail assist handles by

unscrewing the two fasteners that secure it to the roof.
8   Remove the overhead center console (if equipped) (see Section 28).
9   Remove the rear dome light fixture (if equipped).
10   Slide the front seats as far forward as possible and lean the seats back as far as possible.
11   Pull the door seal trim down from around the headliner area.
12   There are two retainer clips on the rear section of the headliner that help hold it up. It's not necessary to remove them, but if needed, unscrew them and set aside for reinstalling.
13   Lower the headliner down and check for any wires that may have been glued to the back side. Pull them off and leave them in place. Disconnect any electrical connectors that lead to the dome light fixtures. The connectors are usually at the edge of the headliner.
14   With the aid of a helper guide the headliner out through a door. On the four-door models, use one of the rear doors.
15   Installation is the reverse of removal.

32 Sunroof - removal and installation

Sunroof shade

1   Remove the headliner (see Section 31).
2   Remove the two screws that secure the stops for the sunroof shade.
3   Pull the sunroof shade rearward to remove.
4   Installation is the reverse of removal.

Sunroof window

5   Open the sunroof to its full vent position.
6   Remove the side curtain trim by pulling in on the lower edge to release the top edge from the track guide.
7   Then pull inward on the top edge and

pull the trim out.
8   Locate the four screws that secure the window to the track. Remove the screws.
9   Lift the window out through the top.
10   Transfer the window seal to the replacement glass (if needed).
11   Installation is the reverse of removal.

Sunroof track

12   Remove the headliner (see Section 31).
13   Disconnect the electrical connector to the sun roof motor.
14   Pull the front and back water drain hoses off of the sunroof track assembly.
15   Loosen the 10 screws that secure the sun roof track to the roof.
16   With the assistance of a helper, finish taking out the screws while holding onto the assembly.
17   Carefully lower the sunroof and guide it out of the vehicle.
18   Installation is the reverse of removal. Tighten the sun roof track screws to 80 in-lbs (9 Nm).

33 Seats - removal and installation

Warning: *The models covered by this manual are equipped with a Supplemental Restraint System (SRS), more commonly known as airbags. Always disable the airbag system before working in the vicinity of any airbag system components to avoid the possibility of accidental deployment of the airbags, which could cause personal injury (see Chapter 12).*
Warning: *Some models are equipped with seat belt pre-tensioners, which are pyrotechnic (explosive) devices that tighten the seat belts during an impact of sufficient force. Always disable the airbag system before working in the vicinity of any restraint system component to avoid the possibility of accidental deployment of the seat belt pre-tensioners, which could cause personal injury (see Chapter 12).*

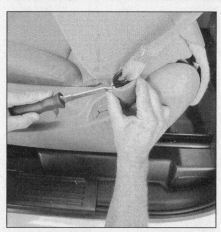

33.1 Remove the trim covers for access to the seat and seat belt mounting fasteners

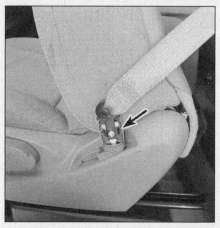

33.2 Location of the seat belt mounting bolt at the seat

33.3 Pull the trim panel straight out to remove

33.4 Mounting fasteners are under the trim plate (one on each seat rail)

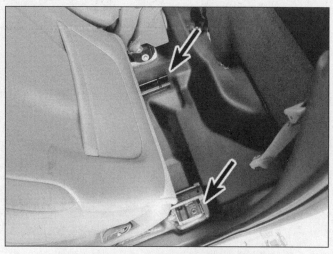

33.5 Location of the rear mounting fasteners

Note: *The removal of seats can be very awkward due to their size and weight. It is best to have an assistant help you with these procedures.*

Note: *Refer to Section 1 for general information on removing trim panels.*

Front seats

1   Remove the plastic trim covers to access the seat and seat belt mounting bolts (see illustration).

2   Detach the seat belt from the seat (see illustration).

3   Remove the side trim panel by grasping onto the edges and pulling straight off (see illustration).

4   Move the seat rearward, pull the plastic trim covering the inboard mounting fastener and remove the front mounting fasteners (see illustration).

5   Move the seat forward and remove the rear mounting fasteners (see illustration).

6   Disconnect the electrical connector then lift the seat out of the vehicle.

Note: *The center seat can only be removed when the seats on each side are removed first. Detach the electrical connector before lifting the center seat out of the vehicle.*

7   Installation is the reverse of the removal procedure.

Rear bench seat

8   The rear seat is removed as an assembly. Remove the seat belt anchor bolt.

9   Remove the seat bracket-to-floor fasteners and lift the rear seat assembly up and out.

Note: *The rear bench seat will have fewer mounting fasteners than the split type.*

10   With the floor mounting bolts removed, lift the assembly up to disengage the seat hooks from the body, then remove it.

Note: *The 60/40 bench-type seats can be divided if necessary.*

11   Installation is the reverse of the removal procedure.

Notes

Chapter 12
Chassis electrical system

Contents

1 General information

1   The electrical system is a 12-volt, negative ground type. Power for the lights and all electrical accessories is supplied by a lead/acid-type battery, which is charged by the alternator.

2   This chapter covers repair and service procedures for the various electrical components not associated with the engine. Information on the battery, alternator and starter motor can be found in Chapter 5.

3   It should be noted that when portions of the electrical system are serviced, the negative battery cable should be disconnected from the battery to prevent electrical shorts and/or fires.

2 Electrical troubleshooting - general information

1   A typical electrical circuit consists of an electrical component, any switches, relays, motors, fuses, fusible links or circuit breakers related to that component and the wiring and connectors that link the component to both the battery and the chassis. To help you pinpoint an electrical circuit problem, wiring diagrams are included at the end of this chapter.

2   Before tackling any troublesome electrical circuit, first study the appropriate wiring diagrams to get a complete understanding of what makes up that individual circuit. Noting whether other components related to the circuit are operating correctly, for instance, can often narrow down the location of potential

trouble spots. If several components or circuits fail at one time, chances are the problem is in a fuse or ground connection, because several circuits are often routed through the same fuse and ground connections.

3   Electrical problems usually stem from simple causes, such as loose or corroded connections, a blown fuse, a melted fusible link or a failed relay. Visually inspect the condition of all fuses, wires and connections in a problem circuit before troubleshooting the circuit.

4   If test equipment and instruments are going to be utilized, use the diagrams to plan ahead of time where you will make the necessary connections in order to accurately pinpoint the trouble spot.

5   For electrical troubleshooting, you'll need a circuit tester, voltmeter or a 12-volt bulb with

a set of test leads, a continuity tester and a jumper wire, preferably with a circuit breaker incorporated, which can be used to bypass electrical components (see illustrations). Before attempting to locate a problem with test instruments, use the wiring diagram(s) to decide where to make the connections.

Voltage checks

6   Voltage checks should be performed if a circuit is not functioning properly. Connect one lead of a circuit tester to either the negative battery terminal or a known good ground. Connect the other lead to a connector in the circuit being tested, preferably nearest to the battery or fuse (see illustration). If the tester bulb lights, voltage is present, which means that the part of the circuit between the connector and the battery is problem free. Continue checking the rest of the circuit in the same fashion. When you reach a point at which no voltage is present, the problem lies between that point and the last test point with voltage. The problem can usually be traced to a loose connection.
Note: Keep in mind that some circuits receive voltage only when the ignition key is in the ACC or RUN position.

Finding a short

7   One method of finding shorts in a live circuit is to remove the fuse and connect a test light in place of the fuse terminals (fabricate two jumper wires with small spade terminals, plug the jumper wires into the fuse box and connect the test light). There should be no voltage present in the circuit. Move the suspected wiring harness from side-to-side while watching the test light. If the bulb lights, there is a short to ground somewhere in that area, probably where the insulation has rubbed through.

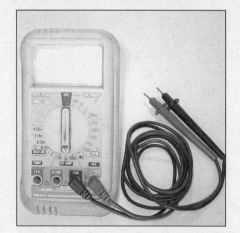

2.5a The most useful tool for electrical troubleshooting is a digital multimeter that can check volts, amps, and test continuity

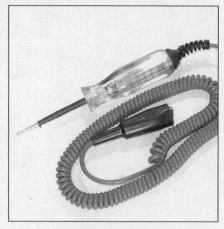

2.5b A simple test light is a very handy tool for testing voltage

Ground check

8   Perform a ground test to check whether a component is properly grounded. Disconnect the battery and connect one lead of a continuity tester or multimeter (set to the ohm scale), to a known good ground. Connect the other lead to the wire or ground connection being tested. If the resistance is low (less than 5 ohms), the ground is good. If the bulb on a self-powered test light does not light, the ground is not good.

Continuity check

9   A continuity check determines whether there are any breaks in a circuit (whether it can no longer carry current from the voltage source to ground). With the circuit off (no power in the circuit), a self-powered continuity tester or multimeter can be used to check the circuit. Connect the test leads to both ends of the circuit (or to the power end and

a good ground), and if the test light comes on the circuit is passing current properly (see illustration). If the resistance is low (less than 5 ohms), there is continuity; if the reading is 10,000 ohms or higher, there is a break somewhere in the circuit. The same procedure can be used to test a switch, by connecting the continuity tester to the switch terminals. With the switch turned to ON, the test light should come on (or low resistance should be indicated on a meter).

Finding an open circuit

10   When diagnosing for possible open circuits, it is often difficult to locate them by sight because the connectors hide oxidation or terminal misalignment. Merely wiggling a connector on a sensor or in the wiring harness may correct the open circuit condition. Remember this when an open circuit is indicated when troubleshooting a circuit. Intermit-

2.6a To use a test light, clip the lead to a known good ground, then use the pointed probe to test connectors, wires or electrical sockets. If the bulb lights, the circuit being tested has battery voltage

2.9 With a multimeter set to the ohm scale, you can check resistance across two terminals. When checking for continuity, a low reading indicates continuity, a high reading indicates high resistance and an infinite reading indicates lack of continuity

3.1a Underhood fuse box

3.1b Driver's side fuse box

3.1c Passenger's side fuse box

tent problems may also be caused by oxidized or loose connections.

11 Electrical troubleshooting is simple if you keep in mind that all electrical circuits are basically electricity running from the battery, through the wires, switches, relays, fuses and fusible links to each electrical component (light bulb, motor, etc.) and to ground, from which it is passed back to the battery. Any electrical problem is an interruption in the flow of electricity to and from the battery.

Connectors

12 Most electrical connections on these vehicles are made with multi-wire plastic connectors. The mating halves of many connectors are secured with locking clips molded into the plastic connector shells. The mating halves of large connectors, such as some of those under the instrument panel, are held together by a bolt through the center of the connector.

13 To separate a connector with locking clips, use a small screwdriver to pry the clips apart carefully, then separate the connector halves. Pull only on the shell; never pull on the wiring harness as you may damage the individual wires and terminals inside the connectors. Look at the connector closely before trying to separate the halves. Often the locking clips are engaged in a way that is not immediately clear. Additionally, many connectors have more than one set of clips.

14 Each pair of connector terminals has a male half and a female half. When you look at the end view of a connector in a diagram, be sure to understand whether the view shows the harness side or the component side of the connector. Connector halves are mirror images of each other, and a terminal that is shown on the right side end-view of one half will be on the left side end-view of the other half.

3 Fuses and fusible links - general information

Fuses

1 The electrical circuits of the vehicle are protected by a combination of fuses, circuit breakers and fusible links. The main fuse/relay panel is in the engine compartment (see illustration), while the interior fuse/relay panel is located inside the passenger compartment (see illustrations). Each of the fuses is designed to protect a specific circuit, and the various circuits are identified on the fuse panel lid. Interior fuse boxes are located on either end of the dash. They are accessed by opening the appropriate door and removing the fuse box panel lid.

2 Several sizes of fuses are employed in the fuse blocks. There are small, medium and large sizes of the same design, all with the same blade terminal design. The medium and large fuses can be removed with your fingers, but the small fuses require the use of pliers or the small plastic fuse-puller tool found in most fuse boxes.

3 If an electrical component fails, always check the fuse first. The best way to check the fuses is with a test light. Check for power at the exposed terminal tips of each fuse. If power is present at one side of the fuse but not the other, the fuse is blown. A blown fuse can also be identified by visually inspecting it (see illustration).

4 Be sure to replace blown fuses with the correct type. Fuses (of the same physical size) of different ratings may be physically interchangeable, but only fuses of the proper rating should be used. Replacing a fuse with one of a higher or lower value than specified is not recommended. Each electrical circuit needs a specific amount of protection. The amperage value of each fuse is molded into

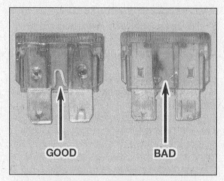

3.3 When a fuse blows, the element between the terminals melts

the top of the fuse body.

Warning: *Avoid using discount store fuses. GM has a service bulletin regarding how to spot these fuses. The bulletin number is 07-08-45-002 "Aftermarket fuses in GM vehicles."*

Note: *If the replacement fuse immediately fails, don't replace it again until the cause of the problem is isolated and corrected. In most cases, this will be a short circuit in the wiring caused by a broken or deteriorated wire.*

Fusible links

5 On these models, large, high-amperage fuses are used instead of traditional fusible links. They are located in the underhood fuse/relay box.

4 Circuit breakers - general information

1 Circuit breakers protect certain circuits, such as the power windows or heated seats. Depending on the vehicle's accessories, there may be one or two circuit breakers, located

in the fuse/relay box in the engine compartment.

2   Because the circuit breakers reset automatically, an electrical overload in a circuit-breaker-protected system will cause the circuit to fail momentarily, then come back on. If the circuit does not come back on, check it immediately.

3   For a basic check, pull the circuit breaker up out of its socket on the fuse panel, but just far enough to probe with a voltmeter. The breaker should still contact the sockets.

4   With the voltmeter negative lead on a good chassis ground, touch each end prong of the circuit breaker with the positive meter probe. There should be battery voltage at each end. If there is battery voltage only at one end, the circuit breaker must be replaced.

5   Some circuit breakers must be reset manually.

5   Relays - general information and testing

General information

1   Several electrical circuits in the vehicle use relays to transmit the electrical signal to the component. Relays use a low-current circuit (the control circuit) to open and close a high-current circuit (the power circuit). If the relay is defective, that component will not operate properly. Most relays are mounted in the engine compartment fuse/relay box, with some specialized relays located above the interior fuse box in the dash (see illustrations 3.1a and 3.1b). If a faulty relay is suspected, it can be removed and tested using the procedure below or by a dealer service department or a repair shop. Defective relays must be replaced as a unit.

Testing

2   Most of the relays used in these vehicles are of a type often called "ISO" relays, which refers to the International Standards Organization. The terminals of ISO relays are numbered to indicate their usual circuit connections and functions. There are two basic layouts of terminals on the relays used in these vehicles (see illustrations).

3   Refer to the wiring diagram for the circuit to determine the proper connections for the relay you're testing. If you can't determine the correct connection from the wiring diagrams, however, you may be able to determine the test connections from the information that follows.

4   Two of the terminals are the relay control circuit and connect to the relay coil. The other relay terminals are the power circuit. When the relay is energized, the coil creates a magnetic field that closes the larger contacts of the power circuit to provide power to the circuit loads.

5   Terminals 85 and 86 are normally the control circuit. If the relay contains a diode, terminal 86 must be connected to battery positive (B+) voltage and terminal 85 to ground. If the relay contains a resistor, terminals 85 and 86 can be connected in either direction with respect to B+ and ground.

6   Terminal 30 is normally connected to the battery voltage (B+) source for the circuit loads. Terminal 87 is connected to the circuit leading to the component being powered. If the relay has several alternate terminals for load or ground connections, they usually are numbered 87A, 87B, 87C, and so on.

7   Use an ohmmeter to check continuity through the relay control coil.

a) Connect the meter according to the polarity shown in illustration 5.2a for one check; then reverse the ohmmeter leads and check continuity in the other direction.

b) If the relay contains a resistor, resistance will be indicated on the meter, and should be the same value with the ohmmeter in either direction.

c) If the relay contains a diode, resistance should be higher with the ohmmeter in the forward polarity direction than with the meter leads reversed.

d) If the ohmmeter shows infinite resistance in both directions, replace the relay.

8   Remove the relay from the vehicle and use the ohmmeter to check for continuity between the relay power circuit terminals. There should be no continuity between terminal 30 and 87 with the relay de-energized.

9   Connect a fused jumper wire to terminal 86 and the positive battery terminal. Connect another jumper wire between terminal 85 and ground. When the connections are made, the relay should click.

10   With the jumper wires connected, check for continuity between the power circuit terminals. Now, there should be continuity between terminals 30 and 87.

11   If the relay fails any of the above tests, replace it.

6   Electrical connectors - general information

1   Most electrical connections on these vehicles are made with multiwire plastic connectors. The mating halves of many connectors are secured with locking clips molded into the plastic connector shells. The mating halves of some large connectors, such as some of those under the instrument panel, are held together by a bolt through the center of the connector.

2   To separate a connector with locking clips, use a small screwdriver to pry the clips apart carefully, then separate the connector halves. Pull only on the shell, never pull on

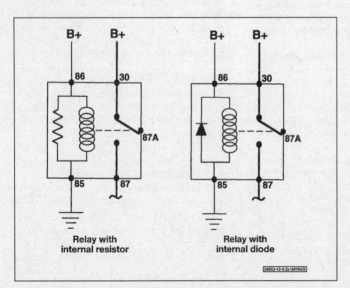

5.2a Typical ISO relay designs, terminal numbering and circuit connections

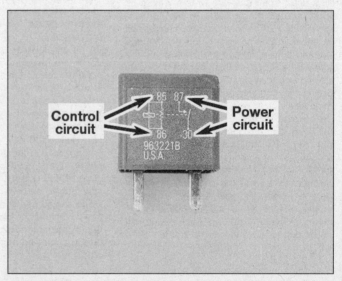

5.2b Most relays are marked on the outside to easily identify the control circuits and the power circuits (four-terminal type shown)

the wiring harness, as you may damage the individual wires and terminals inside the connectors. Look at the connector closely before trying to separate the halves. Often the locking clips are engaged in a way that is not immediately clear. Additionally, many connectors have more than one set of clips.

3   Each pair of connector terminals has a male half and a female half. When you look at the end view of a connector in a diagram, be sure to understand whether the view shows the harness side or the component side of the connector. Connector halves are mirror images of each other, and a terminal shown on the right side end-view of one half will be

on the left side end-view of the other half.

4   It is often necessary to take circuit voltage measurements with a connector connected. Whenever possible, carefully insert a small straight pin (not your meter probe) into the rear of the connector shell to contact the terminal inside, then clip your meter lead to the pin. This kind of connection is called "backprobing." When inserting a test probe into a terminal, be careful not to distort the terminal opening. Doing so can lead to a poor connection and corrosion at that terminal later. Using the small straight pin instead of a meter probe results in less chance of deforming the terminal connector.

7   Turn signals and hazard flashers - general information

1   There is no turn signal and hazard flasher relay on these vehicles. This function is handled by the Body Control Module (BCM).

2   If a bulb on one side of the vehicle flashes much faster than normal but the bulb at the other end of the vehicle (on the same side) doesn't light at all, the bulb that doesn't flash is probably faulty. Replace the bulb (see Section 17).

3   If both the left and right front or rear turn

Electrical connectors

Most electrical connectors have a single release tab that you depress to release the connector

Some electrical connectors have a retaining tab which must be pried up to free the connector

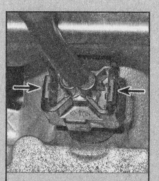

Some connectors have two release tabs that you must squeeze to release the connector

Some connectors use wire retainers that you squeeze to release the connector

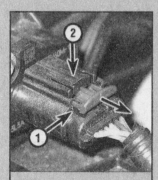

Critical connectors often employ a sliding lock (1) that you must pull out before you can depress the release tab (2)

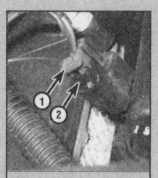

Here's another sliding-lock style connector, with the lock (1) and the release tab (2) on the side of the connector

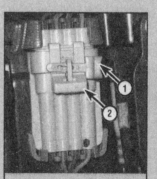

On some connectors the lock (1) must be pulled out to the side and removed before you can lift the release tab (2)

Some critical connectors, like the multi-pin connectors at the Powertrain Control Module employ pivoting locks that must be flipped open

8.3 To disconnect the electrical connectors from the turn signal multi-function switch, use a small screwdriver to disengage the locking tabs on the terminal from the lugs on the connectors

A   Mounting screw locations
B   Multi-function switch electrical connection

9.2 Turn the key to the Start position, insert a thin tool through this hole, depress the lock cylinder release tab and pull out the lock cylinder

9.5a Theft deterrent control module with key lock cylinder removed

signal bulbs are not flashing, the turn signal and hazard flasher relay function in the BCM may be defective, or the turn signal switch is defective, or there is an open circuit between the switch, BCM, or turn signal bulbs and sockets, or faulty grounds. The BCM is not serviceable and must be replaced by a dealer service department or an independent electrical repair facility equipped with the proper tools. Replacing the BCM is not a job that you can do at home because the BCM must be programmed with a factory scan tool when it's replaced.

8   Turn signal/hazard flasher/multi-function switch - replacement

Warning: *The models covered by this manual are equipped with a Supplemental Restraint System (SRS), more commonly known as airbags. Always disarm the airbag system before*

working in the vicinity of any airbag system component to avoid the possibility of accidental deployment of the airbag, which could cause personal injury (see Section 26).
1   Remove the steering wheel (see Chapter 10).
2   Remove the upper and lower steering column covers (see Chapter 11).
3   Disconnect the electrical connectors from the turn signal/hazard flasher/multi-function switch (see illustration).
4   Remove the turn signal/hazard flasher/multi-function switch mounting screws. One screw is horizontal facing you and the other screw is on the top screwed in vertically.
5   Installation is the reverse of removal.

9   Key lock cylinder and ignition switch - replacement

Warning: *The models covered by this manual are equipped with a Supplemental Restraint System (SRS), more commonly known as airbags. Always disarm the airbag system before*

working in the vicinity of any airbag system component to avoid the possibility of accidental deployment of the airbag, which could cause personal injury (see Section 26).

Key lock cylinder
Caution: *The following procedure is included only as a prelude to removing the ignition switch (see below). DO NOT try to replace the key lock cylinder and key at home, unless the original key has been used to set the tumblers in the replacement lock cylinder. If you replace the key lock cylinder and key, you must have the transponder in the new key programmed by a dealer service department or qualified independent repair facility before the engine will start.*
Note: *For additional information on adding keys or key fobs, see Section 27.*
1   Disconnect the cable from the negative terminal of the battery (see Chapter 5). Remove the upper and lower steering column covers (see Chapter 11).
2   Insert the ignition key in the key lock cylinder and turn the key to the START position. Insert a 1/8-inch Allen wrench, awl, punch or a small screwdriver through the hole in the casting that houses the key lock cylinder, then depress the lock cylinder release tab and pull out the lock cylinder (see illustration).
3   Installation is the reverse of removal.

Ignition switch (electrical switch) and theft deterrent module
4   Remove the steering column covers (see Chapter 11).

Theft deterrent module
5   Disconnect the electrical connections from the theft deterrent control module, then remove it from the key lock cylinder housing (see illustrations).

9.5b Detach the theft deterrent control module from the key lock cylinder housing by carefully prying the lock tabs loose from the housing and pulling off the module

9.8 Electrical connection to the ignition switch (Steering column is upside down and removed from the vehicle for clarity)

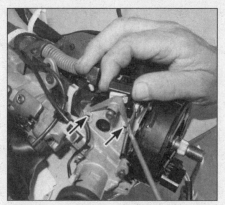

9.9 Steering column shown upside down and removed from the vehicle for clarity. Grasp the switch and pull straight out from the steering column

10.1 Gently pry the trim panel out of the dash

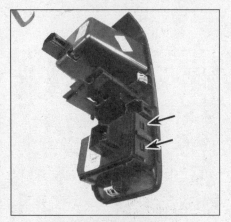

10.2 Gently release the clips on the headlight switch housing (one side shown)

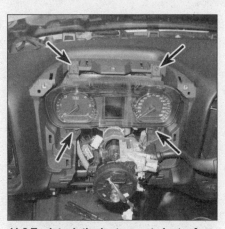

11.2 To detach the instrument cluster from the instrument panel, remove these four screws

11.3 Pull out the cluster, depress the release tab and disconnect the electrical connector from the cluster

Ignition electrical switch

6   Remove the theft deterrent module.

7   Remove the lock cylinder.

8   Disconnect the electrical connector from the ignition switch (see illustration).

9   Remove the ignition switch by inserting a pair of small flat bladed screwdrivers into these slots to free the locking tabs. As you push the tabs in pull the switch free from the steering column (see illustration).

10   When installing the switch, make sure that the gears on top are positioned correctly. Failure to do so will cause a misalignment between the gears on the ignition switch and the gears inside the lock cylinder housing, which could make it impossible to start the engine or could result in a battery current drain. Installation is otherwise the reverse of removal.

10   Dashboard switches - replacement

Warning: *The models covered by this manual are equipped with a Supplemental Restraint System (SRS), more commonly known as air-*

bags. Always disarm the airbag system before working in the vicinity of any airbag system component to avoid the possibility of accidental deployment of the airbag, which could cause personal injury (see Section 26).

Headlight switch/transfer case control switch

Headlight switch and dome light override knob (standard instrument panel)

1   Remove the left side trim panel with a flat trim removal tool (see illustration).

2   Disconnect the electrical connector, then carefully release the locking clips to the headlamp switch and remove the switch (see illustration).

When installing the headlight switch, make sure that it snaps back into place and that the switch is secure in the trim panel.

3   Installation is otherwise the reverse of removal.

Hazard flasher switch

4   The hazard flasher switch, which is located on top of the steering column, is an

integral component of the turn signal/hazard flasher/multi-function switch.

11   Instrument cluster - removal and installation

Warning: *The models covered by this manual are equipped with a Supplemental Restraint System (SRS), more commonly known as air-bags. Always disarm the airbag system before working in the vicinity of any airbag system component to avoid the possibility of accidental deployment of the airbag, which could cause personal injury (see Section 26).*

1   Remove the instrument cluster hood trim panel and the instrument panel trim (see Chapter 11).

2   Remove the instrument cluster retaining screws (see illustration).

3   Pull out the cluster, disconnect the electrical connector (see illustration) and remove the cluster.

Caution: *Replacing the instrument cluster requires programming. See the appropriate repair facility for programming.*

4   Installation is the reverse of removal.

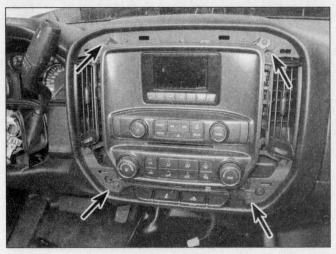

12.2 Radio assembly screw locations

12.3 Tilt the radio assembly down to expose the electrical connections

12.6 Screw locations

12.7 Depress the retaining tab ad disconnect the electrical connector

12.10 Door speaker screw locations

12 Radio and speakers - removal and installation

Warning: *The models covered by this manual are equipped with a Supplemental Restraint System (SRS), more commonly known as airbags. Always disarm the airbag system before working in the vicinity of any airbag system component to avoid the possibility of accidental deployment of the airbag, which could cause personal injury (see Section 26).*

Radio

1   Remove the center trim bezel plate (see Chapter 11).
2   Remove the radio control fasteners (see illustration).
3   Pull the radio assembly out of the dash and disconnect the electrical connections (see illustration).
Note: *Replacing the radio with another stock radio will require programming. See the ap-*
propriate repair facility for programming.
4   Installation is the reverse of removal.

Disc player

5   Remove center trim panel (see Chapter 11).
6   Locate the screws for the disc player and remove them (see illustration).
7   Pull the disc player out and disconnect the electrical connections (see illustration).
8   Installation is the reverse of removal.

Speakers

Door speakers

9   Remove the door trim panel (see Chapter 11).
10   Remove the speaker mounting screws (see illustration).
11   Pull out the speaker and disconnect the electrical connector.
12   When installing the speaker, make sure that the lower mounting flange of the speaker

is aligned with and fits inside the lower edge of the speaker mounting hole in the door.
13   Installation is otherwise the reverse of removal.

Dash speakers

14   Remove the defroster grille (see Chapter 11).
15   Remove the two screws that secure the speaker to the dash.
16   Raise the speaker up to gain access to the wires and disconnect the connector.
Secure the wire and connector from falling back into the dash.
17   Installation is the reverse of removal.

Console speaker

18   Remove the center console (see Chapter 11).
19   Remove the three screws securing the console speaker to the console.
20   Disconnect the electrical connectors.
21   Installation is the reverse of removal.

14.3a Headlamp housing screw locations - front view

14.3b Headlamp housing side screw location

15.1 To turn the headlight housing vertical adjustment screw, insert a Phillips screwdriver into the top

2　Remove the radiator grille and front bumper upper fascia (see Chapter 11).
3　Remove the four headlight housing bolts (see illustrations).
4　Carefully pull out the headlight housing. Note the two locator pins on the outer edge of the housing. When installing the headlight housing, make sure that these locator pins are aligned with their mounting holes in the front fender bracket.
5　If you're replacing either headlight bulb, refer to Section 16. If you're replacing any other bulbs in the headlight housing, refer to Section 17.
6　Installation is otherwise the reverse of removal.
7　Adjust the headlights when you're done (see Section 15).

13　Antenna and cable - removal and installation

Antenna mast
1　Unscrew the antenna mast from the antenna base. Be sure to protect the surrounding painted surfaces.
2　Installation is the reverse of removal.

Antenna mast mounting base and cable
3　Remove the antenna mast. Remove the cowl cover (see Chapter 11).
4　Unbolt the antenna mounting base.
5　Remove the top trim panel from the instrument panel.
6　Disconnect the antenna mast cable from the extension cable.
7　Attach a piece of wire of sufficient length

to the old antenna mast cable and carefully pull out the cable through the grommet located below the antenna mounting base.
8　Attach the new antenna mast cable to the wire and pull it back through the grommet below the antenna mast base.
9　Installation is otherwise the reverse of removal.

Antenna extension cable
10　The antenna extension cable, which connects the antenna mounting base cable to the radio, is routed through the instrument panel, which you must remove to replace it.

14　Headlight housing - removal and installation

1　For headlamp lens refurbishing, see Chapter 11.

15　Headlights - adjustment

Note: *The headlights must be aimed correctly. If adjusted incorrectly they could blind the driver of an oncoming vehicle and cause a serious accident or seriously reduce your ability to see the road. The headlights should be checked for proper aim every 12 months and any time a new headlight is installed or front end bodywork is performed. It should be emphasized that the following procedure is only an interim step that will provide temporary adjustment until a properly equipped shop can adjust the headlights.*
1　The vertical adjustment screws are located behind each headlight housing (see illustration). There are no horizontal adjustment screws.
2　There are several methods for adjusting the headlights. The simplest method requires masking tape, a blank wall and a level floor.

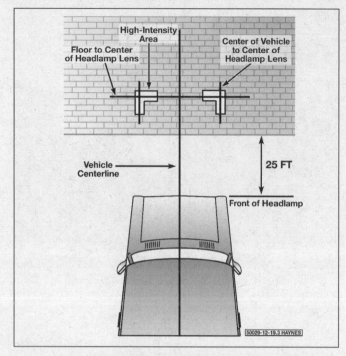

16.2a Twist the dust boot to unlock and remove it from the housing...

15.3 Headlight adjustment details

16.2b... depress the tab and disconnect the electrical connector...

16.2c... then turn the bulb counterclockwise to remove it from the housing

16   Headlight bulb - replacement

Warning: *Halogen gas-filled bulbs are under pressure and can shatter if the surface is scratched or the bulb is dropped. Wear eye protection and handle the bulb carefully, grasping it only by the bulb holder. Do not touch the surface of the bulb with your fingers because the oil from your skin could cause it to overheat and fail prematurely. If you do touch the bulb surface, clean it with rubbing alcohol.*

1   If you're replacing a right-side bulb on a truck model, remove the air filter housing (see Chapter 4). If you're replacing a left-side bulb on a truck model and the vehicle is equipped with an auxiliary battery, remove the battery.

2   Remove the dust boot and disconnect the headlight bulb electrical connector. Rotate the bulb counterclockwise and remove it from the housing (see illustrations).

3   Installation is the reverse of removal.

17   Bulb replacement

Exterior light bulbs

Front parking light/turn signal/ sidemarker/daytime running light bulbs

1   Remove the headlight housing (see Section 14).

2   Turn the bulb holder counterclockwise and pull it out of the headlight housing.

3   Position masking tape vertically on the wall in relation to the vehicle centerline and the centerlines of both headlights (see illustration).

4   Position a horizontal tape line in relation to the centerline of all the headlights.

Note:It might be easier to position the tape on the wall with the vehicle parked only a few inches away.

5   Adjustment should be made with the vehicle parked 25 feet from the wall, sitting level, the gas tank half-full and no heavy load in the vehicle.

6   Starting with the low beam adjustment, position the high intensity zone so it is two inches below the horizontal line. Adjustment

is made by turning the adjusting screw clockwise to raise the beam and counterclockwise to lower the beam.

Note: *It might not be possible to position the headlight aim exactly for both high and low beams. If a compromise must be made, keep in mind that the low beams are the most used and have the greatest effect on safety.*

7   With the high beams on, the high intensity zone should be vertically centered with the exact center just below the horizontal line.

8   Have the headlights adjusted by a dealer service department or service station at the earliest opportunity.

Bulb removal

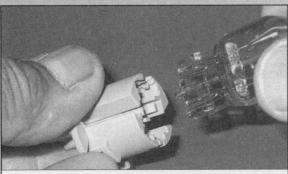

To remove many modern exterior bulbs from their holders, simply pull them out

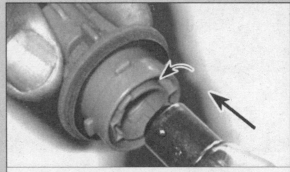

On bulbs with a cylindrical base ("bayonet" bulbs), the socket is spring-loaded; a pair of small posts on the side of the base hold the bulb in place against spring pressure. To remove this type of bulb, push it into the holder, rotate it 1/4-turn counterclockwise, then pull it out

If a bayonet bulb has dual filaments, the posts are staggered, so the bulb can only be installed one way

To remove most overhead interior light bulbs, simply unclip them

3   To remove the old bulb from its holder, pull it straight out. To install a new bulb in the bulb holder, push it straight into the socket until it stops.

4   Install the headlight housing.

Fog light bulbs

Warning: *Halogen gas-filled bulbs are under pressure and can shatter if the surface is scratched or the bulb is dropped. Wear eye protection and handle the bulb carefully, grasping it only by the bulb holder. Do not touch the surface of the bulb with your fingers because the oil from your skin could cause it to overheat and fail prematurely. If you do touch the bulb surface, clean it with rubbing alcohol.*

5   Loosen the front wheel lug nuts, raise the vehicle, place it securely on jackstands and remove the front wheel.

6   Locate the fog light electrical connector and disconnect it.

7   To remove the bulb holder, squeeze the upper and lower tabs on the bulb holder and pull out the holder. The bulb and bulb holder are a single assembly.

8   To install the new bulb, align the ridges on the bulb holder with the slots in the fog light housing and push it into place.

9   Installation is otherwise the reverse of removal.

Center high-mounted brake light bulbs

10   Remove the two center high-mounted brake light housing retaining screws (see illustration).

17.10 To detach the center high-mounted brake light housing, remove these two screws

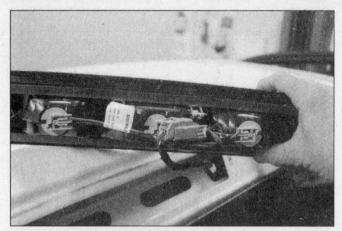

17.11 Center high-mounted brake light housing removed showing the electrical connector and bulb sockets

17.15 Carefully twist the license plate light housing out of the bumper (photo is taken from under the truck looking at the backside of the rear bumper)

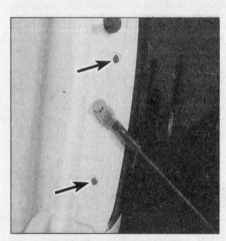

17.20a Remove the taillight housing screws...

11   Remove the center high-mounted brake light housing and disconnect the electrical connector (see illustration).
12   To remove a bulb holder from the center high-mounted brake light housing, turn it counterclockwise and pull it out of the housing.
13   To remove a bulb from the bulb holder, pull it straight out of the holder. To install a bulb in its holder, push it straight into the holder until it stops.
14   Installation is the reverse of removal.

License plate light bulbs

15   Carefully twist the license plate light housing out of the bumper (see illustration).
16   To remove the old bulb from its holder, simply pull it straight out.
17   To install a new license plate light bulb, simply push it straight into the socket until it stops.

18   Installation is the reverse of removal.

Taillight bulbs

19   Open the tailgate or liftgate.
20   Remove the taillight housing retaining screws and remove the taillight housing (see illustrations).
21   Turn the bulb holder counterclockwise to remove it from the housing (see illustration).
22   To remove the bulb from its holder, pull it straight out. Push the new bulb straight into the socket until it stops.
23   When installing the taillight housing, make sure that the locator pins snap into place.

Interior lights

Dome lights/map/reading lights

24   Remove the overhead console (see Chapter 11).

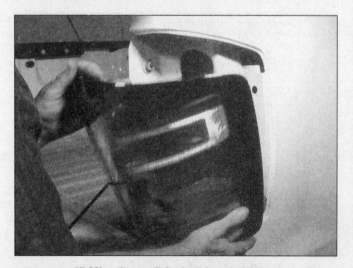

17.20b... then pull the housing straight out

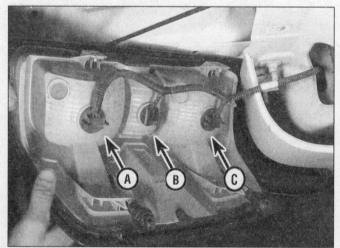

17.21 Typical taillight bulb arrangement (Chevy Silverado shown; refer to your owner's manual for bulb arrangement on other models)

A   *Brake light/turn signal/taillight bulb*
B   *Back-up light bulb*
C   *Brake light/turn signal/taillight bulb*

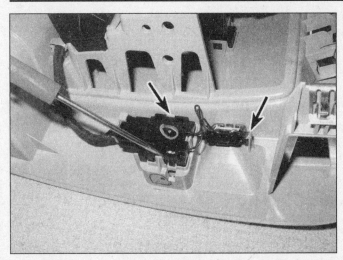

17.25 Gently pry the retaining clips away as you lift the fixture

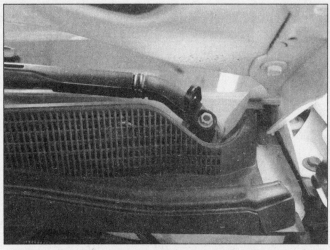

18.1 Pry open each trim cap, remove each wiper arm retaining nut and mark the relationship of each arm to its shaft, then remove the arms

18.5 To detach the windshield wiper motor and linkage assembly from the cowl, remove these three bolts

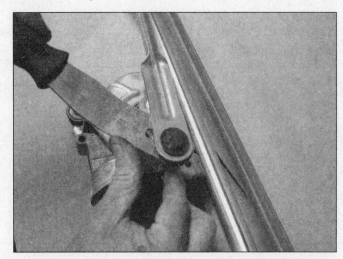

18.7 Carefully pry the linkage arm loose from the crank arm

25   Turn the console over and gently spread the retaining clips from the fixture (see illustration).

26   Installation is the reverse of removal.

18   Windshield wiper and washer system - component removal and installation

Windshield wiper motor

1   Pry off the windshield wiper trim caps (see illustration).

2   Remove the windshield wiper retaining nuts and washers. Mark the position of each wiper arm in relation to its shaft, then remove the wiper arms.

3   Remove the cowl cover (see Chapter 11).

4   Disconnect the windshield wiper motor electrical connector.

5   Remove the three mounting bolts that secure the windshield wiper motor and linkage assembly to the cowl (see illustration).

6   Lift the windshield wiper motor and linkage assembly out of the cowl area.

7   Pry the linkage off the wiper motor crank arm (see illustration).

8   Remove the nut that attaches the actuator arm to the motor shaft (see illustration). Mark the relationship of the actuator arm to the motor shaft, then remove the actuator arm from the shaft.

9   Remove the motor mounting screws and remove the motor.

10   Installation is the reverse of removal. Be sure to align the marks you made on the actuator arm and the motor shaft, and on the windshield wiper arms and the wiper arm shafts.

18.8 Remove the crank arm nut, mark the relationship of the crank arm to the motor shaft, remove the crank arm, then remove the three motor mounting bolts

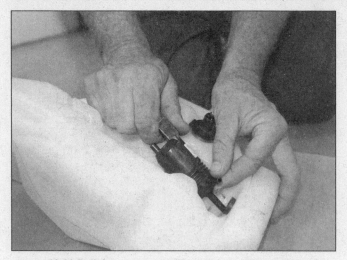

18.20 Pull the pump out with a slight twisting action

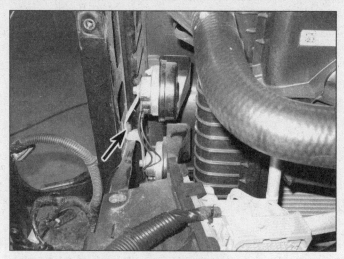

19.2 Disconnect the electrical connector from the horn, then remove the horn mounting bolt

Rear wiper motor (SUV models)

11   Remove the liftgate interior trim panel (see Chapter 11).
12   Remove the wiper arm. (Wiper arm removal is the same as the front wiper arms.)
13   Remove the wiper motor pivot shaft nut and washer, found below the wiper arm on the outside of the liftgate.
14   Remove the two retaining nuts securing the wiper motor to the lift gate.
15   Pull the wiper motor away from the lift gate and disconnect the electrical connector.
16   Installation is the reverse of removal. Tighten the pivot nut to 80 in lbs.

Washer fluid reservoir

17   See Chapter 11, Section 11 for the windshield washer fluid reservoir removal and installation procedure.

Washer fluid pump

18   Remove the washer fluid reservoir (see Chapter 11).
19   Disconnect the electrical connector and remove the hose to the washer pump if you haven't already. Then drain the reservoir.
20   Grasp the washer pump and pull straight out with a bit of a twisting motion (see illustration).
21   Most of the time the rubber grommet will pull out with the pump. With most replacement washer pumps a new grommet will come with it, however if needed, you can reuse the old one.
22   To install the pump, install the grommet first. Then, with a slight twisting motion push the pump back into the reservoir.
Tip: *A bit of silicone spray lubricant will make the installation easier.*
23   The remainder of the installation is the reverse of the removal.

Windshield washer nozzle

24   Remove the cowl panel (see Chapter 11).
25   Twist the windshield washer hose off of the nozzles.
26   Compress the locking tabs on each side of the nozzle and then push the nozzle out of the cowling.
27   Installation is the reverse of removal.
Tip: *Adjusting the nozzle can be accomplished with a sewing needle inserted into the spray tip of the nozzle. A slight movement of the nozzle can result in a great deal of spray pattern change on the windshield. With a few trial and error efforts you can get the spray exactly where you want it on the windshield.*

Windshield wiper switch

28   The wiper switch is part of the multi-function switch mounted on the steering column. See Section 8 for the removal and installation procedure.

19   Horn - replacement

1500 and SUV models

1   Remove the windshield washer reservoir (see Chapter 11).
2   Disconnect the electrical connector from the horn, then remove the bolt securing the horn to the chassis (see illustration).
3   Detach the horn from its mounting bracket.
4   Installation is the reverse of removal.

2500/3500 models

5   Remove the front bumper/impart bar (see Chapter 11).
6   Disconnect the electrical connector.
7   Remove the bolt securing the horn bracket to the frame, then remove the horn assembly.

8   Remove the horn from the bracket.
9   Installation is the reverse of removal.

Horn switch harness replacement

10   Remove the driver's side airbag (see Chapter 10, Section 16).
11   Gently release the retaining clips for the switch housings (right and left side).
12   Remove the switch housings.
13   Disconnect the electrical harness from the steering wheel connector, then remove the harness.
14   Installation is the reverse of removal.

20   Rear window defogger - check and repair

1   The rear window defogger consists of a number of horizontal elements baked onto the glass surface.
2   Small breaks in the element can be repaired without removing the rear window.

Check

3   Turn the ignition switch and defogger system switches to the ON position. Using a voltmeter, place the positive probe against the defogger grid positive terminal and the negative probe against the ground terminal. If battery voltage is not indicated, check the fuse, defogger switch and related wiring. If voltage is indicated, but all or part of the defogger doesn't heat, proceed with the following tests.
4   When measuring voltage during the next two tests, wrap a piece of aluminum foil around the tip of the voltmeter positive probe and press the foil against the heating element with your finger (see illustration). Place the negative probe on the defogger grid ground terminal.

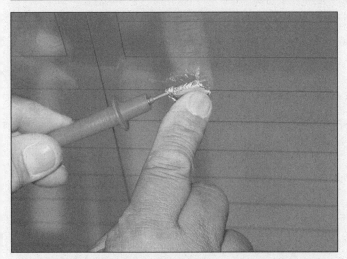

20.4 When measuring the voltage at the rear window defogger grid, wrap a piece of aluminum foil around the positive probe of the voltmeter and press the foil against the wire with your finger

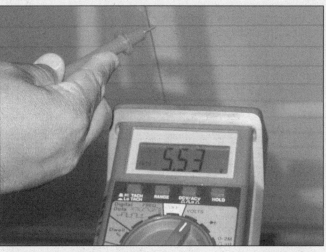

20.5 To determine if a heating element has broken, check the voltage at the center of each element; if the voltage is 5 or 6-volts, the element is unbroken, but if the voltage is 10 or 12-volts, the element is broken between the center and the ground side. If there is no voltage, the element is broken between the center and the positive side

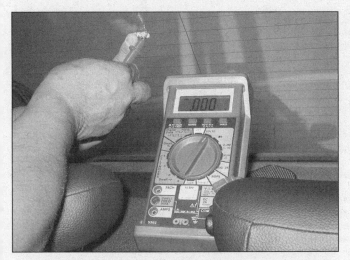

20.7 To find the break, place the voltmeter negative lead against the defogger ground terminal, place the voltmeter positive lead with the foil strip against the heating element at the positive terminal end and slide it toward the negative terminal end. The point at which the voltmeter reading changes abruptly is the point at which the element is broken

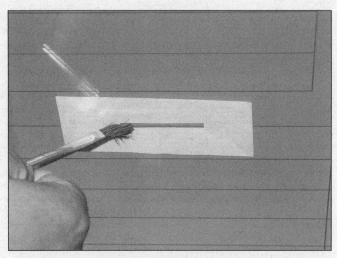

20.13 To use a defogger repair kit, apply masking tape to the inside of the window at the damaged area, then brush on the special conductive coating

5   Check the voltage at the center of each heating element (see illustration). If the voltage is 5 or 6-volts, the element is okay (there is no break). If the voltage is zero, the element is broken between the center of the element and the positive end. If the voltage is 10 to 12-volts the element is broken between the center of the element and ground. Check each heating element.

6   Connect the negative lead to a good body ground. The reading should stay the same. If it doesn't, the ground connection is bad.

7   To find the break, place the voltmeter negative probe against the defogger ground terminal. Place the voltmeter positive probe with the foil strip against the heating element at the positive terminal end and slide it toward the negative terminal end. The point at which the voltmeter deflects from several volts to zero is the point at which the heating element is broken (see illustration).

Repair

8   Repair the break in the element using a repair kit specifically recommended for this purpose, available at most auto parts stores. Included in this kit is plastic conductive epoxy.

9   Prior to repairing a break, turn off the system and allow it to cool off for a few minutes.

10   Lightly buff the element area with fine steel wool, then clean it thoroughly with rubbing alcohol.

11   Use masking tape to mask off the area being repaired.

12   Thoroughly mix the epoxy, following the instructions provided with the repair kit.

13   Apply the epoxy material to the slit in the masking tape, overlapping the undamaged area about 3/4-inch on either end (see illustration).

14   Allow the repair to cure for 24 hours before removing the tape and using the system.

21 Electric side view mirrors - description

Note: *These models are equipped with a Body Control Module (BCM). Several systems are linked to a centralized control module that allows simple and accurate troubleshooting, but only with a professional-grade scan tool. The Body Control Module governs the door locks, the power windows, the ignition lock and security system, the interior lights, the Daytime Running Lights system, the horn, the windshield wipers, the heating/air conditioning system and the power mirrors. In the event of malfunction with this system, have the vehicle diagnosed by a dealership service department or other qualified automotive repair facility.*

1   The electric rear view mirrors use two motors to move the glass; one for up and down adjustments and one for left-right adjustments. Some vehicles are equipped with memory mirrors as well. These mirrors are an integral part of the power seat memory unit as well as incorporated with the Body Control Module (BCM). If there is a problem with these systems it is advised to seek out a qualified independent repair facility or your local dealer.

2   The control switch has a selector portion which sends voltage to the left or right side mirror. With the ignition in the ACC position and the engine OFF, roll down the windows and operate the mirror control switch through all functions (left-right and up-down) for both the left and right side mirrors.

3   Listen carefully for the sound of the electric motors running in the mirrors.

4   If the motors can be heard but the mirror glass doesn't move, there's probably a problem with the drive mechanism inside the mirror. Power mirrors have no user-serviceable parts inside - a defective mirror must be replaced as a unit.

5   If the mirrors don't operate and no sound comes from the mirrors, check for a blown fuse.

6   If the fuses are OK, remove the mirror control switch. Have the switch continuity checked by a dealer service department or other qualified shop.

7   Check the ground connections.

8   If the mirror still doesn't work, remove the mirror and check the wires at the mirror for voltage.

9   If there's not voltage in each switch position, check the circuit between the mirror and control switch for opens and shorts.

If the mirror is inoperative, try holding the switch in one of the directions and swing the door open and closed. If there is a break in the door jamb you may occasionally make contact long enough to avoid removing the mirror from the door for further testing. This will also give you some clue as to where the break is rather than testing things in one given position.

10   If there's voltage, remove the mirror and test it off the vehicle with jumper wires. Before testing check the wiring diagram for the correct leads that have to be used for each position. Applying voltage to the wrong leads can damage the mirror drive motors. Replace the mirror if it fails this test.

22 Cruise control system - general information

1   The Powertrain Control Module (PCM) controls the cruise control system electronically via the electronic throttle control system. If you have problems with the cruise control system, check for the presence of trouble codes stored in the PCM (see Chapter 6). If that doesn't turn up any problems, have it checked by a dealer service department or other qualified repair shop.

23 Power window system - description and check

Note: *These models are equipped with a Body Control Module (BCM) incorporated with the window system. Several systems are linked to a centralized control module that allows simple and accurate troubleshooting, but only with a professional-grade scan tool. The Body Control Module governs the door locks, the power windows, the ignition lock and security system, the interior lights, the Daytime Running Lights system, the horn, the windshield wipers, the heating/air conditioning system and the power mirrors. In the event of malfunction with this system, have the vehicle diagnosed by a dealership service department or other qualified automotive repair facility.*

1   The power window system operates electric motors, mounted in the doors, which lower and raise the windows. The system consists of the control switches, the motors, regulators, glass mechanisms, the Body Control Module (BCM) and associated wiring.

2   The power windows can be lowered and raised from the master control switch by the driver or by remote switches located at the individual windows. Each window has a separate motor that is reversible. The position of the control switch determines the polarity and therefore the direction of operation.

3   The window motor circuits are protected by a fuse. Each motor is also equipped with an internal circuit breaker; this prevents one stuck window from disabling the whole system.

4   The power window system will only operate when the ignition switch has activated the Retained Accessory Power (RAP) relay. In addition, many models have a window lockout switch at the master control switch which, when activated, disables the switches at the rear windows and, sometimes, the switch at the passenger's window also. Always check these items before troubleshooting a window problem related to any of the other windows besides the driver's window. Window lock-out does not affect the driver's window.

5   These procedures are general in nature,

so if you can't find the problem using them, take the vehicle to a dealer service department or to an independent repair facility that specializes in electrical repairs.

6   If the power windows won't operate, always check the fuse and circuit breaker first.

7   If only the rear windows are inoperative, or if the windows only operate from the master control switch, check the rear window lockout switch for continuity in the unlocked position. Replace it if it doesn't have continuity.

8   Check the wiring between the switches and fuse panel for continuity. Repair the wiring, if necessary.

9   If only one window is inoperative from the master control switch, try the other control switch at each individual window.

Note: *This doesn't apply to the driver's door window.*

10   If the same window works from one switch, but not the other, check the switch and/or wiring for continuity.

11   If the switch tests OK, check for a short or open in the circuit between the affected switch and the window motor.

12   If one window is inoperative from both switches, remove the switch panel from the affected door. Check for voltage at the motor (refer to Chapter 11 for door panel removal) while the switch is operated.

Note: *There are voltage and ground signals present at the switch connector. However, on 2010 and later models, there are also two data lines to the BCM that are not true positive/negative signals. Be sure you are testing the correct leads. Do not apply voltage or ground to any leads you are not sure of. Seek professional help in diagnosing any problems with the window circuits if you are unsure.*

13   If voltage is reaching the motor, disconnect the glass from the regulator. Move the window up and down by hand while checking for binding and damage. Also check for binding and damage to the regulator. If the regulator is not damaged and the window moves up and down smoothly, replace the motor. If there's binding or damage, lubricate, repair or replace parts, as necessary.

14   If voltage isn't reaching the motor, check the wiring in the circuit for continuity between the switches and the BCM, and between the BCM (if applicable) and the motors. You'll need to consult the wiring diagram. If the circuit is equipped with a relay, check that the relay is grounded properly and receiving voltage.

15   Test the windows to confirm proper repairs.

To verify if the motor is getting the needed voltage or ground, a simple but effective test is to sit in the car with the ignition on, open a door and look at the dome light. Then operate the switch to the faulty window. If you see the dome light dimming slightly this is a good indication that the motor is getting power and is probably a stuck motor or faulty wiring. Do not hold the switch on for very long when a motor is stuck or wiring is in question or more damage may occur. Finally, in some cases, a good rap on the door panel in the general area of the window motor - while the key is on and the window switch is depressed in the direction the window needs to move - will free up a stuck motor temporarily. You can damage the door panel or more internal components if you hit it too hard or are too aggressive.

Window express down programming

Note: *Any time the battery or window motor are disconnected, you will need to perform this procedure to reestablish the auto feature.*

16 Lower the window to its lowest position, holding the switch in the Down position for an additional five seconds.

17 Raise the window to its highest position, holding the window switch in the Up position for an additional five seconds.

18 Verify proper operation.

24 Power door lock and keyless entry system - description and check

Note: *These models are equipped with a Body Control Module (BCM). Several systems are linked to a centralized control module that allows simple and accurate troubleshooting, but only with a professional-grade scan tool. The Body Control Module governs the door locks, the power windows, the ignition lock and security system, the interior lights, the Daytime Running Lights system, the horn, the windshield wipers, the heating/air conditioning system and the power mirrors. In the event of malfunction with this system, have the vehicle diagnosed by a dealership service department or other qualified automotive repair facility.*

1 The power door lock system operates the door lock actuators mounted in each door. The system consists of the switches, actuators, lock and unlock relays, Body Control Module (BCM) and associated wiring. Diagnosis can usually be limited to simple checks of the wiring connections and actuators for minor faults that can be easily repaired.

2 Power door lock systems are operated by bi-directional solenoids located in the doors. The lock actuators are mounted as part of the door latch. Remove the door latch for access to the door lock actuator. The lock switches have two operating positions: Lock and Unlock. These switches send a signal to the BCM, which in turn sends a signal to the door lock relays, the relays then send the needed voltage to each of the door lock solenoids.

3 If you are unable to locate the trouble using the following general steps, consult your dealer service department or qualified independent repair shop.

4 Always check the circuit protection first. Some vehicles use a combination of circuit breakers and fuses.

5 Check for voltage at the switches. If no voltage is present, check the fuse first. If the fuse is good then check the wiring between the

fuse panel and the switches for an open lead.

6 If voltage is present, test the switch for continuity. Replace it if there's not continuity in both switch positions. There should be a voltage input and, when switch is depressed, voltage should be going out on the appropriate lead. Follow the wiring diagram for the actual wire and position on the switch. To remove the switch, use a flat-bladed trim tool to pry out the door/window switch assembly.

7 If the switch has continuity, check the wiring between the switch, BCM, door lock relay and the door lock solenoid.

8 If all but one lock solenoids operate, remove the trim panel from the affected door and check for voltage at the solenoid while the lock switch is operated. One of the wires should have positive voltage in the Lock position; the other lead should have positive voltage in the Unlock position.

9 If the inoperative solenoid is receiving positive voltage on one lead and negative on the other, the solenoid is most likely defective. Check the connections for good contact; if the connection is good, replace the solenoid.

10 If the inoperative solenoid isn't receiving voltage or ground, check for an open or short in the wire between the lock solenoid and the relay. A good method of non-destructive testing is to squeeze the rubber corrugated tubing and search with your fingers for an individual wire. Follow the wire as far as possible and feel for any breaks in the leads.

Note: *It's not uncommon for wires to break in the portion of the harness between the body and door (opening and closing the door fatigues and eventually breaks the wires).*

11 On the models covered by this manual, power door lock system communication goes through the Body Control Module. If the above tests do not pinpoint a problem, take the vehicle to a dealer or qualified shop with the proper scan tool to retrieve trouble codes from the BCM. Replacing of some components may result in programming issues. To avoid replacing good components always test thoroughly before any parts are deemed faulty.

Keyless entry system

12 The keyless entry system consists of a remote control transmitter that sends a coded infrared signal to a receiver, which then operates the door lock system.

13 Replace the battery when the transmitter doesn't operate the locks at a distance of 10 feet. Normal range should be about 65 feet.

14 For more information on key fob battery replacement, programming and additional keys see Section 27.

25 Daytime Running Lights (DRL) - general information

1 The Daytime Running Lights (DRL) system illuminates the headlights whenever the engine is running. The only exception is with the engine running and the parking brake

engaged. Once the parking brake is released, the lights will remain on as long as the ignition switch is on, even if the parking brake is later applied.

2 The DRL system supplies reduced power to the headlights so they won't be too bright for daytime use, while prolonging headlight life.

26 Airbag system - general information and precautions

General information

1 All models are equipped with two front airbags, formally known as the Supplemental Inflatable Restraint (SIR) system. This system is designed to protect the driver and the front seat passenger from serious injury in the event of a frontal collision. It consists of an array of external and internal (inside the SDM) information sensors (decelerometers), the Inflatable Restraint Sensing and Diagnostic Module (SDM), the inflator modules (a driver's airbag in the steering wheel and a passenger's airbag in the dash) and the wiring and connectors tying all these components together. Optional side-impact airbags, also known as roof rail or side curtain airbags, are available for protection against side impacts. The side-impact airbags, if equipped, are located along the left and right edges of the headliner, above the doors.

Airbag/inflator modules

Driver's airbag/inflator module

2 The airbag inflator module in the steering wheel consists of a housing, the cushion (airbag), an initiating device and a canister of gas-generating material. The initiator is part of the inflator module deployment loop. When a collision occurs, the SDM sends current through the deployment loop to the initiator. Current passing through the initiator ignites the material in the canister, producing a rapidly expanding gas, which inflates the airbag almost instantaneously. Seconds after the airbag inflates, it deflates almost as quickly through airbag vent holes and/or the airbag fabric.

3 When the SDM sends current to the initiator, it travels through the airbag circuit to the steering column. From there, a clockspring on the steering wheel delivers the current to the module initiator. This clockspring assembly, which is the final segment of the airbag ignition circuit, functions as the bridge between the end of the airbag circuit on the (fixed) steering column and the beginning of the circuit on the (rotating) steering wheel. It's designed to maintain a closed circuit between the steering column and the steering wheel regardless of the position of the steering wheel. For this reason, removing and installing the clockspring is critical to the performance of the driver's side airbag. For information on how to remove and install the driver's side airbag, refer to Chapter 10.

**26.4a Passenger airbag connector location
(behind the glove box area)**

**26.4b Passenger airbag module location
(glove box has been removed for clarity)**

Passenger's airbag/inflator module

4   The passenger's airbag/inflator module is mounted above the glove compartment. It's similar in design to the driver's airbag except that it doesn't use a clockspring. When deployed by the SDM, the passenger's airbag bursts through the dashboard above the glove box. Although this area looks like it's simply part of the dashboard, it's actually a trim cover with a perforated seam that allows the cover to separate from the dash when the passenger's airbag inflates (see illustrations).

Side impact airbag/inflator (roof rail) modules

5   The (optional) side-impact airbag/inflator (roof rail) modules are mounted along the outer edges of the headliner, right above the door openings. They extend from the A-pillar (front windshield pillar) to the C-pillar (rear window pillar). Each module consists of a housing, an inflatable airbag, an initiator and a canister of gas-generating material. Each roof rail module employs its own side impact sensor (SIS), which contains a sensing device that monitors changes in vehicle acceleration and velocity. This data is sent to the SDM, which compares it with its program. When the data exceeds a certain threshold, the SDM determines that the vehicle has been hit hard enough on one side or the other to warrant deployment of the roof rail on that side. The SDM doesn't deploy the roof rail airbags on both sides, just on the side being hit. Then the SDM sends current to the roof rail initiator to inflate the airbag, ripping open the headliner trim as it deploys to protect the occupant(s) on the left or right side of the vehicle. Side impact airbag/inflator modules are long enough to protect the driver and a left-side rear-seat passenger, or a front seat passenger and right-side rear-seat passenger.

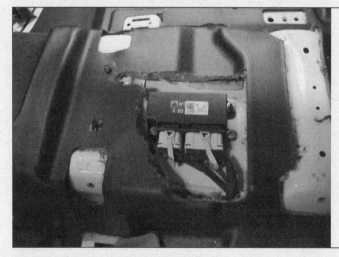

**26.7 SDM location
(seats and center console removed for clarity)**

Inflatable Restraint Sensing and Diagnostic Module (SDM)

6   The SDM is the computer module that controls the airbag system. Besides a microprocessor, the SDM also includes an array of sensors. Some of them are inside the SDM itself. Other external sensors are located throughout the vehicle. All of the sensors, internal and external, send a continuous voltage signal to the SDM, which compares this data to values stored in its memory. When these signals exceed a threshold value (when the SDM determines that the vehicle is decelerating more quickly than the threshold value), the SDM allows current to flow through the circuit to the appropriate airbag module(s), which initiates deployment of the airbag(s).

7   The SDM is located underneath the center console. Once the console is removed (see Chapter 11, Section 27) the carpet padding will need to be removed. The easiest way is to cut around the SDM and remove that section of carpet padding rather than pulling the entire carpet padding up. Just reinstall the cut out piece back into place when you're finished (see illustration).

Disarming the system and other precautions

Warning: *Failure to follow these precautions could result in accidental deployment of the airbag and personal injury.*

8   Whenever working in the vicinity of the steering wheel, instrument panel or any of the other SIR system components, the system must be disarmed. To disarm the system:
a) *Point the wheels straight ahead and turn the key to the Lock position.*
b) *Disconnect the cable from the negative battery terminal. Refer to Chapter 5 for the disconnecting procedure.*
c) *Wait at least two minutes for the back-up power supply to be depleted.*

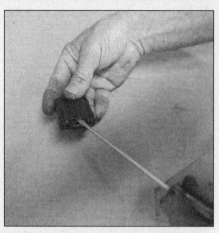

27.1a Carefully pry the two halves apart

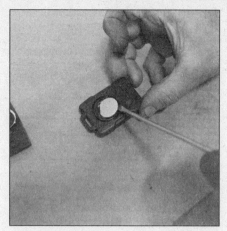

27.1b Pry the battery from the key fob

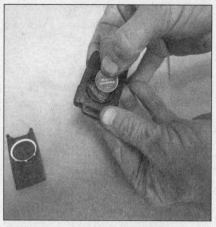

27.3 Remove the battery and observe the correct orientation and polarity

9   Whenever handling an airbag module, always keep the airbag opening (the trim side) pointed away from your body. Never place the airbag module on a bench or other surface with the airbag opening facing the surface. Always place the airbag module in a safe location with the airbag opening (the upholstered side) facing up.

10   Never measure the resistance of any SIR component or use any electrical test equipment on any of the wiring or components. An ohmmeter has a built-in battery supply that could accidentally deploy the airbag.

11   Never dispose of a live airbag/inflator module. Return it to a dealer service department or other qualified repair shop for safe deployment and disposal.

12   Never use electrical welding equipment in the vicinity of any airbag components. The connectors for the system are easy to spot because they're bright yellow. Do NOT disconnect or tamper with these connectors, or you run the risk of setting a Diagnostic Trouble Code (DTC) in the SDM. Like the PCM, the SDM has a malfunction indicator light, known as the AIR BAG indicator light, on the instrument cluster. When you turn the ignition key to ON, the SDM checks out all of the system components and circuits. If everything is okay, the AIR BAG indicator light goes off, just like the PCM's Malfunction Indicator Light (MIL). But if there's a problem somewhere, the light stays on, and will remain on until the problem is repaired and the DTC(s) cleared from the SDM's memory.

Impact seat belt retractors

13   All models are equipped with pyrotechnic (explosive) units in the front seat belt retracting mechanisms for both the lap and shoulder belts. During an impact that would trigger the airbag system, the airbag control unit also

triggers the seat belt retractors. When the pyrotechnic charges go off, they accelerate the retractors to instantly take up any slack in the seat belt system to more fully prepare the driver and front seat passenger for impact.

14   The airbag system should be disabled any time work is done to or around the seats.
Warning: *Never strike the pillars or floor pan with a hammer or use an impact-driver tool in these areas unless the system is disabled.*

---

27   Key fob - battery replacement and adding additional keys

---

Key fob battery replacement

1   Separate the two halves of the key fob by prying them apart at the slot along the edge with a small flat screwdriver or equivalent (see illustrations).

2   Observe the polarity of the battery before removing the old battery.

3   Carefully remove the battery and install the replacement battery. Take care not to bend or disturb any of terminals or leads inside the key fob (see illustration).

4   Snap the two halves of the key fob back together.

5   Check the operation of the key fob by trying the door locks on your vehicle.

Key fob strength testing

Note: *If for some reason your key fob fails to operate even after you've tried a replacement battery, take your key fob to a repair shop that has a tire monitor reset tool. Most of these tools have an RF strength indicator test as part of their diagnostics features. The technician can check whether your key fob is in working order or not. If there is no RF signal, the key fob is more than likely faulty. If the*

signal is weak chances are the battery needs to be replaced.

Adding additional keys

Warning:Up *to eight keys can be stored into the theft system. For USA production vehicles one, properly programmed key must be present. For Canadian models, two properly programmed keys must be present to perform this operation. This procedure will not work unless you already have a programmed key and follow the steps provided.*

USA production vehicle procedure

6   Insert the working key into the ignition and turn the ignition to on (engine off).

7   Turn off the ignition. Within 10 seconds insert the unprogrammed key.

8   Wait five seconds, the new key is programmed.

Canadian production vehicle procedure

9   Insert the working key into the ignition and turn the ignition to on.

10   Remove the key and install the second programmed key into the ignition and turn the ignition to on.

11   Remove the second programmed key and within 10 seconds insert the blank key into the ignition and turn the ignition to on (engine off).

12   Wait five seconds, the unprogrammed key is now programmed.

Replacing a damaged key or stolen key when no programmed key is available

13   This procedure requires the use of a factory scan tool. See the appropriate repair facility with the correct scanner to perform this procedure.

Key fob programming

14   This procedure requires the use of a factory scan tool. See the appropriate repair facility with the correct scanner to perform this procedure.

Garage door opener transmitter replacement

15   Using a flat trim removal tool carefully pry the overhead trim panel by applying pressure to the corners of the trim panel.

16   Disconnect the electrical connectors and remove the panel.

17   The garage door transmitter is mounted on the back of the trim panel by two screws. Remove the screws.

18   Installation is the reverse of removal.

19   Reprogram the garage door transmitter by following the procedure in your owner's manual.

28   Wiring diagrams - general information

1   Since it isn't possible to include all wiring diagrams for every year covered by this manual, the following diagrams are those that are typical and most commonly needed.

2   Prior to troubleshooting any circuits, check the fuse and circuit breakers (if equipped) to make sure they're in good condition. Make sure the battery is properly charged and check the cable connections (see Chapter 1).

3   When checking a circuit, make sure that all connectors are clean, with no broken or loose terminals. When unplugging a connector, do not pull on the wires; pull only on the connectors.

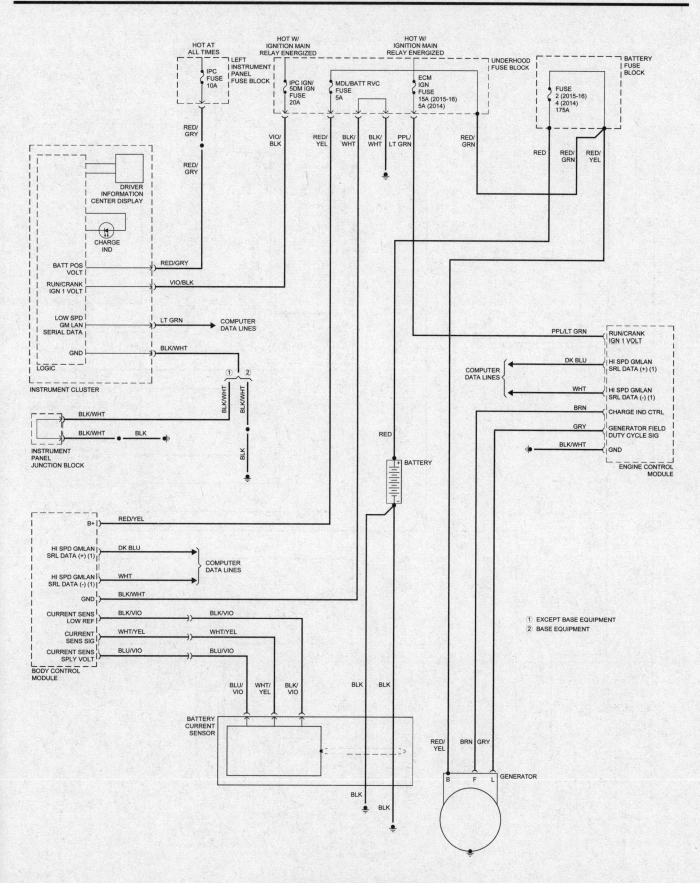

Charging system - Silverado/Sierra

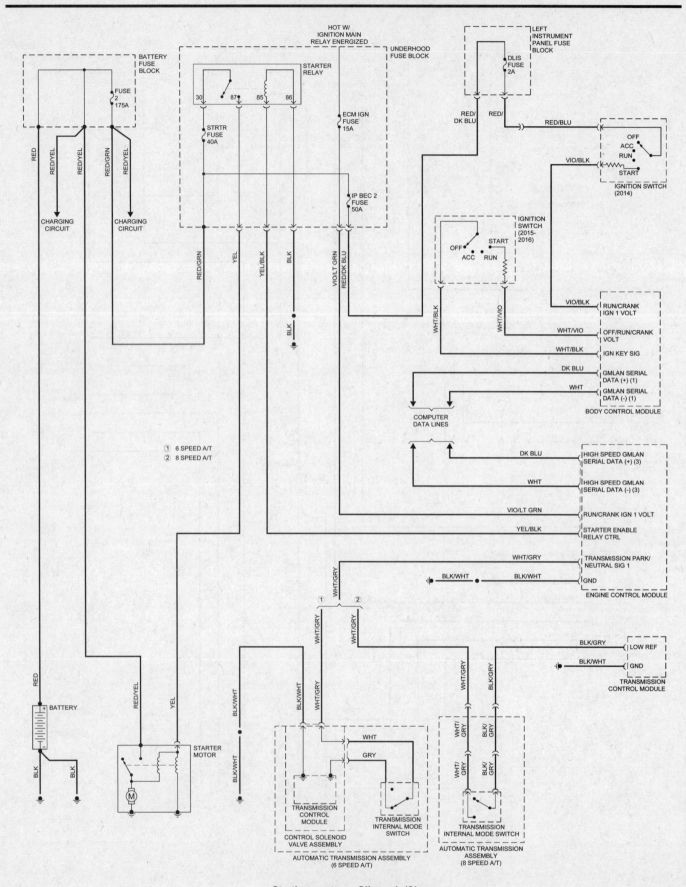

Starting system - Silverado/Sierra

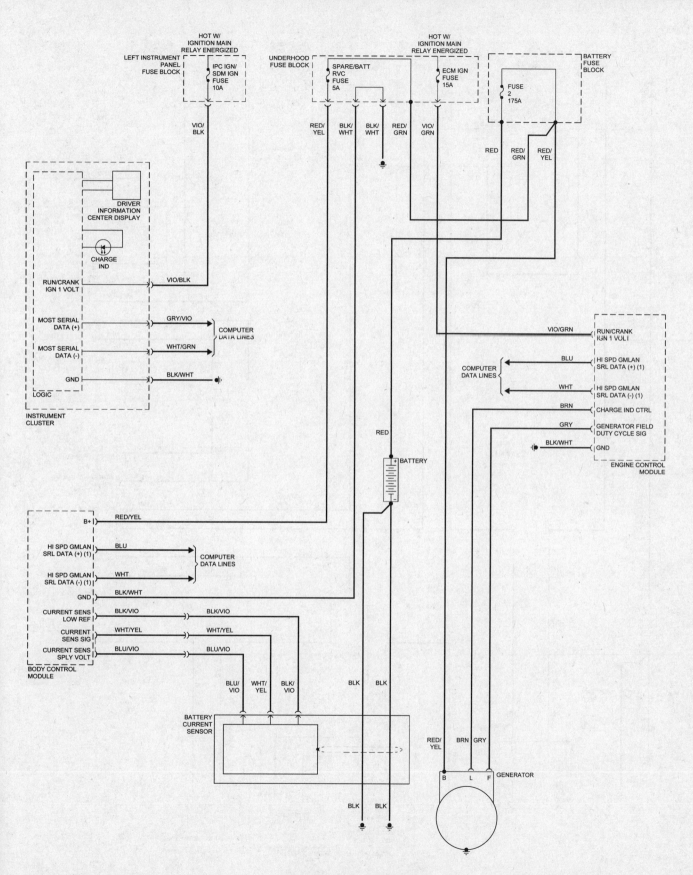

Charging system - SUV models

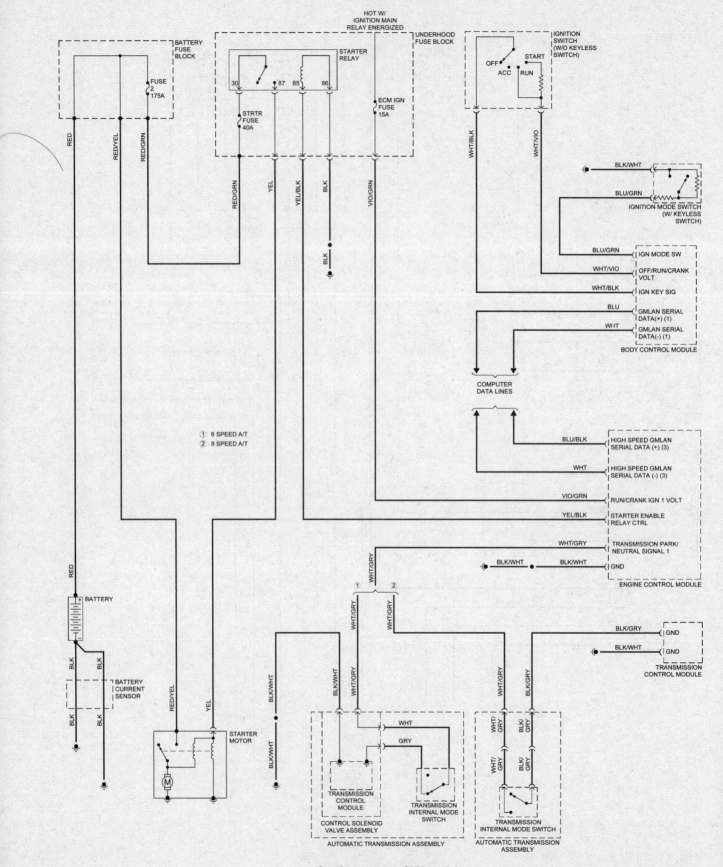

Starting system - SUV models

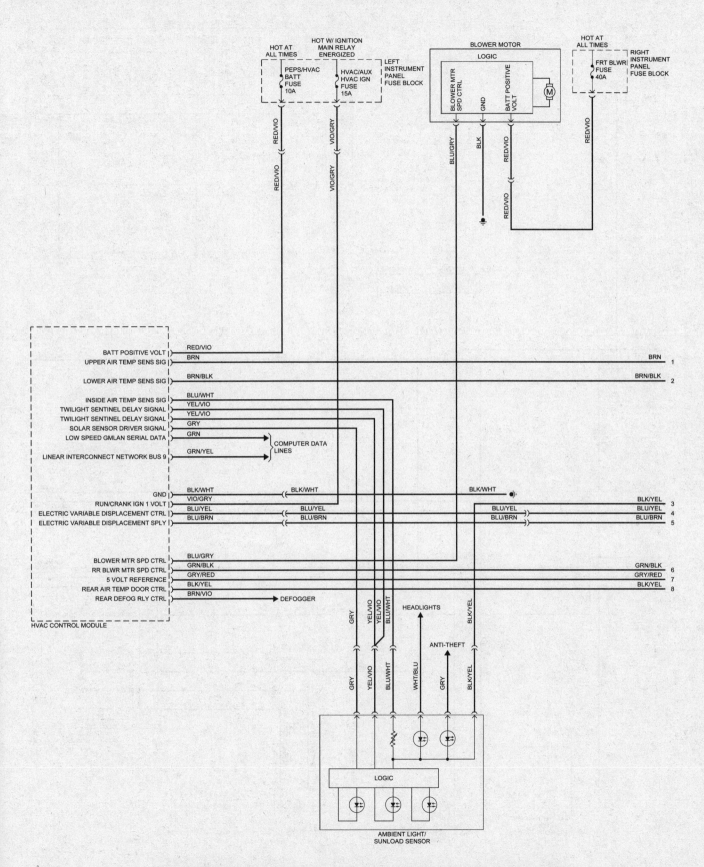

Air conditioning and heating system and engine cooling fans - SUV models (1 of 5)

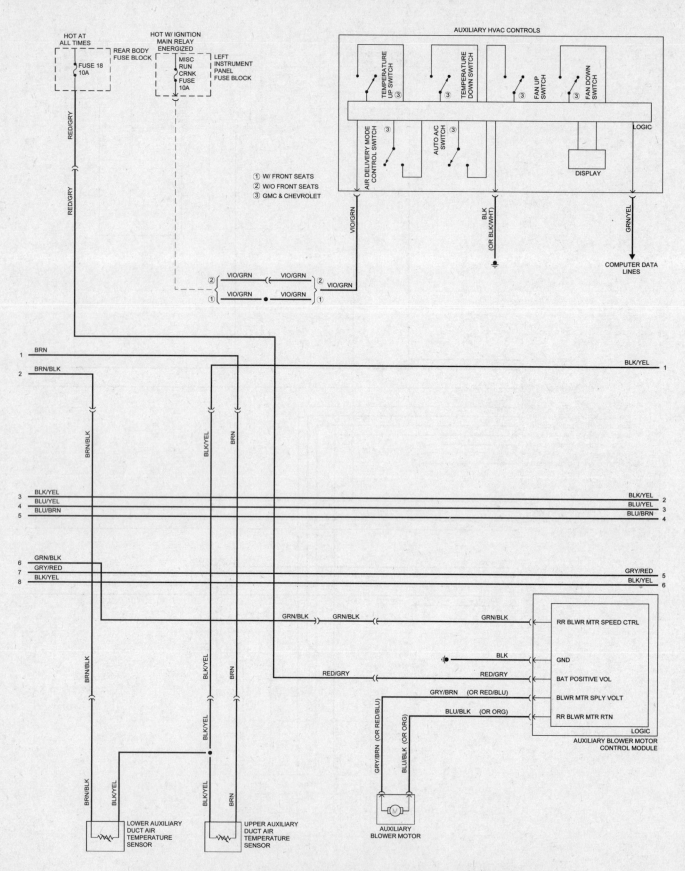

Air conditioning and heating system and engine cooling fans - SUV models (2 of 5)

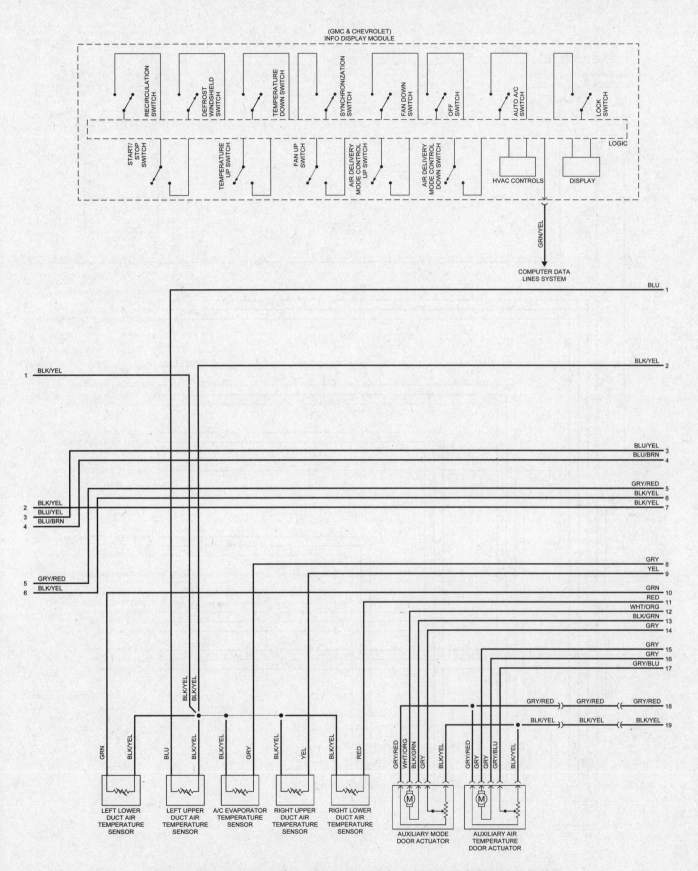

Air conditioning and heating system and engine cooling fans - SUV models (3 of 5)

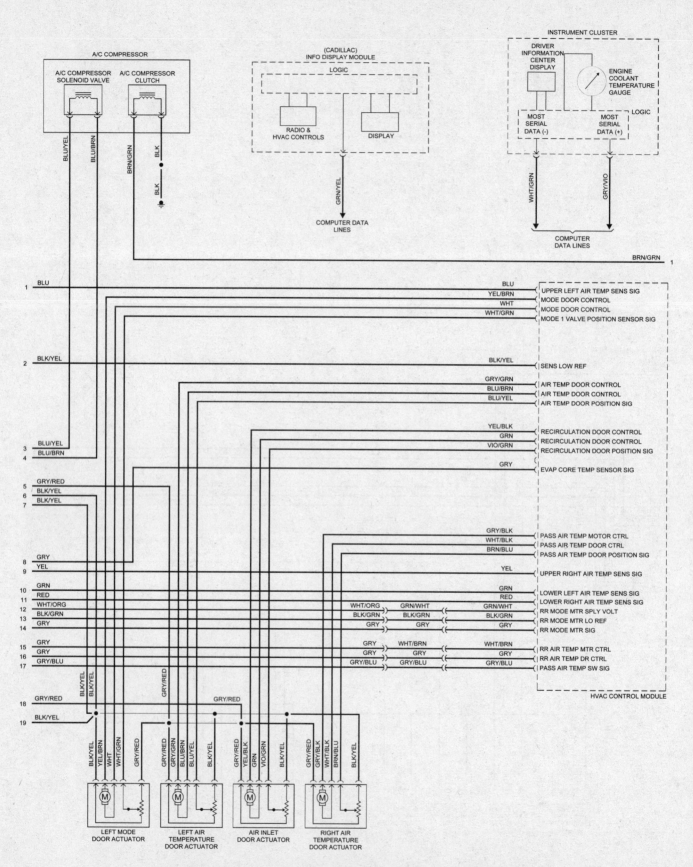

Air conditioning and heating system and engine cooling fans - SUV models (4 of 5)

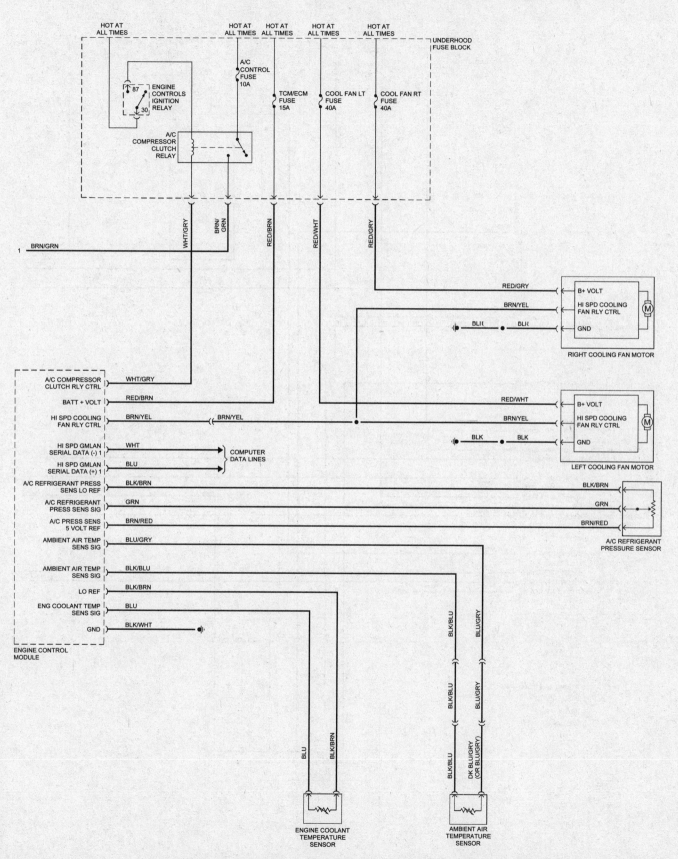

Air conditioning and heating system and engine cooling fans - SUV models (5 of 5)

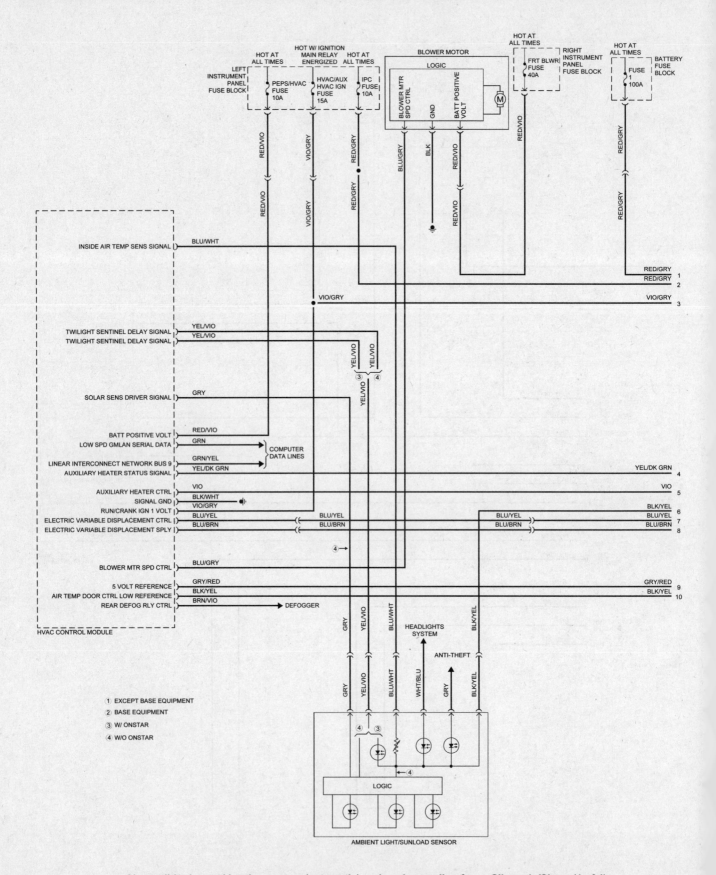

Air conditioning and heating system (automatic) and engine cooling fans - Silverado/Sierra (1 of 4)

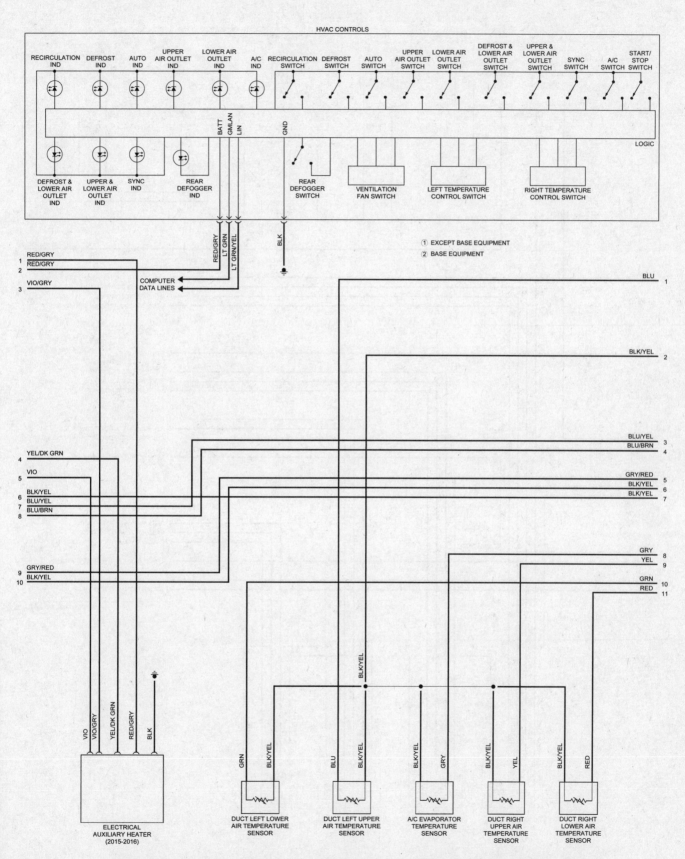

Air conditioning and heating system (automatic) and engine cooling fans - Silverado/Sierra (2 of 4)

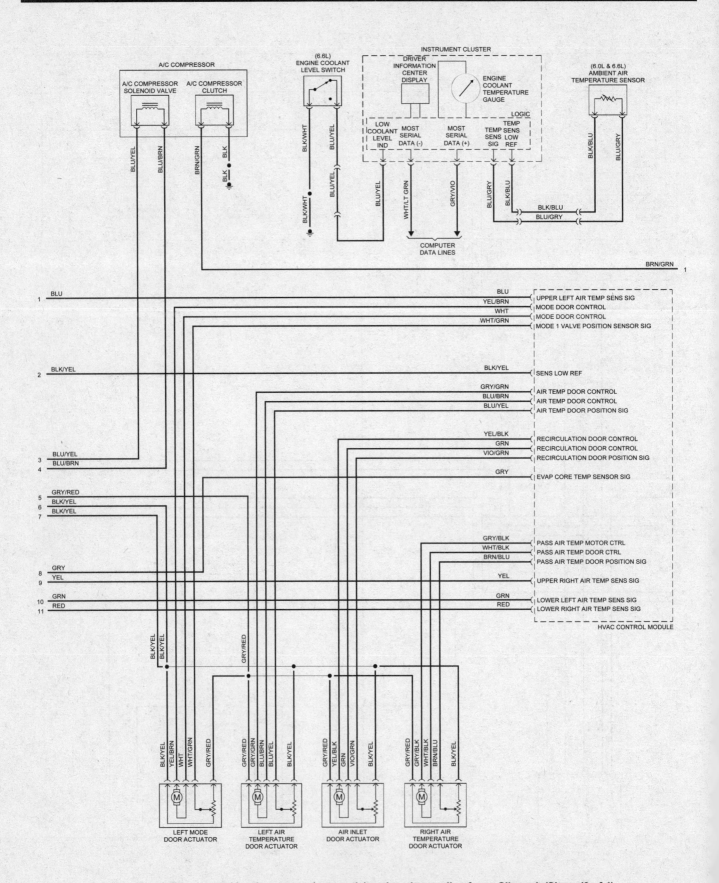

Air conditioning and heating system (automatic) and engine cooling fans - Silverado/Sierra (3 of 4)

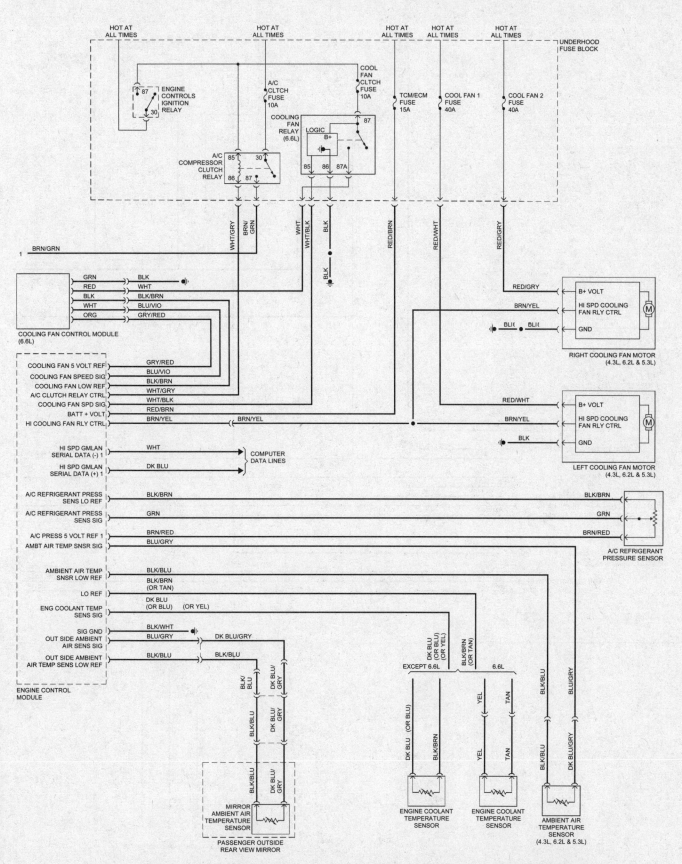

Air conditioning and heating system (automatic) and engine cooling fans - Silverado/Sierra (4 of 4)

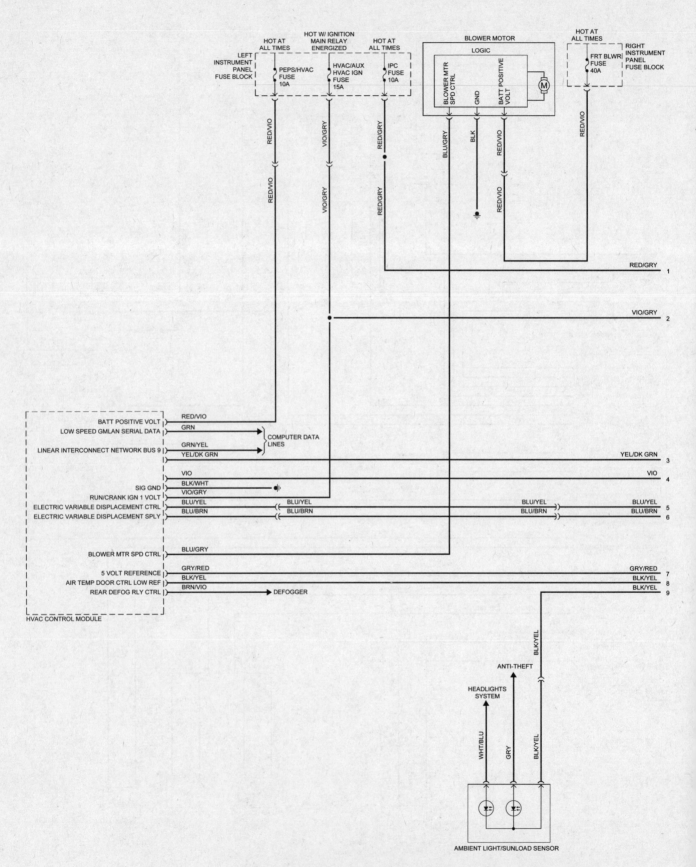

Air conditioning and heating system (manual) and engine cooling fans - Silverado/Sierra (1 of 4)

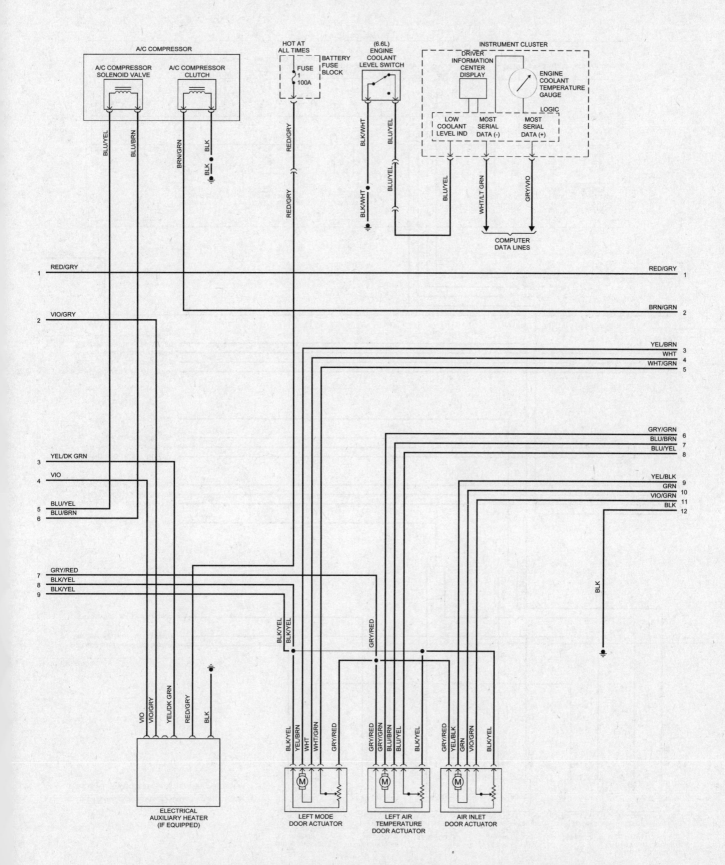

Air conditioning and heating system (manual) and engine cooling fans - Silverado/Sierra (2 of 4)

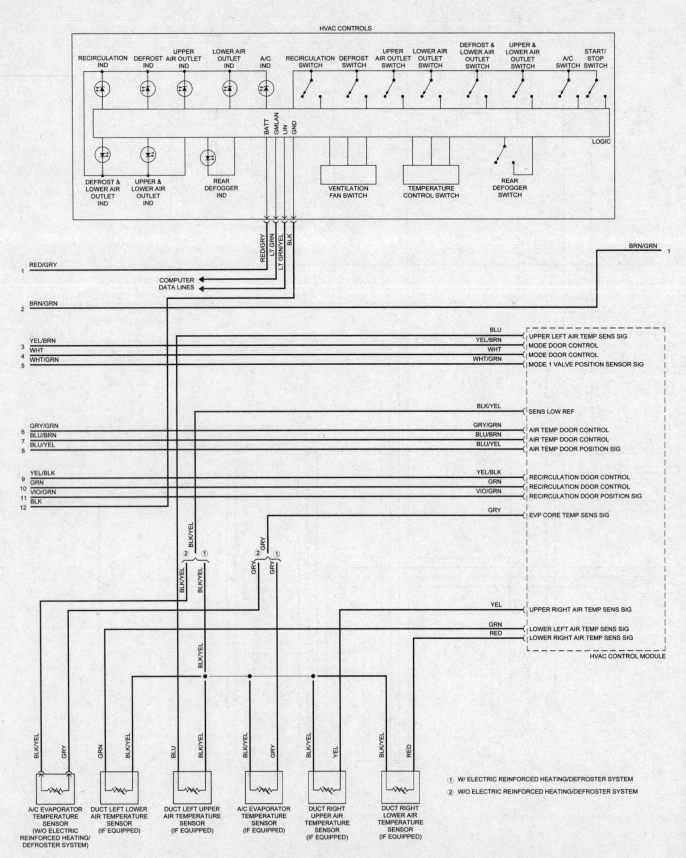

Air conditioning and heating system (manual) and engine cooling fans - Silverado/Sierra (3 of 4)

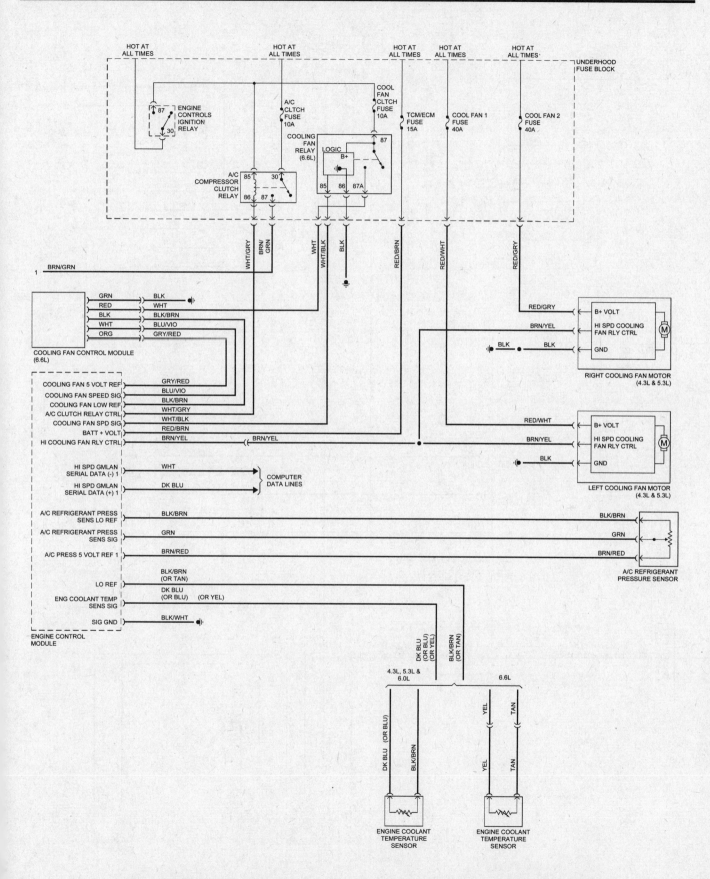

Air conditioning and heating system (manual) and engine cooling fans - Silverado/Sierra (4 of 4)

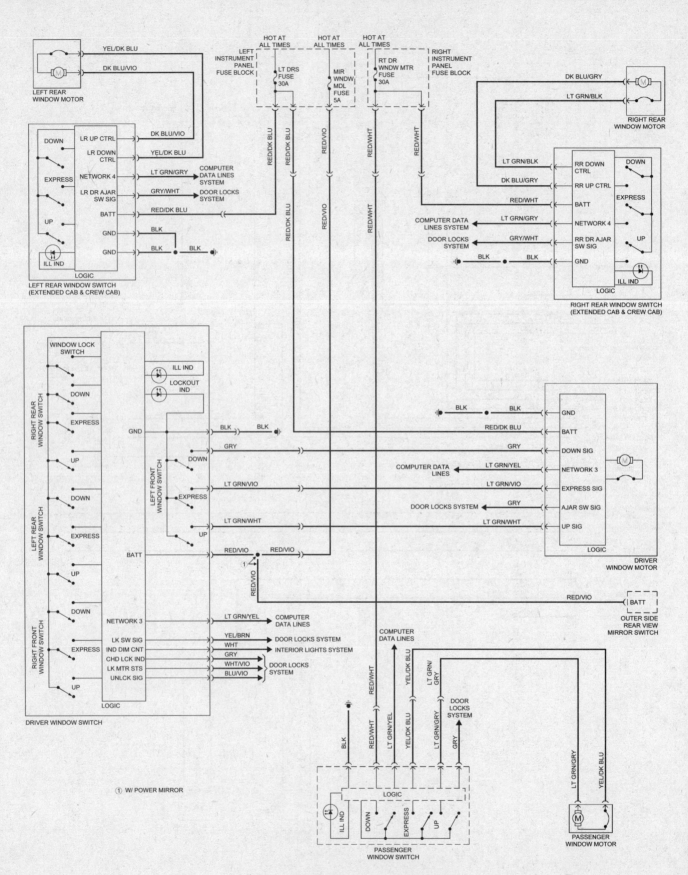

Power window system - Silverado/Sierra

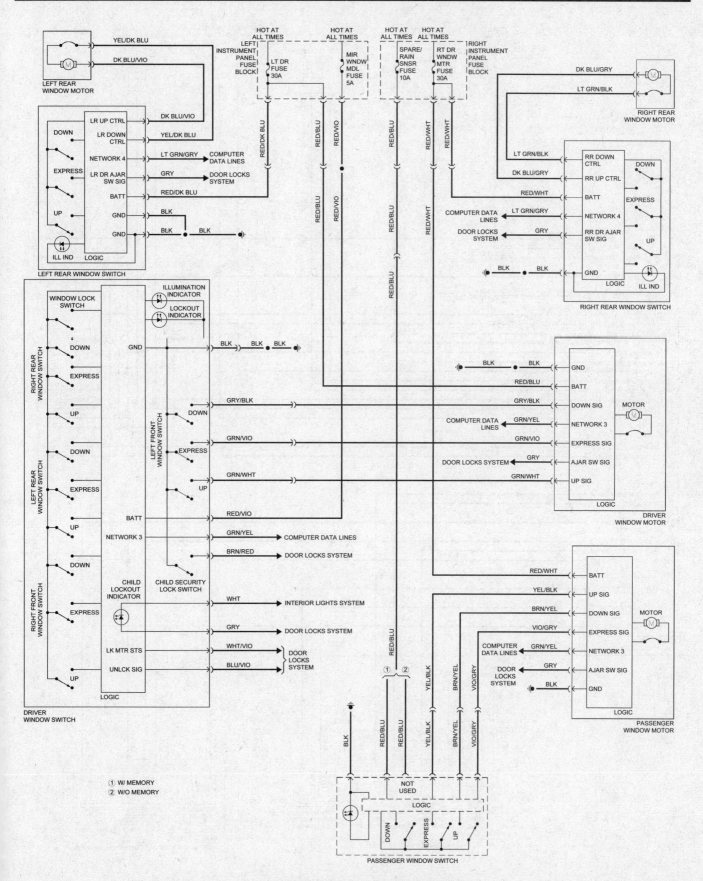

Power window system - SUV models

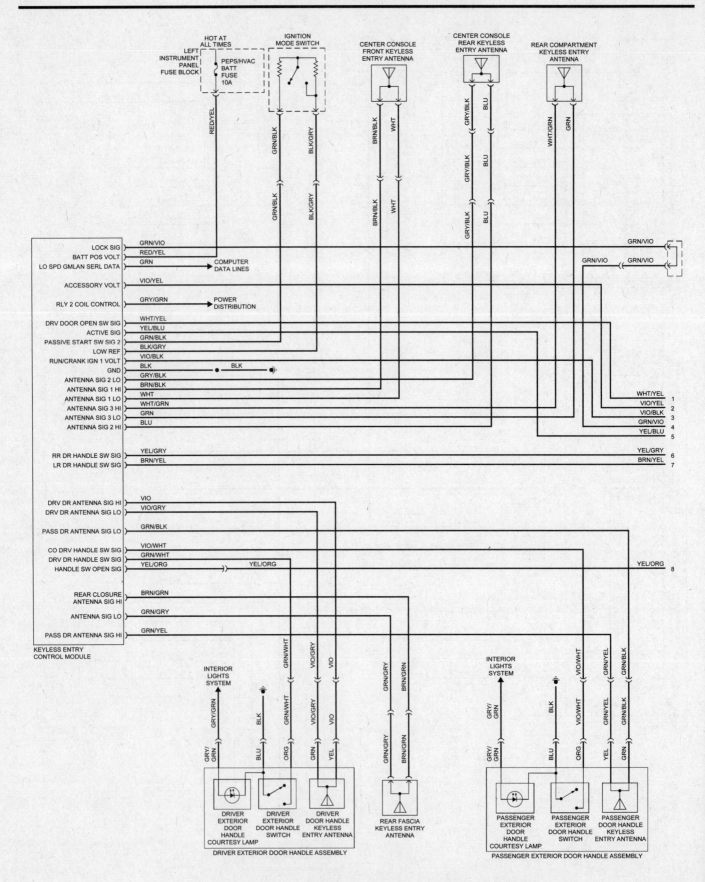

Power door lock system (with passive keyless entry) - SUV models (1 of 7)

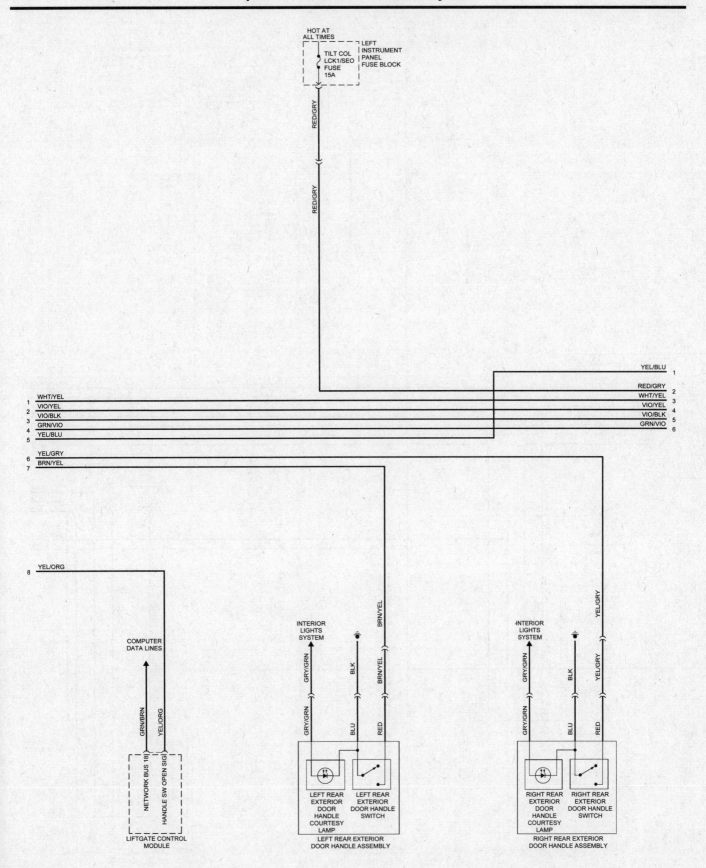

Power door lock system (with passive keyless entry) - SUV models (2 of 7)

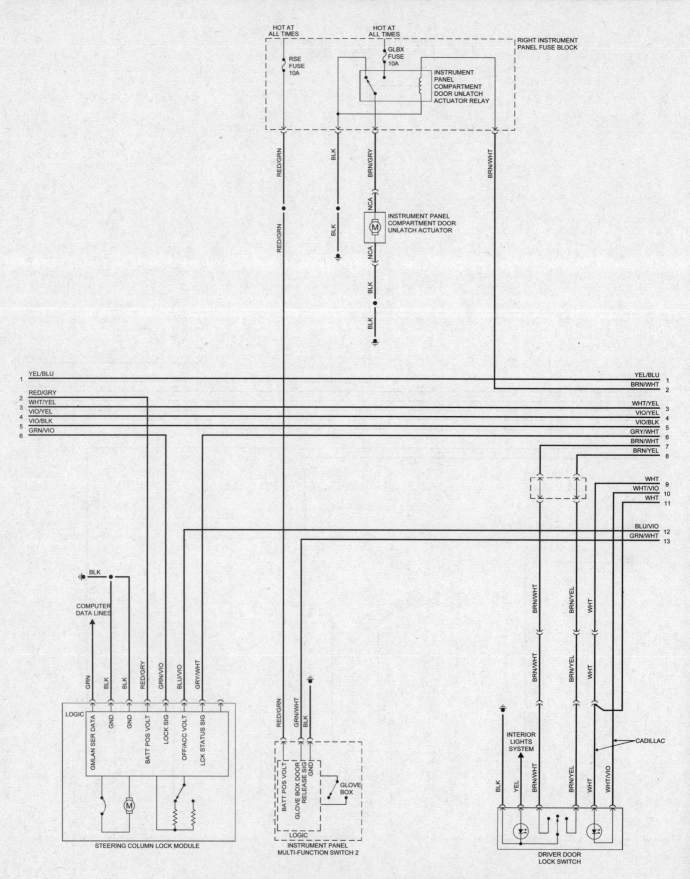

Power door lock system (with passive keyless entry) - SUV models (3 of 7)

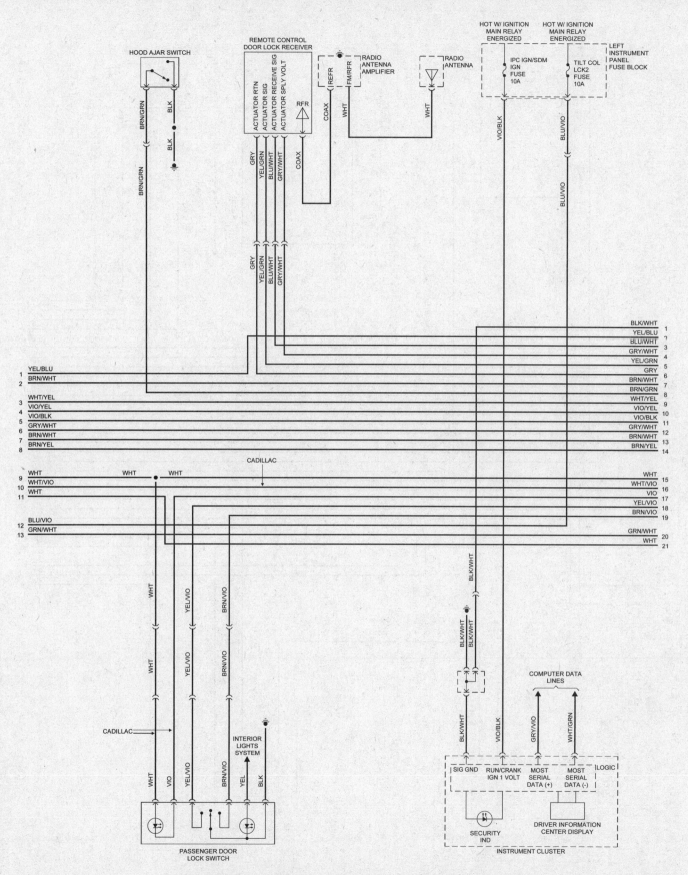

Power door lock system (with passive keyless entry) - SUV models (4 of 7)

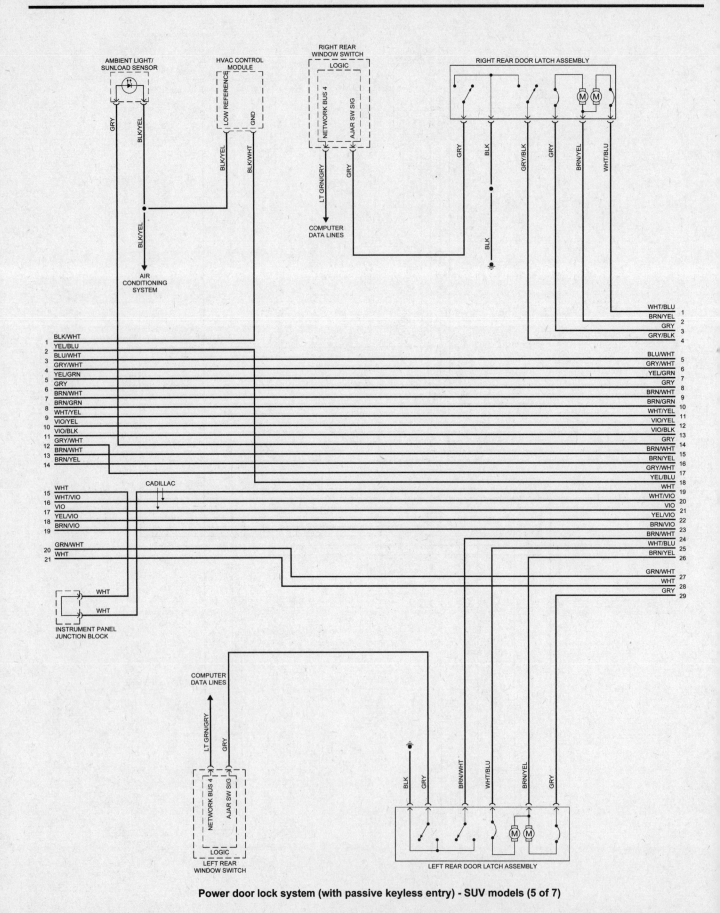

Power door lock system (with passive keyless entry) - SUV models (5 of 7)

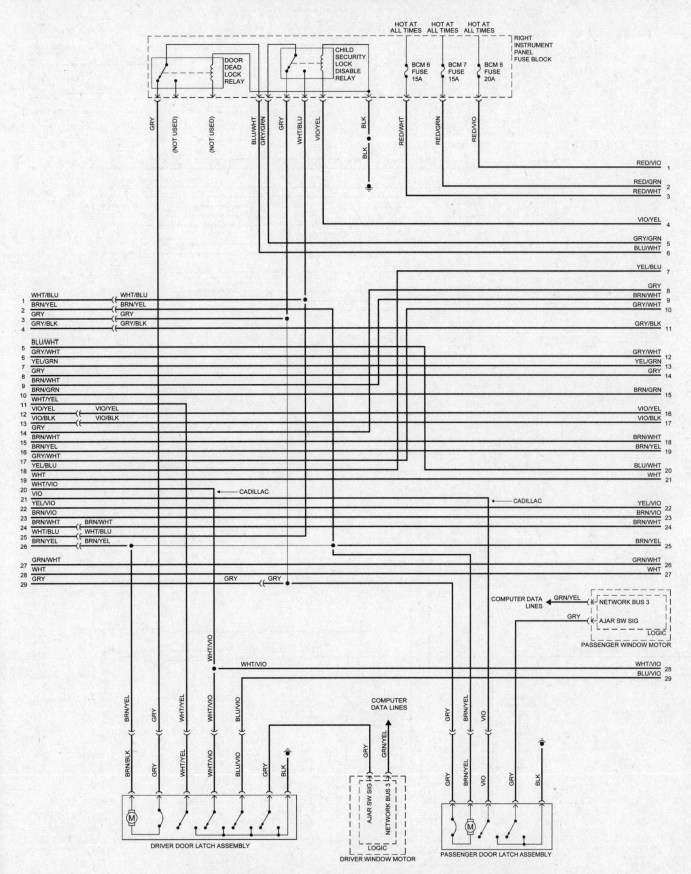

Power door lock system (with passive keyless entry) - SUV models (6 of 7)

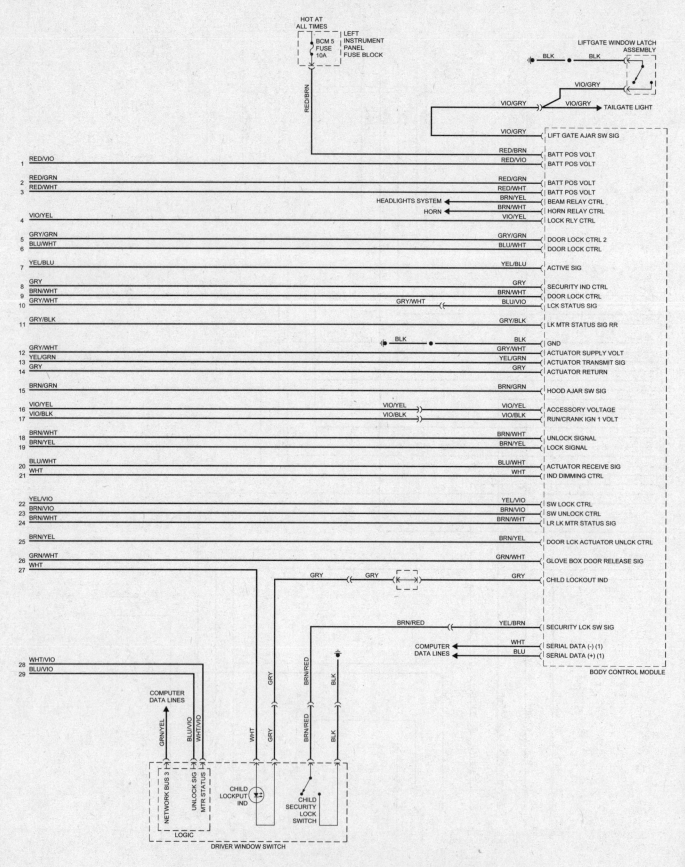

Power door lock system (with passive keyless entry) - SUV models (7 of 7)

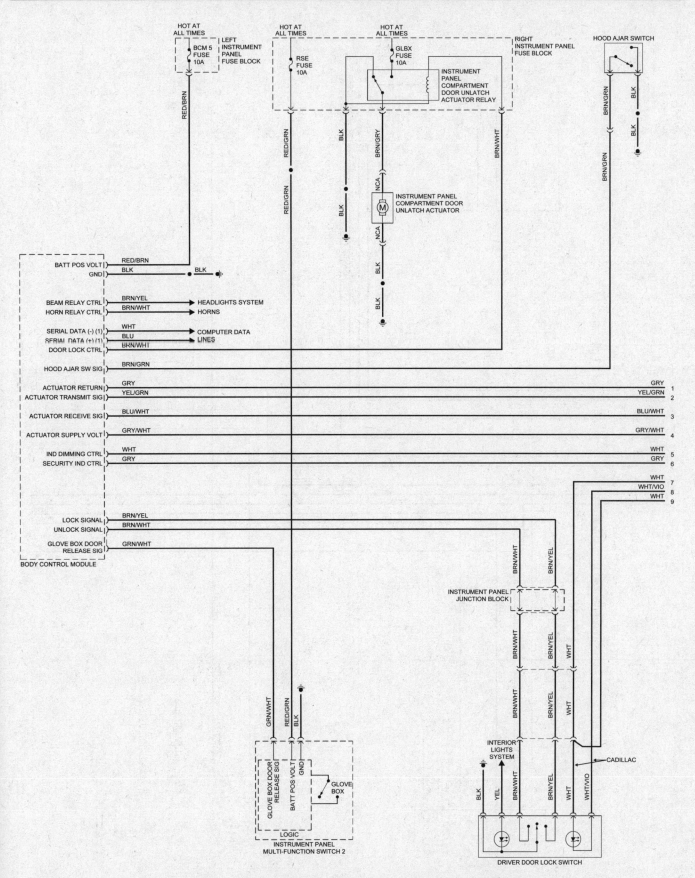

Power door lock system (without passive keyless entry) - SUV models (1 of 4)

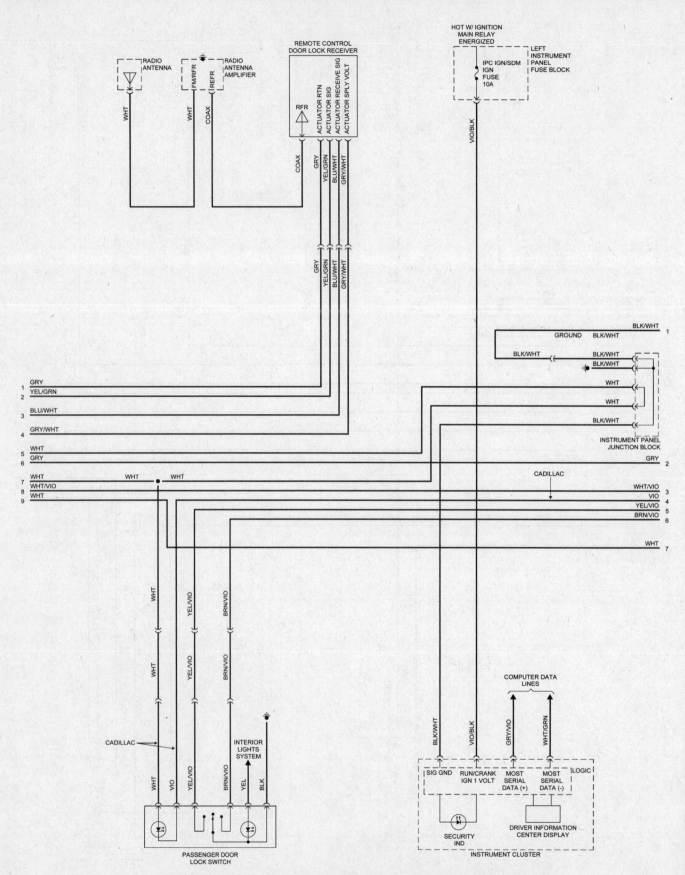

Power door lock system (without passive keyless entry) - SUV models (2 of 4)

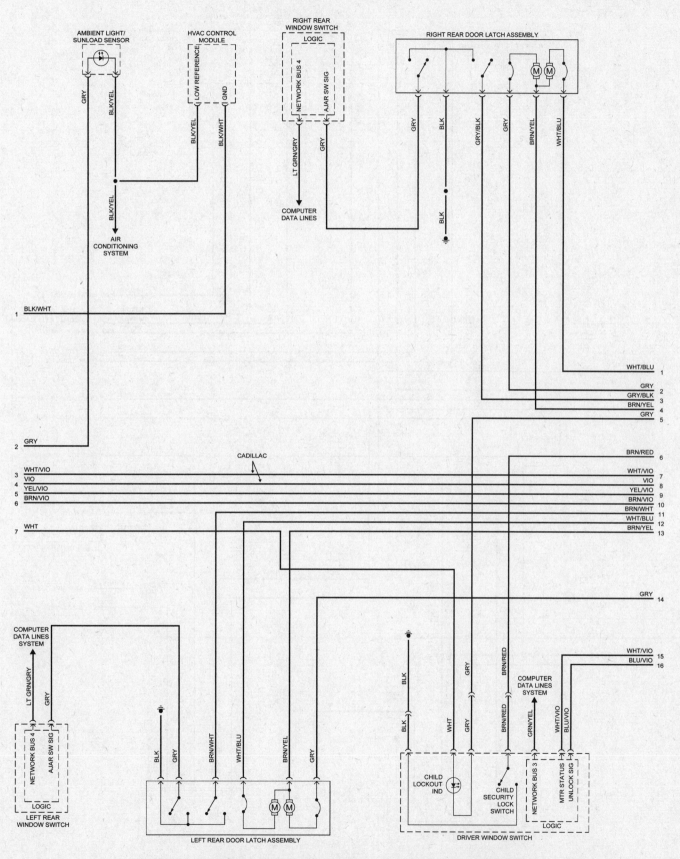

Power door lock system (without passive keyless entry) - SUV models (3 of 4)

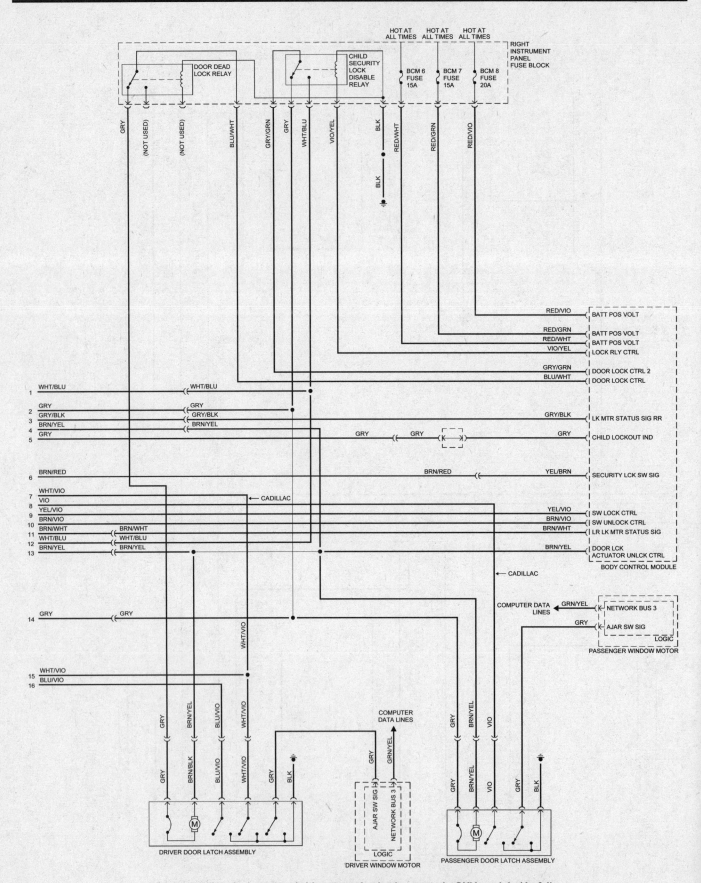

Power door lock system (without passive keyless entry) - SUV models (4 of 4)

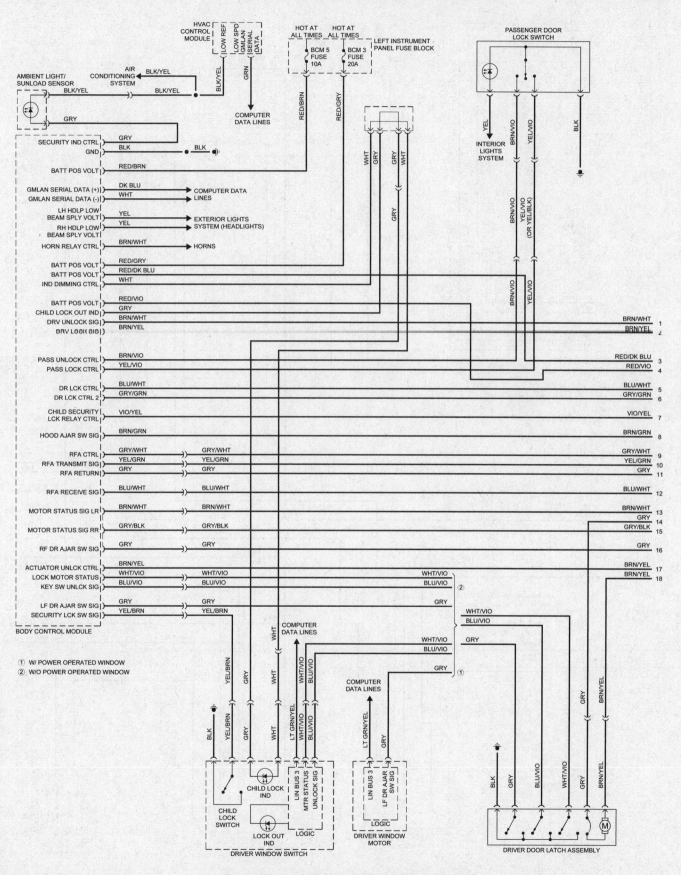

Power door lock system - Silverado/Sierra (1 of 3)

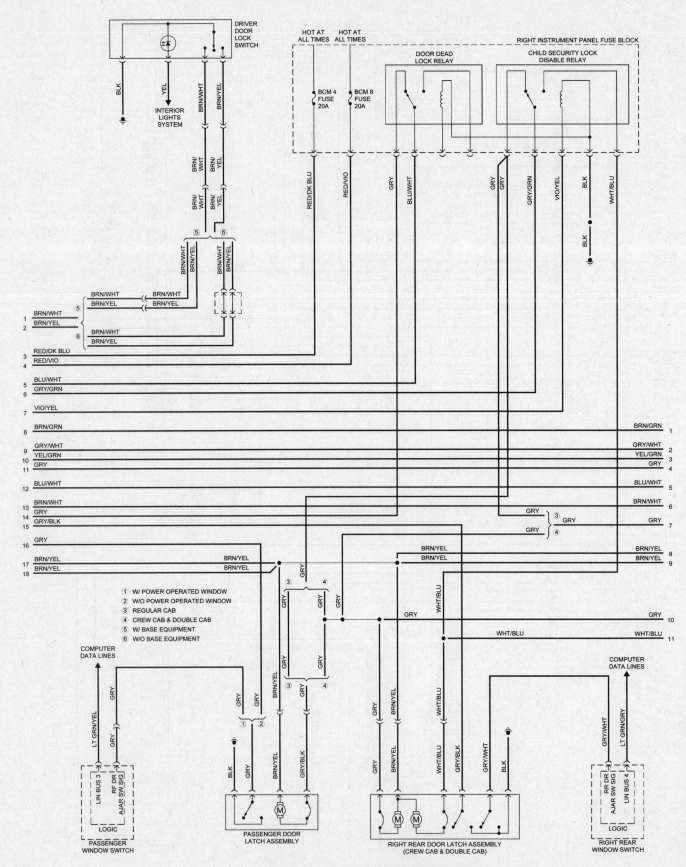

Power door lock system - Silverado/Sierra (2 of 3)

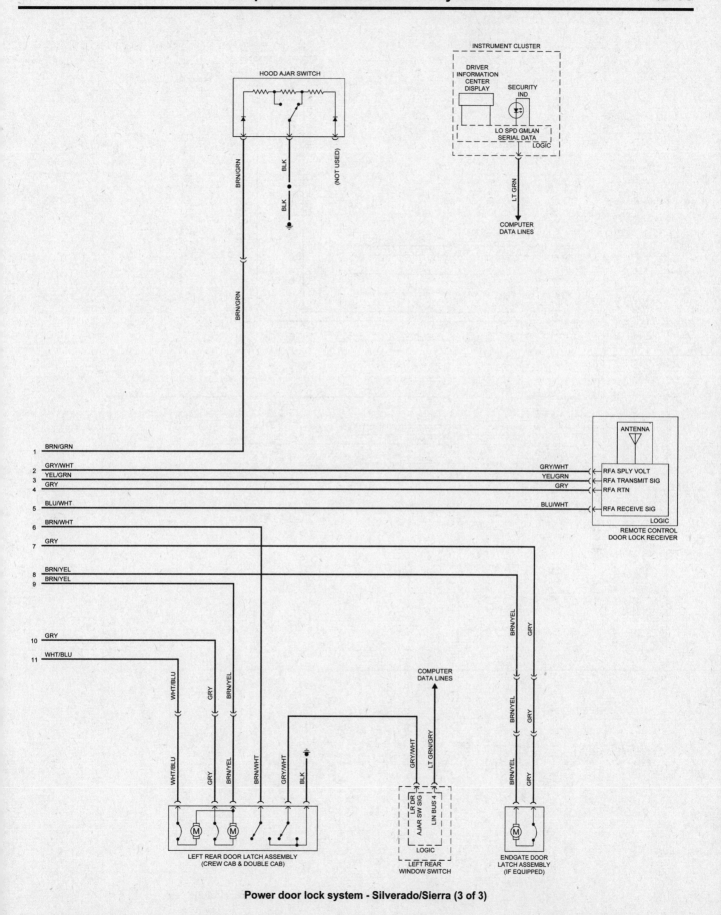

Power door lock system - Silverado/Sierra (3 of 3)

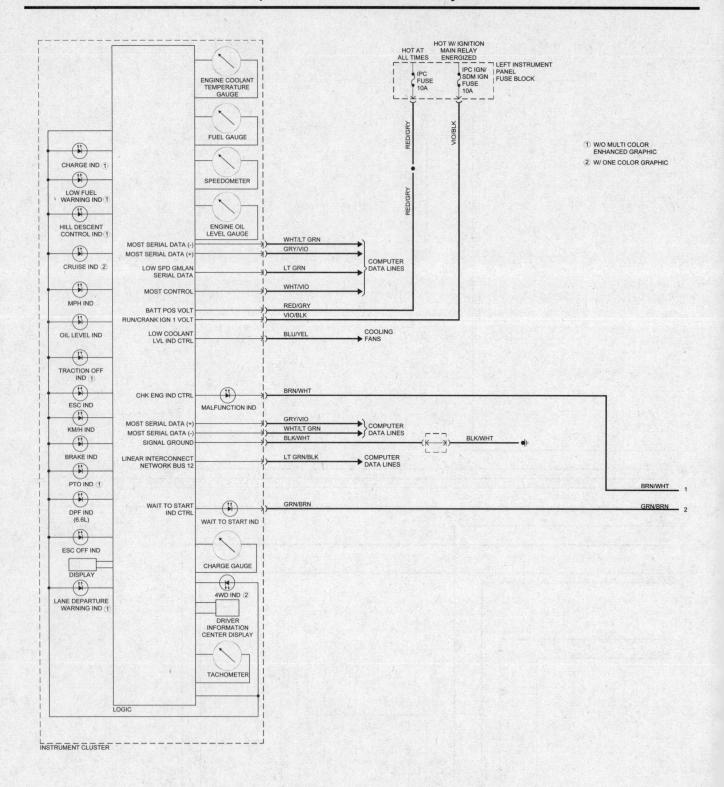

Gauges and warning lights system - Silverado/Sierra (1 of 2)

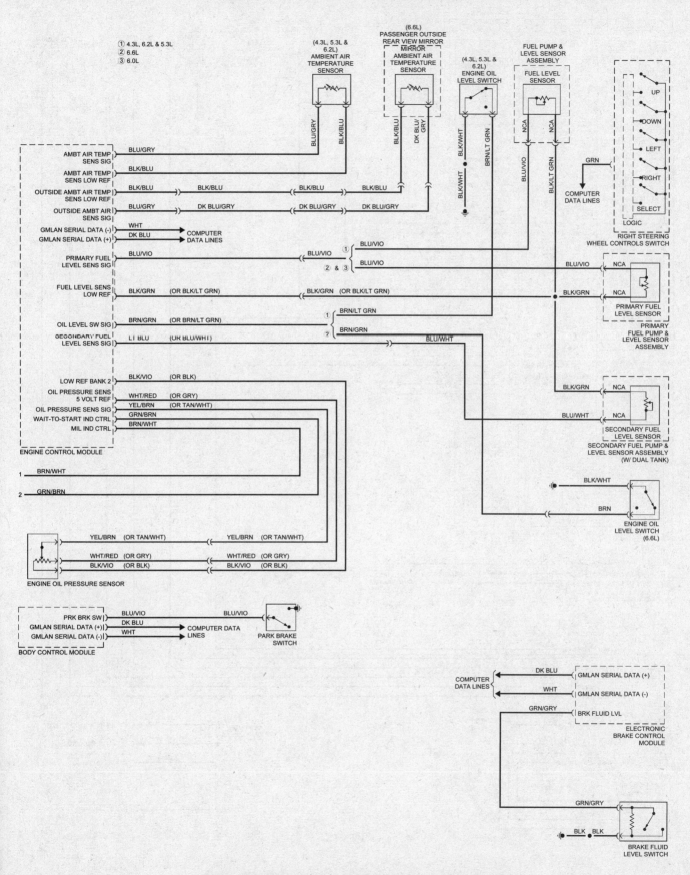

Gauges and warning lights system - Silverado/Sierra (2 of 2)

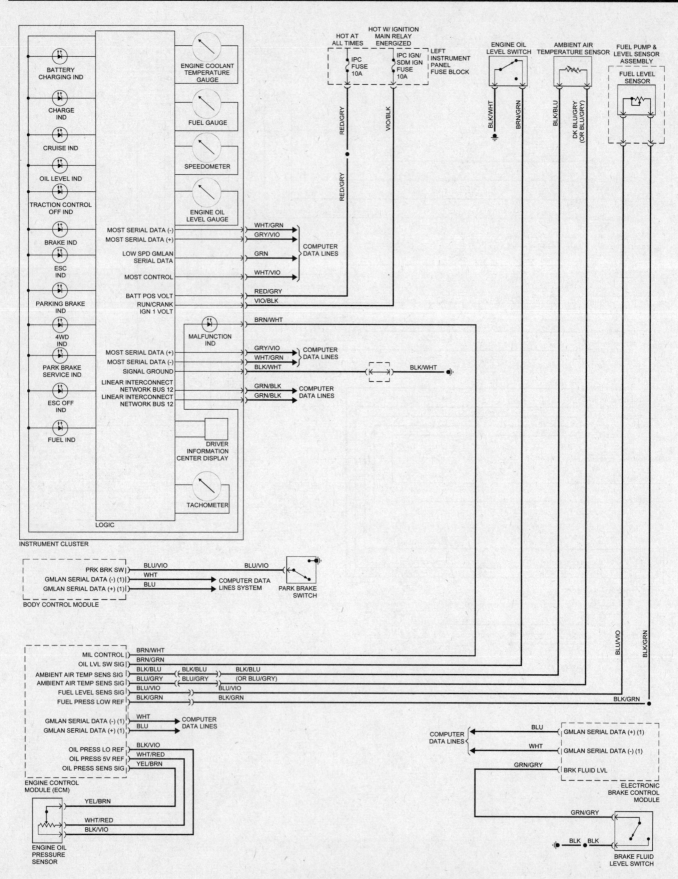

Gauges and warning lights system - SUV models

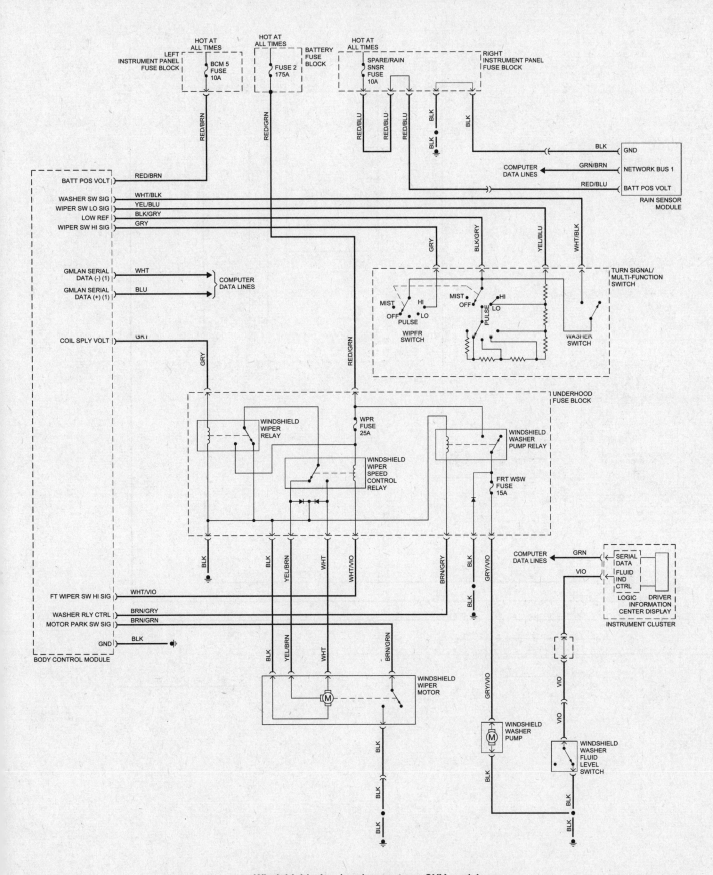

Windshield wiper/washer system - SUV models

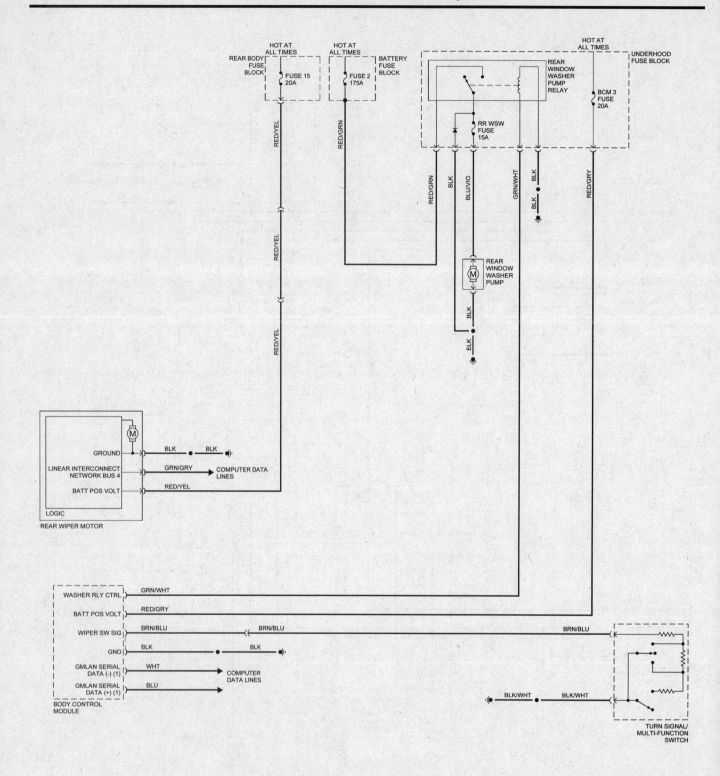

Rear window wiper/washer system - SUV models

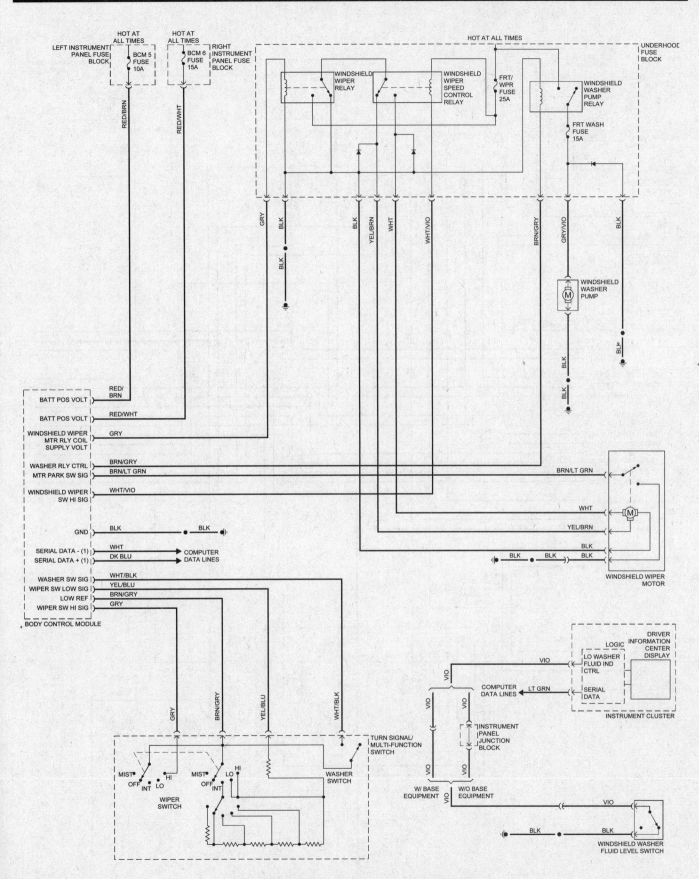

Windshield wiper/washer system - Silverado/Sierra

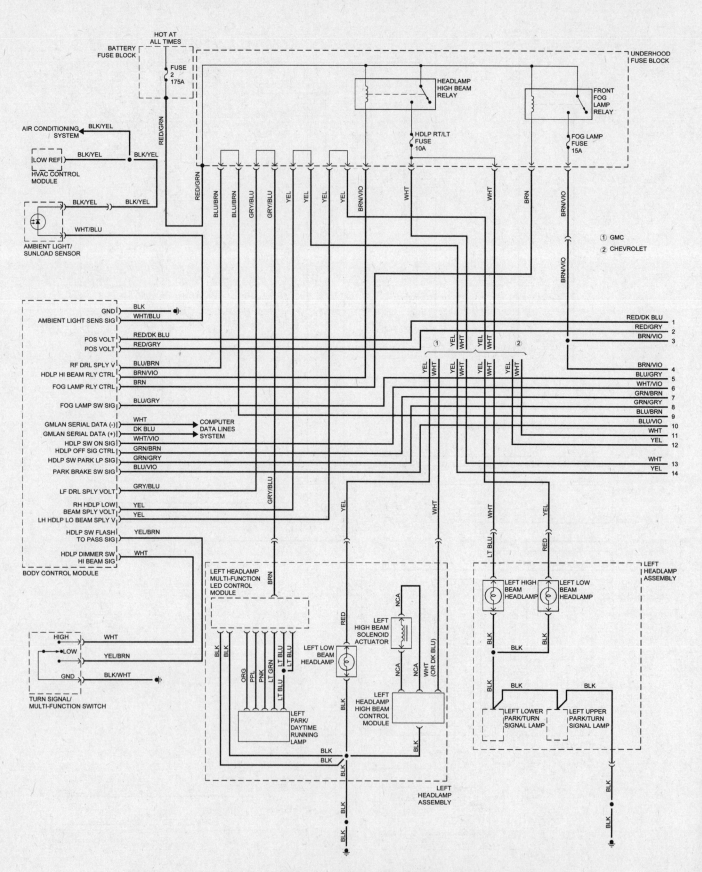

Headlight system - 2014 and 2015 Silverado/Sierra 1500, 2015 Silverado/Sierra 2500/3500 (1 of 2)

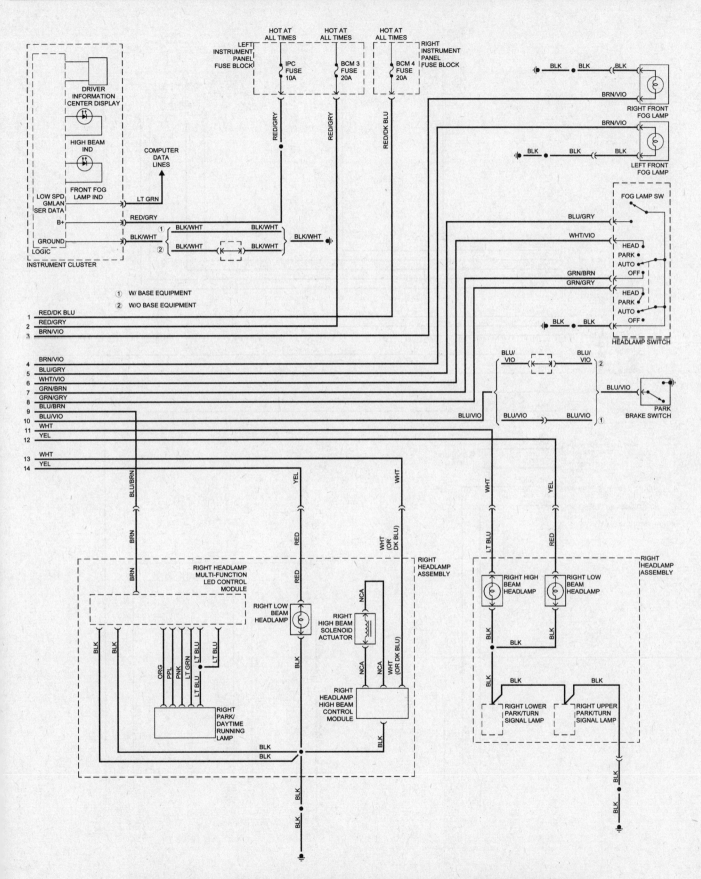

Headlight system - 2014 and 2015 Silverado/Sierra 1500, 2015 Silverado/Sierra 2500/3500 (2 of 2)

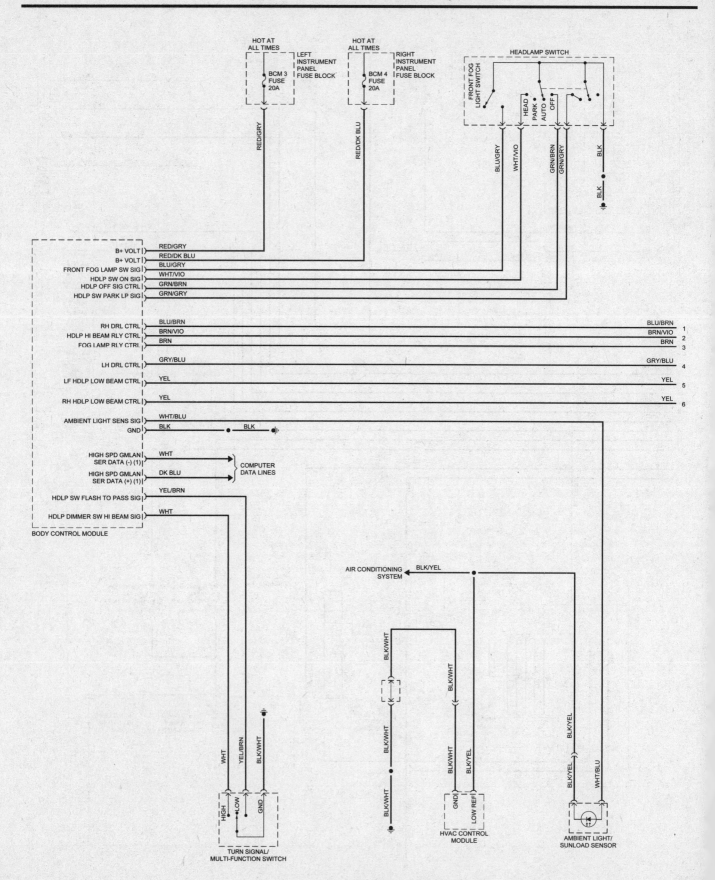

Headlight system - 2016 Silverado/Sierra (1 of 5)

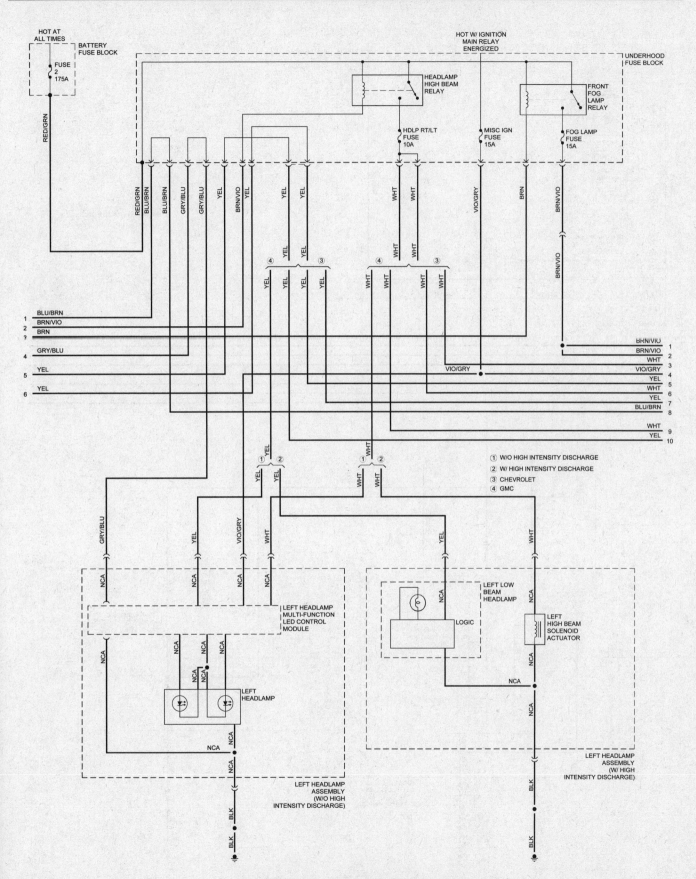

Headlight system - 2016 Silverado/Sierra (2 of 5)

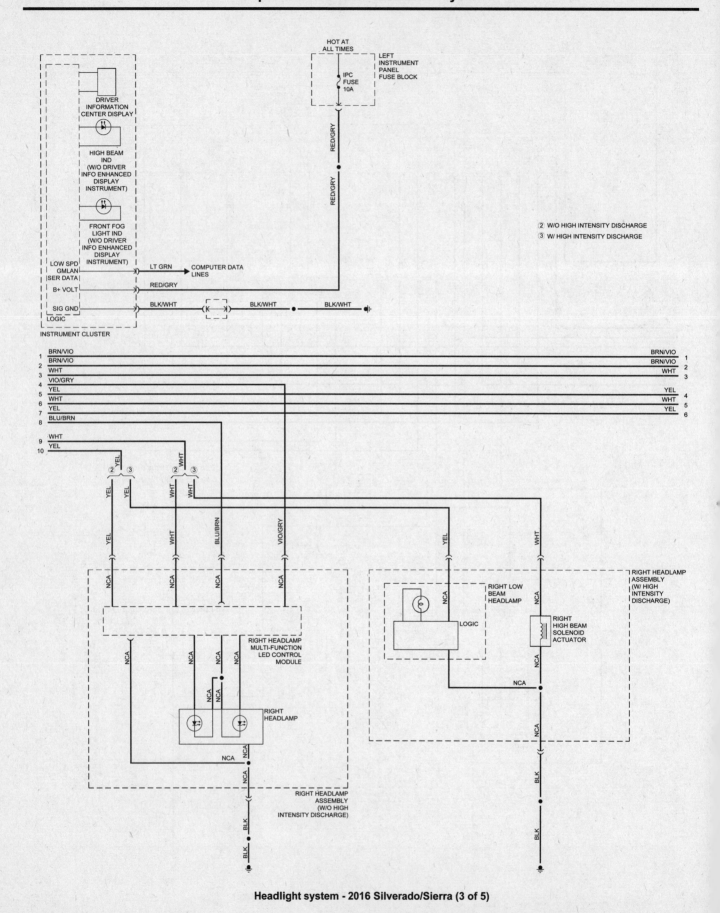

Headlight system - 2016 Silverado/Sierra (3 of 5)

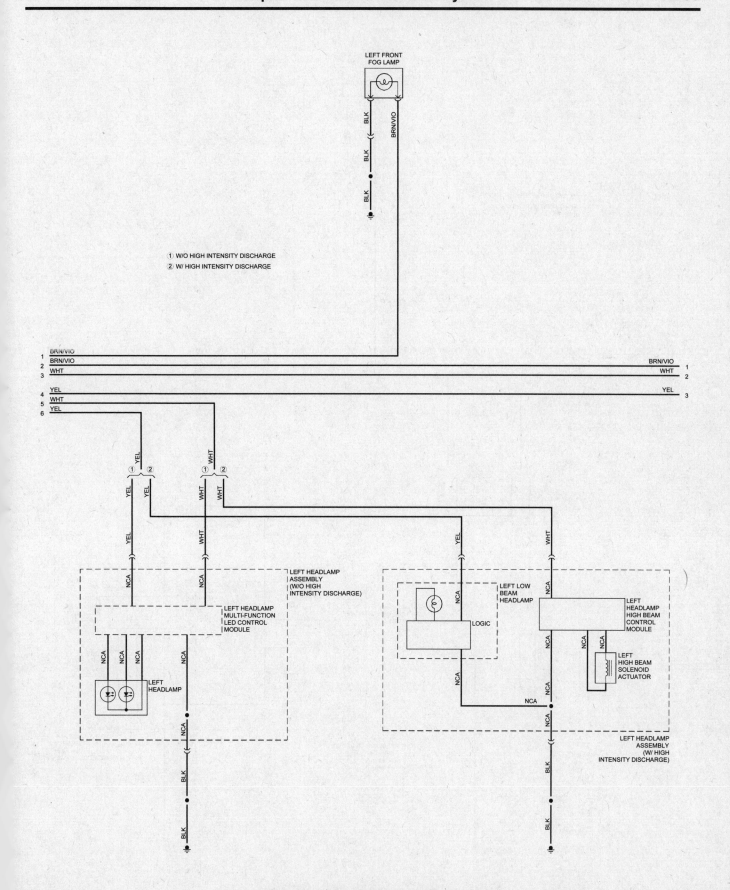

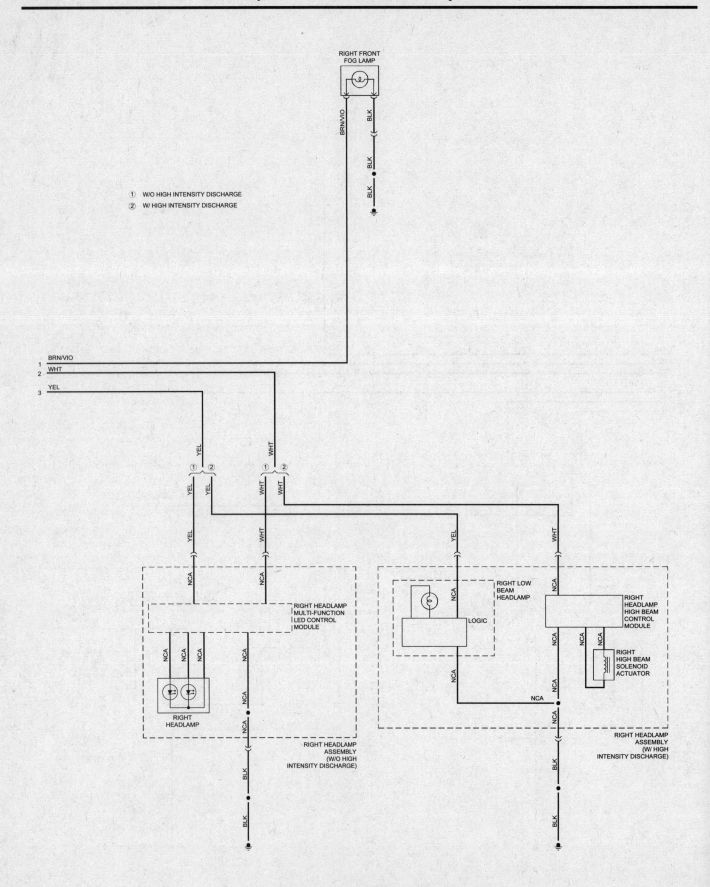

Headlight system - 2016 Silverado/Sierra (5 of 5)

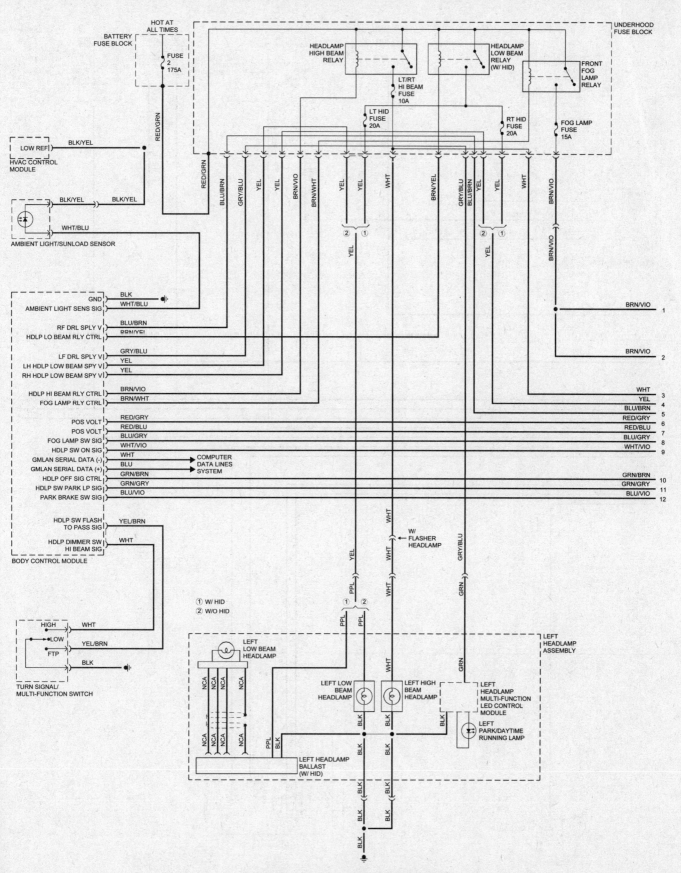

Headlight system - SUV models (1 of 3)

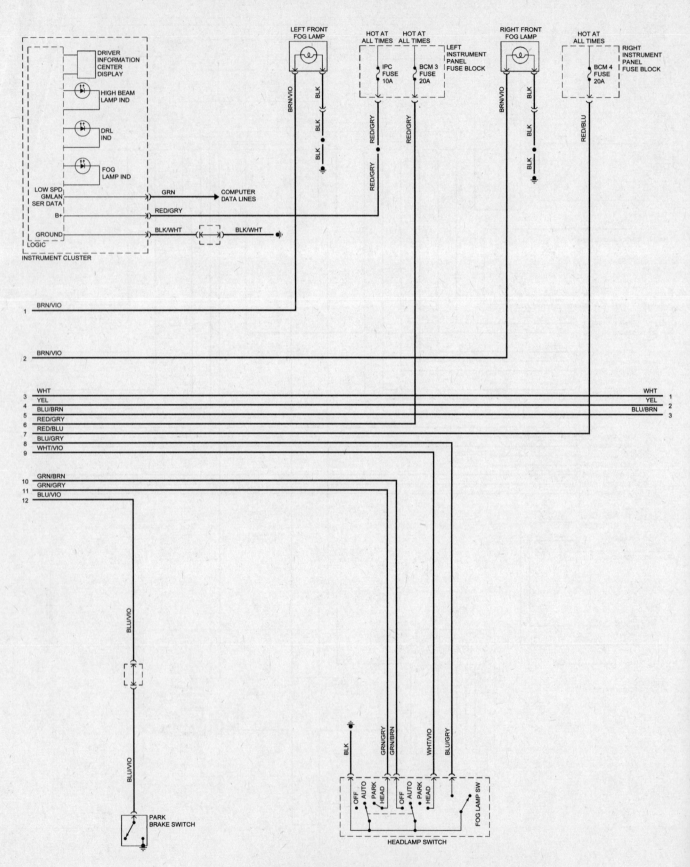

Headlight system - SUV models (2 of 3)

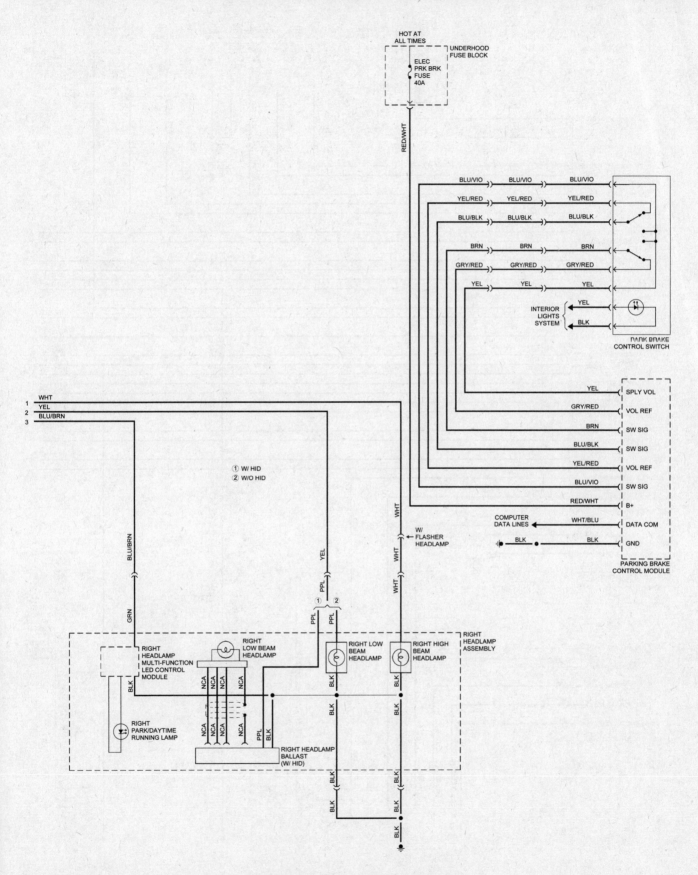

Headlight system - SUV models (3 of 3)

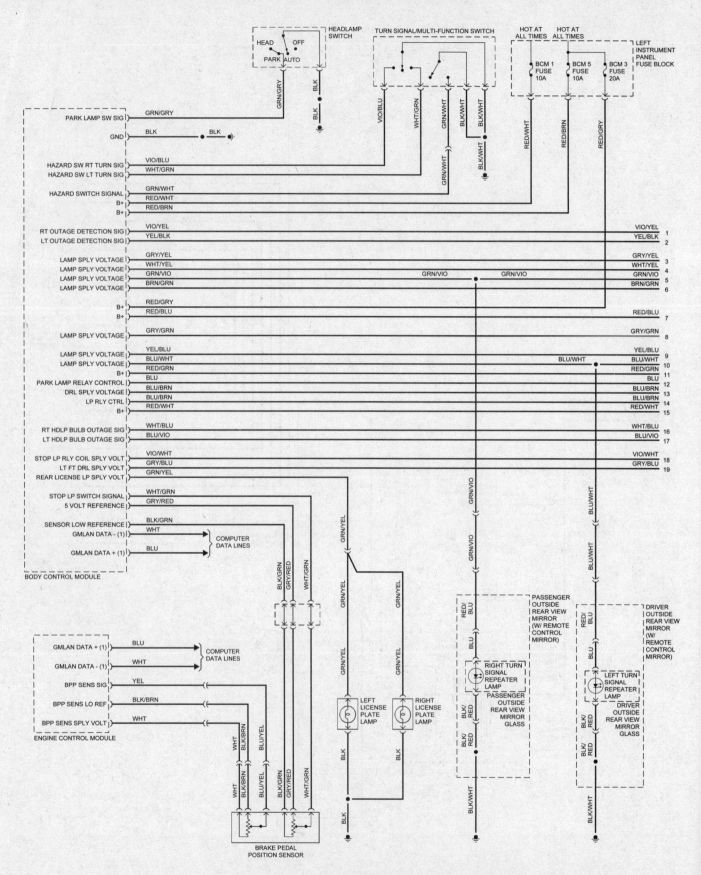

Exterior lighting system (exc. headlights and back-up lights) - SUV models (1 of 6)

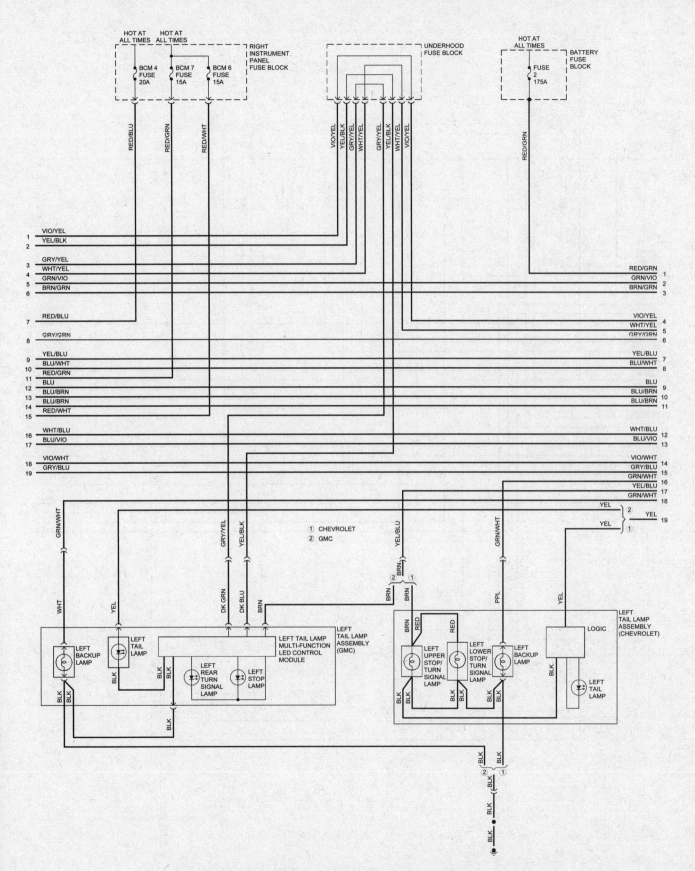

Exterior lighting system (exc. headlights and back-up lights) - SUV models (2 of 6)

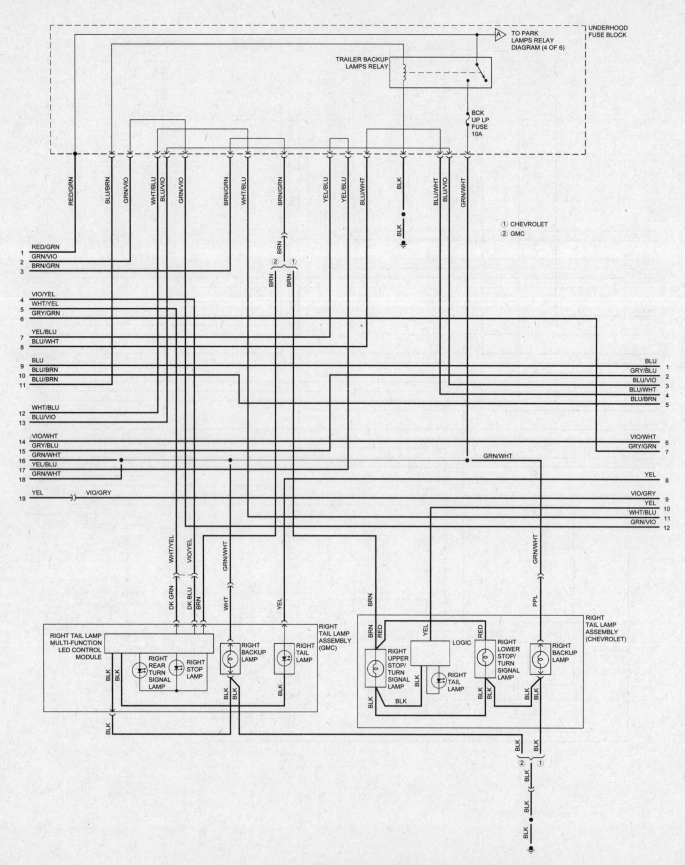

Exterior lighting system (exc. headlights and back-up lights) - SUV models (3 of 6)

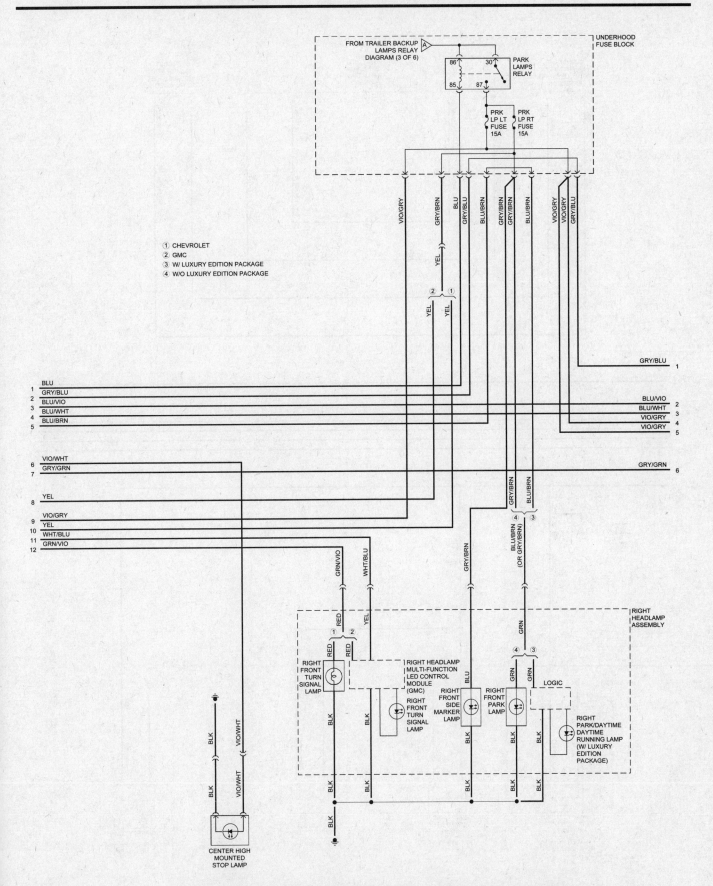

Exterior lighting system (exc. headlights and back-up lights) - SUV models (4 of 6)

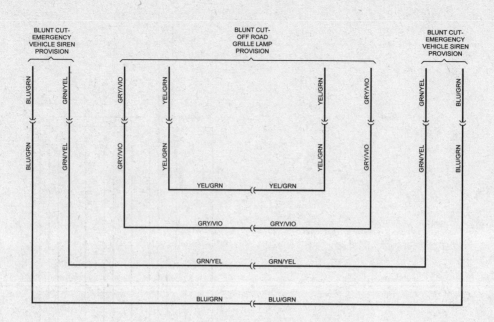

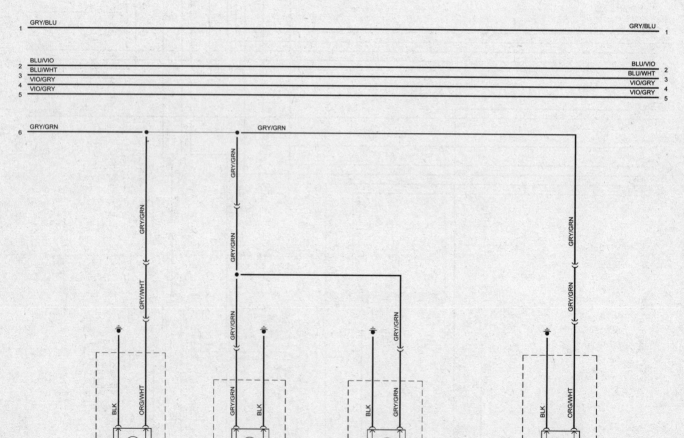

Exterior lighting system (exc. headlights and back-up lights) - SUV models (5 of 6)

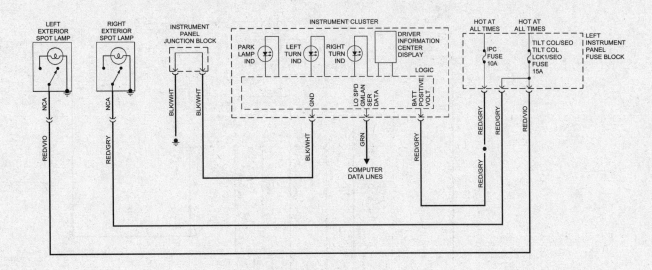

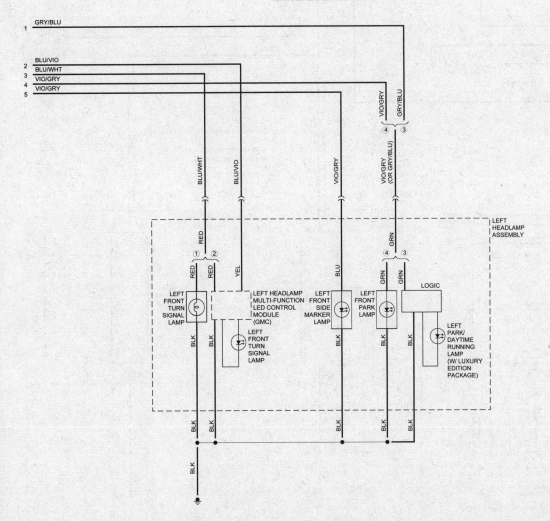

Exterior lighting system (exc. headlights and back-up lights) - SUV models (6 of 6)

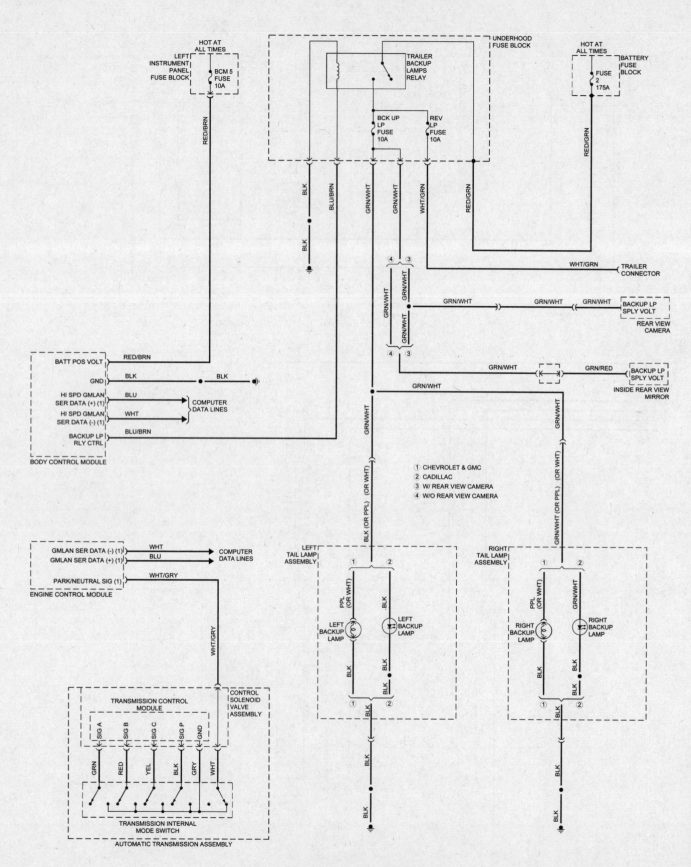

Back-up lights system - SUV models

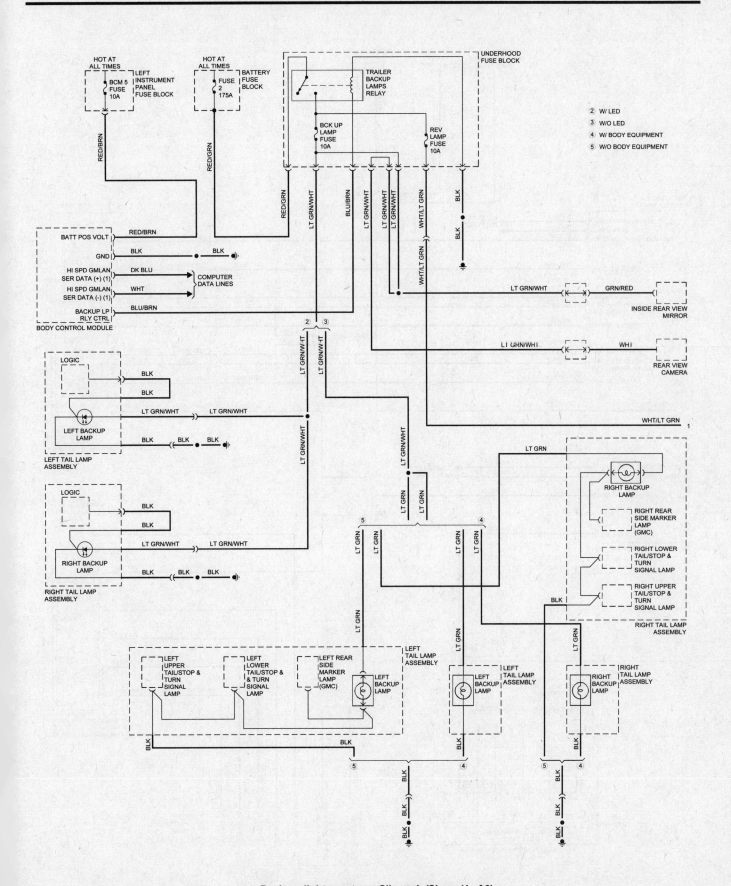

Back-up lights system - Silverado/Sierra (1 of 2)

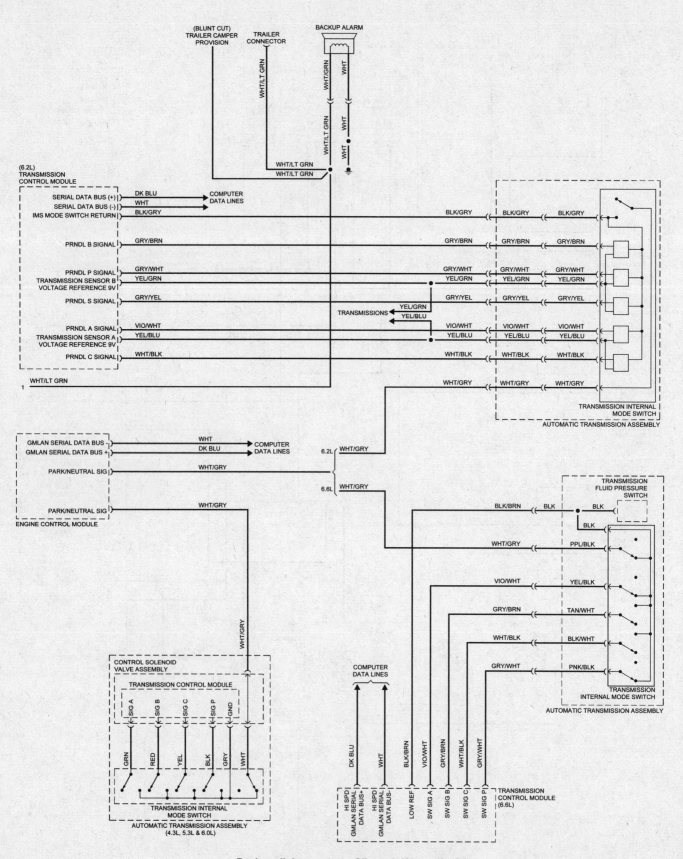

Back-up lights system - Silverado/Sierra (2 of 2)

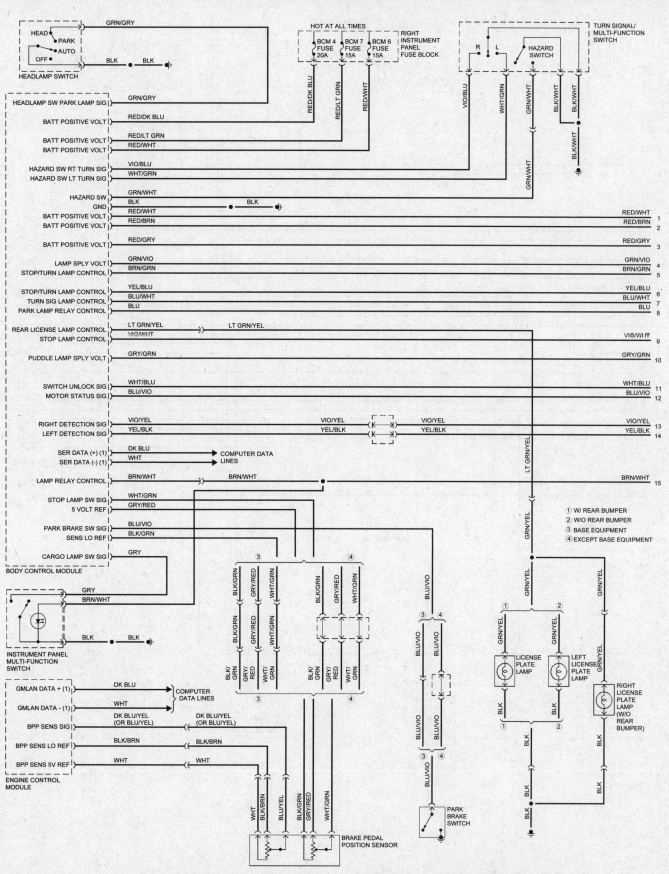

Exterior lighting system (exc. headlights and back-up lights) - Silverado/Sierra (1 of 7)

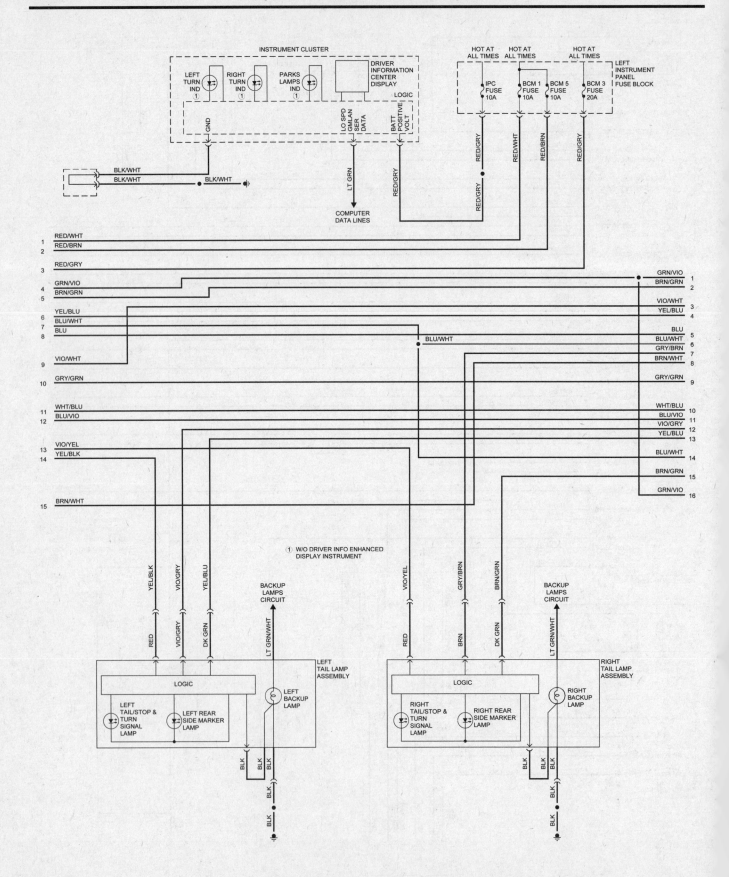

Exterior lighting system (exc. headlights and back-up lights) - Silverado/Sierra (2 of 7)

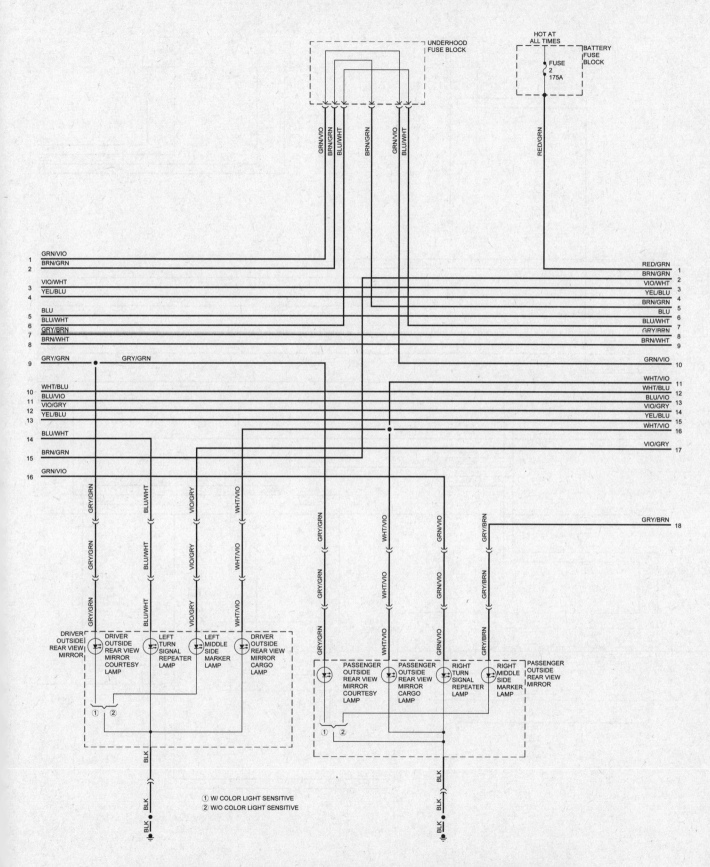

Exterior lighting system (exc. headlights and back-up lights) - Silverado/Sierra (3 of 7)

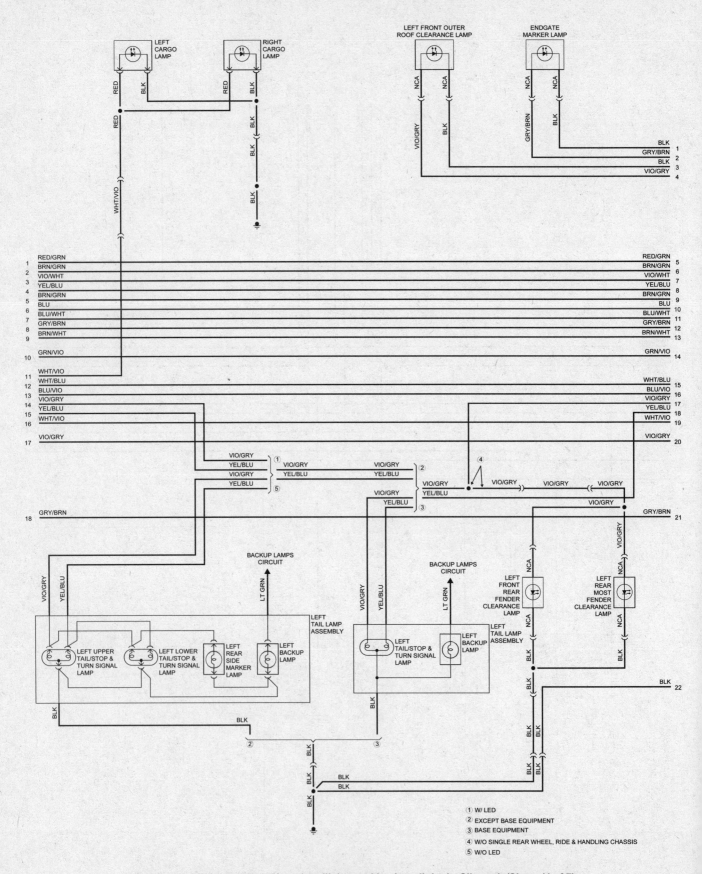

Exterior lighting system (exc. headlights and back-up lights) - Silverado/Sierra (4 of 7)

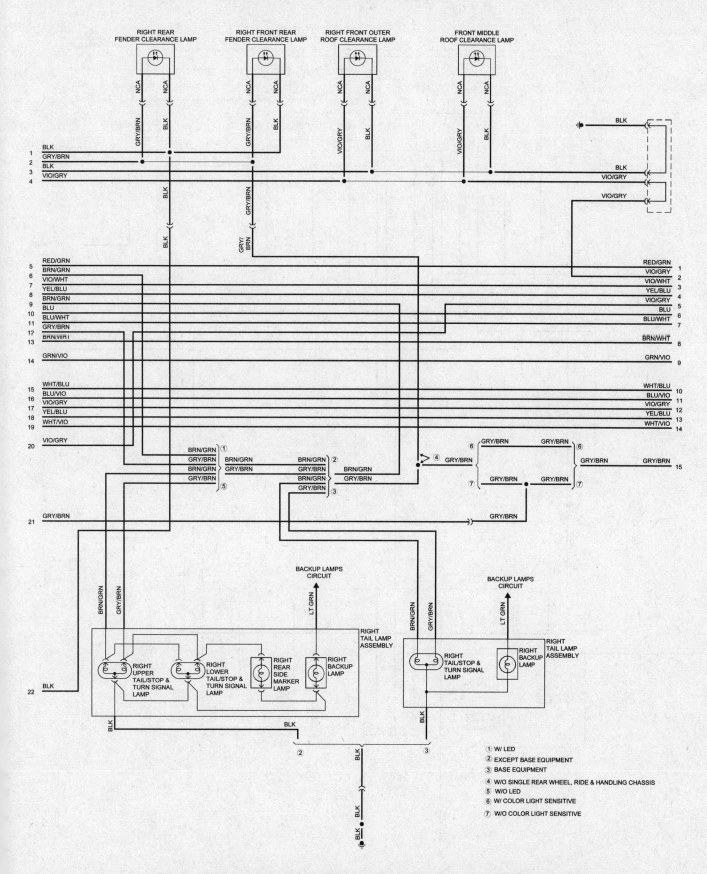

Exterior lighting system (exc. headlights and back-up lights) - Silverado/Sierra (5 of 7)

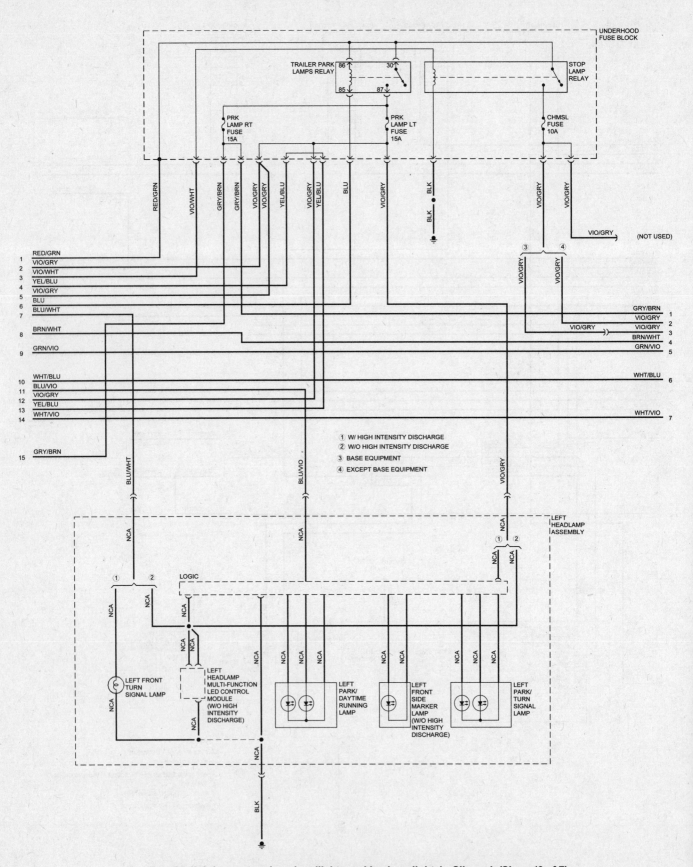

Exterior lighting system (exc. headlights and back-up lights) - Silverado/Sierra (6 of 7)

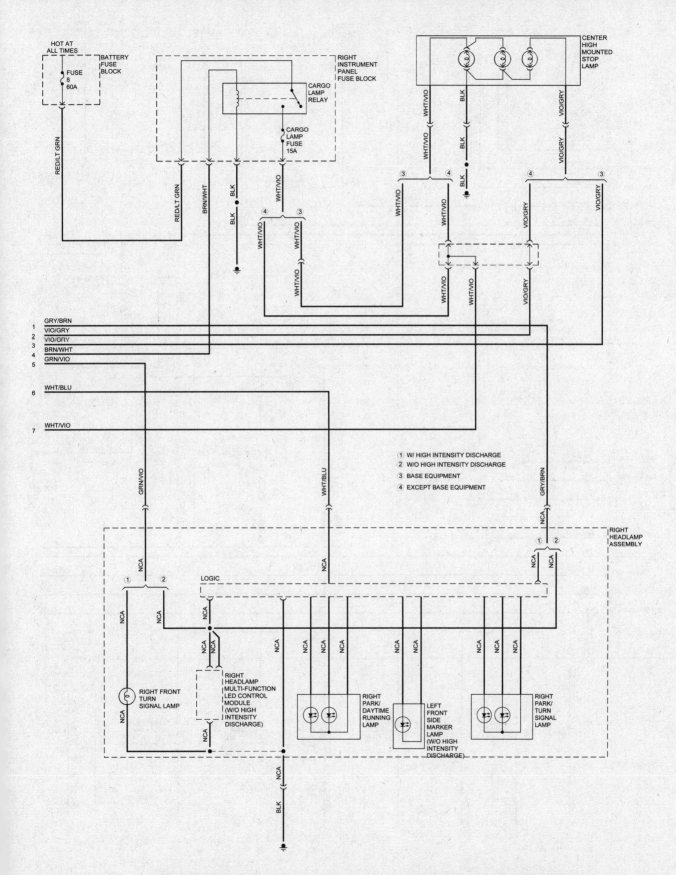

Exterior lighting system (exc. headlights and back-up lights) - Silverado/Sierra (7 of 7)

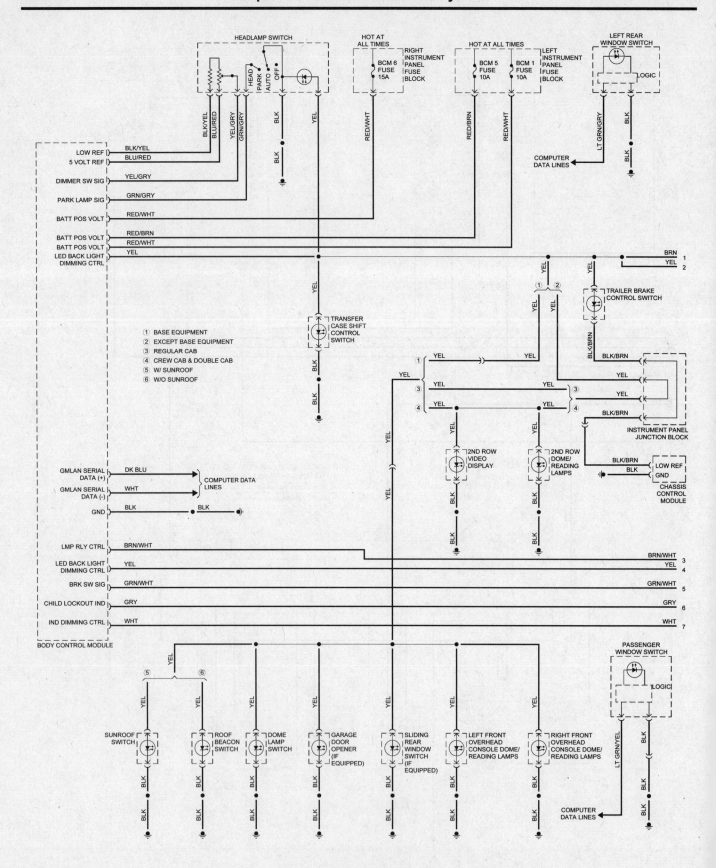

Instruments and switches illumination system - Silverado/Sierra (1 of 3)

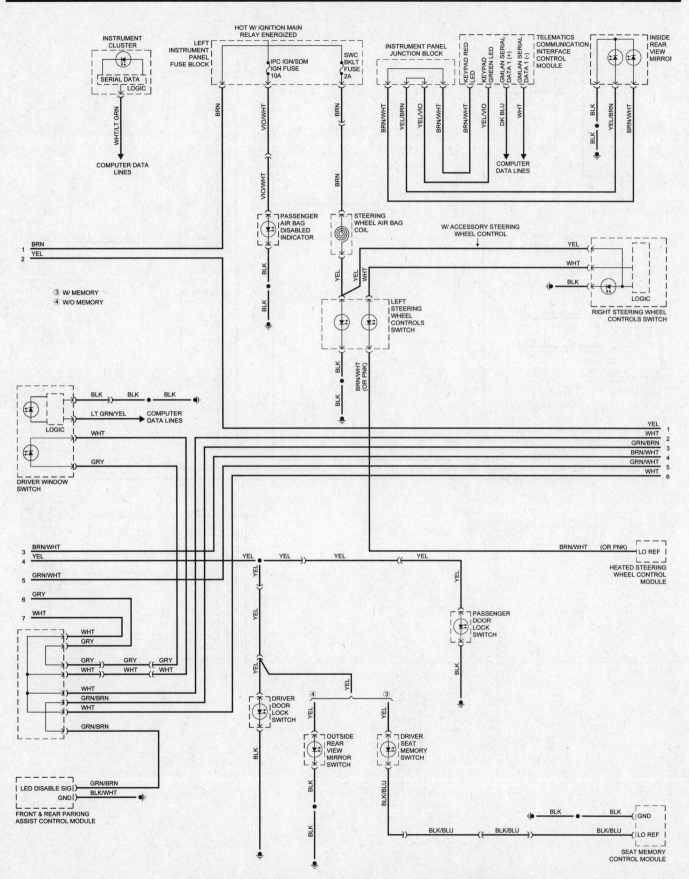

Instruments and switches illumination system - Silverado/Sierra (2 of 3)

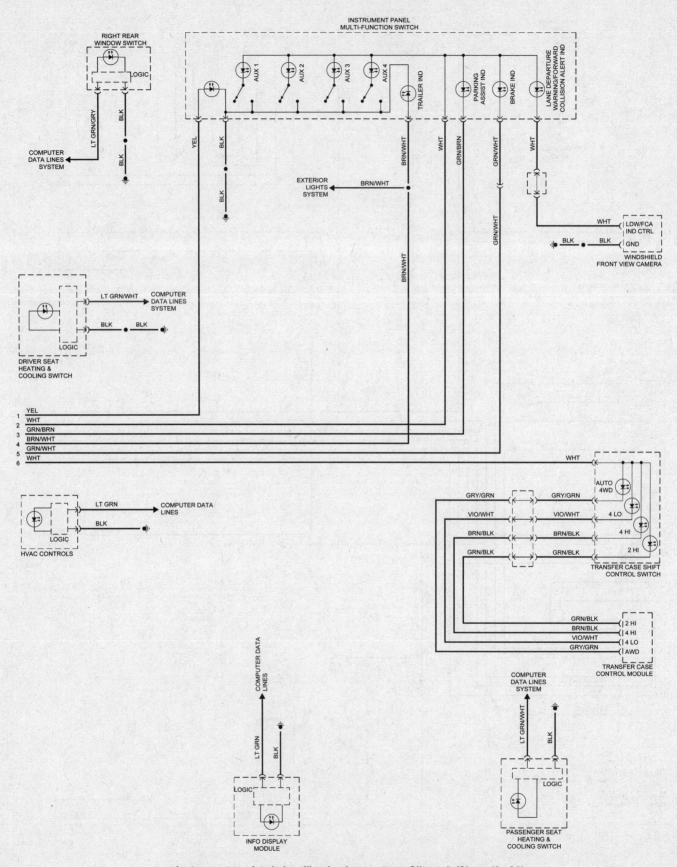

Instruments and switches illumination system - Silverado/Sierra (3 of 3)

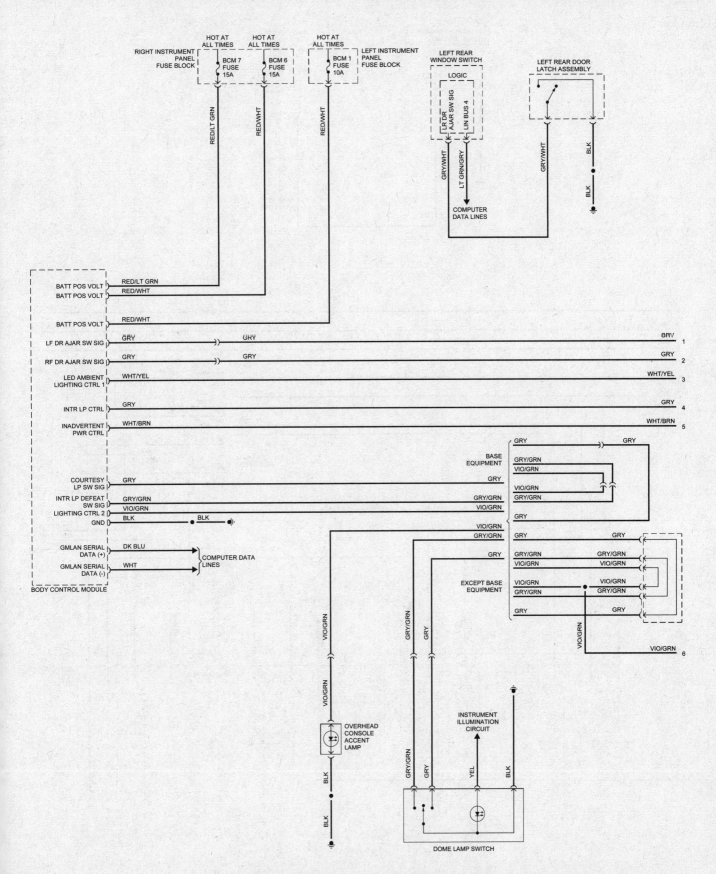

Courtesy lights circuit - Silverado/Sierra (1 of 3)

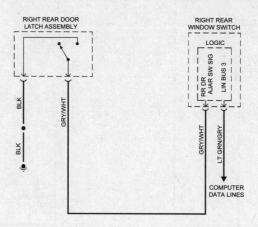

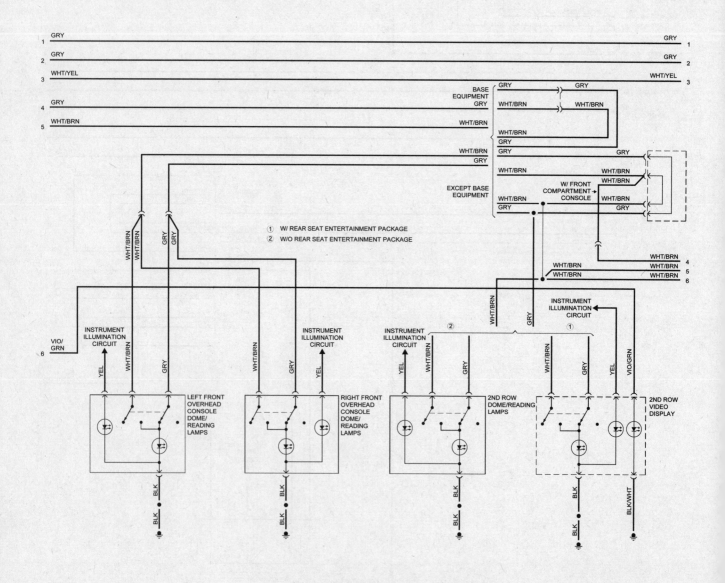

Courtesy lights circuit - Silverado/Sierra (2 of 3)

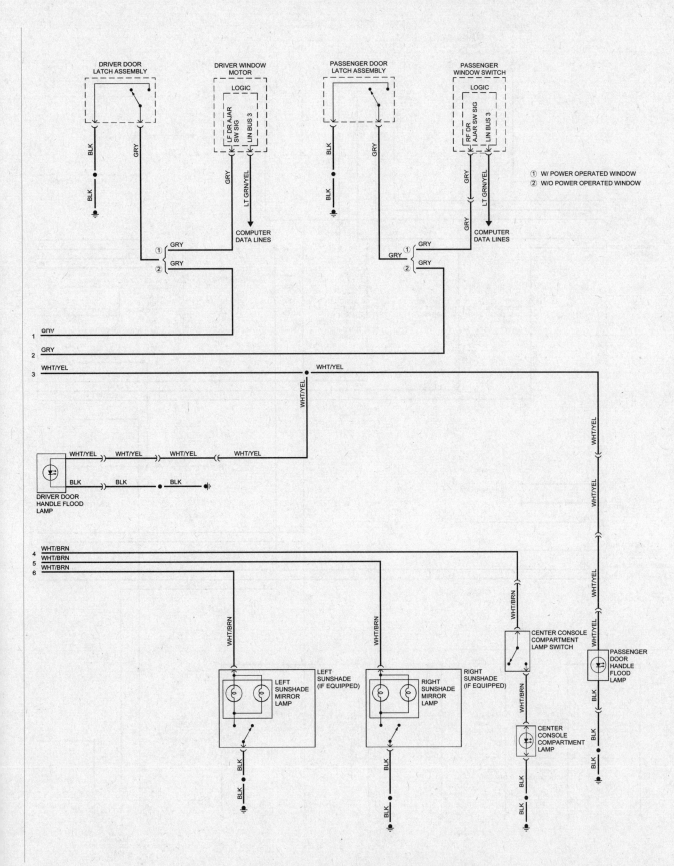

Courtesy lights circuit - Silverado/Sierra (3 of 3)

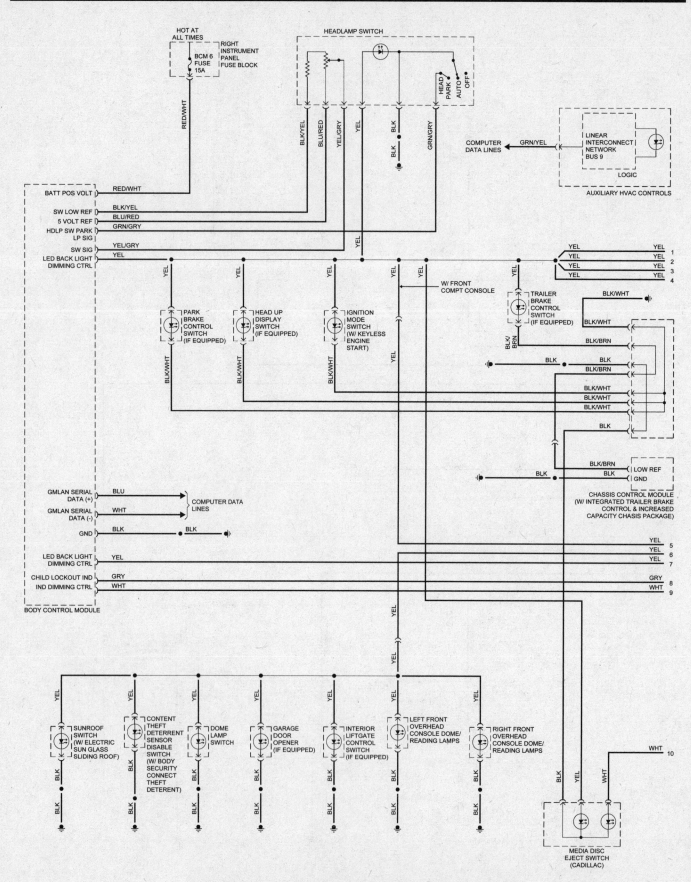

Instruments and switches illumination system - SUV models (1 of 4)

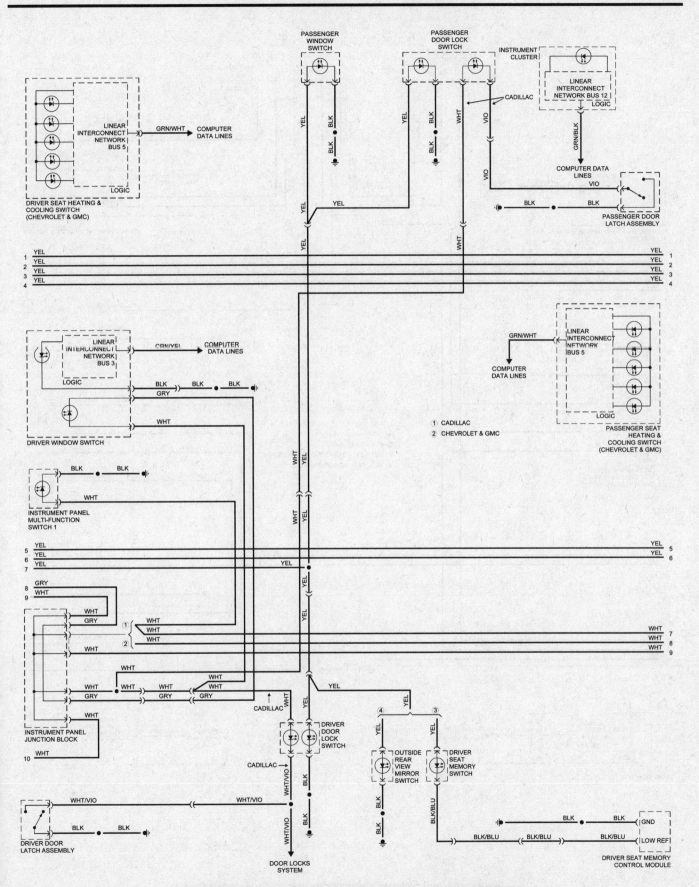

Instruments and switches illumination system - SUV models (2 of 4)

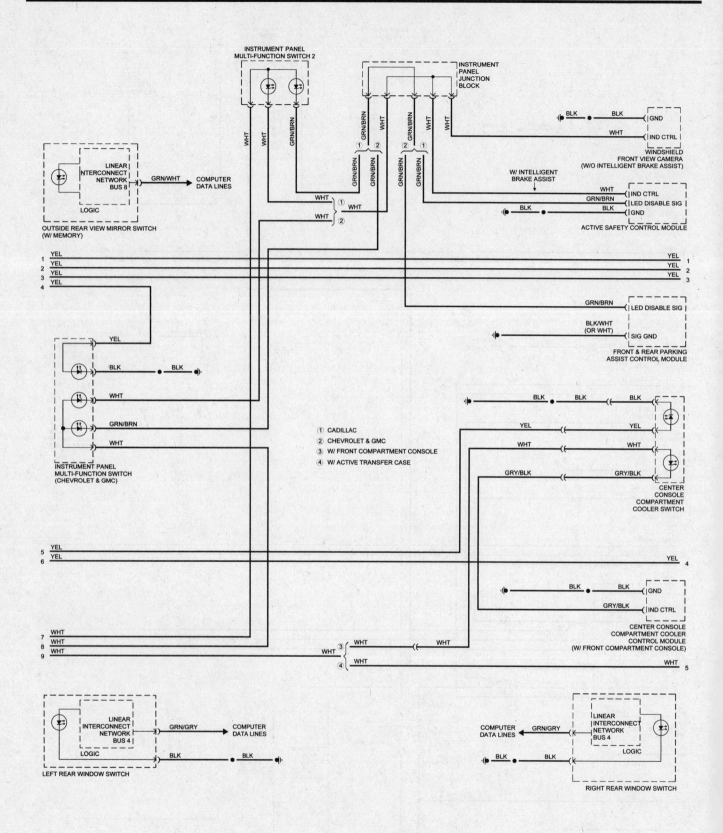

Instruments and switches illumination system - SUV models (3 of 4)

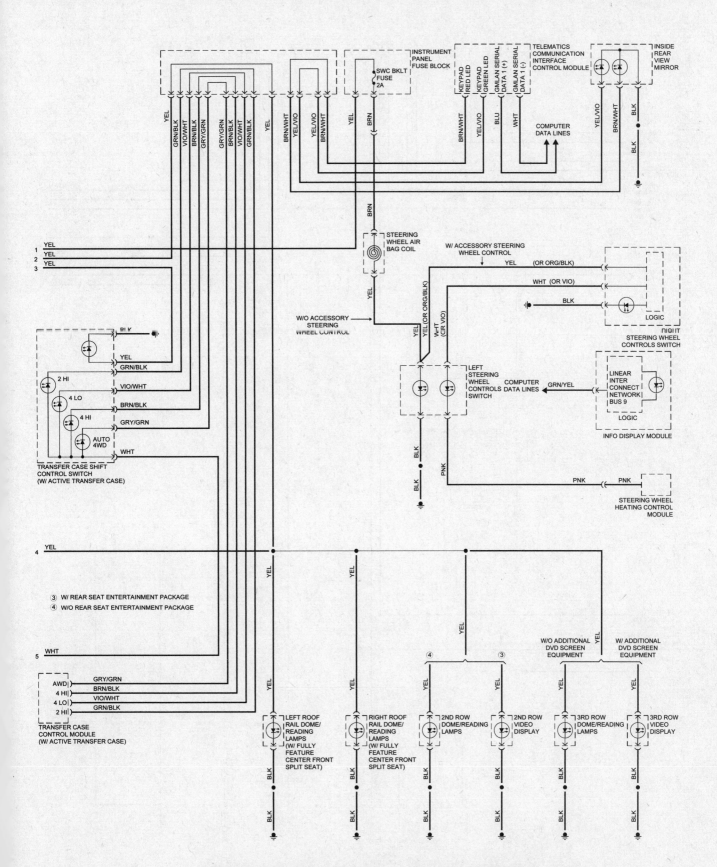

Instruments and switches illumination system - SUV models (4 of 4)

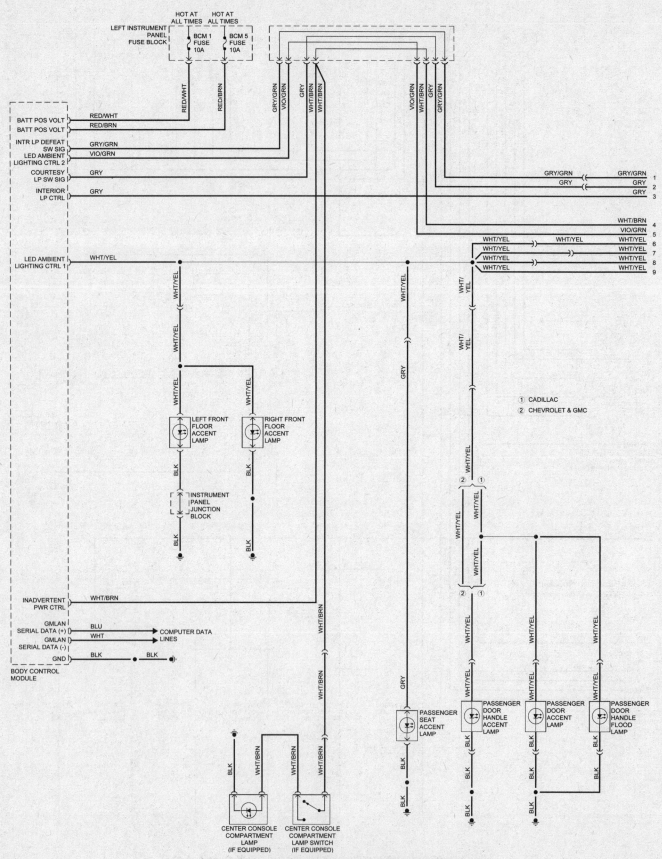

Courtesy lights circuit - SUV models (1 of 4)

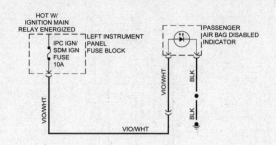

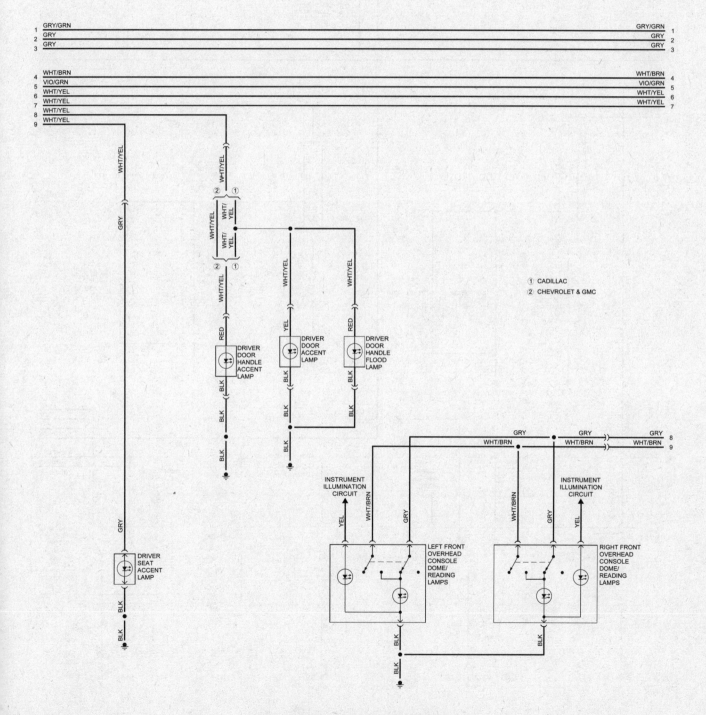

Courtesy lights circuit - SUV models (2 of 4)

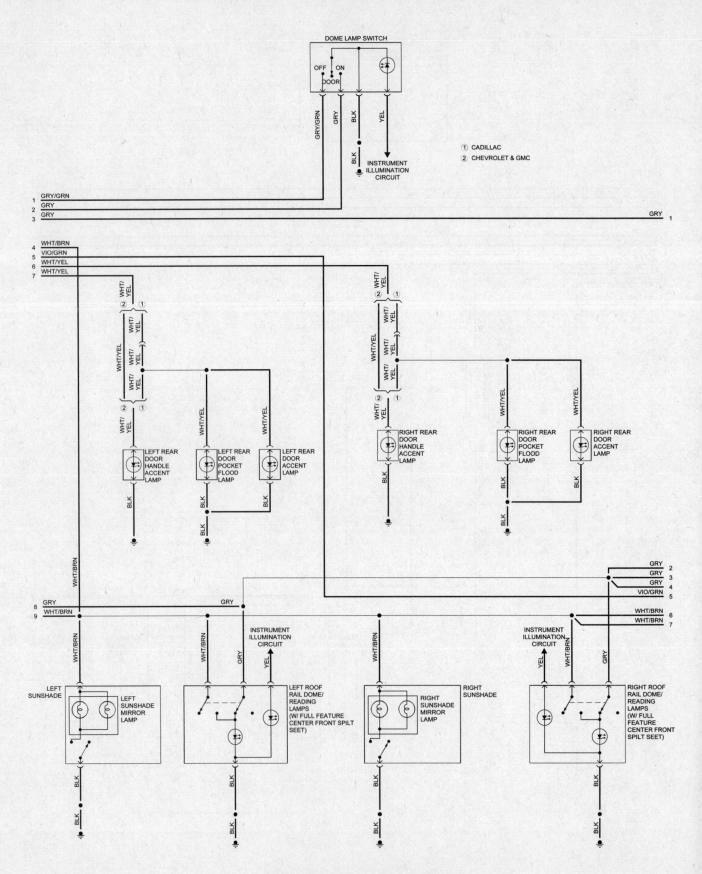

Courtesy lights circuit - SUV models (3 of 4)

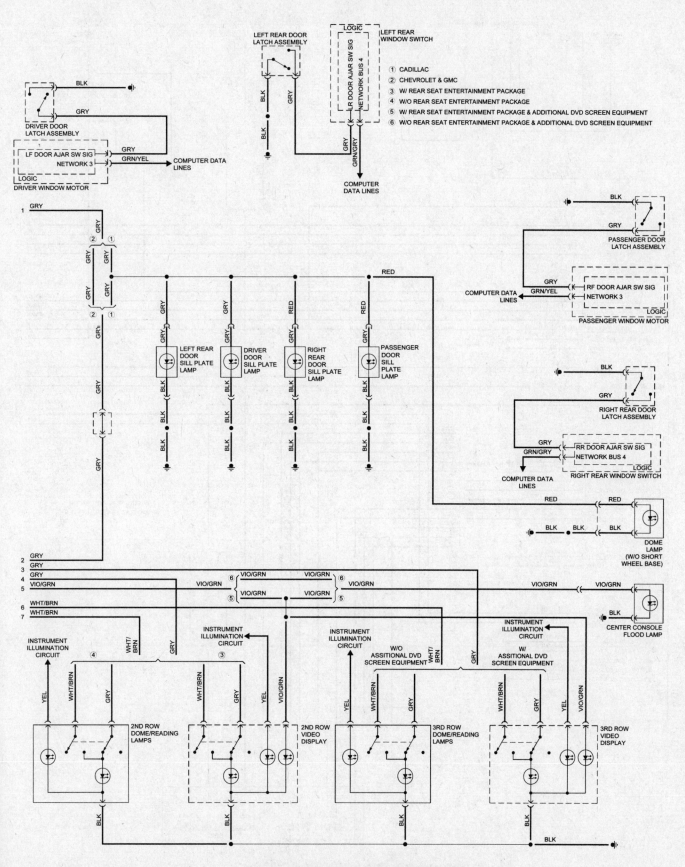

Courtesy lights circuit - SUV models (4 of 4)

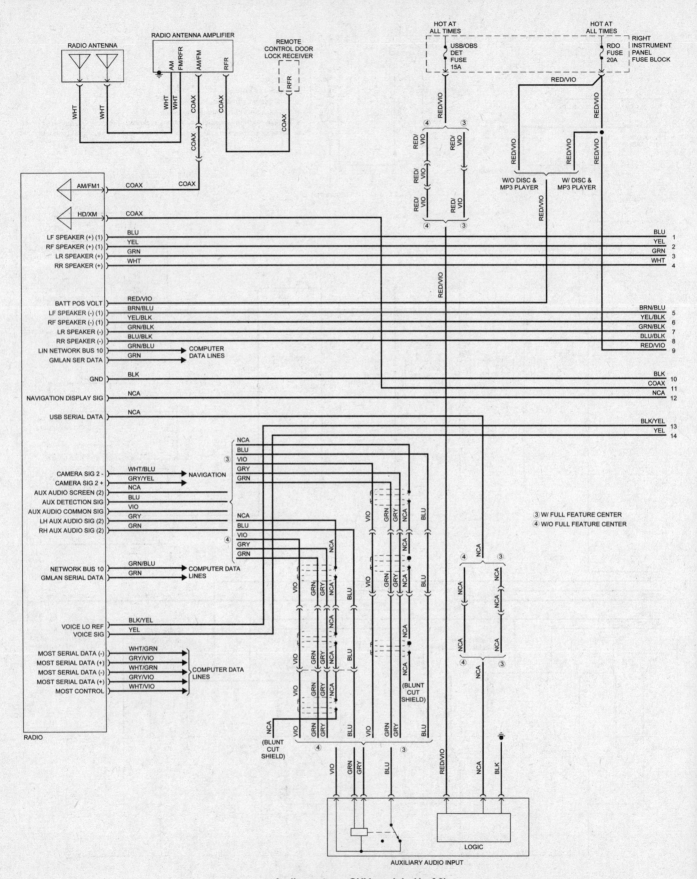

Audio system - SUV models (1 of 2)

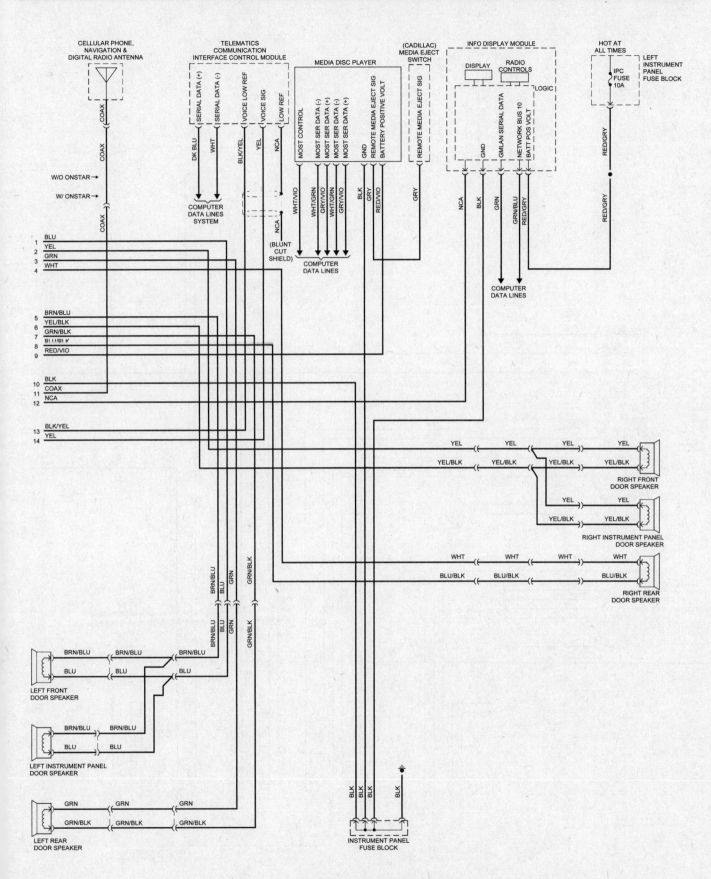

Audio system - SUV models (2 of 2)

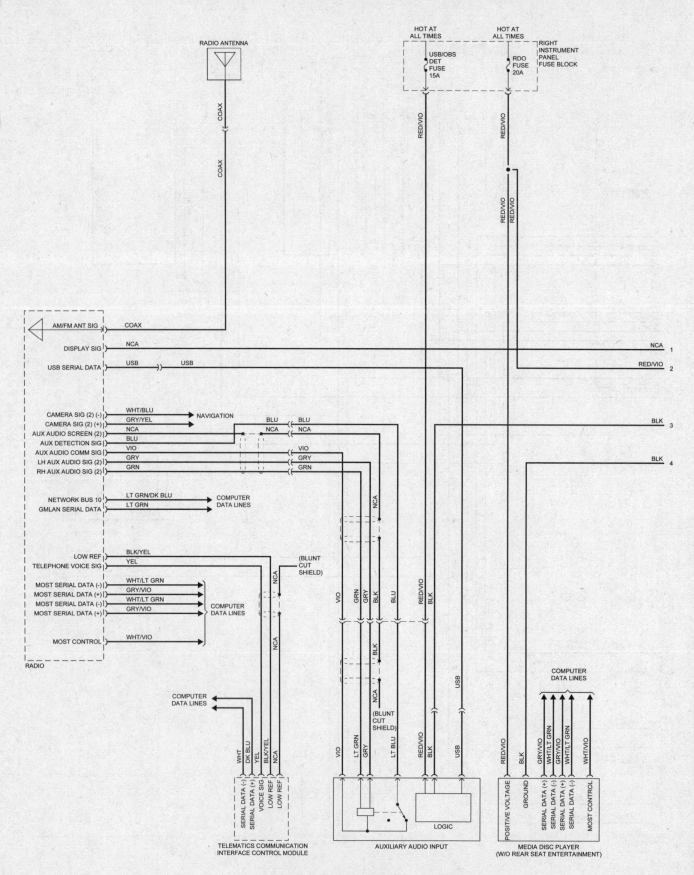

Audio system - Silverado/Sierra (1 of 3)

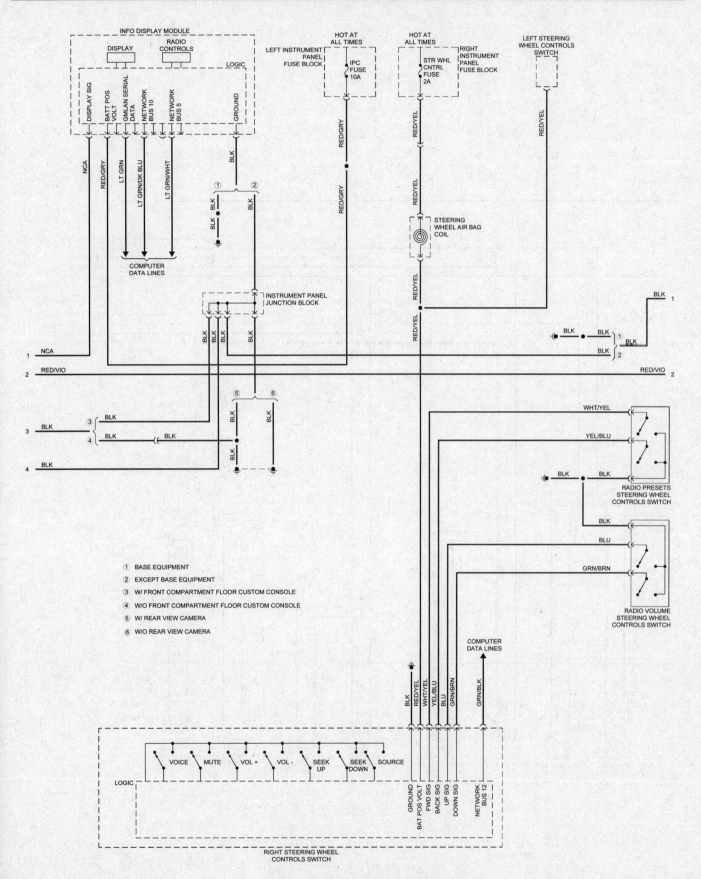

Audio system - Silverado/Sierra (2 of 3)

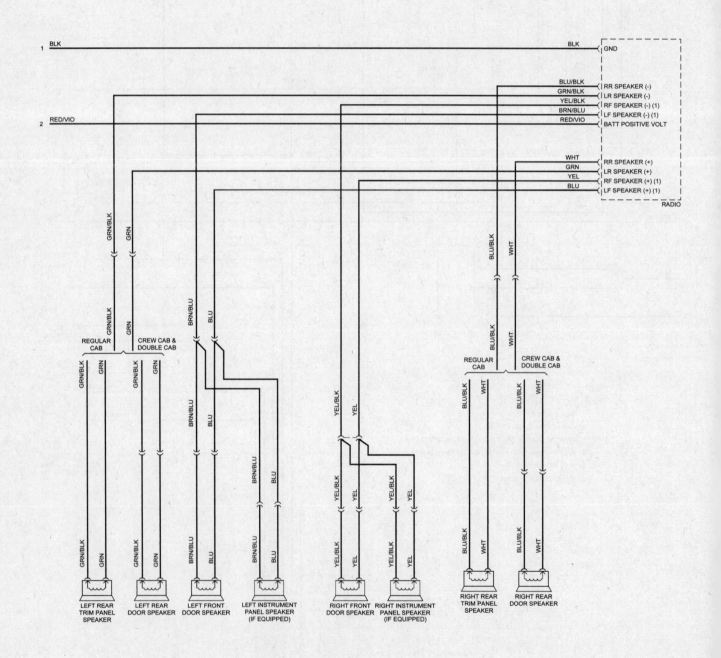

Audio system - Silverado/Sierra (3 of 3)

Index

Haynes Automotive Manuals

NOTE: If you do not see a listing for your vehicle, consult your local Haynes dealer for the latest product information.

ACURA
- 12020 **Integra** '86 thru '89 & **Legend** '86 thru '90
- 12021 **Integra** '90 thru '93 & **Legend** '91 thru '95
  Integra '94 thru '00 - see HONDA Civic (42025)
  MDX '01 thru '07 - see HONDA Pilot (42037)
- 12050 **Acura TL** all models '99 thru '08

AMC
  Jeep CJ - see JEEP (50020)
- 14020 **Mid-size models** '70 thru '83
- 14025 **(Renault) Alliance & Encore** '83 thru '87

AUDI
- 15020 **4000** all models '80 thru '87
- 15025 **5000** all models '77 thru '83
- 15026 **5000** all models '84 thru '88
  Audi A4 '96 thru '01 - see VW Passat (96023)
- 15030 **Audi A4** '02 thru '08

AUSTIN-HEALEY
  Sprite - see MG Midget (66015)

BMW
- 18020 **3/5 Series** '82 thru '92
- 18021 **3-Series** incl. Z3 models '92 thru '98
- 18022 **3-Series** incl. Z4 models '99 thru '05
- 18023 **3-Series** '06 thru '10
- 18025 **320i** all 4 cyl models '75 thru '83
- 18050 **1500 thru 2002** except Turbo '59 thru '77

BUICK
- 19010 **Buick Century** '97 thru '05
  Century (front-wheel drive) - see GM (38005)
- 19020 **Buick, Oldsmobile & Pontiac Full-size**
  (Front-wheel drive) '85 thru '05
  Buick Electra, LeSabre and Park Avenue;
  Oldsmobile Delta 88 Royale, Ninety Eight
  and Regency; **Pontiac** Bonneville
- 19025 **Buick, Oldsmobile & Pontiac Full-size**
  (Rear wheel drive) '70 thru '90
  Buick Estate, Electra, LeSabre, Limited,
  Oldsmobile Custom Cruiser, Delta 88,
  Ninety-eight, **Pontiac** Bonneville,
  Catalina, Grandville, Parisienne
- 19030 **Mid-size Regal & Century** all rear-drive
  models with V6, V8 and Turbo '74 thru '87
  Regal - see GENERAL MOTORS (38010)
  Riviera - see GENERAL MOTORS (38030)
  Roadmaster - see CHEVROLET (24046)
  Skyhawk - see GENERAL MOTORS (38015)
  Skylark - see GM (38020, 38025)
  Somerset - see GENERAL MOTORS (38025)

CADILLAC
- 21015 **CTS & CTS-V** '03 thru '12
- 21030 **Cadillac Rear Wheel Drive** '70 thru '93
  Cimarron - see GENERAL MOTORS (38015)
  DeVille - see GM (38031 & 38032)
  Eldorado - see GM (38030 & 38031)
  Fleetwood - see GM (38031)
  Seville - see GM (38030, 38031 & 38032)

CHEVROLET
- 10305 **Chevrolet Engine Overhaul Manual**
- 24010 **Astro & GMC Safari Mini-vans** '85 thru '05
- 24015 **Camaro V8** all models '70 thru '81
- 24016 **Camaro** all models '82 thru '92
- 24017 **Camaro & Firebird** '93 thru '02
  Cavalier - see GENERAL MOTORS (38016)
  Celebrity - see GENERAL MOTORS (38005)
- 24020 **Chevelle, Malibu & El Camino** '69 thru '87
- 24024 **Chevette & Pontiac T1000** '76 thru '87
  Citation - see GENERAL MOTORS (38020)
- 24027 **Colorado & GMC Canyon** '04 thru '10
- 24032 **Corsica/Beretta** all models '87 thru '96
- 24040 **Corvette** all V8 models '68 thru '82
- 24041 **Corvette** all models '84 thru '96
- 24045 **Full-size Sedans** Caprice, Impala, Biscayne,
  Bel Air & Wagons '69 thru '90
- 24046 **Impala SS & Caprice and Buick Roadmaster**
  '91 thru '96
  Impala '00 thru '05 - see LUMINA (24048)
- 24047 **Impala & Monte Carlo** all models '06 thru '11
  Lumina '90 thru '94 - see GM (38010)
- 24048 **Lumina & Monte Carlo** '95 thru '05
  Lumina APV - see GM (38035)
- 24050 **Luv Pick-up** all 2WD & 4WD '72 thru '82
  Malibu '97 thru '00 - see GM (38026)
- 24055 **Monte Carlo** all models '70 thru '88
  Monte Carlo '95 thru '01 - see LUMINA (24048)
- 24059 **Nova** all V8 models '69 thru '79
- 24060 **Nova and Geo Prizm** '85 thru '92
- 24064 **Pick-ups** '67 thru '87 - Chevrolet & GMC
- 24065 **Pick-ups** '88 thru '98 - Chevrolet & GMC

- 24066 **Pick-ups** '99 thru '06 - Chevrolet & GMC
- 24067 **Chevrolet Silverado & GMC Sierra** '07 thru '12
- 24070 **S-10 & S-15 Pick-ups** '82 thru '93,
  Blazer & Jimmy '83 thru '94,
- 24071 **S-10 & Sonoma Pick-ups** '94 thru '04, including Blazer, Jimmy & Hombre
- 24072 **Chevrolet TrailBlazer, GMC Envoy &**
  Oldsmobile Bravada '02 thru '09
- 24075 **Sprint** '85 thru '88 & **Geo Metro** '89 thru '01
- 24080 **Vans - Chevrolet & GMC** '68 thru '96
- 24081 **Chevrolet Express & GMC Savana**
  Full-size Vans '96 thru '10

CHRYSLER
- 10310 **Chrysler Engine Overhaul Manual**
- 25015 **Chrysler Cirrus, Dodge Stratus,**
  Plymouth Breeze '95 thru '00
- 25020 **Full-size Front-Wheel Drive** '88 thru '93
  K-Cars - see DODGE Aries (30008)
  Laser - see DODGE Daytona (30030)
- 25025 **Chrysler LHS, Concorde, New Yorker,**
  Dodge Intrepid, **Eagle** Vision, '93 thru '97
- 25026 **Chrysler LHS, Concorde, 300M,**
  Dodge Intrepid, '98 thru '04
- 25027 **Chrysler 300, Dodge Charger &**
  Magnum '05 thru '09
- 25030 **Chrysler & Plymouth Mid-size**
  front wheel drive '82 thru '95
  Rear-wheel Drive - see Dodge (30050)
- 25035 **PT Cruiser** all models '01 thru '10
- 25040 **Chrysler Sebring** '95 thru '06, **Dodge** Stratus
  '01 thru '06, **Dodge** Avenger '95 thru '00

DATSUN
- 28005 **200SX** all models '80 thru '83
- 28007 **B-210** all models '73 thru '78
- 28009 **210** all models '79 thru '82
- 28012 **240Z, 260Z & 280Z** Coupe '70 thru '78
- 28014 **280ZX** Coupe & 2+2 '79 thru '83
  300ZX - see NISSAN (72010)
- 28018 **510 & PL521 Pick-up** '68 thru '73
- 28020 **510** all models '78 thru '81
- 28022 **620 Series Pick-up** all models '73 thru '79
  720 Series Pick-up - see NISSAN (72030)
- 28025 **810/Maxima** all gasoline models '77 thru '84

DODGE
  400 & 600 - see CHRYSLER (25030)
- 30008 **Aries & Plymouth Reliant** '81 thru '89
- 30010 **Caravan & Plymouth Voyager** '84 thru '95
- 30011 **Caravan & Plymouth Voyager** '96 thru '02
- 30012 **Challenger/Plymouth Saporro** '78 thru '83
- 30013 **Caravan, Chrysler Voyager, Town &**
  Country '03 thru '07
- 30016 **Colt & Plymouth Champ** '78 thru '87
- 30020 **Dakota Pick-ups** all models '87 thru '96
- 30021 **Durango** '98 & '99, **Dakota** '97 thru '99
- 30022 **Durango** '00 thru '03 **Dakota** '00 thru '04
- 30023 **Durango** '04 thru '09, **Dakota** '05 thru '11
- 30025 **Dart, Demon, Plymouth Barracuda,**
  Duster & Valiant 6 cyl models '67 thru '76
- 30030 **Daytona & Chrysler Laser** '84 thru '89
  Intrepid - see CHRYSLER (25025, 25026)
- 30034 **Neon** all models '95 thru '99
- 30035 **Omni & Plymouth Horizon** '78 thru '90
- 30036 **Dodge and Plymouth Neon** '00 thru '05
- 30040 **Pick-ups** all full-size models '74 thru '93
- 30041 **Pick-ups** all full-size models '94 thru '01
- 30042 **Pick-ups** full-size models '02 thru '08
- 30045 **Ram 50/D50 Pick-ups & Raider and**
  Plymouth Arrow Pick-ups '79 thru '93
- 30050 **Dodge/Plymouth/Chrysler RWD** '71 thru '89
- 30055 **Shadow & Plymouth Sundance** '87 thru '94
- 30060 **Spirit & Plymouth Acclaim** '89 thru '95
- 30065 **Vans - Dodge & Plymouth** '71 thru '03

EAGLE
  Talon - see MITSUBISHI (68030, 68031)
  Vision - see CHRYSLER (25025)

FIAT
- 34010 **124 Sport Coupe & Spider** '68 thru '78
- 34025 **X1/9** all models '74 thru '80

FORD
- 10320 **Ford Engine Overhaul Manual**
- 10355 **Ford Automatic Transmission Overhaul**
- 11500 **Mustang '64-1/2 thru '70 Restoration Guide**
- 36004 **Aerostar Mini-vans** all models '86 thru '97
- 36006 **Contour & Mercury Mystique** '95 thru '00
- 36008 **Courier Pick-up** all models '72 thru '82
- 36012 **Crown Victoria & Mercury Grand**
  Marquis '88 thru '10
- 36016 **Escort/Mercury Lynx** all models '81 thru '90
- 36020 **Escort/Mercury Tracer** '91 thru '02

- 36022 **Escape & Mazda Tribute** '01 thru '11
- 36024 **Explorer & Mazda Navajo** '91 thru '01
- 36025 **Explorer/Mercury Mountaineer** '02 thru '10
- 36028 **Fairmont & Mercury Zephyr** '78 thru '83
- 36030 **Festiva & Aspire** '88 thru '97
- 36032 **Fiesta** all models '77 thru '80
- 36034 **Focus** all models '00 thru '11
- 36036 **Ford & Mercury Full-size** '75 thru '87
- 36044 **Ford & Mercury Mid-size** '75 thru '86
- 36045 **Fusion & Mercury Milan** '06 thru '10
- 36048 **Mustang V8** all models '64-1/2 thru '73
- 36049 **Mustang II** 4 cyl, V6 & V8 models '74 thru '78
- 36050 **Mustang & Mercury Capri** '79 thru '93
- 36051 **Mustang** all models '94 thru '04
- 36052 **Mustang** '05 thru '10
- 36054 **Pick-ups & Bronco** '73 thru '79
- 36058 **Pick-ups & Bronco** '80 thru '96
- 36059 **F-150 & Expedition** '97 thru '09, **F-250** '97
  thru '99 & **Lincoln Navigator** '98 thru '09
- 36060 **Super Duty Pick-ups, Excursion** '99 thru '10
- 36061 **F-150 full-size** '04 thru '10
- 36062 **Pinto & Mercury Bobcat** '75 thru '80
- 36066 **Probe** all models '89 thru '92
  Probe '93 thru '97 - see MAZDA 626 (61042)
- 36070 **Ranger/Bronco II** gasoline models '83 thru '92
- 36071 **Ranger** '93 thru '10 & **Mazda Pick-ups** '94 thru '09
- 36074 **Taurus & Mercury Sable** '86 thru '95
- 36075 **Taurus & Mercury Sable** '96 thru '05
- 36078 **Tempo & Mercury Topaz** '84 thru '94
- 36082 **Thunderbird/Mercury Cougar** '83 thru '88
- 36086 **Thunderbird/Mercury Cougar** '89 thru '97
- 36090 **Vans** all V8 Econoline models '69 thru '91
- 36094 **Vans** full size '92 thru '10
- 36097 **Windstar Mini-van** '95 thru '07

GENERAL MOTORS
- 10360 **GM Automatic Transmission Overhaul**
- 38005 **Buick Century, Chevrolet Celebrity,**
  Oldsmobile Cutlass Ciera & Pontiac 6000
  all models '82 thru '96
- 38010 **Buick Regal, Chevrolet Lumina,**
  Oldsmobile Cutlass Supreme &
  Pontiac Grand Prix (FWD) '88 thru '07
- 38015 **Buick Skyhawk, Cadillac Cimarron,**
  Chevrolet Cavalier, Oldsmobile Firenza &
  Pontiac J-2000 & Sunbird '82 thru '94
- 38016 **Chevrolet Cavalier &**
  Pontiac Sunfire '95 thru '05
- 38017 **Chevrolet Cobalt & Pontiac G5** '05 thru '11
- 38020 **Buick Skylark, Chevrolet Citation,**
  Olds Omega, Pontiac Phoenix '80 thru '85
- 38025 **Buick Skylark & Somerset,**
  Oldsmobile Achieva & Calais and
  Pontiac Grand Am all models '85 thru '98
- 38026 **Chevrolet Malibu, Olds Alero & Cutlass,**
  Pontiac Grand Am '97 thru '03
- 38027 **Chevrolet Malibu** '04 thru '10
- 38030 **Cadillac Eldorado, Seville, Oldsmobile**
  Toronado, Buick Riviera '71 thru '85
- 38031 **Cadillac Eldorado & Seville, DeVille, Fleetwood**
  & Olds Toronado, Buick Riviera '86 thru '93
- 38032 **Cadillac DeVille** '94 thru '05 & **Seville** '92 thru '04
  Cadillac DTS '06 thru '10
- 38035 **Chevrolet Lumina APV, Olds Silhouette**
  & Pontiac Trans Sport all models '90 thru '96
- 38036 **Chevrolet Venture, Olds Silhouette,**
  Pontiac Trans Sport & Montana '97 thru '05
  General Motors Full-size
  Rear-wheel Drive - see BUICK (19025)
- 38040 **Chevrolet Equinox** '05 thru '09 **Pontiac**
  Torrent '06 thru '09
- 38070 **Chevrolet HHR** '06 thru '11

GEO
  Metro - see CHEVROLET Sprint (24075)
  Prizm - '85 thru '92 see CHEVY (24060),
  '93 thru '02 see TOYOTA Corolla (92036)
- 40030 **Storm** all models '90 thru '93
  Tracker - see SUZUKI Samurai (90010)

GMC
  Vans & Pick-ups - see CHEVROLET

HONDA
- 42010 **Accord CVCC** all models '76 thru '83
- 42011 **Accord** all models '84 thru '89
- 42012 **Accord** all models '90 thru '93
- 42013 **Accord** all models '94 thru '97
- 42014 **Accord** all models '98 thru '02
- 42015 **Accord** '03 thru '07
- 42020 **Civic 1200** all models '73 thru '79
- 42021 **Civic 1300 & 1500 CVCC** '80 thru '83
- 42022 **Civic 1500 CVCC** all models '75 thru '79

(Continued on other side)

Haynes North America, Inc., 859 Lawrence Drive, Newbury Park, CA 91320-1514 • (805) 498-6703 • http://www.haynes.com

Haynes Automotive Manuals (continued)

NOTE: *If you do not see a listing for your vehicle, consult your local Haynes dealer for the latest product information.*

42023 **Civic** all models '84 thru '91
42024 **Civic & del Sol** '92 thru '95
42025 **Civic** '96 thru '00, **CR-V** '97 thru '01, **Acura Integra** '94 thru '00
42026 **Civic** '01 thru '10, **CR-V** '02 thru '09
42035 **Odyssey** all models '99 thru '10
Passport - *see ISUZU Rodeo (47017)*
42037 **Honda Pilot** '03 thru '07, **Acura MDX** '01 thru '07
42040 **Prelude CVCC** all models '79 thru '89

HYUNDAI
43010 **Elantra** all models '96 thru '10
43015 **Excel & Accent** all models '86 thru '09
43050 **Santa Fe** all models '01 thru '06
43055 **Sonata** all models '99 thru '08

INFINITI
G35 '03 thru '08 - *see NISSAN 350Z (72011)*

ISUZU
Hombre - *see CHEVROLET S-10 (24071)*
47017 **Rodeo, Amigo & Honda Passport** '89 thru '02
47020 **Trooper & Pick-up** '81 thru '93

JAGUAR
49010 **XJ6** all 6 cyl models '68 thru '86
49011 **XJ6** all models '88 thru '94
49015 **XJ12 & XJS** all 12 cyl models '72 thru '85

JEEP
50010 **Cherokee, Comanche & Wagoneer Limited** all models '84 thru '01
50020 **CJ** all models '49 thru '86
50025 **Grand Cherokee** all models '93 thru '04
50026 **Grand Cherokee** '05 thru '09
50029 **Grand Wagoneer & Pick-up** '72 thru '91
Grand Wagoneer '84 thru '91, Cherokee & Wagoneer '72 thru '83, Pick-up '72 thru '88
50030 **Wrangler** all models '87 thru '11
50035 **Liberty** '02 thru '07

KIA
54050 **Optima** '01 thru '10
54070 **Sephia** '94 thru '01, **Spectra** '00 thru '09, **Sportage** '05 thru '10

LEXUS
ES 300/330 - *see TOYOTA Camry (92007) (92008)*
RX 330 - *see TOYOTA Highlander (92095)*

LINCOLN
Navigator - *see FORD Pick-up (36059)*
59010 **Rear-Wheel Drive** all models '70 thru '10

MAZDA
61010 **GLC Hatchback (rear-wheel drive)** '77 thru '83
61011 **GLC (front-wheel drive)** '81 thru '85
61012 **Mazda3** '04 thru '11
61015 **323 & Protegé** '90 thru '03
61016 **MX-5 Miata** '90 thru '09
61020 **MPV** all models '89 thru '98
Navajo - *see Ford Explorer (36024)*
61030 **Pick-ups** '72 thru '93
Pick-ups '94 thru '00 - *see Ford Ranger (36071)*
61035 **RX-7** all models '79 thru '85
61036 **RX-7** all models '86 thru '91
61040 **626 (rear-wheel drive)** all models '79 thru '82
61041 **626/MX-6 (front-wheel drive)** '83 thru '92
61042 **626, MX-6/Ford Probe** '93 thru '02
61043 **Mazda6** '03 thru '11

MERCEDES-BENZ
63012 **123 Series Diesel** '76 thru '85
63015 **190 Series** four-cyl gas models, '84 thru '88
63020 **230/250/280** 6 cyl sohc models '68 thru '72
63025 **280 123 Series** gasoline models '77 thru '81
63030 **350 & 450** all models '71 thru '80
63040 **C-Class**: C230/C240/C280/C320/C350 '01 thru '07

MERCURY
64200 **Villager & Nissan Quest** '93 thru '01
All other titles, see FORD Listing.

MG
66010 **MGB** Roadster & GT Coupe '62 thru '80
66015 **MG Midget, Austin Healey Sprite** '58 thru '80

MINI
67020 **Mini** '02 thru '11

MITSUBISHI
68020 **Cordia, Tredia, Galant, Precis & Mirage** '83 thru '93
68030 **Eclipse, Eagle Talon & Ply. Laser** '90 thru '94
68031 **Eclipse** '95 thru '05, **Eagle Talon** '95 thru '98
68035 **Galant** '94 thru '03
68040 **Pick-up** '83 thru '96 & **Montero** '83 thru '93

NISSAN
72010 **300ZX** all models including Turbo '84 thru '89
72011 **350Z & Infiniti G35** all models '03 thru '08
72015 **Altima** all models '93 thru '06
72016 **Altima** '07 thru '10
72020 **Maxima** all models '85 thru '92
72021 **Maxima** all models '93 thru '04
72025 **Murano** '03 thru '10
72030 **Pick-ups** '80 thru '97 **Pathfinder** '87 thru '95
72031 **Frontier Pick-up, Xterra, Pathfinder** '96 thru '04
72032 **Frontier & Xterra** '05 thru '11
72040 **Pulsar** all models '83 thru '86
Quest - *see MERCURY Villager (64200)*
72050 **Sentra** all models '82 thru '94
72051 **Sentra & 200SX** all models '95 thru '06
72060 **Stanza** all models '82 thru '90
72070 **Titan pick-ups** '04 thru '10 **Armada** '05 thru '10

OLDSMOBILE
73015 **Cutlass** V6 & V8 gas models '74 thru '88
For other OLDSMOBILE titles, see BUICK, CHEVROLET or GENERAL MOTORS listing.

PLYMOUTH
For PLYMOUTH titles, see DODGE listing.

PONTIAC
79008 **Fiero** all models '84 thru '88
79018 **Firebird** V8 models except Turbo '70 thru '81
79019 **Firebird** all models '82 thru '92
79025 **G6** all models '05 thru '09
79040 **Mid-size Rear-wheel Drive** '70 thru '87
Vibe '03 thru '11 - *see TOYOTA Matrix (92060)*
For other PONTIAC titles, see BUICK, CHEVROLET or GENERAL MOTORS listing.

PORSCHE
80020 **911** except Turbo & Carrera 4 '65 thru '89
80025 **914** all 4 cyl models '69 thru '76
80030 **924** all models including Turbo '76 thru '82
80035 **944** all models including Turbo '83 thru '89

RENAULT
Alliance & Encore - *see AMC (14020)*

SAAB
84010 **900** all models including Turbo '79 thru '88

SATURN
87010 **Saturn** all S-series models '91 thru '02
87011 **Saturn Ion** '03 thru '07
87020 **Saturn** all L-series models '00 thru '04
87040 **Saturn VUE** '02 thru '07

SUBARU
89002 **1100, 1300, 1400 & 1600** '71 thru '79
89003 **1600 & 1800** 2WD & 4WD '80 thru '94
89100 **Legacy** all models '90 thru '99
89101 **Legacy & Forester** '00 thru '06

SUZUKI
90010 **Samurai/Sidekick & Geo Tracker** '86 thru '01

TOYOTA
92005 **Camry** all models '83 thru '91
92006 **Camry** all models '92 thru '96
92007 **Camry, Avalon, Solara, Lexus ES 300** '97 thru '01
92008 **Toyota Camry, Avalon and Solara and Lexus ES 300/330** all models '02 thru '06
92009 **Camry** '07 thru '11
92015 **Celica Rear Wheel Drive** '71 thru '85
92020 **Celica Front Wheel Drive** '86 thru '99
92025 **Celica Supra** all models '79 thru '92
92030 **Corolla** all models '75 thru '79
92032 **Corolla** all rear wheel drive models '80 thru '87
92035 **Corolla** all front wheel drive models '84 thru '92
92036 **Corolla & Geo Prizm** '93 thru '02
92037 **Corolla** models '03 thru '11
92040 **Corolla Tercel** all models '80 thru '82
92045 **Corona** all models '74 thru '82
92050 **Cressida** all models '78 thru '82
92055 **Land Cruiser** FJ40, 43, 45, 55 '68 thru '82
92056 **Land Cruiser** FJ60, 62, 80, FZJ80 '80 thru '96
92060 **Matrix & Pontiac Vibe** '03 thru '11
92065 **MR2** all models '85 thru '87
92070 **Pick-up** all models '69 thru '78
92075 **Pick-up** all models '79 thru '95
92076 **Tacoma, 4Runner, & T100** '93 thru '04
92077 **Tacoma** all models '05 thru '09
92078 **Tundra** '00 thru '06 & **Sequoia** '01 thru '07
92079 **4Runner** all models '03 thru '09
92080 **Previa** all models '91 thru '95
92081 **Prius** all models '01 thru '08
92082 **RAV4** all models '96 thru '10
92085 **Tercel** all models '87 thru '94
92090 **Sienna** all models '98 thru '09
92095 **Highlander & Lexus RX-330** '99 thru '07

TRIUMPH
94007 **Spitfire** all models '62 thru '81
94010 **TR7** all models '75 thru '81

VW
96008 **Beetle & Karmann Ghia** '54 thru '79
96009 **New Beetle** '98 thru '11
96016 **Rabbit, Jetta, Scirocco & Pick-up** gas models '75 thru '92 & Convertible '80 thru '92
96017 **Golf, GTI & Jetta** '93 thru '98, **Cabrio** '95 thru '02
96018 **Golf, GTI, Jetta** '99 thru '05
96019 **Jetta, Rabbit, GTI & Golf** '05 thru '11
96020 **Rabbit, Jetta & Pick-up** diesel '77 thru '84
96023 **Passat** '98 thru '05, **Audi A4** '96 thru '01
96030 **Transporter 1600** all models '68 thru '79
96035 **Transporter 1700, 1800 & 2000** '72 thru '79
96040 **Type 3 1500 & 1600** all models '63 thru '73
96045 **Vanagon** all air-cooled models '80 thru '83

VOLVO
97010 **120, 130 Series & 1800 Sports** '61 thru '73
97015 **140 Series** all models '66 thru '74
97020 **240 Series** all models '76 thru '93
97040 **740 & 760 Series** all models '82 thru '88
97050 **850 Series** all models '93 thru '97

TECHBOOK MANUALS
10205 **Automotive Computer Codes**
10206 **OBD-II & Electronic Engine Management**
10210 **Automotive Emissions Control Manual**
10215 **Fuel Injection Manual** '78 thru '85
10220 **Fuel Injection Manual** '86 thru '99
10225 **Holley Carburetor Manual**
10230 **Rochester Carburetor Manual**
10240 **Weber/Zenith/Stromberg/SU Carburetors**
10305 **Chevrolet Engine Overhaul Manual**
10310 **Chrysler Engine Overhaul Manual**
10320 **Ford Engine Overhaul Manual**
10330 **GM and Ford Diesel Engine Repair Manual**
10333 **Engine Performance Manual**
10340 **Small Engine Repair Manual**, 5 HP & Less
10341 **Small Engine Repair Manual**, 5.5 - 20 HP
10345 **Suspension, Steering & Driveline Manual**
10355 **Ford Automatic Transmission Overhaul**
10360 **GM Automatic Transmission Overhaul**
10405 **Automotive Body Repair & Painting**
10410 **Automotive Brake Manual**
10411 **Automotive Anti-lock Brake (ABS) Systems**
10415 **Automotive Detailing Manual**
10420 **Automotive Electrical Manual**
10425 **Automotive Heating & Air Conditioning**
10430 **Automotive Reference Manual & Dictionary**
10435 **Automotive Tools Manual**
10440 **Used Car Buying Guide**
10445 **Welding Manual**
10450 **ATV Basics**
10452 **Scooters 50cc to 250cc**

SPANISH MANUALS
98903 **Reparación de Carrocería & Pintura**
98904 **Manual de Carburador Modelos Holley & Rochester**
98905 **Códigos Automotrices de la Computadora**
98906 **OBD-II & Sistemas de Control Electrónico del Motor**
98910 **Frenos Automotriz**
98913 **Electricidad Automotriz**
98915 **Inyección de Combustible** '86 al '99
99040 **Chevrolet & GMC Camionetas** '67 al '87
99041 **Chevrolet & GMC Camionetas** '88 al '98
99042 **Chevrolet & GMC Camionetas Cerradas** '68 al '95
99043 **Chevrolet/GMC Camionetas** '94 al '04
99048 **Chevrolet/GMC Camionetas** '99 al '06
99055 **Dodge Caravan & Plymouth Voyager** '84 al '95
99075 **Ford Camionetas y Bronco** '80 al '94
99076 **Ford F-150** '97 al '09
99077 **Ford Camionetas Cerradas** '69 al '91
99088 **Ford Modelos de Tamaño Mediano** '75 al '86
99089 **Ford Camionetas Ranger** '93 al '10
99091 **Ford Taurus & Mercury Sable** '86 al '95
99095 **GM Modelos de Tamaño Grande** '70 al '90
99100 **GM Modelos de Tamaño Mediano** '70 al '88
99106 **Jeep Cherokee, Wagoneer & Comanche** '84 al '00
99110 **Nissan Camioneta** '80 al '96, **Pathfinder** '87 al '95
99118 **Nissan Sentra** '82 al '94
99125 **Toyota Camionetas y 4Runner** '79 al '95

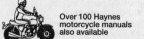
Over 100 Haynes motorcycle manuals also available

7-12

Haynes North America, Inc., 859 Lawrence Drive, Newbury Park, CA 91320-1514 • (805) 498-6703 • http://www.haynes.com